Advanced Algebra Through Data Exploration

A Graphing Calculator Approach

Jerald Murdock
Ellen Kamischke
Eric Kamischke

KEY CURRICULUM PRESS
Innovators in Mathematics Education

Project Editor: Crystal Mills
Editorial Assistants: Caroline Ayres and Jeff Gammon
Historical Researcher: Cathy Kessel
Copyeditor: Dahlia Armon
Production Editor: Deborah Cogan
Production Manager: Luis Shein
Art Direction and Text Design: Mark Ong, Side by Side Studios
Art Development: Elisse Gabriel
Art Coordination: Betty Gee and Suzanna Gee
Illustrators: Ryan Alexiev, Tom Fowler, and Jane McCreary
Technical Artists: Nea Hanscomb, Lisa Hymel, and Kristin Mount
Photo Researcher: Ellen Hayes
Photographers: Greg Ceo and Bonnie Kamin
Composition: Mark Ong and Susan Riley, Side by Side Studios
Prepress: Digital Pre-Press International
Cover Design: Dennis Teutschel, Teutschel Design Services
Printer: R. R. Donnelley & Sons, Willard, Ohio

Publisher: Steve Rasmussen
Editorial Director: John Bergez

10   9   8   7   6   5   4   3   2   1   01   00   99   98   97

Copyright © 1998 by Key Curriculum Press
Key Curriculum Press
P.O. Box 2304
Berkeley, California 94702
editorial@keypress.com
http://www.keypress.com

This material is based upon work supported by the National Science Foundation under award number MDR9154410. Any opinions, findings, and conclusions or recommendations expressed in this publication are those of the authors and do not necessarily reflect the views of the National Science Foundation.

Printed in the United States of America   **ISBN** 1-55953-225-4

Advisors and Contributors

Karen Wootton (Assessment Writer), CPM Educational Program, Terre Haute, Indiana
Bill Medigovich (Consultant), Redwood High School, Larkspur, California
Judy Cubillo (Solutions Writer), Northgate High School, Walnut Creek, California

Multicultural and Equity Reviewers

Edward D. Castillo, Sonoma State University, Rohnert Park, California
Robert Hamada, Los Angeles Unified School District, Los Angeles, California
Marva O. Wilkins, Richmond, California
Claudia Zaslavsky, New York City, New York

Mathematical Reviewers

Mary Barnes, Cremorne, New South Wales, Australia
Tim Erickson, Oakland, California
Warren Page, The Mathematical Association of America, Brooklyn, New York
James W. Wilson, University of Georgia, Athens, Georgia

Field Testers

Margaret A. Bambrick and Candace H. Fernandez, Atlantic High School, Port Orange, Florida
Deborah Berry, Linda A. Jones, and Andrea L. Sukow, Hillsboro High School, Nashville, Tennessee
Barbara Bredel, Crandon High School, Crandon, Wisconsin
Bruce Budzynski, Ludington High School, Ludington, Michigan
Susan H. Burgess, H. H. Dow High School, Midland, Michigan
John Crotty, Career High School, New Haven, Connecticut
Judy Cubillo, Northgate High School, Walnut Creek, California
Carol H. DeCuzzi, Audubon High School, Audubon, New Jersey
Bob Drake and Salvador Quezada, Jr., Roosevelt High School, Los Angeles, California
Steve Eckert, Robert H. Kosztowny, and Michele Mitchell, Fremont High School, Fremont, Michigan
Fred Gerhardt, Kingston High School, Kingston, Michigan
Elizabeth Hales, New School for the Arts, Scottsdale, Arizona
Jane E. Halverson, Grand Canyon High School, Grand Canyon, Arizona
Judy Hicks, Standley Lake High School, Westminister, Colorado
Jane Housman Jones, du Pont Manual High School, Louisville, Kentucky
Carolyn Jordan, Franklin High School, Stockton, California
Jan Kledzik, Centerville High School, Centerville, Ohio
Kim Landeck, Lakeshore Math/Science Center, Stevensville, Michigan
Harry M. Lykens, Mary Institute St. Louis Country Day School, St. Louis, Missouri
Harry E. Mann, Scottsdale School District, Phoenix, Arizona
Diane L. Martling, Illinois Math and Science Academy, Aurora, Illinois
Grant McMicken, San Juan High School, Citrus Heights, California
Bill Medigovich, Redwood High School, Larkspur, California
Denny Miller, Cheshire High School, Cheshire, Connecticut
Jeanette N. Mueller, Traverse City Senior High School, Traverse City, Michigan
Jennifer North Morris, West Hills High School, Santee, California
Marilyn J. Peak, Spencer County High School, Taylorsville, Kentucky
Gary Preto, Folsom High School, Folsom, California
Tara S. Rickart, Nonnewaug High School, Woodbury, Connecticut
Judith L. Zimpfer, Alba Public Schools, Alba, Michigan
Lana Taylor, Siena Heights College, Adrian, Michigan
Tim Trapp, Mountain View High School, Mesa, Arizona
Hugo Trepte, Interlochen Arts Academy, Interlochen, Michigan
Frederick P. Wright, Lakeside School, Seattle, Washington

Author Acknowledgments

Creating a textbook and its supplementary materials is a team effort involving many individuals and groups. We are grateful to the National Science Foundation for their support and the grant that began this process. Through that program the first drafts of this course were created along with workshops and summer institutes presented to more than two hundred teachers from across the country. We are grateful also to those teachers, students, and colleagues who have taken the time to offer suggestions, review materials, locate errors, and act as guinea pigs for new investigations and lessons. Their input and willingness to participate in this project have been invaluable.

Over the course of our careers many individuals and groups have been instrumental in our development as teachers and authors. The Woodrow Wilson National Fellowship Foundation provided an initial impetus for involvement in leading workshops. The documents of the National Council of Teachers of Mathematics have been a guide in the development of this curriculum. Individuals such as Ron Carlson, Helen Compton, Frank Demana, Arne Engebretsen, Paul Foerster, Greg Foley, Heinz-Otto Peitgen, Tara Rickart, James Sandefur, James Schultz, Dan Teague, Tim Trapp, Charles Vonder Embse, Bert Waits, and Mary Jean Winter have inspired us with teaching strategies and innovative activities.

The support we received from representatives of calculator companies such as Texas Instruments, Casio, and Hewlett Packard has helped us to keep up with the latest developments in calculator technology and enabled us to incorporate them in the book.

We are grateful to our colleagues at Key Curriculum Press for working with us to take our project to this final stage. Their confidence, cooperation, and contributions have made this text possible. Our editor, Crystal Mills, has earned a special acknowledgment for her work, perseverance, and friendship.

Finally, but perhaps most importantly, we wish to thank our families and the Interlochen Arts Academy for their support. Our students at Interlochen have played an important part in the development of this book. The support and encouragement we received from them, their parents, our colleagues, and the administration have been invaluable in making this book a reality.

Jerald Murdock
Ellen Kamischke
Eric Kamischke

Foreword

by Glenda Lappan
Michigan State University

One of the challenges we have faced as teachers of mathematics over the past decade is the rapidly changing technology that is available with which to do mathematics. Technology not only has made calculations and graphing easier, but has changed the very nature of the problems important to mathematics and the ways in which mathematicians investigate them. Our biggest challenge as teachers has been to figure out a meaningful response to the impact of technology on the curriculum summarized by the National Council of Teachers of Mathematics:

> *Some mathematics becomes more important because technology **requires** it. Some mathematics becomes less important because technology **replaces** it. Some mathematics becomes possible because technology **allows** it.*

In the 1980s, we were faced with curriculum materials that showed us how technology could help us teach the same things we had been teaching. Teachers and students frequently were left with the feeling that there had to be more to this modern technology than covering the same curriculum with the calculations and graphing supported. We had cannons in our hands, but we were still shooting at gnats. We have also had materials that focused on the calculator, but that lost the coherent, connected study of mathematics. With these curricula, learning to shoot the cannon was the only goal.

Thoughtful curriculum materials that significantly affect the ways in which students explore and learn mathematics have been very slow to be developed. Each of the summary statements from NCTM gives a reason why. It is hard to figure out what is needed, what is not needed, and what is possible in a mathematics education for students who have access to powerful computational and graphics tools. It is even harder, once you have made a set of decisions about what is important for students to know and be able to do, to weave these mathematical ideas into a coherent whole.

Advanced Algebra Through Data Exploration: A Graphing Calculator Approach is a wonderful example of a set of mathematics curriculum materials that uses technology to develop a powerful, coherent, useful mathematics for students. The power of the graphing calculator is directed toward allowing students to investigate real-world problems. The calculator allows students to explore interesting situations that push toward generalizable concepts, and procedures associated with those concepts, *before*

Glenda Lappan is a professor in the department of Mathematics at Michigan State University. She is a co-director of the middle school Connected Mathematics Project and Vice-Chairperson of the Mathematical Sciences Education Board. Dr. Lappan chaired the commission that developed the NCTM Standards for Teaching Mathematics.

the abstractions are made more explicit. The need to develop certain ideas in mathematics comes out of the students' own explorations. As students progress through these carefully sequenced problems, they develop greater understanding of concepts, procedures, processes, and skills. In this way the text supports a very different pedagogy in the classroom without compromising the mathematical expectations we have of students.

Advanced Algebra Through Data Exploration includes important mathematics that is not in traditional texts. These new, more modern strands of mathematics are, for the most part, discrete mathematics topics such as data analysis, Markov processes, and matrices. These are areas in which realizing the power of technology *requires* new mathematics. An example of technology *allowing* different mathematics is the way the text develops functions. I cannot imagine a student failing to understand functions at a fundamentally deeper level with the treatment in this book.

Not only will students coming out of a year with this text have an excellent preparation for continuing in mathematics—or any field of study requiring mathematics—but they also will know the mathematics they know in deeper, more flexible ways. They will have developed a set of what I call mathematical habits of mind that will serve them very well as students or users of mathematics. They will emerge with a sense of mathematics as a search for regularity that allows prediction. They will have gained a sense of mathematics as a tool for investigating important and interesting real-world problems. They will also have developed a sophisticated understanding of that which gives mathematics its power—the language and syntax of a sparse symbol system that allows complex ideas to be represented with clarity and precision and manipulated to allow new insights into real situations. The exciting thing is that these manipulations include graphic and tabular exploration as well as changing symbolic forms.

Those of you who choose to use this text are in for a mathematical treat. You will also recognize that this is a text that has been developed in classrooms by very smart, dedicated teachers. The focus of the text is on teaching students, not on presenting mathematics. I predict that you often will find yourself, as I did, saying "Wow, what a nice way to think about this idea! It will be great for students."

Contents

Chapter 3

Acres of corn

Introduction to Statistics

Chapter 4

Data Analysis

Chapter 5

Functions

Chapter 6

Parametric Equations and Trigonometry

Chapter 7

Exponential and Logarithmic Functions

Chapter 8

Topics in Discrete Mathematics

Chapter 9

Systems of Equations

Chapter 13

Trigonometric Functions   643

A Note to Students

You are about to embark on an exciting mathematical journey. The goal of your trip is to reach the point at which you have gathered the skills, tools, and mathematical power to participate fully as a productive citizen in a changing world. To do so, you need skills that can evolve and adapt to new situations. You need to be able to interpret and make decisions based on numerical information, and to find ways to solve problems that arise in real life, not just in textbooks.

Your trek will not be easy, but you will not be alone in your travels. Your teacher will serve as a guide. You and your classmates will make many discoveries together as you explore new mathematical ideas. In many cases you will be asked to work with other students in a small group. Talk about mathematics with your fellow group members, sharing your ideas and learning from and with each other.

Your graphing calculator will be the tool that enables you to explore new ideas and answer questions that come up along the way. With the calculator you will be able to manipulate large amounts of data very quickly so that you can see the overall picture. Throughout the text you will be referred to Calculator Notes that will provide useful information for your specific calculator.

The text itself will be a guidebook, leading you to explore questions and giving you the opportunity to ponder. Read the book carefully, with paper, pencil, and calculator close at hand. Work through the examples and answer the questions that are asked along the way. Use the Glossary when you encounter a concept or term that you are unsure about. Perform the Investigations as you travel through the course, being careful when making measurements and collecting data. Keep your data and calculations neat and accurate so that your work will be easier and the concepts clearer in the long run. Though the problems in each Problem Set may be few in number, some will require lengthy answers and a great deal of thought. Don't give up. Make a solid attempt at each problem that is assigned. Sometimes you will need to fill in details later after discussing a problem in class or with your group.

Often you will see that concepts and problem situations you have encountered before reappear in slightly altered form. Remembering how you handled the challenges the first time will provide insight when you meet these concepts again. The Take Another Look sections following some Problem Sets provide extensions of work you have done previously. You will also encounter Projects along the way. The Projects provide you with the opportunity to explore concepts and extend your thinking in an open-ended and creative manner. The Geometer's Sketchpad Investigations allow you to explore algebraic concepts visually using a dynamic geometry software program on a computer.

Your notebook will serve as a record of your travels. In it you will record your notes, answers to questions in the text, and solutions for your homework problems.

You may also want to keep a journal of your personal impressions along the way. In many Problem Sets, you will find prompts to spark your journal writing. You can place some of your especially notable accomplishments in a portfolio, which will serve as a kind of photo album of the highlights of your trip. Collect pieces of work in your portfolio as you go, and refine the contents as you make progress on your journey.

From time to time, look back to reflect on where you have been. At the end of each chapter the Assessing What You've Learned section provides suggestions to help you to review your progress and prepare for what comes next. Read these suggestions, and apply them so that they help guide your journey.

We hope that your journey through *Advanced Algebra* will be a meaningful and rewarding experience. And now it is time to begin. Bon voyage!

Jerald Murdock
Ellen Kamischke
Eric Kamischke
Interlochen Arts Academy, Interlochen, Michigan

Introducing the Calculator

Students in this mathematics class are working in groups using technology to solve real-world problems. Graphing calculators and computers are tools that help them develop their mathematical power. They can model situations using real data and use their models to draw conclusions and make decisions. They can graph functions and see what happens when they transform the functions. Throughout the year they will develop a better understanding of how mathematics is useful in their own lives.

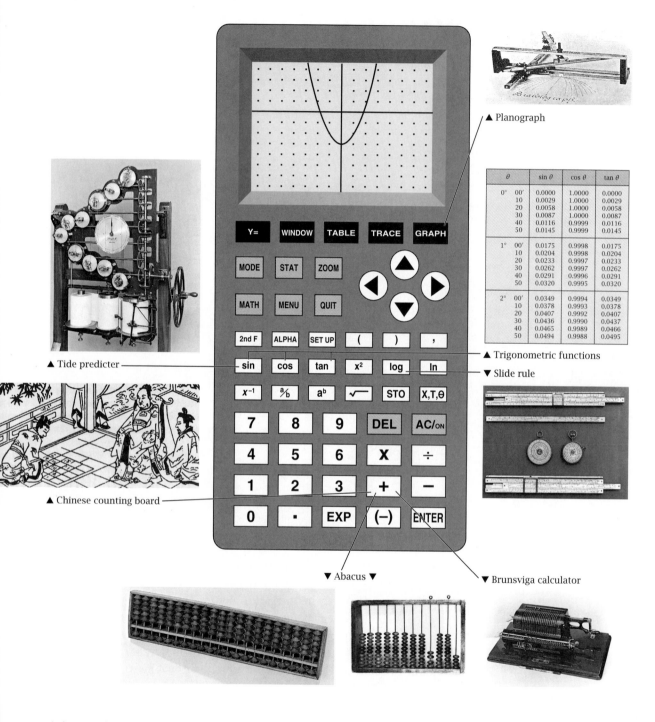

▲ Planograph

θ		$\sin \theta$	$\cos \theta$	$\tan \theta$
0°	00′	0.0000	1.0000	0.0000
	10	0.0029	1.0000	0.0029
	20	0.0058	1.0000	0.0058
	30	0.0087	1.0000	0.0087
	40	0.0116	0.9999	0.0116
	50	0.0145	0.9999	0.0145
1°	00′	0.0175	0.9998	0.0175
	10	0.0204	0.9998	0.0204
	20	0.0233	0.9997	0.0233
	30	0.0262	0.9997	0.0262
	40	0.0291	0.9996	0.0291
	50	0.0320	0.9995	0.0320
2°	00′	0.0349	0.9994	0.0349
	10	0.0378	0.9993	0.0378
	20	0.0407	0.9992	0.0407
	30	0.0436	0.9990	0.0437
	40	0.0465	0.9989	0.0466
	50	0.0494	0.9988	0.0495

▲ Tide predicter

▲ Trigonometric functions

▼ Slide rule

▲ Chinese counting board

▼ Abacus ▼

▼ Brunsviga calculator

The functions performed by a graphing calculator used to require many different machines.

Section 0.1

Using the Calculator for Basic Operations

What we have to learn to do, we learn by doing.
—*Aristotle*

If you were asked to evaluate the expression 4 + 6 – 2, you probably wouldn't reach for your calculator. Many times it is more efficient to use mental or pencil-and-paper calculations to solve a problem. Sometimes you need to decide whether or not to use your calculator. In addition, you must learn not to blindly trust answers that quickly appear on the calculator display. Take a moment to think about the answer, making sure it makes sense in the situation. As a calculator operator, you must know how to enter expressions and what the calculator is doing to the expressions.

How would you evaluate the expression 6 + 4 • 2? If your answer is 14, you are correct. If your answer is 20, you need to review the rules for order of operations. Enter this expression into your calculator to verify that it will give you an answer of 14. The order in which your calculator performs operations can be summarized by the following rules.

Rules for Order of Operations
1. Simplify expressions within parentheses or other grouping symbols.
2. Simplify exponents.
3. Multiply or divide in order from left to right.
4. Add or subtract in order from left to right.

Expressions such as $3n$, 2π, ^-x, and $\frac{2}{5}x$, or the use of parentheses, such as in the expression 4.5(13.864), indicate **implied multiplication.** Some graphing calculators evaluate implied multiplications *before* performing a multiplication or division indicated by an operation sign. Implied multiplication can cause some confusion if you are not careful about how you enter expressions. Experiment by evaluating several expressions that contain implied multiplications. Be sure to check how your calculator evaluates expressions like $\frac{2}{5}x$ and $\frac{1}{2}(2)$. Think about the order in which your calculator evaluates the operations.

The expression $(2 + 3)^2 + 3 \cdot 4^2$ does not contain any implied multiplications. Use the rules for order of operations to evaluate this expression. Then enter it into your calculator and confirm both your interpretation of the correct order of operations and your computed answer. Do you get 73? Do you understand the rules?

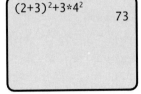

Symbols are an important part of any mathematics course. They are used to denote values, operations, and relationships. When reading a mathematics book, be sure you understand the symbols used. You will be introduced to many new symbols in this book. Some symbols will relate to mathematical concepts; others will be used to denote operations, keys on the graphing calculator, or both.

Many of the symbols used in mathematics have an interesting history, and symbols commonly used today have come from many different cultures. In 1706, William Jones, a mathematics teacher in England, gave the number π (pi) the name by which we know it today. However, this name did not become immediately popular. Some mathematicians had been using the symbol π to denote quantities other than the ratio of the circumference of a circle to its diameter, and for this ratio used instead p or P. Eventually, Jones's symbol became accepted. The determination of the value of π also has an interesting history; in fact, several books have been written on the subject. In about 1650 B.C., Egyptian scribe Ahmes showed that π equals approximately $4(8/9)^2$, or about 3.16049. In A.D. 264, Chinese mathematician Liu Hui showed that π equals approximately 3.14159. Today, some mathematicians and computer scientists are interested in finding ways to compute more and more digits for π. An approximate value for π is stored in your calculator. Can you figure out how to access that value?

Year	Name	Computer	Digits
1949	Reitwiesner	ENIAC	2,037
1954	Nicholson et al.	NORC	3,089
1958	Felton	Pegasus	10,000
1958	Genuys	IBM704	10,000
1959	Unpublished	IBM704	16,167
1961	Shanks, Wrench	IBM7090	100,000
1973	Guilloud, Bouyer	CDC7600	1,000,000
1983	Kanada et al.	Hitachi S-810	16,000,000
1985	Gosper	Symbolics	17,000,000
1986	Bailey	Cray2	29,300,000
1987	Kanada	SX 2	134,000,000
1989	Kanada	HITAC S-820/80	1,073,740,000

Records for calculating the approximate value of π with a computer

Example 1

How do you evaluate $3(2 + 7\pi)$?

NOTE
0A

Solution

First multiply 7 and π (implied). Then add 2 to the product. Finally, multiply by 3 (also implied) to get 71.97344573 . . . . (If your answer is a rounded approximation or looks very different from the answer given here, check **Calculator Note 0A** for settings.) ■

```
3(2+7π)
            71.97344573
```

Example 2

How do you enter $\frac{27 + 39}{4}$ into your calculator to evaluate the expression correctly?

Solution

If you enter $(27 + 39)/4$, you will get the correct answer, 16.5. The fraction bar is a type of grouping symbol. Any operations within the numerator and the denominator must be performed before the division indicated by a fraction bar. ■

```
(27+39)/4
                    16.5
```

■ Example 3

How do you enter $\dfrac{3 + 7^2}{5}(12)$ into the calculator to evaluate the expression correctly?

Solution

NOTE

0B

First enter parentheses around the numerator of the fraction to indicate that it will be divided by 5. Here are two ways to get the correct answer, 124.8. (See **Calculator Note 0B** if you're not sure how to square a number.)

```
(3+7²)/5*12
            124.8
((3+7²)/5)(12)
            124.8
(3+7²)/5(12)
      .8666666667
```

Method 1: Use a multiplication symbol in front of the 12.

   $(3 + 7^2)/5 \cdot 12$

Method 2: Add another layer of parentheses around the entire fraction.

   $((3 + 7^2)/5)(12)$

Perhaps you can find another approach to get the same answer. What is wrong with entering the expression as $(3 + 7^2)/5(12)$? Why doesn't this entry work? ■

The equal sign (=) is probably the most common symbol used in mathematics. In 1557, Welsh physician and mathematician Robert Recorde was the first to use twin lines for the word *equals*. He chose this symbol because ". . . noe .2. thynges, can be moare equalle."

■ Example 4

Evaluate $2L + 2W$ for the given values.
a. $L = 7$, $W = 11$ **b.** $L = 23$, $W = 8$

Solution

NOTE

0B

You can use your calculator's replay (or last-entry) key when you evaluate variable expressions for several different sets of values. This key is helpful because it reprints the previous entry on the screen. (See **Calculator Note 0B**.) Then you can edit the expression by typing over, inserting, or deleting.

Enter the expression, using the first set of values for L and W. Enter $2 \cdot 7 + 2 \cdot 11$ to get 36, the correct answer. To evaluate part b, use the replay key and the arrows to position the cursor on top of the 7. Different combinations of typing over, inserting, and deleting will produce $2 \cdot 23 + 2 \cdot 8$, which will give the answer, 62. ■

```
2*7+2*11
            36
2*23+2*8
            62
```

Using the replay, insert, and delete procedures in this example may seem like more trouble than it's worth. However, these edit functions are extremely helpful with more complicated expressions.

■ **Example 5**

Evaluate $17^2 - 4^3 + 2^5$.

NOTE
0B

Solution

You can enter expressions like this just as they are written. Exponents are entered in two ways: by using special keys for squaring and cubing, or by using keys that allow you to enter any exponent. (See **Calculator Note 0B** for specific instructions.) Be careful to use the *subtract* key rather than the *negative* key (–). ■

$$17^2{-}4^3{+}2{\wedge}5$$
$$257$$

The concepts of positive and negative numbers, and the rules for calculating their sums and differences, were introduced in the Chinese *Nine Chapters on the Mathematical Art*, written around the first century A.D. Rules for multiplying and dividing positive and negative numbers appeared in China around the thirteenth century. In Investigation 0.1.1 you will apply these rules as you practice entering expressions into your calculator.

Investigation 0.1.1

Cross-Number Puzzle

Complete the following cross-number puzzle. Each digit, decimal point, and negative sign will occupy an individual square. Round all answers to the nearest hundredth. If your answer does not fit the squares provided, check your calculation entry and use of parentheses. Learn from your mistakes by working with others in your group, reentering, editing, and discussing what you might have done incorrectly.

Across

1. $12 + 11 \cdot 10$

5. $6543(132 + 329)$

8. $\sqrt{765^2 + 1836^2}$

9. $\left(\frac{1}{2}\right)^4 + 3.7^3$

10. $\dfrac{(3.6 \cdot 10^6)(2.8 \cdot 10^{10})}{2.4 \cdot 10^{12}}$

11. $6\sqrt{11} + \sqrt[3]{4.4} - 1.83^5$

Down

1. $\dfrac{12 + 3}{7 + 5}$

2. $\dfrac{463}{94} \cdot 47$

3. -320^2

4. $-\sqrt{500(17852 + 1993)}$

6. $\sqrt{337 + 504}$

7. $\dfrac{9710}{15(17)}$

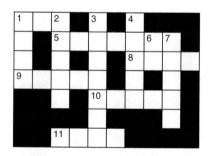

You may be challenged by Investigation 0.1.2 because it is not a five-minutes-or-less type of problem. One objective of this investigation is to give you an opportunity to work with a group in solving a problem. You will participate in many group investigations throughout this course. When working with a group, try a variety of problem-solving approaches. Brainstorm to generate ideas. Try not to make quick judgments. Consider any proposed strategy or solution, asking a group member to explain his or her ideas if someone in the group doesn't understand them. Be sure that each group member can verify whether or not a strategy or proposed solution works.

In this investigation, and throughout this course, each group member has the following responsibilities.

1. Be cooperative and considerate. Never make fun of another person's ideas. Your group will make better progress if members feel free to suggest ideas without worrying about whether others will think they are silly.

2. Listen carefully, without interrupting, while another is talking.

3. Ask questions of others and ask others for help when help is needed. If the group is stuck and can't move on, decide as a group to ask for suggestions or help from your teacher.

4. Help others in your group when asked.

5. Work on a problem until every group member understands it and is ready to describe the solution to the class.

Investigation 0.1.2

Camel Crossing the Desert

A camel is sitting by a stack of 3000 bananas at the edge of a 1000-mile-wide desert. He is going to travel across the desert, carrying as many bananas as he can to the other side. He can carry up to 1000 bananas at any given time, but he eats one banana at every mile. What is the maximum number of bananas the camel can transport across the desert? How does he do it? Be prepared to present your solution to the class. (Hint: The camel doesn't have to go all the way across the desert in one trip.)

Problem Set 0.1

1. Use your calculator to evaluate each expression.

   a. $\sqrt{7^2 + 8^2}$

   b. $\dfrac{2(18 - 2) + 7}{14 + 2 \cdot 3}$

   c. $\sqrt{12(32 + 43)}$

   d. $\pi \cdot \dfrac{1}{2} \cdot 12.6^2$

2. **a.** Evaluate $(^-4)^2$ and $^-4^2$ on your calculator. Compare your answers and explain why they are (or are not) different.

   b. French mathematician and philosopher René Descartes (1596–1650) was the first mathematician to use the notation x^2 to indicate the squaring of a variable. Evaluate the expression x^2 for $x = 17$. Write what you entered into the calculator. What is the answer?

   c. Evaluate the expression $^-x^2$ for $x = 24$. Write what you entered into the calculator. What is the answer?

NOTE

0B

   d. Your calculator can store values for variables. Use this calculator feature to evaluate x^2 and $^-x^2$ for $x = 17$. (See **Calculator Note 0B** for specific instructions.)

3. **a.** For each expression, try to compute the answer in your head.

   i. $2 + \dfrac{3 - \sqrt{169 - 2^3(6)}}{2}$

   ii. $\dfrac{2 + \dfrac{11 - \sqrt{25}}{3}}{\sqrt{6^3 - 20} - \dfrac{18}{2}}$

   b. Write a step-by-step solution showing how to compute each answer without a calculator.

   Example

   $3(2 - 5(4 + 1))^2$

   Solution

   $3(2 - 5(5))^2$
   $3(2 - 25)^2$
   $3(^-23)^2$
   $3(529)$
   1587

   c. Finally, calculate each answer by entering the expression into your calculator.

   d. Write a note to a friend who is absent today that describes each step needed to evaluate expressions like these mentally, with a pencil and paper, and with the calculator. Which method is easiest? Which is most reliable? If there is a combination of methods that makes the evaluation process easier and less susceptible to errors, outline it for your friend.

4. Substitute the given values into each formula and evaluate. If you know what the formula represents, indicate this with your solution.

a. $\frac{1}{2}bh$

  i. $b = 12.3$, $h = 43.7$

  ii. $b = 0.548$, $h = 6.21$

  iii. $b = 4.7$, $h = 2.91$

b. $^-16t^2 + vt + s$

  i. $v = 75$, $t = 3.6$, $s = 24.75$

  ii. $v = 242.8$, $t = 7.72$, $s = 438$

  iii. $v = 28.4$, $t = 2.6$, $s = 47$

c. $\frac{y_2 - y_1}{x_2 - x_1}$

  i. $x_1 = 7$, $y_1 = ^-5.3$, $x_2 = ^-7$, $y_2 = 11.8$

  ii. $x_1 = 12$, $y_1 = 3.9$, $x_2 = 12$, $y_2 = 7.1$

  iii. $x_1 = 4.7$, $y_1 = 2.8$, $x_2 = ^-1.2$, $y_2 = 6$

5. Insert operation signs, parentheses, or both into each string of numbers to create an expression equal to the given answer. You may use the digits as exponents if you desire. Keep the numbers in the same order as they are given. Write an explanation of your answer, including information such as which operation you performed first and which you performed next.

Example

   3 2 5 7 = 18

Solution

   $(3 + 2)(5) - 7 = 18$

First add 3 and 2. Then multiply this sum by 5. Finally, subtract 7.

a. 5 3 8 4 = 16

b. 7 5 3 4 = 602

c. 1 2 3 4 = 28

d. 7 3 2 9 = 18

e. 15 3 7 12 = 30

6. a. Enter a decimal point followed by at least fourteen 4's: 0.44444444444444 (ENTER). What shows on your calculator display? What does this mean?

b. Count the number of digits displayed on your calculator. Call this number n. Enter a decimal point followed by n 4's and several 6's. Press (ENTER). What does your calculator display? What does this mean?

c. Start over again and enter a decimal point followed by n 4's and at least eight 6's. Multiply this number by 10 and subtract the number in front of the decimal. Repeat the procedure in parentheses until you can determine how many digits of a number your calculator actually stores. You can also use this method to *recover* digits of a number that are not displayed on the screen.

Section 0.2

Fractions, Decimal Numbers, and Scientific Notation

We don't know a millionth of one percent about anything.
—Thomas Alva Edison

"Two-thirds of my third-hour class are women."

"One square foot is $\frac{1}{9}$ of one square yard."

"Fifty minutes is $\frac{5}{6}$ of an hour."

"The probability of two consecutive boys being born into a family is about $\frac{1}{4}$."

These are just a few examples of how fractions and ratios are commonly used in the real world. However, the answers your calculator displays will almost always be in decimal form. In this section, you will review how to change fractions to decimal form and vice versa. You will also learn about scientific notation, a special way to express very large and very small numbers efficiently.

■ ### Example 1

a. Convert $\frac{5}{16}$ to decimal form.

b. Convert 42 min to part of 1 hr.

c. What part of a foot is 3 in.?

d. Which is the better deal: a 1 lb tube of cheese for $4.25 or a 10 oz tube of the same product for $2.85?

Solution

a. Because a fraction bar is actually a division sign, divide the numerator by the denominator. Thus $5 \div 16$, or $5/16$, gives 0.3125.

b. Because 1 hr consists of 60 min, enter $42 \div 60$, or $42/60$, to get 0.7 hr.

c. Because 1 ft consists of 12 in., enter $3/12$ to get 0.25 ft.

d. Because 1 lb consists of 16 oz, the unit price for the 1 lb container is $0.266 per ounce; the unit price for the 10 oz container is $0.285 per ounce. ■

```
5/16
                 .3125
42/60
                   .7
3/12
                  .25
```

```
4.25/16
               .265625
2.85/10
                  .285
```

Here are two methods you can use when working with mixed numbers: Convert the mixed number to an improper fraction, then divide; or split the mixed number into an addition problem and a division problem.

■ **Example 2**

    a. Convert $3\frac{8}{25}$ to decimal form.

    b. Convert 2 hr 24 min to hours.

    c. Convert 20 ft 9 in. to feet.

    d. Convert the latitude 16°51′ to an equivalent latitude in decimal degrees.

Solution

    a. First convert the mixed number to $\frac{83}{25}$. Then divide to get 3.32. Alternatively, enter 3 + 8/25 to get 3.32.

    b. 2 hr and 24 min = 2 hr + $\frac{24}{60}$ hr = 2.4 hr

    c. 20 ft and 9 in. = 20 ft + $\frac{9}{12}$ ft = 20.75 ft

    d. $16° + \left(\frac{51}{60}\right)° = 16.85°$ ■

In Example 3, you will convert each number from its decimal form (without repeating digits) to its fractional equivalent. In Investigation 0.2.1, you will discover some techniques to use on decimal numbers with repeating digits.

■ **Example 3**

    a. Convert 0.275 to a fraction.   **b.** Convert 12.125 to a fraction.

Solution

    a. The number 0.275 can also be read as 275 thousandths, so it can be written as $\frac{275}{1000}$. The simplified form of the answer is $\frac{11}{40}$. To verify that these fractions do indeed have the same value, enter 11 ÷ 40 and you will see 0.275. Fractions can also be simplified by dividing the numerator and the denominator by the same number, though you will not often be required to do so in this course.

NOTE

0B

    b. The number 12.125 is equivalent to 12 + 0.125 or
$$12 + \frac{125}{1000} = 12\frac{1}{8} \text{ or } \frac{97}{8}.$$
(See **Calculator Note 0B**; your calculator may have a fraction key.) ■

```
                        12.125
12+125/1000
                        12.125
12+1/8
                        12.125
Ans▸Frac
                          97/8
```

Investigation 0.2.1

Fractions and Decimal Numbers

Though Babylonian and Chinese scholars used decimal fractions, Islamic mathematicians were the first to use a symbol to indicate a decimal fraction. This symbol first appeared in *The Book of Chapters on Indian Arithmetic*, written by Abul Hassan al-Uqlidisi in Damascus, A.D. 952 or 953.

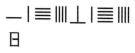

This number, written using Chinese rod numeral notation, is 1.1446154 days. The symbol for days is placed under the digit representing units.

Every fraction can be written in an equivalent decimal form. In some cases, the digits at the end of the number will terminate; in others, a digit or group of digits will begin repeating. (The digits may start repeating near the end of your display. If you are not certain whether or not there is a repeat, try recovering some digits by using the process described in Problem 6 of Section 0.1.)

Part 1 Make up a list of fractions that includes, but is not limited to, those below. Rewrite each in decimal form. If the digits do not appear to end, indicate the repeating unit by placing a bar over those digits that repeat.

$$\left\{ \frac{1}{2}, \frac{7}{16}, \frac{11}{125}, \frac{7}{15}, \frac{8}{31}, \frac{8}{21}, \frac{9}{22}, \frac{11}{30}, \frac{7}{20}, \cdots \right\}$$

a. List the denominators of all fractions that convert to terminating decimal numbers (numbers without a repeating unit).

b. List the denominators of all fractions that convert to decimal numbers with repeating digits.

c. Look at the lists of denominators in a and b above. Describe how you can predict whether a fraction will convert to a decimal number with digits that terminate or with digits that repeat.

Part 2 Use your calculator to convert each number written in decimal form to its fractional equivalent.

a. Multiply each answer from Part 1a by its original denominator. What happens? (If the original decimal number has repeating digits, enter the repeating unit enough times to fill at least 13 decimal places.)

b. This product, $0.\overline{12} \cdot 33$, equals 4. Therefore what fraction equals $0.\overline{12}$?

c. Convert each number to fractional form. (This may require some exploration, using guess-and-check.)

i. $0.\overline{18}$ ii. $1.\overline{72}$ iii. $0.3\overline{571428}$

If you evaluate 345^4, your calculator may display 1.416695063E10, which is in **scientific notation**, and means $1.416695063 \cdot 10^{10}$. It is a rounded-off scientific notation version of the exact answer, 14,166,950,625, a number that has too many digits for most calculator screen displays.

Your calculator moved the decimal point in 14,166,950,625 ten places to the left between the first two digits of the number. This means that the calculator divided the number by 10^{10}. Your calculator will round off the decimal number so that it is short enough to fit your calculator's display screen. A number in scientific notation will always have one nonzero digit to the left of the decimal point.

```
345^4
   1.416695063E10
```

Scientific Notation

Any number written as a number between 1 and 10, multiplied by a power of 10, is said to be in **scientific notation**.

$$25{,}432 = 2.5432 \cdot 10^4$$

$\qquad\qquad$ a number $\quad$ a
$\qquad\qquad$ between $\;$ power
$\qquad\qquad$ 1 and 10 $\;$ of 10

$$0.0039 = 3.9 \cdot 10^{-3}$$

The mass of a hydrogen atom is greater than the mass of an electron. However, both masses are tiny!

The mass of a hydrogen atom is 0.00000000000000000000000017 grams (g).
The mass of an electron is 0.00000000000000000000000000091 grams (g).

Enter the first number above into your calculator, press (ENTER), and you will get the number in scientific notation form. Now find the scientific notation form of the second number above. Can you explain the meaning of the numbers indicated on your calculator?

```
.000000000000000
0000000017
               1.7E-24
.000000000000000
00000000000091
               9.1E-28
```

To change a number from normal (decimal) form to scientific notation, you must determine how far and in what direction to move the decimal point so that there is exactly one nonzero digit to its left. Make a connection between how far and in what direction the decimal point moves and the effect of multiplying by a positive or negative power of ten.

■ Example 4

Write each number in scientific notation.
a. 6,240,000   **b.** 0.004 819

Solution

Refer to **Calculator Note 0C**.
a. $6.24 \cdot 10^6$ **b.** $4.819 \cdot 10^{-3}$ ■

NOTE
0C

Problem Set 0.2

1. Substitute each set of values into the formula and evaluate. Give your answer in scientific notation.

   a. $L \sqrt{1 - \dfrac{v^2}{c^2}}$ i. $L = 12{,}345{,}678$; $v = 5{,}000{,}000$; $c = 300{,}000{,}000$

                          ii. $L = 1$; $v = 299{,}999{,}999$; $c = 300{,}000{,}000$

   b. $\dfrac{eVL}{c}$ i. $e = 1.6 \cdot 10^{-19}$; $V = 40{,}000$; $L = 3.11 \cdot 10^{-11}$; $c = 3 \cdot 10^8$

                          ii. $e = 1.6 \cdot 10^{-19}$; $V = 75{,}000$; $L = 2.79 \cdot 10^{-11}$; $c = 3 \cdot 10^8$

2. Convert each expression to normal (decimal) form.

   a. $3.47895 \cdot 10^8$ **b.** $8.247 \cdot 10^{-12}$ **c.** $\dfrac{(7.952 \cdot 10^{15})(2.5 \cdot 10^{-3})}{(1.42 \cdot 10^8)}$

3. Write a clear but thorough explanation (for a friend who is about to take a quiz) of how to determine when the scientific notation exponent should be positive or negative.

4. The average human brain contains about 8 billion neurons. There are about 250 million people in the United States. About how many total neurons do all these people have?

5. You and eight friends have just ordered Lotza Pizza, the biggest pizza available, and are deciding how to divide it up. Frak Shenwize proposes the following scheme: She will take $\frac{1}{9}$ of the pizza, the next person will take $\frac{1}{8}$ of the remaining pizza, the next will take $\frac{1}{7}$ of the remainder, and so on.

   a. Describe the fairness of this proposal.
   b. How much of the pizza will you get if you are the last one to select?

6. a. Some of your friends claim to have bicycled across the state of Michigan—from Lake Michigan to Lake Erie—at an average speed of 60 ft/sec. Is this possible? Justify your answer. (1 mi = 5280 ft)

b. A Detroit Tiger game announcer recently claimed that an average baseball player could run the bases in 10 sec. Was he right? Justify your answer.

c. The scale on the map of India is listed as 65 km to a centimeter.

    i. Give a quick approximation or estimate for the distance between two cities that are 3.9 cm apart on the map.

    ii. Calculate the actual distance.

    iii. Find the error between the actual distance and your predicted distance.

7. One day it rained 0.1 in., and Harve Ester decided to find out how much water fell on his farmland, which measures 1 sq mi.

a. How many pounds of water fell on his farm? (Water weighs 62.4 lb/ft^3, and 1 ft = 12 in.)

b. If it rains to the depth of one inch, will the water weigh ten times as much as that in 7a? Write a few sentences that describe why or why not.

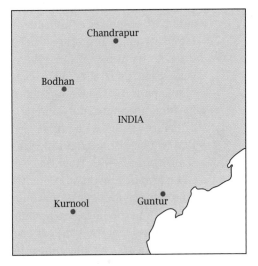

8. Which has the greater mass, the hydrogen atom or the electron? How many times greater? (Find the information needed to solve this problem in this section.)

9. What are the advantages of working in groups in your mathematics class? What are the disadvantages? Completely explain your answers.

Section 0.3

Using the Graphing Calculator

A whole essay might be written on the danger of thinking without images.
—*Samuel Taylor Coleridge*

It is said that a picture is worth a thousand words. The next time you look at a newspaper, a magazine, or a book, remind yourself of the importance of *visual images* in the real world. Throughout this course, you will use graphs to communicate information because a graph can quickly summarize numerical information. As you become more familiar with your graphing calculator, it will allow you to discover patterns, explore relationships, find particular values, and generalize. This technology will enhance your mathematical visualization and provide more depth and meaning to your understanding.

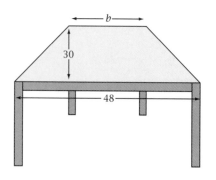

NOTE

0D

Before displaying a graph, set the range of values that will be displayed on the graph. This is similar to figuring out how to label the axes on graph paper when graphing by hand. Determine the lowest (minimum) and highest (maximum) values you want to see on both the horizontal (*x*) and vertical (*y*) axes. You can control the scale for each axis, or at what intervals marks should appear on each axis. This is similar to determining how many units are represented by one square on a piece of graph paper. (See **Calculator Note 0D** for details about your particular graphing calculator.)

■ Example 1

Teacher Fay Silitator is designing tables for her classroom. She wants to use trapezoid-shaped tabletops so that the longer base length is 48 in. and the table width is 30 in. If the shorter base is to be less than 48 in., find a graphing window that displays the relationship between the possible values for the shorter base and the resulting area of the tabletop.

Solution

Recall that the formula for finding the area of a trapezoid is $\frac{1}{2}h(b_1 + b_2)$, where h is the height and b_1 and b_2

represent the lengths of the bases. Because your graphing calculator generally accepts equations in the form "*y* equals an expression involving *x*," rewrite the equation as $y = 0.5(30)(48 + x) = 15(48 + x)$.

Because *x* represents the length of the second base, *x* can be a value between 0 and 48. Set the minimum value of *x* (Xmin) to 0 and the maximum value of *x* (Xmax) to 48. This means your calculator will graph (*base, area*) values so that $0 \le base \le 48$. Set the scale for *x* (Xscl) at 2 to provide 24 tick marks. This means the first mark represents 2, the next 4, the next 6, and so on. An Xscl of 1 would produce 48 very crowded tick marks along the axis.

The *y*-axis represents the area. You can get an idea of a good range for this axis by testing several values for the base (*x*) of the trapezoid. The table below shows several pairs of (*base, area*) values. Remember, the *y*-values represent area values. (See **Calculator Note 0D** to see if your graphing calculator has a table function.)

NOTE
0D

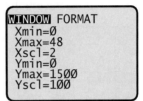

As you look at the table values, you might decide to set the minimum value of *y* (Ymin) at 0—because area can't be negative—and the maximum value of *y* (Ymax) at 1500. Appropriate marks on this axis could be made in increments of 100, so set the scale for *y* (Yscl) at 100. Enter this information and graph the equation to produce a picture like that provided here.

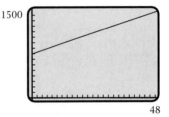

There are other **graphing windows** (Xmin, Xmax, Ymin, and Ymax) that would also work. In Problem Set 0.3, you will practice finding appropriate graphing windows and you'll see how different windows can change the way a graph looks. ∎

NOTE
0E

The distance between any point on a line and the point at 0 is a nonnegative number. If *x* is the coordinate of a point on a number line, the distance from that point to the origin is called the **absolute value** of *x*, written |*x*|. Because distances are always represented by nonnegative numbers, |*x*| is nonnegative. You will explore this function in more detail in Chapter 5. (See **Calculator Note 0E.**)

∎ **Example 2**

Find the distance on a number line between the point at *x* and the point at 0 if

a. $x = 6$

b. $x = {}^-4$

Solution

a. If x is 6, then the distance from x to 0 is 6 units, so $|6| = 6$.

b. If x is $^-4$, the distance from x to 0 is 4 units, so $|^-4| = 4$.

The set of ordered pairs (x, y) that satisfy the equation $y = |x|$ generalize the information pictured on the number lines above. Enter the equation and interpret the meaning of either the table or graph pictured. What is the meaning of $x = ^-1.8$ and $y = 1.8$ as pictured on the graph?

X	Y1
⁻3	3
⁻2	2
⁻1	1
0	0
1	1
2	2
3	3

Y1■abs (X)

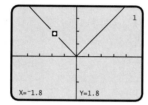

X=⁻1.8   Y=1.8

```
WINDOW FORMAT
Xmin=⁻4.7
Xmax=4.7
Xscl=1
Ymin=⁻3.1
Ymax=3.1
Yscl=1
```

Problem Set 0.3

1. For each set of points, determine values for Xmin, Xmax, Ymin, and Ymax to find an appropriate graphing window for displaying the points.
  a. $(3, 17)$, $(^-2, 21)$, $(2, 12)$ **b.** $(1, 12)$, $(4, 3)$, $(3, ^-4)$

2. Dr. Frank Stein, a famous scientist, is studying the growth of the bacteria *Mathematicus headachus*. He finds that the population of his test-tube bacteria is given by the equation $P = 20 \cdot 1.5^h$, where h is the number of hours since he started the experiment. You can see the growth in the bacteria population over the first 12 hr by setting the Xmin to 0 and the Xmax to 12. Use the settings for Ymin and Ymax given below and record a sketch of each graph.

  a. Ymin = 0, Ymax = 2500, Yscl = 500
  b. Ymin = 0, Ymax = 1500, Yscl = 100
  c. Ymin = 0, Ymax = 500, Yscl = 50
  d. Ymin = 0, Ymax = 125, Yscl = 25
  e. Which of the graphing windows in 2a–d gives the *best* picture of how the bacteria grows? Why?

3. On one midsummer day in Mathtropolis, the temperature over the 12 hr period from 8 a.m. to 8 p.m. varied according to the equation $t = -0.91h^2 + 10h + 65$, where t is the temperature and h is the number of hours after 8 a.m. Set Xmin at 0, Xmax at 12, and Xscl at 1. Use the settings for Ymin and Ymax given below and record a sketch of each graph.

   a. Ymin = 0, Ymax = 80, Yscl = 10
   b. Ymin = 0, Ymax = 160, Yscl = 20
   c. Ymin = 50, Ymax = 100, Yscl = 10
   d. Which of the graphing windows you saw in 3a–c gives the *best* picture of the temperature variance? Why?

4. Find appropriate values for Ymin and Ymax for each equation. In each case, use Xmin = -10, Xmax = 10, and Xscl = 1. Sketch each graph and label the graphing window. Describe why you selected your particular Ymin and Ymax values.

   a. $y = 3x + 5$ **b.** $y = 3x^2 + 5$ **c.** $y = 3|x - 4|$

5. Substitute each set of values into the formula and evaluate.

   a. $\dfrac{2v + at}{2}$ i. $a = -16$, $t = 1.2$, $v = 24$
                         ii. $a = -16$, $t = 0.28$, $v = 36$

   b. $0.2768|f - i|$ i. $f = 3.468$, $i = 3.457$
                         ii. $f = 4.781 \cdot 10^{-4}$, $i = 4.657 \cdot 10^{-4}$

6. Find values for Xmin, Xmax, Ymin, and Ymax that will position this star in the center of the graphing window. You do not need to draw this graph on your calculator.

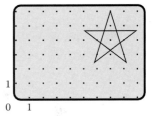

7. Describe a problem that you think is easier to solve with a graphing calculator than with a simpler calculator. Be clear *why* it is easier with the graphing calculator.

8. Describe a problem that some people might *think* requires the graphing calculator to solve but that is actually just as easy to solve with a pencil and paper or with a simpler calculator.

Assessing What You've Learned—Organizing Your Notebook

An essential part of learning is being able to show yourself and others that you understand the concepts you've encountered and that you can do what you were expected to do. The ability to assess your own work is a very valuable skill and isn't limited to what your teacher sees or what makes up your grade. This assessment doesn't come only at the end of a chapter or in the form of tests and quizzes. Every problem you work, every investigation you perform, and every project or exercise you complete gives you a chance to demonstrate to somebody—yourself, at least—that you're learning.

At the end of each chapter in this text, you will find ideas that you can use to help you determine just how well you have understood the material in the chapter.

Sometimes there will be suggestions of things you can put into your portfolio. There may be suggestions for journal entries. You may be asked to organize your notebook. All of the suggested assessment methods will allow you to become more aware of your own learning and understanding in this course.

Organize your notebook so that it will be useful to you. In this course you will be completing investigations, groupwork, homework assignments, and projects. You may want to devote a notebook section to each of these classifications.

You will encounter many new calculator techniques as you progress through this text. Your calculator notes explain some of these techniques, your teacher or classmates may introduce you to a new technique, and you may even discover one yourself. You have probably already learned some new calculator techniques and "tricks" in this chapter. Devote a section of your notebook to calculator methods. Whenever you encounter a new technique or an approach that may differ from one in the textbook, record it in this section of your notebook.

Patterns and Recursion

You have to look closely at this daisy-like pattern to see that it is actually made up of boats docked at a marina. Sometimes you have to look closely at a sequence of numbers, letters, or geometric figures to determine the pattern. Often patterns or sequences can be generated using a recursive definition. Your calculator can generate recursively defined sequences very quickly.

Section 1.1

Recursively Defined Sequences

The mathematical sciences particularly exhibit order, symmetry, and limitation; and these are the greatest forms of the beautiful.
—*Aristotle*

Look around! You are surrounded by patterns and influenced by how you perceive them. You probably recognize visual patterns in tree leaves, flower petals, floor tiles, and windowpanes. In every discipline, people discover, observe, re-create, explain, generalize, and use patterns that are attractive, practical, or predictable. When studying mathematics, you encounter patterns in numbers and shapes. Just as artists, architects, and scientists keep an open dialogue with the natural world, you too can make discoveries and provide appropriate explanations by being alert and observant. Learning about recursively defined sequences will help you visualize and understand some mathematical patterns.

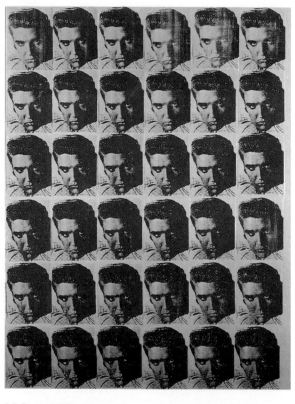

Rózsa Péter (1905–1977) was a leading contributor to the theory of recursion and the first person to propose the study of recursion in its own right. In 1927 she graduated from Eötvös Loránd University in Budapest, and by the 1930s she was a world-famous logician. She was concerned about mathematics education as well as pure mathematics and wrote textbooks in addition to research articles. Her interest in communicating mathematics to nonmathematicians led her to write *Playing with Infinity: Mathematical Explorations and Excursions,* which has been translated into 14 languages. Her mathematical research culminated with her book *Recursive Functions in Computer Theory,* which describes the connections between recursive functions and computer languages. In an interview, she described recursion as follows:

Rózsa Péter

The Latin technical term "recursion" refers to a certain kind of *stepping backwards* in the sequence of natural numbers, which necessarily ends after a finite number of steps. With the use of such recursions the values of even the most complicated functions used in number theory can be calculated in a finite number of steps. The emphasis is on the *finite* number of steps.

■ Example 1

Draw or build the figures pictured below. Make some observations about a pattern suggested by the figures, and continue the pattern.

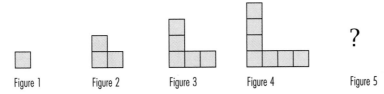

Figure 1 Figure 2 Figure 3 Figure 4 Figure 5

Solution

a. One observation you can make is that each figure is formed by adding two squares to the previous figure. So, the number of squares in Figure 3 is *two* more than the number of squares in Figure 2. This same pattern describes the connection between Figure 1 and Figure 2, as well as that between Figure 3 and Figure 4.

You can organize the information like this:

Figure 2 = Figure 1 + *two* squares.
Figure 3 = Figure 2 + *two* squares.
Figure 4 = Figure 3 + *two* squares.

If you assume that the same pattern continues, then

Figure 10 = Figure 9 + *two* squares.

In general, the pattern is

Figure n = Figure $(n - 1)$ + *two* squares.

The figures are a visual representation of the sequence 1, 3, 5, 7, 9, ... A **sequence** is an ordered list. The tenth term of this sequence, u_{10} (pronounced *u sub ten,* or *the tenth term*), can be compared to the preceding term, u_9, by writing $u_{10} = u_9 + 2$. The nth term, u_n, is called the **general term** of the sequence.

b. You can observe another pattern by looking at the outer perimeter of each figure. The perimeter of Figure 1 is 4. Each time you add a square to the figure, you increase the perimeter by 2. Because you're adding two squares each time, the perimeter increases by 4. So, the perimeter of Figure 2 is that of Figure 1 plus 4, the perimeter of Figure 3 is that of Figure 2 plus 4. In general, the perimeter of Figure n equals the perimeter of the previous figure (Figure $(n - 1)$) plus 4. This means that if n equals 7, the perimeter of Figure 7 equals 4 plus the perimeter of Figure 6. The first few terms of the perimeter sequence are 4, 8, 12, 16, 20, 24, ...

Recursive Definition for a Sequence

A **recursive definition** for a sequence is a set of statements that specifies one or more initial terms and defines the nth term, u_n, in relation to one or more of the preceding terms.

For this perimeter example, $u_1 = 4$ and $u_n = u_{(n-1)} + 4$. This means *the first term is four* and *each subsequent term is equal to the preceding term plus four.* Notice that each new perimeter is described in terms of the previous perimeter. (The notation $u_{(n-1)}$ refers to the preceding term. *It does not mean one less than the term.*)

c. Now consider the total number of segments used to build the shapes. This table display of the sequence is partially completed.

Figure	1	2	3	4	5	...	12	...	32	...	n
Segments	4	10	16	22	–?–	...	–?–	...	–?–	...	–?–

This sequence also appears to be of the form $u_n = u_{(n-1)} + d$, where d is a constant. The constant difference between successive terms is 6. Do you see where the 6 comes from in the table and in the figures? This means each term is six more than the preceding term. Therefore, the sequence representing the total number of segments needed for each figure above is described recursively as $u_1 = 4$, and thereafter as $u_n = u_{(n-1)} + 6$. ∎

Arithmetic Sequence

An **arithmetic sequence** is a sequence in which each term is equal to the preceding term plus a constant. This constant is called the **common difference**.

Arithmetic sequences are of the form $u_n = u_{(n-1)} + d$, where d is a constant. Another way to think of this is that each *answer = preceding answer + d.* Your calculator has an (ENTER) key or an (EXECUTE) key. Each time you press this key, the calculator computes or executes the last command. Your calculator also has a *last answer function.* (In this text, this function is referred to as **Ans,** although it may be different on your calculator.) The purpose of this function is to allow you to use your last answer in the next calculation without retyping the number. In fact, pressing + at the beginning of a line has the effect of entering Ans +. This applies to other operation keys as well.

Using the (ENTER) key and an operation, you can create a recursive routine.

4 (ENTER)	This establishes, or seeds, the first Ans.
Ans + 6 (ENTER)	This calculates the second term and makes it the Ans.
(ENTER)	This establishes the third term as the Ans.
(ENTER)	
and so on.	

Investigation 1.1.1

Shifting Funds

Carlotta "Lotta" Doe has $2,000 in a savings account, while Les Cache has only $470 in his account. Criminal Hollie Hacker gains access to the bank's computer and begins to shift funds around. On the first night, she creates a new account for herself. She takes $50 from Carlotta's account, puts $40 into Les's account, and the remaining $10 is shifted into her own account. Each night after that, she makes the same monetary shifts.

Using your calculators, have one group member model what happens to the balance in Carlotta's account, one group member model Les's account, and another group member model Hollie's account. The fourth group member acts as a recorder, keeping track of how much money is in each account after each night's transactions. Look at your results and answer the following questions.

How many nights did Hollie work until Les had more money than Carlotta?

Hollie was arrested the night that Les's balance first became more than twice Carlotta's balance. How much was in Hollie's account the night she was arrested?

In Example 1 you saw how a recursive sequence can be used to answer questions about a geometric model. In Investigation 1.1.1 you explored how you can solve a problem numerically using recursion. The sequences in Example 1 and Investigation 1.1.1 were both arithmetic sequences. Example 2 further explores the relationship between a geometric model and a sequence that is defined recursively, but you will be introduced to a different kind of sequence—a geometric sequence.

■ Example 2

Waclaw Sierpiński (1882-1969) made significant contributions to number theory, set theory, and topology. He was a major figure in the mathematical community in Poland that flourished between the two world wars. The figure that results from continuing the geometric pattern below is known as the Sierpiński triangle. Count the number of red triangles at each transition. How many red triangles would be in the twentieth such figure?

Solution

The sequence that represents the number of black triangles is 1, 3, 9, 27, ... This pattern can be defined recursively using $u_1 = 1$ and $u_n = 3 \cdot u_{(n-1)}$. On the calculator, start the sequence with 1. Then multiply this last answer by 3. Press (ENTER) repeatedly, and count to the twentieth term. You will find that $u_{20} = 1{,}162{,}261{,}467$. Check this result on your own calculator.

1 (ENTER)	Establishes, or seeds, the first Ans.
Ans × 3 (ENTER)	Calculates the second term and makes it the Ans.
(ENTER)	Establishes the third term as the Ans.
and so on. ■	

The expressions *preceding term, Ans,* and $u_{(n-1)}$ are interchangeable. In the example above, each preceding term was *multiplied* by the same constant. This type of sequence is called a geometric sequence.

Geometric Sequence

A **geometric sequence** is a sequence in which each term is equal to the preceding term multiplied by a constant, or $u_n = r \cdot u_{(n-1)}$. The constant r is called the **common ratio**.

Problem Set 1.1

1. What sequence is generated by this recursive routine?

6 (ENTER)
Ans × 1.5 (ENTER)
(ENTER)
and so on.

Is the sequence arithmetic or geometric? What is the tenth term?

2. Write a calculator routine, similar to the one in Problem 1, to generate an arithmetic sequence with a beginning term of 6 and a common difference of 3.2. What is the tenth term?

3. Write a routine, similar to the one in Problem 1, to generate terms in each sequence. Find the indicated term.

   a. 2, 6, 18, 54, . . .   Find the 15th term.
   b. 10, 5, 2.5, 1.25, . . .   Find the 12th term.
   c. 0.4, 0.04, 0.004, 0.0004, . . .   Find the 10th term.
   d. 2, 8, 14, 20, 26, . . .   Find the 30th term.
   e. 1.56, 4.85, 8.14, 11.43, . . .   Find the 14th term.
   f. 6.24, ⁻15.6, 39, ⁻97.5, . . .   Find the 20th term.

4. A 50 gal bathtub contains 20 gal of water and is being filled at a rate of 2.4 gal/min.

  a. When will the water flow over the top?

  b. Suppose that the bathtub contains 20 gal of water and is being filled at a rate of 2.4 gal/min. The drain is open, and water is draining out at a rate of 3.1 gal/min. How long will it take until the tub is empty?

  c. Write a single recursive routine that shows both the rate of filling and the rate of draining.

5. A car leaves town heading west at 57 kilometers per hour (km/hr).

  a. How far will the car travel in 7 hr?

  b. A second car leaves town 2 hr after the first car, but it is traveling at 72 km/hr. To the nearest hour, when will the second car pass the first?

6. The bathtub in Problem 4 is once again filled to the 20 gal mark. The incoming water is turned off, and the drain allows half of the remaining water to drain out each minute.

  a. How much water will remain after 1 min?

  b. How much will remain after 5 min?

  c. When will the tub be totally empty?

7. The week of February 14, store owner J. C. Nickels ordered hundreds of heart-shaped red vacuum cleaners. The next week, he still had hundreds of heart-shaped red vacuum cleaners, so he told his manager to discount the price 25% each week until they were all sold. The first week the vacuums sold for $80.

  a. What was the price of a vacuum the second week?

  b. What was the price in the fourth week?

  c. When will the vacuum sell for less than $10?

8. Consider again the bathtub containing 20 gal of water. This time, it is draining half the remaining water each minute and, at the same time, is filling at a constant rate of 2.4 gal/min.

  a. Write a recursive routine that incorporates both of these actions.

  b. Using your model, determine how much water will be in the tub after 1 min.

  c. How much water will remain after 5 min?

  d. How much will remain after a long time?

Modeling Growth

Mathematics seems to endow one with something like a new sense.
—Charles Darwin

Have you ever received a chain letter offering you great financial rewards? Typical letters might offer you thousands of cassette tapes, golf balls, or recipes if you would just follow the simple instructions. They ask that you not break the chain. Actually, chain letter schemes are illegal, even though they have been quite common (especially during the 1980s). Carefully read the following letter.

Investigation 1.2.1

Pyramid Investment Plan

Pyramid Investment Plan

Dear Investor:

Become a millionaire! Join the Pyramid Investment Plan (PIP). Send only $20, and return this letter to PIP. PIP will send $5 to the name at the top of the list below. You will receive a new letter, with your name added to the bottom of the list, and a set of 200 names and addresses. Make 200 copies of the letter, mail them, and wait to get rich. Each time a recipient of one of your letters joins PIP, your name advances toward the top of the list. When PIP receives letters with your name at the top, we will start sending you money! A conservative marketing return of 6% projects that you will earn over $1.2 million.

Here is an example of how this works: When we receive your check, we will send $5 to Chris. Then Katie will be #1, and your name will be in position #6. Each time this process is repeated, the names move up on the list. When your name reaches the top, each of the thousands of people who receive that letter will be sending money to PIP, and you will receive your share.

1. Chris
2. Katie
3. Josh
4. Kanako
5. Dave
6. Miranda

Suppose you have just received this letter, along with several quotes from "ordinary people" who have already become millionaires. In your group, prepare a written analysis of this plan. Use the following questions as an outline for your report.

a. If you send copies of this letter to 200 people, the list of names now reads: 1. Katie, 2. Josh, 3. Kanako, 4. Dave, 5. Miranda, 6. **Your Name**. According to the plan's "conservative marketing return of 6%," how many of the 200 people receiving the letter will join the plan?

Round number	1	2	3	4	5	6
Letters sent	200	-?-	-?-	-?-	-?-	-?-
Responses	-?-	-?-	-?-	-?-	-?-	-?-

b. If each new *PIP* investor mails 200 copies of the letter, and 6% of those receiving the letter join *PIP*, how many people will there be in the second round?

c. Continue this process for the third, fourth, fifth, and sixth rounds.

d. Those investors in the sixth round receive a list that may look like this: 1. Your Name, 2. Moira, 3. Elizabeth, 4. Kiku, 5. Bill, 6. Clara. If you receive $5 from each person responding in the sixth round, will you make over $1.2 million? How much will you make?

e. The letter is sent to 200 households in the first round. How many households receive letters in the second round?

f. What is the *total* number of households that receive a letter by the sixth round?

g. Assume that the quotes on the back of the letter are from people who have participated in the plan and are no longer on the list. Receiving this letter places you in at least the seventh round of the plan. How many households will receive the letter by the time it reaches the thirteenth round?

h. According to the 1990 census, how many households were there in the United States?

i. What are your conclusions? Why are chain letter and pyramid schemes illegal?

Each sequence you generated in the above investigation is a geometric sequence that models growth. In many growth models (like those in the next investigation), it is more useful to treat the first term as *term zero,* or u_0. The initial value is usually given at *time zero,* or before the growth begins. However, there are no hard and fast rules. You will have to consider each problem carefully and decide whether you should begin at term one or term zero.

Investigation 1.2.2

Investing with Meg Abux

Meg Abux deposits $2,000 into a bank paying 7% annual interest compounded annually. This means she receives 7% of her bank balance as interest at the end of each year. How can you compute the balance after the first year? The second year? The nth year?

Here is a start to the solution.

NEW BAL = OLD BAL + 0.07 • OLD BAL

or   NEW BAL = OLD BAL • (1 + 0.07)   By the distributive property.

Use the Ans function on your calculator to compute the sequence. Each result will give you a year-end balance.

2000 (ENTER)   This establishes, or seeds, the first Ans.

Ans × (1 + 0.07)   (ENTER)   This establishes $2,140 (the balance after the first year) as the Ans.

(ENTER)   This establishes $2,289.80 (the balance after the second year) as the Ans.

and so on.

As you complete each step, be sure to compare your answers with those of other members in your group

a. Copy and complete the table below.

Elapsed time (yr)	0	1	2	3	...	7	...	10	...	n
Balance ($)	2,000	2,140	2,289.8	$u_3 = -?-$	...	$u_7 = -?-$	...	$u_{10} = -?-$	...	$u_n = -?-$

b. How many years will it take before the original deposit triples in value?

c. Start over with $2,000, and change the annual interest rate to 8.5%.

Elapsed time (yr)	0	1	2	3	...	7	...	10	...	n
Balance ($)	2,000	$u_1 = -?-$	$u_2 = -?-$	$u_3 = -?-$	...	$u_7 = -?-$	...	$u_{10} = -?-$	...	$u_n = -?-$

d. Now how many years will it take for the original deposit to triple in value?

e. Describe the difference between the answers to parts b and d.

f. If 8.5% is the annual interest rate, what is the real-world meaning of 0.085/12?

g. Instead of compounding interest annually, many banks compound it monthly. If this is the case, you would use a recursive routine like the one below. Use this routine to answer each question that follows. (Throughout this course, please label each answer with its proper unit of measurement. For example, these answers could be expressed in dollars, percentages, years, or months.)

2000　(ENTER)
Ans × (1 + 0.085/12)　(ENTER)
and so on.

What is the balance after 1 yr? After 4 yr? After 7 yr? How many years will it take before the original deposit triples in value? How does this compare with the answer to part d?

Problem Set 1.2

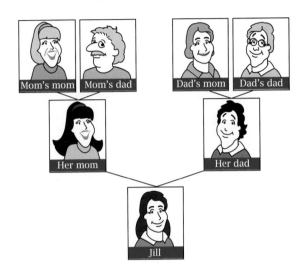

Mom's mom　Mom's dad　Dad's mom　Dad's dad

Her mom　Her dad

Jill

1. Suppose Jill's biological family tree looks like the diagram on the right. Although it is probably an unrealistic assumption, assume there is no common ancestry (that is, assume no two people share an ancestor) so that there will be a pattern you can model.

   a. Copy and complete a table showing the sequence that represents the number of Jill's ancestors in each generation.

Generations back	0	1	2	3	4	–?–	n
Ancestors within a generation	$u_0 = 1$	$u_1 = 2$	$u_2 = 4$	$u_3 = $ –?–	$u_4 = $ –?–	$u_? = 131{,}072$	$u_n = $ –?–

   b. Describe how to find the number of ancestors within a generation if you know the number of ancestors in the preceding generation.
   c. Name the number of the term of this sequence that is closest to 5 million. What is the real-world meaning of this answer?
   d. If a new generation is born every 25 yr, approximately when did Jill have 5 million living ancestors?
   e. Write a few sentences describing any concerns you might have regarding the original assumption of no common ancestors.

2. If the number of people who receive the letter from the Pyramid Investment Plan (Investigation 1.2.1) increases from 200 to 400 at each level, and you still expect 6% of them to respond, will your hypothetical income double? Explain your reasoning.

3. Carbon dating is used to find the age of very old, dead objects. Carbon-14 (C^{14}) is created by the sun and is found naturally in all living things. C^{14} transforms (decays) slowly after death. About 88.55% of it remains after any 1000 yr period of time. Let 100% or 1 be the beginning amount of C^{14}. At what point will less than 5% remain? Write the recursive routine you used.

4. Suppose $500 is deposited into an account that earns 6.5% annually.
  a. If the interest is compounded monthly, what is the monthly rate?
  b. What is the balance after 1 mo?
  c. After 1 yr?
  d. After 29 mo?
  e. What would the annual interest rate (compounded monthly) have to be for the $500 to grow to $600 *during* the 29th month? Write the recursive routine you used.

5. Between 1970 and 1990, the population of Grand Traverse County in Michigan grew from 39,175 to 64,273.
  a. Find the population increase for the 20 yr period.
  b. Find the percentage increase over the 20 yr period by computing the fraction $\frac{\text{actual increase}}{\text{original population}}$.
  c. What do you think the *annual* growth rate was during this period?
  d. Check your answer to 5c by writing and using a calculator recursive routine. Explain why that answer does or does not work out to a population of 64,273 people over the period.

Grand Traverse County

MICHIGAN

  e. Using guess-and-check, find a growth rate, to the nearest 0.1% (0.001), that comes closest to producing the growth experienced.
  f. Use the answer to 5e to estimate the population in 1980. How does this compare with the average of the populations of 1970 and 1990? Why is that?

6. In Problem 5 you looked at the change in population for a county in Michigan. Do some research and find data for your city, county, or state. Answer 5a–f using your data. Write a paragraph summarizing your findings.

Section 1.3

A First Look at Limits

A Mathematician is a machine for turning coffee into theorems.
—Paul Erds

The number of subtriangles at each stage in a Sierpiński triangle, a bank balance that is compounded monthly, and increasing arithmetic and geometric sequences have terms that get larger and larger forever. Is there a limit to how tall a tree can grow? Can people continue to build taller buildings, run faster, jump higher? If you were to record the temperature, at one-minute intervals, of your next cup of hot cocoa as it cooled, this sequence of temperatures would approach the temperature of the room. The amount of water in a bathtub, which is draining half of its remaining water each minute, will slowly stop changing as the bathtub empties. Sequences that slowly stop changing are said to have **limits**. The investigation below introduces another sequence that has a limit. You will revisit variations of this problem, and the limit concept, throughout the year.

Investigation 1.3.1

Color Concentration

A bowl contains a total of 1 liter (L) of liquid. All of the liquid is clear water, except for 16 milliliters (mL), which is a colored fluid.

Part 1   Every hour 250 mL of liquid is removed from the bowl and replaced with 250 mL of clear water.

a. Copy and complete a table like the one following part d, recording the amount of colored fluid in the bowl over several hours.

b. Write a recursive routine to describe this sequence.

c. How many hours will pass before there is less than 1 mL of coloring?

d. What happens in the long run?

Time period	Amount of clear liquid (mL)	Amount of colored liquid (mL)
0	984	16
1	-?-	-?-
2	-?-	-?-
3	-?-	-?-
-?-	-?-	-?-

Part 2 Start over with 1 L of liquid. Again, all of the liquid is clear water, except for 16 milliliters (mL), which is a colored fluid. At the end of each hour, 250 mL of liquid is removed and replaced with a mixture of 234 mL of clear water and 16 mL of coloring.

a. Copy and complete a table like the one below, recording the amount of colored fluid in the bowl over several hours.

b. Write a recursive routine to describe this sequence.

c. Do the contents of the bowl ever turn into pure coloring? Why or why not?

d. What happens in the long run?

Time period	Amount of clear liquid (mL)	Amount of colored liquid (mL)
0	984	16
1	-?-	-?-
2	-?-	-?-
3	-?-	-?-
-?-	-?-	-?-

Source: This investigation is based on an article by James Sandefur in *Mathematics Teacher* 85:2, February 1992, 139–145.

Investigation 1.3.1 illustrates a simplified version of a closed but changing, or dynamic, system. Medicine and its elimination in the human body, or a contaminated lake and cleanup processes, are real-world examples of dynamic systems. Being able to find limits is very important for understanding these systems.

■ **Example 1**

If $u_0 = 450$ and $u_n = 0.75 \cdot u_{(n-1)} + 210$, find u_1.

Solution

$$u_1 = 0.75 \cdot u_{(1-1)} + 210 \qquad \text{Substitute 1 for } n.$$
$$u_1 = 0.75 \cdot u_0 + 210$$
$$u_1 = 0.75 \cdot 450 + 210 \qquad \text{Substitute 450 for } u_0.$$
$$u_1 = 547.50$$

Show that you can use this recursive definition by finding the second and third terms. (The answer for u_2 is 620.625.) At this point, the sequence 450, 547.50, 620.625, . . . has been identified. ∎

The notation below describes the recursive sequence in Example 1.

$$u_n = \begin{cases} 450 & \text{if } n = 0 \\ 0.75 \cdot u_{(n-1)} + 210 & \text{if } n > 0 \end{cases}$$

It is important that you are able to make sense of this kind of mathematical notation. Can you identify the first term? The second term? Given a term, can you see how to get the next term? Do you see the connection between *Ans* and $u_{(n-1)}$? Rewrite this recursive routine using *Ans*.

Problem Set 1.3

1. a. Find u_5 and u_{10} of the sequence defined by the notation below.

$$u_n = \begin{cases} 450 & \text{if } n = 0 \\ 0.75 \cdot u_{(n-1)} + 210 & \text{if } n > 0 \end{cases}$$

b. Invent a situation for which this recursive routine could serve as the model.

c. Describe what happens to this sequence over the long run.

2. a. List the first six terms of the sequence defined by the notation below.

$$u_n = \begin{cases} 1 & \text{if } n = 0 \\ n \cdot u_{(n-1)} & \text{if } n > 0 \end{cases}$$

b. What is u_7? What is u_{14}?

3. Use the notation developed in Problems 1 and 2 to write a recursive definition of each sequence.

a. 49.06, 50.24, 51.42, 52.6, . . .

b. ⁻4.24, ⁻21.2, ⁻106, ⁻530, . . .

4. On October 1, $24,000 is invested, earning 6.4% annually, compounded monthly. Beginning on November 1, a monthly withdrawal of $100 is made, and the withdrawals continue on the first of every month thereafter.

a. Write a recursive routine for this problem.

b. List the first five terms of this sequence of balances.

c. What is the meaning of the fifth term?

d. What is the balance at the end of 1 yr? At the end of 3 yr?

5. The Forever Green Nursery owns 7000 white pine trees. Each year, the nursery plans to sell 12% of its trees and plant 600 new ones.

a. Determine the number of pine trees owned by the nursery after 10 yr.

b. Determine the number of pine trees owned by the nursery after many years (in the long run), and explain what is occurring.

c. Try different starting totals in place of the 7000 trees. Describe any changes to the long-run totals.

d. Rework the problem again, but this time build in a catastrophe of some sort to the nursery in the fifth year. Describe your catastrophe.

e. How does the solution change?

6. Dr. Jeck L. Hyde takes a capsule containing 20 milligrams (mg) of a prescribed medication early in the morning. By the same time one day later, 25% of the medication has been eliminated from his body. Dr. Hyde doesn't take any more medication, and his body continues to eliminate 25% of the remaining medication each day. Write a recursive routine that provides the daily amount of this medication in Dr. Hyde's body. How long will it be before there is less than 1 mg of the medication present in Dr. Hyde's body?

7. Suppose Jeck's doctor prescribes a 20 mg capsule to be taken every morning. As before, 25% of the medication is eliminated from the body each day. Write a recursive routine that provides the daily accumulation of this medication in his body. To what level will the medication eventually accumulate?

8. Consider Part 2 of Investigation 1.3.1. If you double the amount of colored fluid added each time from 16 mL to 32 mL, but continue to add only 250 mL of fluid, will the final concentration be doubled? Write a convincing argument for your position.

9. Suppose you want to buy a new car and need to finance or borrow $11,000. The annual interest rate for a car loan is 9.6% of the unpaid balance, compounded monthly.

a. Write a recursive routine that provides the declining balances of the loan for a monthly payment of $274.

b. List the first five terms of this sequence.

c. When will the loan be paid off?

d. What is the total cost paid for the new car over this time period?

10. a. What happens to the balance in Problem 4 if the same interest and withdrawal pattern continues for a long time?

b. What monthly withdrawal would maintain a constant balance of $24,000?

Take Another Look 1.3

1. Investigate some real data related to buying a car. Find out how much your car will cost. Go to a car dealer, or talk with someone at a bank to learn the down payment required, the monthly payment amount, the interest rate, and how long you can take to repay the loan. Figure out how much you will actually pay for the car.

2. Some people buy or lease a new car every two years. Do some research and compare the costs of buying versus leasing. Which is more economical? You will need to consider such things as the down payment, the interest paid, the depreciated value after two years, and so on. Justify your reasoning.

Project

Automobile Depreciation

Select a particular used automobile that interests you. With help from a car dealer or car collector, gather some data relating the value of the vehicle to its age. Make a graph of your data that covers the life of the vehicle. Find a good mathematical model for this (*age, value*) relationship. Your model may require more than one function. See the following example.

$$u_n = \begin{cases} \$15,000 & \text{if } n = 0 \\ u_{(n-1)}(1 - 0.25) & \text{if } 1 \leq n \leq 3 \\ u_{(n-1)}(1 - 0.18) & \text{if } n > 3 \end{cases}$$

Graphing Sequences

The effort of the economist is to "see," to picture the interplay of economic elements. The more clearly cut these elements appear in his vision, the better; the more elements he can grasp and hold in his mind at once, the better. The economic world is a misty region. The first explorers used unaided vision. Mathematics is the lantern by which what before was dimly visible now looms up in firm, bold outlines. The old phantasmagoria disappear. We see better. We also see further.
—Irving Fisher

Thus far, you have examined several sequences and considered some complicated situations that produce them. By using a recursive routine, you can display a sequence of numbers quickly and efficiently. You can also use your graphing calculator to help you visualize sequences with graphs. These graphs give you a visual spreadsheet of valuable information.

The graph on the right is a visual representation of the first sequence in Section 1.1. Written recursively, this sequence is defined by the notation below.

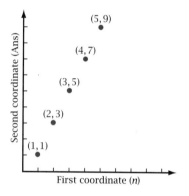

$$u_n = \begin{cases} 1 & \text{if } n = 1 \\ u_{(n-1)} + 2 & \text{if } n > 1 \end{cases}$$

The position of each point is given by two numbers. The first number, or first coordinate, n, provides the horizontal location of the point. The second number, or second coordinate, u_n, provides the vertical location of the point. For example, $u_4 = 7$ is pictured as the point $(4, 7)$.

This means the graph of $u_4 = 7$, or $(4, 7)$, is 4 units to the right, and 7 units up, from the point $(0, 0)$, which is called the origin. Each point in the graph is a geometric representation of (n, u_n) for some choice of n. A table of the early points of this sequence looks like this:

n	1	2	3	4	5
u_n	1	3	5	7	9

Set the graphing window of your calculator to the values [0, 7, 1, 0, 10, 1].

The Xscl and Yscl are not too important, because they do not change the appearance of any graph. They simply provide reference marks on the axes. Refer to **Calculator Note 1A** to learn how to plot the points from a table of values on your calculator screen. Graphs in this section will be collections of points that are not connected. Graphs of sequences are examples of **discrete graphs**, which means they are separate points and are not connected by a line, segment, or curve.

NOTE
1A

The graph of this sequence will appear to be **linear**, that is, the points will appear to lie on a straight line. Do you remember what the slope of a line is? Can you find the slope of the line suggested by this sequence?

You will find that graphs are very useful tools in helping you to understand and explain situations. One of the goals of this book is to help you understand mathematics by providing opportunities for you to "see," or visualize, the mathematics. When you make a graph or look at a graph, look for connections between the graph and the mathematics used to create the graph. Sometimes this will be clear and obvious, and sometimes you will need to look at the graph in a new way to see the connections.

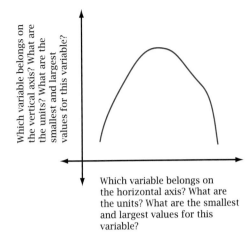

Which variable belongs on the vertical axis? What are the units? What are the smallest and largest values for this variable?

Which variable belongs on the horizontal axis? What are the units? What are the smallest and largest values for this variable?

Investigation 1.4.1

Uncle Scrooge's Investment

An investment plan contains a clause that states that any money in an investment account with a balance over $1,000 cannot be withdrawn all at once. The clause further states that no more than 20% of the investment or $1,000, whichever amount is larger, can be removed in any calendar year. Uncle Scrooge has $50,000 invested in the plan and would like to withdraw his funds. To make the problem simpler, assume that the money remaining in the investment account will not earn any interest.

a. With your group, analyze the situation for Uncle Scrooge. You could start by completing a table like the one below.

Time	Now	After 1 yr	After 2 yr	. . .
Balance	$50,000	–?–	–?–	. . .

NOTE
1B

Then make a graph showing the balance at the end of each year. One way of plotting a number of points is to enter their coordinates into the calculator as a data set. (See **Calculator Note 1B**.) Then the points easily can be replotted with a different window if necessary. Play with the problem to determine an appropriate graphing window. Use your graph and a clear mathematical explanation to help your uncle understand why he cannot have all of his money within five years. Explain how many years it will take him to withdraw all of his money. Explain how the $1,000 limit works and why this is important. Show on the graph when the $1,000 limit "kicks in."

b. What would happen if the balance in the account continued to earn 8% interest? Create another graph of the account balance over time. This graph shows that Uncle Scrooge withdraws 20% at the beginning of each year as above, and that the remaining balance in the account earns 8%. Be sure to note on the graph when the $1,000 limit kicks in. Now explain how long it will take Uncle Scrooge to withdraw all of his money.

Problem Set 1.4

1. a. Copy and complete a table of values generated by the sequence below.

$$u_n = \begin{cases} 2.5 & \text{if } n = 1 \\ u_{(n-1)} + 1.5 & \text{if } n > 1 \end{cases}$$

First coordinate	-?-	-?-	-?-	-?-	-?-	-?-
Second coordinate	-?-	-?-	-?-	-?-	-?-	-?-

b. Provide graphing-window values that give a good picture of these terms.

[Xmin, Xmax, Xscl, Ymin, Ymax, Yscl]

c. Plot the points on your calculator screen.
d. Sketch the graph of the sequence on paper. Remember, this is a discrete graph.

2. The sequence below models the population growth of the United States for each decade since 1790.

$$u_n = \begin{cases} 3929000 & \text{if } n = 0 \\ (1 + 0.24) \cdot u_{(n-1)} & \text{if } n > 0 \end{cases}$$

a. Copy and complete a table of values for the first six terms of the sequence.

n (decades)	0	1	2	3	4	5
u_n	-?-	-?-	-?-	-?-	-?-	-?-

b. What is the meaning of 3,929,000?
c. What is the growth rate over each decade?
d. Is this an arithmetic or geometric sequence, or neither?

How do you think the population growth in Japan compares to that in the United States?

NOTE
1B

e. Using the graphing window provided, list the window dimensions, scatter-plot the points on your calculator screen, and carefully sketch the graph onto your paper.

Graphing window:
[0, 6, 1, 0, 15000000, 5000000].
(See **Calculator Note 1B**.)

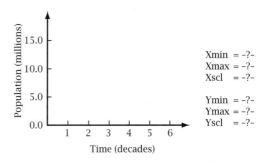

3. Extend Problem 2 so that the graphing window can handle the first 200 yr of the sequence of populations.

  a. Name a graphing window that provides a good picture of the sequence, and sketch a graph of the points involved.

  b. Do the points appear to lie on a straight line?

  c. What is the 200 yr growth rate? Show how you found it.

4. If the original amount of money in the investment described in Investigation 1.4.1 is doubled, will this double the amount of time needed to withdraw all of Uncle Scrooge's money? Write a short note to convince your uncle of your position.

5. Draw a graph or make a scatter plot of the sequence generated in the white pine tree problem (Problem 5, Problem Set 1.3).

Name the graphing window you used.

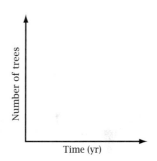

6. The ideal concentration of chlorine in a swimming pool is between 1 and 2 parts per million (ppm). If the concentration gets as high as 3 ppm, the pool is safe, but swimmers are a bit uncomfortable with burning eyes. If the concentration is less than 1 ppm, slime takes over. Suppose 15% of the chlorine present in the pool dissipates (disappears naturally) during a period of one day. Use a graph to answer each question.

  a. If the chlorine content is 3 ppm, how long will it be before the slime takes over?

  b. If the chlorine content starts out at 3 ppm, and 0.5 ppm is added daily, will the concentration be increasing or decreasing? Will the pool ever be pure chlorine? Explain.

  c. Suppose the original chlorine content is 3 ppm, and 0.1 ppm is added daily. Describe what happens.

  d. How much chlorine do you need to add daily for the chlorine content to stabilize at 1.5 ppm?

Take Another Look 1.4

1. In Investigation 1.2.2, you completed a table of increasing balances. Reflect for a moment on the meaning of an annual interest rate of 7%.

   a. Describe how you would use the values listed in the table to discover the related interest rate if the percentage or annual interest rate of 7% wasn't provided.

Elapsed time (yr)	0	1	2	3	. . .
Balance ($)	2,000	2,140	2,289.8	$u_3 = -?-$	. . .

   Think about the recursive procedure that allows you to complete the table. It's likely that you would use some equivalent form of $u_n = (1 + 0.07) \cdot u_{(n-1)}$ to find the next balance (or u_3).

   b. Given only the second-year balance of $2,289.80 and the interest rate of 7%, describe a process to find the balance after three years.

   c. How could you reverse this process? Suppose instead you were given the balance after three years. Describe a recursive process that uses the third-year balance to find the balance after the second year, the balance after the first year, and the initial investment.

   d. Now consider monthly recalculations. Use the recursive procedure below to produce balances after each of the first five months.

   2000 (ENTER)
   Ans × (1 + 0.085/12) (ENTER)
   and so on.

   Then write a recursive procedure that starts with the balance after five months and reverses the process to find the previous balances. Check your answers.

2. In Example 1 of Section 1.3, you were asked to use the recursive routine

   $$u_0 = 450 \quad \text{and} \quad u_n = 0.75 \cdot u_{(n-1)} + 210$$

   to find u_1 and u_2. You were also asked to make sense of the notation

   $$u_n = \begin{cases} 450 & \text{if } n = 0 \\ 0.75 \cdot u_{(n-1)} + 210 & \text{if } n > 0. \end{cases}$$

   Write a paragraph showing that you understand the connection between the two notations. Then write a recursive routine that takes a backward look at the sequence.

The Gingerbread Man

In this project, you will investigate the iteration of different points through the sequences $x_{(n+1)} = 1 - y_n + |x_n|$, $y_{(n+1)} = x_n$. All results will be graphed in the window $^-5 \leq x \leq 10$, $^-5 \leq y \leq 10$.

a. Begin with the point $(0, 0)$ and plot the points resulting from this iteration on graph paper. Describe what happens as you continue to iterate the points. Sequences of points like this are called **periodic**. This sequence has period 6.

b. Begin with the point $(3, ^-1)$ and plot the points resulting from this iteration on graph paper. What is the period of this sequence of points?

c. Begin with the point $(2.5, ^-1)$ and iterate by hand. Plot the points on graph paper. What is the period of this sequence of points?

d. Enter the program in **Calculator Note 1E**. The program will automatically iterate the sequences and plot each point. Set the window to $[^-5, 11.5, 1, ^-1, 8, 1]$.

NOTE

1E

e. Use the program to iterate the function, using each given point as the starting point. Do not clear the screen between program runs.

  i. $(3, 0.5)$ ii. $(1.5, ^-0.2)$ iii. $(1.3, 0.1)$ iv. $(^-0.13, 0)$

  v. $(1, ^-1.8)$ vi. (π, π) vii. $(\sqrt{2}, ^-0.1)$

Describe how the resulting picture relates to the graphs in parts a, b, and c.

f. Use the program to investigate what happens when points within the "belly" are iterated. Describe the periods of the sequences you obtain and any patterns you observe.

g. Use the program to investigate what happens when points within the "head" and "limb" regions are iterated. Describe the periods of the sequences you obtain and any patterns you observe.

h. The points in the shaded region of the gingerbread man belong to sequences with periods of all possible values. Some sequences never repeat themselves. We say that these sequences are not periodic. Investigate what happens when you iterate points just outside the gingerbread man. You may need to iterate several points without clearing the screen to see any pattern. Describe what you see.

A Recursive Routine for Sequences

Mathematical discoveries, small or great, are never born of spontaneous generation. They always presuppose a soil seeded with preliminary knowledge and well prepared by labour, both conscious and subconscious.
—Jules Henri Poincaré

Finding the first six terms of the sequence produced by the calculator recursive routine shown below is easy.

3 (ENTER)
2 × Ans (ENTER)
(ENTER), and so on.

However, many of the longer sequences have probably taxed your patience. Physically pressing the (ENTER) key 48 or 120 times helps you understand what a recursive routine is, but it is not really necessary, because the graphics calculator is a hand-held computer. When routines are not included as features of the calculator, then, as with all computers, routines can be written, edited, stored, and executed when needed. These routines are called programs.

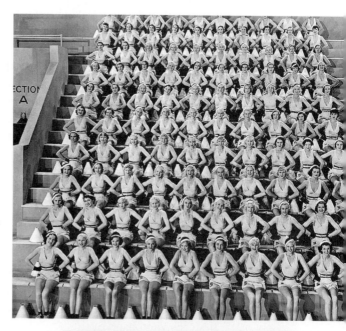

Grace Hopper (1906–1992) was a leader in the field of computer programming. She received a B.A. in mathematics from Vassar College in 1928. In 1934, she received a Ph.D., one of only seven mathematics doctorates awarded by Yale University between 1934 and 1937. In 1944, she learned programming on the Mark I, the world's first large-scale digital computer. "It was 51 feet long, eight feet high, eight feet deep," she said. "And it had 72 words of storage and could perform three additions a second." Hopper originated the idea of making a library of the codes for various computer procedures. When a programmer called on the name of a procedure, the computer located the corresponding code and copied it. Using this idea, Hopper developed the first operational compiler, a major breakthrough

Grace Hopper and colleagues getting the programming language COBOL to run on a UNIVAC computer, circa 1960.

in automatic programming. (A compiler translates a computer programming language into machine language that the computer can understand.) "Nobody believed that," she said. "I had a running compiler and nobody would touch it. They told me computers could only do arithmetic."

Your calculator can certainly do more than simple arithmetic. In fact it is much more powerful than the early computers. In this course, you will encounter a variety of calculator programs. When using a program, try to understand how it works. Many times you will be asked to modify a program, so you need to become comfortable with working in programming mode.

**NOTE
1C**

See **Calculator Note 1C** for help in entering the RECUR program. This program will enable the calculator to perform a recursive routine. The example in the note will seed 3 as the starting term, provide for exactly six terms, and display the results as 3, 6, 12, 24, 48, 96. The display can be a listing of the terms, the plotted points, or both. As with any graph, the graphing window must be set to show what you are interested in seeing. You will need to think carefully about the role of x and y, and how they relate to n and u_n.

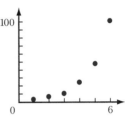

Entering, executing, adjusting, and understanding a new recursive program may be the most complicated process you undertake with your calculator. Do not become frustrated if it doesn't work the first or second time you try. The more you experiment with the calculator, the better you will understand what it is doing.

■ Example 1

Use your new recursive routine to find the balance after 60 mo if $500 is deposited in an account earning 6.5% annual interest compounded monthly.

Solution

The following important modifications are required in the program to arrive at $691.41.

First: The starting value is $500.

Second: Start the sequence at u_0.

Third: The recursive routine is $\text{Ans}(1 + 0.065/12)$.

Fourth: The sequence will end at u_{60}. ■

Investigation 1.5.1

The Tower of Hanoi

Ancient legend has it that Brahma stacked 64 gold disks in order from largest to smallest. According to the legend, the world will end when his priests have transferred all the disks from one tower to another. They are guided by two rules: Only one disk can be moved at a time, and larger disks cannot be placed on top of smaller disks.

The Tower of Hanoi puzzle was actually invented by François Édouard Anatole Lucas (1842–1891) in 1883. He worked at the Paris Observatory and taught high school. He did most of his mathematical research in the field of number theory. He is also responsible for inventing the "legend" about the priests and the end of the world.

Part 1 Frequently this puzzle comes in the form of seven disks stacked on a tower. (If you don't have an actual tower puzzle, you might want to use coins to model the solution.) To find a recursive solution, first simplify the problem.

a. How many moves would you need with just one disk? With two disks? What is the least number of moves with three disks? Keep track of your results in the table below.

Number of disks	1	2	3	4	5	6	7
Number of moves	-?-	-?-	-?-	-?-	-?-	-?-	-?-

b. How can you determine the number of moves required for four disks if you know the number of moves required for three disks? How can you determine the number of moves required for five disks if you know the number of moves required for four disks? How can you determine the number of moves required for n disks if you know the number of moves required for $n - 1$ disks?

c. Look at the sequence of numbers in your table. Write a recursive routine and use it to continue this sequence. Record your start value and your routine.

d. What is the least number of moves required for 64 disks?

Part 2 Suppose the top gold disk has a diameter of 3 in., and the diameter of each lower disk increases by 2 in. from that of the disk above it.

a. List a few terms to represent the sequence of diameters.

b. What is the diameter of the 64th disk?

c. What do you consider to be a reasonable average length of time to move an average disk?

d. Using your last answer, figure out how long it would take to complete the task.

e. If the priests started in 3000 B.C. and worked in 24-hour-a-day shifts, in what year will the world end, according to this legend?

Problem Set 1.5

1. Find the first 30 terms of the sequence 2, 8, 14, 20, 26, ... Write the 10th, 20th, and 30th terms.

2. Find the value of a $1,000 investment, at an annual rate of 6.5% compounded quarterly, for each time period.

    a. 10 yr   **b.** 20 yr   **c.** 30 yr

3. Use what you have learned in this section to solve the white pine tree problem (Problem Set 1.3, Problem 5).

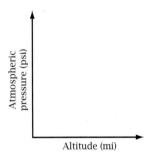

**NOTE
1C**

    a. Draw a graph that represents the number of trees owned by the nursery each year during the first ten years and indicate the graphing window used. (See **Calculator Note 1C.**) Sketch this graph on paper.

    b. Draw graphs for 20 yr and 30 yr.

    c. Describe what happens in the long run.

4. The atmospheric pressure is 14.7 pounds per square inch (psi) at sea level. An increase in altitude of 1 mi produces a 20% decrease in the atmospheric pressure.

    a. Write a recursive routine that will provide atmospheric pressures at different altitudes.

    b. Draw a graph that pictures the relationship between altitude and pressure.

    c. What values do (n, u_n) have when the altitude is 7 mi?

    d. At what altitude does the atmospheric pressure drop below 1.5 psi?

5. Suppose a benevolent grandparent deposits $5,000 in an account for a 10 yr old grandchild. The account pays interest at an annual rate of 8.5% compounded monthly.

    a. What regular monthly deposits are needed to assure that the account will be worth $1 million by the time the youngster is 55 yr old? Write a recursive routine, and use guess-and-check to find the amount of the monthly deposit needed.

    b. Sketch the graph of increasing balances, and indicate the graphing window used.

6. Meg Abux wants to buy a new house and must finance $60,000 at 9.6% annual interest compounded monthly on the unpaid balance.

    a. What monthly payment is needed to pay off the loan in 25 yr?

    b. Sketch the graph of the unpaid balances, and indicate the graphing window used.

7. In 1987, 5% of Americans moved to California and 10% of Californians moved to other states. In 1986, there were 20 million Americans living in California and 220 million living in other states.

    a. Calculate the number of people who left California during 1986.

    b. Calculate the number of people moving into California during 1986.

    c. From these two answers, give the population of California in 1987.

    d. Assume the United States population stays constant at 240 million. What was the population outside of California in 1987?

e. How is this value expressed in terms of California's population?

f. If this trend continues, how many people will be living in California in 1990? In 1995? What will happen in the long run?

8. Suppose a sequence is defined as stated below.

$$u_n = \begin{cases} 1 & \text{if } n = 1 \\ 1 & \text{if } n = 2 \\ u_{(n-1)} + u_{(n-2)} & \text{if } n > 2 \end{cases}$$

a. List the first ten terms of this sequence.

b. Consider the sequence of ratios of the above terms: $\frac{u_2}{u_1}, \frac{u_3}{u_2}, \frac{u_4}{u_3}, \frac{u_5}{u_4}$, and so on. List a few terms of this sequence in decimal form. Describe what is happening.

9. In the previous chapter, you were asked to think about the purpose of working in groups in your classroom. Now think about the role you played in your group while working on one of the investigations in this chapter. Were you a leader? A follower? Were you satisfied with the way you participated in your group? Will you change your role? Does it matter? Be clear and explain your response.

Take Another Look 1.5

In Take Another Look 1.4, you figured out how to find previous balances when you knew the final balance and the interest rate. However, there were no payments involved. Is it possible to find a previous balance if you only know the present balance, the interest rate, and the amount of the monthly payment?

Consider Purchice Newkhar's dilemma. She knows that her unpaid loan balance after making the tenth monthly payment of $294.03 is $12,101.37. The interest rate on her loan is 9.5%.

a. As her financial advisor, explain why the ninth balance wasn't $12,101.37 + $294.03 = $12,395.40.

b. If u_9 represents the balance after the ninth payment, then explain why

$$u_9 \cdot (1 + \frac{0.095}{12}) - 294.03 = 12{,}101.37.$$

c. You tell Purchice to solve this expression for the previous term, u_9. Write a recursive routine that provides the previous unpaid monthly balances for this auto loan.

d. What was the loan balance after the ninth payment?

e. Keep going until you find the initial amount financed. What was it?

f. Carefully explain how Purchice can verify that the previous three answers are correct.

g. Carefully explain how she can find the total amount of interest paid thus far.

Recursive Midpoint Games

GAME 1

Draw a large equilateral triangle on a sheet of paper. Label the vertices *A*, *B*, and *C*. Read the rules of the game and try to predict the outcome before you play.

Start by choosing one of the vertices as your initial point. Roll a die and move according to the following plan.

Die result is 1 or 2:	Move halfway to *A* and plot a new point.
Die result is 3 or 4:	Move halfway to *B* and plot a new point.
Die result is 5 or 6:	Move halfway to *C* and plot a new point.

Connect this new point to the previous point. Starting from this new point, roll the die and repeat the procedure.

What do you think your picture will look like after 50 moves?

Play the game and see if your prediction is correct.

GAME 2

This is exactly like Game 1, but you will not connect the sequence of points as they are generated. Record your prediction for the outcome of this game.

Play the game and make at least 50 moves (more if possible). Describe the result as completely as possible.

NOTE
1F

The calculator is capable of measuring and plotting points much more quickly than you. Enter the program in **Calculator Note 1F** to automate this procedure.

The program uses the window $0 \le x \le 10$ and $0 \le y \le 7$. After running the program once, change the window to view only the top large triangle, and run the program again. How does this picture compare to the one you saw in the full-size window? Zoom in again by changing the window to view only the top large triangle of this new picture, and run the program. You may need to modify the program to plot more points, because many of the points will be plotted outside of the visible window. What do you see? Would the picture change if you had zoomed in on the triangle at the bottom left? How many times can you zoom in and see the same effect? Use these questions to explain what you think the term **self-similarity** means.

Create your own shape that has this same property of self-similarity.

Section 1.6

A Recursive Look at Series

Mathematicians do not study objects, but relations between objects. Thus, they are free to replace some objects by others so long as the relations remain unchanged. Content to them is irrelevant: they are interested in form only.
—Jules Henri Poincaré

Up to 50 tons of garbage has been left by climbers along the routes to the summit of Mount Everest since the first successful climb in 1953. Does this make Mount Everest the world's tallest trash dump? If you think that's a lot of garbage, consider that an average United States resident produces 0.75 tons of solid waste trash each year. At this rate, a community of less than 70 people produces over 50 tons of garbage in just one year. A community of 25,000 Americans produces over 50 tons of solid waste garbage in one day.

According to the *1994 Information Please Environmental Almanac*, each American produced 2.7 lb/day of trash in 1960; this increased to 4.3 lb/day in 1990. Despite attempts to recycle and conserve, our garbage is accumulating. In fact, over a 30-year period, the sum 2.7 + 2.753 + 2.806 + · · · + 4.29 = 108.345 represents the accumulated total. What does this number mean?

Series

A **series** is formed when the terms of a sequence are added. In general, the sum of n terms in a series is written

$$u_1 + u_2 + u_3 + \cdots + u_n = S_n.$$

The notation S_n can be used to represent the sum of the first n terms of a sequence. Thus, S_6 can be used to represent the series $u_1 + u_2 + u_3 + \cdots + u_6$. A simple series, $1 + 3 + 5 + 7 + 9$, the sum of the first five odd integers, can be represented by S_5. A decimal number like 0.44444 is a more complex example. It shows how the geometric series

$$S_5 = 0.4 + 0.04 + 0.004 + 0.0004 + 0.00004$$

is formed by combining five consecutive terms of a geometric sequence with a common ratio $\frac{1}{10}$.

Finding the sum of a series is a problem that has intrigued mathematicians throughout history. Chu Shih-chieh, a renowned thirteenth-century Chinese mathematician, called the sum $1 + 2 + 3 + \cdots + n$ a "pile of reeds" because it can be pictured like the diagram shown at the right.

When the famous mathematician Karl Friedrich Gauss (1777–1855) was 9 years old, his teacher asked the class to find the sum of the numbers from 1 to 100. Historical accounts indicate the teacher was hoping to take a break from his students (things haven't really changed that much since) and expected the students to add the terms one by one. Karl didn't have a calculator (and didn't need one, as you will see later).

To find a recursive definition for S_n, think to yourself—the sum of the first 100 terms is equal to the sum of the first 99 terms, plus the 100th term. Or in general, the sum of the first n terms is equal to the sum of the first $(n - 1)$ terms, plus the nth term. This leads to the equation $S_n = S_{(n-1)} + u_n$, where, in this case, u_n is just n.

NOTE
1D

In **Calculator Note 1D,** you will find directions to modify the recursive routine so that you can sum terms and display the nth sum, or the **partial sum** (the accumulated sum through that term). Refer to the note for help on this example.

■ Example 1

Find the answer to the Gauss problem and make a graph of the partial sums. Be sure to set the graphing window at [0, 110, 10, 0, 5500, 500].

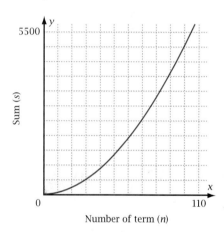

Number of term (n)

Solution

The points are so dense that they appear to form a solid curve, but this is a discrete set of 100 points representing each partial sum from S_1 through S_{100}. Each point is (n, S_n) for integer values of n, $1 \le n \le 100$.

The sum of the first 100 terms is $S_{100} = 5050$. ■

Investigation 1.6.1

Wheat on a Chessboard

A very old Arab legend, recounted by al-Yaqubi in the ninth century, begins, "It is related by the wise men of India that when Husiya, the daughter of Balhait, was queen . . . ," and goes on to tell how the game of chess was invented. The queen was so delighted with the game that she told the inventor, "Ask what you will." The inventor asked for one grain of wheat

on the first square of the chessboard, two grains on the second, four grains on the third, and so on, so that each square contained twice that of the one before.

Part 1 With your group, determine how many grains are needed for the eighth square. How many for the first row? For the 64th square? To fill the board and fulfill the wish?

Part 2 With your group, design a series of *eight* containers.

- The *first* container should be able to hold all of the grains needed for squares 1 through 8 (row 1).
- The *second* container should be able to hold all of the grains needed for squares 1 through 16.
- The *third* container should be able to hold all of the grains needed for squares 1 through 24, the *fourth* for squares 1 through 32, the *fifth* for squares 1 through 40, the *sixth* for squares 1 through 48, the *seventh* for squares 1 through 56, and the *eighth* for the grains from the entire board.

Of course, each container will be a different size. Assume each grain is the size of a small box 1 mm × 1 mm × 4 mm.

Problem Set 1.6

1. Find S_1, S_2, S_3, S_4, and S_5 for this sequence: 2, 6, 10, 14, 18.

2. a. Find S_{15} for the sequence 2, 6, 18, 54, ...
   b. Sketch a graph of the partial sums S_1 through S_{15}, and name the graphing window.

3. a. Find the sum S_{10} for the sequence 0.3, 0.03, 0.003, ...
   b. Find S_{15}. Describe any difficulties encountered.
   c. What is another way of indicating the infinite decimal suggested by the sum of the terms 0.3, 0.03, 0.003, . . . ?

4. a. Find the sum of the first 12 odd positive integers.
   b. Find the sum of the first 20 odd positive integers.
   c. What is the sum of the first n odd positive integers? (Hint: Try several choices for n until you detect a pattern.)

5. Suppose you practiced the piano 45 min on the first day of school and increased your practice time by 5 min each day. How much total time have you devoted to practice if you are now 15 days into the semester? If you are 35 days into the semester?

6. a. Find the sum of the first 1000 positive integers.
   b. Find the sum of the second 1000 positive integers (the numbers from 1001 to 2000).
   c. Make a guess at the sum of the third 1000 positive integers (the numbers from 2001 to 3000).

d. Now find this sum (the sum indicated in 6c).

e. Describe a way to find the sum of the third 1000 positive integers (the numbers from 2001 to 3000) if you know the sum of the first 1000 positive integers.

7. As a contest winner, you are given the choice of two prizes. The first choice will provide you with $1,000 the first hour, $2,000 the second hour, $3,000 the third hour, and so on. For one entire year, you will be given $1,000 more each hour than you were given during the previous hour. The second choice will provide you with 1¢ the first week, 2¢ the second week, 4¢ the third week, and so on. For one entire year you will be given double the amount you received during the previous week. Which of the two prizes will be more profitable, and by how much?

8. Find the sum S_6 of

$$u_n = \begin{cases} 0.39 & \text{if } n = 1 \\ 0.01 \cdot u_{(n-1)} & \text{if } n > 1. \end{cases}$$

9. There are 650,000 people in a city. Every 15 min, the local media broadcasts an important announcement about a huge downtown fire. During each 15 min time period, 42% of the people who had not yet heard the news become aware of the fire.

a. How many people have heard the news about the downtown fire after 1 hr? After 2 hr?

b. Write a news report on the spread of this story through the city's population. Assume the event took place several hours earlier. Be as detailed and as graphic as you wish.

10. Consider again the role of the graphing calculator in this course. Have you discovered new advantages or disadvantages to using the graphing calculator? If so, what are they? Have your feelings or your perspective changed? Be clear and explain your response.

Geometer's Sketchpad Investigation

Constructing a Sequence

You can use The Geometer's Sketchpad to model a recursive sequence. For example, to model the sequence $u_n = 0.6u_{(n-1)} + 1.5$, follow the steps below.

Step 1 Construct vertical segment AB, making it about 10 cm long. (This length will represent u_0.)

Step 2 Open a new script and click Record.

Step 3 Translate point A horizontally by 0.5 cm. Call the new point D. Then translate B horizontally by 0.5 cm and call the new point C.

Step 4 Dilate point D by 60% around the center, C. Call the new point E.

Step 5 Translate point E vertically by 1.5 cm. Call the new point F.

Step 6 Hide points D and E.

Step 7 Construct segment $\overline{CF}$. (This length will represent u_1.)

Step 8 Select point C and then select point F. Click Loop on your script. Hide the labels of C and F, and then click Stop on the script.

Step 9 Open a new sketch and play the script to recursion depth 25. Start by clicking Step, so that you can see how the script is working. Then you can click Play or Fast to finish the construction.

Step 10 Measure segments $\overline{AB}$ and $\overline{CF}$ and the last segment drawn.

Questions

1. With your calculator, verify the lengths of $\overline{CF}$ and the segment with length u_{25} by using as the starting segment value $\overline{AB}$ and the formula $u_n = 0.6u_{(n-1)} + 1.5$ as the basis for verification.

2. Dynamically change the length of $\overline{AB}$ and watch the effect on the length of the last segment. What happens if $\overline{AB}$ is very short? What happens if $\overline{AB}$ is very long? What conclusions can you draw?

3. Use a similar method to model other recursive sequences. Describe what happens if you try to model a sequence that does not converge.

4. Create a sketch that can be used to model any recursive function of the form $u_n = ru_{(n-1)} + d$, where r and d are any constants. Find a sequence that may converge for some initial values, u_0, and not for others.

5. This project uses geometry to model a recursive function. When you dilate the length of a segment, what mathematical operation are you modeling? When you translate a point, what mathematical operation are you modeling?

Section 1.7

Chapter Review

*A mind that is stretched by a new experience can never go back to its
old dimensions.*
—Oliver Wendell Holmes

A sequence is an ordered list. In this chapter you worked with recursively defined
sequences. A recursive definition specifies one or more initial terms and a rule for
generating the nth term by using the previous term or terms. You learned to calculate
terms by hand, by using on-screen recursion, and by using a program. There are two
special types of sequences—arithmetic and geometric. Arithmetic sequences, like 2, 5,
8, 11, 14, . . . , are generated by always adding the same number to get the next term.
Geometric sequences, like 3, 6, 12, 24, 48, . . . , are generated by always multiplying by
the same number to get the next term. The growth of money in a savings account is
one example of a geometric sequence. Many sequences, like mortgage payoffs, do not
fall into either category. Some sequences tend toward a limiting or long-run value
after many, many terms. Sequences can also be pictured graphically by plotting the
points (n, u_n). Looking at a graph may help you see the long-run value or behavior of a
sequence. When you add the terms of a sequence, you get a series. It's challenging at
times to determine whether you need to calculate a term of a sequence or of a series
to solve a problem, so you must read the problem carefully and think about what is
being asked for. Always check for the reasonableness of your answer.

Problem Set 1.7

1. **a.** Mark Ett arranges a display of soup cans as shown in the picture.
   List the number of cans in the top row, in the second row, in the
   third row, and so on, down to the tenth row.
   b. Write a recursive formula for the terms of the sequence in 1a.
   c. If the cans are to be stacked 47 rows high, how many cans will it
   take to build the display?
   d. If Mark uses six cases (288 cans), how tall can he make the
   display?

2. Consider the arithmetic sequence 3, 7, 11, 15, ...
   a. What is the 128th term?   **b.** Which term has the value 159?
   c. Find u_{20}.   **d.** Find S_{20}.

3. Consider the geometric sequence 256, 192, 144, 108, ...
   a. What is the eighth term?   **b.** Which term is the first one smaller than 20?
   c. Find u_7.   **d.** Find S_7.

4. a. If you invest $500 in a bank that pays 5.5% annual interest compounded quarterly, how much money will you have after 5 yr?

   b. Start over and invest $500 at 5.5% annual interest compounded quarterly, and deposit an additional $150 every three months. Now find the balance after 5 yr.

5. The enrollment at the local university is currently 5678. From now on, the university will graduate 24% of its students yearly and add 1250 new ones. What will the enrollment be during the sixth year? What will the enrollment be in the long run?

6. What monthly payment will be required to pay off an $80,000 mortgage at 8.9% interest in 30 yr?

7. List the first five terms of each sequence.

   a. $u_n = \begin{cases} -3 & \text{if } n = 1 \\ u_{(n-1)} + 1.5 & \text{if } n > 1 \end{cases}$ **b.** $u_n = \begin{cases} 2 & \text{if } n = 1 \\ 3 \cdot u_{(n-1)} - 2 & \text{if } n > 1 \end{cases}$

Assessing What You've Learned—Journal Writing

Many students find it useful to reflect on what they're learning by writing in a journal. Like a personal journal or diary, a mathematics journal is a chance to have a conversation with yourself about what's going on in your life. Unlike a personal journal, though, your mathematics journal isn't private—your teacher will probably want to see it. While you might write in your mathematics journal about your feelings toward mathematics, use it primarily to organize your thoughts about what you've learned and what you're still having difficulty with in mathematics. A journal is different from the notebook in which you keep your notes, classwork, and homework. Rather than being a collection of work, a journal contains your reflections on that work.

Throughout the book you will find prompts for journal entries. Many times this prompt will be the last problem in a problem set. Look at the last problems in Problem Sets 1.5 and 1.6. As the year progresses, you'll find other journal prompts in this book. Your teacher may provide journal questions too. But you need not wait to be prompted to write in your journal—write in it any time.

Organize Your Notebook

- This chapter talked about ordered lists of numbers. If a sequence is out of order, you cannot determine the next term. Similarly, if your homework and other papers are out of order, it is much more difficult to review your work. Now that you have finished the assignments in this chapter, go back through them. If there are missing problems, now do them. Also, if you have done any incorrectly, try to fix your errors. By the time you finish, you should have a complete and correct record of your work in this chapter. Going back over old work and correcting your errors is a helpful step in making sure that your understanding is complete.

- You probably learned many techniques for using recursion to solve problems in this chapter. You will continue to encounter these kinds of problems throughout the text, so take a few minutes and record in your notebook any calculator techniques you found to be especially useful.

2

Sequences and Explicit Formulas

These fractured ocean ice blocks resemble a fractal-like geometric pattern.
Fractal patterns in nature often result from seemingly random events.
Likewise in mathematics, an orderly pattern can emerge out of a random
process. Often you can use either a recursive definition or an explicit rule
to generate the same sequence. There are many surprising connections
between fractal patterns, sequences, and series.

Section 2.1

Explicit Formulas for Arithmetic Sequences

Education's purpose is to replace an empty mind with an open one.
—Malcolm S. Forbes

Matias wants to call his aunt in Chile on her birthday. He learned that the first minute costs $2.27, and each additional minute costs $1.37. How much would it cost to talk for 30 minutes?

   If you're thinking recursively, the answer is easy: It costs $2.27 for 1 minute; $1.37 more, or $3.64, for 2 minutes; $5.01 for 3 minutes, and so on. Just keep adding $1.37. It's an arithmetic sequence with a first term of 2.27 and a common difference of 1.37. But you don't want to carry that sequence all the way out to 30 terms. So what does the recursive definition tell you about the 30th term of the sequence? Only that it's 1.37 more than the 29th term—not much help if you don't know the 29th term. But you can find the 29th term: It's 1.37 more than the 28th term, and that's . . . hmm. Can you see the limitations of a recursive definition? You want to be able to find the value of *any* term in the sequence without having to start at (or work back to) the beginning of the sequence. Explicit formulas allow you to do that.

Explicit Formula for a Sequence

The **explicit formula** for a sequence defines u_n with an expression that does not involve previous terms. Individual terms are defined in terms of *n*, where *n* is a nonnegative integer.

   Fortunately, Matias found a direct way to calculate the cost of a 30-minute call. He figured he'd pay $2.27 for the first minute and $1.37 for each of the next 29 minutes. So he calculated $2.27 + (29)(1.37)$. The call would cost $42. You can use this method to find the cost of a phone call of any length. Can you write an expression for calculating the cost of an *n*-minute call?

   You may find some patterns easier to define explicitly than recursively. Consider the sequence 1, 4, 9, 16, 25, . . . , 225. There is no *common difference,* so this sequence is not arithmetic. It isn't geometric, because consecutive terms have no *common ratio.* This sequence isn't even a combination of the two. Yet, chances are you can see a pattern and you can find the missing terms between 25 and 225. In this case, you can easily relate the term number *n* and the term value u_n.

n	1	2	3	4	5	6	7
u_n	1	4	9	16	25	-?-	-?-

To find the term value, just square the number of the term. Thus, $u_8 = 8^2 = 64$, and $u_{15} = 15^2 = 225$. What is u_{10}? Find n so that $u_n = 289$.

The formula $u_n = n^2$ is an example of an explicit formula for a sequence. You can calculate any term by substituting that particular term number for n. You don't need to know any previous terms, as you would with a recursive definition.

■ Example 1

Complete a table of values for the sequence defined by the explicit formula $u_n = 2(1 + 3n)$.

n	1	2	3	4	...	11	...	-?-	n
u_n	-?-	-?-	-?-	-?-	...	-?-	...	52	$2(1 + 3n)$

Solution

The solution involves substitution, which is typical of most work with explicit formulas. To find u_1, substitute 1 for n in the formula and simplify.

$$u_1 = 2(1 + 3 \cdot 1)$$
$$u_1 = 2(4)$$
$$u_1 = 8 \qquad \text{Likewise for } n = 2, 3, 4, \text{ and } 11.$$

Finding the missing value of n when $u_n = 152$ also involves substitution.

$$152 = u_n$$
$$152 = 2(1 + 3n) \qquad \text{Substitute } 2(1 + 3n) \text{ for } u_n.$$
$$76 = 1 + 3n \qquad \text{Divide by 2.}$$
$$75 = 3n \qquad \text{Subtract 1.}$$
$$25 = n \qquad \text{Divide by 3.}$$

This means that $u_{25} = 152$. ■

The greatest difficulty occurs when the formula is unknown and you are to describe a relation between n and u_n. Some relations will require creative solutions. Here is an unusual sequence. Can you complete it?

n	1	2	3	4	5	6	...	10	...	18	19
u_n	O	T	T	F	F	S	...	-?-	...	E	-?-

Try this next one.

n	1	2	3	4	...	11	...	-?-	...	n
u_n	2	5	10	17	...	-?-	...	401	...	-?-

Hint: The formula involves squaring.

The real purpose of this section, however, is for you to learn to write and use explicit formulas for *arithmetic sequences* like the one given in the phone call example. Although you can use creative thinking or guessing to find these formulas, you can also use what you know about writing equations for lines.

■ Example 2

Find an explicit formula for the arithmetic sequence 2, 8, 14, 20, 26, . . . , and use it to find u_{22} and the value of n to make $u_n = 86$.

Solution

Notice that the common difference is 6. First create a data set representing the sequence as pairs of numbers, with n representing the number of the term and u_n representing the term itself.

n	1	2	3	4	5	...	22	...	-?-	...	n
u_n	2	8	14	20	26	...	-?-	...	86	...	-?-

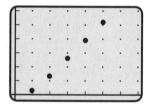

Graph the sequence. The graphing window shown at right is [0, 7, 1, 0, 30, 5].

The common difference between terms is 6. The points appear to lie on a line. What is the slope (rate of increase) of this line?

The vertical intercept of this line would be ⁻4. Do you see why?

The explicit formula of the sequence using the slope and vertical intercept is $u_n = 6n - 4$.

NOTE

2A

Now you can use this formula to find u_{22}. By substitution, $u_{22} = 6 \cdot 22 - 4$. Therefore, $u_{22} = 128$. (See **Calculator Note 2A**.)

Find n when $u_n = 86$. Again, by substituting in the formula $86 = 6n - 4$, you get $n = 15$.

The equation of the line $y = 6x - 4$ will also contain all of the points in the sequence. ■

What is the relationship between the common difference of an arithmetic sequence and the slope of the line that connects the points representing the sequence? Will the graph of every arithmetic sequence be a set of points that appear to lie on a line? Why or why not?

Problem Set 2.1

1. a. Find the first five terms of the sequence whose nth term (the **generator**) is given by

$$u_n = \frac{n(n + 1)(2n + 3)}{6}.$$

b. Is this sequence arithmetic, geometric, or neither?

2. Complete the table and write an explicit formula for the sequence. (Hint: Experiment with different calculator keys.)

n	1	2	3	4	5	6	...	-?-	...	n
u_n	1	1.41	1.73	2	2.24	-?-	...	3.87	...	-?-

3. a. Graph the sequence $u_n = \begin{cases} 18 & \text{if } n = 1 \\ u_{(n-1)} - 3 & \text{if } 1 < n \le 6. \end{cases}$

   b. What is the common difference?
   c. What is the slope of the line that contains the points?
   d. What is the vertical or u_n-intercept?
   e. Write the explicit formula for the sequence.
   f. Use this formula to find u_{10}.
   g. Write the equation of the line that contains these points.

4. a. What are the terms of the sequence pictured?
   b. What is u_3?
   c. What is the common difference?
   d. If the pattern is continued, what is u_5? What is u_0?
   e. What is the slope of the line through the points?
   f. What is the u_n-intercept?
   g. Write the explicit formula for the sequence.
   h. Write the equation of the line that contains these points.

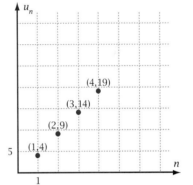

5. Find the four arithmetic means between 7 and 27. In other words, find an arithmetic sequence that reads 7, -?-, -?-, -?-, -?-, 27.

   a. Name two points on the graph of this sequence, (-?-, 7) and (-?-, 27).
   b. Plot the two points you named in 5a, and find the slope of the line connecting the points. (You can assume the points lie on a line, because the sequence is arithmetic.)
   c. Use the slope to find the missing terms and the term just prior to the 7.
   d. Plot all the points, and write the equation of the line that contains them.
   e. What equation gives the explicit formula for the sequence u_n?
   f. What is the connection between the slope and the common difference in this sequence?

6. a. Write an explicit formula for an arithmetic sequence with a first term of 6.3 and a common difference of 2.5.
   b. Use the formula to figure out which term is 78.8.

7. Suppose you drive from Interlochen (which is 15 mi from Traverse City) toward Detroit at a steady 54 mi/hr.

  a. What is your distance from Traverse City after driving 4 hr?

  b. Write an equation that represents your distance from Traverse City after x hours.

  c. Graph the equation.

  d. Does this equation model an arithmetic sequence? Why or why not?

8. Les Cache's older brother, Noah, sells cars for a living. If he sells only three cars, he is still in debt by $2,050. If Noah sells seven cars, he makes a profit of $1,550. Assume that d (the number of dollars of profit) is related to c (the number of cars sold) and that the possible profits form an arithmetic sequence.

  a. List a few terms of this sequence of profits.

  b. Sketch a graph of possible profits.

  c. What is the real-world meaning of the common difference?

  d. What is the real-world meaning of the slope of a line drawn through the points?

  e. What is the real-world meaning of the horizontal and vertical intercepts?

  f. What is the explicit formula relating profit to cars sold?

9. The points on the graph on the right represent the first five terms of an arithmetic sequence. The height of each point can be described as its distance from the x-axis, or the value of the second coordinate of the point.

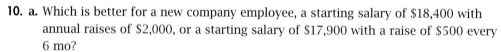

  a. Find u_0, the second coordinate of the point preceding those given.

  b. How many common differences (d's) are needed to get from the height of $(0, u_0)$ to the height of $(5, u_5)$?

  c. How many d's would be needed to get from the height of $(0, u_0)$ to the height of $(7, u_7)$?

  d. Explain why the height from the x-axis to $(7, u_7)$ can be found using the equation $u_7 = u_0 + 7d$.

  e. The height of $(13, u_{13})$ is $u_{13} = u_0 + (?)d$.

  f. In general, for an arithmetic sequence, $u_n = $ –?–.

10. a. Which is better for a new company employee, a starting salary of $18,400 with annual raises of $2,000, or a starting salary of $17,900 with a raise of $500 every 6 mo?

  b. Is there ever a time when one choice is better than the other? Explain.

Take Another Look 2.1

Several times in Chapter 1 you were asked to find a monthly payment for a loan or a mortgage. At this point you can probably use techniques involving guess-and-check to help someone determine if they can afford to finance a new house.

a. Describe a technique that you could use to find the correct monthly payment for a 25 yr mortgage of $84,000 with an annual interest rate of 7.4%.

b. Explain how you would verify that the payment found in part a was correct.

The next few questions suggest another technique for finding the correct monthly payment for the mortgage described above. Once mastered, very little guess-and-check will be necessary. This strategy, which requires very little time to master or to use, was discovered by an algebra student. Please share any discoveries that you make during the year with your teacher and classmates.

The bank or mortgage owner makes money by charging interest. Typically, most of the money collected for early mortgage payments is used to pay the interest—very little of the payment remains to reduce the balance.

c. Explain how to find the amount of money needed to cover only the first month's interest (in other words, the entire payment would be used to pay the interest).

d. Describe what would occur to the mortgage balance if someone made monthly payments of the amount you found in part c.

e. Describe what would occur if someone were to make monthly payments less than the amount found in part c.

f. Create a table similar to the one below. In the first column list the payment you calculated in part c and four more monthly payment amounts. (The five payments should form an increasing arithmetic sequence with a common difference of $1.) Compute and record the final loan balance to the nearest penny for each payment.

Monthly payment	Final balance after 25 yr	Common difference
-?-	-?-	-?-
-?-	-?-	-?-
-?-	-?-	-?-
-?-	-?-	-?-
-?-	-?-	-?-

g. Complete the third column and describe any patterns that you find.

h. Think about what would happen if you continued entering payments in the table. Describe a process (using the pattern you discovered in parts f and g) that will provide the correct monthly mortgage payment for the new house.

i. What is the correct monthly payment for this mortgage? Describe a process you could use to verify that this amount is correct.

j. How many rows in your table were really necessary? Explain your thinking.

k. Use the new strategy introduced here to solve Problem 6 in Problem Set 1.7.

Explicit Formulas for Arithmetic Series

*If I am given a formula, and I am ignorant of its meaning, it cannot teach me
anything, but if I already know it, what does the formula teach me?*
—St. Augustine

Suppose a family friend just told you the
story of her life and the history of her
current job. Her original, or first-year,
salary was $18,400, with annual raises
averaging about $2,000. How much did
she make during the first 15 years? The
series $S_{15} = 18{,}400 + 20{,}400 + 22{,}400 +$
$\cdots + u_{15}$ provides this income total. One
disadvantage of computing this sum
recursively is that you, or the calculator,
must compute each of the individual
salaries. Is there any way to compute the
income total without finding all 15
numbers and adding?

If you can find an explicit formula, you
will be able to compute the sum directly.
Explicit formulas allow you to compute
sums very quickly, and the process that
is involved helps you develop more
mathematical power. The following
example and activities will give you an
opportunity to discover at least one
explicit formula for summing terms of an
arithmetic series.

■ **Example 1**

Recall the problem given to Gauss when he was 9 years old. He was asked to find the
sum of the first 100 counting numbers.

$$1 + 2 + 3 + \cdots + 98 + 99 + 100 = S \text{ (the total sum)}$$

Solution

His ingenious solution was to add the terms in pairs. Consider the series written
normally and written backwards.

1	+	2	+	3	+	$\cdots$	+	98	+	99	+	100	=	S_{100}
100	+	99	+	98	+	$\cdots$	+	3	+	2	+	1	=	S_{100}
101	+	101	+	101	+	$\cdots$	+	101	+	101	+	101	=	$2S_{100}$

The sum of each column shown is 101. In fact, the sum of *every* column is 101. There are 100 columns. Thus, the sum of the integers 1 through 100 is $\frac{100 \cdot 101}{2}$. The 2 as a divisor is the tricky part; it is necessary because the series was added twice (forward and backward). ■

Investigation 2.2.1

Arithmetic Series Formula

Write your own arithmetic series, one that is different from those written by other group members. Select a start value, a common difference, and a number of terms (between 10 and 20).

a. Use Gauss's method, as shown in Example 1, to compute the sum of your series.

b. Check your sum by using a method from Chapter 1.

c. Work together with other members of your group to develop a formula for the sum of an arithmetic series. (Hint: Think about the information you'll need in order to use Gauss's method.) Test your formula by finding $S_{15} = 18{,}400 + 20{,}400 + 22{,}400 + \cdots + u_{15}$. (Your answer should be 486,000.)

Another way to write the sum of the terms of a sequence is to use the symbol Σ. The letter Σ (sigma) is a capital S in the Greek alphabet, and it stands for "sum." The expression

$$\sum_{n=1}^{15} u_n$$

is a shorthand way of writing $u_1 + u_2 + u_3 + \cdots + u_{15}$. For example, the notation

$$\sum_{n=1}^{15} (18{,}400 + 2{,}000(n-1))$$

tells you to substitute the values $[1, 2, 3, \ldots, 15]$ for n in the expression $u_n = 18{,}400 + 2{,}000(n-10)$, and then sum the resulting 15 values.

Investigation 2.2.2
Toothpick Trapezoids

It takes five toothpicks to build the top trapezoid figure pictured at the right. Nine toothpicks are enough to build a two-in-a-row configuration of trapezoids, because the two trapezoids share one side. Thirteen toothpicks are needed to build a three-in-a-row configuration of trapezoids.

Build several more rows of trapezoids, each containing one more trapezoid than the preceding row.

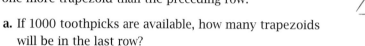

a. If 1000 toothpicks are available, how many trapezoids will be in the last row?

b. How many rows will there be?

c. How many toothpicks will be used?

d. Use the numbers in this investigation to carefully describe the difference between a sequence and a series.

There are times when adding individual terms or numbers together is questionable. For example, consider this sign posted at the city limits of a small town.

Problem Set 2.2

1. Find the sum of the first 50 multiples of 6.
(Hint: $6 + 12 + 18 + \cdots + u_{50}$.)

2. Find the sum of the first 75 even numbers, starting with 2.

3. a. Find u_{75} if $u_n = 2n - 1$.

b. Find $\displaystyle\sum_{n=1}^{75} (2n - 1)$.

c. Find $\displaystyle\sum_{n=20}^{75} (2n - 1)$.

4. a. Find S_{67} for the sequence $125.3 + 118.5 + 111.7 + 104.9 + \cdots$.

b. Write an equivalent expression for S_{67} using sigma (Σ) notation.

5. a. What is the 46th term of the sequence shown at the right?

b. Write a general expression for u_n.

c. Find the total sum of the heights from the horizontal axis of the first 46 points of the sequence pictured.

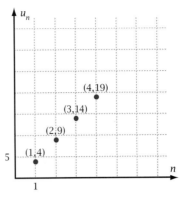

6. A large barrel contained 12.4 gal of oil 18 min after a drain was opened. How many gallons of oil were in the barrel initially, if it drained at 4.2 gal/min?

7. Make several different graph sketches, each representing a generic arithmetic sequence. What graph shapes are possible? (Hint: Use what you know about different kinds of slopes.)

8. Your friend buys you a concert ticket for seat 995 in a concert hall with 65 seats in row one, 67 seats in row two, 69 seats in row three, and so on. The seats are numbered from left to right, so the first seat in row one is 1, the first seat in row two is 66, and so on. The concert hall has 40 rows of seats.

a. How many seats are in the last row?

b. How many seats are in the concert hall?

c. Describe the location of your seat.

9. a. Find the area of the trapezoid bounded by the x-axis, vertical segments at $x = 5$ and $x = 6$, and the line containing points of the sequence $u_n = 1.8n + 2.6$.

b. Find the total area between the line through the sequence points, and the x-axis from $x = 0$ to $x = 10$.

c. Explain how you can find the area from 9b using a series of ten terms.

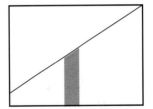

Section 2.3

Explicit Formulas for Geometric Sequences

I wish to God these calculations had been executed by steam.
—Charles Babbage

Have you and your classmates tried linking calculators, or transferring data from one calculator to another using some electronic method? Suppose there are a sufficient number of link cables in a classroom and that it takes 20 seconds to link and then transfer a program from one calculator to another. During the first time period, the program is transferred to one calculator; during the second time period, to two more calculators; during the third time period, to four more calculators; and so on. How long before everyone in a class of 25 students has the program? How long before everyone in a lecture hall of 250 students has the program? You could answer these questions very quickly if you knew an explicit formula for the sequence involved.

Over uniform time periods (like 20 seconds, 1 day, 1 year, or 1 decade), many increasing populations produce a sequence that often can be modeled approximately by a geometric sequence.

Decade	1890	1900	1910	1920	1930	1940	1950	1960
California population (millions)	1.213	1.485	2.378	3.427	5.677	6.907	10.586	15.717

Source: The Universal Almanac 1994.

This table of figures lists California's census populations for the years 1890, 1900, 1910, . . . , 1960. (If you investigate the growth after 1960, you will find a different pattern.) You can create an approximate model for this growth in successive decades by finding a common ratio and multiplying. (Use 0, 1, 2, . . . 7 to represent the decades 1890, 1900, 1910, . . . , 1960 respectively.)

1.213 u_0, or the initial population (in 1890).

$1.213 \cdot 1.45$ Population one decade later = 1.759 (approx).

$(1.213 \cdot 1.45) \cdot 1.45 = 1.213 \cdot 1.45^2$ Population two decades later = 2.550 (approx).

$(1.213 \cdot 1.45^2) \cdot 1.45 = 1.213 \cdot 1.45^3$ Population three decades later = 3.698 (approx).

and so on.

Can you write a similar expression for u_7, the population seven decades later?

The 1.45 used in the solution is the average ratio of any two consecutive populations, $\frac{\text{next decade population}}{\text{present decade population}}$, found in the table. By graphing the actual data and the values generated by the model, you can see how well the model fits the data.

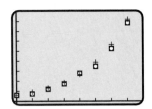

Investigation 2.3.1

Bouncing a Superball

In this investigation, you will work with your group to gather data from an experiment. Your group needs to decide upon a good experimental procedure. Try to collect data that are as accurate as possible. Your group may have to be imaginative and creative to obtain accurate measurements. Do not oversimplify the experiment by making assumptions that you have not tested.

a. Carefully drop a superball from a starting height of 200 cm. Record the height of the first rebound, then of the second rebound, and so on, to the sixth rebound. Repeat the experiment five times. Copy and complete a table like the one below to show the results of all five trials for each rebound number.

First rebound

Trial number	Rebound height
1	–?–
2	–?–
3	–?–
4	–?–
5	–?–

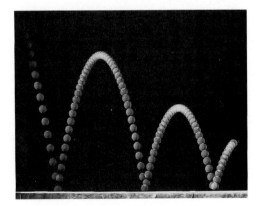

b. Find and record the average height of all the first rebounds in the five trials. Do the same for the second rebounds, the third rebounds, and so on. Complete a table like the one at the top of the next page.

Rebound number	Average height	Reound ratio
0	200	
1	-?-	-?-
2	-?-	-?-
3	-?-	-?-
4	-?-	-?-
5	-?-	-?-
6	-?-	-?-

c. Compute the rebound ratio, the fraction representing $\dfrac{\text{height of rebound}}{\text{distance of previous fall}}$ for the ball you are using. Call this fraction r (for *ratio*.)

d. Describe some of the factors that might affect the ratio in this experiment.

Because the original height term zero, the term number, n, is equal to the number of rebounds. For example, u_0 is after no rebounds, u_5 is after five rebounds.

Ideally, the ratios in your table will be the same for each rebound number.

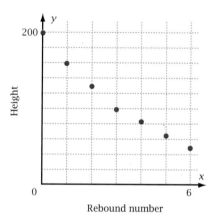

e. Write a recursive formula that uses this common ratio. The value for the first term should be nearly equal to $200 \cdot r$.

f. Express the value of the second term using only 200 and your value of r.

g. Express the value of the fifth term (the height of the fifth rebound) using only 200 and r.

h. Express the value of the nth term using only 200 and r.

i. Write an explicit formula using only u_0 and the variable r.

■ Example 1

An automobile depreciates as it gets older. This means it becomes less valuable. Suppose that every year it loses one-fifth of its value (or maintains four-fifths of its value). Find the value of a six-year-old automobile that initially cost $14,000.

Solution

The geometric sequence of annual values shown at the top of the next page represents the pattern of the car's depreciation.

CHAPTER 2   SEQUENCES AND EXPLICIT FORMULAS

Original value	Value after 1 yr	Value after 2 yr
$14,000	$14,000(0.8)	$14,000(0.8)^2

Therefore, the six-year-old car has a value of $14,000(0.8)^6, or $3,670.02. ∎

Problem Set 2.3

1. Use an explicit formula to find the fifteenth term of the sequence 2, 6, 18, 54, ...

2. Suppose $1,500 is deposited in an account earning 5.5% annually, compounded annually. What is the balance after 8 yr? (Remember that the multiplier must be greater than 1 for the balance to grow.) How long before the balance is at least $5,000?

3. What could be a real-world meaning for these expressions? Use the value of the expression in a sentence.
   a. $4000(1 + 0.072)^{10}$

   b. $4000\left(1 + \dfrac{0.072}{12}\right)^{48}$

   c. Write an explicit formula for the solution to Problem 2.

4. Without using your calculator, match each sequence in the second column to an explicit formula in the first column. After you have done this, check your answer with your calculator.

   a. $u_n = 2(5)^n$ i. 7, 9, 11, 13, 15, . . .

   b. $u_n = 2 + 5n$ ii. 10, 20, 40, 80, . . .

   c. $u_n = 5(2)^n$ iii. 7, 12, 17, 22, 27, . . .

   d. $u_n = 5 + 2n$ iv. 10, 50, 250, 1250, . . .

5. Try different values of r in the expression $u_n = 60 \cdot r^n$. Try negative numbers, fractions, 0, 1, and −1. Make sketches of the different graphs that are possible as n gets larger. Write a paragraph describing at least two discoveries you made.

6. Without using your calculator, match each explicit formula to a graph. After you have done this, check your answers by graphing each equation on your calculator.

   a. $u_n = 10(0.75)^n$ **b.** $u_n = 10(1.25)^n$ **c.** $u_n = 10(1.00)^n$

   i.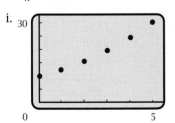

   ii.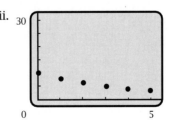

   iii.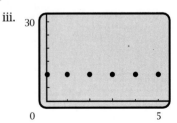

7. Suppose the rebound heights (in inches) of an ideal rebounding ball are 80, 64, 51.2, 40.96, ... The initial height from which the ball is dropped is 100 in.

  a. What is the height of the tenth rebound?

  b. How far in the sequence do you have to go until the height becomes less than 1 in.? Less than 0.1 in.?

8. The week of February 14, store owner J. C. Nickels ordered hundreds of heart-shaped red vacuum cleaners. The next week, he still had hundreds of heart-shaped red vacuum cleaners, so he told his manager to discount the price 25% each week until they were all sold. The first week they sold for $80.

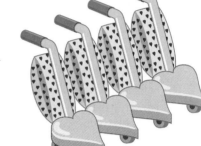

  a. Write an explicit formula you can use to find the price of the vacuum cleaners in successive weeks.

  b. What was the price in the second week?

  c. What was the price of the vacuums in the fourth week?

  d. When will the vacuum sell for less than $10? (You may need to use guess-and-check to answer this question.)

9. Suppose $u_n = \begin{cases} 0.39 & \text{if } n = 1 \\ 0.01 \cdot u_{(n-1)} & \text{if } n > 1. \end{cases}$ Find $\displaystyle\sum_{n=1}^{6} u_n$.

10. In Chapter 1, you studied sequences by looking at recursive definitions. In this chapter you have been learning about explicit definitions for sequences. Write a letter to a new student in the class explaining how these approaches differ. Discuss the advantages and disadvantages of each approach.

Project

Instant Money

Recently, an advertisement came through the mail offering a low-payment loan. The advertisement claimed the loan was ideal for paying off high-interest-rate credit card debts or for consolidating all debts. The promoters claimed to offer low monthly payments, which are always 2% of the loan balance. With even a mediocre credit history, an interested individual could borrow up to $5,000 instantly. The first monthly payment would only be $100, and the dollar amount of each payment after that would decrease, as long as you didn't borrow more money. The loan had no initial fees (another "plus") and charged an annual percentage interest rate of 21.9% compounded monthly. Analyze the proposal mathematically, and offer your own conclusions about whether or not this is a good offer. Be very detailed in your analysis (as if you were writing to someone who is not very knowledgeable about loans and interest).

Section 2.4

Explicit Formulas for Geometric Series

For the things of this world cannot be made known without a knowledge of mathematics.
—Roger Bacon

In the last section, you were asked, "If a pair of calculators can be linked and a program transferred from one calculator to the other in 20 seconds, how long before everyone in a lecture hall of 250 students has the program?" During the first time period, the program is transferred to one calculator; during the second time period, to two calculators; during the third time period, to four more calculators; and so on. Do you see that the problem involves determining the maximum value of n before $S_n = 1 + 2 + 4 + \cdots + u_n$ exceeds 250?

You have developed recursive tools for finding the sum of geometric series. For some series, those involving a large number of terms, an explicit formula is very accurate, and faster to compute. This investigation will help you develop an explicit formula for summing terms of geometric sequences.

Investigation 2.4.1

Explicit Geometric Series

Let the month you were born be called r, and the day you were born be called u_1. (Note: If you were born in January, choose any number between 2 and 12 for r.)

a. List the first six terms of the geometric sequence defined by u_1 and r.

b. Multiply each term of this sequence by r, and write a new sequence.

c. Cancel any values that appear in both lists.

d. Subtract those terms remaining in the sequence you wrote in part b from those remaining in the sequence in part a.

e. Find the value of $(1 - r)$, and divide this into the answer from part d.

f. Find the sum of the original six numbers.

g. Working together with your group, write an explanation for what happened. Find an explicit formula that gives the sum of the terms of a geometric series. Test your formula on another group member's series.

h. Why will the formula you wrote in part g not work when r is equal to one?

There are many ways to express the explicit formula for the sum of a geometric series. You need to be familiar with different symbolic forms of the formula. The information you gather will determine which form you need to use. In Example 1 below, the formula uses only three pieces of information—the first term, the common ratio, and the number of terms. This explicit formula may look different from your version, but it does not require you to find any other terms before you find the sum.

■ Example 1

Find S_{10} for the series defined by $16 + 24 + 36 + \cdots + u_{10}$.

Solution

The first term, u_1, equals 16; the common ratio, r, equals 1.5; and the number of terms, n, equals 10.

$$S_{10} = \frac{16(1 - 1.5^{10})}{1 - 1.5} = 1813.28125 \quad ■$$

Try using the explicit formula used in Example 1 to find S_6 in Investigation 2.4.1.

■ Example 2

Each day, the now-extinct Caterpillarsaurus would eat 25% more leaves than it did the day before. If a 30-day-old Caterpillarsaurus has eaten 151,677 leaves in its brief lifetime, how many will it eat the next day?

Solution

In this problem the first term is unknown, but $r = (1 + 0.25) = 1.25$, and $n = 30$. This means

$$\frac{u_1(1 - 1.25^{30})}{1 - 1.25} = 151{,}677$$

$$3227.17u_1 = 151{,}677$$

$$u_1 = \frac{151{,}677}{3227.17} = 47.$$

Knowing this, you can predict that on its 31st day the Caterpillarsaurus will consume no less than $47(1.25)^{30} = 37{,}966$ leaves. ■

Problem Set 2.4

1. Find the missing value in each set of numbers. This may require some guess-and-check work.

   a. $u_1 = 3$ $r = 2$ $n = 10$ $S_{10} = $ -?-

   b. $u_1 = 4$ $r = 0.6$ $n = $ -?- $S_? = 9.999868378$

   c. $u_1 = $ -?- $r = 1.4$ $n = 15$ $S_{15} = 1081.976669$

   d. $u_1 = 5.5$ $r = $ -?- $n = 18$ $S_{18} = 66.30642497$

2. Sue Perntendant has been offered a 7 yr contract totaling $2.7 million. Her first-year salary is $200,000. Assume she is to get the same percentage raise each year. What is that percentage?

3. Consider the geometric series $5 + 10 + 20 + 40 + \cdots$.

   a. Create a table of the first seven partial sums, $S_1, S_2, S_3, \ldots, S_7$.

   b. Do the sums found in 3a also form a geometric sequence?

   c. If $u_1 = 5$, find a value(s) of r so that consecutive partial sums also form a geometric sequence.

4. Find each sum for $u_n = \begin{cases} 40 & \text{if } n = 1 \\ 0.60u_{(n-1)} & \text{if } n > 1. \end{cases}$

   a. S_5 **b.** S_{15} **c.** S_{25}

5. $\dfrac{1}{1} + \dfrac{1}{2} + \dfrac{1}{3} + \dfrac{1}{4} + \cdots + \dfrac{1}{8} = \displaystyle\sum_{n=1}^{8} \dfrac{1}{n}$.

   (Notice that $1, 2, 3, \ldots, 8$ replace n in the expression $\dfrac{1}{n}$ to form the series.)

   a. Is this series arithmetic, geometric, or neither?

   b. Find the sum of this series.

6. **a.** List the terms of the series indicated by $\displaystyle\sum_{n=1}^{7} n^2$ and find the sum.

   b. List the terms of the series indicated by $\displaystyle\sum_{n=3}^{7} n^2$ and find the sum.

7. Remember the chess inventor and his wish in Investigation 1.6.1?

   a. How many grains of wheat are on that 64th square?

   b. How many grains of wheat are there on the entire chessboard?

   c. Write the series using sigma (Σ) notation.

8. Suppose $u_n = \begin{cases} 8 & \text{if } n = 1 \\ 0.5 \cdot u_{(n-1)} & \text{if } n > 1. \end{cases}$

   a. Find $\displaystyle\sum_{n=1}^{10} u_n$.   **b.** Find $\displaystyle\sum_{n=1}^{20} u_n$.   **c.** Find $\displaystyle\sum_{n=1}^{30} u_n$.

   d. Explain what is happening to these partial sums as you add more terms.

Living in the City

In a recent article, Sonya Ross of the Associated Press stated: "The world's big cities are growing by 1 million people a week and will hold more than half the earth's population within a decade. . . . Urban populations are growing by 3.8% a year, and it is projected that by 2020, 3.6 billion people will inhabit urban areas while about 3 billion will remain in rural areas. . . . In 1990, there were 1.4 billion people living in the world's urban areas." There are several statements here about the population of large cities. Some of them contradict each other, and some just don't work out. Write a response to these statements showing the formulas you used and the conclusions you reached based on the facts and predictions in the article. Try viewing the information from different perspectives. Use two or three "facts" from the article to set up equations and to draw more conclusions.

New York City, New York, USA

Kassala, Sudan

Section 2.5

In the Long Run

We used to think that if we knew one, we knew two, because one and one are two.
We are finding that we must learn a great deal more about "and."
—Sir Arthur Eddington

In preceding sections, you developed some useful explicit formulas for sequences and series. These formulas are expressed in more formal mathematical notation below.

Explicit Formulas for Arithmetic and Geometric Sequences and Series

The **explicit formula for the general term of an arithmetic sequence** is

$$u_n = u_0 + nd,$$

where d represents the common difference between the terms and $n = 1, 2, 3, \ldots$.
The explicit formula can also be given as

$$u_n = u_1 + (n - 1)d.$$

The **sum of an arithmetic series** is given by the formula

$$S_n = \frac{n(u_1 + u_n)}{2},$$

where n is the number of terms, u_1 is the first term, and u_n is the last term.

The **explicit formula for the general term of a geometric sequence** is

$$u_n = u_0 \cdot r^n,$$

where r represents the common ratio between the terms and $n = 1, 2, 3, \ldots$.
The explicit formula can also be given as

$$u_n = u_1 \cdot r^{(n-1)}.$$

The **sum of a geometric series** is given by the formula

$$S_n = \frac{u_1(1 - r^n)}{1 - r},$$

where u_1 is the first term, r is the common ratio ($r \neq 1$), and n is the number of terms.

These formulas work when you have a specific number of terms. But what happens "in the long run"? How can you find out what would happen if n, the number of terms, grew without bound? Some series, called **convergent series**, have a limiting value as the number of terms gets larger.

The Portuguese scholar José Anastácio da Cunha (1744–1787) was one of the first to give a criterion for a convergent series in his book *Principios Matemáticos,* which was published in sections beginning in 1782. He wrote:

A **convergent** series, so Mathematicians say, is one whose terms are similarly determined, each one by the number of the preceding terms, in such a way that the series can always be continued, and finally it need not matter whether it does or does not because one may neglect without considerable error the sum of any number of terms one might wish to add to those already written or indicated.

Da Cunha had some ups and downs before he published his book. He was a military officer during the French and Spanish invasion of Portugal and was appointed to the chair of geometry at the University of Coimbra in 1773. He gained a reputation as a freethinker and, after the death of the king of Portugal in 1777, was arrested and convicted by the Inquisition. He was pardoned in 1781 and spent the remainder of his life as a teacher of mathematics in a Lisbon school for poor children.

In Section 2.6, you will consider the **Sierpiǹski triangle**. This figure begins as an equilateral triangle with each segment one unit in length. The recursive procedure is to replace the triangle with three congruent smaller equilateral triangles in such a way that each smaller triangle shares a vertex with the larger triangle. What do you expect to happen to the area in the long run? What is the long-run sum of the segments? Some sequences and series have a **limiting value**, and some do not. In this section, you will find more long-run answers and make some initial classifications.

Investigation 2.5.1

Counting Beans

Begin this investigation by assigning tasks in your group. There are four jobs that need to be done. They will be carried out by the bean counter, the bean taker, the bean giver, and the recorder. Your group will be given some beans to be kept in the "bank."

Before beginning the investigation, the *bean giver* gives the *bean counter* 10 beans from the bank. Repeat the steps below until the number of beans in the pile stops changing or until it becomes obvious that the number of beans in the pile will never stop changing.

- On each turn, it is the task of the *bean taker* to take 20% of the bean counter's beans (rounded off to the nearest bean) and return them to the bank.

CHAPTER 2 SEQUENCES AND EXPLICIT FORMULAS

- It is the job of the *bean giver* to give the bean counter 10 beans from the bank, after the bean taker has taken the correct share.
- It is the job of the *bean counter* to keep careful count of all the beans in the pile.
- It is the job of the *recorder* to record all transactions and inventories in a table.

a. Now start over. In this run, the bean counter will begin with 150 beans. Repeat the investigation as before.

b. Answer the following questions.

    i. If the bean taker did not round off, what values do you think you would have had for these two runs?

    ii. Does rounding off affect the final outcome?

    iii. How did you know that the value would not start changing again if you were to resume the investigation?

The remainder of this investigation can be done either by using beans or by using a calculator to simulate the movements. Do not be concerned with whether or not you round off the numbers.

c. Begin again with 10 beans and repeat the investigation, but this time the bean giver will give only 5 beans.

d. For the fourth run, start with 150 beans. The bean taker takes 20%, and the bean giver gives 5 beans.

e. Start again with 10 beans. The bean giver gives 10 beans, but the bean taker removes 25% of the beans.

f. Analyze your information, and summarize your findings in a way that allows you to predict what will happen with any start value, take percentage, and give value. Present your findings as a formula or a procedure in your conclusion.

Consider the ideal bouncing ball again. If the distances the ball falls can be represented by 200, 200(0.80), 200(0.80)^2, 200(0.80)^3, and so on, then the distance it falls after the tenth bounce is 200(0.80)^{10}, or almost 11 inches. What about after the 25th bounce? How long before the molecules are just shrugging their shoulders? Mathematicians say the **limiting value** of this sequence is zero (as n gets larger), because in the long run the values become so close to zero that you cannot measure the difference.

How will the sum of all the distances be affected as the value of successive distances gets closer and closer to zero? Do you agree that the total grows? Try bigger and bigger values of n in the formula

$$S_n = \frac{u_1(1 - r^n)}{1 - r} = \frac{200\,[1 - (0.80)^n]}{1 - 0.80}.$$

What limiting value does this sum seem to approach for larger and larger values of n? Can you make the sum larger than that value?

Problem Set 2.5

1. Consider the geometric sequence with $u_1 = 6$ and $r = 1$. What is the sum of the first ten terms? The first n terms? An infinite number of terms?

2. a. Consider the infinite geometric sequence with $u_1 = 4$ and $r = 0.7$. What is the sum of the first ten terms? The first 40 terms?

b. Change r to 1.3 and answer the same questions.

c. Change r to 1 and answer the same questions.

d. Sketch a graph of each of the partial sums described in parts a–c.

e. For what values of r does the sum appear to approach a limiting value?

3. Use the results from Investigation 2.5.1 to find the limiting value of the sequence in the white pine tree problem (Problem Set 1.3, Problem 5).

4. a. What is the sum of the first five terms of $\frac{1}{10} + \frac{1}{30} + \frac{1}{90} + \frac{1}{270} + \cdots$?

b. The first ten terms?

c. The first n terms, as n gets larger than the biggest number your mathematics teacher can name?

d. Give an argument why the limiting value for the partial sums of an infinite geometric series is $S = \frac{u_1}{1 - r}$ when the value of r is between 1 and $^-1$ (that is, when $|r| < 1$).

5. A mathematics conference descends upon a city, and the teachers spend $1 million "on the town." The money is received by the "townies," and they spend 90% of it in their city. Suppose 90% of that amount is again spent in the city, and so on. Show that the total impact is ten times as great as the original amount spent.

6. A flea jumps $\frac{1}{2}$ ft, then $\frac{1}{4}$ ft, then $\frac{1}{8}$ ft, and so on. Its first jump was to the right, its second jump was to the left, then to the right, and so on.

a. Which way and how far is its seventh jump?

b. Which way and how far is its eighteenth jump?

c. What point is the flea zooming in on?

7. Two trains are 60 mi apart and heading toward each other on the same track. Each train is traveling at 30 mi/hr. A bee buzzes back and forth between them at 50 mi/hr until it is squished by the two trains. How far did the bee travel?

    The Hungarian mathematician John von Neumann was famous for the speed at which he could calculate. According to one story, when he was asked to solve a problem similar to the bee problem above, he solved it instantly. The person who asked him the problem said, "Oh, you must have heard the trick before!" "What trick?" said von Neumann. "All I did was sum the infinite series."

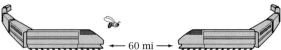

8. Prudence and Charity are identical 20 yr old twins with identical jobs and identical salaries, and they receive identical bonuses of $2,000 yearly.

Prudence is immediately concerned with saving. She invests her $2,000 bonus each year at 9% interest compounded annually. At age 30, she decides it is time to see the world, and from that point on she spends her annual bonus on a trip.

Charity is immediately concerned with saving the world. She gives her $2,000 bonus to charitable causes every year until she reaches 30. On her 30th birthday, her friends start telling her stories about what happens to people who haven't saved any money for their retirement. She gets so worried about what will happen when she retires that she starts saving her bonus money at 9% compounded annually.

How much will they each have when they are 30 yr old? Compare the value of each investment account when Prudence and Charity are 65 yr old.

9. Suppose a square *ABCD* with side length 8 in. is cut out of paper. Another square *EFGH* is placed with its corners at the midpoints of *ABCD*, as pictured at the right. A third square is placed with its corners at midpoints of *EFGH*, and so on.

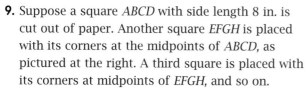

a. What is the perimeter of the tenth square?
b. What is the area of the tenth square?
c. If the pattern could be repeated forever, what would be the total perimeter of the squares? What would be the total area?

10. a. List the terms of $\sum_{n=1}^{12} 96(0.25)^{(n-1)}$.

b. Find the sum of $\sum_{n=1}^{12} 96(0.25)^{(n-1)}$.

c. Find the sum of $\sum_{n=1}^{\infty} 96(0.25)^{(n-1)}$. This sum has an infinite number of terms.

d. Draw a sketch of the graph of partial sums for $n \geq 1$ in 10b.

11. Find three problems in this chapter that you feel are representative of the first five sections. Write out the problems and the solutions. Explain why you chose each problem.

Take Another Look 2.5

**NOTE
0D**

Many graphing calculators will produce table values for the equations listed in *y=* or stored in the calculator. (If you haven't been using this feature, refer to **Calculator Note 0D** where you will find directions for setting and viewing table values.) Table values can provide you with a powerful and efficient method of calculating term values or partial sums for any of the explicit formulas given in Section 2.5.

a. Enter the equation $y_1 = 200(0.80)^{(x-1)}$ and set up your table so that you can see the values listed at the right. (Notice that the variable *x* replaces the variable *n* listed in Section 2.5.) Assume that these values apply to a bouncing ball, and write a sentence or two that explains the meaning of the pair (3, 128).

x	y_1
1	200
2	160
3	128
4	102.4
5	81.92
6	65.536

b. Assume that the values in the accompanying bottom table apply to a bouncing ball, and write a sentence or two that explains the meaning of the entries in the row with (3, 128, 488). What equation would you enter for y_2 so that the third-column entries look like these?

c. What happens to the entries in the columns headed by y_1 and y_2 as *x* gets very large? Complete your explanation using the example of a bouncing ball.

d. What alternative equation could you write that provides the same entries as $y_1 = 200(0.80)^{(x-1)}$? Explain why.

x	y_1	y_2
1	200	200
2	160	360
3	128	488
4	102.4	590.4
5	81.92	672.32
6	65.536	737.856

Use the process described above to look again at the concert seat problem (Problem 8, Problem Set 2.2).

e. Write equations for y_1 and y_2. One equation will provide the number of seats in each row (u_n), and the other will keep track of the total number of seats (S_n). Describe how you can use the equations and table values to find how many seats are in the last row and how many seats are in the concert hall. Describe the location of your seat.

f. Suppose you buy two concert tickets for seats 879 and 880 in another concert hall that has 25 seats in row one, 29 seats in row two, 33 seats in row three, and so on. The seats are numbered from left to right, so the first seat in row one is 1, the first seat in row two is 26, and so on. The concert hall has 36 rows of seats. How many seats are in the last row? How many seats are in the concert hall? Describe the location of your seats.

Geometer's Sketchpad Investigation

Seeing the Infinite Sum

The sum of an infinite geometric sequence is sometimes hard to visualize. Some sums clearly converge, while other sums do not. In this investigation, you will use Sketchpad to simulate an infinite sum of a geometric series.

Step 1   Construct horizontal segment *AB*, making it about 4 cm long.

Step 2   Open a new script and click Record.

Step 3   Dilate point *A* by 60% around center *B*. Label the new point *C*.

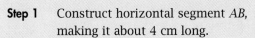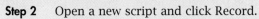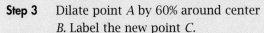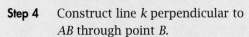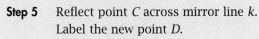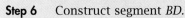

Step 4   Construct line *k* perpendicular to *AB* through point *B*.

Step 5   Reflect point *C* across mirror line *k*. Label the new point *D*.

Step 6   Construct segment *BD*.

Step 7   Select point *B*, then select point *D*. Next, select segment *BD*. Click Loop on your script, then click Stop.

Step 8   Open a new sketch and play the script to recursion depth 25. Start by clicking Step, so that you can see how the script is working. Then you can click Play or Fast to finish the construction.

Step 9   Measure *AB* and the total length from *A* to the last point drawn.

Questions

1. What infinite sum does your model represent? Write your answer in summation notation. (Hint: Figure out what each step does with the information from the previous step.) Using the lengths you measured, verify the sum with your calculator.
2. Vary the length of segment *AB*. What conclusions can you draw? Does the sum always converge for this constant ratio?
3. Repeat steps 1–9, but this time change step 3 and dilate point *A* by 120% around center *B*. How does this new value of the dilation affect the sum?
4. How would you create a script to model the action of any infinite sum of the form

$$\sum_{n=1}^{\infty} xa^{n-1},$$

where *x* is the initial length of the segment and *a* is the constant ratio?

Section 2.6

Fractal Patterns

Everything should be made as simple as possible, but not simpler.
—Albert Einstein

A map of the United States' major highways is a fairly complex drawing. If you concentrate your view on only one of the states pictured on such a map, the drawing seems less complex. A part of the map showing a rural county of that state would be simpler yet. This phenomenon is typical of most of the graphs you will investigate this year. That is, if you look at some small portion of the total graph, it looks much simpler and probably does not look much like a larger view of the graph.

However, the graphs you will investigate in this section do not become simpler as you move, or zoom, in. These graphs are called **fractals**. When you take a very close look at some small area of a fractal graph, you find that it is just as complex as the greater view and that there is a marked similarity between this close view and the total view. In the upcoming problems, you will explore some very interesting and mysterious patterns. Each figure in this section is generated by applying a recursive transformation to a given figure. Like sequences, some of these patterns will grow larger and larger forever, and some of them will shrink at each step of the recursion.

Problem Set 2.6

1. **Geome Tree:** This figure begins as a vertical segment one unit in length. The recursive procedure is to create two new segments at the end of each previously drawn segment. Each new segment is half as long as the previously drawn segment(s) and is rotated 135° clockwise and counter-clockwise, respectively. Copy the table shown on page 85 onto your paper, and fill in each missing value. It may be helpful to draw each figure accurately and to measure carefully to verify your results.

a. The length of the last segment drawn at each stage.
b. The total length of each path, beginning at the base of the tree and proceeding to the end of a branch.
c. The total number of segments that make up the tree.
d. The sum of the lengths of all segments in the tree.
e. The height of the tree from the base to the topmost branch. (Hint: The formula for n may have two forms, depending on whether n is even or odd.)
f. The width of the tree at its widest point. (See the diagram on page 84.)

	1	2	3	4	...	n	...	∞
a. Length of the last segment	1	-?-	-?-	-?-	...	-?-	...	-?-
b. Total length of a path	1	-?-	-?-	-?-	...	-?-	...	-?-
c. Total number of segments	1	-?-	-?-	-?-	...	-?-	...	-?-
d. Sum of the lengths of all segments	1	-?-	-?-	-?-	...	-?-	...	-?-
e. Height of the tree	1	-?-	-?-	-?-	...	-?-	...	-?-
f. Width of the tree	0	-?-	-?-	-?-	...	-?-	...	-?-

2. **Koch snowflake:** Helge von Koch (1870–1924) was a Swedish mathematician. His principal research involved problems of infinitely many linear equations in infinitely many unknowns. (You will learn about linear equations with a finite number of unknowns in Chapter 9.) He invented what is called the Koch curve in 1904. This figure begins as an equilateral triangle, with each segment one unit in length. The recursive procedure is to trisect each segment and replace the middle segment with two sides of an equilateral triangle. Copy the table at the top of page 86 onto your paper, and fill in each missing value. It may be helpful to draw each figure accurately and to measure carefully to verify your results.
a. The length of each segment.
b. The total number of segments.
c. The perimeter, or sum of the lengths of all segments in the snowflake.
d. The area enclosed by the snowflake.

	1	2	3	4	...	n	...	∞
a. Length of each segment	1	-?-	-?-	-?-	...	-?-	...	-?-
b. Total number of segments	3	-?-	-?-	-?-	...	-?-	...	-?-
c. Perimeter	3	-?-	-?-	-?-	...	-?-	...	-?-
d. Area	0.43301	-?-	-?-	-?-	...	-?-	...	-?-

3. Sierpiński triangle: This figure begins as an equilateral triangle, with each segment one unit in length. The recursive procedure is to replace the triangle with three smaller congruent equilateral triangles such that each smaller triangle shares a vertex with the larger triangle. Draw each figure below and copy the table. Complete the table by finding the requested information in a–f.

a. The length of each side of the triangle drawn at any recursion.
b. The number of new triangles drawn at each stage.
c. The perimeter of each new triangle.
d. The area of each new triangle.
e. The total perimeter of all new triangles.
f. The total area of all triangles.

Wacław Sierpiński

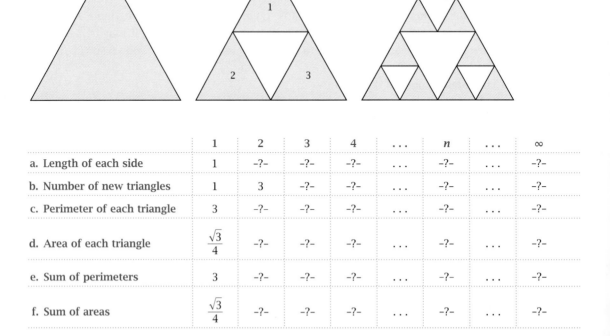

	1	2	3	4	...	n	...	∞
a. Length of each side	1	-?-	-?-	-?-	...	-?-	...	-?-
b. Number of new triangles	1	3	-?-	-?-	...	-?-	...	-?-
c. Perimeter of each triangle	3	-?-	-?-	-?-	...	-?-	...	-?-
d. Area of each triangle	$\frac{\sqrt{3}}{4}$	-?-	-?-	-?-	...	-?-	...	-?-
e. Sum of perimeters	3	-?-	-?-	-?-	...	-?-	...	-?-
f. Sum of areas	$\frac{\sqrt{3}}{4}$	-?-	-?-	-?-	...	-?-	...	-?-

4. Create your own recursively defined pattern. Choose a simple polygon. Define some type of procedure to copy the figure (or the sides of the figure) to new locations, new lengths, or new orientations. Construct several stages. It may be very difficult to create a figure that does not grow incredibly large very quickly or shrink out of existence too fast. Give it your best effort. Keep it simple. Identify at least two sequences formed by your pattern, such as length and area.

Take Another Look 2.6

In Problem 6 of Problem Set 2.5, a flea is jumping back and forth along a line. Suppose the flea reconsiders and always jumps to the right, first $\frac{1}{2}$ ft, then $\frac{1}{4}$ ft, then $\frac{1}{8}$ ft, and so on. There are many different strategies for solving this problem. Some involve recursive procedures and others involve explicit formulas.

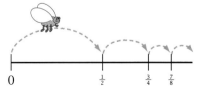

a. Decide which strategy to use and then explain why you think this is an arithmetic (or geometric) jumping flea.

b. How long is its eighth jump and where is the flea after its eighth jump?

c. How long is its 20th jump? Where is the flea after its 20th jump?

d. What equations in y_1 and y_2 will provide the jump length and flea location for any requested jump?

e. What point is the flea zooming in on? Explain your answer by using information from a table of values.

Project

Sierpiński Carpet

To create a Sierpiński carpet, begin with a square. (A 27-by-27 square grid on graph paper works well.) Divide the whole into nine equal-sized squares, and remove the center square. (See the middle diagram.) Divide each of the remaining eight squares into nine parts and remove their centers. There are several patterns involved if you continue this process. Find mathematical expressions that generate these patterns of numbers. Be sure to look at the remaining carpet area, the perimeter, and the area removed at each stage. You can even look for other patterns that emerge. Make predictions about what will happen to these patterns after *n* stages, and in the long run. Your project should include a drawing of the next stage of this carpet, an explanation of all mathematical expressions you find, and a prediction of what the carpet would look like if the process continued forever.

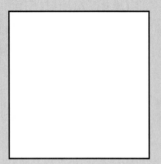 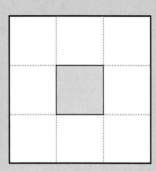 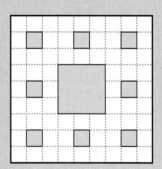

Chapter Review

How can it be that mathematics, being after all a product of human thought
independent of experience, is so admirably adapted to the objects of reality?
—Albert Einstein

Sequences can sometimes be defined recursively, as in Chapter 1, and sometimes they can also be defined explicitly. With an explicit definition you can find any term of a sequence without having to know the preceding term(s). Terms of an arithmetic sequence are defined by $u_n = u_0 + nd$, where d is the common difference and u_0 is the initial, or "zero," term. Terms of a geometric sequence are defined by $u_n = u_0 r^n$, where r is the common ratio or multiplier. There are several versions of the formula for a geometric series. One of these is

$$S_n = \frac{u_1(1 - r^n)}{1 - r}.$$

If the geometric series is tending toward a long-run or limiting value, then the sum of all the terms in the sequence will approach the value given by

$$S = \frac{u_1}{1 - r}.$$

The sum of an arithmetic series is given by the formula

$$S_n = \frac{n(u_1 + u_n)}{2}$$

Many times it is difficult to determine which formula to use. You may find it helpful to write out a few of the terms before trying to apply a formula. Next identify whether the sequence is arithmetic or geometric. Be sure to read the problem carefully to determine if you are being asked for a term or a sum. If you think about what you are being asked to find and do some experimenting before choosing a formula, you will usually gain some insight into the problem and find that solving the problem is much easier.

Problem Set 2.7

You may notice that some of these problems are the same as the problems in Problem Set 1.7. As you rework these problems, use explicit formulas unless you are asked to do otherwise.

1. **a.** Mark Ett must arrange a display of soup cans as shown in the picture. List the number of cans in the top row, in the second row, in the third row, and so on, to the tenth row.
   b. Write a recursive formula for the terms of the sequence from 1a.
   c. Write an explicit formula for the terms of the sequence from 1a.
   d. How many cans will it take to make a display 47 layers high?
   e. If Mark must use six cases (288 cans), how many layers will be in the display?

2. Consider the arithmetic sequence 3, 7, 11, 15, ...
   a. What is the 128th term?
   b. Which term has the value 159?
   c. Find u_{20}.
   d. Find S_{20}.

3. Given plenty of food and space, the biological specimen *Grossus Buggus* will reproduce geometrically, with each pair hatching 24 young every five days. Initially, there are 12 bugs.
   a. How many are born in 5 days? In 10 days? In 15 days? In 35 days?
   b. Write a recursive formula for the terms of the sequence from 3a.
   c. Write an explicit formula for the terms of the sequence from 3a.
   d. Find the *total* number of bugs after 60 days.

4. Consider the geometric sequence 256, 192, 144, 108, ...
   a. What is the eighth term?
   b. What is the term number of the first term smaller than 20?
   c. Find u_7.
   d. Find S_7.
   e. What happens to S_n as n gets very large?

5. a. If you invest $500 in a bank that pays 5.5% annual interest compounded quarterly, how much money will you have after 5 yr?
   b. Start over and invest $500 at 5.5% annual interest compounded quarterly, and deposit an additional $150 every 3 mo. What will the balance be after 5 yr?

6. A university currently has an enrollment of 5678. They predict that from now on, 24% of their students will graduate yearly, and 1250 new students will enroll each year.
   a. What will be the university enrollment after 5 yr?
   b. What will be the enrollment in the long run?

7. A super-duper ball will rebound to 95% of the height from which it is dropped.
   a. If it is originally dropped from a height of 200 cm, how high will it bounce on the seventh bounce?
   b. Considering only the downward trips made by the ball, what will be the total distance traveled in seven falls?
   c. What will be the total falling distance traveled in the long run?

8. Birdie Parr's golf ball is lying 12 ft away from the eighteenth hole on the golf course. She putts and, unfortunately, the ball rolls to the other side of the hole, two-thirds as far away from the hole as it was before. On her next putt, the same thing happens. If this pattern continues, how far will her ball travel in seven strokes? How far will it travel in the long run?

9. What monthly payment will be required to pay off an $80,000 mortgage at 8.9% interest in 30 yr?

10. Georg Cantor (1845–1918) was born in St. Petersburg, Russia, to parents who had migrated from Denmark. When Cantor was 11, he and his family moved to Germany, where Cantor spent most of his life. His mathematical work led him to establish a new mathematical discipline, the field of set theory.

Pomo Indian basket. Can you see the relationship between the design on the basket and the Cantor set?

One of his contributions is a set of numbers called the Cantor set. To generate this set, consider a line segment between 0 and 1, inclusive. Call this line segment C_1.

$$\overline{\hspace{6cm}}$$
0   1

C_1

Remove the middle third of the line segment (and the numbers) to get C_2.

0          $\frac{1}{3}$ $\frac{2}{3}$ 1

C_2

Remove the middle third of each line segment in C_2 to get C_3.

0   ?   ? $\frac{1}{3}$ $\frac{2}{3}$?   ?   1

C_3

    a. Name the sequence of numbers that represents the sum of the segment lengths for C_1, C_2, C_3, ...

    b. What is the long-run value of the terms of this sequence?

11. a. Use your calculator to find the sequence of partial sums S_{10}, S_{20}, S_{30}, . . . , S_{90} for the sequence $u_n = \frac{1}{n}$.

    b. Describe what you think is happening to this sequence of partial sums over the long run.

Assessing What You've Learned—Portfolios

When applying for a job or applying to a college or a university, you may be asked to submit a portfolio of your work. Usually portfolios are associated with artists, but any collection of your work can also be a portfolio.

A portfolio is different from a notebook. Your notebook might contain everything from scratch work to completed problems, investigations, and projects. A portfolio is reserved for your most significant or best work so that you can demonstrate what you are capable of doing. The portfolio can also show how your work has changed over time.

Review all the work you've done so far and choose one or more examples of your best work for inclusion in your portfolio. Your teacher may have specific suggestions on how to select and document your work. One way to document your work is to write a paragraph or two about each item you select, addressing the following questions:

- What is the item? Is it a homework problem? A project? A group investigation?
- What makes it representative of your best work?
- What mathematics did you learn or apply in this work?
- How would you improve this work if you were to redo or revise it?

Journal Entries

- Write in your journal. Look for journal prompts in Problem Sets 2.3 and 2.5.

Organize Your Notebook

- Take a few minutes to organize your work for this chapter, and be sure to update your list of calculator techniques.

3 Introduction to Statistics

You can draw different kinds of graphs to help describe either a large population or a smaller group like the crowd of people shown above on the lawn of the United States Capitol. Box plots, histograms, and scatter plots will provide you with different views of data. Summary values like the mean and the mean absolute deviation also provide you with more information about the data.

Section 3.1

Box Plots and Measures of Center

Science is made up with facts, as a house is with stones. But a collection of facts is no more a science than a heap of stones is a house.
—*Jules Henri Poincaré*

Gottfried Achenwall, a professor at the Universities of Göttingen and Marburg, invented the word *statistics* ("state arithmetic") in 1749. What he meant by "state arithmetic" was counting and calculating activities, such as census-taking, which governments find useful. One of the earliest large-scale statistical surveys was that of the fourteenth-century Hawaiian king Umi. He is said to have collected all his people on a small plain, afterward called the Plain of Numbering, and to have asked each to deposit a stone in an area encircling the temple on that plain. The stones were to be placed in piles according to district and the piles were located in the direction of the districts. The result showed the relative sizes of the districts' populations.

John Sinclair, in 1794, was the first English writer to use the term *statistics*. During the 1800s, the development of statistical ideas and concepts continued. Francis Galton, Gustav Fechner, and Karl Pearson are a few of the names associated with this movement. In 1931, the first master's degree in statistics at Iowa State College was awarded to

In the fifteenth century, the Incas used quipus to record numerical information. The word *quipu* means "knot."

Gertrude Cox, who later became head of the Department of Experimental Statistics at North Carolina State College. She made many contributions to the field of experimental design. John Tukey, another twentieth-century statistician, is responsible for developing several new kinds of graphs used to interpret data.

Today, newspapers, magazines, the evening news, commercials, government bulletins, almanacs, and sports publications bombard you daily with data and statistics. If you are to be an informed citizen who makes intelligent decisions, you will need to be able to interpret this information. Studying statistics will help you learn how to collect, organize, analyze, and interpret data. In this chapter, you will learn how to make several kinds of graphs that picture data. In addition, you will study some numerical measures of data, which also help you to better understand what the numbers are telling you.

The following table lists 20 toothpaste brands. They are ranked on a 100-point scale on their ability to clean stained teeth. A score of 100 indicates perfectly clean unstained teeth. The cost per month is an estimate based on brushing twice a day with one-half inch of toothpaste.

Product	Size (oz)	Price ($)	Cost per month ($)	Rank
Ultra brite Original	6.0	1.56	0.58	86
Gleem	7.0	2.23	0.66	79
Caffree Regular	5.9	2.96	1.02	77
Crest Tartar Control Mint Gel	6.4	1.99	0.53	75
Colgate Tartar Control Gel	6.4	2.04	0.57	74
Crest Tartar Control Original	6.4	2.00	0.53	72
Ultra brite Gel Cool Mint	6.0	1.53	0.52	72
Colgate Clear Blue Gel	6.4	2.06	0.71	71
Crest Cool Mint Gel	6.4	1.99	0.55	70
Crest Regular	6.4	2.01	0.59	69
Crest Sparkle	6.4	2.03	0.51	64
Close-up Tartar Control Gel	6.4	1.94	0.67	63
Close-up Anti-Plaque	6.4	1.97	0.62	62
Colgate Tartar Control Paste	6.4	2.04	0.66	62
Tom's of Maine Cinnamint	6.0	3.29	1.07	62
Aquafresh Tartar Control	6.0	1.97	0.80	60
Aim Anti-Tartar Gel	6.4	2.24	0.79	58
Aim Extra-Strength Gel	6.4	1.70	0.44	57
Slimer Gel	3.0	1.79	1.04	57
A & H Baking Soda Mint	6.3	3.26	1.12	55

Source: Consumer Reports, September 1992.

First, you might want to see if your favorite toothpaste is listed and how it compares with others. Many people seek out useful information when they are changing products, making a purchase, or trying to influence the decisions of others. Sometimes it's easy to find information about a particular product, but patterns, relationships, tendencies, and general observations are frequently hidden in a large table of numbers like this one.

This set of data clearly does not include every type and brand of toothpaste. You have to be careful when drawing conclusions from a set of data. Summaries of data like this may not tell much about toothpaste in general. In order to draw general conclusions from a set of data, you must have data that represent a random sample. The following investigation will help you understand something about random sampling.

Investigation 3.1.1
Random Samples

For this investigation you will need a standard deck of playing cards with the aces removed. Jacks, queens, and kings are each valued at ten, and other cards are valued according to their number.

a. Show mathematically that the average value of all the cards is seven.

b. Shuffle the deck well and select ten cards at random. Find the average of these ten cards.

c. Return the cards to the deck and repeat five more times the process of finding the average of ten cards.

d. What is the average of the ten lowest-value cards?

e. What is the average of the ten highest-value cards?

f. How does the average value of all the cards compare to the average value of your random samples? Use the results of this investigation to write a paragraph comparing the average value of a random sample to the average value of the entire population.

In the above investigation you were asked to "shuffle the deck well and select ten cards at random." Certainly, a classmate (even a friend) would feel obligated to challenge the process and the results if the cards were not first shuffled. Why? Selecting nonrandom samples or conducting experiments that are not randomized may produce results and conclusions that are not true in general. To help ensure that results are not biased, sample data must be collected randomly.

If you assume the table of toothpaste data is from a random sample of *all* toothpaste brands, then you can make some statements about all brands with some degree of accuracy. What is the typical toothpaste tube size? Is there a single number that can serve as the representative tube size for the population? The size that occurs most frequently, the **mode**, is 6.4 oz. Karl Pearson (1857–1936), a mathematician at University College in London, originated the term *mode* in 1895, writing, "I have found it convenient to use the term *mode* for the abscissa corresponding to the ordinate of maximum frequency." Gustav Fechner (1801–1887), an early experimental psychologist, had used the expression *der dichteste Werth* (the densest value) for the mode in 1878. The **median** is another single number that can be used to represent an average value. Fechner described the properties of the median, which he called *der Centralwerth* (the central value), in 1874. In 1882, Francis Galton gave this concept the English name of *median.*

Karl Pearson

Gustav Fechner

Francis Galton

Median

In a set with an odd number of elements, the **median** is the middle number when the elements are listed in order (ascending or descending). If the set has an even number of elements, then the median is the average of the two middle values.

NOTE 3A

NOTE 3B

Because there are 20 values, the median tube size is the average of the tenth and eleventh values, $\frac{6.4 + 6.4}{2} = 6.4$. (See **Calculator Note 3A** for help with entering the data into the calculator and **Calculator Note 3B** for help in finding the median.)

3.0, 5.9, 6.0, 6.0, 6.0, 6.0, 6.3, 6.4, 6.4, $\boxed{6.4, 6.4}$, 6.4, 6.4, 6.4, 6.4, 6.4, 6.4, 6.4, 7.0

If you consider the cost per month, you will find two modes at $0.53 and $0.66 (each occurs twice), and a median cost per month of $0.64. Remember to arrange the data in order (either ascending or descending) to find the median.

The **box-and-whisker plot** (or box plot) provides a visual tool for analyzing information about a set of data. John Tukey, a professor at Princeton University, introduced the use of box-and-whisker plots in his 1970 book *Exploratory*

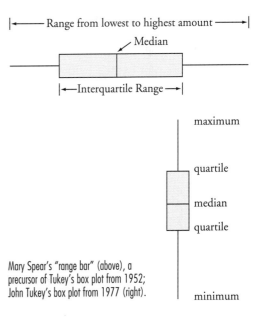

Mary Spear's "range bar" (above), a precursor of Tukey's box plot from 1952; John Tukey's box plot from 1977 (right).

Sources: Mary Eleanor Spear, *Charting Statistics.* (New York, 1952), p. 166; John W. Tukey, *Exploratory Data Analysis* (Reading, Mass., 1977).

Data Analysis. He explained, "One of the simplest errors in graphing, particularly for those fortunate enough to have convenient graphical output from their computers, is to plot *too many points.*" The box plot gives you a good idea of how the data are distributed, or spread, and how symmetric the distribution is by graphing only five summary values.

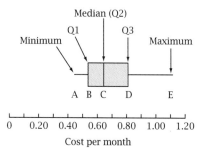

The lines emanating from the box are called whiskers. The whisker endpoints at A and E identify the smallest and largest values of the data. The median, point C, of the data is at the vertical line within the box. The left edge of the box, B, is the median of all the values below C; and D, the right edge of the box, is the median of the values above C. The value B marks the **first,** or **lower, quartile,** the value C marks the **second,** or **middle, quartile,** and the value D marks the **third,** or **upper, quartile.** Explain why 50% of the data are contained in the box. (See **Calculator Note 3C** to learn how to create a box plot on your calculator.)

NOTE
3C

■ **Example 1**

   a. What percentage of the cost-per-month toothpaste data are represented by the lower whisker?

   b. What are the values for the first, second, and third quartiles?

   c. What are the five summary values for this data?

Solution

   a. One-quarter, or 25%, of the data are represented by the lower whisker. As a matter of fact, one-quarter of the data are represented by the upper whisker, one-quarter are represented by the upper part of the box, and one-quarter are represented by the lower part of the box.

   b. The first quartile is the average of the fifth and sixth values, or $0.54, the median is the average of the tenth and eleventh values, or $0.64, and the third quartile is the average of the fifteenth and sixteenth values, or $0.795.

   c. The five summary values {minimum, first quartile, median, third quartile, maximum} are {0.44, 0.54, 0.64, 0.795, 1.12}. ■

NOTE
3B

   A balance point, called the **mean,** is another single number used to represent the typical data value in a set of data. **Calculator Note 3B** explains how you can find the mean using your calculator.

Mean

The **mean,** represented by the symbol $\bar{x}$, is the ratio $\dfrac{\text{sum of the data values}}{\text{number of values}}$.

Frequently the symbol Σ (sigma) is used to indicate a sum. The Σ symbol tells you to sum the individual values. So

$$\frac{\sum_{i=1}^{n} x_i}{n}$$

would represent the mean, where n is the number of values and $x_1, x_2, x_3, \ldots,$ $x_i, \ldots, x_n$ are the individual data values. Of the three measures of central tendency (mean, median, mode), the mean is the most sensitive to individual values, because every value in the list is used to compute it. You will investigate the effect of individual values on the mean in the problems.

Investigation 3.1.2
Pulse Rates

Measure and record your resting pulse rate for one minute. Then exercise for two minutes by doing jumping jacks or by running in place. Afterwards, measure and record your pulse rate again. Collect the data from each student in the class. Prepare a box plot picturing the resting pulse rate measurements and a box plot of the pulse rate measurements after exercising. Analyze, interpret, and compare the graphs, measures of central tendency, and measures of spread. Write a few sentences that summarize your results.

Problem Set 3.1

1. Fay Silitator uses a variety of methods to assess her students. The lists below represent scores for various assignments that she has recorded for two of her students during a semester.

Connie Sistant   82, 86, 82, 84, 85, 84, 85

Ozzie Laiting   72, 94, 76, 96, 90, 76, 84

Find the median and mean for each set of scores, and explain why they do not tell the whole story about the differences between Connie's and Ozzie's scores.

2. The two box plots pictured represent Connie's and Ozzie's scores.

Write a paragraph describing the information pictured in the box plots. Use the plots to help you draw some statistical conclusions. Include in your description answers to such questions as: What does it mean that the second box plot is longer? Where is the left whisker of the top box plot? What does it mean when the median isn't in the middle of the box? What does it mean when the left whisker is longer than the right whisker?

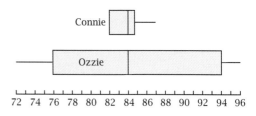

3. a. Homer Unn has played in the minor leagues for 11 yr. His home run totals, in order, for each of those years are 56, 62, 49, 65, 58, 52, 68, 72, 25, 51, and 64. Construct a box plot showing these data.

   b. List the five summary values.

   c. Find $\dfrac{\sum\limits_{i=1}^{n} x_i}{n}$.

   d. How many home runs would Homer need to hit next season to have a 12 yr mean of 60?

4. The difference between the lower and upper quartiles (the length of the box) is called the **interquartile range.** Sometimes there are one or more data points that are extremely different from the others. If the distance of a data point from the box is more than 1.5 times the length of the box, that point is called an **outlier.** This definition is somewhat arbitrary, and other texts may define it slightly differently. But the basic idea is that an outlier is a value that lies far away from the majority of the values.

   a. Look at the box plots shown in Problem 2. Do there appear to be any outliers? What high and low scores would be outliers for Connie? For Ozzie?

   b. Show that there is only one outlier (using our definition) with Homer's home run data in Problem 3.

5. Refer to the toothpaste data listed at the beginning of this section.

   a. Compute the mean toothpaste cost per month.

   b. Draw the graph at right on your own paper. Draw a vertical line at the mean cost per month.

   c. Compare the mean and median values for the data. Which is greater? Explain why it is greater.

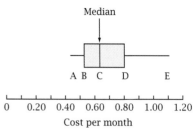

6. It is estimated that people spend between 25% and 35% of their income for shelter. This amount can be in the form of rent or a mortgage payment. In Chapters 1 and 2, when learning about sequences, you explored how to compute mortgage payments. Although interest rates are usually fairly uniform throughout the United States, the price of a home varies considerably. The data in the list below give the median price of a home in various metropolitan areas in the United States.

a. Make a box plot and list the five summary values for the data. Are there any outliers? Explain why or why not.

b. Make another box plot after eliminating all of the median home prices greater than $135,000. List the summary values.

c. Divide the data into two lists and construct a box plot for each list. You decide what criteria to use for dividing the list. You could choose metropolitan areas east of the Mississippi River and areas west of the Mississippi River. Another possibility might be metropolitan areas in coastal states and those not in coastal states. Describe any similarities or differences you observe.

City	Median home price ($)	City	Median home price ($)
Atlanta, GA	93,200	Milwaukee, WI	106,500
Baltimore, MD	115,700	Minneapolis-St. Paul, MN	100,000
Boston, MA	170,600	New York City, NY	170,300
Chicago, IL	135,500	Philadelphia, PA	116,800
Cincinnati, OH	93,600	Phoenix, AZ	89,200
Cleveland, OH	94,200	Pittsburgh, PA	80,000
Dallas, TX	95,100	St. Louis, MO	83,100
Denver, CO	111,200	San Diego, CA	177,800
Detroit, MI	84,500	San Francisco Bay Area, CA	246,900
Houston, TX	84,800	Seattle-Tacoma, WA	152,900
Kansas City, MO, KS	84,900	Tampa-St. Petersburg, FL	74,300
Los Angeles, CA	188,500	Washington, D.C.	154,900
Miami-Hialeah, FL	105,000		

Source: The Universal Almanac 1995.

7. While it is difficult to actually count the number of homeless people in the United States, the federal government, as well as independent agencies, have made attempts to do so. The estimates range from 50,000 to a million or more. One night during the 1990 census, census workers did attempt to count as many homeless people as they could by visiting shelters and street sites. On that night, a total of 228,621 homeless persons were counted. The list below contains estimates of the total number of

homeless persons in selected cities in 1990. The second column indicates how many people, out of the total number, sleep in official shelters.

City	Total number of homeless people	Number in shelters
New York City, NY	33,830	23,383
Los Angeles, CA	7,706	4,597
Chicago, IL	6,764	5,180
San Francisco, CA	5,569	4,003
San Diego, CA	4,947	2,846
Washington, D.C.	4,813	4,682
Philadelphia, PA	4,485	3,416
Newark, NJ	2,816	1,974
Seattle, WA	2,539	2,170
Atlanta, GA	2,491	2,431
Boston, MA	2,463	2,245
Houston, TX	1,931	1,780
Phoenix, AZ	1,786	1,710
Portland, OR	1,702	1,553
Sacramento, CA	1,552	1,287
Baltimore, MD	1,531	1,144
Dallas, TX	1,493	1,200
Denver, CO	1,269	1,169
Oklahoma City, OK	1,250	1,016
Minneapolis, MN	1,080	1,052

Source: The Universal Almanac 1995.

a. What is the mean number of homeless persons in these cities? What is the median number? Which cities, if any, are outliers?

b. Omit the number of homeless persons in New York City and recompute the mean and the median. Which was more affected by this one extreme score, the mean or the median?

c. Give an argument for using the median score when discussing the average number of homeless persons in major cities. Give an argument for using the mean score.

d. How would the mean and the median values be affected if 1000 more people were added to each number in the list?

e. Calculate the percentage of homeless people in each of these cities who stay in shelters. Make a box plot of these percentages. Write a paragraph describing the results. Be sure to include a discussion of the median and the mean in your description.

8. a. Invent a data set with seven values and a mean of 12. (This is more interesting if all the values aren't 12.)

b. Invent a data set with seven values, a mode of 70, and a median of 65.

c. Invent a data set with seven values that will create the box plot at right.

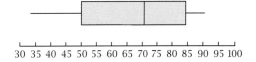

30 35 40 45 50 55 60 65 70 75 80 85 90 95 100

9. The table below shows the average amount of per capita taxes paid in the countries listed. These numbers include national, local, and social security taxes.

Country	Per capita taxes ($)	Country	Per capita taxes ($)
Australia	5,050	Luxembourg	11,976
Austria	8,830	Netherlands	9,064
Belgium	8,985	New Zealand	4,481
Canada	8,190	Norway	11,701
Denmark	12,219	Portugal	2,487
Finland	9,366	Spain	4,693
France	9,255	Sweden	14,628
Germany	8,279	Switzerland	10,489
Greece	2,635	Turkey	549
Ireland	4,623	United Kingdom	6,341
Italy	7,907	United States	6,550
Japan	8,419		

Source: The American Almanac 1994–95.

a. Make a box plot of these tax amounts.

b. Are there any outliers? If so, what are they? If not, what tax amounts would be outliers? What does it mean to be an outlier?

c. What are the mode, the median, and the mean tax amounts?

d. In what quartile is the United States?

10. a. Find the median and the mean toothpaste price, and the median and the mean cleaning rank, for the products listed at the beginning of this section.

b. Create two box plots: one representing the toothpaste prices and one representing the cleaning ranks.

c. Based on the information in the table, write a brief review or analysis of these toothpaste products. Use the vocabulary developed in this section in your review.

Project

Stem-and-Leaf Plots

John Tukey introduced stem-and-leaf plots in a 1972 article about displaying information. He thought better displays were needed for certain kinds of data, and he was trying to stimulate the ideas of others by providing new examples. The idea behind stem-and-leaf plots was to display a collection of numbers "in a form that is appropriately compact and easy to look over."

The stem-and-leaf plot offers another way to represent one-variable data. Something like a sideways histogram, it is more detailed because individual data values can be found in the graph. Consider the scores that your good friends Connie and Ozzie got in their mathematics class.

Connie Sistant   82, 86, 82, 84, 85, 84, 85
Ozzie Laiting   72, 94, 76, 96, 90, 76, 84

Two different stem-and-leaf plots of these data are given here.

```
       Connie    Ozzie              Connie    Ozzie
                 7 | 2  6  6                  7 | 2
6 5 5 4 4 2 2  8 | 4                          • | 6  6
                 9 | 0  4  6          4 4 2 2  8 | 4
                                       6 5 5   • |
         Key:  7 | 2  = 72                     9 | 0  4  6
```

To create the display, first order the data, and then divide it into groups (similar to histogram displays discussed in Section 3.3). The left graph is divided into ranges of ten points, and the right graph is divided into ranges of five points. A key to the graph must be provided so that one can interpret the magnitude of the data. In other cases, 7|2 could mean 7200, 7.2, or even 0.0072.

Sometimes a stem-and-leaf plot does not maintain the same level of accuracy that is provided by the data. For example, consider how a data set of calories—320, 340, 410, 344, 570, 614, 500, 935—appears in each of these displays.

3	2 4 4
4	1
5	0 7
6	1
7	
8	
9	3

Key: 3 | 2 = 320

3	20 40 44
4	10
5	00 70
6	14
7	
8	
9	35

Key: 3 | 20 = 320

The left plot shows that there are two values in the 340s, but we cannot see that one is 340 and one is 344. Both options are correct. You must decide whether that greater level of accuracy is important, or whether the information is sufficiently clear without it.

Create stem-and-leaf plots for the data given in Problem 6, Problem Set 11.4. Remember to provide a key. Explain how the data have been organized and what insight can be obtained from your stem-and-leaf plots.

Measures of Variability

Research is the process of going up alleys to see if they are blind.
—Marston Bates

If you ask two or more people to describe their recollections of events or places, their descriptions will usually differ. People vary in their interests, in their habits, and in the way they perceive things. When two people independently measure the same object, their measurements will probably vary. In this section, you will investigate different ways to measure and describe variability.

Investigation 3.2.1
A Typical Student

Each group should choose a different set of three body measurements, such as height, length of an ear, and wrist circumference. Collect these data from each member of your class. Determine the median and the mean values for each measurement. Share your results with other groups in your class.

Now write a report carefully explaining your procedures and conclusions. Use the questions below as a guide.

a. How would you describe the "mean student" and the "median student" in your class?

b. Do you think there is any one person that fits either description? Why or why not?

c. Which do you think is a better description of a "typical" or "average" student in your class?

d. Is your class representative of every class in your school?

A box plot is a visual display of the way data vary. One measure of spread, the range, is the distance between the whisker endpoints. Another measure of spread is the length of the box, or the interquartile range (IQR). There are ways to obtain numerical measures of data that indicate inconsistency, variation, or spread within data. One way to do this is to find the **deviation**, or directed distance, from each data value to the mean.

■ Example 1

Connie and Ozzie volunteered for an experiment in biology class. Every other Wednesday for 14 weeks, they had their cholesterol levels checked. Find the difference (deviation) between each data point and the mean of the data, for both Connie and Ozzie.

Connie Sistant 182, 186, 182, 184, 185, 184, 185

Ozzie Laiting 152, 194, 166, 216, 200, 176, 184

Solution

The mean for each student is 184. The individual deviations, $x_i - \bar{x}$, for each data value x_i, are in the table below.

Connie	Level	Deviation	Ozzie	Level	Deviation
x_1	182	182 – 184 = ⁻2	x_1	152	152 – 184 = ⁻32
x_2	186	186 – 184 = 2	x_2	194	194 – 184 = 10
x_3	182	182 – 184 = ⁻2	x_3	166	166 – 184 = ⁻18
x_4	184	184 – 184 = 0	x_4	216	216 – 184 = 32
x_5	185	185 – 184 = 1	x_5	200	200 – 184 = 16
x_6	184	184 – 184 = 0	x_6	176	176 – 184 = ⁻8
x_7	185	185 – 184 = 1	x_7	184	184 – 184 = 0

■

These deviations indicate more variation in Ozzie's levels than in Connie's. Do you think the sum of Ozzie's deviations should be larger than the sum of Connie's? If you think of the mean as a balance point in a data set, what do you expect will happen when you sum the positive and negative deviations for either Connie or Ozzie?

Connie's deviation sum = ⁻2 + 2 + ⁻2 + 0 + 1 + 0 + 1 = 0
Ozzie's deviation sum = ⁻32 + 10 + ⁻18 + 32 + 16 + ⁻8 + 0 = 0

The deviation sum for both students is zero. Therefore, the average deviation in both lists is also equal to zero.

$$\frac{⁻2 + 2 + ⁻2 + 0 + 1 + 0 + 1}{7} = 0 \quad \text{and} \quad \frac{⁻32 + 10 + ⁻18 + 32 + 16 + ⁻8 + 0}{7} = 0$$

Because the mean is a balance point in a list of values, the deviation sum, or average deviation, doesn't reflect the variation differences, or spread, in the two lists. Look at the table below. It suggests another possibility that provides a numerical approach to variability, or spread, in data.

Connie Sistant			Ozzie Laiting		
Level	Deviation	Absolute deviation	Level	Deviation	Absolute deviation
182	⁻2	2	152	⁻32	32
186	2	2	194	10	10
182	⁻2	2	166	⁻18	18
184	0	0	216	32	32
185	1	1	200	16	16
184	0	0	176	⁻8	8
185	1	1	184	0	0
Sum		8			116
Mean		1.14			16.57

Did you notice that, instead of summing the deviations, you can sum the absolute values of the deviations, and that the sum is no longer zero? The sum of the absolute values of the deviations, divided by the number of values, is called the average absolute deviation or the **mean absolute deviation (MAD),** and it provides one way to judge the "average difference" between data values and the mean.

Formula for the Mean Absolute Deviation

The **mean absolute deviation** is represented by the formula

$$\frac{\sum_{i=1}^{n} |x_i - \bar{x}|}{n}.$$

The variable x_i represents an individual score, n represents the number of individual scores, and $\bar{x}$ is the mean.

The larger mean absolute deviation for Ozzie indicates that his levels generally lie much further from the mean than do Connie's. A large value for the mean absolute deviation tells you that the data values are not as tightly packed around the mean. As a general rule, a distribution with more data near the mean will have less spread and a smaller mean absolute deviation.

■ Example 2

The data in the table on page 109 represent the student-to-teacher ratios for elementary and secondary schools, listed by region, in the continental United States.

Calculate the mean and the mean absolute deviation for each region. What does this tell you about the distribution of each set of ratios? Which region has the most consistent ratios?

Northeast		Midwest		South		West	
ME	13.9	MI	19.8	VA	15.7	WA	20.1
NH	16.2	WI	16.2	NC	16.9	OR	18.5
VT	13.2	MN	17.3	SC	16.8	CA	22.8
MA	15.4	OH	17.2	GA	18.3	NV	19.4
RI	15.4	IN	17.5	FL	17.2	ID	19.6
CT	13.6	IL	16.7	AL	19.9	UT	25.0
NY	14.6	IA	15.6	MS	17.9	AZ	19.4
PA	17.0	MO	15.5	TN	19.2	MT	15.9
NJ	15.6	KY	19.9	AR	16.8	WY	14.5
DE	13.6	ND	15.5	LA	18.6	CO	17.8
MD	16.8	SD	15.2	OK	15.6	NM	18.1
WV	16.5	NE	14.6	TX	15.4	KS	15.0

Solution

NOTE
3D

The mean student-to-teacher ratios of the Northeast, Midwest, South, and West are 15.15, 16.75, 17.36, and 18.84, respectively. Likewise, the mean absolute deviations are 1.14, 1.33, 1.18, and 2.21 students per teacher. (See **Calculator Note 3D** to learn how to find the mean absolute deviation using your calculator.) There are many conjectures and questions that you can propose. The greater spread of the values in the West compared to those in the other three regions reflects a wider variety of student-teacher ratios in that part of the country. ■

Problem Set 3.2

1. The average (mean) diameter measurement of a Purdy Goode Compact Disc is 12 cm, with a mean absolute deviation of 0.12 cm. No CDs can be shipped that are more than one mean absolute deviation from the mean. What does this imply from the perspective of the company's quality control engineer?

2. Invent a data set with seven length measurements such that both the mean and the median are 84 cm, the range is 23 cm, and the interquartile range is 12 cm.

3. Without calculating, use the mean and the mean absolute deviation to sketch what you think a graph of the four box plots for Example 2 would look like. Find the five summary values and draw the actual box plots.

4. The following information was collected during a mathematics lab by a group of students. The mean measurement was 46.3 cm, and the deviations of the eight individual measurements were 0.8 cm, ⁻0.4 cm, 1.6 cm, 1.1 cm, ⁻1.2 cm, ⁻0.3 cm, ⁻0.6 cm, and ⁻1.0 cm.

a. What were the original eight measurements collected?

b. Find the mean absolute deviation of the original measurements.

c. Which measurements were more than one mean absolute deviation from the mean?

5. The students in four classes recorded their pulse rates. The class averages and mean absolute deviations are given below. Each class has an equal number of students.

Class	Mean	Mean absolute deviation
First period	79.4	3.2
Third period	74.6	5.6
Fifth period	78.2	4.1
Sixth period	80.2	7.6

a. Which class has students with pulse rates most alike? How can you tell?

b. Can you tell which class has the students with the fastest pulses? Why or why not?

c. Using the same scale for each class, sketch your best estimate of a box plot for each class.

6. Each year many earthquakes occur throughout the world. Most earthquakes can only be detected by very sensitive instruments. An earthquake of magnitude 7.0 or greater is considered to be a major quake and is capable of causing widespread damage. The table on the facing page gives the number of earthquakes of magnitude 7.0 or greater that have occurred in the years between 1900 and 1989.

Damage to the Dawai Department Store in Fukui, Japan, as the result of a magnitude 7.3 earthquake on August 28, 1948.

a. Choose one column of the data. Describe how you could find the mean number of earthquakes for this column if you didn't have a calculator. Use your calculator to find the mean number of earthquakes for the column you chose.

b. Describe how you could find the mean absolute deviation for the column you chose if you didn't have a calculator. Use your calculator to find the mean absolute deviation for the column you chose.

c. Draw the figure at the right and label the mean. Point A and point B indicate distances of one mean absolute deviation from the mean; point C and point D indicate distances of two mean absolute deviations from the mean. Find the numerical value for each of the points A, B, C, and D.

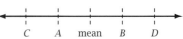

C A mean B D

Year	Earthquakes	Year	Earthquakes	Year	Earthquakes
1900	13	1930	13	1960	22
1901	14	1931	26	1961	18
1902	8	1932	13	1962	15
1903	10	1933	14	1963	20
1904	16	1934	22	1964	15
1905	26	1935	24	1965	22
1906	32	1936	21	1966	19
1907	27	1937	22	1967	16
1908	18	1938	26	1968	30
1909	32	1939	21	1969	27
1910	36	1940	23	1970	29
1911	24	1941	24	1971	23
1912	22	1942	27	1972	20
1913	23	1943	41	1973	16
1914	22	1944	31	1974	21
1915	18	1945	27	1975	21
1916	25	1946	35	1976	25
1917	21	1947	26	1977	16
1918	21	1948	28	1978	18
1919	14	1949	36	1979	15
1920	8	1950	39	1980	18
1921	11	1951	21	1981	14
1922	14	1952	17	1982	10
1923	23	1953	22	1983	15
1924	18	1954	17	1984	8
1925	17	1955	19	1985	15
1926	19	1956	15	1986	6
1927	20	1957	34	1987	11
1928	22	1958	10	1988	8
1929	19	1959	15	1989	7

Source: National Earthquake Information Center, U.S. Geological Survey.

d. Identify each year in your column in which the number of major earthquakes fell within one mean absolute deviation of the mean.

e. Were there any years in which the number of earthquakes was at least two mean absolute deviations away from the mean? If so, identify them.

7. Use the data in Problem 6 to answer the questions below.

   a. Choose a different column of earthquake data from the one you chose in Problem 6 and compute the mean for this column.

   b. Compute the mean absolute deviation for this column.

   c. Draw the figure at the right and label the mean. Point A and point B indicate distances of one mean absolute deviation from the mean; point C and point D indicate distances of two mean absolute deviations from the mean. Find the numerical value for each of the points A, B, C, and D.

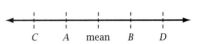

   d. Were there any years in which the number of earthquakes was at least two mean absolute deviations away from the mean? If so, identify them.

   e. Describe any similarities or differences between the two columns of data you chose, basing your description on the means and the mean absolute deviations for the two sets of data.

8. The normal daily mean temperatures for Juneau, Alaska, and New York, New York, are given below.

Month	Juneau	New York
January	24	32
February	28	34
March	33	42
April	40	53
May	47	63
June	53	72
July	56	77
August	55	76
September	49	68
October	42	58
November	32	48
December	27	37

Source: The American Almanac 1994-95.

Juneau, Alaska

New York, New York

   a. Find the mean absolute deviation and the interquartile range for each city; then draw a box plot for each city.

   b. Which city has more consistent temperatures? Justify your conclusion.

   c. Does the interquartile range or the mean absolute deviation give a better measure of the spread? Justify your conclusion.

9. Members of the school mathematics club sold packages of hot chocolate mix to raise funds for their club activities. The numbers of packages sold by individual members are given below.

65	76	100	67	44
147	82	94	92	79
158	77	62	85	71
69	88	80	63	75
62	68	71	73	74

a. Find the median and the interquartile range for this set of numbers.
b. Find the mean and the mean absolute deviation for the individual sales numbers.
c. Draw a box plot for this set. Name any numbers that are outliers.
d. Remove the outliers from the data set and draw another box plot.
e. With the outliers removed, recalculate (i) the mean and the mean absolute deviation, and (ii) the median and the interquartile range.
f. Which is more affected by outliers, the mean or the median? The mean absolute deviation or the interquartile range? Explain why you think this is so.

10. Since the beginning of the school year, you have been working with your group, or perhaps you have worked with several different groups. How has your attitude toward group work changed since the beginning of the school year? Has your role in your group changed? Explain in detail.

Take Another Look 3.2

The table below lists the numbers of packages of hot chocolate mix sold by individual members of the school math club (Problem 9 of Problem Set 3.2).

65	76	100	67	44
147	82	94	92	79
158	77	62	85	71
69	88	80	63	75
62	68	71	73	74

If you have already completed this problem, refer to your answers. (The answers are also provided in the back of the book.) The purpose of this second look at the data set is (1) to review how you use your calculator to find statistical information, (2) to make certain you understand how to find statistical values without using calculator shortcuts, and (3) to compare statistical information for related data sets.

a. Review again the techniques listed in the appendices that allow you to find the median, the interquartile range, the five-number summary, the mean, and the mean absolute deviation. In other words, be certain you know how to use your calculator to find this information. Be certain you know how to enter and plot data and how to find the data-related statistics.

b. Now describe how to find the median, the interquartile range, the five-number summary, the mean, and the mean absolute deviation without using calculator shortcuts, menus, or designated keys. Then draw a box plot of the data provided.

c. If each package sold for a net profit of 28¢, then each club member produces some income for the club. Find the median, the interquartile range, the five-number summary, the mean, and the mean absolute deviation—and draw a box plot for the incomes generated by each club member. Describe any calculator-efficient methods that you have used.

d. Compare your income statistics with the original statistics describing the numbers of packages sold. The two sets of statistics and the graphs are related by the number 0.28. Explain this relationship. Predict net profit statistics if the net profit per package is 35¢.

e. Suppose that in an attempt to "look good," the club secretary over-reported the original values, and the school audit finds that each individual member actually sold 20 fewer packages than those originally listed. Now describe a process you could use to find the corrected results for all of the information requested in part a. Look for relationships between these two sets of statistics, and explain any that you discover. Predict the statistical results if instead there were 10 fewer packages than those originally listed.

You were asked to make several measurements within Investigation 3.2.1. If you have that information, then use those measurements. Otherwise, use the following student heights (measured in inches).

69	64	62	72	67	63	73	70
67	75	66	71	77	64	64	68
70	70	69	60	64	67	70	68

f. Form a second table by converting the measurements to centimeters. Find the median, the interquartile range, the five-number summary, the mean, and the mean absolute deviation of each data set. On paper, graph box plots for both data sets.

g. Describe the relationships that exist between the two sets of data. Compare the graphs and describe any relationships that exist.

Geometer's Sketchpad Investigation

Comparing the Mean and the Mean Absolute Deviation

In this investigation, you will use the Sketchpad to create a model of the mean absolute deviation (MAD).

Step 1 Draw a vertical segment, *AB*, and place four points on one side of the line. The measure of the horizontal distance between each point and the vertical line will represent the value of each data point.

Step 2 Find a way to create a segment that has a length equal to the mean value of your data points. There is more than one method for doing this. (Hint: Think about how you would calculate the mean of four numbers.)

Step 3 Create a segment that has a length equal to the MAD of your data points. Be sure to review the formula for the MAD before calculating the length of the segment that represents this measurement. If you are having difficulty, make use of the hints given below, but first try doing the task without looking at the hints.

This diagram shows five data points. The distance between each point and the vertical line represents the value of the data point. In this model, it does not matter on which side of the vertical segment the point lies. In this case the value of the MAD is less than the mean.

Hints: To calculate the mean, measure the distance between each data point and the vertical segment *AB*. Use the Sketchpad calculator to find the mean of these values, and translate a point by that marked distance to calculate the mean. To calculate the MAD, you may wish to calculate or construct each of the deviations. Then proceed as you did with the mean.

Questions

1. Try changing the distance between your data points and the line. What happens to the mean and the MAD?
2. What conditions make the MAD move toward zero? When is the MAD greater than the mean? When is it less than the mean? When are the mean and the MAD equal? Make one or more conjectures based on your study.
3. What information does the MAD give you about the data that is not given by the mean? Why is it useful to calculate the MAD?
4. Use your knowledge of geometry to create a model that does not use the calculator to determine the MAD, but instead uses geometric properties of the segments.

Project

Collecting Data

In this project you will design an experiment and collect your own data. You will need to explain the factors you considered when setting up your experiment. Note as many other possible variables as you can, no matter how unlikely they seem to you, such as the temperature, the day and the time the data were collected, and any other factors that you think may or may not affect the data. Be prepared to describe in detail the method you used for collecting the data. Record the data neatly and clearly, labeling variables and units. When summarizing the results of your experiment, use graphs and statistical measures that look at the data in different ways. In your conclusions, provide some analysis of the data and an interpretation of the results. Finally, draw some generalizations from the experiment and attempt to explain any outliers.

The list below contains some possible ideas for collecting data, but you may choose to come up with your own idea.

- For how many seconds can you balance a ball on your head?
- How far can you roll a penny before it falls over?
- Roll a die once and record the outcome. How many more rolls does it take for you to get the same number?
- Conduct a study and a ratings survey of a selection of radio stations in your area. In your study, list the type of music played by each station. Ratings should be determined for different age groups.

Section 3.3

Histograms and Percentiles

Numbers are intellectual witnesses that belong only to mankind.
—Honoré de Balzac

A box plot gives you a good picture of a data distribution, but in some cases you might want to see other information and details that a box plot doesn't show. The term *histogram* was introduced by Karl Pearson in an 1895 lecture, in which he described it as "a common form of graphical representation, that is, by columns marking as areas the frequency corresponding to the range of their base." Histograms give vivid pictures of distribution features, clusters of values, or gaps in data. They are especially useful for displaying large data sets.

City	1980 population	1990 population	Growth rate (%)	City	1980 population	1990 population	Growth rate (%)
Mesa, AZ	152,404	288,091	89.0	Glendale, AZ	97,172	148,134	52.4
Cucamonga, CA	55,250	101,409	83.5	Mesquite, TX	67,053	101,484	51.3
Plano, TX	72,331	128,713	77.9	Ontario, CA	88,820	133,179	49.9
Irvine, CA	62,134	110,330	77.6	Virginia Beach, VA	262,199	393,069	49.9
Escondido, CA	64,355	108,635	68.8	Scottsdale, AZ	88,622	130,069	46.8
Oceanside, CA	76,698	128,398	67.4	Santa Ana, CA	204,023	293,742	44.0
Bakersfield, CA	105,611	174,820	65.5	Stockton, CA	148,283	210,943	42.3
Arlington, TX	160,113	261,721	63.5	Pomona, CA	92,742	131,723	42.0
Fresno, CA	217,491	354,202	62.9	Irving, TX	109,943	155,037	41.0
Chula Vista, CA	83,927	135,163	61.0	Aurora, CO	158,588	222,103	40.1
Las Vegas, NV	164,674	258,295	56.9	Raleigh, NC	150,255	207,951	38.4
Modesto, CA	106,963	164,730	54.0	San Bernardino, CA	118,794	164,164	38.2
Tallahassee, FL	81,548	124,773	53.0				

Source: The Universal Almanac 1994.

The histogram on the right pictures the 25 fastest-growing major cities in the United States between 1980 and 1990. Growth rates for these cities range from 38.2% for San Bernardino, California, to 89% for Mesa, Arizona. The width of each bar represents a range of 5%. The gap between 70% and 75% means no major United States city grew at a rate between 70% and 75%. How can you know if the graph accounts for all 25 cities?

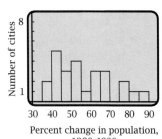

Percent change in population, 1980-1990

The individual bar width is arbitrary. However, in the histograms you will deal with in this course, all the bars should have the same width. You can see that a histogram with bar widths of 10% (shown at right) presents a different look than one with bar widths of 5%. Notice that the columns are taller in this graph because each category is made up of two categories from the previous graph. (Look at the vertical scale to confirm that these bars are indeed taller.) Use the information in the table above to create the same graphs on your calculator. (See **Calculator Note 3E.**)

NOTE
3E

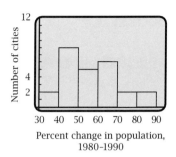

■ **Example 1**

The annual tuition costs of 50 different public colleges are shown in the histogram below. This distribution is said to be stretched, or **skewed**, to the right, toward the outliers.

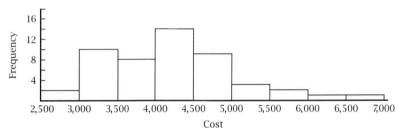

a. How many colleges represented in this graph have tuitions that are between $3,000 and $3,500?

b. In what interval is the median tuition?

c. What percent of these tuitions are less than $5,000?

Solution

a. The height of the second bar from the left indicates that 10 of the 50 college tuitions are between $3,000 and $3,500.

b. This histogram represents 50 college tuitions. (Find the sum of the bar heights.) The median, which is between the 25th and 26th number, is found by adding up the frequencies, or heights, of each column from the left until you get to 25. The median must be in the $4,000 to $4,500 range,

but it can't be determined any more closely than this. You do know that 50% of all the values in a data set are below or at the median value.

c. The college tuitions in 43 of the 50 colleges are less than $5,000. These 43 represent $\frac{43}{50} \cdot 100$, or 86% of the schools. This means $5,000 has a **percentile rank** of about 86, because 86% of the school tuitions are less than $5,000. Percentile ranks are frequently used to describe very large distributions. ■

Francis Galton, who originated the term *percentile* around 1885, said, "The value that is unreached by *n* percent of any large group of measurements, and surpassed by 100 – *n* of them, is called the *n*th percentile." You can use the somewhat simpler definition below.

Percentile Rank

The **percentile rank** of a data value in a large distribution is the percent of scores that are below the given value.

Suppose a large number of students take a standardized test like the SAT. Students at point A are at the 30th percentile, because their scores are better than 30% of the tested students.

Likewise, students at point B are at the 80th percentile, because 80% of the tested students have results that are lower.

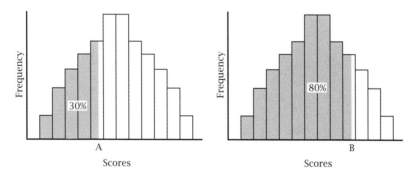

A percentile rank gives a good indication of how one individual's SAT score compares to other scores across the country. So many individual scores are involved that it would be impossible to look at all of the actual numbers.

■ Example 2

Make a histogram of the flight duration for space flights between 1961 and 1972, based on the table of data on the next page. Round off each flight time to the nearest hour.

Launch of
Apollo 11

Date	Mission name	Duration (hrs)	Date	Mission name	Duration (hrs)
4/12/61	Vostok 1	1.8	11/11/66	Gemini-Titan XII	94.6
8/6/61	Vostok 2	25.3	4/23/67	Soyuz 1	26.7
2/20/62	Mercury-Atlas 6	4.9	10/11/68	Apollo-Saturn 7	260.2
5/24/62	Mercury-Atlas 7	4.9	10/26/68	Soyuz 3	94.9
8/11/62	Vostok 3	94.4	12/21/68	Apollo-Saturn 8	146.0
8/12/62	Vostok 4	71.0	1/14/69	Soyuz 4	71.2
10/3/62	Mercury-Atlas 8	9.2	1/15/69	Soyuz 5	72.7
5/15/63	Mercury-Atlas 9	34.3	3/3/69	Apollo-Saturn 9	241.0
6/14/63	Vostok 5	119.1	5/18/69	Apollo-Saturn 10	192.1
6/16/63	Vostok 6	70.8	7/16/69	Apollo-Saturn 11	195.3
10/12/64	Voskhod 1	24.3	10/11/69	Soyuz 6	118.7
3/18/65	Voskhod 2	29.0	10/12/69	Soyuz 7	118.7
3/23/65	Gemini-Titan III	4.9	11/14/69	Apollo-Saturn 12	244.6
6/3/65	Gemini-Titan IV	97.9	4/11/70	Apollo-Saturn 13	142.9
8/21/65	Gemini-Titan V	190.9	1/31/71	Apollo-Saturn 14	216.0
12/4/65	Gemini-Titan VII	330.6	6/6/71	Soyuz 11	569.7
12/15/65	Gemini-Titan VI-A	25.9	7/26/71	Apollo-Saturn 15	295.9
3/16/66	Gemini-Titan VIII	10.7	4/16/72	Apollo-Saturn 16	265.9
6/3/66	Gemini-Titan IX-A	72.4	12/7/72	Apollo-Saturn 17	301.9
7/18/66	Gemini-Titan XI	71.3			

Source: The World Almanac and Book of Facts 1994.

Solution

There is not necessarily one right way to group these numbers, but you want to divide them so that there won't be too many columns. If you group them by 48's, then each column will show a time period of two days. The first column will show the number of flights from 0 to 47 hours, the next from 48 to 95 hours, and so on. If you are drawing the graph on your calculator, you'll need to estimate the maximum bar height in order to determine the value for Ymax.

In the histogram on the far right, each bar represents an interval of 24 hours, which gives a slightly different perspective of the totals.

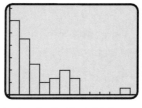

Window [0, 600, **48,** 0, 14, 2]

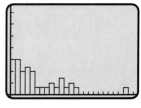

Window [0, 600, **24,** 0, 14, 2]

Investigation 3.3.1

Fast Food

How conscious are you of good nutrition? Do you often eat at a fast-food restaurant? If you do, this investigation may help you become more aware of what you are eating and whether it is good for you.

Most adults require about 1800 to 2400 calories per day. It is generally recommended that 50% to 60% of your calories come from carbohydrate food sources. Your diet should include approximately 63 grams of protein per day if you are an adult male over the age of 25. For a female, the recommendation is 50 grams of protein per day. Less than 30% of your daily intake of calories should come from fat. Cholesterol should be limited to between 13 and 20 grams per day. Your daily intake of sodium should not exceed 3000 milligrams (about one and a half teaspoons). That's a lot to think about when planning your diet.

Examine the information given below about the nutritional content of fast foods. (All items are sandwiches unless noted by an asterisk.) With your group, select either a type of food (burger, chicken, or fish) *or* one of the nutritional elements (calories, carbohydrates, protein, fat, cholesterol, or sodium). If your group chooses a type of food, investigate the nutritional elements of that type of food. If your group chooses a nutritional element, compare the amount of that element in the burger, chicken, or fish items. Prepare a report that uses box plots and histograms. Use all of the measures of central tendency and spread in your investigation. Draw attention to items that might be classified as outliers. Write a report discussing your conclusions. Prepare a short oral presentation for the class to accompany your report.

Company	Food	Serving size (oz)	Total calories	Carbohydrate (g)	Protein (g)	Fat (g)	Cholesterol (mg)	Sodium (mg)
Arby's	Roast Beef	5.5	383	35	22	18	43	936
Burger King	Whopper Jr.	4.7	300	29	14	15	35	500
Carl's Jr.	Carl's Original Hamburger	6.8	460	46	25	20	50	810
Dairy Queen	Hamburger	5	310	29	17	13	45	580
Hardee's	Big Deluxe Burger	7.6	500	32	27	30	70	760
Jack in the Box	Hamburger	3.4	267	28	13	11	26	556
McDonald's	Hamburger	3.6	255	30	12	9	37	490
Rax	Regular Rax	4.7	262	25	18	10	15	707
Wendy's	Single Hamburger	4.7	350	31	25	15	70	510

(table continued on next page)

Company	Food	Serving size (oz)	Total calories	Carbohydrate (g)	Protein (g)	Fat (g)	Cholesterol (mg)	Sodium (mg)
Whataburger	Whataburger Jr.	5.4	304	31	15	12	30	684
Arby's	Chicken Breast Fillet	7.2	445	42	22	23	45	958
Burger King	Chicken	8	620	57	26	32	45	1430
Carl's Jr.	Charbroiler BBQ Chicken	11	310	34	25	6	30	680
Chick-Fil-A	Chick-Fil-A Deluxe	7.5	369	30	41	9	66	1178
Church's Fried Chicken	Fried Chicken Breast	2.8	200	4	19	12	65	510
Dairy Queen	Grilled Chicken Fillet	6.5	300	33	25	8	50	800
Hardee's	Chicken Fillet	6	370	44	19	13	55	1060
Jack in the Box	Chicken and Mushroom	7.8	438	40	28	18	61	1340
KFC	Original Recipe Breast	3.6	260	8	25	14	92	609
Long John Silver's	Batter-dipped Chicken	4.5	280	39	14	8	15	790
McDonald's	McChicken	6.5	415	39	19	20	50	830
Popeyes	Chicken Breast	3.7	270	9	23	16	60	660
Rax	Grilled Chicken	6.9	402	26	25	23	69	872
Wendy's	Grilled Chicken	6.25	290	35	24	7	60	360
Whataburger	Whatachicken	10	671	61	35	32	71	1460
Arby's	Fish Fillet	7.8	526	50	23	27	44	872
Carl's Jr.	Carl's Catch	7.5	560	54	17	30	5	1220
Dairy Queen	Fish Fillet	6	370	39	16	16	45	630
Hardee's	Fisherman's Fillet	7.5	480	50	23	21	70	1210
Jack in the Box	Fish Supreme	7.7	510	44	24	27	55	1040
Long John Silver's	Batter-dipped Fish	5.6	340	40	18	13	30	890
McDonald's	Fillet-O-Fish	5	370	38	14	18	50	730
Wendy's	Fish	6.4	460	42	18	25	55	780
Whataburger	Whatacatch	6.2	475	43	14	27	34	722

Source: Marion J. Franz, *Fast Food Facts* (Chronimed Publishing, 1994).

Problem Set 3.3

1. Recently Fay Silitator's students spent the class period rolling pairs of dice and recording the results. They kept track of the sum of the two dice on each of 1000 rolls. The number of times (**frequency**) each different sum came up is listed below.

Total on dice	Number of rolls (frequency)
2	26
3	56
4	83
5	110
6	145
7	162
8	149
9	114
10	73
11	61
12	21

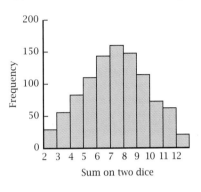

NOTE
3E

a. Graph the histogram above on your calculator. List the window values needed for it to look like the histogram pictured. (See **Calculator Note** 3E for help.)
b. Explain why the histogram has a mound-like shape.
c. Describe how you would find the mean sum and the median sum for the pairs of dice rolled.

2. Rita and Noah are working on a report for their economics class. They surveyed 95 farmers in their county to see how many acres of sweet corn the farmers had planted. The results are summarized in the histogram on the right.
   a. The distribution is skewed to the right. Explain what this means.
   b. Graph the histogram on your calculator.
   c. Describe what you think a box plot of this information would look like, and then check your conjecture with your calculator.

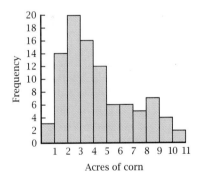

3. Describe a situation and sketch a histogram to reflect each condition named below.
   a. mound-shaped and quite symmetric   b. skewed to the left
   c. skewed to the right   d. rectangular

4. At a large university, 1500 students took a final exam in chemistry. Frank Stein learned that his score of 76 (out of 100) placed him at the 88th percentile.

  a. How many students had lower scores than Frank? How many had higher scores?

  b. Mary Curie had a score of 82, which placed her at the 95th percentile. Describe how Mary's performance compared to that of others in the class.

  c. What percentile is associated with the best test score of 91?

  d. If every student who scored above the 90th percentile received an A, how many students earned this grade?

5. Ozzie kept a log of the amount of time he spent doing homework and watching television during 20 days in October.

October date	3	4	5	6	7	8	10	11	12	13
Homework (min)	4	10	40	11	55	46	46	23	57	28
TV (min)	78	30	15	72	25	30	90	40	35	56

October date	14	15	17	18	19	20	21	22	24	25
Homework (min)	65	58	52	38	38	39	45	27	41	44
TV (min)	12	5	95	27	38	50	10	42	60	34

  a. Draw two box plots, one showing the amount of time spent doing homework, and one showing the amount of time watching television. Name the five summary values for each. Which distribution has the greatest spread? What is the spread value of each?

  b. Make an educated guess at the histogram shape for each set of data. Will either, or both, be skewed or mound-shaped? Describe what you think each will look like. Confirm your guesses by constructing each histogram.

  c. Calculate all three measures of spread—interquartile range, range, and mean absolute deviation—for either the homework data or the television data. Which measure of spread is least affected by outliers? Which measure of spread best represents the data?

6. a. Given that the deviations from the mean for Penny Saved's bank account during the last eight months are 0, ‾40, ‾78, ‾71, 33, 36, 42, and 91, how do you know that at least one of the deviations is incorrect?

  b. If it turns out that 33 is incorrect, while the others are correct, what should that deviation be?

  c. For the corrected list, find the mean absolute deviation, the actual data values, the median, and the interquartile range for each given mean value.

  i. The mean value is 747.   **ii.** The mean value is 850.

  d. Write a paragraph describing what you discovered in this problem.

7. Use the information in the table about major-league baseball stadium capacities, 1992 average home attendance, and the year the stadium was built, when answering the questions.

Team	Stadium	Year built	Capacity	1992 average attendance
Baltimore	Orioles Park	1992	48,041	44,598
Boston	Fenway Park	1912	34,142	31,648
California	Anaheim Stadium	1966	64,593	25,499
Chicago	Comiskey Park	1991	44,702	33,101
Cleveland	Cleveland Stadium	1931	74,483	15,694
Detroit	Tiger Stadium	1912	52,416	18,256
Kansas City	Royals Stadium	1973	40,625	23,642
Milwaukee	County Stadium	1953	53,192	23,511
Minnesota	H.H.H. Metrodome	1982	55,883	30,647
New York	Yankee Stadium	1923	57,545	21,859
Oakland	Coliseum	1966	47,313	30,792
Seattle	The Kingdome	1976	59,702	20,387
Texas	Arlington Stadium	1965	43,521	27,478
Toronto	SkyDome	1989	50,516	49,732
Atlanta	County Stadium	1965	52,007	38,468
Chicago	Wrigley Field	1914	38,710	26,584
Cincinnati	Riverfront Stadium	1970	52,952	28,949
Colorado	Mile High Stadium	1948	76,100	Not available
Florida	Joe Robbie Stadium	1987	48,000	Not available
Houston	The Astrodome	1965	54,816	14,956
Los Angeles	Dodger Stadium	1962	56,000	32,120
Montreal	Olympic Stadium	1976	43,739	20,864
New York	Shea Stadium	1964	55,601	23,415
Philadelphia	Veterans Stadium	1971	62,382	24,711
Pittsburgh	Three Rivers Stadium	1970	58,729	22,585
St. Louis	Busch Stadium	1966	56,227	30,231
San Diego	Jack Murphy Stadium	1967	59,700	21,252
San Francisco	Candlestick Park	1960	62,000	19,759

Source: The 1993 Information Please Sports Almanac.

a. Compute the mean absolute deviations of both the stadium capacities and the average attendance. Which has the larger mean absolute deviation? In your own words, explain what this means.

b. How does knowledge about the mean absolute deviation help you predict the shape of a histogram? Of a box plot?

c. Based on your answer to part b, predict what the two box plots and the two histograms will look like. Confirm your predictions by drawing each of the four graphs on your calculator.

d. Write a short paragraph to a sports-minded friend about something that interests you in this table. Support your writing with statistical information.

8. Explain how the information shown in a box plot differs from that shown in a histogram. Describe a situation in which a box plot would be the better choice for presenting data. Describe a situation in which a histogram would be the better choice.

Dodger Stadium, Los Angeles

Take Another Look 3.3

1. Expressions like

$$\frac{\sum_{i=1}^{n} x_i}{n} \quad \text{and} \quad \frac{\sum_{i=1}^{n} |x_i - \bar{x}|}{n}$$

are often difficult to understand. Take another look at the pulse-rate data collected in Investigation 3.1.2. If that information is not available, then use the pulse rates given below of 50 people.

66	75	83	73	87	94	79	93	87	64
80	72	84	82	80	73	74	80	83	68
86	70	73	62	77	90	82	85	84	80
80	79	81	82	76	95	76	82	79	91
82	66	78	73	72	77	71	79	82	88

a. With reference to the pulse rates, carefully explain the meaning of every number, variable, and operation in the expression

$$\frac{\sum_{i=1}^{n} x_i}{n}.$$

Then find the value of this expression.

b. With reference to the pulse rates, carefully explain the meaning of every number, variable, and operation in the expression

$$\frac{\sum_{i=1}^{n} |x_i - \bar{x}|}{n}.$$

Then find the value of this expression.

c. With reference to the pulse rates, carefully explain the meaning of every number, variable, and operation in the expression

$$\sqrt{\frac{\sum_{i=1}^{n}(x_i - \bar{x})^2}{n}}.$$

Then find the value of this expression. This expression represents a measure of spread called standard deviation. One of the projects in this chapter is devoted to this measure.

2. Example 2 of Section 3.2 contains data about student-to-teacher ratios.

a. Do some research and find out how the student-to-teacher ratio for your school or your district, or both, compares to the ratio given for your state.

b. How does this ratio compare to the mean ratio for your region? The mean for the entire data set? Describe the ratio for your school in terms of the mean absolute deviation for your region and for the data set as a whole.

c. Compute the standard deviation for your region using the expression given in Problem 1c. Describe the ratio for your school in terms of the mean absolute deviation for your region.

d. Interview at least three teachers and get their opinions about the student-to-teacher ratio in your school.

e. Pretend that you are a student member of the school board and have been asked to submit a report concerning the student-to-teacher ratio in your school. Write a report summarizing your findings, and be sure to include a discussion of some of the statistical measures you used.

Project

Standard Deviation

You will need a meterstick and a string a little longer than 1.5 m. Ask between 30 and 50 people to measure the cord as accurately as they can and to give you its length in centimeters. Enter these data into your calculator and construct several histograms using different interval widths. Decide which interval width gives the best picture

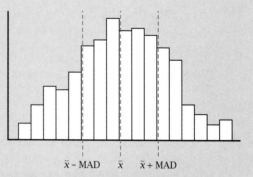

$\bar{x} - \text{MAD}$ $\bar{x}$ $\bar{x} + \text{MAD}$

of the data and make a sketch of this histogram. Find the mean value of the data set and the deviation of each measurement from the mean. Calculate the mean absolute deviation (MAD). Add three vertical lines to your sketch—one at the mean, one at one mean absolute deviation above the mean, and one at one mean absolute deviation below the mean.

Square each deviation instead of taking the absolute value. The mean value of the squares of the deviations is called the **variance** of the data. The units of the variance for this project are centimeters squared, which is a little confusing because it is not a measure of area, but a squared measure of length. The square root of the variance is called the **standard deviation** of the data. Karl Pearson coined the term *standard deviation* around 1893, denoting it by the lowercase Greek letter sigma (σ), which is still used today. The units of the standard deviation for this project are centimeters. Find the standard deviation for these data and add two more vertical lines to your sketch—one that is one standard deviation above the mean, and another that is one standard deviation below the mean.

NOTE
11E

One advantage of the standard deviation is that it is a built-in function in many calculators, computer spreadsheets, and other analysis tools. (See **Calculator Note 11E** for instructions on how to calculate standard deviation on your calculator.) Research and identify other advantages to using standard deviation. (See Section 11.4 for definitions of variance and standard deviation.)

Chapter Review

Errors using inadequate data are much less than those using no data at all.
—Charles Babbage

Lists of data, such as temperatures, the sugar content of breakfast cereals, and the number of hours of television watched weekly by the members of your class, can be analyzed and pictured using tools that you learned about in this chapter. The mean and the median value of a list are called measures of center. They are the average and middle values, respectively. But they do not tell the whole story. You also need to look at how the values are spread. The mean absolute deviation (MAD) helps you determine the spread, or variation, of the data. To visually display the data, you can use a box plot or a histogram. A box plot shows the median of the data and the range of the entire set, along with the range that includes the middle 50% of the data. The bars of a histogram show how the data are spread throughout the entire range. However, no set percentages or subsets of the data are specifically shown. By changing the width of the bars, you can get a different perspective on the distribution. Percentiles can be used to show how one value in the list compares to the list as a whole. For example, if a cereal with 16 grams of sugar is at the 90th percentile in the set of cereals examined, that means it contains more sugar than 90 percent of the cereals examined. By using a combination of these statistical tools, you can better understand the meaning and implications of the data.

Problem Set 3.4

1. Which box plot (A or B pictured at the right) has the larger mean absolute deviation? Support and explain your answer.

2. **a.** Draw two different histograms that might represent the information pictured in the two box plots C and D below.
   b. How many data values are represented in each lower whisker? How many are represented in the upper whisker in plot D?
   c. Which plot represents the data set with the larger mean absolute deviation? Explain how you know this.

3. Invent two data sets, each with seven values, such that data set A has the greater MAD and data set B has the greater IQR.

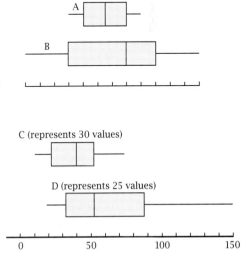

C (represents 30 values)

D (represents 25 values)

4. The table contains the recorded extreme temperatures (in degrees Fahrenheit) for each of the seven continents. Find the mean and the mean absolute deviation of the extreme high temperatures. Then find the mean and the mean absolute deviation of the extreme low temperatures. Which values, if any, are more than two mean absolute deviations from the mean?

Continent	High	Low
Africa	136	⁻11
Antarctica	59	⁻129
Asia	129	⁻90
Australia	128	⁻8
Europe	122	⁻67
North America	134	⁻87
South America	120	⁻27

Source: Information Please Almanac 1996.

5. a. Create a histogram that has a mean absolute deviation close to zero.
   b. Create a histogram with the same number of values as in part a, but with a mean absolute deviation of about 5.

6. Enter the space flight data from Example 2 in Section 3.3 into your calculator. You may round off the flight duration to the nearest hour.
   a. Make a prediction as to which is longer, the median flight duration or the mean flight duration. List some reasons for your prediction. Then use the calculator to compute each statistic.
   b. Divide the data into two lists, one representing Soviet space flights and one representing United States space flights. Construct a histogram for each list.
   c. Predict which data set—the United States flights or the Soviet flights—will have the greater mean absolute deviation. Check your prediction using your calculator.

7. The 1991 United States plant passenger-car production totals are shown below.

Plymouth	143,963	Cadillac	228,419	Dodge	275,613
Saturn	95,821	Ford	771,354	Honda	451,199
Lincoln-Mercury	400,326	Mazda	165,314	Chevrolet	786,012
Nissan	133,505	Pontiac	509,080	Subaru	57,945
Oldsmobile	439,752	Toyota	298,847	Buick	436,922

Source: The World Almanac and Book of Facts 1993.

a. Make a box plot of the production totals.
b. Make a histogram using a bar width that provides meaningful information about the data.

c. Write a short news article describing the information in these data.

d. Suppose the total number of cars produced in a different year is 400,000 greater than the 1991 total. Describe how this could affect the shape of your box plot and histogram.

8. Examine the information in the following table about the percentage of the population over five years old in the United States that does not speak English.

Percent of Population over Five Years Old in the United States That Is Non-English Speaking

State	Percent non-English	State	Percent non-English
Alabama	2.9	Montana	5.0
Alaska	12.1	Nebraska	4.8
Arizona	20.8	Nevada	13.2
Arkansas	2.8	New Hampshire	8.7
California	31.5	New Jersey	19.5
Colorado	10.5	New Mexico	35.5
Connecticut	15.2	New York	23.3
Delaware	6.9	North Carolina	3.9
Florida	17.3	North Dakota	7.9
Georgia	4.8	Ohio	5.4
Hawaii	24.8	Oklahoma	5.0
Idaho	6.4	Oregon	7.3
Illinois	14.2	Pennsylvania	7.3
Indiana	4.8	Rhode Island	17.0
Iowa	3.9	South Carolina	3.5
Kansas	5.7	South Dakota	6.5
Kentucky	2.5	Tennessee	2.9
Louisiana	10.1	Texas	25.4
Maine	9.2	Utah	7.8
Maryland	8.9	Vermont	5.8
Massachusetts	15.2	Virginia	7.3
Michigan	6.6	Washington	9.0
Minnesota	5.6	West Virginia	2.6
Mississippi	2.8	Wisconsin	5.8
Missouri	3.8	Wyoming	5.7

Source: The World Almanac and Book of Facts 1994.

a. Prepare a histogram and a box plot that best picture the information. Describe the information you can get from looking at the graphs.

b. Prepare histograms and box plots that compare information from states east of the Mississippi River with those west of the Mississippi River. Describe and explain the similarities and differences between the two regions.

c. Compare histograms and box plots of data from different geographic regions of the United States as defined in Example 2 of Section 3.2.

d. Prepare a report that uses box plots, histograms, and each of the measures of central tendency and spread. What information could you provide to someone who is making a decision related to these data? Prepare a short oral presentation to the class to accompany your report.

Assessing What You've Learned—Performance Assessment

In this chapter you learned how to use your calculator as a tool to do many new things related to statistical data and graphs. Part of the assessment for this chapter is evaluating what you can do with this tool. Do you know how to store data in your calculator? Can you construct box plots and histograms? Can you display data in some form and make conjectures based on these data? Demonstrating that you can do tasks like these is sometimes called performance assessment.

Look over the steps for constructing box plots and histograms, and make sure that you know how to construct each type of graph. Practice making these graphs until you're absolutely certain that you know how to do them. Choose some data and demonstrate to a classmate, a family member, or your teacher, that you know how to construct box plots and histograms. Do every step from start to finish and explain what you're doing. Be sure to describe any information provided by the graph that may not be in the raw data.

Organize Your Notebook

- Is your notebook still organized? Have you organized your work for this chapter? Did you complete all of the assignments? Take a few minutes to complete any missing problems.
- Be sure to add any notes about new calculator techniques you've learned.

Write in Your Journal

- At the end of Problem Sets 3.2 and 3.3, you will find suggestions for journal entries.

Update Your Portfolio

- If you completed a project in this chapter, document your work and add it to your portfolio.
- Choose a problem from this chapter with a box plot or a histogram that you found particularly interesting or challenging. Describe your work on each step of the problem, including the way you figured out how to move from step to step. Add this description to your portfolio.

Data Analysis

Have you ever watched a large "people wave" at a sporting event? How long would it take for all the soccer fans in this Mexico City stadium to participate in the wave if they all agreed to do it in some orderly fashion? Can you predict the time needed? What information would you need? By gathering some data with several smaller groups of people, you might be able to make a prediction about a stadium full of people. To make this prediction, first you will need to find a mathematical model—an equation and its graph— that "fits" the data.

Section 4.1

The Best-Fit Line

It isn't that they can't see the solution. It is that they can't see the problem.
—G. K. Chesterton

Data is a name for numerical information. In Chapter 3, you learned how to make a graph to display a set of data, and how to calculate summary statistics to describe it. **Data analysis** is a process of deriving information from data that helps you to answer the questions that interest you. This often involves describing a relationship that closely fits your data. Such a relationship is called a **mathematical model**. Once you define a model, you may be able to extract other information from the data. Data analysis is not an exact science, however, and often there is more than one way to find a mathematical model; sometimes there may be several different models that appear to fit the data.

The study of statistics and the search for mathematical models to fit data is a relatively new field in mathematics. In the late 1800s, Francis Galton's interest in evolution and natural selection led him to study heredity and to try to find general laws of inheritance. One of his first projects was to study the weight of sweet-pea seeds. He analyzed the data comparing the weights of original seeds and the weights of seeds of their offspring using a linear model. In this chapter, you will look at different methods for finding models, and you will also explore methods for determining how good a model is.

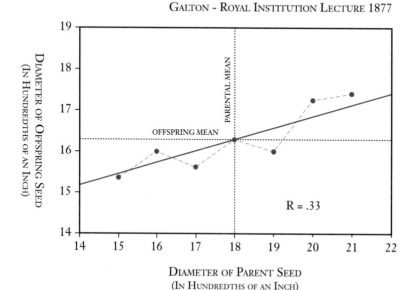

INHERITANCE IN SIZE OF SWEET PEA SEEDS.

GALTON - ROYAL INSTITUTION LECTURE 1877

Galton's line of best-fit for his sweet-pea seed data

Suppose you collect data from several thousand adult males selected at random. You make a table showing the height of each man (in inches) and his weight (in pounds). From your information, you might estimate that a man's weight increases by about 3.7 pounds for each inch of increase in height. You know that there are factors other than weight that affect height, so it is not unreasonable to expect that the data will not fit the pattern exactly. The challenge is to find the best model that fits the data you have. As your search for a more exact model becomes more sophisticated, you will refine your model so that it includes the influence of these other factors.

Investigation 4.1.1

Car Data

With members of your group, measure the lengths and widths of at least 12 cars. Be sure to measure cars that are all the same type, such as two-door sedans, pick-up trucks, or station wagons. Record this information in a table. You don't need to record the make or model of each car. Next, plot the points representing these pairs of numbers on graph paper. Draw a line that seems to fit your data. Save the data and the graph for a problem in the problem set.

Length of car	Width of car
–?–	–?–
–?–	–?–

How would you describe the **best-fit line** for a set of data? Ideally, you might want every point to lie on the line, but in real life this will rarely occur (and you probably will be suspicious if it does happen). There is no single list of rules that will obtain the *best* line in every instance, but by observing the four guidelines that follow, you will usually end up with a reasonably good fit.

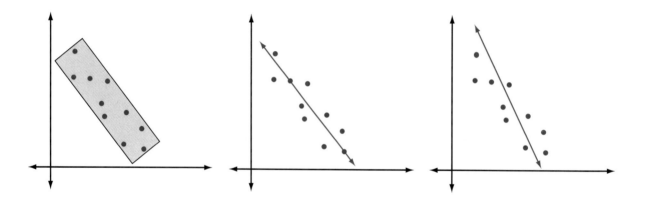

1. The line should show the direction of the points. The smallest rectangle that contains the points shows the general direction of the line.
2. The line should divide the points equally. There should be about as many points above the line as below the line.
3. As many points as possible should be *on* the line, but the previous two guidelines are more important.
4. The points above the line should not be concentrated at one end, nor should the points below the line.

These four guidelines may seem confusing at first, but the following problems will help clarify their meanings.

Problem Set 4.1

1. Look at each graph below, and choose the *one* with the line that best satisfies the guidelines above. (That was the easy part.) For each of the other graphs, explain which guidelines were violated.

a.

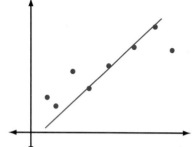

b.

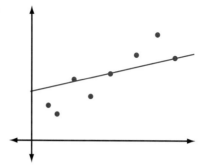

c.

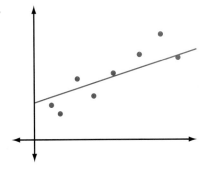

d.

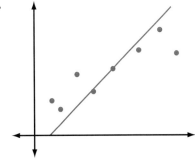

e.

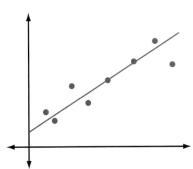

f.

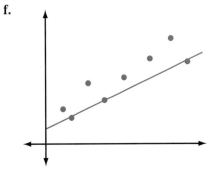

2. For each graph below, lay your ruler along your best-fit line. Assuming a scale of 1 on both axes, give an approximate value for the *y*-intercept and name one other point that the line goes through (it need not be one of the given points).

a.

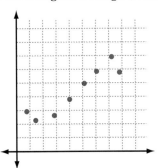

b.

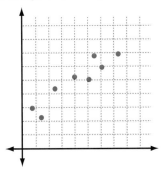

c.

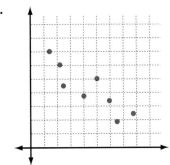

d.

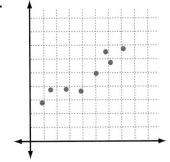

e.

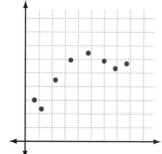

f.

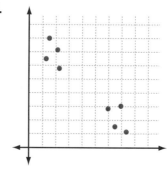

For Problems 3 and 4, graph the data and draw your best-fit line.

3.

Planet	Mean distance from the sun (AU)	Time of one revolution (yr)
Mercury	0.387	0.241
Venus	0.723	0.615
Earth	1.000	1.000
Mars	1.523	1.881
Jupiter	5.203	11.861
Saturn	9.541	29.457
Uranus	19.190	84.008
Neptune	30.086	164.784
Pluto	39.507	248.350

Note: 1 AU ≈ 93 million mi.

4.

Taxable income ($)	Tax ($)
12,000	2,260
16,000	3,260
20,000	4,380
24,000	5,660
28,000	7,100
32,000	8,660

5. Look at the best-fit line you drew in the Investigation 4.1.1. Analyze your line using the four guidelines given in this section. Does your line satisfy these guidelines? If you think you can draw a line that fits better, do so.

6. Listed below are the dimensions (in inches) used by pattern manufacturers. These are supposed to represent the measurements of an average adult woman.

Misses size	6	8	10	12	14	16	18	20
Bust	$30\frac{1}{2}$	$31\frac{1}{2}$	$32\frac{1}{2}$	34	36	38	40	42
Waist	23	24	25	$26\frac{1}{2}$	28	30	32	34
Hips	$32\frac{1}{2}$	$33\frac{1}{2}$	$34\frac{1}{2}$	36	38	40	42	44

a. How many graphs are needed to show all the possible relationships between the data?

b. Choose two relationships from the table, and plot them on separate graphs.

7. Have you discovered any new advantages of working in groups in your mathematics class? New disadvantages? Explain these completely.

Take Another Look 4.1

With many calculators, it's possible to create a histogram using two separate lists. One list contains the data and the other records the frequency of each data value. If possible, determine how this can be done with your calculator. Now take another look at Problem 2 of Problem Set 3.3. If you haven't done so already, graph the histogram using this technique.

Then find the mean number of acres planted and the mean absolute deviation (MAD) for this information. Describe how you found these values using data stored in two separate lists.

Acres of corn	Frequency	Acres of corn	Frequency
0	3	6	6
1	14	7	5
2	20	8	7
3	16	9	4
4	12	10	2
5	6		

Equation of a Line

He who wonders discovers that this in itself is wonder.
—M. C. Escher

Suppose you are taking a long trip in your car. At
5 p.m., you notice that the odometer reads 45,623
miles. At 9 p.m., you note that it reads 45,831.
What was your average speed during that time
period? The answer, 52 miles per hour, is a rate.
If you graph the information, 52 is the slope of
the line connecting the two points. You use the
definition of slope when you calculate the speed.

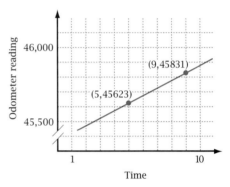

$$\text{Average speed} = \frac{45831 - 45623}{9 - 5} \quad \text{or} \quad \frac{d_2 - d_1}{t_2 - t_1}$$

Slope is one of the most important mathematical concepts that you will study. In
trigonometry, it is used to help find the heights of objects like trees and buildings,
and the distances across lakes or canyons. In calculus, it is used to determine how
fast populations are growing, or to help in designing soda cans that can be
manufactured with the least cost. Slope is just as important in physics and chemistry.
In application problems, slope is often called **rate of change**.

Slope

The slope of a line is $\dfrac{\text{change in } y}{\text{change in } x}$ or $\dfrac{\text{rise}}{\text{run}}$.

The formula for the **slope** from point 1 (x_1, y_1) to point 2 (x_2, y_2) is

$$m = \frac{y_2 - y_1}{x_2 - x_1}.$$

The letter m is usually used to represent slope. The
ratio of *the change in the y-values* over *the change in the
x-values* will be constant for any two points selected on the
line. This means that the ratio is invariant on a line. In
other words, a line has only one slope.

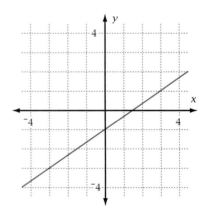

■ **Example 1**

Find the slope of the line shown at the right.

Solution

First, identify two points on the line, such as the points $(^-3, ^-3)$ and $(3, 1)$. Then use the formula to find the slope.

$$m = \frac{1 - (^-3)}{3 - (^-3)} = \frac{2}{3}$$

In many cases, you may not be able to identify the coordinates of the points as easily as in the example above. To increase your accuracy when calculating the slope, choose your points carefully, and select them from opposite ends of the line segment. Then choose a third point, and find the slope between it and one of the first two points to serve as a check on your work.

Check: Points $(0, ^-1)$ and $(3, 1)$: $\quad \frac{1 - (^-1)}{3 - 0} = \frac{2}{3}$ ■

You can use the slope formula to find the equation of a line containing two points. Select one point, and let the second point be a "generic" point (x, y).

■ Example 2

In the automobile trip example, the points are $(5, 45623)$ and $(9, 45831)$. Use the first of these points and the generic point (x, y) to write an equation for the line. You will also need the rate (slope), which is 52 mi/hr.

Solution

$\dfrac{y_2 - y_1}{x_2 - x_1} = m$	Formula for slope.
$\dfrac{y - 45623}{x - 5} = 52$	Substitute (x, y) for (x_2, y_2), $(5, 45623)$ for (x_1, y_1), and 52 for m.
$y - 45623 = 52(x - 5)$	Multiply both sides by $(x - 5)$.
$y = 52(x - 5) + 45623$	Add 45,623 to both sides.

(The result can also be rewritten as $y = 52x - 260 + 45623$ or $y = 52x + 45363$.) ■

Point-Slope Form

The **point-slope form** of the equation of a line with slope m containing point (x_1, y_1) is

$$y = m(x - x_1) + y_1.$$

■ Example 3

Find the equation of the line shown at right.

Solution

Select the points: (⁻3, 1) and (3, ⁻2).

Find the slope: $m = \dfrac{-2 - 1}{3 - (-3)} = \dfrac{-1}{2}$

Then choose either of the points and substitute the *x*- and *y*-values into the point-slope form. If you choose the first point, (⁻3, 1), then

$$y = -\frac{1}{2}(x + 3) + 1.$$

NOTE

4A

Check your answer by repeating the procedure, using the point (⁻1, 0). When you simplify, you should get an equivalent equation. You can do a visual check by graphing the line and the points on your calculator. (See **Calculator Note 4A** for help in graphing points and lines.) Another quick check, if your calculator has a table feature, is to make a table for your equation and see if each point satisfies the equation. ■

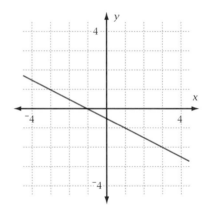

Investigation 4.2.1

Financing a Car

You plan to borrow $12,000 to purchase a new car. The bank advertises an interest rate of 11%. Use the following method to determine how much your payment needs to be for you to pay off the loan in 5 yr (60 mo).

Payment	Balance remaining
–?–	–?–
–?–	–?–

a. Have each group member try a different payment amount. For each payment amount, record the payment and the balance remaining, positive or negative, after 60 mo. Make a table like the one shown above.

b. Graph these ordered pairs on your calculator, or on graph paper. What do you observe about the points?

c. Each group member needs to select a different pair of points, and then find the equation of the line that contains them. Compare your equation with those of other members of your group. What do you notice?

---

d. Locate the point where the balance (the *y*-value) is zero. What is the payment (the *x*-value) for this point?

e. Try the payment you found in part d to verify that the balance is zero.

f. What is the *y*-intercept of your line? What is its real-world meaning?

g. What is the slope of your line? What is its real-world meaning?

Problem Set 4.2

Sketch a graph next to your solution for each of Problems 1–3.

1. Find the slope of the line containing each pair of points.
   a. $(3, {}^-4)$ and $(7, 2)$ **b.** $(5, 3)$ and $(2, 5)$

2. Find the slope of each line.
   a. $y = 3x - 2$ **b.** $y = 4.2 - 2.8x$ **c.** $y = 5(x - 3) + 2$
   d. $y - 2.4x = 5$ **e.** $4.7x + 3.2y = 12.9$

3. Find the equation of the line that passes through each pair of points.
   a. $(4, 0)$ and $(6, 3)$ **b.** $({}^-4.33, 7.51)$ and $(1.58, 0.87)$

4. Find the equation of each line.

  a. 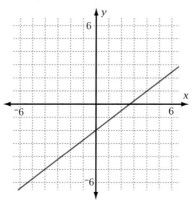   **b.**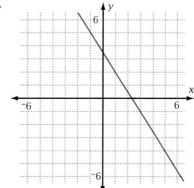

5. Find the equation for the line you drew in Problem 3, Problem Set 4.1.

6. Find the equation for the line you drew in Problem 4, Problem Set 4.1.

7. Find the equation for the line you drew in Problem 5, Problem Set 4.1.

8. Use the method from Investigation 4.2.1 to find the payment needed to pay off a 25-yr mortgage on a new house if you finance $60,000 at 9.6% on the unpaid balance.

Section 4.3

Real-World Meanings

Nature conceals her mystery by means of her essential grandeur, not by her cunning.
—Albert Einstein

Evelyn Boyd Granville, one of the first African American women to receive a Ph.D. in mathematics, calculated orbits and worked on computer procedures for Project Vanguard and Project Mercury at IBM. The Mercury Project was the first mission to put United States astronauts in space. Granville also worked as a research specialist on the Apollo Project, which sent astronauts to the moon. Much of her work was in the areas of celestial mechanics, trajectory and orbit computation, numerical analysis, and digital computer techniques.

Evelyn Boyd Granville

Before launching satellites and sending astronauts into orbit, space scientists must first collect and analyze data. An important component of data analysis is finding a **mathematical model**. Finding the equation of a line to fit data that appear to be linear is one way of creating a mathematical model. Understanding the real-world meaning of the variables and terms in the equation is also important. What does the equation mean, and how can it be used? In this section you will explore the answers to these questions.

Planet	Mean distance from the sun (AU)	Time of one revolution (yr)
Mercury	0.387	0.241
Venus	0.723	0.615
Earth	1.000	1.000
Mars	1.523	1.881
Jupiter	5.203	11.861
Saturn	9.541	29.457
Uranus	19.190	84.008
Neptune	30.086	164.784
Pluto	39.507	248.350

Note: 1 AU ≈ 93 million mi.

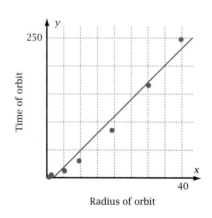

By analyzing data giving the mean distance from the sun and the time for one revolution for each planet, you might find an equation that looks like $y = 6.1x - 12.4$. (Your equation might be a bit different, depending on the points you chose.)

Whenever you use measurements, you need to name the unit of measure. Otherwise, the measurements are meaningless. What are the units in this problem?

The units of x are astronomical units (AU), and the units of y are years. What are the units of the slope? The y-values represent years. The slope is the change in y over the change in x. So the slope must be measured in years per astronomical unit, that is, 6.1 yr per AU. So what does a slope of 6.1 mean in this example?

Neptune is currently orbiting at about 30 AUs from the sun. If Neptune's orbit increased to 31 AUs, the time for its orbit would change from 164.8 yr to about 170.9 yr, increasing 6.1 yr for an increase of 1 AU.

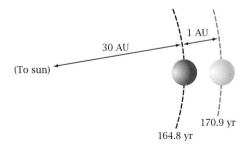

Radius (AU)	Time (yr)
30	164.8
31	170.9
32	177

If Neptune's orbit increased by another AU, then it would take another 6.1 yr to complete its orbit. So the slope, 6.1, is the increase in the time of revolution for each increase of 1 AU in a planet's distance from the sun.

When you begin to analyze a set of data, you must decide which information will be represented by the x-values and which will be represented by the y-values. The set of x-values is called the **domain,** and x is called the **independent** variable. The set of y-values is called the **range,** and y is called the **dependent** variable.

Domain and Range

The **domain** is the set of values for the independent variable.
The **range** is the set of values for the dependent variable.

The x-values can be any number within the domain (they are independent), and the y-values must in some way correspond to the chosen x-values (the y-values are dependent). After you have determined the domain and range variables, consider what domain and range values will be meaningful for a particular situation.

In the example above, mean distance from the sun is the independent variable, and time for one revolution is the dependent variable. In this case, you can think of the relationship between the independent and dependent variables as one of cause and effect. If you change the distance, the time for one revolution will change. The time of orbit cannot change without a change in the distance. In the next example, you will deal with the amount of tax you pay compared to the amount of money you earn. Which of these variables depends on the other? It is clear that you have to earn the money before it is taxed, so money earned precedes tax paid. In other cases, the choice may be arbitrary. There is obviously a relationship between the dimensions used by dressmakers for waist measurements and for hip measurements, but does one of these depend on the other? In this case, your choice of the independent and dependent variables may be different from someone else's, but each may be correct.

■ Example 1

An equation of a best-fit line for the data shown in the table below is $y \approx 0.32x - 1820$. If x is dollars earned and y is tax paid, then the slope is 0.32 dollars (or 32¢) paid as tax for each dollar earned.

Taxable income ($)	Tax ($)
12,000	2,260
16,000	3,260
20,000	4,380
24,000	5,660
28,000	7,100
32,000	8,660

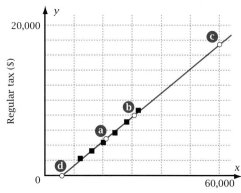

a. Figure out the tax you must pay if your expected income is $21,000.

b. Tex Peyar reported that he paid $8,000 in taxes this year. Estimate his income.

c. What would you expect the tax to be for Noah Cache, whose income was $60,000?

d. When could you expect to pay *no* taxes?

Solution

a. Because $21,000 is between $20,000 and $24,000, the tax will be between $4,380 and $5,660, and should be closer to the lower value. If you use the model and substitute the value $21,000 for x, you find $y = 0.32(21000) - 1820 = \$4,900$. Finding a value between those given in a table is called **interpolation.**

b. You can estimate Tex Peyar's income by interpolating the taxable income with the model. Solving $8000 = 0.32x - 1820$ gives you an x-value of about $30,700. (Check this result.)

c. An income of $60,000 is well beyond the incomes listed in the table. Because you have no other information, you will have to assume that the model does not change at higher incomes, even though this may be a poor assumption. The equation predicts that Noah Cache will pay $17,380 in taxes. (Can you work this equation through and come up with this result?) This use of a model to extend beyond the present range of values is called **extrapolation.**

d. You would expect to pay no taxes when $0 = 0.32x - 1820$, or when your income is about $5,690. The accuracy of extrapolating values far from your data will depend on the accuracy of the data, the accuracy of the model, and the likelihood that no other factors come into play. ■

Investigation 4.3.1
The Wave

This is a class investigation. The objective is to determine how much time it takes for a given number of people to do "the wave." The wave is a sociological phenomenon that sometimes occurs at sporting events. Spectators simulate an ocean wave by rising quickly in sequence with their arms upraised and then quickly sitting down again in a continuous rolling motion. You will need a watch with a second hand to time each wave. Using different-sized groups, determine the time for each group to complete the wave. Collect at least nine pairs of data and put the numbers into a table like the one below.

Number of people	3	5	6	8	...	15
Time (sec)	–?–	–?–	–?–	–?–	–?–	–?–

Plot the points and find the equation of a best-fit line. Write a paragraph about your results. Be sure to include the following information:

a. What is the slope of your line, and what is its real-world meaning?

b. What is the *y*-intercept for your line, and what is its real-world meaning?

c. What is the *x*-intercept for your equation, and what is its real-world meaning?

d. What is a reasonable domain for this equation? Why? (Keep these data and the equation. You will be using them in a later section.)

Problem Set 4.3

Problems 1–4 are review questions about slopes and special types of lines.

1. a. Graph the line $y = 5$.
   b. Identify two points on it.
   c. What is the slope of this line?

2. Write the equation of the line that contains the points $(3, {}^-4)$ and $({}^-2, {}^-4)$. Write three statements about horizontal lines and their equations.

3. Write the equation of the line that contains the points $(3, 5)$ and $(3, 1)$. Your calculator can only graph equations for which *y* can be written in terms of *x*. This is not the case for a vertical line. Find a way to graph a vertical line on your calculator. (There is more than one way.)

4. a. Graph the line $x = {}^{-}3$ on paper.
   b. Identify two points on it.
   c. What is the slope of this line?
   d. What is the y-intercept of this line?

5. The graph at the right shows the relationship between the height of some tall buildings in Los Angeles and the number of stories in those buildings. The best-fit line drawn has the equation $y = 13.02x + 20.5$.

Los Angeles

   a. What is the meaning of the slope?
   b. What is the meaning of the y-intercept?
   c. According to the graph, what is a reasonable domain and range?

6. Consider the equation used to model the salary of Anita Raze for the last seven years: $y = 847x + 17109$. The variable x represents the number of years of experience she has, and y represents her salary in dollars.
   a. What did she earn the fifth year?
   b. What is the slope of this line?
   c. What is the real-world meaning of the slope?
   d. What is the y-intercept of this line?
   e. What is the real-world meaning of the y-intercept?
   f. What is a reasonable domain for this problem? Justify your answer.

In Problems 7–10 you must choose how to represent x accurately. There may be more than one correct choice. There are many correct answers for each problem. Your answers may differ from the answers provided. If so, graph both your answer and the text answer, and compare. The graphs should look similar.

7. The photography studio offers several packages to students posing for yearbook photos, as shown in the following table.

Number of pictures	44	31	24	15
Total cost	$19.00	$16.00	$13.00	$10.00

a. Plot the data, and find an equation of a best-fit line.
b. Use a complete sentence to explain the real-world meaning of the slope.
c. Find the point where your line crosses the *y*-axis.
d. Use a complete sentence to explain the real-world meaning of the *y*-intercept.
e. If the studio offers a 47-print package, what do you think they should charge?
f. If you have only $14.50, how many prints do you think they should sell you?

When entering data involving years, you can either enter the whole year, such as 1986, or work from a reference year, such as 1900. If you use 1900 as the reference year, then enter the years in the form 86, 87, and so on. You could also use a reference year of 1986, so that 1986 would be entered as 0, 1987 would be entered as 1, 1988 would be entered as 2, and so on. In order to obtain answers that match those provided, use 1900 as a reference year unless otherwise noted.

8. In the 1980s and early 1990s, a downward trend was noticed in average SAT verbal scores.

Year	1986	1987	1988	1989	1991
Score	431	430	428	427	422

a. Plot the data, and find the equation of a best-fit line.
b. What are the units of the domain (*x*-values)?
c. Use complete sentences to explain the real-world meaning of the slope.
d. Use the model to predict the average score last year.
e. Use the model to predict the average score in 1980.
f. How can you explain the fact that in 1980 the average verbal score was actually 424? Make an observation about the data and the use of this model.

9. The percentage of American students in grades 9 through 12 using a computer at home is shown below, for different family incomes.

Family income ($)	5,000–9,999	10,000–14,999	15,000–19,999	20,000–24,999	25,000–29,999	30,000–34,999	35,000–39,999
Percent using computers	4	7	14	14	17	20	25

a. Draw a histogram of these data.
b. Find a best-fit line that represents the trend shown by the histogram.
c. Use complete sentences to explain the real-world meaning of the slope.
d. Use the model to predict the percentage of students using a computer at home in families with an income of $62,000.

10. The percentage of unmarried males by age group is given in the table below.

Age	15–19	20–24	25–29	30–34
Percent unmarried	96.2	73.2	38.2	19.6

a. Plot the data, either as points or as a histogram, and find a best-fit line.
b. What are the units of the dependent variable (the *y*-values)?
c. Use complete sentences to explain the real-world meaning of the slope.
d. Use the model to predict the percentage of men that are not married at age 40.
e. What is the real-world meaning for the result in part d?

Project

Talkin' Trash

The amount of trash that this country produces is staggering. And with the growing population, we have a growing problem! It is estimated that 190 million tons of trash were placed in United States landfills during the year 1993. Even as you read this, landfills are eating up more and more space. There are already over 9,000 of them in the United States; more than 80% of them will have to be closed within the next 20 years

Year	Waste (million tons/yr)	Population (millions)
1960	88	179
1965	103	190
1970	122	203
1975	128	214
1980	152	227
1985	164	238
1990	196	249

Source: The Universal Almanac 1995.

because they are full. It is becoming more difficult to locate new sites; people don't want them in their communities because they leak, stink, and pollute!

How much trash do you think you and your family generate each day? Does your family recycle and try not to waste? Is recycling our only solution? What are some alternatives to landfills and recycling? As you complete this project, keep your own habits of trash disposal in mind.

1. Use the data in the table to find best-fit models for (*year, waste*) and (*year, population*). Select a domain and a range to view all the data and graphs. Describe how you find or select your models, and provide real-world meanings for all equation values. Use your equations to predict the population and the amount of waste that you might expect in the years 1995 and 2000. Use your graphs and equations to help you decide if the amount of waste is

increasing because of the increase in population or if there is more to this situation. Justify your answer. Use complete sentences as you write up your results.

2. Calculate a new column of data that contains pounds per person per day. Explain how you calculated these values. Analyze and sketch a graph of these data. Predict the number of pounds of garbage per person per year for the years 1995 and 2000. Do some research to find out if this prediction applies to other countries.

3. Investigate the total amount of trash from your household for some convenient time period. Calculate the pounds per person per day from your household. Compare your result to the data provided in the table.

The Median-Median Line

An expert is a man who has made all the mistakes, which can be made, in a very narrow field.
—Niels Henrik David Bohr

Have you noticed that you and your classmates frequently find different equations for the same data? You may be wondering what makes one equation a better (more accurate) model than another. Answering this question is difficult, and you will spend part of this chapter looking at ways to judge just how well a line represents the data, or if indeed there is any line that fits. First, you will learn a procedure for finding a possible best-fit line for a set of data that will enable each member of the class to get the same equation for the same set of data.

There are a variety of techniques for finding the best-fit line. One method, though it may be long, is quite simple in concept and in computation. The procedure for finding the median-median line involves a "chunking" process. Three points are selected to represent the entire data set, and the equation that best fits these three points is taken as the best fit for the entire set of data. This is similar to the method Francis Galton used in 1888 to estimate what he was then calling "the index of co-relation." His data were the length of the left cubit (forearm) and the stature (height) of 348 adult males.

To select the three points that will represent an entire data set, you must first order them by their domain value (the *x*-value) and then divide the data into three equal groups. If the number of points is not divisible by three, then split them so that the first and last groups are the same size. For example:

18 data points:	split into groups of 6 – 6 – 6
19 data points:	split into groups of 6 – 7 – 6
20 data points:	split into groups of 7 – 6 – 7

Then order the *y*-values within each of the groups. The representative point for each group has the coordinates of the **median** *x* of that group and the **median** *y* of that group. Carefully study the following example to see how this is done.

x	y	(median x, median y)
4.0	23	
5.2	28	
5.8	29	(5.8, 29)
6.5	35	
7.2	35	
7.8	40	
8.3	42	(8.6, 44.5)
8.9	50	
9.7	47	
10.1	52	
11.2	60	(11.9, 60)
11.9	58	
12.5	62	
13.1	64	

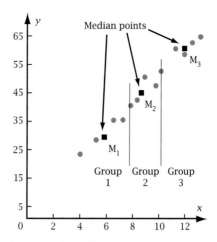

Note: The median point need *not* be one of the data points. Don't forget to order the y-values in each group when finding the median y-values.

Use the first and last of the three representative points (M_1 and M_3) to find the slope of the median-median line. To find the intercept, slide the line one-third of the way toward the middle point. Study the following example to see how this works.

First find the equation of the line containing the points $M_1(5.8, 29)$ and $M_3(11.9, 60)$:

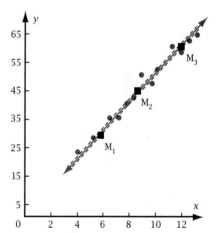

$$\text{slope} = \frac{60 - 29}{11.9 - 5.8} \approx 5.08.$$

Using M_1,

$$y = 5.08(x - 5.8) + 29 \quad \text{or}$$
$$y = 5.08x - 0.46.$$

Check to see that you will get the same equation if you use M_3.

A line that is parallel and passes through the middle representative point $M_2(8.6, 44.5)$ is

$$y = 5.08(x - 8.6) + 44.5 \quad \text{or}$$
$$y = 5.08x + 0.81.$$

The median-median line will be parallel to both of these lines, so it will also have 5.08 as its slope. To find the equation of the line that is one-third the distance from the line containing two points, you can average the intercepts for the lines. This is tricky. You have to use the value -0.46 twice, because this line goes through two of the points and therefore represents two-thirds of the data.

$$\text{Average of the } y\text{-intercepts} = \frac{-0.46 + -0.46 + 0.81}{3} \approx -0.04$$

Therefore, the final median-median equation is $y = 5.08x - 0.04$.

■ Example 1

In the graph at the right, the original data are not shown, only the three summary points are pictured. Find the equation of the median-median line.

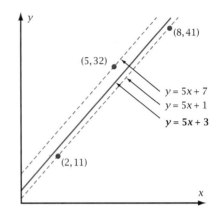

Solution

The first and third points lie on the line $y = 5x + 1$. Parallel to (having the same slope as) this line and passing through the second point is the equation $y = 5(x - 5) + 32$ or $y = 5x + 7$. Average the intercepts, $\frac{1 + 1 + 7}{3} = \frac{9}{3} = 3$, and write the equation of the median-median line as $y = 5x + 3$.

The median-median line is closer to the first line, because the line going through two points represents two-thirds of the data. ■

Investigation 4.4.1

Spring Experiment

Attach a mass holder to a spring. Hang the spring from a spring stand, and the mass holder from the spring. Measure the length of the spring (in centimeters) from the first coil to the last coil. Add different amounts of mass to the mass holder, recording the corresponding length of the spring each time. Collect about 20 data points.

Mass	Length
-?-	-?-
-?-	-?-
-?-	-?-
-?-	-?-

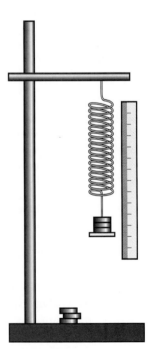

Graph the data on graph paper. Calculate and draw the median-median line through the data. Write the equation of this line. Answer the questions below in your write-up of the investigation.

a. How much does your measured length for the third point differ from the value given by your equation for that mass?

b. Which two points differ the most from your equation? Can you explain why?

c. Give the real-world meaning of your slope.

d. Find the *y*-intercept, and give the real-world meaning of this value.

e. Assume that the spring will stretch forever. According to your model, how long would the spring be if you were to hang 4.7 kg from it?

f. What is wrong with the assumption in part e?

g. What mass should make your spring stretch 20 cm? Show how you determined this.

Finally, summarize what you have learned in this investigation. List any difficulties that you experienced.

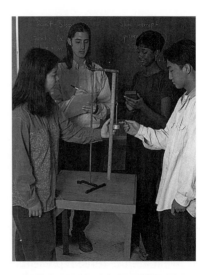

Problem Set 4.4

1. a. How would you divide a set of 31 elements into three groups for the median-median line procedure?
  b. How would you divide a set of 50 elements into three groups for the median-median line procedure?

NOTE 4B

After completing each problem below, construct the graph for a visual confirmation that your equation is correct. Sketch your graph onto your paper beside your solution. (See **Calculator Note 4B** if you have forgotten how to graph both data points and lines with your graphing calculator.)

2. Find the equation of the line passing through each pair of points.
  a. $(8.1, 15.7)$ and $(17.3, 9.5)$ **b.** $(3, 47)$ and $(18, 84)$

3. Find the equation of the line parallel to $y = 0.75x - 12.2$ that passes through the point $(14.4, 0.9)$.

4. Find the equation of the line one-third of the way from $y = {}^-1.8x + 74.1$ to $y = {}^-1.8x + 70.5$.

5. Find the equation of the line one-third of the way from $y = 0.65x + 19.3$ to $y = 0.65x + 26.7$.

6. Find the equation of the line one-third of the way from $y = 4.7x + 2.8$ to the point $(12.8, 64)$.

7. The questions that follow will help you find the equation for the median-median line for the data on male life expectancy in the United States. (Enter 20, 25, and so on as *x*-values.)

Year of birth	1920	1925	1930	1935	1940	1945	1950	1955
Male life expectancy	53.6	56.3	58.1	59.4	60.8	62.8	65.6	66.2

Year of birth	1960	1965	1970	1975	1980	1985	1990
Male life expectancy	66.6	66.8	67.1	68.8	70.0	71.2	72.0

a. How many points are there in each of the three groups?

b. What are the three representative points for these data? Graph these points.

c. Draw the line through the first and third points. What is the slope of this line? What is the real-world meaning of the slope?

d. What is the equation of the line through the first and third points?

e. Draw the line parallel to the line in 7d that passes through the second point. What is the equation of this line?

f. Average the *y*-intercepts and write the equation of the median-median line. Graph this line. (Note: Remember that you have to use one of the *y*-intercepts twice.)

g. The year 1978 is missing from the table. Using your model, what would you predict the life expectancy to be for children born in 1978?

h. Use your model to predict the life expectancy of children born in 1991, and those born in 1954.

i. Using this model, when would you predict the life expectancy to exceed 80 years?

8. Find the error for each data point in Investigation 4.1.1. Display these errors with a histogram or box plot. Using the information in your histogram or box plot, describe how good you think your model is. Justify your conclusion.

9. Refer to your data from Investigation 4.3.1 and find the equation for the median-median line. (See **Calculator Note 4C** for a way to use your calculator to find this equation.) Compare this equation to the one you found previously. Which equation do you feel is a better model for the data? Why?

NOTE
4C

10. Use the table data on world records for the one-mile run to answer the questions below.

Year	Runner	Time	Year	Runner	Time
1875	Walter Slade, Britain	4:24.5	1942	Arne Andersson, Sweden	4:06.2
1880	Walter George, Britain	4:23.2	1942	Haegg	4:04.6
1882	George	4:21.4	1943	Andersson	4:02.6
1882	George	4:19.4	1944	Andersson	4:01.6
1884	George	4:18.4	1945	Haegg	4:01.4
1894	Fred Bacon, Scotland	4:18.2	1954	Roger Bannister, Britain	3:59.4
1895	Bacon	4:17.0	1954	John Landry, Australia	3:58.0
1911	Thomas Connett, U.S.	4:15.6	1957	Derek Ibbotson, Britain	3:57.2
1911	John Paul Jones, U.S.	4:15.4	1958	Herb Elliott, Australia	3:54.5
1913	Jones	4:14.6	1962	Peter Snell, New Zealand	3:54.4
1915	Norman Taber, U.S.	4:12.6	1964	Snell	3:54.1
1923	Paavo Nurmi, Finland	4:10.4	1965	Michel Jazy, France	3:53.6
1931	Jules Ladonumegue, France	4:09.2	1966	Jim Ryun, U.S.	3:51.3
1933	Jack Lovelock, New Zealand	4:07.6	1967	Ryun	3:51.1
1934	Glen Cunningham, U.S.	4:06.8	1975	Filbert Bayi, Tanzania	3:51.0
1937	Sydney Wooderson, Britain	4:06.4	1975	John Walker, New Zealand	3:49.4
1942	Gunder Haegg, Sweden	4:06.2			

Source: Information Please Almanac 1996.

a. What is the equation of the median-median line?

b. What is the real-world meaning of the slope? What are the units of the slope?

c. Use the equation to predict what new record might have been set in 1992.

d. Describe some problems you might encounter with this type of extrapolation. Answer in complete sentences.

e. Has a new world record been set since 1975? Find more recent information on this subject and compare it to the predictions of your model.

11. The median-median line procedure divides the data into three groups and uses the median x- and y-values. Devise a mean-mean line procedure and use it on the data in Problem 10. Compare this model to the median-median model.

12. Find a problem that you cannot solve (from this chapter or a previous chapter). Write out the problem and as much of the solution as you can. Then clearly explain what is keeping you from solving the problem. Be as specific and clear as you can.

Take Another Look 4.4

The three representative points pictured here and in Example 1 of Section 4.4 are used to find the two parallel lines and, finally, the median-median line for data points that are not pictured.

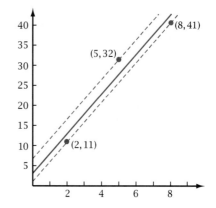

The line represented by the equation $y = 5x + 1$ passes through the first and last points.

A parallel line represented by the equation $y = 5x + 7$ passes through the middle point.

The weighted average, $\frac{1 + 1 + 7}{3} = 3$, provides the y-intercept of the median-median line, $y = 5x + 3$. If you focus on the y-axis, the vertical distance between the top line and the median-median line is four units, while the vertical distance between the median-median line and the bottom line is two units. This means the median-median line is two-thirds of the vertical distance from the top line to the bottom line.

Now find the centroid, or balance point, of the triangle formed by the three representative points. Remember, the centroid is the point $(\bar{x}, \bar{y})$. Will the three representative points always form a triangle? Explain.

a. What is the centroid of the points with coordinates $(2, 11)$, $(5, 32)$, and $(8, 41)$? Write an equation of a line that passes through the centroid and has a slope of 5. Compare this equation with the given equation, $y = 5x + 3$, and with the median-median equation given by your calculator. Describe your results.

b. Write a careful explanation of how you could use the technique in this Take Another Look to find the median-median best-fit model for the data collected in Investigation 4.1.1.

c. Look through your geometry notes or search through a geometry text for more information about centroids. Try to find conjectures or theorems that are related to this particular investigation. Write a few sentences about your discoveries.

Counting Forever

How long would it take you to count to 1 million? Some numbers require more time to say; some numbers have one digit, some have two digits, and so on. Collect data by recording the time required to say different numbers. Prepare a table showing the number of digits and the time it takes to say the number. Explain the procedure you used to collect these data. Describe the approach you used to determine how long it will take to count to 1 million; include graphs, data, and equations. Extend the problem by predicting the time it would take to count to 1 billion, 1 trillion, and to the federal debt amount.

Section 4.5

The Residuals

The measure of our intellectual capacity is the capacity to feel less and less satisfied with our answers to better and better problems.
—*C. W. Churchman*

The median-median line method is not perfect. In some cases, you can find a more accurate model if you draw a line by hand rather than by following all the steps in the median-median line procedure. However, having a line that "looks better" is not a very convincing argument that it really is better. You must look at the differences between the points in your data set and the points generated by your model.

Look at the point on your best-fit line directly below (or above) each of the data points. The distance between the data point and the point on the line is called the **residual**. The residual is a **signed distance**; that is, it can be positive or negative. The residual is similar to the deviation from the mean you learned about in the previous chapter. Positive deviations meant the value was above the mean, and negative deviations meant the value was below. Here, a positive residual indicates that the point is above the line, and a negative residual indicates that the point is below the line. The line should have about as many points above it as below. You can state this more clearly by saying that the sum of the residuals should be near zero. In other words, if you connect each point to the line, the sum of the lengths of the vertical connectors above the line should be about equal to the sum of those below the line.

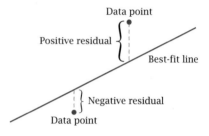

The manager of Cicero's Pizza must order supplies for the month of November. She looks at her records and finds the sales for the past four years. She decides to use the previous years' November sales figures to guide her purchases. November sales have been 512, 603, 642, and 775 pizzas. She graphs these, using x-values of 1 through 4 to represent the last four years, and draws her best-fit line. Her equation is $y = 63.5x + 474$.

If you evaluate her equation at 1, 2, 3, and 4, you will find y-values of 537.5, 601, 664.5, and 728. The first residual is $512 - 537.5 = {}^-25.5$. The remaining residuals are $+2$, $^-22.5$, and $+47$, respectively. The sum of these residuals is $({}^-25.5 + 2 + {}^-22.5 + 47) = 1$, which is very close to zero. By the way, how many pizzas should she be prepared to sell this November?

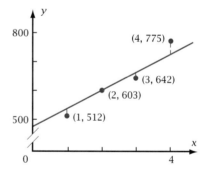

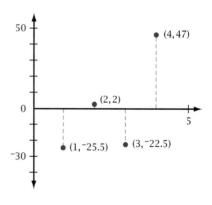

NOTE

4D

By looking at the residual plot, you will sometimes be able to improve the equation of the line. In addition to a sum of nearly zero for the residuals, there should not appear to be a pattern in the graph. If there is a pattern, it is almost certain that there is a better equation that fits the data. You will learn more about residual patterns in later chapters. You can use your calculator to make a graph of the residuals. (See **Calculator Note 4D** for help with residual plots.)

The data below have a median-median line of $y = 0.067x - 2.359$, as shown in the graph to the right of the table.

Table of Coronary Heart Disease (CHD) per 100,000 people per year ages 35–64

Country	Cigarettes per adult per year	CHD mortality per 100,000
United States	3900	265
Canada	3350	212
Australia	3220	238
New Zealand	3220	212
United Kingdom	2790	194
Switzerland	2780	160
Ireland	2770	187
Iceland	2290	111
Finland	2160	208
West Germany	1890	150
Netherlands	1810	125
Greece	1800	41
Austria	1770	182
Belgium	1700	118
Mexico	1680	32
Italy	1510	114
Denmark	1500	120
France	1410	60
Sweden	1270	127
Spain	1200	44
Norway	1090	90

Source: American Journal of Public Health, Vol. 60, 1970, p. 119.

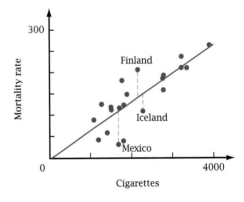

The residuals for these data are plotted to the right. Notice that the scale of the residuals is from ⁻100 to 80. The sum of the residuals is ⁻1.022. In some cases, you might be able to shift the line slightly and get a better distribution of the residuals.

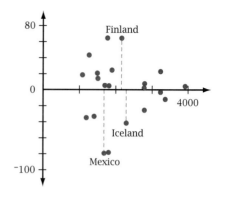

In addition to helping you determine whether or not a model is a good fit for a data set, residuals can help you find points that are not true to the data. The data below were gathered in a lab by measuring the current through a circuit with constant resistance as the voltage was varied.

Volts	5.000	7.500	10.000	12.500	15.000	17.500	20.000
Milliamps	2.354	3.527	4.698	5.871	7.151	8.225	9.403

On the left, below, is the graph of the data and a best-fit line. On the right is the graph of the residuals.

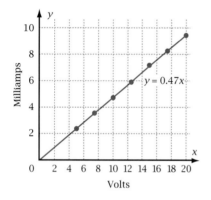
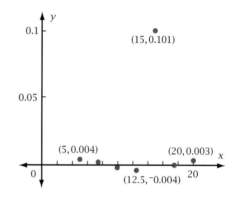

The scale of the *y*-axis of the first graph is from 0 to 10, while the range of the residuals is from ⁻0.004 to ⁺0.101. From the first graph, you only have confirmation that the line is a good fit. From the second, you can see that six of the seven data points are within 0.004 of a milliamp of the line, but one point is about 25 times as inaccurate as the worst of the others. This point is called an **outlier**; it could indicate that this particular measurement was inaccurate, or that some unusual phenomenon occurred. Either way, it is worth further investigation back in the lab.

Examining the residuals can help you find a "better" line. Look at the graphs at the top of the next page. The graph on the left shows the residuals for a set of data with respect to a preliminary "best-fit" equation. Because most of the residuals are positive, you can improve the fit of the equation by increasing the *y*-intercept, thus raising the line. The graph on the right shows the result of doing so.

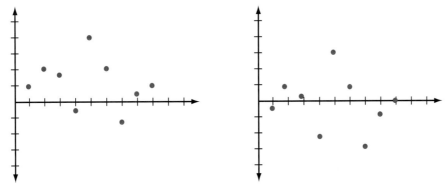

Graph A below shows another set of hypothetical residuals with respect to some preliminary line. Because there seems to be a definite slope to the residuals, you could change the slope of the line. Graph B shows the new residuals for an adjusted line with steeper slope. Now a line drawn through the residuals would have a zero slope, but this line needs to be moved down in order to be centered among the points. Graph C shows the results of decreasing the y-intercept.

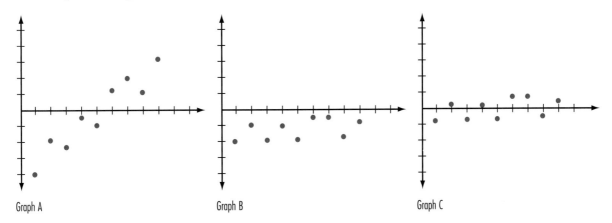

Graph A   Graph B   Graph C

Knowing how to make these changes is a matter of practice. In the upcoming problems, you will have the opportunity to improve on some "best-fit" lines. If you think the slope needs to be changed, do this before changing the intercept. Don't try to change both the slope and the y-intercept at the same time.

Investigation 4.5.1
Airline Schedules

For this investigation, you will need an airline timetable that includes both flight times and distances. You will also need a time zone map. Decide as a class which major city in the continental United States is going to be the starting point.

a. Have each group record the flight time and distance to at least eight other continental United States cities from the chosen starting point. Choose only nonstop flights.

b. Plot the (*time, distance*) pairs for all the data.

c. Find the median-median line for the data.

d. What is the real-world meaning of the slope?

e. What is the meaning of the *y*-intercept?

f. Find the value of the *x*-intercept and explain its real-world meaning.

g. Have each group member calculate the residuals by completing a table like the one below. The first two columns contain the original data. The third column is found by calculating the *y*-value of the equation (found in part c) for time *x*. The last column is found by subtracting the third column from the second.

From: *Name of city*

Destination	Time (min)	Distance (mi)	Computed distance (mi)	Residual (mi)
Name of city	90	402	417	⁻15

h. When you have completed the table, find the greatest positive and negative residuals. Check those points again in the airline table. See if a particular flight time is different at other times of the day. Are there any flights that would fit your model better? Why do you suppose the flight times vary? When does the actual flight time start and end? Is the flight time from east to west the same as the flight time from west to east? What other interesting observations can you share?

Problem Set 4.5

1. The median-median line for a set of data is $y = 2.4x + 3.6$. Find the residual for each given point.
  a. $(2, 8.2)$ **b.** $(4, 12.8)$ **c.** $(10, 28.2)$

2. Return to Problem 7, Problem Set 4.4 (about life expectancy). Using the equation you found for the median-median line, plot the residuals on your calculator.
  a. Describe the residuals.
  b. What must be done to better balance the residuals?
  c. Make a small change in the *y*-intercept of your equation to see if you can improve the fit by splitting the data points more evenly.
  d. How much does this change in the *y*-intercept change your prediction of the life expectancy of a child born in 1991?

3. The average height in centimeters of United States children from ages 7 to 15 is given in the table below.

Age	7	8	9	10	11	12	13	14	15
Height (cm)	119.3	127.0	132.0	137.1	142.2	147.3	152.4	157.5	162.2

Source: 1990 Physicians Handbook.

   a. Plot the data and find the median-median line.
   b. Plot the residuals and label the range.
   c. Which points stand out in the residual plot?
   d. Give an argument why the points represented by these residuals do not fit the model.

4. Consider the residuals from Problem 3.
   a. Make a box plot of these values.
   b. Write a paragraph that conveys the information about the residuals that is shown in the box plot.

5. The following readings were taken from a display outside the First River Bank. The display alternated between °F and °C. However, there was an error within the system that calculated the temperatures.

°F	18	33	37	25	40	46	43	49	55	60	57
°C	⁻6	2	3	⁻3	5	8	7	10	12	15	13

   a. Plot the data and find the median-median line.
   b. Plot the residuals.
   c. You will see that the residuals are low on the left and high on the right. To correct this distortion, first adjust the slope of your line, then adjust the y-intercept.
   d. Using your new equation, what temperature do you expect to be paired with 85°F? (Remember, the bank will round off temperatures to the nearest degree.)
   e. What temperature do you expect to be paired with 0°C on the bank's thermometer?

6. A circle can be circumscribed around any regular polygon. Consider a set of regular polygons whose side lengths are one unit. The lengths of the radii of the circumscribed circles are given in the table.

Polygon	Number of sides	Radius
Triangle	3	0.577
Square	4	0.707
Pentagon	5	0.851
Hexagon	6	1.000
Heptagon	7	1.152
Octagon	8	1.306
Nonagon	9	1.462
Decagon	10	1.618
Undecagon	11	1.775
Dodecagon	12	1.932

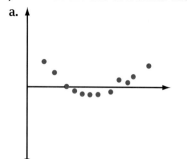 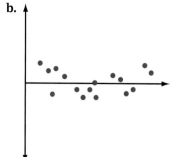 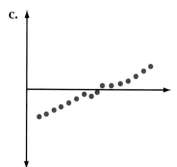

a. Trace each polygon and sketch its circumscribed circle. Draw and label the radius of each circle.

b. Plot the data and find the median-median line.

c. Plot the residuals.

d. Even though the line appears to fit the data, you will see a pattern in the residuals that tells you that, although this line may serve as a rough model, there is a better model that is not a line.

Replace the linear equation with $y = \dfrac{0.5}{\sin \dfrac{180}{x}}$ and check the residuals again.

(Be certain your calculator is in *degree* mode.) What is the range of the residuals?

e. Use your knowledge of geometry to derive the formula given in part d.

7. Each graph below shows the residuals for a linear equation. What does each plot tell you about the use of a linear model for the data?

a. **b.** **c.**

Section 4.6

The Least-Squares Line

A formal manipulator in mathematics often experiences the discomforting feeling that his pencil surpasses him in intelligence.
—Howard W. Eves

In the eighteenth century there was great interest in an accurate account of the moon's movements, primarily for navigational purposes, but also for scientific reasons—astronomers were interested in finding out how the moon and other planets moved in order to refine Isaac Newton's theory of gravitation. Even Newton thought that developing a theory of lunar movement was a difficult problem, saying repeatedly that it made his head ache and kept him awake so often that he would think of it no more.

The observations gathered by different astronomers were contradictory. Newton's theory provided a general model of what was going on, but more observations were needed to find equations of motion for the planets and to create tables of the moon's movement that could be used for navigation. A natural question was: What should be done with the observations? Johann Tobias Mayer (1723-1782), an astronomer and cartographer, came up with a method of combining observations rather than simply choosing "good" ones, but it was not justified mathematically. Mayer's method was something like the median-median method; it was easy to use and generally gave sensible results, so it became popular among astronomers and geodesists. (Geodesists use mathematics to determine the size and shape of the earth and the exact position of points on its surface.) His idea of combining observations encouraged others to search for a way to do so that *could* be justified mathematically.

The outcome was the criteria of least-squares deviations and the derivation of a system of equations for finding least-squares lines. This was first published in 1805 by the French mathematician Adrien Marie Legendre in a book entitled *New Methods for Determining the Orbits of Comets.* Gauss had also developed the method of least squares in 1795 and had used it to devise a scheme for computing the orbits of planets from a limited number of observations. This method, known as Gauss's method, is still used to track satellites. Mayer's method remained in use, however, because Mayer's tables of the moon were

An artist's drawing showing a comet that appeared over Rome in 1680

among the most accurate available, and furthermore the method required less computation than least-squares. But it was never given mathematical justification and gradually faded from use as least-squares computations were simplified.

You might wonder why Francis Galton didn't use least squares when he was analyzing his sweet pea and cubit data in the late 1800s. A short answer is that biometricians and astronomers viewed data analysis very differently. A synthesis of their statistical ideas took place around the end of the nineteenth century and formed the foundation of modern statistics.

So how do you use the least-squares criteria to determine how well a line fits data? Begin with some data points and a best-fit line. Draw the residuals and find the length (value) of each one. If the residual sum is a large number, then either a linear model does not fit the data very well, or the line was not well placed, or both. Knowing that the sum of the residuals is small may mean the line fits the points well. Still, it is possible for the sum of the residuals to be zero even when the line is a poor fit.

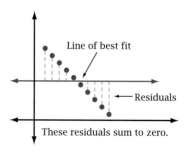

However, the **square** of each residual will be a positive number. So, to keep both the sum of the residuals small, and the residuals themselves small, you'll need to find a line where the sum of the squares of the residuals is a small number.

x	y
4	7
6	15
9	17
12	25

■ Example 1

Determine which of the models, $y_1 = 1 + 2x$ and $y_2 = {}^-3 + 2.5x$, best fits the four-point data sample.

Solution

From the graph at the right, both appear to be good lines of best fit. The table below shows the residuals and their squares for each of these equations. Note that the residual sum for y_2 is closer to zero, but y_1 has the smaller sum of the squared residuals. So y_1 is considered the better of the two models. According to the calculator, the line with the smallest sum of the squared residuals is $y_3 = 0.18 + 2.04x$. Find the sum of the squares of the residuals for y_3. Did you get 10.94?

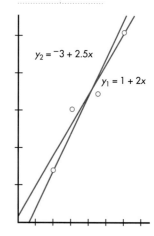

x	y	y_1	Residual	Residual^2	y_2	Residual	Residual^2
4	7	9	${}^-2$	4	7	0	0
6	15	13	2	4	12	3	9
9	17	19	${}^-2$	4	19.5	${}^-2.5$	6.25
12	25	25	0	0	27	${}^-2$	4
Total			${}^-2$	12		${}^-1.5$	19.25

You can picture the squares of the residuals in a drawing such as those on the right. Imagine summing the areas of all the squares on each graph. The squares in the first graph cover a smaller area than the squares in the second graph.

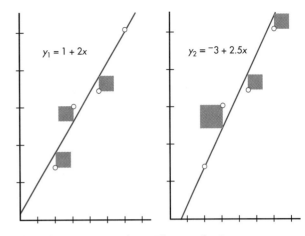

Finding the equation where the squares of the residuals have the smallest sum isn't much fun with four points, and becomes unmanageable with more. With the help of some calculus, the procedure can be simplified to a series of basic calculations that provide the equation of the least-squares line. The graphs in this example were created using The Geometer's Sketchpad. If you want to explore further how the least-squares line of best fit works, try the Geometer's Sketchpad Investigation following this section. Fortunately, your calculator can do these calculations with lightning speed and accuracy. ■

■ **Example 2**

Consider these data, which were used in a previous section. Is the median-median line "better" than the least-squares line?

Volts	5.000	7.500	10.000	12.500	15.000	17.500	20.000
Milliamps	2.354	3.527	4.698	5.871	7.151	8.225	9.403

Solution

Use your calculator to find the least-squares line. (See **Calculator Note 4E**.) The slope is 0.4714 and the y-intercept is -0.0023. These values are close to, but not the same as, the values for the median-median line ($y = 0.4699x + 0.0017$).

NOTE
4E

Look at the graph of the residuals for each of the two lines. The median-median line (indicated by circles on the graph) has smaller residuals for all but one point, so it might be considered the better line. The median-median line is sometimes called the **resistant line** because it is not influenced as much by one or two "bad" data points. The least-squares line uses every point in its calculation, so it is affected by outliers. ■

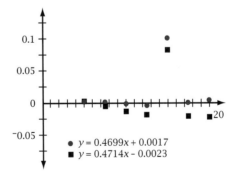

Investigation 4.6.1

Relating Body Lengths

As a group, decide upon two different lengths that you can measure on your body (for example, the length of an ear and the distance from the back of the knee to the bottom of the heel). Have each group member measure these lengths on his or her body and also on at least two other people. (Each group needs to collect at least twelve measurements.)

a. Record all the data collected by the group in a table.

b. Find the median-median line to fit the data.

c. Make a plot of the data and of the residuals for this line.

d. Name the range of your residuals.

e. Find the least-squares line for these data.

f. Make a plot of the residuals for this line and name the range.

g. Compare the two models and write a paragraph summarizing which one is better, and why. Write a sentence or two describing the relationship between the body parts measured.

Problem Set 4.6

1. Each graph below shows similar data sets. The graph on the right has two points that are different. These points might be considered outliers for the set. Copy the graphs onto your paper. On each grid, identify the three groups of points for the median-median line procedure. Then plot the three representative points. How do these summary points compare in the two graphs? How will the median-median line be affected by the outliers? Will this always be the case when there are outlying points?

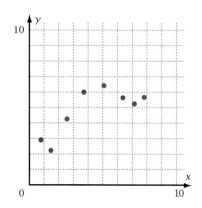
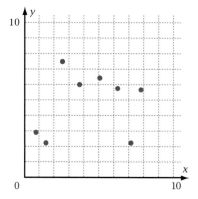

2. What are the major differences (name at least two) between the median-median method and the least-squares method for finding the best-fit line?

3. Use the data from Example 2 with the outlying point removed, and calculate the new least-squares line. Compare this to the least-squares equation that used all of the data. Calculate a new median-median line. Compare it to the median-median line that used all of the data. Explain what it means to be a *resistant line,* and why the median-median line has this property.

4. Why is it important to minimize the sum of the **squares** of the residuals? Try to think of another method you could use to find a best-fit line. Explain what advantage or disadvantage the squares of the residuals have over the other method.

5. Use the data in Problem 3, Problem Set 4.5.
   a. Find the equation of the least-squares line.
   b. Verify that the least-squares line passes through the mean x-value and the mean y-value.
   c. Decide which of the two equations, the median-median line or the least-squares line, is a better model, and write a paragraph defending your choice.

6. Use the data in Problem 5, Problem Set 4.5.
   a. Find the equation of the least-squares line.
   b. Verify that the least-squares line passes through the mean x-value and the mean y-value.
   c. Decide which of the two equations, the median-median line or the least-squares line, is a better model, and write a paragraph defending your choice.

7. A 20-year $60,000 mortgage on a new home has an annual interest rate of 9.5%.
   a. Find the final balance that results from each of several different monthly payments. What is the minimum number of points needed to find the equation of the least-squares line?
   b. Find the least-squares line that fits the data in part a.
   c. Use the equation of the line to find the payment that gives a balance of nearly zero after 20 yr.

8. Look back at the definition of deviation in Chapter 3. Compare this measure of error to the residual. How do they relate to each other? How are they different?

9. Another measure of error is the mean absolute residual. This is the mean of the absolute values of all the residuals. Determine this value for the model in Investigation 4.6.1. Describe how you could use this value to determine if the line is a good fit.

10. The following table gives the average daily maximum temperatures in April for various cities in North America, and the corresponding latitudes in degrees and minutes north.

Place	Lat.	Temp. (°F)	Place	Lat.	Temp. (°F)
Acapulco, Mex.	16°51′	87	Mexico City, Mex.	19°25′	78
Bakersfield, CA	35°26′	73	Miami, FL	25°49′	81
Caribou, ME	46°52′	50	New Orleans, LA	29°59′	77
Charleston, SC	32°54′	74	New York, NY	40°47′	60
Chicago, IL	41°59′	55	Ottawa, Ont.	46°26′	51
Dallas, TX	32°54′	75	Phoenix, AZ	33°26′	83
Denver, CO	39°46′	54	Quebec, Que.	46°48′	45
Duluth, MN	46°50′	52	Salt Lake City, UT	40°47′	58
Great Falls, MT	47°29′	56	San Francisco, CA	37°37′	65
Juneau, AK	58°18′	39	Seattle, WA	47°27′	56
Kansas City, MO	39°19′	59	Vancouver, BC	49°18′	58
Los Angeles, CA	33°56′	69	Washington, DC	38°51′	64

a. Find the equation of the least-squares line. (Note: You will need to convert the latitudes to decimal degrees; for example, $35°26′ = 35\frac{26}{60} \approx 35.43°$.)

b. What is an appropriate domain for this model?

c. Which cities appear not to follow the pattern? Give a reason for each case.

d. Choose two cities not on the list, and find the latitude for each. Use your model to predict the average daily maximum temperature in April for each city. Compare your result with the official average April temperature for the city. (An almanac is usually a good source for this information.)

11. The table below shows the percentage of women in the United States labor force.

Year	1950	1960	1970	1980	1990
Percent	29.6	33.4	38.1	42.5	45.3

1950   1960   1970   1980   1990

a. Find the least-squares line for these data. (Use 1900 as the reference year.)

b. What is the real-world meaning of the slope? Of the y-intercept?

c. According to your model, what percentage of the labor force is currently made up of women? Check with an almanac to see how accurate your prediction is.

12. Consider again the role of the graphing calculator in this course. In this chapter, have you discovered new advantages, or disadvantages, to using the graphing calculator? If so, what are they? Have your perspective or your feelings changed towards the use of the graphing calculator? Be clear and explain your response.

Project

Linear Extrapolation

Look through magazines and newspapers to find a case when someone has used a linear mathematical model to project into the future. (This is usually identifiable by a graph in which the rightmost portion is drawn with a dashed line.) Study the data and make your best guess as to the method used by the author to find the line. Offer other models with the same data and give projections using those models. What would you guess is the degree of accuracy of the forecast? Give your reasons for this measure of accuracy. If you are using an old article, try to find recent data to determine if the model remains nearly accurate today.

Geometer's Sketchpad Investigation

Least Squares

In this investigation you will use Sketchpad to investigate the least-squares line. First you will create a script that constructs the residual and draws squares whose areas represent the squares of the residuals.

Step 1 Open a new sketch. Choose Create Axes from the Graph menu. Draw line *l*. Draw and label point *A*, placing it near, but not on, line *l*.

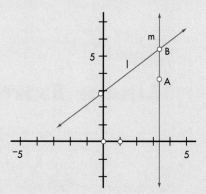

Step 2 Open a new script and click Record.

Step 3 Construct line *m* through point *A* parallel to the *y*-axis. Construct point of intersection *B* of line *l* and line *m*. Draw segment *AB*. Hide line *m*.

Step 4 Construct line *n* perpendicular to segment *AB* through point *A*.

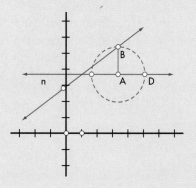

Step 5 Construct a circle with center *A* and radius *AB*. Construct the points of intersection of circle *A* and line *n*. Select one of the points as point *D*. Hide circle *A*, line *n*, and the point of intersection that you didn't select.

Step 6 Construct line *s* parallel to segment *AB* through point *D*. Similarly, construct line *t* perpendicular to segment *AB* through point *B*. Construct point of intersection *C* of line *s* and line *t*.

Step 7 Construct polygon interior *ABCD*. Measure the area of *ABCD*. Hide points *B*, *C*, and *D*, and lines *s* and *t*.

Step 8 Click Stop on your script.

To play your script, you will need to draw a new data point, select it, select the *y*-axis, and then select line *l*. As you can see, the script creates and measures the area of the square of the residual of a data point. Add four or more data points and use your script to create the square of the residual for each point. Use the Sketchpad calculator to sum the areas of all the squares.

Make sure that the Snap To Grid option on the Graph menu is turned off. Change the slope and the position of line *l*. Observe the effect that the slope of the line has on the sum of the areas of the squares. Try to find the line that minimizes the total area of the squares.

Questions

1. Minimize the total area of the squares by adjusting the slope and position of line *l*. Display the equation of line *l*, and record the slope and intercept of the line for which the sum of the squares is the least. Record the values of your data points.

NOTE
4E

2. Using the coordinates of your data points from Question 1, your graphing calculator, and the method presented in **Calculator Note 4E**, determine the slope and intercept of the least-squares line. Compare your results with your equation from Question 1. How close are the two equations?

3. Plot the point that is the mean of all five *x*-values and the mean of all five *y*-values. This is the mean point. How does it relate to the least-squares line?

4. Position one point of line *l* on the mean point and move the other point on line *l* to find the line that minimizes the sum of the squares.

Coefficient of Correlation

Mathematics is not a careful march down a well-cleared highway, but a journey into a strange wilderness, where the explorers often get lost.
—W. S. Anglin

Two students, Woody and Forrest, collected data on tree diameters and heights. They plotted the data on graph paper. Woody put the diameters on the *x*-axis and the heights on the *y*-axis. Forrest squared the diameters and plotted them on the *x*-axis, and he put the heights on the *y*-axis. Each found a best-fit line for his data. Their graphs are shown above.

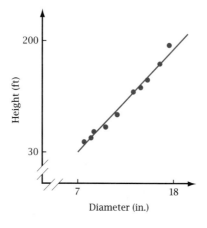

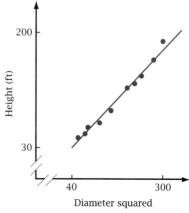

Which student found the better relationship? How good is the fit for each line? Each student believes he has found the best-fit line for his data. But is a line the appropriate model? Is there a linear relationship between Woody's data, or is there a better linear relationship between Forrest's data using the squares of the diameters?

To answer this question, you could look at the sum of the residuals, but you have seen that even a very poor fit can have a zero sum. You can give the range of the residuals, but this is misleading in data sets that have one or two outliers falling much farther from the line than the rest of the data. A measure that is sometimes used to determine how well a line fits the data is the mean absolute value of the residuals. (See **Calculator Note 4F.**)

NOTE
4F

There are many other measures of fit. The most commonly used measure is called the **correlation coefficient,** denoted by the letter *r*. In 1896, Karl Pearson gave a formula for calculating correlation coefficients and

The Chandelier Drive-Thru Tree in northern California is 315 feet high. At its base the diameter is 21 feet. Many of its branches are 4 to 8 feet in diameter, larger than many mature trees.

a justification for why his formula should give the best value, given that the data came from normal distributions (you will learn about normal distributions in Chapter 11). Using this formula was a lot of work. A researcher remarked in 1972:

Those who began their statistical apprenticeship later than the early 1920s can scarcely imagine the many hours previously spent by high-powered research men [and women] in the drudgery of computing correlation coefficients one by one. Only the most tenacious and devoted could come through those ordeals with enough enthusiasm and time left to do the real work of finding the basic biological, economic, or physical mechanisms which were causing their data to behave as they did. (Jay Lush, in *Statistical Papers in Honor of George W. Snedecor,* edited by T. A. Bancroft, 219–220. Ames, IA: Iowa State University Press, 1972.)

Karl Pearson

Today you can easily calculate the coefficient of correlation with your calculator. But you want to make sure that you understand what this coefficient means. Values of r range from $^-1$ to 1. A value of zero shows absolutely no linear correlation between the values of x and y. The sign of r will be the same as the sign of the slope of the best-fit line. A value of ± 1 shows a perfect correlation between x and y, meaning that the data pairs fall exactly on a line. A correlation coefficient of 0.94 for one data set and of $^-0.94$ for another are equally accurate. For Woody's data, the correlation coefficient is 0.992. That's pretty good. For Forrest's data, the correlation coefficient is 0.999. That's even better. So, for the trees measured, a linear model relating the heights to the squares of the diameters gives a better fit.

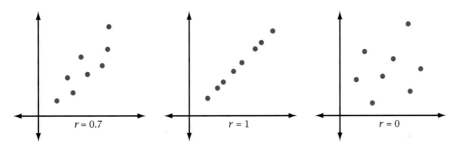

The formal definition of r is too complex for this course, so we will use a simpler, more workable definition based on the square of the correlation coefficient. The value of r^2 is a measure of the fraction of the total variation in the values of y (the dependent variable) that is explained by the regression equation. The rest of the variation in y-values is due to other factors, some of which may be random. This means that if $r = 0.5$, then $r^2 = 0.25$, and 25% of the variation in y-values can be explained by the regression equation. If $r = 0.7$, then $r^2 = 0.49$, so a coefficient of 0.7 is almost twice as good as a coefficient of 0.5 would be. You may find it helpful to think of r^2 as a measure of how closely the data points are clustered into a narrow band.

In a recent election, eight candidates ran for class president. Two "scores" were recorded for each candidate. The first was the candidate's combined SAT score. The second was the candidate's popularity, measured by the number of students who considered the candidate a friend, in a random poll of 100 students. The third column shows the number of votes that each candidate received. Which of these two measures seems to have a greater influence on the number of votes received?

Name	SAT score	Popularity	Votes
Ajene	1210	65	60
Benny	1450	40	26
Caron	1380	58	47
Doug	1580	21	40
Erica	940	61	29
Fuyu	1320	51	71
Gert	1470	78	104
Hector	1320	47	52

Solution

The (*SAT score, votes*) data pairs have an *r*-value of 0.25. The (*popularity, votes*) data pairs have an *r*-value of 0.61. Of the two factors, popularity seems to have more vote-getting potential than SAT scores. Further investigation shows that $r^2 = 0.06$ in the (*SAT score, votes*) case, or that only 6% of the variance in the votes can be attributed to the candidates' SAT scores. In other words, there is no linear relationship for (*SAT score, votes*). In the case of (*popularity, votes*), $r^2 = 0.38$. There is a very weak (38%) linear relationship between these two variables. So it appears that voting depends on some factor (or combination of factors) other than those presented here.

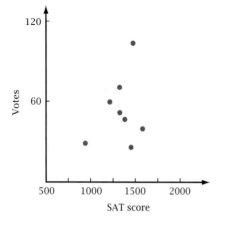
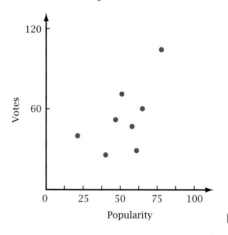

Example 2

The table at the right shows the normal monthly temperatures for New York City. Is there a linear correlation between the month and the temperature?

Month	Temp. (°F)
January	32
February	33
March	41
April	53
May	62
June	71
July	77
August	75
September	68
October	58
November	47
December	36

Solution

It seems easy to say, "Yes, look at the way the numbers rise and fall." But this is neither precise nor conclusive. If you number the months consecutively, you can name 12 ordered pairs to analyze: $(1, 32), (2, 33), (3, 41), (4, 53), (5, 62), \ldots, (12, 36)$. For this set of data, (*month, temp*), $r = 0.31$ and $r^2 = 0.10$. There is hardly any correlation at all. The meaning of linear correlation is that as the values of the domain increase, then the values of the range *must react in direct response* to that change, either always increasing or always decreasing. But, in this example, going from February to March has the opposite effect of going from August to September. While there is probably a relationship of some kind between the month and the temperature, it is not linear. ■

Example 3

The following table shows the average height (in centimeters) of U.S. children from ages 7 to 15. How linear are these data?

Age	7	8	9	10	11	12	13	14	15
Height (cm)	119.3	127.0	132.0	137.1	142.2	147.3	152.4	157.5	162.2

Source: 1990 Physicians Handbook.

Solution

The least-squares model is *height* $= 84.3 + 5.235(age)$. The coefficient of correlation is 0.99864796, or, to three digits, $r = 0.999$. This is a highly accurate model in which r^2 is equal to 0.997. A linear model fits the data very well through the domain given. Do you suspect it will be linear much outside this domain? Explain why, or why not. ■

Be careful that you don't confuse the ideas of correlation and causation. There may exist a strong correlation between two sets of data, but this does not necessarily imply causation. For example, there may be a strong correlation between year of birth and life expectancy, but the year of birth does not cause life expectancy rates to change. Even though there may appear to be a strong correlation between some element in people's diet and cancer risk, there may be other environmental factors that actually cause the cancer risk to be higher or lower.

Investigation 4.7.1

Analyzing Cereals

The following table lists some information written on cereal boxes.

a. Compare the categories to find which have the strongest linear relationships.

b. Which of the cereals' characteristics are most related? Can you explain the reason for any of these relationships?

c. Write a paragraph describing the relationships you discover. Include any nonrelationships that you find surprising.

Percent of Recommended Daily Allowance

	Thiamine	Riboflavin	Iron	Phosphorus	Magnesium
Shredded Wheat, Spoon Size	4	0	4	10	8
100% Bran	25	25	45	30	30
Shredded Wheat 'n Bran	4	0	8	10	10
Grape-Nuts	25	25	45	6	6
Banana Nut Crunch	25	25	10	8	6
Golden Crisp	25	25	10	4	4
Post Raisin Bran	35	35	35	15	15
Marshmallow Alpha-Bits	25	25	15	6	4
Fruity Pebbles	25	25	10	0	0
Honey-Comb	25	25	15	2	2
Total	100	100	100	20	6
Fiber One	25	25	25	15	15
Trix	25	25	25	2	2
Cocoa Puffs	25	25	25	4	0
Special K	35	35	25	0	4
Corn Flakes	25	25	10	0	0
Frosted Flakes	25	25	10	0	0
Corn Pops	25	25	10	0	0
Product 19	100	100	100	4	2
Fruit Loops	25	25	25	2	2

	Thiamine	Riboflavin	Iron	Phosphorus	Magnesium
Rice Krispies	25	25	10	4	2
Life	30	30	45	0	0
Cheerios	25	25	45	10	10

Problem Set 4.7

1. What is the slope of the line that passes through the point $(4, 7)$ and is parallel to the line $y = 12(x - 5) + 21$?

2. Find the equation of the line passing through $(4, 0)$ and $(6, {}^-3)$.

3. Find the point on the line $y = 16.8x + 405$, where x is equal to ${}^-19.5$.

4. This table shows the percentage of the African American population that dropped out of high school in the years from 1970 through 1990.

Year	1970	1975	1980	1985	1987	1988	1989	1990
Percent	22.2	18.5	16.0	13.8	12.7	12.0	11.4	11.2

Source: The World Almanac and Book of Facts 1993.

   a. What is the least-squares model for this data?
   b. What is the coefficient of correlation for this model?
   c. Using complete sentences, explain what this correlation coefficient tells you about the model.
   d. Use the model to predict what the percentage was in 1972.
   e. How accurate do you think your prediction is? (On a scale of 1 to 10, with 10 being *very* accurate.)

5. These data list the number of bound volumes, the annual circulation, and the annual operating cost for randomly selected public libraries. Each of the numbers in the table is in thousands.

City	Volumes	Circulation	Cost ($)	City	Volumes	Circulation	Cost ($)
Atlanta, GA	1,600	2,183	9,453	Detroit, MI	2,446	1,441	14,690
Baton Rouge, LA	493	1,641	2,631	Kansas City, MO	1,346	875	5,091
Boston, MA	4,916	1,454	11,500	Memphis, TN	1,535	2,500	8,726
Buffalo, NY	3,426	6,228	12,344	Oakland, CA	779	1,633	5,869
Columbus, OH	1,353	4,320	11,500	Philadelphia, PA	3,038	5,205	22,379
Dallas, TX	1,777	3,874	14,847	Portland, OR	1,179	3,237	5,526
Denver, CO	1,178	2,570	11,398	St. Paul, MN	657	1,942	4,640

Source: The World Almanac and Book of Facts 1986.

a. How strongly is each measure, volumes and circulation, tied to operating cost?

b. Which of the two seems to have the stronger correlation to cost? Explain your reasoning using complete sentences.

6. This table shows the number of seats on various types of airplanes, the planes' cruising speeds, and their operating costs per hour.

Plane	Seats	Speed (mph)	Cost ($)
B747-400	403	534	7,098
B747-100	399	520	5,905
L-1011-100/200	293	495	4,072
DC-10-10	282	488	4,056
A300-600	266	474	3,917
DC-10-30	265	522	4,595
B767-300	224	489	3,384
B757-200	188	458	2,293
B767-200	187	483	2,956
A320-100/200	149	441	1,868
B727-200	148	430	2,263
B737-400	145	400	1,743
MD-80	142	419	1,842
B737-300	131	415	1,768
DC-9-50	122	387	1,640
B727-100	117	429	2,220
B737-100/200	112	387	1,735
DC-9-30	102	381	1,658
F-100	99	361	1,445
DC-9-10	77	361	1,439

Source: The World Almanac and Book of Facts 1994.

a. How strongly is each measure, seats and speed, related to operating cost?

b. Which of the two seems to have the stronger correlation to cost? Explain your reasoning using complete sentences.

7. What is the coefficient of correlation for the data from Investigation 4.6.1? How does that affect the conclusions you made?

8. Consider the following data that shows (*number of students, number of faculty*) at selected colleges and universities. (Be sure to save these data in your calculator. You will need them in the next section.)

College	Number of students	Number of faculty	College	Number of students	Number of faculty
Agnes Scott College	600	66	Penn State	37,269	1,986
Alfred University	2,593	175	Princeton University	6,140	800
Bennington College	613	78	Rhode Island Sch. of Design	1,916	275
Boston University	28,557	2,707	Rhodes College	1,346	149
Bowling Green State Univ.	17,882	845	St. John's College	1,998	156
Brandeis University	3,689	496	St. Olaf College	3,121	382
Brown University	7,612	548	Spelman College	2,075	116
Bryn Mawr College	1,849	137	Stanford University	13,224	1,315
California College of Arts	1,119	167	Stockton State College	5,297	243
Carleton College	1,885	151	Swarthmore College	1,333	179
College of William & Mary	7,372	716	Syracuse University	16,821	1,050
Cornell University	18,088	1,597	Tufts University	7,868	589
De Paul University	2,480	218	Tuskegee University	3,371	254
DePauw University	14,699	734	University of Central Florida	18,094	754
Drake University	6,618	256	University of Cincinnati	26,475	1,457
Duquesne University	6,370	479	University of Colorado	10,090	624
Eastman School of Music	1,232	122	University of Delaware	11,090	693
Florida State University	23,883	1,434	University of Hawaii at Manoa	19,836	1,249
Gallaudet University	2,031	300	University of Houston	30,372	2,025
Hampshire College	1,232	112	University of Iowa	29,230	1,600
Howard University	10,538	1,195	University of Massachusetts	25,216	1,412
Illinois Wesleyan University	1,750	157	University of Miami	11,397	1,934
Lehigh University	6,569	487	University of Michigan	35,220	3,619
Maryland Institute, C. of Art	1,285	112	University of Minnesota	38,172	2,836
Miami Univ. of Ohio	16,044	840	University of Nevada	15,000	521
Michigan State University	42,695	3,990	University of South Florida	30,003	1,422
Mills College	1,141	74	University of Tulsa	4,431	400
Morehouse College	3,150	150	University of Utah	23,626	924
Mt. Holyoke College	1,947	203	University of Virginia	17,198	1,804
New England Conservatory	781	191	Webster University	9,049	353
New Mexico State University	15,788	651	Wesleyan University	2,938	346
New York University	31,690	5,428	Western Michigan University	24,861	1,223
Northwestern University	11,337	729	Wheaton College	2,445	236
Oakland University	12,254	617	Yale University	10,998	718

Source: The World Almanac and Book of Facts 1993.

a. Find an equation that relates the number of students to the number of faculty, and another equation that relates faculty to students.

b. Describe the correlation in these data. Use complete sentences and discuss r and r^2.

9. Consider only schools from the above list that have less than 2000 students.

a. Find an equation that relates the number of students to the number of faculty, and another equation that relates faculty to students.

b. Describe the correlation in these data. Use complete sentences and discuss r and r^2.

10. What ideas or topics have been introduced in this chapter that you feel you do not yet understand or see the purpose of? Give examples and explain why you feel this way.

Take Another Look 4.7

The data in the table describe a relationship between the number of minutes played and total points scored during the 1987–1988 season by Chicago Bulls basketball players.

Take a look at the scatter plot of (*minutes played, total points*). Draw a best-fit line. Which point do you think should have the greatest residual for any given best-fit model? What information is represented by this point?

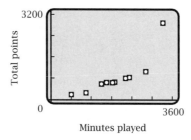

Player	Minutes played	Total points
Brown	591	197
Corzine	2328	804
Grant	1827	622
Jordan	3311	2868
Oakley	2816	1014
Paxon	1888	640
Pippen	1650	625
Sellers	2212	777
Sparrow	1044	260
Vincent	1501	573

The two graphs below show the lines determined by the median-median line criterion and the least-squares criterion. Try to determine which is which before you test out your conjecture with your calculator. Write a paragraph that supports your conjecture and identifies the better model for these data. Why do you think one model is better than the other in this situation? What are the equations of the two models? Explain why the models are so different.

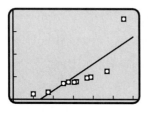
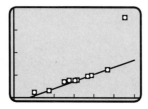

Source: Adapted from Helen Compton, "Teaching Contemporary Secondary Mathematics." *NCSSM* 6:1 (December 1994).

Project

Least-Squares Formulas

Where do the numbers come from in a least-squares analysis? Given n points of data, $\sum_{i=1}^{n} x_i$ is equal to the sum of all the x-values in the data. Likewise, $\sum_{i=1}^{n} y_i$ is equal to the sum of the y-values from 1 to n. The sum of the squares of the x-values is $\sum_{i=1}^{n} x_i^2$, and $\sum_{i=1}^{n} x_i y_i$ is the sum of the products of the x- and y-values.

Year	1965	1970	1975	1979	1980	1981	1982
Households (in thousands)	1,181	1,239	1,499	1,655	1,733	1,933	1,986

Find the values in the table for each data pair. Use 1900 as the reference year. Sum the values in each column. Use these sums to evaluate each formula given below.

n	x	y	x^2	y^2	xy
1	–?–	–?–	–?–	–?–	–?–
2	–?–	–?–	–?–	–?–	–?–
. . .	. . .	. . .	. . .	. . .	. . .
Sum	–?–	–?–	–?–	–?–	–?–

$$y\text{-intercept} = \frac{\left(\sum_{i=1}^{n} x_i^2\right)\left(\sum_{i=1}^{n} y_i\right) - \left(\sum_{i=1}^{n} x_i\right)\left(\sum_{i=1}^{n} x_i y_i\right)}{n\left(\sum_{i=1}^{n} x_i^2\right) - \left(\sum_{i=1}^{n} x_i\right)}$$

$$\text{slope} = \frac{n\left(\sum_{i=1}^{n} x_i y_i\right) - \left(\sum_{i=1}^{n} x_i\right)\left(\sum_{i=1}^{n} y_i\right)}{n\left(\sum_{i=1}^{n} x_i^2\right) - \left(\sum_{i=1}^{n} x_i\right)}$$

$$r = \frac{n\left(\sum_{i=1}^{n} x_i y_i\right) - \left(\sum_{i=1}^{n} x_i\right)\left(\sum_{i=1}^{n} y_i\right)}{\sqrt{n\left(\sum_{i=1}^{n} x_i^2\right) - \left(\sum_{i=1}^{n} x_i\right)^2} \sqrt{n\left(\sum_{i=1}^{n} y_i^2\right) - \left(\sum_{i=1}^{n} y_i\right)^2}}$$

Enter the data in your calculator and locate the values for Σx, Σy, Σx^2, Σy^2, and Σxy.

Verify the values for the y-intercept, the slope, and r (the correlation coefficient) by using the built-in least-squares regression.

Section 4.8

Accuracy

Standard mathematics has recently been rendered obsolete by the discovery that for years we have been writing the numeral five backward. This has led to reevaluation of counting as a method of getting from one to ten.
—Woody Allen

"Nine out of ten dentists recommend. . . ." "Prices expected to rise 4% over the next year. . . ." "Health care costs to double in the next ten years. . . ."

Many numerical claims such as these appear in news releases or in advertisements. Use of data or statistics can inform *or* mislead you. The purpose of this section is to help you understand the accuracy of predictions. Your answers should be based both on mathematics and on a commonsense understanding of the situation.

The accuracy of any model used to study a phenomenon or to make a prediction is largely dependent on two factors. The first is the accuracy of the data that were used to create the model. For example, if all of your data were temperatures rounded to the nearest degree, then it would be misleading and unscientific to use a model to predict temperatures to the tenth of a degree. Proper use of significant digits is a major concern in scientific applications.

The second factor that affects the accuracy of any model is how well or accurately the equation fits the data. Consider two sets of data gathered with very similar accuracy. From each data set a model is derived. In Model A the coefficient of correlation (*r*) is 0.995, and in Model B the *r*-value is 0.647. You can certainly use model A for predictions with much greater accuracy than Model B.

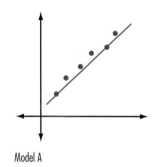

Model A

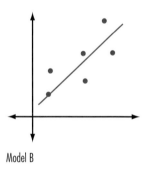

Model B

A low *r*-value does not always mean disaster. You may look at the residuals and see a case such as that shown at the right. If the three points far below the line can be traced to measurements made by one person, or with one piece of equipment, you may have reason to disregard them. The accuracy of your model will then be much higher.

Is it important for you to specify the accuracy of a model? In routine usage of a model, a little less accuracy will not hurt. However, if it is a medical model that involves lives, or a financial model that is critical to the existence of a company and its employees, accuracy can be very important. For example, if a mathematical model predicts a patient can undergo radiation for 10.785 minutes before there is damage to healthy cells, then the doctor may decide to give a 10-minute treatment. But if it is known that there is a 2.5-minute error factor in the model, then the treatment might be shortened to as a 2.5-minute error factor in the model, then the treatment might be shortened to as little as 8 minutes, to be safe.

There are several ways to estimate the accuracy of a model. One way is to look at the range of the residuals: their maximum and minimum values. A second way to estimate the accuracy is to consider the average size of the residuals. In the following examples, you will examine both of these methods.

■ Example 1

Consider the data collected from the U.S. Bureau of the Census showing the number of one-parent families headed by a male, from 1965 through 1990.

Year	1965	1970	1975	1980	1985	1990
Households (in thousands)	1,168	1,228	1,485	1,733	2,228	2,884

The least-squares regression, using 1900 as the base year, is $y = 67.589x - 3450.448$, and $r = 0.9558141192$. Predict the number of one-parent families in 1972 that were headed by a male.

Solution

Using 72 for x in the regression equation gives a value of 1,415,929.52 families. Because it is difficult to picture what 0.52 of a family would look like, you can give the answer as 1,415,930 families. However, because your data do not include this much accuracy, you need to round to 1,416,000. The square of the correlation coefficient is 0.914, or about 91%. The residuals range between ⁻224,000 and ⁺251,000 families. The "residual range" gives a range of 1,192,000 to 1,667,000 families. Your best answer to this problem may be 1,400,000 ± 200,000 families.

Year	1965	1970	1975	1980	1985	1990
Households	1,168	1,228	1,485	1,733	2,228	2,884
Residual	225	⁻53	⁻134	⁻224	⁻67	251 ■

The range of the residuals in the last problem was a useful guide for determining a reasonable range for the answer. The actual residuals are 225, ⁻53, ⁻134, ⁻224, ⁻67, and 251. Three of the six residuals have magnitude greater than 200. What if you have a case where one residual is ⁺200 units and the remaining points are within ±30 units of the best-fit line? Would you be compelled to think that any prediction you make is, at best, within 200 units of the line? You would likely find that you have a higher r^2 value for this case, so you could justify a more accurate result.

NOTE
4F

Another technique to measure the accuracy of your prediction is to use the mean (average) absolute value of the residuals. (This is similar to using the mean deviation in Chapter 3.) In Example 1, this mean absolute value is 159. So your answer might be 1,416,000 ± 159,000. (See **Calculator Note 4F**.) There are many possible answers, depending on the method used for determining the accuracy. Being able to justify your answer is the important thing.

Example 2

The contamination of Lake Michigan trout by the insecticide DDT decreased steadily between 1970 and 1984. The following data represent the mean concentration of DDT found in lake trout caught and tested by the Great Lakes National Program Office of the Environmental Protection Agency for the years from 1970 to 1984. Use the least-squares line to estimate when the fish would show no concentration of the DDT. (Use a reference year of 1900.)

Year	1970	1971	1972	1973	1974	1975	1976
DDT level (mg/kg)	19.1	13.4	11.5	10.1	8.3	7.5	5.5

Year	1977	1978	1979	1980	1981	1982	1984
DDT level (mg/kg)	6.0	4.7	6.9	4.9	3.1	3.0	2.7

Solution

The equation of the least-squares line is $y = 81.3 - 0.962x$, where y is the concentration in milligrams of DDT per kilogram of fish, and x is the number of years since 1900. Setting y equal to zero, you find x equals 84.5, which indicates the year 1985. The residuals for the points are 5.2, 0.42, ⁻0.52, ⁻0.96, ⁻1.8, ⁻1.6, ⁻2.7, ⁻1.2, ⁻1.5, 1.6, 0.58, ⁻0.26, 5.99, and 2.22. Taking the absolute values of these residuals and averaging them gives the mean absolute residual of 1.5 mg/kg. If you think of a band of this width along both sides of your best-fit line, you'll see that the boundaries of your range are from 1983 to 1986. These boundary values can be found by setting y equal to zero in the two boundary equations $y = 81.3 - 0.962x \pm 1.5$.

If you study the residual plot, you might conclude that a line might not be the best model for this data, as there seems to be a pattern to the residuals. ∎

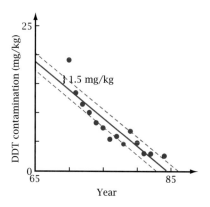

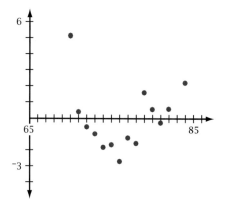

It is risky to try to extrapolate or forecast far into the future with any model. In the last example, the model predicts a negative concentration of DDT if you try to use it too far into the future. Weather predictions may be very accurate for one or two days into the future, but few people would rely on predictions made six months in advance. The accuracy of any prediction drops off quickly as you move into uncharted data. In Example 2, you could show the increase in inaccuracy on the graph by flaring away from the best-fit line as you pass the final data point. The bands on both sides of the data will become wider as you use the model to extrapolate further and further from your data.

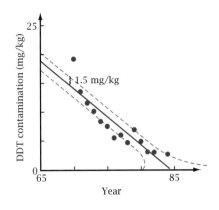

Problem Set 4.8

1. Examine the three scatter plots below.

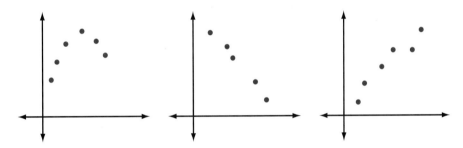

a. Which is the plot with the least linear correlation? Why?
b. Which is the plot with the most linear correlation? Why?
c. Which plots, if any, show negative correlation? How can you tell?

2. Copy the following table onto your paper.

x	4	7	11	12.9	16	18.5
y	22	47	74	87	111	128
$y_1(x)$	-?-	-?-	-?-	-?-	-?-	-?-
Residual	-?-	-?-	-?-	-?-	-?-	-?-
Residual^2	-?-	-?-	-?-	-?-	-?-	-?-

a. Find the least-squares line (y_1), and complete the table.
b. What is the range of the residuals?
c. Find the sum of the absolute values of the residuals.
d. Find the mean absolute residual.
e. Find the sum of the squares of the residuals.
f. Use the information calculated to analyze just how good y_1 is as a best-fit line.

3. Give a specific example (different from those given in the text) when overstating the accuracy of a prediction based on a mathematical model would be cause for concern.

4. Make a residual plot for the data in Example 1. Discuss the appropriateness of using a least-squares model.

5. The data below were collected from students doing "the wave."

Number of students	3	5	6	10	12	16	20	24
Time (sec)	1.5	2.3	2.7	2.5	4.2	5.8	7.1	7.8

a. Find the least-squares line for this data.
b. Using your model, predict the time for 13 people.
c. In a complete sentence, explain the accuracy of your prediction using the mean absolute residual.

6. You are given a model $y = 12.5 + 4.17x$, using values of x between 11 and 28, with a coefficient of correlation $r = 0.940$. The residuals range from -18.5 to $+15.8$, with a mean absolute residual of 11.2.
a. What would you predict for y when $x = 19$?
b. What accuracy can you give for your prediction? Describe how you might change this reported accuracy depending on what the model represented.

7. Return to the data in Problem 8, Problem Set 4.7.
a. Determine the mean absolute deviation for the residuals.
b. List the schools that have residuals greater than one mean absolute deviation from the mean. What do these schools have in common?
c. Which schools have residuals greater than two mean absolute deviations from the mean? What do these schools have in common?
d. Explain why you think the schools in each of these lists lie so far from the model.

8. The following table gives the weights of transmitters used in some animal studies in the 1960s.
a. Using the average of the weight range for each animal, find a relationship between the animal weights and the transmitter weights.

Deer mouse

b. Use your model to predict the proper weight of a transmitter for tracking an animal, whose weight range is from 10,000 to 25,000 grams.

c. Describe the accuracy of this prediction. Explain how you determined this.

d. How might you improve this measure of accuracy using the same data?

Study	Species	Weight of animal (g)	Weight of transmitter package (g)
Rawson & Hartline (1964)	*Peromyscus sp.* (deer mouse)	10–35	2.6
Beal (1967)	*Sciurus carolinensis* (gray squirrel)	340–680	21
Beal (1967)	*S. niger* (fox squirrel)	545–1,360	21
Cochran et al. (1965)	*Sylvilagus floridanus* (cottontail rabbit)	900–1,800	32
Mech et al. (1965)	*Lepus americanus* (snowshoe hare)	900–1,800	50
Merriam (1963, 1966)	*Marmota monax* (woodchuck)	2,300–4,500	45
Moore & Kluth (1966)	*Dasypus novemcinctus* (nine-banded armadillo)	3,400	40
Cochran et al. (1965)	*Vulpes fulva* (red fox)	4,500–6,800	130
Cochran et al. (1965)	*Taxidea taxus* (badger)	5,900–11,300	140
Mech et al. (1965)	*Procyon lotor* (raccoon)	5,400–15,900	115
Tester et al. (1964)	*Odocoileus virginianus* (white-tailed deer)	34,000–91,000	180
Cochran et al. (1965)	*Odocoileus virginianus* (white-tailed deer)	34,000–91,000	300
Craighead & Craighead (1965)	*Ursus arctos* (polar bear)	147,000–385,000	906

Source: Robert H. Giles, *Wildlife Management Techniques,* 3rd ed. rev. (Washington, DC: The Wildlife Society, 1971), p. 97.

Chapter Review

It is a capital mistake to theorize before one has data.
—Sir Arthur Conan Doyle

In this chapter you analyzed sets of two-variable data, which, when plotted, tended to lie on a line. Then you explored different methods for finding the equation of a best-fit line. First, you drew the best line you could and found the equation of this line by calculating the slope between two points on the line. You used this slope along with the coordinates of one point to write the equation in point-slope form, $y = m(x - x_1) + y_1$. The slope of the line is the rate of change of the dependent variable, y, with respect to the independent variable, x. Then you learned about two methods that can be used to determine an equation of best fit—the median-median line and the least-squares line. Using either of these methods, everyone will get the same equation. When using your calculator to find the least-squares line, you also get the correlation coefficient, which helps determine whether or not a line is a good model for the data. Whatever method you choose, you should examine the residuals to decide if it is a good model. With a good model, the graph of the residuals should appear completely random: both positive and negative values should occur, and there should be no visible pattern. A linear pattern to the residuals indicates that a better linear model is possible. A curved pattern to the residuals indicates that the data are not linear and a different sort of relationship should be investigated. Finally, you explored different ways to evaluate the accuracy of a model. Your concerns about the accuracy of a model may depend on the source of the original data, the correlation coefficient, how you are going to use the model, or a combination of factors.

Problem Set 4.9

1. Find the slope of the line containing the points $(16, 1300)$ and $(^-22, 3250)$.

2. What is the slope of the line $y = {^-}5.0247 + 23.45x$?

3. Find the point on the line $y = 16.8x + 405$, where y is equal to 740.

A table of health indicators for some Asian and African countries appears on pages 194–195. As you will notice, an indicator may be quite high (or low) compared to the same indicator for other countries in the list. You might want to do some research or have a discussion with your group concerning the social and political factors that contribute to these figures. Use these data when working on Problems 4–27.

4. Determine good windows for viewing points given by each data pair.
   a. (*daily calorie supply, life expectancy*)
   b. (*availability of health services, infant mortality*)
   c. (*safe water, sanitation*)

5. Refer to the (*daily calorie supply, life expectancy*) data. What is the slope of the line connecting the points associated with Rwanda and Kuwait?

6. Find the equation of the line using the points from Problem 5.

7. Graph the (*daily calorie supply, life expectancy*) data points and the line from Problem 6 on your calculator. Experiment by changing the *y*-intercept, the slope, or both, until you find an equation that appears to be a better fit for the data.

8. What is the domain for the line in Problem 7? What are the units of the domain?

9. What are the units of the slope for the equation you found in Problem 7?

10. Give a real-world meaning for both the slope and the *y*-intercept for the line in Problem 7.

11. Use your equation from Problem 7 to predict the daily calorie supply for a country whose people have a life expectancy of 57 years.

12. What life expectancy would you predict for a country whose average daily calorie value is 2012?

13. What is the median of the life expectancy values?

14. Name the three points you would use to find the equation of the median-median line for the (*safe water, life expectancy*) data.

15. What is the slope of the median-median line, based on the three points you named in Problem 14?

16. What is the equation of the median-median line?

17. Draw a graph of the residuals on your calculator. What does this graph tell you about your model?

18. What is the residual for the point representing Ethiopia? Explain how you calculated this number.

19. Which point most poorly fits the median-median line you found in Problem 16?

20. Find the least-squares line for the (*health services, infant mortality*) data.

21. Write a sentence explaining the real-world meaning of the slope.

22. Find the median-median line for the data in Problem 20. Compare this equation to the one for the least-squares line. Which line seems to be the best fit for the data?

23. What infant mortality rate would each of the models predict for a health services rate of 55%?

24. What is the coefficient of correlation for the least-squares line in Problem 20? Explain the significance of this value.

25. Sort the data in ascending order according to the residuals for the least-squares line. Delete the first three data points and the last three data points. Find the least-squares line and the coefficient of correlation for this altered set of data points. Describe how removing these points changes the equation of the least-squares line and the coefficient of correlation.

26. How would you describe the accuracy of your solution to Problem 23?

27. Describe at least three conclusions you can make based on your analysis in Problems 4–26.

Country	Life expectancy (yr)	Daily calorie supply	Infant mortality rate	Health services (%)	Safe water (%)	Sanitation (%)
Algeria	66	2866	61	90	70	60
Angola	46	1807	125	30	34	18
Benin	51	2305	110	30	54	42
Botswana	68	2375	35	89	60	42
Cambodia	51	2166	116	53	37	15
Central African Republic	47	2036	105	30	12	21
China	71	2639	38	90	83	97
Egypt	62	3336	57	99	88	51
Ethiopia	49	1667	168	46	28	16
Ghana	55	2248	81	60	54	42
Guinea	44	2132	133	40	64	24
Indonesia	60	2750	72	80	51	44
Iran	65	3181	65	87	61	51
Iraq	64	2887	58	99	91	70
Jordan	70	2634	47	97	99	76
Kenya	59	2163	66	77	50	43
Kuwait	75	3195	14	100	100	98
Liberia	55	2382	131	39	54	15
Libya	63	3324	68	100	93	95
Madagascar	51	2158	113	65	20	5
Malaysia	71	2774	14	90	72	94
Mongolia	64	2479	60	100	79	73
Mozambique	47	1680	147	39	24	24

Country	Life expectancy (yr)	Daily calorie supply	Infant mortality rate	Health services (%)	Safe water (%)	Sanitation (%)
Niger	46	2308	123	30	55	10
Nigeria	52	2312	84	72	50	15
Papua New Guinea	56	2403	54	97	32	56
Philippines	65	2375	40	75	82	69
Rwanda	46	1971	110	80	66	58
Saudi Arabia	69	2874	31	98	93	82
Senegal	48	2369	80	40	47	54
Singapore	75	3198	6	100	100	96
Somalia	49	1906	127	27	60	17
Sri Lanka	72	2277	18	90	71	60
Sudan	52	1974	99	60	45	70
Tanzania	51	2206	115	80	51	66
Thailand	69	2316	26	70	76	74
Togo	54	2214	85	60	59	21
Zaire	52	1991	91	40	33	25
Zambia	48	2077	108	74	48	43
Zimbabwe	60	2299	47	83	36	42

Source: The Universal Almanac 1995.

Note: The life-expectancy column gives numbers for life expectancy predicted at birth. The numbers for infant mortality are the death rates among children under age 5 per 1000 live births. The numbers in the last three columns are the percentages of people who have access to health services, safe water, and sanitation.

Assessing What You've Learned—Open-ended Investigations

Now that you are becoming more familiar with your calculator and the content of this course, you may be ready to devise investigations of your own or to pursue challenging extensions to the investigations. That's what the Take Another Look section is about. You'll find Take Another Look suggestions at the end of many sections, just after the problem sets. Your teacher may already have assigned some of them. You can use these open-ended investigations to assess the depth of your understanding of the guided investigations in the lesson.

Take Another Look activities can be quite challenging—you certainly wouldn't want to try all of them. In consultation with your teacher, choose one or more activities to try. Most of these activities call for an investigation or an explanation. Make sure you communicate clearly what you've done and what you've discovered, either in writing or in a presentation or performance assessment. If you write up your Take Another Look work, choose one or more of those write-ups that you think are most significant and add them to your portfolio.

Whether or not you choose to add Take Another Look activities to your portfolio, don't overlook other assessment opportunities in the investigations, problems, and projects.

Organize Your Notebook

- However you've decided to organize your notebook, it should contain virtually all of your mathematical output for the year: homework, class notes, investigations, projects, calculator techniques, and now, possibly Take Another Look activities. Review your notebook to be sure it's complete and well organized.

Write in Your Journal

- Look for journal prompts in Problem Sets 4.1, 4.4, 4.6, and 4.7.
- If you've done a Take Another Look activity, how did that experience differ from doing an investigation? Did you work with a group or by yourself? Did you find the Take Another Look easier or harder than an investigation? Do you think Take Another Look adds to your understanding of the concepts in the lesson? Explain why or why not.

Update Your Portfolio

- As mentioned above, your work on an open-ended Take Another Look activity is an excellent candidate for your portfolio. Choose one, explain what you did, and add it to your portfolio.
- Choose another piece of work to add to your portfolio—an investigation, a project, a problem set, a test—whatever you think best represents your work.

Performance Assessment

- Your teacher may actually want to observe you doing an open-ended investigation from one of the Take Another Look sections, especially if you worked in a group. Show your teacher what you did, explain why you did it that way, and describe your findings.

5 Functions

These teenagers are riding a roller coaster at Six Flags Mid America in St. Louis, Missouri. If you know the shape of a roller coaster, you can draw a graph showing the relative speeds at which the train travels during the trip. The next time you take a roller coaster ride, you might want to think about the relationship between where you are on the roller coaster and how fast the car is traveling. Graphs of relations and functions provide visual information that can help you understand what is happening.

Interpreting Graphs

Common sense is the collection of prejudices acquired by age eighteen.
—*Albert Einstein*

Students at Central High School have been complaining that the soft drink machine is empty too often. Student council members Rita and Noah have decided to study this problem. First, they recorded information and made a graph showing the number of cans in the soda machine at various times during a typical school day. Their graph gives them a lot of information about the use of the soda machine.

   The school cafeteria doesn't open until 7 a.m., so no one can use the machine before that time. Rita and Noah figured out from the graph that Jake, who maintains the machine, fills it to capacity just before the first lunch period, then quickly recharges it before the last lunch period is complete. (A recharge fills the machine to 75% capacity.) Jake told them that it takes him about five minutes to do a recharge and ten minutes to completely fill the machine. Although it was difficult for Rita and Noah to provide a minute-by-minute analysis from the graph, the overall picture was very useful, and they could observe definite tendencies. Each horizontal segment indicates a time interval when the vending area is closed, when the machine is empty, or when no one is drinking soda. Rita and Noah reported to the student council that the machines are filled overnight, again at 10:30 a.m., and again just after school lets out. The machines are filled to 75% capacity during the last lunch period. The greatest consumption is pictured by the steep, declining slopes during the lunch periods and

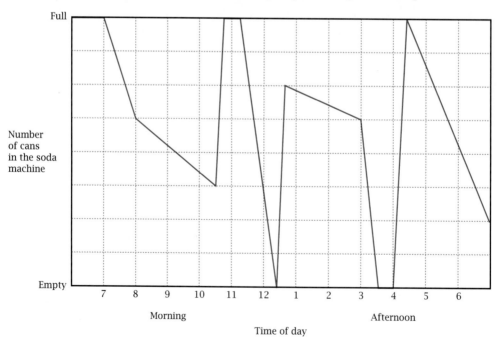

when school lets out. By studying the graph, the student council was able to determine whether or not a change in the refill schedule was needed. What do you think their recommendation was?

Although Rita and Noah were interested in solving a problem related to soda consumption, they also could have used the graph to answer many other questions about Central High School. When do students arrive at school? What time do classes begin? When is lunch? When do classes let out for the day?

There is a dynamic relationship between a graph and a real-world situation. In this section, you will investigate this relationship. A picture can be worth a thousand words *if you can interpret the picture.*

■ Example 1

What is the real-world meaning of this graph picturing the relationship between the number of people getting haircuts and the amount charged for each haircut?

Solution

The number of haircuts depends on what is charged for each haircut. As the price increases, the number of haircuts decreases linearly. The slope indicates the number of haircuts lost for each dollar increase. The *x*-intercept represents the haircut cost that is too expensive for everyone. The *y*-intercept indicates the number of haircuts when they are free. Why isn't the *y*-intercept bigger? Do you think this should be a linear graph? Why or why not? ■

■ Example 2

Which of these graphs pictures a student's walking speed from the time she realizes she might be tardy for class until she arrives at class?

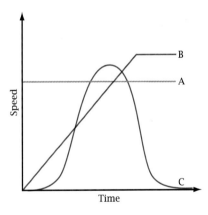

Solution

Graph B is probably the best answer.

Graph A isn't a good answer, because it is unlikely that anyone can instantly get up to speed and maintain that exact speed.

Graph C indicates she knows she will be late and has given up trying to beat the clock. Notice, however, that her speed isn't zero. ■

Investigation 5.1.1

Invent a Story

Part 1   The graph at the right tells a story. It could be a story about a lake, a bathtub, or whatever your imagination can create. Spend some time with your group discussing all the information contained in the graph. Write a story that conveys all of this information.

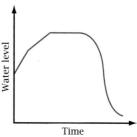

Part 2   Sketch a graph that reflects all the information given in the story below.

    "It was a dark and stormy night. The old bucket stood empty in the yard before the torrents of rain came. As day broke on the horizon, the rain subsided. The bucket stood quietly through the morning until Old Dog Trey arrived as thirsty as a dog. The sun shone brightly through the afternoon when Billy, the kid next door, arrived. He noticed two plugs in the side of the bucket. One of them was about a quarter of the way up, and the second one was near the bottom. As fast as you could blink an eye, he pulled out the plugs and quickly ran away."

Problem Set 5.1

1. Birdie Parr's brother, Hawkeye, describes himself as an inconsistent golfer. His concentration often wanders from the mechanics of golf to the mathematics involved in his game. His scorecard frequently contains mathematical doodles and graphs.

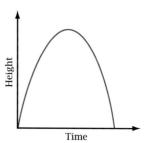

   a. What is a real-world meaning for this graph found on one of his recent scorecards?
   b. What units might he be using?
   c. Describe a realistic domain and range for this graph.
   d. Does this graph show how far the ball traveled? Explain.

2. Make up a story to go with this graph.

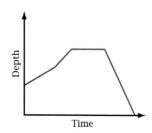

3. Trace the section of roller-coaster track pictured by the graph below.

    a. Sketch a graph of the roller-coaster car's speed over this portion of the track to compare the speeds at each of the points A through K. No numbers are needed on your graph.

    b. At which lettered point is the roller-coaster car moving the fastest?

    c. At which lettered point is the roller-coaster car moving the slowest?

    d. Name two points where the speeds are about the same.

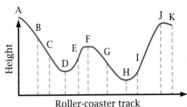

Roller-coaster track

Sketch what you think is a reasonable graph for each relationship described in Problems 4–20. If one variable is clearly dependent on the other, put it on the vertical axis. Put the independent variable on the horizontal axis. Label the units. Decide whether each graph should be a distinct set of points or points connected by a smooth curve. The graph doesn't need to be detailed, but *do justify* the shape you have chosen by writing one or two complete sentences.

4. The amount of money you have in an account that is compounded annually, over a period of several years.

5. The same amount of money you started with in Problem 4, hidden in your mattress over this time period.

6. The distance it takes to stop a car, compared to the car's traveling speed at the start.

7. The height of a baseball after it leaves the bat.

8. The temperature of a hot drink sitting on your desk.

9. The temperature of an iced drink sitting on your desk.

10. Your height above the ground as you ride a Ferris wheel.

11. The money you earned in a week, compared to the number of hours you worked in the week.

12. The speed of a falling acorn after it is dropped by a squirrel from the top of an oak tree.

13. Your height over your entire life span.

14. Your speed as you cycle up a hill and down the other side.

15. Your distance from Detroit, during a flight from Detroit to Newark, if your plane is directed to circle Newark in a holding pattern.

16. The daily maximum temperature over a period of time.

17. The amount of postage charged for different weights of letters.

18. Adult shoe sizes as related to the adult's foot length.

19. The intensity of light available for reading, and your distance from the reading lamp.

20. The altitude of a hot dog wrapper after it is released by your little brother from the top row in the football stadium.

21. Describe a relationship of your own and draw a graph to go with it.

Take Another Look 5.1

Real estate guides for prospective home buyers are available as newspaper supplements at grocery stores, real estate offices, and many other community locations. Select ten or more different houses that are listed for sale. Try to select only one type of house—three-bedroom ranch, townhouse, New England style, and so forth. Then cut out the house advertisements you selected and attach them to a sheet of paper to be turned in with your work.

a. Do a one-variable analysis of the asking prices for the homes selected. Find the mean, the median, and the mean absolute deviation, and provide a box plot and a histogram of your data. Write several sentences describing your analysis.

b. Do a two-variable analysis of (*square footage, asking price*). Scatter plot the data and decide on a best-fit model for your data. Defend or explain why you chose the particular best-fit model. Provide a real-world meaning for the slope of your best-fit model. Use your model to estimate the cost of a 2800 sq ft house. Use your model to predict the cost of a house outside of your data set. Write several sentences describing your analysis.

c. Select one of the house advertisements and find the monthly payment for a 25 yr mortgage at 9.5%. Determine the actual cost of the house over the 25 years.

Section 5.2

Connections with Sequences

Coming together is a beginning; keeping together is progress; working together is success.
—Henry Ford

Frequently, you are given information or data that can be pictured as a **discrete** graph made up of distinct points. Suppose the *mileage* on your family car's short-trip odometer reads as shown in the following table.

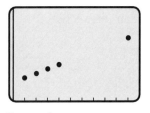

Discrete graph

Time (min)	2	3	4	5	. . .	10
Mileage	104.4	105.1	105.8	106.5	. . .	110

What was the odometer reading before the car started moving? What was the average speed during the trip to school? What is the equation of the line pictured? How do you put a continuous graph on a sequence, or set, of discrete points? This section will help you answer such questions.

Many things—such as growth, changes in speed, or distance from home—really happen in a continuous way. Graphs of these relationships are not made up of separate distinct points, but will be smooth lines or curves. The line pictured at the right shows a distance in miles for every possible time from zero minutes through ten minutes.

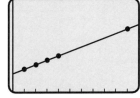

Continuous graph

Investigation 5.2.1

Distance from Home

Draw a graph that shows your distance from home between 7 a.m. and 9 p.m. on a typical Friday. Exchange graphs with another person in your group. Try answering each of the following questions by looking at your partner's graph: When did your partner leave home? How far is home from school? When was your partner the furthest from home? What was your partner's greatest distance from home? At what times during the day was your partner not traveling? When was your partner traveling the fastest? When did your partner get home?

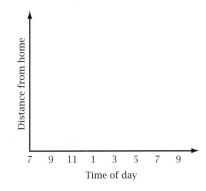

Up to now in this book, sequences and their terms have been identified with subscripts, as in the sequence $u_1, u_2, u_3, \ldots, u_n$. You will make a simple notation change in the next example. The term u_1 will be identified as $u(1)$, u_2 will be identified as $u(2)$, and so on. This means that the sixth term of the sequence in Graph A will be called $u(6) = 25$ instead of $u_6 = 25$. This transition will help prepare you for the function notation introduced in this section.

■ Example 1

Write an explicit formula for each sequence graph.

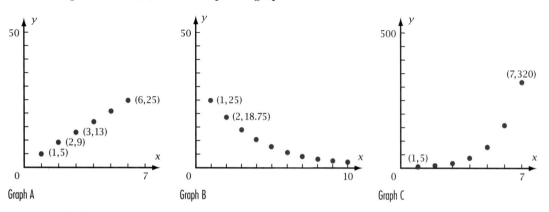

Graph A   Graph B   Graph C

Solution

Graph A represents an arithmetic sequence, {5, 9, 13, . . . }, because the set of points appears to be linear. The term $u(1)$ equals 5, and the slope between any two points is

$$\frac{y_2 - y_1}{x_2 - x_1} = 4.$$

The sequence point that precedes the first pictured point is $(0, 1)$, which means that $u(0) = 1$. The point $(0, 1)$ is also the vertical intercept. Therefore, the explicit formula is $u(n) = 4n + 1$.

The next two graphs represent geometric sequences. An explicit formula for a geometric sequence is given by $u(n) = u(0) \cdot r^n$.

In Graph B, you know that $r < 1$, because the sequence is decreasing.

In Graph C, you know that $r > 1$, because the sequence is increasing.

In Graph B, the common ratio is $\frac{u(2)}{u(1)} = \frac{18.75}{25} = \frac{3}{4}$. To find $u(0)$ you must back up one term from $u(1)$. Because $u(0)$ times $\frac{3}{4}$ will be 25, you can divide 25 by $\frac{3}{4}$ to get

$u(0) = \frac{100}{3}$. An explicit formula for this graph is $u(n) = \frac{100}{3} \cdot \left(\frac{3}{4}\right)^n$. Confirm that this formula is correct by using it to find $u(2)$.

In Graph C, $u(1) = 5$ and $u(7) = 320$. Therefore, $5r^6 = 320$ or $r^6 = 64$, which means $r = 2$. The vertical intercept is 2.5 and the explicit formula is $u(n) = 2.5 \cdot 2^n$. Confirm that this formula is correct by using it to find $u(7)$. ■

You have used u_n or $u(n)$ notation for sequences because you can only substitute nonnegative integers for n. Sequence formulas generate discrete points. If you wish to show what would happen for real-number values of the independent variable, like 2.3 or $^-1.9$, then the graphs will need to show that the points are connected. For these nondiscrete functions, change the variable notation from n to x, and write the equation in the form $y = \textit{some expression in } x$.

■ **Example 2**

Write an equation in the form $y = \textit{some expression in } x$ for each graph pictured below. Use the graphing calculator to plot the given points on the screen and then enter the equation into $y=$ to draw the graph that contains the points. The graph will be a smooth, unbroken (*continuous*) curve indicating that x can be any real number.

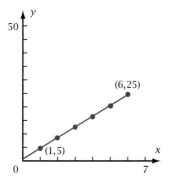
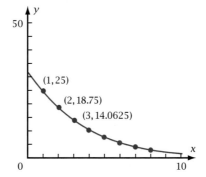

Solution

Equations for the continuous graphs are

$$y = 4x + 1 \quad \text{and} \quad y = \frac{100}{3} \cdot \left(\frac{3}{4}\right)^x.$$

Trace the graphs to locate values of y at other real-number choices of x. (Your calculator is able to calculate values of $\left(\frac{3}{4}\right)^x$ when x is not a positive integer. You will learn in Chapter 7 what this means mathematically. Meanwhile, try graphing this function to see how it behaves.) ■

In a sequence $(1, u(1)), (2, u(2)), (3, u(3)), \ldots$, the value of $u(n)$ is a **function** of n because exactly one value is produced for any choice of n. Another way of expressing this is that there is a single output for each input.

The equation $y = 4x + 1$ contains the sequence points and an infinite number of other points. The variable y is a function of x. The function $f(4)$, read as "f of 4," means the *y*-value, or the height of the graph, when *x* = 4. Because this function is continuous, it also makes sense to consider numbers other than positive integers, like 4.5. The value of *y* when *x* = 4.5 will be 4(4.5) + 1, or 19. If *y* is a function of *x*, then *f*(*x*) is the function value of *y* at that choice of *x*. This means *y* = *f*(*x*). For this reason, functions like *y* = 4*x* + 1 are frequently written *f*(*x*) = 4*x* + 1. This notation means *y* is a function of *x*, and it gives you a convenient notation for evaluating the function at particular choices of *x*, like 4.5.

Function Notation

A **function** *y* = *f*(*x*) is a description relating the variables *x* and *y* to each other. For each specified value of *x*, the description allows you to define a single value of *y*.

This is a fairly simple definition of a very important concept in mathematics. One of the first definitions of "function" was given by the Swiss mathematician Leonhard Euler (1707–1783) in 1755. He said:

> If some quantities so depend on other quantities that if the latter are changed the former undergo change, then the former quantities are called functions of the latter. This denomination is of the broadest nature and comprises every method by means of which one quantity could be determined by others. If, therefore, *x* denotes a variable quantity, then all quantities which depend on *x* in any way or are determined by it are called functions of *x*.

Which definition do you prefer?

In the next investigation you will explore the concept of a function by looking at the relationship between Fahrenheit and Celsius temperature scales. Daniel Gabriel Fahrenheit (1686–1736) patterned his thermometers after those of the Danish astronomer Olaus Roemer, whom he had visited in 1708. Roemer probably used his thermometers for meteorological purposes because their scales were calibrated using the temperature of melting ice (7.5° on the Roemer scale) and that of boiling water (60°). While making the thermometers, Roemer put them in *blutwarm* (blood-warm) water that registered 22.5° on his scale. Fahrenheit mistakenly thought that this was part of the calibration process and that *blutwarm* meant the temperature of the human body. (By *blutwarm*, Roemer had meant simply the temperature of tepid water.) Fahrenheit took the upper fixed point of Roemer's scale, 22.5°, as the temperature of the human body, later changing it to 96°, and he changed the lower measure to 32° in order to eliminate "inconvenient and awkward fractions." He reported that the boiling point on his scale was 212°, which is several degrees higher than it should be. After his death, Fahrenheit thermometers were calibrated by setting 212° as the temperature of boiling water. On these thermometers normal body temperature is 98.6°.

Investigation 5.2.2

Temperature Scales

The objective of this investigation is to find a relationship between the Fahrenheit and Celsius temperature scales.

a. With your group, collect data by taking temperatures, in °F and °C, in several different environments, such as in the classroom, outdoors, or water flowing from the water cooler. (If your group has several thermometers, then each member can collect several different data pairs, and you can combine the data into a group data set.) Be certain that the thermometer stays in the medium long enough to stabilize the temperature before you record the value.

°C	°F	Location of reading
–?–	–?–	–?–

b. Plot all data on an appropriately scaled graph. Use degrees Celsius as the independent variable.

c. Find a best-fit line using the method of your choice. Be prepared to explain why you selected that method. Compare your best-fit line with those of other members of your group.

d. Decide as a group on an equation to use for $F(c)$.

e. Convert this equation to a function that finds Celsius in terms of Fahrenheit, $C(f)$.

f. Predict the temperature in °C for 95°F. Plot this point on your graph.

g. Predict the temperature in °F for ⁻5°C. Plot this point on your graph.

h. What is the possible error in part f? In part g? Explain how you found these errors.

i. Give a real-world meaning for the y-intercept of the graph.

j. Give a real-world meaning for the slope of the graph.

k. Find a temperature where both scales give the same reading.

Problem Set 5.2

1. Find the coordinates for each unlabeled point pictured in Graph A, Graph B, and Graph C of Example 1.

In Problems 2–4, complete the following three steps:
a. Plot the first three discrete points of the sequence.
b. Write the explicit equation of the associated continuous function, using $f(x)$ notation.
c. Draw its graph through the points. (The domain should include all numbers that make sense.)

2. $u(n) = n^2$ **3.** $u(n) = \sqrt{n}$ **4.** $u(n) = \begin{cases} 4 & \text{if } n = 1 \\ 1.3 \cdot u(n-1) & \text{if } n > 1 \end{cases}$

5. Complete 5a–d for the sequence in Problem 4.

    a. Mark the point $(4, f(4))$ on your graph and describe, in complete sentences, its location relative to the point $(0, 0)$.

    b. What are the coordinates of the point $(7.25, f(7.25))$?

    c. What is the height of the point determined by $f(6.5)$?

    d. Draw a segment on your graph that represents $f(6.5)$.

6. Suppose $f(x) = \dfrac{-3}{5}x + 25$.

    a. Draw a graph of this function.

    b. Identify the point $(7, f(7))$ by marking it on your graph.

    c. What is $f(7)$?

    d. Draw a segment on your graph that identifies $f(7)$.

    e. Find the value of x when $f(x) = 27.4$. Mark this point on your graph.

7. Frequently, wild economic behavior occurs in a country experiencing a dramatic change in philosophy or government. The fallout of this behavior might be in the form of inflation. A 10% annual inflation rate means that at the end of a year, it will cost $110 for goods or services that cost $100 at the beginning of the year. A 1992 report indicated that the inflation rate in Russia was 3% per week.

    a. Given the above data about the economy in Russia, write an explicit equation and draw a continuous graph that illustrates the inflationary growth of $100.

    b. What will the height of the graph be after 10.5 weeks?

    c. What will the height of the graph be after one year?

    d. What is the real-world meaning of the last answer?

    e. When will the inflationary value reach $295?

8. Dr. Igota Cure has prescribed a new medication for her patient Anna Geezic. Suppose she starts by taking a pill containing 200 mg of the medication. Assume that her body eliminates 10% of the medication daily.

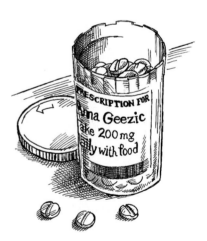

    a. Write an explicit equation and draw a continuous graph that illustrates this situation.

    b. How much of the medication remains in Anna's body after 4 days? After 10.5 days?

    c. What are the heights of each point named in 8b?

    d. When will her medication level reach 5 mg?

    e. When will the medication be totally eliminated from Anna's body?

    f. What happens if Anna continues to take 200 mg of the medication each morning?

    g. How many pills should the doctor prescribe if the medication has detrimental side effects after it builds up to 1900 mg in the body?

9. Sketch a graph showing the oven temperature after you turn off an oven that has been on for an hour.

Take Another Look 5.2

As you darken the screen of your calculator you can see the pixels (picture elements). They are the square dots that make up the calculator's rectangular display screen. Graphs are drawn as x takes on the values from Xmin to Xmax, the two window values that are centered in the leftmost and rightmost pixels used in the graphing window. The extreme vertical graph values are listed as Ymin and Ymax.

Horizontal and vertical distances between adjacent pixels will vary depending on your calculator model. Set the graphing window at [0, 100, 0, 0, 100, 0] and turn off all stat plots and equations. As you move the cursor about the screen, coordinates of adjacent pixels are displayed on the screen. These coordinates are not convenient or "friendly" values because you are unable to locate integer horizontal or vertical coordinates.

Your task is to find Xmax and Ymax values for a window of [0, Xmax, 0, 0, Ymax, 0] so that the change, or distance, between consecutive x-values (Δx) is 1 and the distance between consecutive y-values (Δy) is also 1 as you move the cursor about the graphing window. This is certainly a "friendly window" because the integer coordinates are one unit apart.

You can accomplish this task by making a few trial-and-error choices for Xmax. If you move the cursor to the left-hand edge of the graphing screen, and then move it one space to the right, the x-coordinate value is the same as Δx. Don't worry about the Ymax choice at this point. You will know that you are correct when your choice for Xmax gives an x-value of 1 when the cursor is one space to the right of the left-hand edge. When this has been accomplished, use similar substitutions to find the Ymax value so that $\Delta y = 1$.

The horizontal difference that you just discovered, Xmax − Xmin, is a value that you should remember. This value, H, is significant because

$$\frac{\text{Xmax} - \text{Xmin}}{H}$$

gives a Δx value of 1. Likewise, the vertical value you discovered, V, always gives

$$\frac{\text{Ymax} - \text{Ymin}}{V} = \Delta y = 1.$$

Determine a window setting where the origin is at the center of the screen, and the distance between pixels is one unit.

Section 5.3

The Linear Family

Try to be one of the people on whom nothing is lost.
—Henry James

What do you remember about the slope of a horizontal line? What makes one line steeper than another? How do the slopes compare if two lines are parallel? What can you say about the slopes of two lines that are perpendicular? In this section you will look for answers to these questions as you review and learn more about linear functions.

Linear Function

A function is **linear** if it can be put in either of the forms

$$y = mx + b \quad \text{or} \quad y = m(x - x_1) + y_1$$

where m is the **slope** of the line, b is the **y-intercept**, and (x_1, y_1) is a **point** on the line.

■ Example 1

The equation $4x - 2y = 16$ describes a linear relation, but it can't be entered directly into your calculator without correctly solving for y (putting the equation in $y=$ form). What is $y=$ form for this example?

Solution

$$
\begin{aligned}
4x - 2y &= 16 \\
-2y &= {}^-4x + 16 & \text{Add } {}^-4x. \\
y &= ({}^-4x + 16)/{}^-2 & \text{Divide by } {}^-2. \\
y &= 2x - 8 & \text{An alternate form.}
\end{aligned}
$$

(You can graph this function on your calculator using either of the $y=$ forms given above.) ■

Investigation 5.3.1

Special Slopes

René Descartes (1596–1650) was interested in solving geometry problems such as those posed by the ancient Greeks. He developed a new method, which he first described in 1628, of solving geometry problems by giving two coordinates to each point of a curve in the plane and working with the equations that described the relationships between the coordinates of each curve. In this activity you will explore some geometric relationships using coordinates of points and slopes of lines.

René Descartes

Part 1 Have each group member choose a different set of four points, each with integer coordinates.

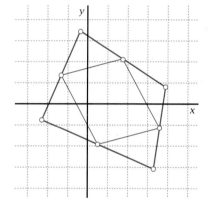

    a. Plot your four points on graph paper.

    b. Connect the points to form a quadrilateral. Locate and label the midpoints of each side.

    c. Connect these midpoints in order.

    d. What shape appears to have been created?

    e. Which sides, if any, seem to be parallel?

    f. Calculate the slopes of a pair of sides that appear to be parallel.

    g. Are these two sides indeed parallel? How can you tell?

    h. What kind of figure was created by connecting the midpoints of the quadrilateral?

    i. Compare your results with those of other members of your group.

Part 2 Take a right-angled corner of a piece of paper and place it on top of a piece of graph paper. Line it up so that the corner is at a point with integer coordinates, and the sides pass through other points with integer coordinates.

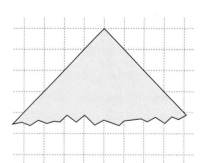

    a. Trace along the edges of the paper to form two perpendicular lines.

    b. Calculate the slope of each line. Is there a relationship between the slopes?

    c. Compare your slopes with those of other members in your group.

    d. What can you conclude about the slopes of perpendicular lines?

NOTE
5A

The SQUARE option in the ZOOM menu adjusts the window so that it is "square." This means the ratio of the height of the window to its width has been adjusted so that one unit in the x direction is the same as one unit in the y direction. Perpendicular lines will look perpendicular, circles will look like circles, 45° angles will look like 45° angles, and so on. Your calculator will change the y-values or the x-values or both. Experiment by entering some odd-shaped windows in your calculator and trying the SQUARE option. See **Calculator Note 5A.**

Problem Set 5.3

1. Example 1 in this section shows algebraically that $4x - 2y = 16$ and $y = 2x - 8$ are equivalent equations.
   a. Name an x-value and a y-value that make $4x - 2y = 16$ a true statement.
   b. Show that the same values make $y = 2x - 8$ a true statement.
   c. Find another pair (x, y) and show that it works in both forms of the equation.
   d. Explain what it means to say that two equations are equivalent.

2. Graph the equation $2.8x + 5.1y = 22$. Identify the slope, the y-intercept, and the x-intercept of the line.

3. a. Write the equation of the line shown at the right. Check your equation by graphing the line on your calculator and using the trace function.
   b. Write the equation and graph the function that is two units above, and parallel to, the pictured line.

4. Graph each function in this problem on the same set of coordinate axes. (Be certain that your calculator graphing window accurately pictures perpendicular lines.)
   a. Rewrite the equation for function f, $3x + 2y + 12 = 0$, in $y=$ form and graph it.
   b. Write the equation for a line that is perpendicular to f at its y-intercept. Suppose this is function g. (Hint: Perpendicular lines have slopes that multiply to $^-1$.)
   c. Write the equation for a line that is perpendicular to f at its x-intercept. Suppose this third line is function h.
   d. Write the equation for a fourth line that is perpendicular to g at its x-intercept.
   e. Name the geometric figure outlined by the four lines.

(Graph shows a line passing through the points $(^-5.2, 3.18)$ and $(1.4, ^-4.4)$, with axes labeled x and y, and gridlines marked at 6 and $^-6$.)

5. When graphing equations, it is often convenient to use a graphing window in which the pixel coordinates are set at "friendly" values. This means that when you trace a graph, you will get integer values for x. **Calculator Note 5A** explains how to get a friendly window on your calculator and how to automatically set your window to these values.

NOTE
5A

a. Determine a window setting where the origin is at the center of the screen and the distance between pixels is 0.1. (This means that when you use the trace function, the x- and y-values will increase or decrease by 0.1.)

b. Determine a window setting where the origin is at the lower left corner of the screen and the distance between pixels is 0.1.

6. Write an equation for each line pictured below. In each case, the grid spacing is one unit. (For more practice, see **Calculator Note 5B**.)

NOTE
5B

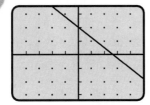 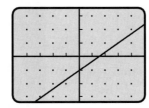

7. When *y varies directly with x,* you can write a special linear function, $y = kx$. The constant of variation, k, is just another name for slope, and the graph passes through the origin. Draw several different-sized squares on graph paper. For each square, measure the length of the side and the length of the diagonal. Collect data from other students until you have at least twelve data points.

a. Plot the points (*side length, diagonal length*) and find the equation of a best-fit line. Remember that the point $(0, 0)$ is also on your line.

b. Your equation is of the form $d = ks$, where d is the length of the diagonal and s is the length of the side. This is a direct variation. What is your constant of variation, k, for $d = ks$?

c. If a square has a side length of 6.4 cm, what is the length of its diagonal?

d. What is the side length of a square with diagonal $14\sqrt{6}$?

8. The Internal Revenue Service has approved ten-year linear depreciation as one method for determining the value of business property. This means the value declines to zero over a ten-year period.

Suppose a piece of equipment costs $12,500 originally and is depreciated over a ten-year period.

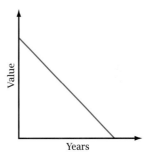

a. What is the y-intercept? Give a real-world meaning for this value.

b. What is the x-intercept? Give a real-world meaning for this value.

c. What is the slope? What is the real-world meaning of the slope?

d. Write an explicit equation that describes the value of the equipment during the ten-year period.

e. When is the equipment worth $6,500?

9. Suppose that your basketball team's scores in the first four games of the season were 86 points, 73 points, 76 points, and 90 points.

   a. What will your team's scoring average be if the next game score is 79 points?

   b. Write a function and draw a graph that compares the next-game score and the average score.

   c. What score will give a five-game average of 84 points?

10. Mr. and Mrs. De La Cruz want to buy a new house and must finance $60,000 at 9.6% on the unpaid balance.

    a. Make several guesses for a monthly payment that will pay off the loan in 25 yr.

    b. Plot the points determined by your guesses (*monthly payment, balance after 25 yr*).

    c. Find a best-fit line for the points.

    d. What is the *y*-intercept? What is the real-world meaning of the *y*-intercept?

    e. What is the *x*-intercept? What is the real-world meaning of the *x*-intercept?

    f. What is the slope? What is the real-world meaning of the slope?

11. Use the data and the equation from Problem 8 to determine the average value of the equipment over the ten-year period. To figure this out, determine the starting value, the value each year, and the final value. Then average these numbers.

Section 5.4

The Parabola Family

The pure and simple truth is rarely pure and never simple.
—Oscar Wilde

What would this graph look like if a teacher decides to add five points to each of the numerical scores pictured in the histogram below? Have any of your teachers ever done that?

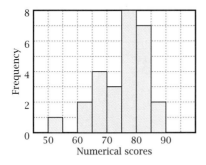

What change, or transformation, will move the triangle on the left to its position on the right? Did you do transformations like this in your geometry class?

Transformations are a natural feature of the real world, including the world of art. Music can be transposed from one key to another. Melodies are often shifted by a certain interval within a composition.

Can you name other examples of transformations?

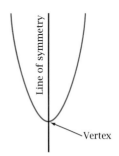

In this section you will experiment with alterations to the equation and graph of the function pictured at the right. The **parabola** $y = x^2$ is a simple building-block function. One variation of this function models the height of a projectile from the ground as a function of time. Another variation gives the area of a square as a function of the length of a side.

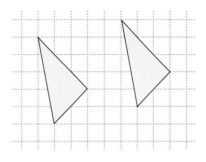

■ Example 1

If you are given a stick that is 100 cm in length, is there a way you can break it so that the pieces form a rectangle with the largest possible area?

Solution

Make a table of values $(x, y) = (side\ length,\ area)$ that can represent this situation. Invent several possible side lengths and then compute the associated areas.

Length (x)	5	10	15	20	25	30	35	40	45
Width	45	40	35	30	25	20	15	10	5
Area (y)	225	400	525	600	625	600	525	400	225

The graph of (*side length, area*) is a parabola that is upside-down and translated from its usual position. Do you see that the **vertex** is at the highest point and shows that a side length of 25 cm gives the greatest area, which is 625 cm²? For this example, what geometric shape has maximum area? ■

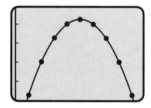

Set a "friendly" graphing window in which the distance between the pixels is 0.2 on both the x- and y-axes. Enter this y-symmetric graph on your calculator as $y = x^2$. Some of the points not shown on the screen include $(^-3, 9)$, $(3, 9)$ and $(^-4, 16)$, $(4, 16)$.

All parabolas are related to this simple parent function: $y = x^2$ with the **vertex** at $(0, 0)$. The major focus of this section will be for you to (a) slide, or translate, this graph to a new position, (b) write the equation of a parabola based on its shape and the position of its vertex, and (c) predict the graph of a parabola given its equation. Locating the vertex and connecting it to an equation is your key to success with parabolas.

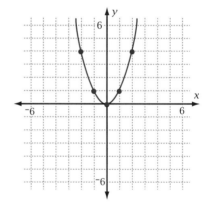

Investigation 5.4.1
Make My Graph

The function $y = x^2$ is shown on each graph below. Experiment by changing this equation to find out how you can slide the parabola up and down. Use a combination of calculator guess-and-check, logic, and common sense. Try to learn from your mistakes. When you have succeeded, write the equation that worked.

a.

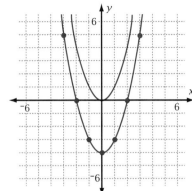

b.

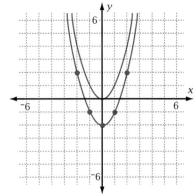

c.

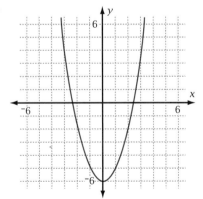

d.

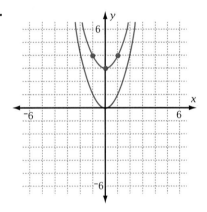

Problem Set 5.4

1. Use your calculator to find the equation for each parabola. Each parabola is congruent to $y = x^2$.

a.

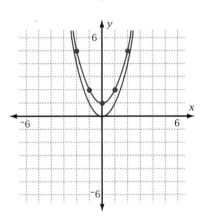

b.

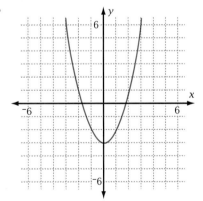

c. 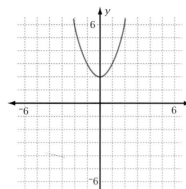   **d.**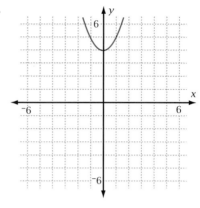

2. In each part of this problem, the graph will be a parabola that is congruent to the parent function $f(x) = x^2$.

   a. Write the equation and draw the graph of a parabola that is congruent to $f(x) = x^2$ with the given translation.

   i. six units down from $f(x)$ ii. two units up from $f(x)$

   b. Write an equation in $y=$ form and describe the location of each parabola relative to $f(x)$.

   i. $f(x) - 5$ ii. $f(x) + 4$

   c. In general, $y = x^2 + c$ means the same thing as $f(x) + c$ when $f(x) = x^2$. Describe the location of $f(x) + c$.

3. Now that you have discovered how to move the parabola up and down, experiment to find out how to move it from side to side. Write the equation you used to slide the parabola, $y = x^2$, to the right or left.

   a. 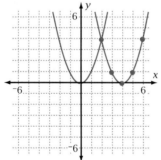   **b.** 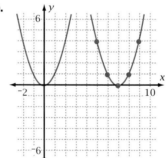   **c.**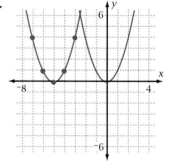

4. Describe what happens to the graph of $y = x^2$, pictured at right, in the following situations.

   a. x is replaced by $(x - 3)$.
   b. x is replaced by $(x + 3)$.
   c. y is replaced by $(y - 2)$.
   d. y is replaced by $(y + 2)$.

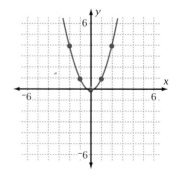

5. Write an equation for each parabola pictured at the right. (See **Calculator Note 5C** for additional practice.)

NOTE
5C

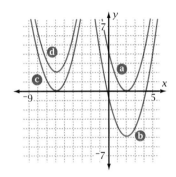

6. a. Describe a two-step process for sliding $f(x) = x^2$ to the location of $f(x - 5) - 3$, as pictured at the right.
  b. Write the equation of this parabola in $y=$ form.
  c. Where is the vertex of this parabola?
  d. What are the coordinates of the other four points if they are one and two horizontal units from the vertex?
  e. What is the length of segment b? Of segment c?

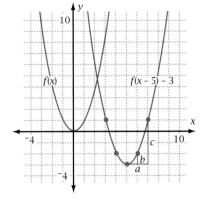

7. Write the equation and graph each parabola on your calculator. (Each parabola is congruent to $y = x^2$.)

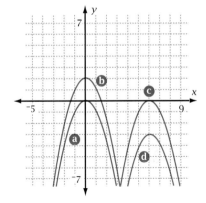

8. Write the equation of a graph that is congruent to $y = {}^-1(x + 3)^2 + 4$, but shifted five units right and two units down.

9. The **graphing form** of the equation of a parabola is often written as $y = \pm 1(x - h)^2 + k$. Based on your work in the previous problems, explain the effect of ± 1, h, and k on the graph of the parent function. Be as explicit as possible.

10. Write an equation of the form $y = \pm 1(x - h)^2 + k$ that provides the table values for the (*length, area*) data of Example 1 in this section. Graph your equation to check your answer.

11. Make a table of values that compares the number of teams in a league and the number of games required for each team to play every other team twice (once at home and once away from home).

Number of teams	1	2	3	. . .	10
Number of games	0	2	6	. . .	–?–

Plot each point and describe the graph produced. Write an explicit function for this graph.

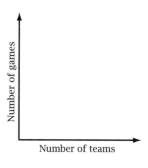

Number of games

Number of teams

12. The height of a bowling ball dropped from the top of a 64-foot tower is given by $h = {}^-16t^2 + 64$, where t is the number of seconds after the ball has been dropped, and h is the height of the ball in feet. The questions here will look at the average height of the ball during the first two seconds.

a. Make a table showing the time and the height of the ball when it is dropped, when it hits the ground, and every $\frac{1}{2}$ sec in between. Then average these heights.

b. Find the average height by using the heights every $\frac{1}{4}$ sec.

c. Find the average height by using the heights every $\frac{1}{10}$ sec.

d. Explain the differences in your answers to 12a, b, and c. Which best answers the question, "What is the average height?" Why?

Take Another Look 5.4

How familiar are you with the Periodic Table of Elements? Have you or will you soon take a chemistry course? Make a scatter-plot of (*atomic number, atomic mass*) for the first 12 elements listed. Find the least-squares model for this information. Find the residuals for the first 12 elements using this model. Then use your model to predict the atomic mass of mercury, copper, lead, silver, and gold. Find the residuals for these five elements and discuss the accuracy of this model. Ask a chemistry teacher or chemistry-aware friends to help you find the information you need.

Project

Even and Odd Functions

Graph each of the functions $y = x^2$, $y = \sqrt{4 - x^2}$, and $y = |x|$. Describe any symmetry appearing in these graphs. These functions are examples of **even functions**. A function f is even when $f(^-x) = f(x)$ for all defined values of x. Explain how this definition relates to the symmetry you see in the graphs.

Graph these examples of **odd functions**: $y = x^3$, $y = \frac{1}{x}$, and $y = \sqrt[3]{x}$. Now rotate your calculator 180°. Each graph will look the same as it looked before the rotation. This property is called symmetry with respect to the origin. Odd functions are defined as those functions f where $^-f(x) = f(^-x)$ for all defined values of x. Explain how this definition relates to the symmetry you see in the graphs.

Give an example of a function that is neither even nor odd. Graph your example and explain why you think it qualifies.

When functions are combined, the symmetry may change. Use functions from the examples given for even and odd functions above to investigate what happens when even and odd functions are combined. Is the result even, odd, or neither? Make a table like the one below and record your results. The notation $f(g(x))$, which is used to combine functions, may be unfamiliar to you. If so, be sure to read Section 5.9 for an explanation.

	$f(g(x))$	$g(f(x))$	$f(x) + g(x)$	$f(x)g(x)$	$\frac{f(x)}{g(x)}$
$f(x)$ even, $g(x)$ even	–?–	–?–	–?–	–?–	–?–
$f(x)$ even, $g(x)$ odd	–?–	–?–	–?–	–?–	–?–
$f(x)$ odd, $g(x)$ odd	–?–	–?–	–?–	–?–	–?–

Choose three entries from the table and prove your result. A sample proof is given below.

Prove: If $f(x)$ is even and $g(x)$ is odd, $f(g(x))$ is even.

If $g(x)$ is odd, then $g(^-x) = ^-g(x)$. This means $f(g(^-x)) = f(^-g(x))$.

If $f(x)$ is even, then $f(^-g(x)) = f(g(x))$.

Therefore, $f(g(^-x)) = f(g(x))$ and hence $f(g(x))$ is even.

The Square Root Family

*The pursuit of pretty formulas and neat theorems can no doubt quickly
degenerate into a silly vice, but so can the quest for austere generalities which are
so very general indeed that they are incapable of application to any particular.*
—Eric Temple Bell

The square root graph is another parent
function that can be used to illustrate
transformations. Both the domain and range of
$f(x) = \sqrt{x}$ are real numbers that are zero or
greater. If you trace the graph, there are no
function values for y unless x is at least zero.
Trace to show that $\sqrt{3}$ is approximately 1.732 and
that $\sqrt{8}$ is approximately 2.828. Describe how you
would use the graph to find $\sqrt{31}$. What happens
when you try to trace for values of $x < 0$? What is
$\sqrt{-4}$?

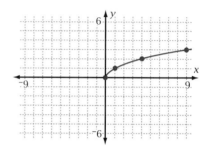

Investigation 5.5.1

Pendulum Experiment

For this investigation, the group will need some string and an object to use as a
weight. You will also need a stopwatch or a watch with a second hand.

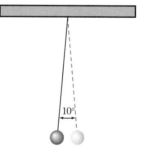

a. Tie the weight at one end of a length of string. Firmly hold the other end of the
string or tie it to something, so that the weight hangs freely.

b. Measure the length from the center of the weight to the point where the string is
held.

c. Carefully extend and release the weight so that it swings back and forth in a short arc of about 10°. Time ten complete swings; forward and back is one swing.

d. Find the period by dividing by ten. The period of your pendulum is the time for one complete swing (forward and back).

e. Repeat the experiment for several different string lengths and complete a table of values like the one below. Use a variety of short, medium, and long string lengths. Save these data for one of the problems in Problem Set 5.5.

Length (cm)	–?–	–?–	–?–	–?–	–?–	–?–
Period	–?–	–?–	–?–	–?–	–?–	–?–

You can use the square root function when finding the height of a falling object. Example 1 shows you how to do this.

■ Example 1

An object falls to the ground because of the influence of gravity. When an object is dropped from a height of d meters, the height after t seconds is given by $h(t) = {}^-4.9t^2 + d$. If an object is dropped from a height of 1000 meters, the height of the object at any given time (in seconds) is given by the function $h(t) = {}^-4.9t^2 + 1000$. How long does it take for the object to reach the ground?

Solution

You are finding the time until the height will be 0.

$$0 = {}^-4.9t^2 + 1000 \qquad \text{Set the height} = 0.$$

$$4.9t^2 = 1000 \qquad \text{Add } 4.9t^2 \text{ to both sides.}$$

$$t^2 = \frac{1000}{4.9} \qquad \text{Divide both sides by 4.9.}$$

$$t = \sqrt{\frac{1000}{4.9}} \approx 14.3 \text{ seconds} \qquad \text{Take the square root of both sides.} \quad ■$$

Certainly the falling time depends on the starting height. How long will it be until an object reaches the ground, if it is dropped from 800 meters? From 650 meters? From d meters? This is just one of many functional relationships involving the square root function.

Problem Set 5.5

1. Write the equation for each transformed graph. The parent function is $y = \sqrt{x}$. Verify each answer by graphing it on your calculator.

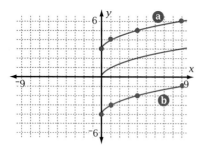
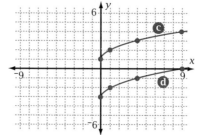

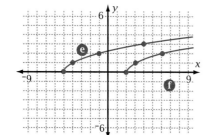
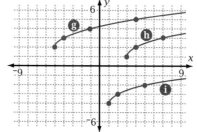

2. **a.** What happens to the graph $y = \sqrt{x}$ if x is replaced with $(x - 3)$? With $(x + 3)$?

   b. What happens to the graph $y = \sqrt{x}$ if y is replaced with $(y - 2)$? With $(y + 2)$?

3. Write an equation for each of the three graphs below.

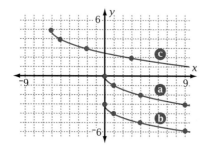

4. Consider the parent function $f(x) = \sqrt{x}$.

   a. Name three pairs of integer coordinates that are on the graph of $f(x + 4) - 2$.

   b. Write $f(x + 4) - 2$ in $y=$ form and graph it.

   c. Write $^-f(x - 2) + 3$ in $y=$ form and graph it.

5. a. Graph this parabola (shown at right) on your own calculator. (Hint: You will need to graph two functions.)

b. Combine the two functions in 5a and write the equation in condensed form, $y = \pm\sqrt{x}$. When both sides of this equation are squared, what is the resulting equation?

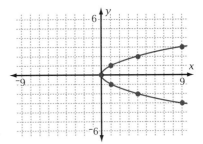

6. Refer to the two parabolas at the right.

a. Explain why neither graph represents a function.

b. Write equations for each parabola in the condensed form $y = \pm$(a square root expression).

c. Square both sides of each equation in 6b. What is the resulting equation for each parabola?

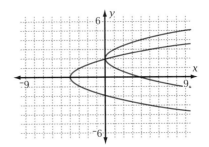

7. Graph the parabola $(y - 2)^2 = x + 3$.

8. Write the equation for each graph.

a.

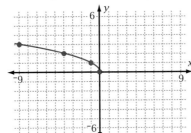

b.

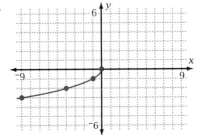

9. a. Enter the data collected during Investigation 5.5.1 into your calculator.

b. Plot the data, and write an equation that best fits the data. Graph the residuals.

c. Use your model to predict the period for a 10-meter pendulum length.

d. Find the length for a clock pendulum that has a period of one second.

10. The following table provides information about the (*distance, velocity*) relationship for an object dropped near the earth's surface. The distance the object has fallen is measured in feet, and velocity is in feet per second. Use guess-and-check to write a square root function that provides a good fit for the data.

Distance (ft)	0	2.5	5	10	15	20	25
Velocity (ft/sec)	0	12.65	17.89	25.30	30.98	35.78	40.00

11. Using **Calculator Note 5C** as a guide, write a program that will randomly generate graphs of square root functions. Give a line-by-line explanation describing how the program works.

NOTE
5C

Take Another Look 5.5

Example 1 in this section describes the height of a falling object dropped from a height of 1000 meters. You will now use similar functions to describe a ball that is thrown vertically at 32 m/sec. How high do you think it will get before falling back to the ground? How long will it take before the ball hits the ground? Make two sketches that show (*time, height*) and (*time, velocity*) of the thrown ball. (The velocity of the moving ball is the ratio $\frac{\text{difference in height}}{\text{difference in time}}$ for two different positions. Positive, zero, and negative velocity values can help you interpret the ball's movement.)

a. The functions $h(t) = {}^-4.9t^2 + 32t + 2.1$ and $v(t) = {}^-9.8t + 32$ can be used to predict the height and velocity at any time while a thrown object is moving. Graph the two functions simultaneously.

Time (sec)	Height (m)	Velocity (m/sec)
0	–?–	–?–
1	–?–	–?–
2	–?–	–?–
3	–?–	–?–
4	–?–	–?–
5	–?–	–?–
6	–?–	–?–
7	–?–	–?–

 i. Complete a table like the one above, giving the height and velocity for each time listed.

 ii. Find the maximum height of the ball and the time it takes to reach that height. What is the velocity when the ball is at its maximum height? Describe the velocity before and after that time.

 iii. Explain the relationship between the two graphs before the maximum height, at the maximum height, and after the maximum height.

 iv. Describe realistic domains and ranges for the two functions.

 v. In the context of this activity, describe the real-world meaning of every variable, number, operation, and expression term in each of the two functions provided.

b. Find the velocity of the ball at the time it hit the ground and explain how you determined this.

c. The graph of the (*time, height*) relationship is symmetrical. Carefully explain the height and velocity implications of this symmetry.

Section 5.6

The Absolute Value Family

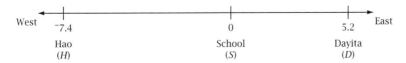

The test of a first-rate intelligence is the ability to hold two opposed ideas in the mind at the same time, and still retain the ability to function.
—F. Scott Fitzgerald

Hao and Dayita ride the subway to school each day. They live on the same east-west subway route. Hao lives 7.4 miles west of the school, and Dayita lives 5.2 miles east of the school. This information is shown on the number line below.

West ◄─────┼──────────────────────┼──────────────────┼─────► East
         −7.4   0   5.2
         Hao   School   Dayita
         (H)   (S)   (D)

The distance from Hao's stop to school, *HS,* is 7.4 units. The distance from Hao's stop to Dayita's stop, *HD,* is 12.6 units. When you talk about distance, you usually don't mention direction, unless you're interested in the directed distance. Therefore, a distance will be either positive or zero.

This is exactly what the **absolute value** function does. It makes numbers positive or zero. The job is easy when the number is zero or a positive number, and not difficult when the number is negative. The mathematical notation for the absolute value of ⁻3, or the distance from ⁻3

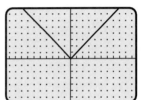

to the origin, is |⁻3|. What is the value of |⁻3|? What is the value of |5.2 − ⁻7.4|, the distance from *D* to *H*? What is the value of |13.4|?

The absolute value function was first described by the French mathematician Augustin-Louis Cauchy in the 1820s. The symbol used today for absolute value was introduced by the German mathematician Karl Weierstrass in 1841.

When you determined the absolute deviation, or the distance from a data point to the mean, you were using the absolute value function. You also used this function when finding the mean absolute value of the residuals.

In this section you will learn about the graph of $y = |x|$ as another example of a function that can be transformed. The parent function $y = |x|$ is shown at the right. Graph this equation on your calculator. In the upcoming problems, you will find equations of the form $y = a|x - h| + k$. What you have learned about moving other graphs will work with this function as well.

Problem Set 5.6

In Problems 1–6, write the equation of each graph. Be sure to check each equation by graphing it on your calculator.

1.

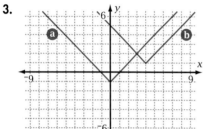

2.

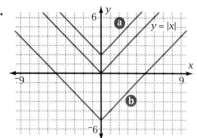

3.

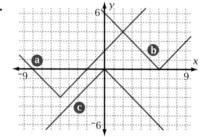

4.

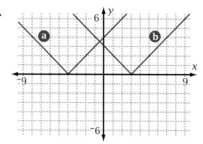

5.

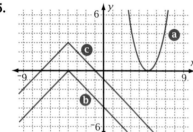

6.

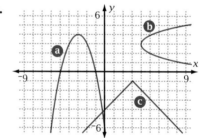

7. a. If $f(x) = |x|$, what is the equation in $y=$ form for $^-f(x - 2) + 3$?
   b. Describe the transformations needed to move $f(x)$ into this position.

8. a. What is the graphic result when x is replaced by $(x - 5)$ in an equation?
   b. What is the graphic result when x is replaced by ^-x in an equation?
   c. What is the graphic result when y is replaced by $(y - 3)$ in an equation?
   d. What is the graphic result when y is replaced by ^-y in an equation?

9. At the right is an illustration of how to solve the equation $|x - 4| = 3$ graphically. The equations $y_1 = |x - 4|$ and $y_2 = 3$ were graphed on the same coordinate axes.

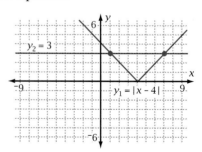

What is the x-coordinate of each point of intersection? What x-values are solutions of the equation $|x - 4| = 3$?

10. Solve the equation $|x + 3| = 5$ using the method shown in Problem 9. Sketch the graph on your paper, and indicate where the solutions are on the graph.

11. Graph two equations that show the x-value(s) when $-(x + 3)^2 + 5 = |x - 1| - 4$. Sketch a graph on your paper and indicate where the solutions are on your graph. Trace and zoom to find these values to the nearest 0.1.

12. Sketch the graphs of $y = x$, $y = -x$, and $y = |x|$ on the same axes. Use a different colored pen or pencil for each equation. Study the three graphs, especially where they overlap, and write a definition of $|x|$ in terms of x and $-x$.

13. Each year the local school district schedules a mathematics and science fair. A panel of judges rates each exhibit. The ratings for the top 20 exhibits are shown in the table.

Exhibit	1	2	3	4	5	6	7	8	9	10
Rating	68	71	73	77	79	79	81	83	83	84

Exhibit	11	12	13	14	15	16	17	18	19	20
Rating	85	86	88	89	89	90	92	92	92	94

The judges decide that the top rating should be 100, so they add 6 points to each rating score.

a. What was the mean and the mean absolute deviation of the ratings before raising them? After raising them? What do you notice about the change in the mean? In the mean absolute deviation?

b. Plot the original ratings, using the exhibit number as the x-coordinate.

c. Plot the raised ratings on the same graph. Describe how the alteration of the ratings affected the graph.

14. You can use a single receiver to find the distance to a homing transmitter by measuring the strength of the signal, but you cannot determine the direction from which the signal is emanating. The following distances were measured while driving east along a straight road. Find a model that closely fits the data. Where do you think the homing transmitter might be located?

Miles traveled	0	4	8	12	16	20	24	28	32	36
Distance to object	18.4	14.4	10.5	6.6	3.0	2.6	6.0	9.9	13.8	17.8

Section 5.7

Stretching a Curve

My method to overcome a difficulty is to go around it.
—George Polya

You have explored several functions and moved them around the plane. You know that a horizontal translation occurs when x is replaced by $(x - h)$, and a vertical translation occurs when y is replaced by $(y - k)$. You have flipped, or reflected, graphs over the y-axis and x-axis by replacing x with (^-x), and y with (^-y), respectively. In each case, however, the final image was the same size and shape as (or congruent to) the original graph.

You can also distort a graph so that the image isn't congruent to the original graph. One of the easiest ways to do this is to stretch the y-values, or the x-values, or both. In Section 5.5 you stretched the graph of $y = \sqrt{x}$ to fit the (*distance, velocity*) relationship for an object dropped near the earth's surface. Using guess-and-check, you were able to show that $v = 8\sqrt{d}$ provides a good fit with the data.

Distance (ft)	0	2.5	5	10	15	20	25
Velocity (ft/sec)	0	12.65	17.89	25.30	30.98	35.78	40.00

The graph that shows distortions most clearly is the circle. Suppose P is a point on a unit circle with center at the origin. A **unit circle** has a radius of one unit.

You can derive the equation of a circle from this diagram by using the Pythagorean theorem. The equation is $x^2 + y^2 = 1$, because the legs of the right triangle are of lengths x and y and the length of the hypotenuse is one unit.

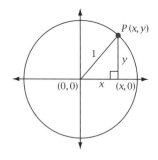

Equation of a Unit Circle

$x^2 + y^2 = 1$ is the equation of a **unit circle** with center $(0, 0)$.

What is the domain and range of this circle? If a value, like 0.5, is substituted for x, what are the output values of y? Is the graph a function? Why or why not?

In order to draw the graph of a circle on your calculator, you will need to solve the above equation for y. When you do this, you will get two equations, $y = {}^+\sqrt{1 - x^2}$ and $y = {}^-\sqrt{1 - x^2}$. By graphing both of these equations, you will be able to draw the complete circle. Be sure to use a "friendly" graphing window so that the circle will look like a circle and not an ellipse.

Problem Set 5.7

When possible, verify your work by graphing each equation on your calculator. Be sure to use a "friendly" graphing window.

1. The equation $y = \sqrt{1 - x^2}$ is the equation for the top half of the unit circle with center at $(0, 0)$ shown on the left. Alter this equation to graph the figure on the right below. What is the equation of the semicircle after it has been stretched vertically?

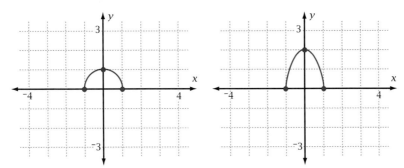

2. Write the equation of each graph. The graph will be a **stretched** or **compressed** version of $y = \sqrt{1 - x^2}$.

a.

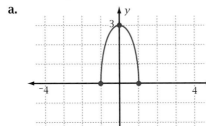

b.

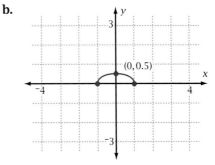

3. Consider the function $f(x) = \sqrt{1 - x^2}$, and graph each of the functions below.
   a. $^-f(x)$
   b. $^-2f(x)$
   c. $2f(x) - 3$

4. Write an equation in *y*= form for each graph.

a.

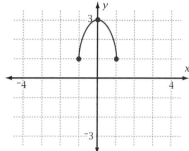

b.

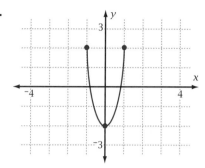

5. Suppose the top half of the unit circle with center $(0, 0)$ is named $f(x)$.

a. Write the equation of each graph below in terms of $f(x)$.

b. Write the *y*= form of each graph.

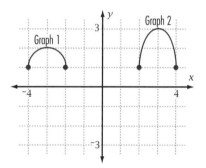

6. Write an equation in *y*= form for each graph below.

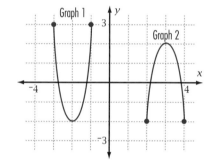

7. Write an equation, and graph each distortion of the unit semicircle.

a. Replace *y* by $(y - 2)$.

b. Replace *x* by $(x + 3)$.

c. Replace *y* by $\frac{y}{2}$.

d. Replace *x* by $\frac{x}{2}$.

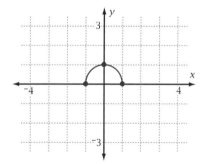

8. a. Write the equation of the distorted semicircle shown below. The *x*-coordinate of each point has been stretched by a factor of three.

b. What term did you use to replace *x* in the parent equation?

c. If $f(x)$ was the original semicircle, then what is this new function in $f(x)$ notation?

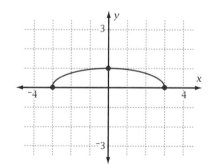

9. In the figure below, the *y*-coordinate of each point of the semicircle has been stretched by a factor of two, and the *x*-coordinate has been stretched by a factor of three.

   a. What is the equation of this set of points?

   b. What is the equation of the reflection image over the *x*-axis?

10. Given the semicircle pictured below, write the equation that generates each distortion.

   a. Each *y*-value is half the original *y*-value.

   b. Each *x*-value is half the original *x*-value.

   c. Each *y*-value is half the original *y*-value, and each *x*-value is twice the original *x*-value.

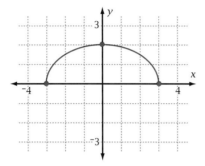

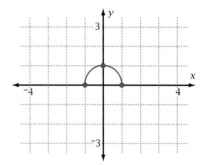

11. a. Write two equations that can be used to graph this relation.

   b. Write one equation in $y = \pm$ form that could be used to replace the two equations in 11a.

   c. Write another equation by squaring both sides of the equation in 11b.

12. Write the equation of the transformed semicircle, pictured below, in the following forms.

   a. In *y*= form

   b. In $f(x)$ form

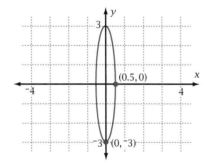

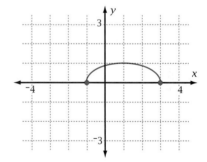

13. Refer to Problem Set 5.6, Problem 13. After the judges raised the rating scores by adding the same number to each score, one of the judges suggested that perhaps they should have multiplied the original scores by a factor that would make the highest score equal 100. They decided to try this method.

Exhibit	1	2	3	4	5	6	7	8	9	10
Rating	68	71	73	77	79	79	81	83	83	84

Exhibit	11	12	13	14	15	16	17	18	19	20
Rating	85	86	88	89	89	90	92	92	92	94

a. By what factor should they multiply the highest score, 94, to get 100?

b. Use this same multiplier to alter all of the scores, and record the altered scores.

c. What is the mean and the mean absolute deviation of the original scores? Of the altered scores?

d. Plot the original and altered scores on the same graph. Describe what happened to the scores visually. How does this explain what happened to the mean and the mean absolute deviation?

e. Which method do you think the judges should use? Explain your reasoning.

14. What is the average value of the function $y = \sqrt{1 - x^2}$ in the interval between $x = {}^-1$ and $x = 1$?

a. Find the value of the function at $^-1$, $^-0.5$, 0, 0.5, and 1. Then average these values.

b. Find the value of the function at $^-1$, $^-0.8$, $^-0.6$, . . . , 0.8, and 1. Then average these values.

c. Repeat this process once more using more closely spaced x-values.

NOTE
5D

d. Compare the answers from 14a, b, and c. If you continue this process with more and more closely spaced x-values, what would you expect to get for an average value? You can use a program that will compute the average value of a function. (See **Calculator Note 5D.**)

e. Give a line-by-line explanation of how the average value program works.

15. You probably used your graphing calculator quite a bit in this chapter to explore several families of graphs. Some people might think it isn't necessary to study these families because graphing calculators are available. What do you think? Support your opinion with clear statements and examples.

Project

The Greatest Integer Function

In this chapter you have studied in detail five parent functions and several generic functions. You have shifted, flipped, and stretched functions. In this project you will look at a quite different, but important, parent function known as the greatest integer function. Its full name is the "Greatest Integer Less Than or Equal To Function." The symbol $[\![x]\!]$ is used for this function, but most computers and calculators use int(x) in the same way abs(x) is used for absolute value. Change the calculator mode to *disconnected* or *dot graphs* to study this function, because the function is not always smooth and it jumps at times. (See **Calculator Note 5E** for specific notes on your calculator.)

NOTE 5E

Your task is to explain what the function does, to describe its graph with both words and pictures, and to give a detailed account using complete sentences of how this function behaves with shifts, flips, and stretches (both vertical and horizontal). Look at both the overall nature of the function and at what happens at specific x-values, such as 2.5, 4.7, ⁻3.1, 5, ⁻4, and so on.

Geometer's Sketchpad Investigation

Transforming a Point and a Line

It is sometimes difficult to see exactly what happens when you apply transformations to a line. However, by using Sketchpad and by looking at a point on the line and then tracing its locus, you can better visualize these transformations.

Part 1   In Part 1 of this investigation you will explore how translations affect the equation and the graph of a line.

Step 1   Choose Create Axes from the Graph menu, and draw line n anywhere.

Step 2   Construct point E on line n and measure its coordinates.

Step 3   Translate point E horizontally 3 cm. Label this new point F. Measure the coordinates of point F.

Step 4   Select point F and choose Trace Point. Move point E along line n and observe the path of point F.

Step 5   Construct another point on line n and label this point G. Translate point G to point H by using the same transformation that was used in Step 3.

Step 6   Construct a line through point F and point H. Label this line m.

Step 7   Measure the equations of line n and line m.

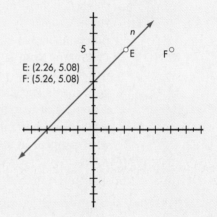

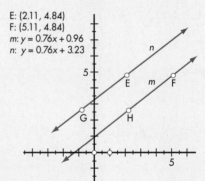

Questions

1. Observe how the coordinates of point F change with respect to the coordinates of point E. Describe the locus of point F with respect to point E.

2. Compare the equations for line n and line m. How did the transformation affect the slope and the y-intercept of the original line?

3. What happens as you rotate the original line? When does the translated line become concurrent with the original line?

4. Experiment with other horizontal and vertical translation components. What happens when you do both a horizontal and a vertical transformation at the same time? Summarize your discoveries.

Part 2   In this part of the investigation you will see how stretches affect the equation and the graph of a line.

Step 1   Start with a new sketch. Choose Create Axes from the Graph menu, and draw line *n*.

Step 2   Construct point *E* on line *n* and measure its coordinates.

Step 3   Construct a line through point *E* that is perpendicular to the *x*-axis. Construct the point of intersection of this line with the *x*-axis. Label this point *F*.

Step 4   Mark point *F* as a center, and dilate point *E* around this center by 60%. Label this dilated point *G*. Measure the coordinates of point *G*. Hide the perpendicular line and point *F*.

Step 5   Select point *G* and choose Trace Point. Move point *E* along line *n* and observe the path of point *G*.

Step 6   Calculate the ratio of the *y*-coordinate of point *G* to the *y*-coordinate of point *E*.

Step 7   Construct another point on line *n* and label this point *H*. Construct a line through point *H* that is perpendicular to the *x*-axis. Construct the point of intersection of this line with the *x*-axis. Label this point *K*.

Step 8   Mark point *K* as a center and dilate point *H* around this center by 60%. Label this dilated point *J*. Measure the coordinates of point *J*. Hide the perpendicular line and point *K*.

Step 9   Construct a line through point *G* and point *J*. Label this line *m*.

Step 10   Measure the equations of line *n* and line *m*.

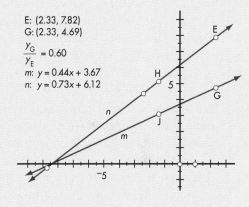

E: (2.33, 7.82)
G: (2.33, 4.69)

$$\frac{y_G}{y_E} = 0.60$$

m: y = 0.44x + 3.67
n: y = 0.73x + 6.12

Questions

1. Try dynamically changing the position and slope of line *n*. Does the relationship between the equations of the two lines stay the same? What is the relationship?

2. Unless the two lines are parallel to the *x*-axis, both of the lines intersect at a point where *y* = 0. Use algebra to show why.

3. Open a new sketch and do a similar construction to show the effect of a dilation on the *x*-coordinate of a point. Explore what happens if you apply a horizontal stretch on a line.

Section 5.8

A Summary

In this chapter, you have studied a variety of graphs. You have learned how to recognize a graph and match it with its basic, or parent, equation.

Graph	Parent equation
line	$y = mx + b$
square root	$y = \sqrt{x}$
absolute value	$y = |x|$
parabola	$y = x^2$
semicircle	$y = \sqrt{1 - x^2}$

A **function** is a relationship between two variables in which there is exactly one value of the dependent variable (y) for each value of the independent variable (x). You see functions as graphs, equations, two-variable data, or verbal descriptions. Function equations can be defined recursively or explicitly. The data might be in the form of points (x, y) or tables of information. But in each instance where y is a **function** of x, exactly one output value is paired with each input value. Graph A displays this quality. If you draw a vertical line at any x-value, it will not intersect the graph at more than one point. This is called the **vertical line test** to determine if a graph is a graph of a function.

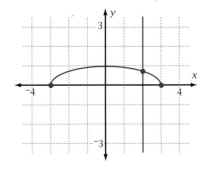

Graph A

Graph B doesn't qualify as a function because it's possible to find an instance where there is more than one output value for an input value, as shown by the vertical line intersecting the graph in more than one point. The graph fails the vertical line test. The graph still qualifies as a relation, however. Every graph is a **relation**, or correspondence, between variables.

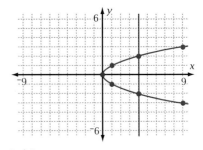

Graph B

The **domain of a function** is the set of allowable input values for the independent variable, while the **range of a function** is the set of resulting output values. The domain of the function described by the graph at the top of page 239 is all real numbers, and the range is real numbers greater than or equal to $^-1$.

The notation $f(x)$ has been used to identify a relation as a function. It offers an easy and standard way of identifying points and indicating transformations. For example, the graph of $y = 2(x + 3)^2 - 1$ is a function, and the equation can be written in function form like this: $f(x) = 2(x + 3)^2 - 1$. The graph is a parabola with the **vertex** at $(-3, -1)$ and a **line of symmetry** at $x = -3$. The graph is congruent to the graph of $y = 2x^2$ (a stretched version of $y = x^2$). The notation $f(-2)$ represents the y-coordinate when x is -2. So $f(-2) = 1$.

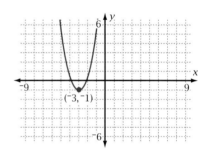

Translations, reflections, stretches or compressions of graphs, and combinations of these, all qualify as transformations. Translations and reflections produce images that remain congruent to the original image. However, with stretches and compressions (like the vertical distortion caused by $af(x)$) the original graph and the new graph are *not* congruent.

In many of the following problems, you will combine translations with stretches or compressions. At times the order won't make any difference. You will always be correct, however, if you perform any stretches *before* you translate points vertically.

Problem Set 5.8

1. Suppose the function pictured is $f(x)$.
   a. $f(3) = -?-$
   b. $f(-2) = -?-$
   c. When is $f(x) = 0$?
   d. When is $f(x) = 2$?
   e. What is the range, R_f, of f?
   f. What is the domain, D_f, of f?

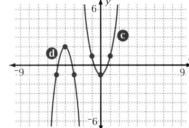

2. Using the graph in Problem 1 as function f, carefully sketch a separate graph of each transformation.
   a. $f(x) - 3$ **b.** $f(x - 3)$ **c.** $-f(x)$
   d. $2f(x) - 3$ **e.** $f(-x)$ **f.** $f\left(\dfrac{x}{2}\right)$

3. Use what you know about translations and stretches to write an equation for each graph a–h. Then check your answer by graphing each equation on your calculator.

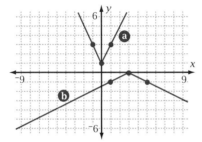

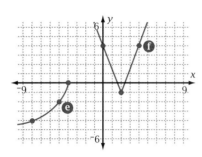
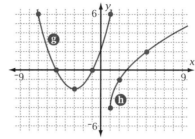

4. Respond to each of the following with a selection from {all, some, none}. If your choice is some or none, then draw an instance where the graph isn't a function.
  a. Circles are functions.
  b. Parabolas are functions.
  c. Lines are functions.

5. Suppose $f(x) = x^2$. Name a sequence of transformations, in a correct order, that will change $f(x)$ into each equation below.
  a. $y = 2x^2 - 3$ **b.** $y = (x - 4)^2 - 2$
  c. $y = ^-(x + 3)^2 + 1$ **d.** $y = 0.5(x - 2)^2 - 3$

6. Rewrite each equation without parentheses. Graph both forms of the equation to check your work.
  a. $y = 2(x - 4)^2 + 1$
  b. $y = ^-(x + 3)^2 + 2$
  c. $y = 0.5(x - 2)^2 - 3$

NOTE
5D

7. In previous problems you found the average value of a function. The value of a function at any point can be thought of as the height of the graph above the x-axis. Therefore, the average value can be considered the average height of the graph. Draw the graph of $y = ^-(x - 3)^2 + 4$ for $x = 1$ to $x = 5$. (See **Calculator Note 5D**.)
  a. Calculate the average value of the function over this interval. Evaluate the function at each endpoint, and at every 0.2 units in between. Average these values.
  b. Calculate the average value again using values of x every 0.1 unit.
  c. What do you think the average value would be if you used extremely closely spaced x-values? Support your answer.
  d. Draw a rectangle using the interval on the x-axis as the base, and the average height of the function as the height of the rectangle. What is the area of this rectangle?
  e. How do you think this compares with the area enclosed by the curve? Explain.

8. Describe a procedure to find the area indicated in the graph at the right.

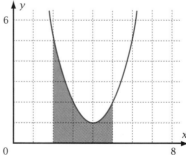

9. The Canz4U Container Corporation receives 450 drums of plastic packing pellets every 30 days. The inventory function (drums on hand as a function of days) is

$$I(d) = 450 - \frac{d^2}{2}.$$

Find the average daily inventory. If the cost of keeping one drum is two cents per day, find the average daily holding cost.

10. Solve each equation for y, and draw the graph.

    a. $2x - 3y = {}^-12$ **b.** ${}^-2(x + 1.5) + 3(y - 2) - 3 = 0$

    c. $\frac{y}{2} = (x - 3)^2 - 2$ **d.** ${}^-y + \frac{(x - 3)^2}{2} = 1$

11. Suppose f is a linear function. What is its equation if $f(2) = 6$ and $f({}^-3) = {}^-4$?

12. The distances needed to stop a car on dry pavement in a minimum length of time for various speeds are shown in the table below. Reaction time is considered to be 0.75 sec.

Speed (mi/hr)	10	20	30	40	50	60	70
Stopping distance (ft)	19	42	73	116	173	248	343

    a. Construct a scatter plot for this data.

    b. Use guess-and-check to find the equation of a parabola that "best" fits the points; graph it.

    c. Find the residual sum for this equation.

    d. Predict the stopping distance from 56.5 mi/hr.

    e. How fast are you traveling if you need a stopping distance of 385 ft?

13. You have studied several families of functions (parabolas, square roots, absolute value, semicircles) and transformations of these functions. Discuss the similarities and differences of these transformations among the families.

Project

Boolean Graphs

The self-taught English logician George Boole (1815–1864) described Boolean expressions in his book *An Investigation into the Laws of Thought*. (He didn't call them "Boolean expressions" though; they were later named after him.) The aim of *The Laws of Thought* was to "investigate the fundamental laws of those operations of the mind by which reasoning is performed; to give expression to them in the symbolical language of a Calculus, and upon this foundation to establish the science of Logic and construct its method."

George Boole

A Boolean expression is interpreted to be true or false. If you divide an expression by another expression like ($x \geq 3$), the graph of the function will "disappear" when x is less than three because this value will make the expression false (= 0). Because the calculator cannot divide by zero, it will ignore that part of the graph.

Write a program that will draw a picture on the graphics screen of your calculator. Incorporate all five of the functions that have been covered in this chapter. The example below is of a car drawn in the window $0 \leq x \leq 9.4$ and $0 \leq y \leq 6.2$ on a TI-82 graphics calculator. The domains for some functions have been limited, or restricted, by using Boolean expressions that specify x-values over which to graph that function.

Prgm6:CAR
:ClrDraw
:DrawF $1/(x \geq 1)(x \leq 9)$
:DrawF $(1.2\sqrt{(x - 1)} + 1)/(x \leq 3.5)$
:DrawF $(1.2\sqrt{-(x - 9)} + 1/(x \geq 6.5)$
:DrawF $(-.5(x - 5)^2 + 4)/(x \geq 3.5)(x \leq 6.5)$
:DrawF $-\sqrt{(1 - (x - 2.5)^2)} + 1$
:DrawF $-\sqrt{(1 - (x - 7.5)^2)} + 1$
:DrawF $(abs(x - 5.5) + 2)/(x \geq 5.2)(x \leq 5.8)$

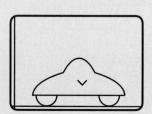

Include at least one example of each of the five functions when drawing your picture. Use translations, stretches, and vertical and horizontal flips. In your project report, explain each line of program code in terms of the transformations made on the parent function, and also explain which part of the picture was created by each equation.

Section 5.9

Compositions of Functions

One cannot escape the feeling that these mathematical formulas have an independent existence and an intelligence of their own, that they are wiser than we are, wiser even than their discoverers, that we get more out of them than was originally put into them.
—Heinrich Hertz

Many times, you will encounter two functions that are related, and you may need both functions in order to answer a question or analyze a problem. Graph A shows the radius of a spreading oil slick, from a leaking offshore well, growing as a function of time, $r = f(t)$. Graph B shows the area of the circular oil slick as a function of its radius, $a = g(r)$. Time is measured in hours, the radius is measured in kilometers, and the area is measured in square kilometers.

■ **Example 1**

Use the graphs to find the area of the oil slick after 4 hr.

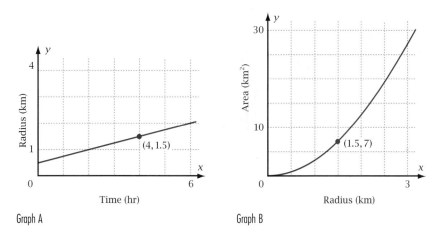

Graph A   Graph B

Solution

From Graph A, you find the radius is 1.5 km when $t = 4$ hr. From Graph B, you find that a radius of 1.5 km indicates an area of approximately 7 km². ■

In the example above, two different functions, represented by their graphs, helped you find the solution. You actually used the output from one function as an input in the other function. This is an example of the composition of two functions to form a new functional relation between area and time, area $= g(f(t))$. Notice that $f(t)$ is the output from Graph A and the input in Graph B.

The symbol $g(f(x))$, read "g of f of x," is a **composition** of the two functions f and g. The composition $g(f(x))$ gives the final outcome when an x-value is substituted into the inner function f, and its value $f(x)$ is then substituted into the outer function g.

You have actually been composing functions when you transformed graphs using two or more steps. The function $3f(x) - 1$ is obtained by first stretching a function $f(x)$ by a factor of three to get a new image, and then subtracting 1 from these new y-values to slide the graph down one unit. (Remember to perform stretches before you do any vertical translations.)

■ **Example 2**

Consider the line pictured on the left below as an inner function, perhaps

$$f(x) = \frac{3x}{4} - 3.$$

Suppose g is the absolute value function. Then $g(f(x))$ will be the absolute value of the inner linear function $f(x)$. What will $g(f(x))$ look like?

Solution

The solution is the composition graph on the right. Take a minute or so to make sure you understand why this graph shows the solution.

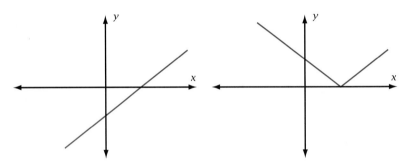

■

■ **Example 3**

Suppose $g(x) = 3x - 7$ and $f(x) = \frac{1}{x}$.

Determine the value for each function composition.

a. $f(g(4))$ **b.** $f(g(x))$ **c.** $D_{f(g(x))}$ **d.** $g(f(4))$

Solution

a. First, $g(4) = 3(4) - 7 = 5$. Therefore, $f(g(4)) = f(5) = \frac{1}{5}$.

b. By definition, $g(x) = 3x - 7$. Therefore, $f(g(x)) = f(3x - 7) = \frac{1}{3x - 7}$.

c. The domain required will contain all real numbers except $\frac{7}{3}$, because you cannot allow the denominator of $\frac{1}{3x - 7}$ to be zero.

d. First, $f(4) = \frac{1}{4}$. Therefore, $g\left(\frac{1}{4}\right) = 3\left(\frac{1}{4}\right) - 7 = -6\frac{1}{4}$. ∎

One way to visualize what is happening when you do a composition of functions is to use a three-part graphing procedure. Graph A shows $g(x) = -0.5(x - 5)^2 + 8$, Graph B shows the line $y = x$, and Graph C shows $f(x) = 4(x - 3)^2$.

- Choose an x-value. In this example, an x-value of 2 has been chosen.
- Evaluate $g(2)$ by drawing a vertical line from the x-axis to the function on Graph A.
- Then draw a horizontal line from that point to the line $y = x$ on Graph B. The point where this line intersects the graph has x- and y-coordinates that are the same.
- Now draw a vertical line from this point so that it intersects the graph of the parabola in Graph C. The y-value of this point gives the same result as evaluating f at the y-value of the original function.
- Draw a horizontal line from the intersection point to the y-axis.
- The y-value is $f(g(2))$, or 1.

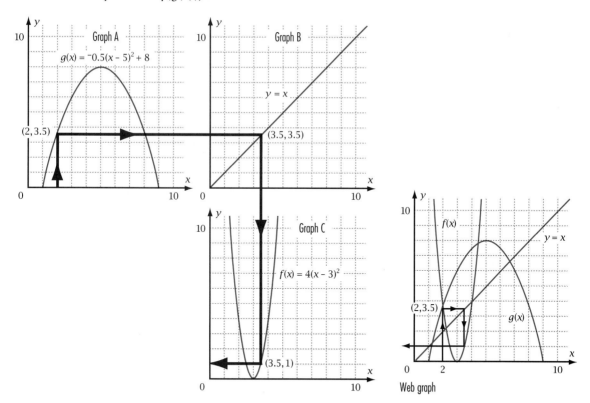

Use the method demonstrated to find $f(g(1.5))$ and $f(g(8.5))$. Trace the path for each composition and estimate the answer. Confirm the result by first calculating $g(x)$ and then substituting this answer into $f(x)$.

This procedure can be shortened by placing each graph on the same axes. When you do this, the graph is called a **web graph**, as shown above. The path then moves from the x-axis to $g(x)$ to the line $y = x$ to $f(x)$ to the y-axis. The order is very important. A modification of this procedure allows you to graphically show $f(f(x))$. In the following investigation, you will explore this process for a specific function.

Investigation 5.9.1

$$f(f(f(f(\ldots f(x)\ldots))))$$

You will need a worksheet with graphs of $y = ax(1 - x)$ for various values of a. Begin with an x-value of 0.3. Use a graphical method similar to the one described above to find $f(f(f(f(\ldots f(x)\ldots))))$. Carefully draw each web graph. Repeat the graphical steps enough times to be able to predict what is going to happen. Did everyone in your group draw the same types of graphs? Describe what happened in each case.

Problem Set 5.9

1. Graph A shows a swimmer's speed as a function of time. Graph B shows the swimmer's oxygen consumption as a function of her speed. Time is measured in seconds, speed in meters per second, and oxygen consumption in liters per minute.

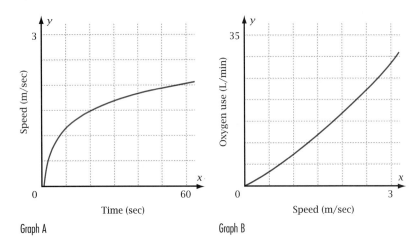

Graph A   Graph B

   a. Use the graphs to find the swimmer's oxygen consumption after 20 sec of swimming.
   b. Sketch the graphs on your paper and draw segments on both graphs that verify your thinking.
   c. How many seconds have elapsed if the swimmer's oxygen consumption is 15 L/min?

2. a. Write the equation in *y*= form for the graph pictured at the right.

   b. Invent two functions *f* and *g* so that the figure is the graph of *f*(*g*(*x*)).

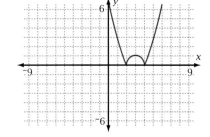

3. A, B, and C are thermometers with different linear scales. When A reads 12 and 36, B reads 13 and 29, respectively. When B reads 20 and 32, C reads 57 and 84, respectively.

   a. Sketch a separate graph for each function. Label the axes.

   b. If A reads 12, what does C read?

   c. Write a function with B depending on A.

   d. Write a function with C depending on B.

   e. Write a function with C depending on A.

4. A graph of the function is shown at the right. Draw a graph of each related function, *h*(*x*), given below.

   a. $h(x) = \sqrt{g(x)}$

   b. $h(x) = |g(x)|$

   c. $h(x) = g(x)^2$

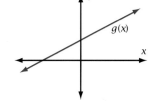

5. Suppose $g = \{(1, 2), (^-2, 4), (5, 5), (6, ^-2)\}$ and $f = \{(0, ^-2), (4, 1), (3, 5), (5, 0)\}$.

   a. Find $g(f(4))$.　　　　　　**b.** Find $f(g(^-2))$.

6. Suppose $g = \{(1, 2), (^-2, 4), (5, 5), (6, ^-2)\}$ and $f = \{(2, 1), (4, ^-2), (5, 5), (^-2, 6)\}$.

   a. Find $g(f(2))$.　　　　　　**b.** Find $f(g(6))$.

   c. Select any number from the domain of either *g* or *f* and find its composite value by using the two functions. Describe what is happening.

7. The two graphs pictured at the right are $f(x) = 2x - 1$ and $g(x) = \frac{1}{2}x + \frac{1}{2}$. Begin by making an accurate copy of the graph. Solve each problem both graphically and numerically.

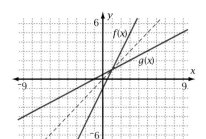

   a. Start with *x* = 2, and find $g(f(2))$.

   b. Start with *x* = ⁻1, and find $f(g(^-1))$.

   c. Pick your own starting *x*-value in the domain of *f*, and find $g(f(x))$.

   d. Pick your own starting *x*-value in the domain of *g*, and find $f(g(x))$.

   e. Carefully describe what is happening in these compositions.

8. Suppose $f(x) = ^-x^2 + 2x + 3$ and $g(x) = (x - 2)^2$. Find each value below, both graphically and algebraically.

   a. $f(g(3))$　　　　**b.** $f(g(2))$　　　　**c.** $g(f(0.5))$　　　　**d.** $g(f(1))$

9. Your calculator can create graphical compositions like those in Investigation 5.9.1. (See **Calculator Note 5F** for specific instructions.) Use your calculator to verify your conclusions from the investigation. Determine the value that each function appears to approach in the long run as you continue the process.

10. Aaron and Davis are both studying the graph shown at the right. They need to write the equation that will produce this graph.

> "This is impossible!" Aaron exclaims. "How are we supposed to know if the parent function is a parabola or a semicircle? If we don't know the parent function, there is no way to write the equation."

> "Don't panic yet," Davis replies. "I am sure we can determine its parent function if we study the graph carefully."

Who is correct? Explain completely and, if possible, write the equation of the graph.

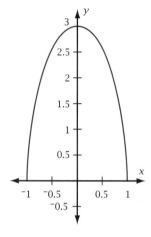

Section 5.10

Chapter Review

I cannot judge my work while I am doing it. I have to do as painters do, stand back and view it from a distance, but not too great a distance. How great? Guess.
—Blaise Pascal

In the first part of this chapter you learned how linear equations and arithmetic sequences are related. The concept of a function was also introduced. You explored several families of functions—linear, quadratic, square root, and absolute value, and you learned how to move and stretch these functions. For example, in the equation $y = 3((x - 1)/2)^2 + 4$, the parent function, $y = x^2$, has been stretched by a factor of three vertically, stretched by a factor of two horizontally, moved to the right one unit, and moved up four units. When applying transformations to a parent function, remember to apply the stretches before moving the graph out of its original position. The same rules of transformation apply to all functions.

Finally, you looked at the composition of functions. Many times solving a problem involves two or more related functions. You can find the value for a function composition by using algebraic or numeric methods or by graphing. Be sure that you understand how to use the different methods.

Problem Set 5.10

1. Sketch a graph showing the relationship between the number of pops per second and the time since you plugged in the popcorn popper. Describe in words what your graph is showing.

2. If $f(x) = {}^-2x + 7$, $g(x) = x^2 - 2$, and $h(x) = (x + 1)^2$, find each value.
  a. $f(g(3))$ **b.** $g(h({}^-2))$ **c.** $h(f({}^-1))$
  d. $f(g(x))$ **e.** $h(f(x))$ **f.** $g(f(x))$

3. For each function pictured below, draw the indicated transformation.
  a. $f(x) - 3$ **b.** $f(x - 3)$

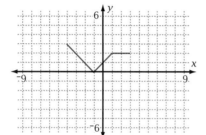
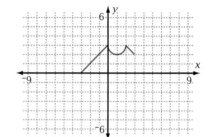

4. Describe the correct order for performing the combination of transformations on each function $f(x)$ given below.

   a. $f(x + 2) - 3$ **b.** $^-f\left(\dfrac{x}{2}\right) + 1$ **c.** $2f\left(\dfrac{x-1}{0.5}\right) + 3$

5. Solve for y.

   a. $2x - 3y = 6$ **b.** $(y + 1)^2 - 3 = x$ **c.** $\sqrt{1 - y^2} + 2 = x$

6. The graph of $y = f(x)$ is given. Draw each transformation, or combination of transformations, of this function on a separate axis.

   a. $f(x) - 2$ **b.** $f(x - 2) + 1$

   c. $^-f(x)$ **d.** $2f(x + 1) - 3$

   e. $f(^-x) + 1$ **f.** $f\left(\dfrac{x}{2}\right) - 2$

   g. $^-f(x - 3) + 1$ **h.** $^-2f\left(\dfrac{x-1}{1.5}\right) - 2$

7. For each graph, name the parent function and write an equation of the graph.

   a.

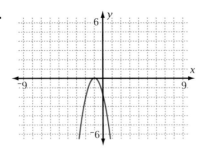

   b.

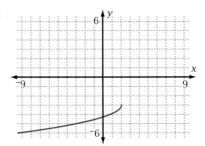

   c.

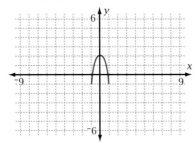

   d.

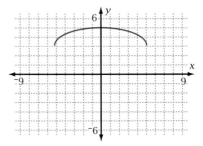

   e.

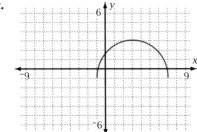

   f.

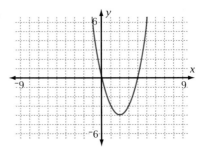

g.

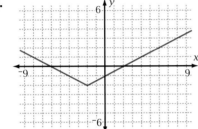

h.

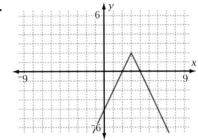

Project

Melting Ice

Algebra student Will Melt carefully crafted a device from a wire coat hanger and a rubber band. He placed this device on a scale and attached an ice cube to the rubber band. He then carefully read the mass every 10 minutes for 100 minutes, at which time the ice cube dropped off the rubber band. Because melting occurs on the surface of the ice and surface area is measured in square centimeters, he was sure the relationship would be quadratic. The data he collected is in the table below. Time is recorded in minutes and mass is recorded in grams.

Time (min)	0	10	20	30	40	50	60	70	80	90	100
Mass (g)	52.4	51.9	50.8	49.4	47.9	46.4	45	43.3	42.1	40.6	39.2

Much to his dismay, he discovered the data was quite linear. Plot the data and draw the least-squares line. (Be sure to label the scale and units in each graph you create in this project.)

Upon reflection, Will recalled that he needed to subtract the mass of the hanger and the rubber band, which totaled 34.3 grams. Subtract this from the original y-values and plot the points with the new y-values on the same graph. Find the equation that fits this new data.

Will then decided that, because little significant melting happened in the first 10 minutes, he would subtract 10 from each of the x-values. Graph the data and the equation for this set of data.

Things still weren't working out as he thought they should, so he converted grams to ounces by dividing each y-value by 28.35. He then repeated his analysis. Add this graph and equation to your report.

Still not satisfied, Will decided to convert the time to seconds, so he multiplied all the x-values by 60. He thought again about the coat hanger and wondered if he should subtract its weight first and then change to ounces, or change to ounces and then subtract the weight. Try these two to determine which is correct.

(continued on next page)

Even after all this, he was not content, so he thought he would check the mass of the melted water. He made all the y-values negative and added the mass of the original cube.

Write a summary of what Will, and you, learned at each step of this analysis. Explain how each step relates to the transformation of functions.

Assessing What You've Learned—Constructing Test Questions

Have you ever wondered how your teacher decides what to put on a test or which questions to ask in order to assess what students have learned? One thing that teachers may consider is the amount of time spent on each topic. Other considerations may include the importance of a topic, its application, or perhaps the special interest that it generated during class discussions. Writing good test items is not an easy task, but it is another way for you to assess what you have learned.

Think about the investigations and problems you have completed in this chapter. By yourself or with your group, write at least five problems that you think could be used to assess what a student should have learned. Some of the questions you create may pertain to specific skills you have acquired, but try to write a few that require a student to apply problem-solving strategies. Your teacher may even choose some of your problems to include on the next test.

Continue using the other methods that have been described to assess what you've learned. You might not be using them all, but it's a good idea to assess yourself using a variety of methods.

Organizing Your Notebook

• By taking just a few minutes each day, you can keep your notebook in shape and avoid the hassle of having to locate and organize your work when you complete a chapter.

Keeping a Journal

• Look in Problem Sets 5.7 and 5.8 for journal prompts.

Portfolio

• Have you done any work in this chapter that you would like to include in your portfolio? If so, document it, and put it in.

Performance Assessment

• Demonstrate to someone that you know how each of the transformations introduced in this chapter will affect the graph of a function.

Open-ended Investigations

• Choose one of the Take Another Look investigations or a project, or design your own investigation. Share your results with a classmate, your group, or your teacher.

6 Parametric Equations and Trigonometry

Not only do these parachutists require a great deal of teamwork to make this maneuver, but they must also have an understanding of distance, rate, and time relationships. These parachutists are falling at a rate of 120 miles per hour, thousands of feet high in the sky. They will break their formation and open their parachutes when they are about 2,000 feet from the ground. You can use your parametric equations to model the relationships among distance, rate, and time.

Graphing Parametric Equations

What lies behind us and what lies before us are tiny matters compared to what lies within us.
—Ralph Waldo Emerson

As you walk around school each day, you probably cross paths with many of your friends. But does this necessarily mean that you meet them each time? Look at the map, or drawing, below. It shows the paths that Noah and Rita traveled during a recent school day. You can see that their paths crossed several times during the day. What other information do you need to have in order to know whether they actually did bump into each other?

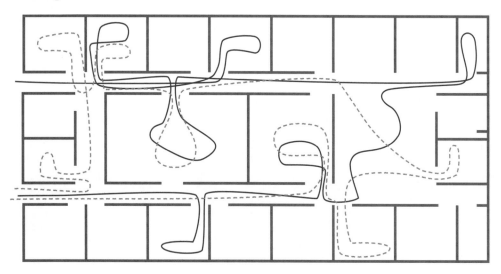

Without knowing when they were at each of the intersections, you can't determine if they actually met. Similar situations involving time-related intersections arise often in the real world.

In your previous work with graphs and functions, you dealt with relationships between two variables, such as x and y. The graphs below are representations of x- and y-values that are related by the equation $y = x^2$. The graph on the right shows some additional restrictions that you will soon learn how to control.

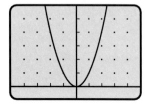
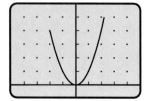

In this chapter, you will also investigate some other interesting graphs and geometric figures. Two variables are often not enough to easily describe graphs like these.

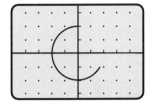

You can use **parametric equations** to separately describe the *x*- and *y*-coordinates of a point. In a parametric equation, the *x*- and *y*-variables are each written as a function of a third variable, *t*, called the **parameter**. Now you will have better control over which points are plotted. In the next example, the variable *t* represents time. You will see how *t* controls the *x*- and *y*-values.

■ Example 1

Two tankers leave Corpus Christi at the same time, traveling toward St. Petersburg, which is 900 mi east. Tanker A travels at 18 mi/hr and Tanker B travels at 22 mi/hr. Establish a coordinate system and use your calculator to simulate the motion involved in this situation.

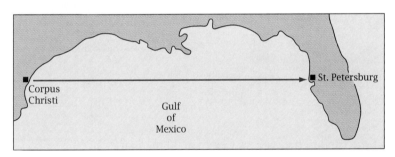
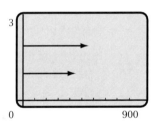

Solution

Establish the coordinate system by locating the origin at Corpus Christi. The *x*-coordinate for each plotted point is the distance of a tanker from Corpus Christi. Because St. Petersburg is directly east, the *y*-coordinate for each path will remain constant.

NOTE
6A

The graphing window (see **Calculator Note 6A**) will accommodate the time, the distance traveled (*x*-coordinate), and the path (*y*-coordinate) on which each tanker travels. For this problem, use parameter settings of [0, 50, 0.5] and window settings [0, 900, 100, ⁻1, 3, 1]. The first values in this window are parameter values for the variable *t*. As you work through this example, try to figure out what each value means.

Assume that each tanker moves at a constant speed. After 2 hr, traveling at 18 mi/hr, the slower tanker will be 36 mi from Corpus Christi. After 3 hr, it will be

54 mi away; after 10 hr, it will be 180 mi away; and after t hr, it will be $18t$ mi away, or $x = 18t$. (Enter this equation into x_{1t}.) This equation provides the distance traveled and locates the position of Tanker A at any given time. You can see that the x-value is dependent on the time, or t-value. Position the starting point of Tanker A 1 mi north of Corpus Christi by setting $y_{1t} = 1$. (It is difficult to see the tanker move if it travels along the x-axis.) These two equations ($x_{1t} = 18t$ and $y_{1t} = 1$) are examples of a pair of parametric equations. The t-values selected will determine which (x, y) points are plotted.

The motion and position of the second tanker can be simulated with $x_{2t} = 22t$ and $y_{2t} = 2$. What real-world meaning can you give to $22t$, and what reason supports using $y_{2t} = 2$? ■

Investigation 6.1.1

Simulating Motion

Be sure the equations and graphing window from Example 1 above are entered into your calculator before you begin this activity.

Part 1 Trace the path of the appropriate tanker to help you answer each question.

    a. How long does it take the faster tanker to reach St. Petersburg?

    b. Where is the slower tanker when the faster tanker reaches its destination?

    c. When, during the trip, is the faster tanker exactly 82 mi in front of the slower tanker?

    d. During what part of the trip are the tankers less than 60 mi apart?

Part 2 Have each group member describe another tanker situation. Write at least four questions related to your description. Be sure to state your assumptions. Write an explanation and answer for each of your questions on a separate paper. Exchange your questions with another member of your group, and try to answer each other's questions.

Parametric equations allow you to simulate motion and to picture related paths when the location of the points is dependent on time. A parametric representation lets you see the dynamic nature of the motion. You can even adjust the plotting speed by changing the Tstep value. However, the parameter t doesn't always have to represent time. It can be a number just like x and y. Sometimes you may want to control which x-values or y-values or both are plotted. You can do this by defining a range for the t-values.

■ Example 2

Graph the curve described by the parametric equations $x = t + 2$ and $y = t^2$ for $0 \leq t \leq 4$ on graph paper.

t	x	y
0	2	0
1	3	1
2	4	4
3	5	9
4	6	16

Solution

The problem states that you may only use values of t between 0 and 4. Use the given equations to calculate the x- and y-values that correspond to each value of t. Next, graph the points. Graph the point with the lowest value of t first. Then graph the rest of the points as t increases, connecting each point to the previous one as you graph them. Add arrows to indicate the direction of increasing values of t. When you look at the graph on paper, you can only see the x- and y-coordinates. Values of t are used to determine x and y, but they do not appear in the actual plot of the graph. Verify this graph on your calculator. ■

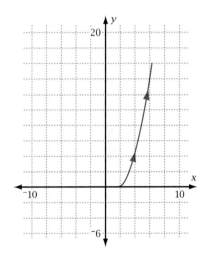

Investigation 6.1.2

Exploring Parametrics

Set your graphing window so that $^-14 \leq x \leq 14$ and $^-10 \leq y \leq 10$. Use the interval $0 \leq t \leq 4$ for the values of t with a Tstep of 0.1. The objective of this investigation is to explore parametric equations of the form

$$x_{1t} = x_0 + at \quad \text{and} \quad y_{1t} = y_0 + bt.$$

You can choose values for x_0 and y_0 from the set $\{^-3, ^-2, ^-1, 0, 1, 2, 3\}$ and values for a and b from $\{^-1, 0, 1\}$. By changing the value of only one of these variables (for example, the variable a) several times, you can see what effect the changes have on the graph.

a. Assign each group member the task of investigating one of the variables, a, b, x_0, or y_0, to see what effect changing the value of the variable has on the graph. Each person starts with the equations $x_{1t} = {}^-3 + {}^-1t$ and $y_{1t} = {}^-3 + {}^-1t$. Be sure to trace the graphs and look at the x- and y-values. Make conjectures that describe the effects of changing the value of your variable. Describe similarities and differences in the graphs. Calculate the slope of each graphed line, and indicate at least one endpoint. Make a connection between the slope and the values of a and b.

b. Share your conjectures with your group. Be sure that everyone in the group understands what effect changing each variable has on the graphed equation. Prepare a group report that describes the results of your investigation.

c. Change the interval for t to $^-4 \le t \le 0$, and graph some of the same equations again. Have each group member check to see if his or her earlier conjectures are still true. What is the same and what has changed?

d. Discuss your discoveries with your group. Summarize everyone's discoveries, and add these results to your group report.

e. Investigate each of the following questions. Be sure to divide the tasks among the group members. Share your results with each other, and add your discoveries to your group report.

   i. Describe what happens if you don't restrict the values of x_0 and y_0 to those suggested.

   ii. Describe what happens if you don't restrict the values of t.

   iii. Is it possible to write two sets of parametric equations that graph perpendicular segments? What is the relationship between the equations?

In the example below you will see how you can adjust the values for Tmin and Tmax so that you will see a complete graph in your viewing window.

■ Example 3

Find values of t that generate the graph described by the parametric equations $x = t - 1$ and $y = \frac{1}{2}t + 2$ shown in the window pictured below.

t	x	y
$-?-$	$^-5$	0
$-?-$	$^-3$	1
$-?-$	$^-1$	2
$-?-$	1	3
$-?-$	3	4

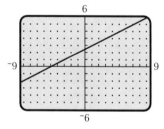

Solution

Substitute an *x*- or *y*-value into the appropriate equation and solve for *t*.

$$^-5 = t - 1 \quad \text{or} \quad 0 = \tfrac{1}{2}t + 2$$

Either substitution will give you $t = {}^-4$ when $(x, y) = ({}^-5, 0)$. Complete the table for each of the other pairs of *x* and *y*.

To find the *t*-value that gives the point at the left edge of your "friendly" calculator window, solve the equation $x = t - 1$ by substituting the Xmin value for *x*. For a "friendly" window defined by $^-9.4 \le x \le 9.4$ and $^-6.2 \le y \le 6.2$, you will find that when $x = {}^-9.4$, $t = {}^-8.4$. Use the Xmax to find the *t*-value at the other edge of the screen. You will find that $t = 10.4$ when $x = 9.4$. These *t*-values, or a range that includes them, can be used as Tmin and Tmax to generate a graph like the one shown. In this example, part of the screen on the right-hand side was not used because the *y*-coordinates of the points were outside the range. If you don't want to graph that part of the line, you will need to reduce the range of *t*-values. Because the graph reaches the Ymax value before it reaches the Xmax value, set $\tfrac{1}{2}t + 2 = 6.2$ (Ymax) and solve for *t*. Use this *t*-value as your new Tmax. ■

Problem Set 6.1

1. Graph each pair of parametric equations. Be careful to account for any restrictions on *t* that are included. Indicate (with arrows) the direction of increasing *t*-values along the graph. If an interval for *t* isn't listed, then find one that shows all of the graph that fits in a window with $^-10 \le x \le 10$ and $^-6 \le y \le 6$.

   a. $x = 3t - 1$, $y = 2t + 1$ 　　　　　**b.** $x = t + 1$, $y = t^2$

   c. $x = t^2$, $y = t + 3$, $^-2 \le t \le 1$ 　　**d.** $x = t - 1$, $y = \sqrt{4 - t^2}$, $^-2 \le t \le 2$

2. In the last chapter, you learned how to transform functions. You can do these same transformations with parametric equations. Parametric transformations are probably easier and may seem more natural to you. Use a *t*-interval equal to your *x*-interval, and a Tstep of 0.1 when drawing each graph.

   a. Graph $x = t$, $y = t^2$.

   b. Graph $x = t + 2$, $y = t^2$. How does this compare to the graph in 2a?

   c. Graph $x = t$, $y = t^2 - 3$. How does this compare to the graph in 2a?

   d. Predict what the graph of $x = t + 5$, $y = t^2 + 2$ will look like compared to the graph in 2a. Graph the equations to verify your conjecture.

   e. Predict what the graph of $x = t + a$, $y = t^2 + b$ will look like compared to the graph in 2a. Graph the equations to verify your conjecture.

3. **a.** Graph $x = t$, $y = |t|$.

   b. Graph $x = t - 1$, $y = |t| + 2$. How does this graph compare to the graph in 3a?

   c. Write a pair of parametric equations that will move the graph in 3a four units left and three units down.

   d. Graph $x = 2t$, $y = |t|$. How does this graph compare to the graph in 3a?

e. Graph $x = t$, $y = 3|t|$. How does this graph compare to the graph in 3a?

f. Describe how the numbers 2, 3, and 4 in the equations $x = t + 2$ and $y = 3|t| - 4$ change the graph in 3a.

4. Write parametric equations of the form $x = f(t)$, $y = g(t)$ for each graph. (Hint: You can always invent a parametric equivalent of a function by setting $x = t$ and changing y to a function of t by substituting t for x in the $y=$ equation.)

a.

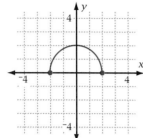

b.

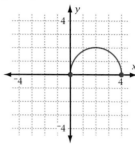

c.

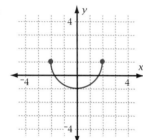

d.

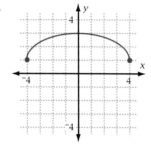

5. The graph of the parametric equations
$x = f(t)$ and $y = g(t)$ is pictured below.

a. Sketch a graph of $x = f(t)$ and $y = {}^-g(t)$ on paper. Describe the transformation that you have just completed.

b. Sketch a graph of $x = {}^-f(t)$ and $y = g(t)$ on paper. Describe the transformation that you have just completed.

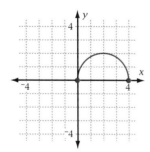

6. At the right is a graph of the parametric equations $x = f(t)$ and $y = g(t)$. Write the parametric equations for each graph below in terms of $f(t)$ and $g(t)$.

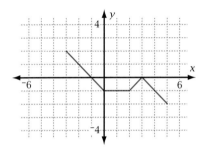

a.

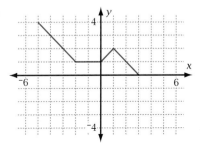

b.

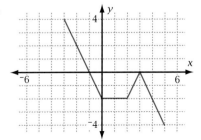

c.

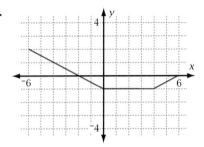

d.

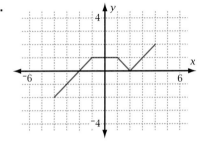

Parametric to Nonparametric

The truth of a theory is in your mind, not in your eyes.
—Albert Einstein

In the last set of problems, you learned that you can always find a parametric equivalent of a function by setting $x = t$ and making y a function of t instead of a function of x. This means $y = x^2$ can be graphed in parametric form using $x = t$ and $y = t^2$.

If you know the parametric equations of a graph, you can write an equation *eliminating the parameter.* In other words, you can change the equation so that it no longer contains t, by solving either the x- or the y-equation for t and substituting the result into the other equation. Generally, you start by choosing the equation in which it is easier to solve for t. Do this with the equations in Example 2 from Section 6.1.

$x = t + 2$ and $y = t^2$	Given equations.
$t = x - 2$	Solve the x-equation for t.
$y = (x - 2)^2$	Substitute for t in the y-equation.

NOTE
6B

The graph of the function $y = (x - 2)^2$ is a parabola whose vertex is at $(2, 0)$. (See **Calculator Note 6B.**) Notice that in this case you get the entire parabola, whereas the parametric form gives only a portion of the parabola because of the domain restrictions that were placed on t.

■ **Example 1**

Graph the curve described by the parametric equations $x = t^2 - 4$ and $y = \dfrac{t}{2}$, for $-10 \le t \le 10$. Then eliminate t from the equations and graph the result.

Solution

Plot the points, connecting them as t increases. Verify this graph on your calculator. Notice that the graph is not a function, even though both x and y are functions of t.

Eliminate the parameter, and solve for y.

$x = t^2 - 4,\ y = \dfrac{t}{2}$	Given equations.
$t = 2y$	Solve the y-equation for t.
$x = (2y)^2 - 4$	Substitute into the x-equation.
$x = 4y^2 - 4$	Expand.
$4y^2 = x + 4$	Add 4 to both sides.

$$y^2 = \frac{x+4}{4}$$ Divide both sides by 4.

$$y = \pm\sqrt{\frac{x+4}{4}}$$ Take the square root of both sides.

$$= \frac{\pm\sqrt{x+4}}{2}$$

You can also solve the original x-equation for t and substitute into the y-equation.

$$x = t^2 - 4, \; y = \frac{t}{2}$$ Given equations.

$$t^2 = x + 4$$ Add 4 to both sides.

$$t = \pm\sqrt{x+4}$$ Take the square root of both sides.

$$y = \pm\sqrt{\frac{x+4}{4}}$$ Substitute into the y-equation.

$$= \frac{\pm\sqrt{x+4}}{2}$$

Notice that both methods result in the same equation.

You might recognize this as the equation of a "sideways" parabola, similar to the equations you studied in the previous chapter. Check the result by graphing to show that the graphs of

$$y = \pm\sqrt{\frac{x+4}{4}} \quad \text{and} \quad x = t^2 - 4, \; y = \frac{t}{2}$$

are the same. ■

Problem Set 6.2

1. Eliminate the parameter in each pair of equations and solve the resulting equation for y. Graph this new relation in a "friendly" graphing window in which the distance between pixels is 0.2 on both the x- and y-axes. Verify that the graph of the new equation is the same (except for restrictions forced on t) as the graph of the parametric equation.

   a. $x = t + 1, \; y = t^2$ **b.** $x = 3t - 1, \; y = 2t + 1$

   c. $x = t^2, \; y = t + 3, \; {}^-2 \le t \le 1$ **d.** $x = t - 1, \; y = \sqrt{4 - t^2}, \; {}^-2 \le t \le 2$

2. Write a nonparametric equation that is equivalent to each pair of parametric equations.

   a. $x = 2t - 3, \; y = t + 2$ **b.** $x = t^2, \; y = t + 1$

   c. $x = \frac{1}{2}t + 1, \; y = \frac{t-2}{3}$ **d.** $x = t - 3, \; y = 2(t - 1)^2$

3. a. Graph $x = t + 5$ and $y = 2t - 1$.

   b. Write parametric equations that produce a graph with coordinates that are the reverse of the coordinates graphed in 3a. For example, if $(6, 1)$ is a point on the original graph, then $(1, 6)$ will be a point on the new graph. Use a "friendly" graphing window.

   c. Describe the relationship between the two graphs.

4. Set a "friendly" graphing window in which the distance between pixels is 0.2 on both the x- and y-axes. Find the smallest interval for t that produces the same graph for the parametric equations $x = t + 2$ and $y = t^2$ and the nonparametric form, $y = (x - 2)^2$.

5. The slides and stretches in Problem Set 6.1 are transformations. Graph $x(t) = t + 2$ and $y(t) = \sqrt{1 - t^2}$. Then graph the parametric equations below. Test your conclusions by experimenting with other parametric equations, and use them to support your answers, or to come to a new conclusion.

   a. Graph $x = x(t)$, $y = {}^-y(t)$ and identify any transformations of the original equations.

   b. Graph $x = {}^-x(t)$, $y = y(t)$ and identify any transformations of the original equations.

   c. Graph $x = {}^-x(t)$, $y = {}^-y(t)$ and identify any transformations of the original equations.

6. Write parametric equations for two perpendicular lines that intersect at the point $(3, 2)$. One of the lines should have a slope of $^-0.5$.

7. Tanker A moves at 18 mi/hr and Tanker B moves at 22 mi/hr. Both are traveling from Corpus Christi to St. Petersburg, which is 900 mi directly east. Simulate the tanker movements if Tanker A leaves Corpus Christi at noon and Tanker B leaves at 5 p.m.

   a. Write the equations you used to simulate the motion.

   b. Name the window you used to graph the equations in 7a.

   c. When and where does Tanker B overtake Tanker A?

   d. Simulate the tanker movements if both tankers leave at noon, but Tanker A leaves from Corpus Christi and Tanker B leaves from St. Petersburg, each heading toward the other. Record your equations and determine the time interval during which they are within 50 mi of each other.

Take Another Look 6.2

NOTE

6B

Calculator Note 6B explains how to graph a function in $y=$ form when your calculator is in *parametric* mode in order to verify that the $y=$ form and the parametric form are equivalent. If you haven't tried this yet, do so now.

Another verification possibility was suggested in Problem 4 of Problem Set 6.1. Instead of using DrawF, you can always invent a parametric equivalent of a function by setting $x = t$ and changing y to a function of t by substituting t for x in the $y=$ equation. You can then graph both pairs of equations to verify that their graphs are the same.

Use this substitution strategy to graph $y = \dfrac{\pm\sqrt{x+4}}{2}$, the result of Example 1.

Show that this graph and the graph of $x = t^2 - 4$, $y = \dfrac{t}{2}$ are the same. (If you do this, you will note that the graphs are the same even though the same t-values result in different points in each graph.)

Section 6.3

Right Triangle Trigonometry

A human being should be able to change a diaper, plan an invasion, butcher a hog, conn a ship, design a building, write a sonnet, balance accounts, build a wall, set a bone, comfort the dying, take orders, give orders, cooperate, act alone, solve equations, analyze a new problem, pitch manure, program a computer, cook a tasty meal, fight efficiently, die gallantly. Specialization is for insects.
—Lazarus Long

Panama City is 750 miles from Corpus Christi on a heading, or bearing, of 73°. How can you simulate the movement of Tanker A from Corpus Christi to Panama City? (As pictured below, a heading of 73° refers to the 73° angle measured clockwise from north.) Now you have to model a motion that isn't strictly left-to-right or up-and-down.

Panama City, Florida

Parametric equations are especially useful for modeling motion that is at an angle to the horizontal. In these situations, you will be working with right triangles in which one of the acute angles is between the horizontal axis and the line of motion. To solve these problems you will use **trigonometric ratios**.

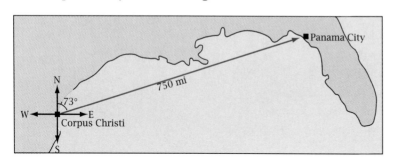

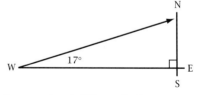

Do you see where the 17° comes from?

Investigation 6.3.1

Trigonometric Ratios

In this investigation you will learn more about how trigonometric ratios are found. Each group member needs to complete the steps in Part 1. In Part 2, you will share your results.

Part 1 **a.** Choose an angle measure between 0° and 90° and carefully draw angle *A* using a protractor. (Be sure that each group member chooses a different angle measure.)

b. Carefully draw six vertical lines to form a set of six overlapping right triangles with the long leg (base) of each triangle on the same horizontal line. (See the diagram at the right.)

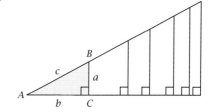

c. Make a table like the one below, but with six empty rows. In the table, record the lengths of a, b, and c, where a is the height, b is the base, and c is the hypotenuse. Measure to the nearest 0.1 cm. Compute each ratio, $\frac{a}{c}$, $\frac{b}{c}$, and $\frac{a}{b}$, to the nearest hundredth. Do this for all six triangles.

d. Make sure your calculator is set in *degree* mode. Find the values of sin A, cos A, and tan A, rounding each to the nearest 0.01. Look for relationships between the calculator ratios and the values of sin A, cos A, and tan A.

Measure of angle A –?–

sin A –?–   cos A –?–   tan A –?–

a	b	c	$\dfrac{a}{c}$	$\dfrac{b}{c}$	$\dfrac{a}{b}$
–?–	–?–	–?–	–?–	–?–	–?–
–?–	–?–	–?–	–?–	–?–	–?–

Part 2 Share your results with other group members. Look for relationships between the calculated ratios and the sine, cosine, and tangent values. Carefully describe any relationships you think might be true.

In the similar right triangles pictured below, the ratio of the length of the shorter leg to the length of the longer leg is always 0.75, and the ratios of the lengths of other pairs of corresponding sides are also equal. In right triangles, there are special names for each of these ratios.

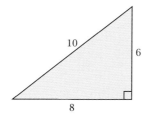

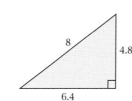

Trigonometric Ratios

The **sine** of an acute angle in a right triangle is the ratio of the length of the opposite leg to the length of the hypotenuse.

The **cosine** of an acute angle in a right triangle is the ratio of the length of the adjacent leg to the length of the hypotenuse.

The **tangent** of an acute angle in a right triangle is the ratio of the length of the opposite leg to the length of the adjacent leg.

In triangle *ABC*, the sine, cosine, and tangent are defined as follows.

sine $A = \dfrac{a}{c}$

cosine $A = \dfrac{b}{c}$

tangent $A = \dfrac{a}{b}$

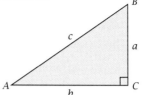

If, instead, you refer to angle *B,* then the ratios are the following.

sine $B = \dfrac{b}{c}$ cosine $B = \dfrac{a}{c}$ tangent $B = \dfrac{b}{a}$

The word *sine* has a curious history. The Sanskrit term for sine in an astronomical context was *jya-ardha* ("half-cord"). This was later abbreviated to *jya.* Islamic scholars, who learned about the sine from the Indians, called it *jiba.* One Islamic mathematician, Muhammad ibn Musa al-Khwārizmī (A.D. 780–850), wrote *Hisab al-jabr wa'l-muqabala* (*The Book of Restoration and Confrontation*). In Segovia, around 1140, Robert of Chester read *jiba* as *jaib* when he was translating al-Khwārizmī's book from Arabic into Latin. One meaning of *jaib* is "indentation" or "gulf." So *jiba* was translated into Latin as *sinus* ("fold" or "curve"), and from that we get the word *sine.* The Latin translation began "Dixit algoritmi," or "al-Khwārizmī says," and from that came the word *algorithm.*

You can use the sine and the other trigonometric ratios to find the unknown side lengths of a right triangle when you know the measure of one acute angle and the length of one of the other sides.

■ Example 1

Find the length of the indicated side in each triangle.

a.

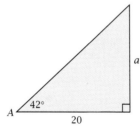

b.

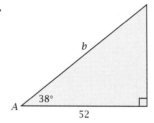

Solution

a. The sides involved with respect to angle *A* are the two legs. Therefore, you will use the tangent ratio. (You can't use sine or cosine, because the hypotenuse isn't involved.)

$$\tan 42° = \dfrac{a}{20}$$
$$a = 20 \tan 42°$$
$$a \approx 18.008$$

(Be sure your calculator is in *degree* mode.)

b. The sides involved with respect to angle A are the adjacent leg and the hypotenuse. Therefore, you will use the cosine ratio.

$$\cos 38° = \frac{52}{b}$$

$$b \cos 38° = 52$$

$$b = \frac{52}{\cos 38°}$$

$$b \approx 65.689 \quad \blacksquare$$

■ **Example 2**

Find the measure of angle A.

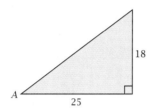

Solution

The sides involved with respect to angle A are the two legs. Therefore, you will use the tangent ratio; $\tan A = \frac{18}{25}$. You know the lengths of the sides but not the angle measures, so $A = \tan^{-1}\left(\frac{18}{25}\right) \approx 35.75°$. The $^{-1}$ in this case indicates that you are using the **inverse tangent function**. This is a function that tells you the angle when you know the tangent ratio. Inverse trigonometric functions are written $\sin^{-1} x$, $\cos^{-1} x$, and $\tan^{-1} x$. Although the $^{-1}$ looks like an exponent, it isn't. It doesn't mean $\frac{1}{\tan x}$. The equation $A = \tan^{-1}\left(\frac{18}{25}\right)$ means A is the angle that has a tangent ratio of $\frac{18}{25}$. ■

Investigation 6.3.2
Finding the Height of a Tree

Assign a task to each group member. The four tasks are the walker, the hugger, the VAMD operator, and the recorder. Your group will need a length of string, a meter stick, and a VAMD (Vertical Angle Measuring Device).

Step 1 Determine the length of the walker's step by having the walker pace off a given marked distance, then calculating the average length of a step.

Step 2   Choose a tree to measure.

Step 3   The VAMD operator locates the point where he or she needs to stand in order to sight the top of the tree.

Step 4   The walker paces off the distance between the tree and the spot where the VAMD operator is standing.

Step 5   The VAMD operator measures the angle between the horizontal and the top of the tree, with the recorder's assistance.

Step 6   Meanwhile the hugger measures the circumference of the tree using the string and the meter stick.

Step 7   The recorder records the measurements provided by the hugger, the walker, and the VAMD operator.

Repeat Steps 2–7 for at least six trees of the same species. Be sure to measure the circumference at the same height on each tree. When you have the data, organize them in a table like the one below. Calculate the height and diameter of each tree and add this information to your table. Show in detail an example of each of the two calculations. Plot the heights and diameters, and find the best-fit line for these data.

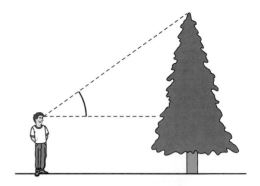

Distance	Angle	Circumference	Height	Diameter
–?–	–?–	–?–	–?–	–?–
–?–	–?–	–?–	–?–	–?–

Problem Set 6.3

1. Find the length of the indicated side of each triangle.

a.

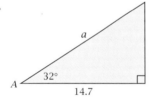

b.

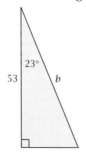

c.

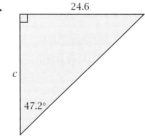

d.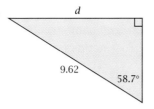

e.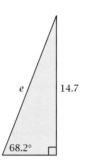

f.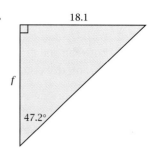

2. Find the measure of each indicated angle.

a.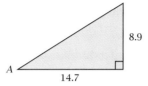

b.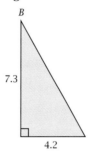

c.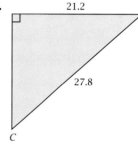

d.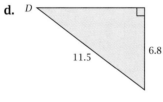

e.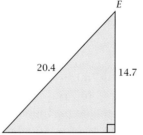

f.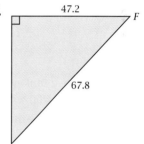

3. Two ants leave the nest. One walks east 28.5 cm and the other walks south 60.3 cm.

   a. After the ants get where they're going, what is the heading of the line of sight from the southern ant to the eastern ant?

   b. How far apart are the ants?

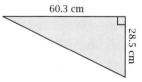

4. a. Graph the parametric equations $x = t \cos 39°$ and $y = t \sin 39°$. Use a graphing window with $0 \le x \le 10$ and $0 \le y \le 6.5$. Describe the graph.

   b. In order to determine the angle between this line and the x-axis, trace to a point on the line and find the coordinates. Make a triangle by drawing a vertical line from the point to the x-axis. Label the lengths of the legs of the triangle. What is the angle between the line and the x-axis?

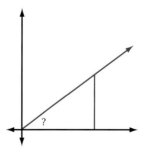

5. Graph the parametric equations $x = t \cos 45°$ and $y = t \sin 45°$. Use a graphing window with $0 \le x \le 10$, $0 \le y \le 6.5$, and $0 \le t \le 10$. Describe the graph and name the angle between the graph and the x-axis. What is the relationship between this angle and the parametric equations?

6. What parametric equations could you use to graph a line that makes a 57° angle with the x-axis? Find an interval for t that gives a complete graph in the window with $^-4.7 \le x \le 4.7$ and $^-3.1 \le y \le 3.1$.

7. What parametric equations could you use to graph a line that makes a 29° angle with the x-axis?

8. Write parametric equations, involving the tangent ratio, that will graph a line that makes a 29° angle with the x-axis.

9. Write parametric equations for each graph and indicate the t-interval that you used.

a.

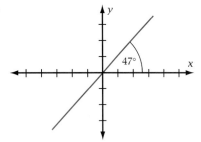

b.

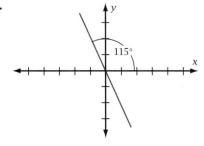

10. Suppose a tanker is moving at 10 mi/hr on a bearing of 60°.

a. Use the right triangle pictured to write equations for x and y, in terms of t, that simulate the motion.

b. What t-values are required to picture 100 mi of tanker motion?

c. What is the real-world meaning of the numerical values and variables you used in your equations?

d. What is the real-world meaning of the graph produced with these equations?

11. Simulate the movement of Tanker A at 18 mi/hr from Corpus Christi to Panama City. Panama City is 750 mi from Corpus Christi on a heading of 73°. Make a sketch of the tanker's motion, showing the coordinate axes you used.

a. How long does the tanker take to get to Panama City?

b. How far east and how far north is Panama City from Corpus Christi?

12. a. Simulate the movement of Tanker B at 22 mi/hr from St. Petersburg to New Orleans on a heading of 285°. The distance between the two ports is 510 mi. Make a sketch of the tanker's motion, showing the coordinate axes you used.

A band playing original jazz at Preservation Hall in New Orleans

b. How long does it take to get to New Orleans?

c. How far west and how far north is New Orleans from St. Petersburg?

d. Suppose Tanker A in Problem 11 leaves at the same time as Tanker B. Describe where the ships' paths intersect. St. Petersburg is 900 mi east of Corpus Christi.

Geometer's Sketchpad Investigation

Trigonometric Ratios

You can use Sketchpad to investigate the sine, cosine, and tangent functions.

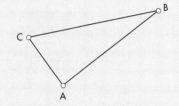

Step 1 Draw segment *AB.* Construct line *l* perpendicular to *AB* through point *A.*

Step 2 Construct any point on line *l* and label it *C.* Construct segment *AC* and segment *BC.* Hide line *l.* You should now have right triangle *ABC.*

Step 3 Measure the lengths of each side of your triangle, and use the ratio of the lengths to calculate the sine, cosine, and tangent of angle *B.* Measure angle *ABC.*

Vary the size, shape, and orientation of your triangle. Try moving each of the three corners. Observe when the values of sine, cosine, and tangent change and when they stay fixed.

Questions

1. In what ways can you change your triangle without varying the values of the sine, cosine, and tangent?

2. When are the values of the sine and cosine of your triangle equal? How do you make the value of the tangent increase? How can you make it decrease? When is it zero?

3. When is the sine greater than the cosine? When is the tangent greater than the sine? When is the tangent greater than the cosine?

4. Measure angle *B.* Move the points until segment *AB* has a length of 4 cm and angle *B* has a measure of 40°. (Check that the precision of length measurements is set to tenths and that the precision for angle measurements is set to units.) What are the lengths of the other sides? Can you find a triangle with a different shape or size that has the same measures for segment *AB* and ∠*B*?

Geometric Shapes

Few are lacking in capacity. They fail because they are lacking application.
—Calvin Coolidge

Besides representing time, the variable *t* in parametric equations can represent an angle. When it does, you can write equations that create a wide variety of different geometric shapes. The mathematical ideas that you'll use to create these shapes are based on the equation of a circle and on some trigonometric definitions.

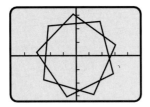 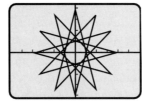

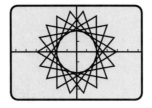

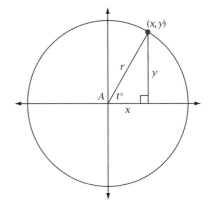

A **circle** is the set of all the points in a plane that are the same distance from a given point called the **center**. This distance is called the **radius**. When you graph a circle, it is apparent that it is not a function. To graph a complete circle on your calculator, you will have to write two separate function equations: one for the top half of the circle, and one for the bottom half. This task becomes much simpler with parametric equations. With parametric equations, you can draw some very interesting geometric shapes based on a circle.

In a circle with radius *r* and *t* degrees at the central angle *A*, $\sin t = \frac{y}{r}$ and $\cos t = \frac{x}{r}$. Solve these equations for *x* and *y* to get the **parametric equations for a circle**: $x = r \cos t$ and $y = r \sin t$.

■ **Example 1**

Use parametric equations to draw the graph of a circle of radius 3 centered at (0, 0).

Solution

The parametric equations for a circle of radius 3 centered at $(0, 0)$ are $x = 3 \cos t$ and $y = 3 \sin t$. The variable t represents the central angle of the circle. What does the 3 represent in the equations? Be sure your calculator is in *parametric* mode, and set a "friendly" window in which the distance between the pixels is 0.1. (The first three numbers in the window setting don't actually affect the window size, but they will affect how the graph itself appears.) What would you do to graph a circle of radius 2? Of radius 1? What happens if you use a Tstep of 120°? ■

Investigation 6.4.1

Drawing Polygons

In this investigation you will explore what happens to a graph when you change the parameter t. Have each group member work individually on the exploration in Part 1a. Then share your conjectures with a partner. Finally, work together with your group to prepare a summary of your discoveries.

Part 1 **a.** Start with the equations $x = 3 \cos t$ and $y = 3 \sin t$. Experiment with the parameter t, changing Tmin, Tmax, and Tstep. Use the following questions to guide your exploration.

    i. What effects do each of these changes have on the graph?

    ii. Can you make a square? A hexagon? An octagon? A triangle?

    iii. What would it take to make a square with sides parallel to the axes?

    iv. How can you rotate a polygon shape about the origin by altering the equation?

    v. Be sure you can graph each shape shown below. Try to find more than one way to draw each figure. (Each grid mark represents one unit.)

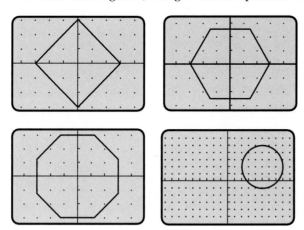

b. Share your conjectures with your partner.

c. Work together with your group to write a paragraph summarizing your discoveries.

Part 2 **a.** Working with your partner, discuss how you might translate the circle $x = 3 \cos t$ and $y = 3 \sin t$ so that it is centered at $(5, 2)$. Do this.

b. Reflect this graph over the y-axis, the x-axis, the line $y = x$, and the line $x = {}^-1$. Describe the method you used for each of these reflections.

c. Graph the equations $x = 3 \cos t$ and $y = 3 \sin t$, but this time set your Tstep to 125°. You will also need to increase Tmax, so that $0° \le t \le 3600°$, to get a good picture. Then try other values, such as 100°, 150°, and 185°, for Tstep. (You may also need to change Tmax to get a better picture.) Write a paragraph explaining what happens in each case.

If you look at a special right triangle with a 1-unit hypotenuse, the definitions for sine and cosine give you the equations $\sin A = y$ and $\cos A = x$. Applying the Pythagorean theorem yields the equation $x^2 + y^2 = 1$. If you substitute the trigonometric ratios for x and y, you'll get $(\cos A)^2 + (\sin A)^2 = 1$. This equation will be true for any angle A. You can use your calculator to verify that it's true for $A = 47°$.

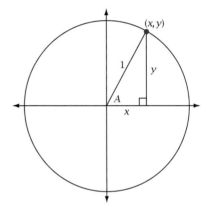

$\cos 47° \approx 0.6820$, $(\cos 47°)^2 \approx 0.4651$
$\sin 47° \approx 0.7313$, $(\sin 47°)^2 \approx 0.5349$
$(\cos 47°)^2 + (\sin 47°)^2 \approx 0.4651 + 0.5349 = 1$

Try substituting other angle values for A, and convince yourself that the equation will always work.

Problem Set 6.4

1. Write parametric equations for each figure. Indicate the range used for t, and the increment. (Each grid mark represents one unit.)

a.

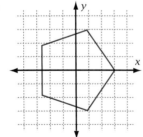

b.

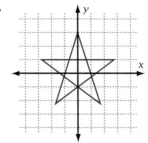

c.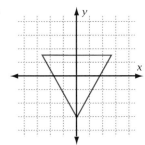

d.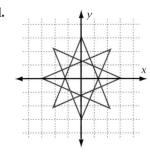

2. a. Write parametric equations for a circle of radius 1, centered at the origin. Graph the equations using a Tstep of 15°.

   b. Use the trace function to complete a table like the one below.

Angle A	0°	30°	45°	60°	90°	120°	135°
$\cos A$	-?-	-?-	-?-	-?-	-?-	-?-	-?-
$\sin A$	-?-	-?-	-?-	-?-	-?-	-?-	-?-

   c. Write an alternative definition for $\cos A$ that uses the following words: coordinate, unit circle, perimeter, central angle.

   d. Write an alternative definition for $\sin A$ that uses the following words: coordinate, unit circle, perimeter, central angle.

3. Experiment with your calculator to find parametric equations for each circle. Each one has a 2-unit radius and has been translated from the origin.

a.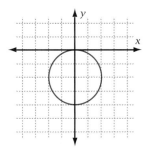

b.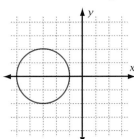

c.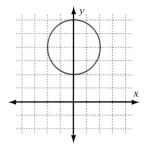

d.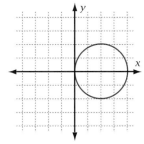

e.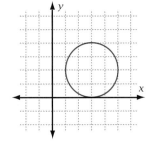

4. Complete the following steps to eliminate the parameter t in the equations $x = 3 \cos t$ and $y = 3 \sin t$.

   a. Divide both sides of each equation by 3 to isolate the t parts of the expressions. This means one equation will be solved for $\cos t$ and the other will be solved for $\sin t$.

   b. Square both sides of each equation.

   c. Add the equations together. Make sure the terms involving t are on one side of the final equation, and the terms involving x and y are on the other.

   d. Because $(\sin t)^2 + (\cos t)^2 = 1$ for any angle, use this to simplify the t side of the equation.

   e. Multiply your final equation by 9 to eliminate the fractions.

   f. The standard form of the equation of a circle in nonparametric form, when the center is at the origin, is $x^2 + y^2 = r^2$, where r is the radius. What is the value for r in your equation?

5. Use your equations from Problem 3e, and complete each step to eliminate the parameter t.

   a. Isolate the t part of each equation as in Problem 4a.

   b. Square both sides of each equation, and add them together.

   c. Use the fact that $(\sin t)^2 + (\cos t)^2 = 1$ to simplify the t side of the equation.

   d. Multiply by the appropriate number to eliminate any fractions.

   e. The standard nonparametric form of the equation of a circle that is not centered at the origin is $(x - h)^2 + (y - k)^2 = r^2$. The center is at (h, k) and the radius is r. What are the values for $h, k,$ and r in your equation?

   f. Graph this new equation to see if it matches the parametric graph. You will have to solve for y first.

6. Experiment to find parametric equations for each figure. The center of each figure is at the origin. (Each grid mark represents one unit.)

   a. 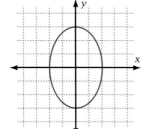   **b.** 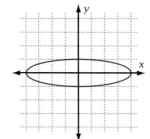   **c.**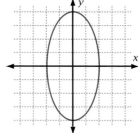

7. The figures in Problem 6 are called ellipses. They can be thought of as having two different radii: a horizontal radius and a vertical radius. Write the equation of each ellipse described below in parametric form.

   a. Horizontal radius = 4, vertical radius = 3, center $(0, 0)$

   b. Horizontal radius = 3, vertical radius = 2, center $(4, 0)$

   c. Horizontal radius = 2.5, vertical radius = 1.5, center $(0, 2)$

   d. Horizontal radius = 2, vertical radius = 3.5, center $(1, 3)$

8. a–b. Follow the steps described in Problem 5a–c to eliminate the parameter *t* from the equations you wrote in Problems 7a and 7c.

   c. The standard nonparametric form of the equation of an ellipse is

$$\frac{(x - h)^2}{a^2} + \frac{(y - k)^2}{b^2} = 1.$$

The center is at (h, k), and *a* and *b* represent half the length of each axis. Find the center of the ellipse and the length of each axis for 8a and 8b.

9. Write parametric equations and give values for Tmin, Tmax, and Tstep that will result in each graph or shape. (Each grid mark represents one unit.)

   a.

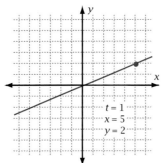

$t = 1$
$x = 5$
$y = 2$

   b.

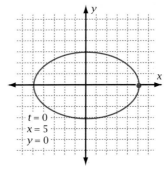

$t = 0$
$x = 5$
$y = 0$

   c.

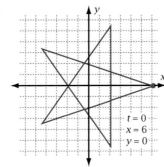

$t = 0$
$x = 6$
$y = 0$

   d.

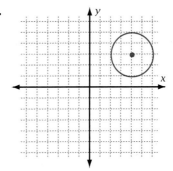

10. a. Create the shape in the figure to the right.
   b. Reflect the shape over the *x*-axis.
   c. Reflect the shape over the *y*-axis.
   d. Rotate the shape 180° about the origin.
   e. Name the values of Tmin, Tmax, and Tstep that you used in 10a, b, and c.
   f. Describe another way to rotate the shape.

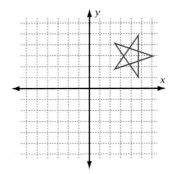

Viewing Angle

When classrooms are arranged, one thing that should be considered is how well all students will be able to see the chalkboard. Those students who sit toward the center of the room will have no difficulty. However, those who sit on the sides, along the walls, will have a more limited view. Consider the classroom design below. Determine the angle of view for the student sitting at each desk shown.

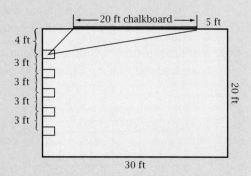

Which seat will have the best view of the chalkboard? Show all of your calculations and justify your conclusions.

For the desks in your classroom, determine an arrangement that you believe will provide all students with the best view possible. Present your plan, along with its justification, to your teacher.

Section 6.5

Wind and River Problems

To Thales the primary question was not what do we know, but how do we know it.
—*Aristotle*

Navigators have always steered by the stars. One method of navigation, going back to at least 1722, was developed by the navigators of the Caroline Islands in Micronesia. This method doesn't use any instruments, diagrams, or charts at all. At night, during their voyages in outrigger canoes between tiny islands in the open ocean, the navigators knew where they were from by observing the North Star, which the Skidi Pawnee call Star-which-does-not-move, and from watching "moving" stars rise and set. The North Star is also known as the Pole Star or Polaris.

The British learned about oceanic navigation primarily by translating Portuguese manuals, and by the 1570s they had developed a method of calculating a ship's speed. Using a compass to find the heading and the log line to find speed (you'll learn about these in Chapter 7), a navigator could find a ship's latitude by calculating one of the sides of what was called the nautical triangle.

The course of a sailing ship is usually not a straight line unless the wind happens to be blowing in the direction of the ship's course. European navigators had to calculate, or plot, the results of this "traverse sailing" in order to estimate where they were.

Winds and air currents affect the direction and speed a plane will travel. A pilot flying an airplane often has to compensate for these effects. Parametric equations are very useful in modeling these situations.

Loxodromes were used by navigators in the 1600s for creating maps. The quadrants formed by the north-south and east-west lines are bisected, and these four lines with the original axes represent the eight principal winds. The quadrants are further divided to show the half-winds and quarter-winds.

Investigation 6.5.1

Modeling Motion

You will need to do this investigation with a partner. Place a piece of paper lengthwise in front of you. Lightly hold a 12-inch ruler so that you will be able to draw a straight line across the paper toward yourself. (See the picture at the right.) Your partner will hold the end of the paper and slowly pull it under the ruler as you draw the line.

After you have drawn your line, answer each question below. You may want to exchange tasks and repeat the experiment.

a. Is the line you drew parallel to one of the sides of the paper? Is it diagonal on the paper?

b. How does the position of your line change when the paper is pulled at a faster rate? At a slower rate?

c. What could you do to make the line more perpendicular to the direction of the paper's motion?

d. What will happen if your partner pulls the paper at an increasing rate? (You might want to try this.)

The investigation above simulates what happens when you try to swim across a river with a strong current. The current sweeps you downstream, and when you reach the other side you will not be directly across from the point where you began. This movement is also similar to what happens to an airplane or a bird when the wind blows at them from the side.

Consider three toy cars on a large piece of plywood that is moving to the right across the floor at a rate of 60 cm/sec. Each car is moving 40 cm/sec in the direction indicated. After 1 second, car A is 100 cm to the right of its original position. It is at the 200 cm mark after 2 seconds and at the 300 cm mark after 3 seconds. During the same time intervals, car B is located 20 cm,

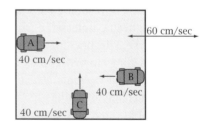

40 cm, and 60 cm to the right of its original position. The velocities of car A and car B relative to the floor are 100 cm/sec and 20 cm/sec, respectively.

The motion of car C is more complicated. After 1 second, it is 60 cm to the right and 40 cm above its original position. After 2 seconds, it is 120 cm to the right and 80 cm above its original position. Using the Pythagorean theorem, you can determine that the car is moving at $\sqrt{60^2 + 40^2} \approx 72.1$ cm/sec relative to the floor.

■ Example 1

Pat Dulbote heads her boat directly across a river which is 2 mi wide in this stretch. Her ancient motor can move the boat at a speed of 4 mi/hr on water where there is no current. However, the river current flows at 3 mi/hr. How far downstream is she by the time she gets across? How far did her boat actually travel? What was the actual velocity of her boat? What was the angle of the actual path, relative to a trip straight across the river?

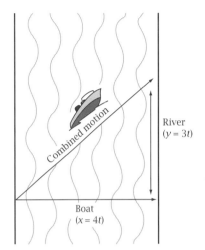

Solution

The first step is to establish a coordinate system. Assume that Pat starts at $(0, 0)$ and heads in the positive x-direction. The distance an object travels is given by the equation $d = rt$, where r is the rate of speed and t is time. If there were no current, the distance Pat's boat would travel would be $x = 4t$, where t is measured in hours. Assume that the current flows toward the positive y-direction. The equation representing the water current would be $y = 3t$. The combined effect of these two equations will represent the distance she actually travels.

To choose an appropriate window to graph this situation, you need to be sure to include the starting point of the boat and to adjust the x- and y-values so that you can see where the boat is going. In this case, a window that shows the upper right quadrant of the coordinate plane is appropriate. Because neither the boat nor the current travels very fast, the window does not need to extend very far in either direction. Graph $x = 4t$ and $y = 3t$ on your calculator using parameter settings of $[0, 0.5, 0.01]$ and $[0, 2, 1, ^-1, 2, 1]$. Trace to find the point on the other side of the river when $x = 2$. The corresponding y-coordinate is 1.5. This means that the boat traveled 1.5 mi downstream during the time it took the boat to move 2 mi across the river. The t-value of this point is 0.5, so it took $\frac{1}{2}$ hr to make the trip.

To determine the actual distance traveled by the boat, look at the triangle formed with the horizontal. Use the Pythagorean theorem to determine this distance.

$$2^2 + 1.5^2 = d^2$$
$$4 + 2.25 = d^2$$
$$d^2 = 6.25$$
$$d = \sqrt{6.25} = 2.5$$

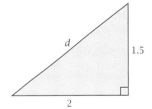

Therefore, Pat traveled 2.5 mi as she crossed the river.

Because *distance* = *rate* • *time,* and you know she traveled 2.5 mi in 0.5 hr, her rate can be determined using substitution.

2.5 = *rate* • 0.5   or   *rate* = 5 mi/hr

Several different methods could be used to find the angle of motion. Trace to any point (*x, y*) on the actual path. Then find the inverse tangent (tan⁻¹) of the ratio $\frac{y}{x}$. (Why does this work?) The angle of motion is about 36.9°.   ■

An airplane is affected by the wind in the same way a boat is affected by the current. The following situation illustrates what happens when a pilot does not compensate for this wind effect.

■ Example 2

A pilot heads a plane due west from Memphis, Tennessee, toward Albuquerque, New Mexico. The cities are 1000 mi apart, and the pilot sets the plane's controls to fly at 250 mi/hr. However, there is a constant 20 mi/hr wind blowing from the north. Where does the plane end up?

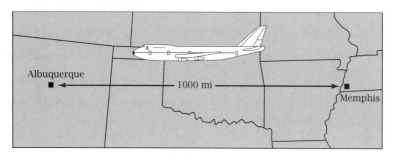

Solution

Set up a coordinate system with Memphis at the origin. The plane's motion can be described by the equation *x* = ⁻250*t*. (Why is ⁻250*t* used rather than 250*t*?) The wind's force can be described by *y* = ⁻20*t*. (Why is ⁻20*t* used rather than 20*t*?) Choose an appropriate graphing window and watch the result of the combined motions.

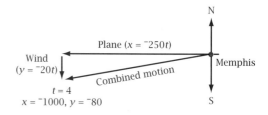

Tracing this graph will show that after 4 hr the plane has traveled the necessary 1000 mi west, but it is 80 mi south of Albuquerque, somewhere in the White Sands Missile Range!

The Pythagorean theorem indicates that the plane has actually traveled $\sqrt{1000^2 + 80^2}$, or about 1003 mi in 4 hr; this is a rate of 250.8 mi/hr.

The actual angle of motion between the plane's path and due west is $\tan^{-1}\left(\frac{80}{1000}\right)$, or about 4.6°.   ■

Problem Set 6.5

1. Convert each angle of motion in Example 1 and Example 2 to a compass heading. (Remember, the heading is the angle measured clockwise from north.)

2. Pa Pye heads his boat directly across the 1.5 mi wide Whett River to his friend Ollie Voyl's house. His boat can go 6 mi/hr and the river flows at 2 mi/hr.
   a. Write the equation that describes the effect of the river current.
   b. Write the equation that describes the boat's contribution to the motion.
   c. Graph these equations.
   d. How far downstream does Pa land?
   e. How far has his boat traveled?

3. A pilot wants to fly from Toledo to Chicago, which lies 280 mi directly west. Her plane can fly at 120 mi/hr. She ignores the wind and heads directly west. However, there is a 25 mi/hr wind blowing from the south.
   a. Write the equation that describes the effect of the wind.
   b. Write the equation that describes the plane's contribution to the motion.
   c. Graph these equations.
   d. How far off course is the plane when it has traveled 280 mi west?
   e. How far has the plane actually traveled?
   f. What was the plane's actual speed?

4. Fred points his small boat directly across a river, which is 4 mi wide. There is a 5 mi/hr current. When he reaches the opposite shore, Fred finds that he has landed at a point 2 mi downstream.
   a. Write the equation that describes the effect of the river current.
   b. If Fred's boat can go 3 mi/hr, what equation will describe his contribution to the motion?
   c. Graph these equations and then change Fred's speed (using guess-and-check) until he reaches the correct point 2 mi downstream on the opposite shore.
   d. How far did Fred actually travel?
   e. How long did it take him?
   f. What was Fred's actual speed?
   g. As the boat travels down the river, what angle does it make with the river bank?

5. A plane takes off from Orlando, Florida, heading 975 mi due north toward Cleveland, Ohio. The plane flies at 250 mi/hr. There is a 25 mi/hr wind blowing from the west.
  a. Where is the plane after it has traveled 975 mi north?
  b. How far did the plane actually travel?
  c. How fast did the plane actually travel?
  d. At what angle from the horizontal did the plane actually fly?
  e. What was the heading?

Problems 6–9 deal with the motion of a falling object. The height of the object is affected by the force of gravity. An equation for the height is $y = {}^-16t^2 + s_0$. Here t is the time (measured in seconds) and s_0 is the initial height of the object (measured in feet.) The coefficient $^-16$ is related to the *acceleration* of the object caused by the force of gravity.

6. A ball is rolled off the end of a table with a horizontal velocity of 1.5 ft/sec. The table is 2.75 ft high.
  a. If there were no gravity, what equation would describe the x-direction motion of the ball?
  b. Gravity will affect the vertical motion of the ball. Use the equation given above, with the appropriate value for the initial height, to model the vertical motion of the ball.
  c. Enter these two equations in your calculator and graph them.
  d. How far from the table does the ball hit the floor? Give your answer to the nearest hundredth of a foot.
  e. How long does it take for the ball to hit the floor? Give your answer to the nearest hundredth of a second.

7. A ball is rolled off a 3 ft high table and lands at a point 1.8 ft away from the table.
  a. How long did it take for the ball to hit the floor? Give your answer to the nearest hundredth of a second.
  b. How fast was the ball traveling when it left the table? Give your answer to the nearest hundredth of a second. (Hint: You can find this answer by guess-and-check, or by using the answer from 7a.)

8. A wildlife biologist sees a deer standing 400 ft away. Her gun is loaded with tranquilizer darts that leave her gun traveling at 650 ft/sec. The biologist is holding the gun level, at a height of 5.5 ft above the ground.
  a. Record the equations you used to model this motion.
  b. Does she hit the deer? If not, by how much did she miss?
  c. Use guess-and-check to determine how high the biologist would have to hold the gun to hit the deer at a height somewhere between 3 ft and 4.5 ft above the ground. (The gun is held level with the ground.)

d. How far does the dart travel before it drops 1 ft in height? Does the original height make a difference? Does the original velocity of the dart make a difference? Explain.

9. A golf ball rolls off the top step of a flight of 14 stairs with a horizontal velocity of 5 ft/sec. The stairs are each 8 in. high and 8 in. wide. On which step does the ball first bounce? (To solve this problem, you may want to convert everything to inches, including the gravity constant of $^-16$ ft/sec^2, the vertical-component equation for the motion.)

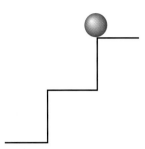

10. You have studied parametric equations in several different contexts. Explain some advantages and disadvantages of using parametric equations. Include examples if appropriate.

11. Create your own problem that is related to something you have studied so far in this chapter. Write out the complete solution to your problem and explain why you think it is a good problem. (Note: Please make sure that it is a problem or a question, and not just an explanation or a description.)

Take Another Look 6.5

When a graph is reflected over the y-axis, the corresponding x-coordinates of the graph and its image are opposites of each other ($x_{2t} = {^-x_{1t}}$). This means $\frac{x_{1t} + x_{2t}}{2} = 0$ (the average is 0) for each value of the parameter t, and the y-axis ($x = 0$) is the line of reflection.

What if the corresponding x-coordinates of a graph and its reflection always average to $^-2$? Does this mean $x = {^-2}$ is the line of reflection for these two graphs? Morever, how can you write an x_{2t} equation that will provide the needed reflection for any given x_{1t} equation? You can find the answer by solving for x_{2t} in the equation

$$\frac{x_{1t} + x_{2t}}{2} = {^-2}.$$

You will find that $x_{2t} = {^-4} - x_{1t}$.

a. Take another look at this graph from Problem 10 of Problem Set 6.4. Write parametric equations whose graph is the given shape. Then write another pair of equations whose graph is a reflection image over the line $x = {^-2}$. Verify your work by checking several of the required averages. Explain your procedure for doing this.

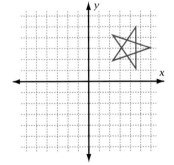

b. What parametric equations will reflect the pictured shape over the line $x = {^-2}$ and then reflect that image over the line $y = {^-1}$? Explain.

c. Take another look at the graph in Example 2 of Section 6.1. Write one pair of parametric equations for the original graph and another pair for its image after a reflection over the line $x = 5$. Explain how you know that you are correct.

d. Using what you've learned in a–c above, create a symmetric drawing by graphing parametric images and their reflections. Set a friendly window with $(0,0)$ at the lower left corner and distances of one unit between pixels on both the x- and y-axes.

Project

Projectile Motion

In this chapter, you have considered motion at an angle A, using the parametric equations $x(t) = vt \cos A$ and $y(t) = vt \sin A$. You have also looked at motion affected by gravity, using the equations $x(t) = vt + x_0$ and $y(t) = {}^-at^2 + y_0$. In this project, you will combine these two ideas to consider motion at an angle relative to the ground that is affected by gravity. Explain in detail with words, equations, graphs, and diagrams how you would solve the following problem.

Great Gonzo, the human cannonball, is fired out of a cannon at a speed of 40 ft/sec. The cannon is tilted at an angle of 60°. A 10 ft diameter net is hung 10 ft above the floor, at a distance of 30 ft from the cannon. Does Gonzo land in the net?

Section 6.6

Using Trigonometry to Set a Course

Every new body of discovery is mathematical in form, because there is no other guidance we can have.
—Charles Darwin

In Section 6.5, you solved problems in which a plane or a boat was moving in a direction perpendicular to a wind or a current. Planes and boats actually travel at a variety of angles with respect to the wind and water flow. These situations can also be modeled with trigonometric ratios and by breaking a motion into vertical and horizontal components.

■ Example 1

An object is moving at a speed of 10 units/sec, at an angle of 30° to the *x*-axis. What are the horizontal and vertical components of this motion?

Solution

Draw a triangle with a 30° angle. The hypotenuse represents the path of the object and its length represents the distance traveled by the object; label it $10t$. Now you can use trigonometry to calculate the lengths of the legs of the triangle, which are the horizontal and vertical components of the motion.

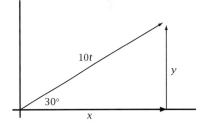

$$\sin 30° = \frac{y}{10t} \qquad \cos 30° = \frac{x}{10t}$$

$$y = 10t \sin 30° \qquad x = 10t \cos 30°$$

Check to see that these equations will provide the motion required. ■

In general, the horizontal component is $x = v_0 t \cos A$, where v_0 is the initial velocity, A is the angle, and the vertical component is $y = v_0 t \sin A$.

■ Example 2

A pilot heads from Memphis, Tennessee, toward Albuquerque, New Mexico. The cities are 1000 mi apart; Memphis is due east of Albuquerque. The plane flies at 250 mi/hr, and there is a constant 20 mi/hr wind blowing from the north. What angle and heading should the pilot set so that he actually lands in Albuquerque and is not blown off course?

Solution

Set up a coordinate system with Memphis at the origin, and sketch the plane's path slightly to the north. The plane's distance along the hypotenuse can be described by

$250t$. The east-west component is $x = {}^-250t \cos A$, where A is the tiny angle toward the north that the pilot must set. (The negative sign directs the motion to the west.)

The wind's velocity can be described by $y = {}^-20t$ because it is blowing south. The north-south component of the plane's course, $y = 250t \sin A$, must exactly match the velocity of the wind (add up to zero) if the pilot hopes to land in Albuquerque.

$250t \sin A + {}^-20t = 0$

or $20t = 250t \sin A$

$20 = 250 \sin A$

$\sin A = \frac{20}{250} = 0.08$

$\sin^{-1} A = 4.59$, so A is about $4.59°$

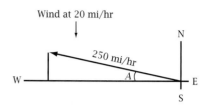

Turn off the axes on your calculator and graph
$x = {}^-250t \cos 4.59°$ and $y = 250t \sin 4.59° - 20t$ to see the plane move directly west. Be sure to use an appropriate graphing window.

Because a compass bearing is measured as an angle clockwise from due north, the pilot would actually set his instruments at $270° + 4.59°$, or $274.59°$. ∎

■ Example 3

A plane is headed from Memphis to Albuquerque, which is 1000 mi due west. The plane flies at 250 mi/hr. On this trip the pilot encounters a 20 mi/hr wind blowing in from the northwest. Where will the plane end up if the pilot does not compensate for the wind?

Solution

You will begin by setting up the same type of coordinate system as before. Because the plane is headed directly west, you use the equation $x = {}^-250t$ to model the plane's contribution to the motion. Because the wind is blowing at an angle, it will affect both the east-west and north-south directions of motion. You must break the velocity of the wind into these two components. A picture such as the one below is helpful.

Memphis, Tennessee

The problem now is to find the lengths of the two legs of the triangle.

To find the southward leg, use the sine ratio.

$\sin 45° = \frac{{}^-y}{20t}$ $y = {}^-20t \sin 45°$

To find the eastward leg, use the cosine ratio or the Pythagorean theorem.

$\cos 45° = \frac{x}{20t}$ $x = 20t \cos 45°$

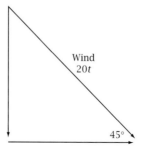

CHAPTER 6   PARAMETRIC EQUATIONS AND TRIGONOMETRY

Notice that the signs of these equations are determined by the directions of the arrows in the diagram.

Both the plane's motion and the wind contribute to the actual path of the plane, so you add the *x*-contributions together and the *y*-contributions together to form the final equations.

$$x = {}^-250t + 20t \cos 45° \quad \text{and} \quad y = {}^-20t \sin 45°.$$

(You may also use the decimal forms of these equations, $x = {}^-250t + 14.14t$, or $x = {}^-235.86t$, and $y = {}^-14.14t$, but you will lose some accuracy in your calculations.)

By graphing and tracing, you will find that it takes the plane about 4.24 hr to fly 1000 mi west, and it is then about 60 mi south of Albuquerque. ∎

■ Example 4

What angle adjustment should the pilot in Example 3 make in the flight so that he will land in Albuquerque?

Albuquerque, New Mexico

Solution

For the plane to actually fly straight west, it must head a bit north. It must have a north-south component to its motion that will exactly counteract the north-south effect of the wind. The northern component of the plane's motion will be $y = 250t \sin A$, where A is that unknown little angle to the north. The wind's contribution will remain $y = {}^-20t \sin 45°$. For the plane to fly directly west, these must add up to zero.

$$250t \sin A + {}^-20t \sin 45° = 0$$

$$250t \sin A = 20t \sin 45° \qquad \text{Add } 20t \sin 45° \text{ to both sides.}$$

$$\sin A = \frac{20}{250} \sin 45° \qquad \text{Divide by } 250t.$$

$$A = \sin^{-1}\left(\frac{20}{250} \sin 45°\right) \approx 3.24° \qquad \text{Take the inverse sine.}$$

By adjusting for this angle, the plane will fly directly west. To model the motion on the calculator, you must also use this angle to modify the *x*-equation.

$$x = {}^-250t \cos 3.24° + 20t \cos 45°$$
$$y = 250t \sin 3.24° + {}^-20t \sin 45°$$

Plane without wind

Plane and wind together

Wind without plane

Enter these two equations and graph. (Turn off the axes or you may see nothing happening, because the graph is being drawn on top of the *x*-axis.) A trace of the graph will show that after 4.28 hr, the plane has traveled the 1000 mi west, and is only about a tenth of a mile north of its destination. (This slight error could be reduced by using a more accurate measure for the angle.) Therefore, the pilot must set an instrument heading of 270° + 3.24°, or 273.24°. ∎

Problem Set 6.6

1. Beau Terr wants to travel directly across the Wyde River, which is 2 mi wide in this stretch. His boat can move at a speed of 4 mi/hr. The river current flows at 3 mi/hr. At what angle upstream should he aim the boat so that he ends up going straight across?

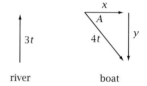

   a. Write an equation for the upstream component of the boat's motion.
   b. Write an equation for the river's motion.
   c. Equate these components and solve for A.
   d. Write equations for the horizontal components of motion.
   e. Model the motion on your calculator, and verify that Beau will travel directly across the river. Record your equations.

2. A plane is flying on a heading of 310° at a speed of 320 mi/hr. The wind is blowing directly from the east at a speed of 32 mi/hr.

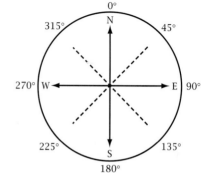

   a. Make a drawing to indicate the plane's motion.
   b. Write equations that model the plane's motion without the wind.
   c. Make a drawing to indicate the wind's motion.
   d. Write equations that model the wind's motion.
   e. What are the resulting equations that model the motion of the plane with the wind?
   f. Where is the plane after 5 hr?

3. **a.** Use guess-and-check to find the angle adjustment the pilot must make in Problem 2 so that the plane is not blown off course during this flight. (Hint: What are the x- and y-coordinates of the plane in Problem 2 if it isn't blown off course? Use this point as a target on your screen.)
   b. Write the final equations that combine both the plane's and the wind's contributions to the flight.
   c. Test your equations by graphing and tracing.

4. A plane is flying on a heading of 250° at a speed of 220 mi/hr. The wind is blowing 40 mi/hr toward a heading of 160°. Where is the plane after 5 hr?
   a. Make separate diagrams for the plane and the wind. Find the angle each path makes with the x-axis.
   b. Write equations for the east-west and north-south components for the wind and the plane.
   c. Write combined equations for x and y, and graph them.
   d. Where is the plane after 5 hr?
   e. How far has it traveled from its starting point?
   f. At what heading did it actually travel?

5. a. Describe how you can find the angle adjustment the pilot must make in Problem 4 so that the plane is not blown off course during the flight.

   b. Write the final equations you used that combine both the plane's and the wind's motion contributions to the flight.

   c. Test your equations by graphing and tracing.

6. Superman takes off from Metropolis to fly to Central City, which is 800 mi directly west; he flies at a leisurely rate of 75 mi/hr. The wind is blowing toward a heading of 300° at a speed of 32 mi/hr. Follow the steps below to find the correct heading and the length of time it will take Superman to reach Central City.

   a. Write an equation showing the relationship between the north-south components of the wind and Superman's flying speed. Solve this for the angle at which Superman must fly to arrive in Central City. Convert this to a heading.

   b. Write an equation showing the relationship between the east-west components of the wind and Superman's flying speed, and the 800 mi he needs to travel.

   c. How long does it take him to fly to Central City?

7. A bird is starting its annual migration from northern Michigan to Florida. It takes off on a heading of 165°. The bird flies at an average speed of 10 mi/hr. On the day it takes off, there is an 8 mi/hr breeze blowing toward a heading of 100°.

   a. Make a diagram showing the effect of the wind. Label the east-west and north-south components. Write equations for the east-west and north-south components.

   b. Make a diagram showing the bird's contribution to the motion. Write equations for the east-west and north-south components.

   c. Write the combined equations for the motion and graph the equations. Where is the bird after 8 hr of travel?

   d. At what heading has the bird actually traveled?

   e. How do birds actually stay on course during migration? Investigate this subject and write a paragraph summarizing the theories.

8. a. A new plane is proposed that will fly 12,000 mi in 3 hr. How fast will the plane have to travel?

   b. Suppose this plane flies on a heading of 270° (straight west) and there is a 30 mi/hr wind blowing from the north. How far off course will the plane be after traveling 12,000 mi?

   c. At what heading should the plane fly to correct this? How practical is this? Explain your answer.

9. Is there a problem in this section that you are having difficulty solving? If so, write out the problem and as much of the solution as you can. Then, clearly explain what is keeping you from solving the problem. Be as specific as you can.

Take Another Look 6.6

Take another look at Problems 6–9 of Problem Set 6.5. Did you find the time it took for the ball to hit the floor in Problem 6 by graphing, by tracing, or by zooming in on table values? Another possibility would be to solve for t after replacing y by 0 in the equation $y = {}^-16t^2 + 2.75$. (Solve $0 = {}^-16t^2 + 2.75$ for t.) You may have discovered this strategy, or your teacher may have encouraged it at the time you worked on the problems.

Confirm that the appropriate value of t is $\sqrt{\dfrac{2.75}{16}}$.

Now find the x-position of the ball at this particular time. Your answers should agree with your original conclusions.

No single solution strategy is being advocated here. In each instance, drawing graphs, looking at table values, and using algebraic manipulations combine to help you make sense of the situation.

a. Use algebraic manipulation to solve the problem in Example 2 of Section 6.5. In other words, answer the questions asked after first solving $^-1000 = {}^-250t$.

b. Use algebraic manipulation as a strategy for solving Problem 7 of Problem Set 6.5.

Project

Boolean Expressions

Boolean expressions, often used by programmers, are mathematical statements that are either true or false. In 1938, a century after Boole first described these expressions in *The Laws of Thought*, Claude Shannon (1916–), who was a graduate student at the Massachusetts Institute of Technology, wrote a paper describing how Boole's system could be used in the design of relay and switching circuits. This idea had already been presented in earlier articles written in Russian by Paul Ehrenfest and V. I. S. Sestakov, and in Japanese by Akira Nakasima and Masao Hanzawa. However, mainly because Shannon's paper was in English and because it gave a detailed delineation of the connection between Boole's system and circuit design, it received wide attention and was followed by hundreds of other papers. Designers began to use Shannon's methods and still use them today.

In Boolean expressions, *true* has a value of one, and *false* has a value of zero. If you type 4 = 7 on your calculator, it will give you 0. If you enter 4 = 4, it will give you 1. Try this now.

If you enter $x > 3$ in your calculator and it gives you 1, you know that the current value stored in x is greater than 3. Try graphing the function $y = (x > 3)$. The graph will look like the one below on the left if you are in *connected* mode. If you are in *dot* mode, it will look like the one on the right. Be sure you can explain what is happening. (Each grid mark represents one unit.)

You can use Boolean expressions when you simulate motion that changes at a particular time. For example, Trodd Myles walks at 3 mi/hr at a bearing of 210° for 2 hr

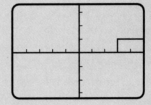
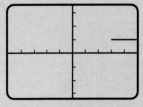

30 min, then turns and walks due east for 1 hr 45 min.

$$x(t) = {}^-3t \cos 60° \cdot (t \le 2.5) + ({}^-7.5 \cos 60° + 3(t - 2.5) \cos 0°) \cdot (t > 2.5)(t \le 4.25)$$
$$y(t) = {}^-3t \sin 60° \cdot (t \le 2.5) + ({}^-7.5 \sin 60° + 3(t - 2.5) \sin 0)° \cdot (t > 2.5)(t \le 4.25)$$

Write a paragraph detailing the meaning of each of the parts and numbers in the equations above. Then find the third leg of the journey to return back to the starting point, and adjust the equations to show the complete trip.

Chapter Review

> *The bottom line for mathematicians is that the architecture has to be right. In all
> the mathematics that I did, the essential point was to find the right architecture.
> It's like building a bridge. Once the main lines of the structure are right, then the
> details miraculously fit. The problem is the overall design.*
> —Freeman Dyson

Parametric equations describe the locations of points by using a third variable. In
many cases this third variable can be thought of as time. In other cases it can be
interpreted as an angle. The third variable, t, is called a parameter. By controlling the
range of t-values, you can graph part of a function. To convert from parametric form
to regular form, solve either the x- or the y-equation for t. Then substitute this
expression into the other equation. The result is an equation involving only x and y.

One use of parametric equations is to simulate motion. This often involves the use
of right triangle trigonometry. If the object, such as a plane or a boat, is traveling in a
direction that is not straight north, south, east, or west, you have to break the motion
into east-west and north-south components. The east-west component is $x = vt \cos A$,
where A is the angle the object makes with the x-axis and v is the velocity of the
object. The north-south component is $y = vt \sin A$. If the motion is directed below the
x-axis, then a negative sign should be placed at the front of the y-equation. If the
motion is directed to the left of the y-axis, a negative should be placed in front of the
x-equation. Sometimes the wind or a current is present and influences the motion. If
this is the case, the motion of the wind or current also needs to be broken into its
components and these added to the equations for the object's motion. Parametric
equations can also be used to model the motion of a falling object.

Another use of parametric equations is to graph geometric shapes. In this case the
parameter t indicates an angle. The number of sides of the shape will be determined
by the Tstep. To create a figure with n sides, the Tstep should be $360/n$. If the Tstep
is not a factor of 360, then by using a larger range for t you can create patterns that
resemble string art.

Problem Set 6.7

1. a. Make a (*time, distance*) graph that represents motion at 20 m/sec for 5 sec and
then at 30 m/sec for 8 sec.
   b. What does the (*time, speed*) graph of this motion look like?

2. Use the parametric equations $x = {}^-3t + 1$ and $y = \dfrac{2}{t + 1}$ to answer each question.
   a. Find the x- and y-coordinates of the points that correspond to the values of $t = 3$,
   $t = 0$, and $t = {}^-3$.
   b. Find the y-value that is paired with $x = {}^-7$.

c. Find the *x*-value that is paired with $y = 4$.

d. Sketch the curve for $^-3 \leq t \leq 3$, showing the direction of movement. Trace the graph and explain what happens when $t = ^-1$.

3. Complete the following tasks for each set of parametric equations below.
   i. Graph them.
   ii. Eliminate the parameter and solve for *y*.
   iii. Graph the resulting nonparametric equation and describe how it compares with the original graph.

   a. $x = 2t - 5, y = t + 1$ **b.** $x = t^2 + 1, y = t - 2, ^-2 \leq t \leq 6$

   c. $x = \dfrac{t + 1}{2}, y = t^2, ^-4 \leq t \leq 3$ **d.** $x = \sqrt{t + 2}, y = t - 3$

4. Write parametric equations that will result in each transformation below for the equations in Problems 3a and 3c.
   i. Reflect the curve across the *y*-axis.
   ii. Reflect the curve across the *x*-axis.
   iii. Slide the curve three units up.
   iv. Slide the curve four units left and two units down.

5. Solve to find the measure of the angle or the length of the side, as indicated in each triangle.

a.

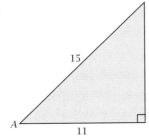

b.

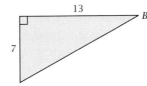

c.

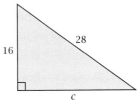

d.

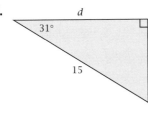

e.

f.

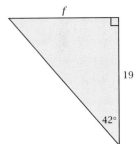

6. Sketch a graph of $x = t \cos 28°, y = t \sin 28°$. What is the angle between the graph and the *x*-axis?

7. A diver runs off a 10 m platform with an initial horizontal velocity of 4 m/sec. The edge of the platform is directly above a point 1.5 m from the pool's edge. How far from the edge of the pool will she hit the water? (Use $h = {}^-4.9t^2 + s_0$ for the vertical-component equation.)

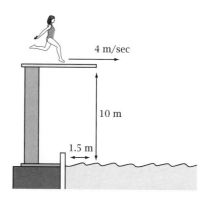

8. Speedo the Duck paddles 2.4 ft/sec aiming directly for the other bank of a 47 ft wide river. When he lands, he finds himself 28 ft downstream from the point across from where he started. What is the speed of the current?

9. Wildlife biologist R. E. Searcher sees a monkey in a tree that is 94 ft away from him. He is also in a tree, at the same height as the monkey. The muzzle velocity of his tranquilizer gun is 150 ft/sec. If he holds his gun horizontally when he fires, will he hit the monkey? (Locate the monkey by entering its coordinates as a pair of parametric equations.)

10. If R. E. Searcher knows that the monkey will drop from the branch the moment the gun is fired, describe what will happen.

11. A pilot wishes to fly his plane to a destination 700 mi away at a bearing of 105° from north. The cruising speed of the plane is 500 mi/hr, and the wind is blowing between 20 mi/hr and 30 mi/hr toward a bearing of 30°. At what angle should he steer the plane to compensate for the wind? With the variation in the wind, what is the widest margin of error by which the pilot could miss the airport?

12. If you had to choose a favorite problem from this unit, what would it be? Why?

Baseball Pitcher

Model the path of a ball thrown by a major-league baseball pitcher. The speed of the ball will depend on the type of pitch, as well as on how hard the ball is thrown.

For example, a fastball might be released at 98.5 mi/hr, while a forkball change-up pitch might be released at 80 mi/hr. Suppose the pitches are thrown parallel to the ground directly across home plate. In your model, be sure to consider the height of the pitcher's mound, and take into account the height at which the ball will be released. Determine the speed of the strike pitches. Determine how long it takes for these pitches to reach the plate. Justify all assumptions you have made.

Assessing What You've Learned—Group Presentations and Tests

Throughout this course you have worked on investigations, and most likely problem sets, with your group. You may have even been asked to make a group presentation or to take a group test. Several of the journal prompts have asked you to write about your experiences when working in your group. Being able to work in a group is a very important skill to learn. If you go to college, you will probably be doing group projects; and when you get a job, you will find that you will have to work with others to solve problems. You have probably found that it's often easier to solve a problem when working with others.

It is important for you to be able to assess how you function in a group. Are you the organizer? The one who summarizes? The idea generator? The one who keeps others on task? Probably your role is a combination of these things. Being able to analyze your role in a group is another means of assessing yourself.

What else have you done in this chapter to assess what you've learned?

Organizing Your Notebook
- It's time to check your notebook again. Have you completed all of the assignments and reworked problems that were difficult for you?

Keeping a Journal
- Look in Problem Sets 6.5, 6.6, and 6.7 for journal prompts.
- Look back at an investigation you did in this chapter. Write a paragraph or two about your function in the group, your strengths, and what you need to do to improve.

Portfolio

• Have you done some work in this chapter that you would like to include in your portfolio? If so, document it, and put it in.

Performance Assessment

• Demonstrate to someone that you know how to model a motion problem on your calculator using parametric equations.

Open-ended Investigations

• Choose one of the Take Another Look investigations or a Project, or design your own investigation. Share your results with a classmate, your group, or your teacher.

Constructing Test Questions

• Write several test problems that you think would be useful in determining whether or not a student understands the concepts presented in this chapter.

7

Exponential and Logarithmic Functions

As the images of the chess pieces recede, the height of each piece is a percentage of the height of the previous piece. This percentage remains constant, so the height is an exponential function of the distance. This is similar to what happens when you observe fence posts receding into the distance.

Section 7.1

The Exponential Function

"Obvious" is the most dangerous word in mathematics.
—Eric Temple Bell

Every two seconds, nine babies are born and three people die. The net increase of three people each second results in a growth in world population of 10,600 per hour, 254,000 per day, 1.8 million per week, 7.7 million per month, and 93 million per year. It is estimated that by the year 2000, annual population growth will increase to 94 million; by 2020, it will be 98 million. Social scientists who study long-range population trends often use exponential functions to model the growth.

In previous chapters, you found that geometric sequences of the form

$u_n = u_0 r^n$ are used to model discrete **growth** of money, trees, populations, and a variety of other natural phenomena. In this section, you will focus on situations involving *continuous* growth. Growth (or its opposite, **decay**) often occurs exponentially and continuously. The continuous exponential function form $f(x) = ab^x$ follows naturally from the explicit geometric sequence model. In general, **exponential functions** are functions with a variable in the exponent.

The idea of using the exponential model for population growth was inspired by the writings of Thomas Malthus (1766–1834), a professor of modern history and political economy in England. He published a long pamphlet in 1798 called *An Essay on the Principle of Population.* In it he discussed the idea that human populations would eventually exhaust their food supplies. This was not a new idea, though it has come to be associated with Malthus's name. What was new was the forcefulness of the way in which it was stated. Malthus argued that human (and other) populations increase exponentially, but food supplies increase linearly. He concluded that while food supplies might conceivably be doubled in 25 years, it was impossible to imagine that they would be quadrupled in another 25 years. His original conclusions, however, did not draw on much data. In 1803, Malthus published a second edition of his *Essay* that incorporated observations he had made during his travels in Europe as well as data from published sources.

■ Example 1

In 1989, the population of India was 835 million people. The annual growth rate was about 1.9%. Use this information to predict future populations of the world's second most populous country.

Solution

You have frequently found discrete or yearly totals using recursive routines:

835   (ENTER)

Ans (1 + 0.019)   and press (ENTER) repeatedly.

The explicit formula $y = 835(1 + 0.019)^x$ provides the same results as the recursive routine when x represents the number of years since 1989. To predict the population for 1991, use an x-value of (1991 – 1989), or 2. The explicit function implies that the growth is continuous. Populations actually grow discretely, because there are no fractional people. However, because the numbers are so large and you are measuring in millions of people, the discrete graph is nearly continuous, so you can use a continuous function to model the growth.

This model predicted $y = f(2) = 835(1.019)^2 = 867$ million people in 1991. What x-value gives the population in 1995?   ■

If you assume a constant growth rate, you can see that millions more people will soon be living in India. (Look at the table that follows.) The population graph also suggests a little of the curvature that you will soon recognize as a characteristic of exponential relations. Enter the data in your calculator and make a scatter plot that looks like the one below.

Year	Population (in millions)	Year	Population (in millions)
1989	835	1998	989.1
1991	867	1999	1007.9
1992	883.5	2000	1027.1
1993	900.3	2001	1046.6
1994	917.4	2002	1066.5
1995	934.8	2009	1216.7
1996	952.6	2014	1336.7
1997	970.7	2018	1441.2

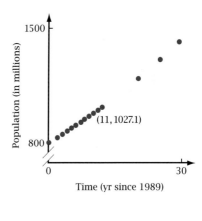

The population of India is constantly growing. If you assume that the growth rate will remain constant, then from 1989 to 2018 the graph will show a continuous population growth from 835 million to 1441.2 million people.

For example, when $x = 4.6$ years, $y = 835(1.019)^{4.6} = 910.5$ million people. A smooth curve drawn through the indicated table values is a better graphic representation of

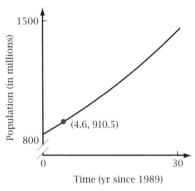

the increasing population of India from 1989 to 2018 than a discrete graph showing only points.

■ Example 2

Most automobiles depreciate as they get older. Suppose that an automobile that originally costs $14,000 loses one-fifth of its value every year.

a. What is the value of this automobile after two and one-half years?

b. Approximately when is this automobile worth $7,000 (half of its initial value)?

Solution

a. The recursive solution to this problem only furnishes automobile values after one year, two years, three years, and so on.

> 14000   (ENTER)
> Ans(1 – 0.2)   press (ENTER) repeatedly to get the values.

Original investment	After 1 yr	After 2 yr	After 2.5 yr	After 3 yr	After 4 yr
$14,000	$11,200	$8,960	–?–	$7,168	$5,734.40

Looking at the table you can see that if $2 \leq year \leq 3$, then $8960 \geq auto\ value \geq 7168$. You can verify the table entries by using the explicit formula $y = 14000(1 - 0.2)^x$.

$$y = 14000(1 - 0.2)^2 = \$8,960$$
$$y = 14000(1 - 0.2)^3 = \$7,168$$

You can also assign noninteger values, like 2.5, to x.

$$y = 14000(1 - 0.2)^{2.5} = \$8,014.07$$

b. Experimenting with exponents between 3 and 4 can produce a value as close to $7,000 as you want. The value of $14000(0.8)^{3.10628372}$ is very close. This means that after 3.10628372 years (about 3 years and 39 days), the value of the auto is half of its original value. This is

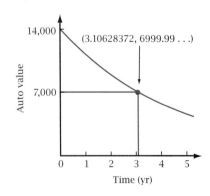

       CHAPTER 7   EXPONENTIAL AND LOGARITHMIC FUNCTIONS

the **half-life** of the value of the automobile, or the amount of time needed for the value to decrease to half of the original amount. ■

When the **base**, b, of the exponential function $y = ab^x$ is less than one ($b < 1$), the value of the function decreases (or decays) as the value of x increases. Decay is a way of describing growth in reverse. In the example of declining auto values described by $y = 14000(0.8)^x$, the base (0.8) was less than one.

Investigation 7.1.1

Radioactive Squares

Radioactive decay occurs when an unstable atom is bombarded with energy and the atom breaks apart into a different form. Energy bombardment can strike any atom at random. If it strikes a stable atom, then no change occurs.

Part 1   In this investigation, you will simulate what happens when a sample of 900 radioactive (unstable) atoms are randomly bombarded with energy. The sample is represented by 900 (uncolored) small squares, in a 30-by-30 configuration. You will color each "atom" as it decays to a more stable form. Your group will need a sheet of acetate and a 30-by-30 square grid, numbered horizontally and vertically from 0 to 29. (See the drawing at the right.)
Divide the tasks as follows:

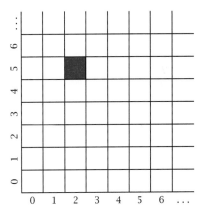

a. The *recorder* will lay the clear acetate over the grid and carefully outline the area. Be sure to mark the "top" on the acetate. The recorder will be responsible for coloring squares as coordinates are generated.

NOTE
7A

b. The *technical advisor* will enter the routine found in **Calculator Note 7A** into a calculator. The technical advisor is responsible for generating the pairs of coordinates.

c. The *data monitor* will keep track of the number of pairs generated. This person, with the help of the *checker*, will also be responsible for sharing the group's data with the class in Part 2 of the investigation.

d. The *checker* will check that the recorder is indeed coloring the correct square and will help the data monitor when recording the data on the class chart.

The technical advisor announces the coordinates of a square, such as (2, 5). The recorder colors that square (if it is not already colored), and the data monitor keeps track of how many coordinate pairs have been generated. (If the square represented by a pair of coordinates has already been colored, the data monitor still counts that pair as one of the 50 pairs.)

When each group has finished collecting data and coloring squares, the recorder and checker will place the group's acetate on an overhead projector and count how many squares have not yet been colored. Each group will lay its acetate on top of the previous one, and will record its data in a chart like the one below.

Group		1	2	3	4	. . .
Number of points generated	0	50	100	150	200	. . .
Number of points not colored	900	–?–	–?–	–?–	–?–	. . .

Part 2 After the class data have been collected, discuss the following questions with your group members.

a. What does an uncolored square represent?

b. What does a colored square represent?

c. Find a geometric sequence that models the recorded data.

d. Find a continuous function that models the data.

e. What is the approximate half-life of this simulated radioactive decay?

■ **Example 3**

Radioactivity is measured in units called rads. A sample of phosphorus-33 is found to give off 480 rads initially. The half-life of phosphorus-33 is 25 days.

a. What continuous function represents the radioactivity measure of this sample?

b. What is the radioactivity measure after 225 days?

Solution

a. A half-life of 25 days means that during each 25-day period the radiation is decreased by half. This leaves $Ans(1 - 0.5)$ after every 25-day period. A function that models this behavior is $f(x) = 480(1 - 0.5)^x$, where x is the number of 25-day periods, 480 is the initial value, and 0.5 is the rate of decay every 25 days.

b. During 225 days, you have nine 25-day periods. Use your calculator to show that $f(9) = 0.9375$ rads. ■

Problem Set 7.1

1. In 1991, the population of the People's Republic of China was 1.151 billion (or 1151 million), with a growth rate of 1.5% annually.

Year	Population (in billions)
1991	1.151
1992	–?–
1993	–?–
1994	–?–
1995	–?–
1996	–?–
1997	–?–
1998	–?–
1999	–?–
2000	–?–

  a. Write an explicit equation that models this growth.
  b. Complete the table for the years indicated.
  c. Use the population growth equations for India and China to predict the year (and population) when the populations of the two countries will be about equal.
  d. What assumptions allow you to make this prediction? How much confidence do you place in the prediction? Why?

2. A lad by the name of Jack Fum made a shrewd trade of an undernourished bovine for a start in a new experimental crop, *Legumen magikos*. With the help of his mother he planted the bean just outside his kitchen window. It immediately sprouted 2.56 cm above the ground. Contrary to popular legend, it did not reach its full height in one night. Being a student of mathematics and the sciences, Jack kept a careful log of the growth of the sprout. On the first day at 8:00 a.m., 24 hr after planting, he found the plant to be 6.4 cm tall. At 8:00 a.m. on the second day, the growing bean sprout was 16 cm in height. At 8:00 a.m. on the third day, he recorded 40 cm. At the same time on the fourth day, he found it to be 1 m (100 cm) tall.

Time (days)	Day 0	Day 1	Day 2	Day 3	Day 4
Height (cm)	2.56	6.4	16	40	100

a. Write an explicit formula for this pattern. If the pattern were to continue, what would be the heights on the fifth and sixth days?

b. Jack's younger brothers Phee and Fy measured the plant at 8:00 p.m. on the third day, and found it to be about 63.25 cm tall. Show how this value can be found mathematically. You may need to experiment with your calculator.

c. Find the height that Jack's youngest brother, Foe, tried to measure at 12:00 noon on the sixth day.

d. Experiment with the equation to find the day and time (to the nearest hour) when the stalk reached its final height of 1 km (1,000 m or 100,000 cm).

3. Use your calculator to find each number. (Express answers to four decimal places unless the answer is a whole number.)

a. 7^2 **b.** $7^{2.25}$ **c.** $7^{2.5}$ **d.** $7^{2.75}$ **e.** 7^3

f. Find the difference between 3b and 3a, between 3c and 3b, between 3d and 3c, and between 3e and 3d. What do these differences tell you?

g. Find the ratios of the results of 3b to 3a, 3c to 3b, 3d to 3c, and 3e to 3d. What do these values tell you?

h. What observation can you make about decimal powers?

4. Given that $f(x)$ is an exponential function and that $f(4) = 1229$ and $f(5) = 3442$, give your best guess for the value of $f(4.5)$. Justify your answer.

5. In Example 3, you are given the function $f(x) = 480(0.5)^x$, where x is the number of 25-day periods and $f(x)$ is the number of rads.

a. Find $f(3)$ and provide a real-world meaning for it.

b. Find $f(3.2)$ and provide a real-world meaning for it.

c. Find $f(0)$ and provide a real-world meaning for it.

d. Find $f(^-1)$ and provide a real-world meaning for it.

e. For what value of x does $f(x)$ equal 240? What does this mean?

f. How many rads will be measured after 110 days? (Hint: Find the x-value first.)

6. Five thousand dollars is invested in an account that pays interest at a rate of 6.5% compounded annually.

a. Name the function that furnishes the account balance after x years.

b. Find $f(5)$.   **c.** What is the real-world meaning of $f(5)$?

d. Find $f\left(4\frac{1}{3}\right)$.   **e.** What is the real-world meaning of $f\left(4\frac{1}{3}\right)$?

f. Find $f(0)$ and give its real-world meaning.

g. What is the value of the account after 7 yr 9 mo? If the account is closed at this time, do you expect the bank would pay this amount?

7. Ice is added to a glass of water. If not stirred, the water at the bottom cools according to the formula $g(x) = 23(0.94)^x$, where x is the number of minutes since the ice was added and g is the temperature in Celsius.

a. What is the real-world meaning of 0.94? (Hint: The number 0.94 can be written as $(1 - 0.06)$.)

b. What is the initial temperature of the water?

c. Find $g(7.4)$ and give its real-world meaning.

d. Find the temperature after 5 min 45 sec.

e. Find x to make $g(x) = 10$. What is the real-world meaning of your answer?

f. How long (to the nearest hundredth of a minute) will it take until the water has cooled to 5°C?

Project

Baseball for Bucks

The table contains minimum and average salaries for professional baseball players. Look in an almanac to find more recent salary information, and make some predictions about salaries ten years from now, based on mathematical models. What assumptions are you making?

Find similar data for professional basketball players and professional football players. Does a similar model fit these sets of data? How do salaries compare for players in different sports?

Year	Minimum	Average
1967	6,000	19,000
1970	12,000	29,303
1973	15,000	36,566
1976	19,000	51,501
1979	21,000	113,558
1982	33,500	241,497
1985	60,000	371,571
1988	62,500	438,729
1991	100,000	851,492

Source: Data compiled by Major League Baseball Players Association.

Dean Chance, of the Minnesota Twins, 1967

Ozzie Smith, of the St. Louis Cardinals, 1991

Section 7.2

Rational Exponents and Roots

Thought is only a flash between two long nights, but this flash is everything.
—Jules Henri Poincaré

Noninteger x-values are meaningful and useful. In the last section, you used noninteger x-values in the model $f(x) = 14000(0.8)^x$ to predict declining values of an automobile. You used fractional x-values to represent parts of a day in $f(x) = 2.56(2.5)^x$ to find beanstalk heights. Now you are ready to discover important connections and properties involving fractional exponents.

Investigation 7.2.1

Fractional Exponents

In this investigation work with a partner. If questions or problems arise, check your results with the other pair of partners in your group.

NOTE
7B

a. Use your calculator to set up a list of pairs $(x, x^{0.5})$. (See **Calculator Note 7B**.) As you view the list, there are a few pairs that will help you discover a relationship between x and $x^{0.5}$. (Note: The values of $x^{0.5}$ have been rounded.)

x	21	22	23	24	25	26	27
$x^{0.5}$	4.5826	4.6904	4.7958	4.899	5	5.099	5.1962

b. Set your grapher to a "friendly" window so that the distance between the pixels for both the x- and y-values is 0.2, and graph $y_1 = x^{0.5}$. Does this graph look familiar? What is another equation of this function? Enter this equation in y_2 and verify that the equation gives the same y-value at each x-value as the original equation.

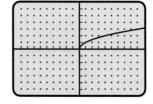

c. The list suggests that when 25 is raised to the one-half power, you get 5. What other operation on 25 gives you 5? Check a few more pairs in your list to verify this relationship.

d. Write a true statement about raising a number to the one-half power. Include an example with your statement.

e. Use your calculator to calculate values for $f(x) = 25^x$ in a table like the one below. (Don't forget that a fractional exponent will need to be enclosed in parentheses— like this, $25^{(1/2)}$—when you enter the expression into your calculator.)

---

x	$\frac{1}{2}$	$\frac{2}{2}$	$\frac{3}{2}$	$\frac{4}{2}$	$\frac{5}{2}$	$\cdots$	$\frac{11}{2}$
25^x	5	25	125	–?–	3125	$\cdots$	–?–

f. Values in the second row in the table above are also powers of 5. In particular, because 125 is 5^3, $25^{3/2}$ is $(25^{1/2})^3$. Explain why $25^{3/2} = \left(\sqrt{25}\right)^3$.

g. Write an equation (y_2) involving a root that is equivalent to $y = x^{3/2}$.

h. Copy and complete the table below. Sketch a graph of each equation.

x	$y_1 = x^{3/2}$	$y_2 = $ –?–
5	11.18	–?–
8	–?–	–?–
10	–?–	–?–
11	36.483	–?–

i. Name an equation that produces the same graph as $y = x^{5/3}$ over the domain of $x \geq 0$. Write a statement, using the word *root*, that defines $27^{n/3}$. Use your calculator to confirm your statement. Explain why the domain was restricted.

j. As a group, write a paragraph or two summarizing what you learned in this investigation.

Other roots, such as the fifth root $\sqrt[5]{}$, the sixth root $\sqrt[6]{}$, and so on, can be written using fractional exponents like $\frac{1}{5}$ and $\frac{1}{6}$. For fractional exponents with numerators other than one, the numerator is interpreted as the power to which to raise the root. Below is a general definition of fractional exponents.

Definition of Fractional Exponents

$$a^{m/n} = \left(\sqrt[n]{a}\right)^m \quad \text{or} \quad \sqrt[n]{a^m} \quad \text{for } a \geq 0$$

■ **Example 1**

What does $9^{5/2}$ mean?

Solution

The number $9^{5/2}$ means the square root of 9 raised to the fifth power, or $\left(\sqrt{9}\right)^5 = 3^5 = 243$. Therefore, $9^{5/2} = 243$. The definition also indicates that $9^{5/2} = \sqrt{9^5}$. Evaluate $\sqrt{59049}$ to verify that it is also 243. ■

The square root of 9 raised to the fifth power, $\sqrt{9^5}$, can also be written $9^{1/2}$ raised to the fifth power, or $(9^{1/2})^5$. This means $9^{5/2} = (9^{1/2})^5$. Because the nth root, $\sqrt[n]{}$, can be written using the fractional exponent $\frac{1}{n}$, another way of expressing the definition of $a^{m/n}$ is

$$a^{m/n} = (a^{1/n})^m = (a^m)^{1/n}.$$

Verify these results with your calculator.

■ Example 2

Rewrite each expression using the radical (root) definitions. Use your calculator to evaluate each expression. Be sure to enclose fractional exponents in parentheses.

a. $64^{2/3}$ **b.** $4096^{3/4}$ **c.** $\left(\dfrac{9}{49}\right)^{3/2}$

Solution

Convert the expressions to radical, or root, form and evaluate.

a. $64^{2/3} = \left(\sqrt[3]{64}\right)^2 = 4^2 = 16.$

Or, $64^{2/3} = \left(\sqrt[3]{64^2}\right) = \sqrt[3]{4096} = 16.$

Therefore, $64^{2/3} = 16.$

b. $4096^{3/4} = \left(\sqrt[4]{4096}\right)^3 = 8^3 = 512.$

Or $4096^{3/4} = \sqrt[4]{4096^3} = \sqrt[4]{68,719,476,736} = 512$

NOTE
7C

Therefore, $4096^{3/4} = 512.$ (See **Calculator Note 7C.**)

c. $\left(\dfrac{9}{49}\right)^{3/2} = \left(\sqrt{\dfrac{9}{49}}\right)^3 = \left(\dfrac{3}{7}\right)^3 = \dfrac{27}{343}$

Or $\left(\dfrac{9}{49}\right)^{3/2} = \sqrt{\left(\dfrac{9}{49}\right)^3} = \sqrt{\dfrac{729}{117,649}} = \dfrac{27}{343}.$

Therefore, $\left(\dfrac{9}{49}\right)^{3/2} = \dfrac{27}{343}.$ ■

Example 3

Solve the following equation for x: $4^x = 8$.

Solution

Enter the left side of the equation in y_1 and the right side of the equation in y_2. Graph the functions in a "friendly" window so that the distance between the pixels for both the x- and y-values is 0.1. Trace along the curve to locate the point of intersection. The coordinates are $(1.5, 8)$. Therefore, $x = \dfrac{3}{2} = 1.5$ is the solution to the equation. ■

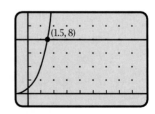

Example 4

Solve the equation $2 \cdot 125^x = 50$.

Solution

NOTE

7D

The equation is equivalent to $125^x = 25$. Do you see why? What will you enter as y_1 and y_2? Trace to locate the point where the curves intersect. In this case, you will not be able to locate the exact intersection without zooming in (either graphically or with a table). (See **Calculator Note 7D**.) Zoom in on this point until you are satisfied that the x-coordinate is 0.666. . . . Therefore, $x = \frac{2}{3}$ is the solution to the equation. ■

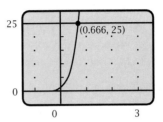

Problem Set 7.2

1. Write a complete sentence that relates each expression to a power of a root. Then find the numerical value in two different ways.
   a. $49^{5/2}$ **b.** $16^{3/4}$ **c.** $64^{5/3}$ **d.** $32^{2/5}$

2. From ages one to seven, Hannah's weight (in kg) was equal to her height (in cm) to the 2/3 power.
   a. At one year of age, Hannah was 64 cm tall. What was her weight?
   b. She was 125 cm tall at age seven. What was her weight?
   c. At age four, she weighed 20.25 kg. What was her height?

3. Convert each radical expression to exponent form.
   a. $\sqrt[4]{x}$ **b.** $\sqrt[5]{x^3}$ **c.** $\left(\sqrt[3]{x}\right)^7$ **d.** $\sqrt[5]{x^4}$

4. Evaluate each of these expressions on your calculator.
   a. $\left(\sqrt[3]{8}\right)^7$ **b.** $\sqrt[5]{243^4}$
   c. $\sqrt[3]{25^6}$ **d.** $(9^5)^{3/10}$

5. **a.** Lieutenant Bolombo found a cryptic message containing a clue about where the money was hidden. After consulting his high school algebra book, he knew where to look. The clue was

   $^{1/2}\sqrt{cin}$ *nati.*

   Find the location and explain how you knew.
   b. Invent a cryptic message of your own like the clue that Lieutenant Bolombo found.

6. Rewrite each exponential expression in radical (root) form.
   a. $x^{2/3}$ b. $x^{2.75}$

7. Solve each equation for x.
   a. $9^x = 27$ b. $32^x = 128$

8. One dollar is invested at 4% annual interest, compounded once each year.
   a. Write a recursive formula for the balance.
   b. Write an explicit formula for the balance after x years.
   c. Find when the account will reach $50.

9. Explain how you would instruct your calculator to graph $y = \sqrt[5]{x}$.

10. Consider the equation $y = 4000\left(1 + \frac{0.072}{12}\right)^x$,

    where y represents the amount in a bank account and x represents the number of months since the original amount was deposited. Explain the real-world meaning of each number in parts a–f below.

    a. 4000   b. 0.072   c. $\frac{0.072}{12}$

    d. $x = 1$ e. $x = 0$ f. $x = {}^-1$

    g. Find the value of x when $y = 8000$.

11. Graph the parametric equations $x(t) = t^4$ and $y(t) = t^3$ for $t \geq 0$. Find a function, $f(x)$, that gives the same graph.

Take Another Look 7.2

NOTE
8A

NOTE
7A

Each student in the class will need to generate a random number so that $0 < random\ number < 1$. (In Chapter 8, you will find several methods of generating random numbers, including one using your calculator. See **Calculator Note 8A.** Be sure each calculator has been seeded according to the procedure in **Calculator Note 7A.**) All students should stand with their calculators in hand.

On a command from the teacher, each student produces a random number with the calculator. Those students with a random number of $0 <$ $random\ number < 0.15$ will sit down. (This means that students with a random number of $0.15 \leq$ $random\ number < 1$ will remain standing.) Record the number of students standing at this stage.

Time period	Students standing
0	*(Number of students in class)*
1	–?–
2	–?–
3	–?–
4	–?–
5	–?–
6	–?–
7	–?–
8	–?–

Repeat the process outlined in the previous paragraph several times, and record the number of students still standing at each stage. Quit the simulation when a small number of standing students remain standing through several trials.

Do you see the results of this activity as a geometric sequence or as a radioactive decay simulation? Find a recursive model and an explicit model for your data. Use your model to predict the number of students standing at any given time period. What is the theoretical common ratio? What is the half-life of this simulation? How would you change the activity so that at any stage, 20% would decay?

Section 7.3

Properties of Exponents

A certain amount of opposition is a great help. . . . Kites rise against, not with the wind.
—John Neal

Often you will need to rewrite a mathematical expression in a different form. Changing from fractional-exponent form to an equivalent radical form is one example. If you get an answer like $\sqrt[5]{x^3}$, and find a different looking expression in the answer section, you need to be able to recognize whether the two answers are equivalent. Many equivalent expressions might be listed as the answer, including $x^{3/5}$ or $\sqrt[10]{x^6}$, when $x \geq 0$. In this section, you will use the calculator to discover, and verify, other ways to write an exponential expression.

In Investigation 1.6.1, the inventor asked for one grain of wheat on the first square of the chessboard, two grains on the second, four grains on the third, and so on, with each square containing twice the number of grains as its predecessor. The third square contained $2 \cdot 2 = 2^2$ grains, the fourth square contained $2 \cdot 2 \cdot 2 = 2^3$ grains, and so on, and the last square contained $2 \cdot 2 \cdot 2 \cdot \ldots \cdot 2 = 2^{63}$ grains. Exponents are used to indicate repeated multiplication of a base.

■ **Example 1**

a. What does $2^3 \cdot 2^4$ mean?

b. Name another pair of factors that provide an equivalent product.

Solution

a. By definition, $2^3 \cdot 2^4$ means $(2 \cdot 2 \cdot 2) \cdot (2 \cdot 2 \cdot 2 \cdot 2)$.

b. The exponential expression 2^7 can be written as $(2 \cdot 2 \cdot 2 \cdot 2 \cdot 2 \cdot 2 \cdot 2)$, which is the same as $(2 \cdot 2) \cdot (2 \cdot 2 \cdot 2 \cdot 2 \cdot 2)$, or $2^2 \cdot 2^5$. This is just one way to write 2^7 as a product of two factors. ■

Name two different combinations of exponents that make each equation correct.

$$2^m \cdot 2^n = 2^{50} \qquad\qquad 3^c \cdot 3^d = 3^{63} \qquad\qquad a^x \cdot a^y = a^{17}$$

Test $a^m \cdot a^n = a^{(m+n)}$ for enough different values of m, n, and a ($a > 0$) to convince yourself that the following property is true.

$$a^m \cdot a^n = a^{(m+n)} \quad \text{for } a > 0$$

Another property of exponents helps you rewrite expressions such as $(x^3)^2$. You already know that you can write $(x^3)^2$ as $x^3 \cdot x^3$, and the multiplication property allows you to write this product as x^{3+3}, or x^6. Therefore, $(x^3)^2 = x^6$.

Nested Power Property of Exponents

$$(a^m)^n = a^{mn} \quad \text{for } a > 0$$

■ Example 2

Use the nested power property to rewrite each expression as a power of a smaller positive base.

a. 8^x **b.** 16^x **c.** $\left(\dfrac{49}{9}\right)^{3/2}$

Solution

a. Because $2^3 = 8$, $8^x = (2^3)^x = 2^{3x}$

b. $16^x = (2^4)^x = 2^{4x}$

c. $\left(\dfrac{49}{9}\right)^{3/2} = \left(\dfrac{7^2}{2^2}\right)^{3/2} = \left(\dfrac{7}{3}\right)^{2 \cdot 3/2} = \left(\dfrac{7}{3}\right)^3$

What graphs could you examine to verify that $(2^3)^x = 2^{3x}$? ■

Investigation 7.3.1

Ratios and Exponents

In this investigation, you will explore how some ratio expressions can be written as exponential expressions. You will also learn about another property of exponents.

a. Have each group member choose one of the problems below. For each problem, use exponents to express the ratio described. Then share your expression with other group members and justify why you think the expression represents the situation.

   i. Each square on the chessboard contains twice as many grains of wheat as the

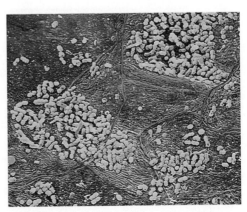

Unidentified colonies of bacteria growing on a human tongue. Sometimes bacteria grow exponentially.

previous square. Write an exponential expression representing the ratio of the number of grains on the last square of the chessboard to the number of grains on the tenth square.

ii. A $1 investment grows at a rate of 8% annually. Write an exponential expression representing the ratio of the investment's value after 20 yr to its value after 6 yr.

iii. A ball with a rebound ratio of 0.65 is dropped from a height of 300 cm. Write an exponential expression representing the ratio of the height of the second bounce to that of the fifth bounce.

iv. A bacteria population grows according to the model $y = 25 \cdot 2^x$, where x represents the number of hours that have elapsed. Write an exponential expression representing the ratio of the population at 15 hr to the population at 7 hr.

b. Each group member needs to find at least two combinations of exponents m and n, so that $\dfrac{2^{20}}{2^n} = 2^m$. Make a group list of eight different combinations that work.

c. Write an equivalent equation in exponential form that represents this relationship:
$$\frac{(4)(4)(4)(4)(4)}{(4)(4)} = \frac{(4)(4)(4)(4)(4)}{(4)(4)}.$$

d. Have each group member choose one of the problems below. Work the problem, and explain your results to the other group members.

If possible, rewrite each expression using a single exponent. If it's not possible, explain why.

i. $\dfrac{8^5}{8^2}$ ii. $\dfrac{x^{5.5}}{x^3}$ iii. $\dfrac{240 \cdot (0.94)^{15}}{240 \cdot (0.94)^5}$ iv. $\dfrac{x^3 + x^7}{x^2}$

e. Have all the group members use their calculators to test $\dfrac{a^m}{a^n} = a^{(m-n)}$ for several different values of m, n, and a ($a > 0$).

f. As a group, write a paragraph summarizing what you learned in this investigation.

In the previous investigation, you explored the division property of exponents. This property can be generalized as follows.

Division Property of Exponents

$$\frac{a^m}{a^n} = a^{(m-n)} \quad \text{for } a > 0$$

Investigation 7.3.2

Negative Exponents

In this investigation, you will explore the concept of a negative exponent and see how it can be related to real-world applications.

a. In Section 7.1, you used the model $f(x) = 835(1.019)^x$ to represent the population growth in India from the year 1989. You can use a negative exponent to compute the population for a year prior to 1989. Have each group member find the function value and provide a real-world meaning for one of the values below. Share your results.

    i. $f(^-4)$ ii. $f(^-3)$ iii. $f(^-2)$ iv. $f(^-1)$

b. You can rewrite $\dfrac{x^3}{x^5}$ as $\dfrac{xxx}{xxxxx}$. If you divide out common factors, you will get $\dfrac{1}{x^2}$.
Using the division property of exponents, how would you express this answer? As a group, carefully describe why $x^{-2} = \dfrac{1}{x^2}$.

c. As a group, decide on an example, similar to the one in part b, that shows $x^{-1} = \dfrac{1}{x^1}$.

d. Have each group member choose one of the problems below. Share your results with your group.

    For each equation, write another, equivalent equation. Verify that your new equation is equivalent to the original one by graphing.

    i. $y = x^{-3}$ ii. $y = \dfrac{1}{2^x}$ iii. $y = 10.5(1 + 0.035)^{-4x}$ iv. $\dfrac{1}{x^{-2}}$

e. Have each group member choose one of the problems below. Share your results with your group.

    Rewrite each complex fraction as a simple fraction.

    i. $\dfrac{\frac{1}{2}}{3}$ ii. $\dfrac{\frac{1}{3}}{2}$ iii. $\dfrac{1}{\left(\frac{2}{3}\right)^2}$ iv. $\dfrac{\frac{1}{a}}{b}$

f. A ball with a rebound factor of 0.65 is dropped from a height of 300 cm. As a group, find the ratio of the height of the fifth bounce to that of the second bounce.

g. Have each group member choose two pairs of values for a and b (a, $b > 0$). For each pair of values, use your calculator to verify that $a^{-n} = \dfrac{1}{a^n}$ for $a > 0$ and that $\left(\dfrac{a}{b}\right)^{-n} = \left(\dfrac{b}{a}\right)^n$. Did everyone in the group get the same results?

h. As a group, determine what x-value in the function $f(x) = 835(1.019)^x$ gives the original population? Carefully show or describe how you found this x-value.

i. With your group, write a reason for each step in the logical argument that follows.

$$x^3 \cdot x^{-3} = x^0$$

$$x^3 \cdot x^{-3} = x^3 \cdot \left(\frac{1}{x^3}\right)$$

$$x^3 \cdot \left(\frac{1}{x^3}\right) = 1$$

Therefore, $x^0 = 1$.

j. A solution manual will not list $\frac{2^5}{2^5}$ as an answer. Using the division property of exponents, you can rewrite $\frac{2^5}{2^5}$ as $\frac{2 \cdot 2 \cdot 2 \cdot 2 \cdot 2}{2 \cdot 2 \cdot 2 \cdot 2 \cdot 2}$ and divide out common factors. What is the result? Based on this result, how would you define 2^0?

k. As a group, write a paragraph summarizing what you learned in this investigation.

In Investigation 7.3.2, you explored two additional exponent properties. The general form of these properties is summarized below.

Definition of Negative and Zero Exponents

$a^{-n} = \dfrac{1}{a^n}$ for $a > 0$ or $\left(\dfrac{a}{b}\right)^{-n} = \left(\dfrac{b}{a}\right)^n$ for $a, b > 0$

$a^0 = 1$ for $a > 0$

■ Example 3

Rewrite $\left(\dfrac{9}{49}\right)^{-3/2}$ without an exponent.

Solution

$$\left(\frac{9}{49}\right)^{-3/2} = \left(\frac{49}{9}\right)^{3/2}$$ Definition of negative exponents.

$$= \left(\sqrt{\frac{49}{9}}\right)^3$$ Definition of fractional exponents.

$$= \left(\frac{7}{3}\right)^3$$ Take the square root.

$$= \frac{343}{27}$$ Cube the number.   ■

The preceding example shows another property of exponents, the power of a product property, which is generalized below.

Power of a Product Property

$(ab)^n = a^n b^n$ for $a > 0$ and $b > 0$

Be careful that you don't apply this property to powers of binomials. In other words,

$$(a + b)^n \neq a^n + b^n \quad \text{(except when } n = 1\text{)}.$$

This is a common error made by many students. What expression is equivalent to $(a + b)^2$?

■ Example 4

Rewrite $0.94^x \cdot 0.5^x$ using the power of a product property.

Solution

$0.94^x \cdot 0.5^x = (0.94 \cdot 0.5)^x$

Verify the result by graphing

$y_1 = (0.94)^x \cdot (0.5)^x$ and $y_2 = (0.94 \cdot 0.5)^x$. ■

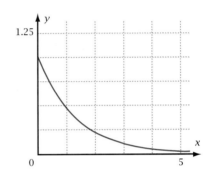

■ Example 5

Solve $5^x = \dfrac{1}{25}$ without graphing.

Solution

If you can write both sides of the equation with exponents of the same base, you can solve this problem by inspection.

$5^x = \dfrac{1}{25}$ Given.

$5^x = \dfrac{1}{5^2}$ Because $5^2 = 25$.

$5^x = 5^{-2}$ Definition of negative exponents.

$x = {}^-2$ By inspection. ■

Problem Set 7.3

1. Rewrite each expression in fractional form without using exponents or radicals. Then verify that the new expression is equivalent to the original one by evaluating each expression on your calculator.

   a. 3^{-3}
        b. $25^{-1/2}$
        c. ${}^-36^{3/2}$
        d. $({}^-12)^{-2}$

   e. $\left(\dfrac{3}{4}\right)^{-2}$
        f. $\left(\dfrac{2}{7}\right)^{-1}$
        g. ${}^-\left(\dfrac{8}{27}\right)^{-1/3}$
        h. $\left(\dfrac{4}{9}\right)^{-5/2}\left(\dfrac{2}{3}\right)^5$

2. Find an alternate way to write each expression.

   a. $(2x)^{-3}$
        b. $2x^{-3}$
        c. $x^{(1/2)}x^{(2/3)}$
        d. $(4x)^{(-1/2)}(8x^3)^{(2/3)}$

3. Mr. Higgins told his wife, the mathematics professor, that he would make her breakfast. She handed him this message:

$$\text{I want } \frac{(\text{Eas})^{-1}(\text{ter})^0 \text{ Egg}}{y}.$$

What should Mr. Higgins fix his wife for breakfast?

4. Indicate whether each equation is true or false. If it is false, explain why.

a. $3^5 \cdot 4^2 = 12^7$ **b.** $100(1.06)^x = (106)^x$

c. $\sqrt{a^2 + b^2} = a + b$ **d.** $\frac{a+b}{a} = b$

e. $\sqrt[4]{16x^{20}} = 2x^5$ **f.** $\frac{6.6 \cdot 10^{12}}{8.8 \cdot 10^{-4}} = 7.5 \cdot 10^{15}$

5. Solve each equation by using exponent properties.

a. $3^x = \frac{1}{9}$ **b.** $\left(\frac{5}{3}\right)^x = \frac{27}{125}$ **c.** $\left(\frac{1}{3}\right)^x = 243$ **d.** $5 \cdot 3^x = 5$

6. Graph the following equations on the same screen: $y_1 = 1.5^x$, $y_2 = 2^x$, $y_3 = 3^x$, $y_4 = 4^x$. Then sketch each graph on paper. How do the graphs compare? What points (if any) do they have in common? Predict what the graph of $y = 6^x$ will look like. Verify your prediction by using your calculator.

7. Graph the following equations on the same screen: $y_1 = 0.2^x$, $y_2 = 0.3^x$, $y_3 = 0.5^x$, $y_4 = 0.8^x$. Then sketch each graph on paper. How do the graphs compare? What points (if any) do they have in common? Predict what the graph of $y = 0.1^x$ will look like. Verify your prediction by using your calculator.

8. Refer to the graphs and equations in Problems 6 and 7. What do all the equations in Problem 6 have in common? What do all the equations in Problem 7 have in common? Guess the function that produces each graph shown below.

a.
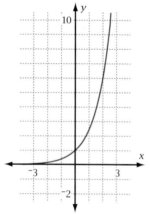

b.
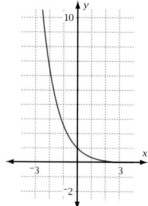

9. Some functions can be classified as increasing or decreasing functions. The first graph in Problem 8 is an example of an increasing function. The second graph is an example of a decreasing function. A function is an **increasing function** if, and only if, for each $x_1 > x_2$, $f(x_1) \geq f(x_2)$. This means that as the x-values increase, the y-values also increase.

   a. Which of the functions in Problems 6 and 7 are increasing?

   b. Write a definition for a decreasing function that is similar to the definition of the increasing function given above.

10. a. Describe and compare the graphs if x is replaced with ^-x in the equation $y = ab^x$. What is another way to write this equation?

   b. Describe and compare the graphs if y is replaced with ^-y in the equation $y = ab^x$.

   c. Describe and compare the graphs if x is replaced with $(x - 2)$ in the equation $y = ab^x$.

11. Indicate whether each statement is true or false. Justify your answers.

   a. A negative number raised to a negative power is always positive.

   b. When a number larger than one is raised to a positive power that is less than one, the number becomes larger.

   c. A positive number raised to the zero power is equal to zero.

   d. If $a < b$, and a and b are both positive, then $a^n < b^n$ for any number n.

Building Inverses of Functions

It is unwise to be too sure of one's own wisdom.
—*Gandhi*

Rita and Noah are each making a graph for a project in their science class. They are both using the same data, but their graphs look different. "I know my graph is right!" exclaims Rita. "I've checked and rechecked it. Yours must be wrong, Noah." Noah disagrees. "I've entered these data in my calculator, and I made sure I entered the correct numbers." Can you explain what's happening?

Sometimes it makes sense for either one of two related variables to be used as the independent variable. This occurred, for example, when you studied the (°C, °F) and (°F, °C) temperature relationships. Two related but different looking functions can be used to model this temperature relationship.

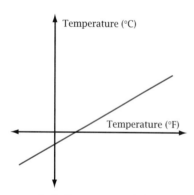

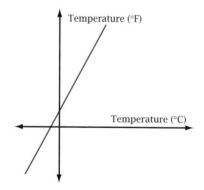

x is in °F	y is in °C
32	0
68	20
95	35
212	100
239	115

x is in °C	y is in °F
0	32
20	68
35	95
100	212
115	239

Convince yourself that the table values are correct. Do you recognize both the freezing and boiling temperatures for water? Try other values for °F and °C that are not already listed in the tables to see if the coordinates are always reversed.

NOTE
7E

In this figure, both temperature graphs are drawn in the same graphing window ($^{-}50 \leq x \leq 150$, $^{-}50 \leq y \leq 150$). The graphing window was "squared up," and the graph of $y = x$ was added. (See **Calculator Note 7E.**)

The two temperature functions,

$$y = 1.8x + 32 \quad \text{and} \quad y = \frac{(x - 32)}{1.8},$$

are inverses of each other. This means that every point (a, b) on one graph has a corresponding point (b, a) on the other. In a correctly sized window, they appear as reflection images of each other over the line $y = x$. This will happen for any pair of inverse relations.

Inverse of a Relation

The **inverse** of a relation is obtained by exchanging the x- and y-coordinates of all points. The graph of an inverse relation will be a reflection of the original relation over the line $y = x$.

In this section, you will learn how to find the inverse of a function or relation, and you will learn about some other important connections between relations and their inverses.

■ **Example 1**

At the right is a graph of $y = 6.34x - 140$, which models a relationship between time and distance for continental United States flights. There is no reason why *time* must be the independent variable and *distance* the dependent variable. Find a model representing the inverse relation (*distance, time*).

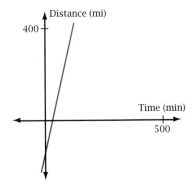

Solution

There are at least three methods that you can use to find the inverse relation.

Method 1

Find some points on the graph of $y = 6.34x - 140$. Then name some points on the inverse relation by switching the x- and y-coordinates.

Points on original function		Points on inverse function	
Time (min)	Distance (mi)	Distance (mi)	Time (min)
50	177	177	50
80	367.2	367.2	80
100	494	494	100
150	811	811	150

These new points also lie on a line. (Check to see if this is true.) Choose two points and find the equation of the line that represents the inverse relation.

$$y = \frac{(150 - 50)}{(811 - 177)}(x - 177) + 50, \quad \text{or} \quad y = \frac{100}{634}x + \frac{14000}{634}$$

Method 2

To find the equation of the inverse, you must find the equation that will *undo* what the original equation does. In the original function, x is multiplied by 6.34, and then 140 is subtracted from this value. Therefore, to find the inverse relation, you need to do the opposite operations in reverse order. Thus, you would add 140 to x and divide by 6.34. One form for the inverse relation will be

$$y = \frac{(x + 140)}{6.34}.$$

Check to see that this form is equivalent to the inverse relation you found when you used the first method.

Method 3

Switch the x- and y-variables in the original equation, and solve for y.

$$y = 6.34x - 140 \qquad \text{Original equation.}$$
$$x = 6.34y - 140 \qquad \text{Inverse equation.}$$
$$y = \frac{(x + 140)}{6.34} \qquad \text{Inverse equation solved for } y. \quad \blacksquare$$

What is the real-world meaning of the slope, x-intercept, and y-intercept of the inverse equation in $y=$ form?

■ Example 2

a. Find and graph the inverse of the parametric equations $x = t + 2$ and $y = t^2$.

b. Write the nonparametric equations of the function and its inverse.

Solution

a. You can easily find the inverse relations for parametric equations by switching the x- and y-variables in the equations. (See the equations and graphs at the right.) If possible, set your calculator so that both graphs are

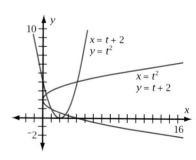

drawn simultaneously. Trace both curves and examine the corresponding coordinates.

b. $x = t + 2, y = t^2$ Original equations.

$t = x - 2$ Solve the *x*-equation for *t*.

$y = (x - 2)^2$ Substitute this value into the *y*-equation, which is the function form required.

$x = t^2, y = t + 2$ Inverse equations.

$t = \pm\sqrt{x}$ Solve the *x*-equation for *t*.

$y = \pm\sqrt{x} + 2$ Substitute this value into the *y*-equation to get the equation of the inverse. ■

NOTE 7F

Notice that in this case the inverse of the original function is not a function. Do you see why? Check the nonparametric graphs to make certain you have correctly represented the same points. (See **Calculator Note 7F**.) When the original function, written as $f(x)$, has an inverse that is a function, you write the inverse as $f^{-1}(x)$. For example, the temperature functions could be written as

$$f(x) = 1.8x + 32 \quad \text{and} \quad f^{-1}(x) = \frac{(x - 32)}{1.8}.$$

The next investigation considers the composition of inverse functions $f^{-1}(f(x))$ and $f(f^{-1}(x))$.

Investigation 7.4.1

Compositions of Inverse Functions

You will now explore what happens when you form a new function that is a composition of a function and its inverse. You may want to work with a partner, but be sure each person does the exploration and graphing on his or her calculator.

a. Set your graphing window at $^-50 \le x \le 150$, $^-50 \le y \le 150$, and then "square up" the window.

NOTE 7G

b. Enter $f(x) = 1.8x + 32$ as y_1 and its inverse, $f^{-1}(x) = \frac{(x - 32)}{1.8}$, as y_2. Choose five different *x*-values from the suggestions listed below, and determine values for $f(x)$, $f^{-1}(x)$, and $f^{-1}(f(x))$, either from a table or by evaluating the functions. (See **Calculator Note 7G**.) Use values from the following list as your *x*-values: today's temperature, the coldest day during the last month, the warmest day during the last month, the coldest day since school started, the warmest day since school started, the temperature at which you feel the most comfortable, the coldest day you have ever experienced, the hottest day you have ever experienced. (If you're not sure about one of these temperatures, you can use an estimate.) Carefully describe the relationship between each *x* and $f^{-1}(f(x))$.

c. Describe what the graph of $f^{-1}(f(x))$ will look like by looking at the values you have generated. What function can you enter into your calculator that generates this graph?

d. What will you do differently to find values for $f(f^{-1}(x))$? Describe a graph of $f(f^{-1}(x))$ by looking at the values of $f(f^{-1}(x))$. What function can you enter into your calculator that generates the graph $f(f^{-1}(x))$?

e. Enter a new function, $y_1 = x^3$. What inverse relation should you enter into y_2? Investigate by trying enough values so that you can describe what $f(f^{-1}(x))$ and $f^{-1}(f(x))$ will look like.

Problem Set 7.4

1. Find the inverse of each pair of parametric equations. Graph the original pair of equations and the inverse equations on the same set of axes.

a. $x = 2t - 3$, $y = t + 2$ **b.** $x = t^2$, $y = t + 1$

c. $x = \frac{1}{2}t + 1$, $y = \frac{t-2}{3}$ **d.** $x = t - 3$, $y = 2(t - 1)^2$

e. Describe the relationship between the graph of the original parametric equations and the graph of the inverse equations.

f. How do you graph the line $y = x$ in *parametric* mode?

2. Which graph below is the inverse of the graph at the right? Explain how you know.

a.
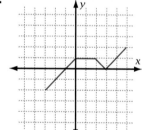

b.
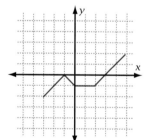

c.
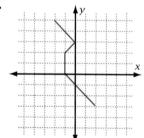

d.
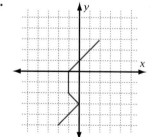

e.
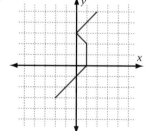

3. **a.** Eliminate the parameter from $x = t + 5$, $y = 2t - 1$ by solving the x-equation for t and substituting the result into the y-equation.
   b. Find parametric equations for the inverse relation of the equations given in 3a.
   c. Eliminate the parameter in the inverse by solving the y-equation for t and substituting the result into the x-equation.
   d. Compare the nonparametric equations for the original relation and the inverse. Describe any similarities and differences between the original relation and its inverse.

4. **a.** Eliminate the parameter from $x = t^2 + 2$, $y = t + 3$ by solving the y-equation for t and substituting the result into the x-equation.
   b. Write parametric equations for the inverse of the relation in 4a.
   c. Eliminate the parameter in the inverse by solving the x-equation for t and substituting the result into the y-equation.
   d. Compare the nonparametric equations for the original relation and the inverse. Describe any similarities and differences between the original relation and its inverse.

5. Find a range of t-values so that both $x = t - 1$, $y = (t - 3)^2$ and its inverse are functions.

6. Find a range of t-values so that both $x = t^2 + 2$, $y = \dfrac{t - 3}{4}$ and its inverse are functions.

7. **a.** Use your knowledge of transformations to write parametric equations for $y = (x + 1)^2 - 2$.
   b. Write parametric equations for the inverse of the function in 7a.
   c. Eliminate the parameter and solve the resulting equation for y. (It doesn't matter whether you start with the x-equation or with the y-equation.)
   d. Write the original and inverse equations in nonparametric form.

8. Write each function using $f(x)$ notation and find its inverse. If the inverse is a function, write it using $f^{-1}(x)$ notation.
   a. $y = 2x - 3$ **b.** $3x + 2y = 4$ **c.** $x^2 + 2y = 3$

9. For each function find:
   i. $f^{-1}(x)$ ii. $f(f^{-1}(15.75))$ iii. $f^{-1}(f(15.75))$ iv. $f(f^{-1}(x))$ and $f^{-1}(f(x))$

   a. $f(x) = 6.34x - 140$
   b. $f(x) = 1.8x + 32$

10. The data in the table describe the relationship between altitude and air temperature.
    a. Write a best-fit equation for $f(x)$ that describes the relationship (*altitude in meters, temperature in °C*). Use at least three decimal places in your answer.
    b. Use your results from 10a to write the equation for $f^{-1}(x)$.

Feet	Meters	°F	°C
1,000	300	56	13
5,000	1,500	41	5
10,000	3,000	23	⁻5
15,000	4,500	5	⁻15
20,000	6,000	⁻15	⁻26
30,000	9,000	⁻47	⁻44
36,087	10,826	⁻69	⁻56

c. Write a best-fit equation for $g(x)$, describing (*altitude in feet, temperature in °F*).

d. Use the results of 10c to write the equation for $g^{-1}(x)$.

e. What would the temperature in °F be at the summit of Mount McKinley, which is 6194 m high?

f. Write a composition of functions that will provide the answer for 10e. (Choose your functions from this problem and from Investigation 7.4.1.)

11. Anders Celsius (1701-1744) was a Swedish astronomer. His thermometric scale used the freezing and boiling temperatures of water as reference points, where freezing corresponded to 100° and boiling to 0°. His colleagues at the Uppsala observatory reversed his scale five years later, giving us the current version. This thermometer was known as the Swedish thermometer until the 1800s when people started referring to it as the Celsius thermometer.

Anders Celsius

a. On Celsius's original scale, freezing corresponded to 100° and boiling corresponded to 0°. Write a formula that converts a temperature given by today's Celsius scale into the scale that Celsius invented.

b. Explain how you would convert a temperature given in degrees Fahrenheit into a temperature on the original scale that Celsius invented.

12. Rewrite the expression $125^{2/3}$ in as many different ways as you can.

13. Here is the paper Anisha turned in for a recent quiz in her mathematics class.

If it is a four-point quiz, what is Anisha's score? For each problem that Anisha did not answer correctly, provide the correct answer and explain to her what she did wrong, so that next time she will get it right!

Name: *Anisha*   Score: _____

1. Rewrite x^{-1}.
   Ans: $\dfrac{1}{x}$

2. What does $f^{-1}(x)$ mean?
   Ans: $\dfrac{1}{f(x)}$

3. Rewrite $9^{-1/5}$
   Ans: $\dfrac{1}{9^5}$

4. $0^0 = ?$
   Ans: 0

Take Another Look 7.4

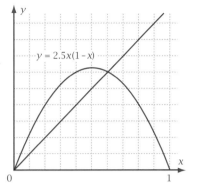

Take a minute or so to refer back to web graphs in Example 3 of Section 5.9 and in Investigation 5.9.1. Web graphs give you an interesting perspective on sequence values, long-run patterns, and the long-run behavior of a function of itself or $f(f(x))$.

NOTE
5F

Investigation 5.9.1 allowed you to explore the behavior of $f(x) = ax(1 - x)$ for various values of a and an initial seed value of 0.3 for x. (See **Calculator Note 5F** for help with web graphs.) The sequence of values produced is called the orbit of the initial term $x_0 = 0.3$. What appears to be the limit of this orbit?

Part 1 If you haven't worked with web graphs, then you might do Investigation 5.9.1 at this time. Your teacher will provide you with the investigation worksheet. As you work your way through the investigation, determine what happens when you use different initial values for x_0. Look at consecutive table values far into the sequences. Try to make sense of the long-run orbit limit or limits. Your explanations might include such words as *input*, *output*, *previous answer*, *cycle*, and *period length*.

Part 2 Use your calculator to investigate the long-run limit of $f(x) = \sqrt{x}$ for $x_0 = 2$. This means you will iterate and investigate the sequence

$$2, \sqrt{2}, \sqrt{\sqrt{2}}, \sqrt{\sqrt{\sqrt{2}}}, \ldots$$

What is the apparent limit? What happens if you use $x_0 = 10$? Or $x_0 = 0.5$?

Part 3 Make a web graph of successive iterates of the exponential growth determined by $u_n = 1.15 \cdot u_{(n-1)}$. Start with $u_0 = 100$. Explain the long-run behavior of this graph. Describe what occurs at a particular stage or iteration. What would happen if the model showed a 15% decay rather than a 15% increase? Explain.

Geometer's Sketchpad Investigation

Inverse Functions

Part 1   Choose the Create Axes option. Draw the line for the function $y = x$. Mark this line as a mirror. Draw a line anywhere on the plane. Label this line k. Reflect line k across the mirror. Label this new line m. Show the equations of both lines.

Questions

1. Move line k and observe what happens with line m.
2. Demonstrate algebraically that one equation is the inverse of the other.

Part 2   Create a new sketch. Choose the Create Axes option, and draw the line for the function $y = x$. Mark this line as a mirror. Draw a circle anywhere on the plane. Reflect the circle across the mirror. Show the equations of both circles in center radius form. Create a point F on the first circle and reflect this point across the mirror also. Measure the coordinates of F and F'.

Questions

1. Move point F and observe what happens to the coordinates of F'.
2. Move circle 1 and observe what happens to the equations and the points of circle 2.
3. Make some conjectures about inverses, the equations, and the points.

Section 7.5

Equations with Rational Exponents

But if adventure has a final and all-embracing motive it is surely this: We go out because it is our nature to go out, to climb mountains and to sail the seas, to fly to the planets and plunge into the depths of the oceans. By doing these things we can make touch with something outside or behind, which strangely seems to approve our doing them.
—Wilfred Noyce

Rita's economics teacher has convinced her that if she starts saving money now, she will have a sizable "nest egg" when she gets older, so Rita decides to invest $500. She has been investigating several options. One investment advisor told her that if she puts her money into a Save-a-Lot Account, her investment will double in eight years. Rita would like to be able to figure out whether this is a good deal. Fortunately, in her mathematics class, she is learning to solve exponential equations.

Frequently, exponential growth situations are described in terms of doubling time. Rita has been told that her investment of $500 compounded annually will double in eight years. What is the annual rate of interest for this account? She knows that she will have $1,000 in eight years, so she needs to find r in the equation $1000 = 500(1 + r)^8$. This is equivalent to solving $2 = (1 + r)^8$. Do you see why? Can you help Rita solve this equation?

r	$(1 + r)^8$
0.08	1.8509
0.09	1.9925
0.091	2.0072
0.0905	1.9998

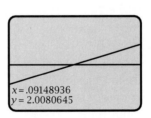

Using substitution and experimentation, you can come as close as you want to the solution in a short time. Another way to find the solution would be to zoom in on the intersection of $y_1 = (1 + x)^8$ and $y_2 = 2$.

You can also use an algebraic process to solve an equation in which the base is unknown but the power, or exponent, is given. This process involves finding an inverse operation, or "undoing" the power applied to the base. How do you undo a power?

$$2 = (1 + r)^8$$ The given equation.

$$2^{1/8} = ((1 + r)^8)^{1/8}$$ Power property of equality (see below).

$$2^{1/8} = 1 + r$$ Nested power property of exponents.

$$2^{1/8} - 1 = r$$ Subtract 1 from both sides.

Therefore, $r \approx 0.0905077327$.

This means that if Rita were to put her money into a Save-a-Lot account it would earn 9% interest.

The procedure to find inverses of a given power, or to solve an equation by "undoing" an exponent, is generalized in the property below.

Power Property of Equality

If $a = b$, and a, b are positive real numbers, then $a^n = b^n$ for all values of n.

■ Example 1

Solve each equation for x.

a. $x^2 = 49$ **b.** $\sqrt{x} = 6$ **c.** $x^{5/2} = 243$

Solution

a. You can solve this problem by "inspection." One solution is $x = 7$. A standard strategy, involving the power property of equality, is to raise each side of the original equation to the one-half power (or to take the square root of each side). Then $\sqrt{x^2} = \sqrt{49}$ gives you the positive solution, $x = 7$.

b. Again, solve by inspection. The answer is $x = 36$. You can also get this solution by squaring both sides, $\left(\sqrt{x}\right)^2 = 6^2$.

c. Raise both sides to the power that is the reciprocal of the power on x, so that the exponent on x becomes one: $(x^{5/2})^{2/5} = 243^{2/5}$. Therefore, $x = 9$. ■

Each equation in Example 1 was solved by "undoing" an exponent. Graphs of $y = x^{5/2}$ and $y = x^{2/5}$ show that these functions are inverses of one another. In solving the equation in part c, you actually used a composite of the two functions, $y = (x^{5/2})^{2/5}$, to arrive at the identity function $y = x$. The power property of equality is true for all *positive* bases. Many fractional exponents, such as $\frac{1}{2}$, do not give real solutions when applied to negative numbers. Can you explain why?

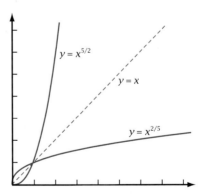

If you use the power property of equality to solve an equation, you will *only* get the positive solution. This is because you are working with functions, and there can be only one output for any input in a function. It is standard practice to choose a positive answer if presented with a choice.

■ Example 2

To predict the likelihood of snow on an overcast day, you are given the following formula with temperature, T, in degrees Fahrenheit.

Percent chance of snow $= 100 - \dfrac{(T - 15)^2}{4}$

What temperature would indicate that there is a 5% chance of snow?

Solution

$$5 = 100 - \frac{(T - 15)^2}{4} \qquad \text{Set equation equal to 5.}$$

$$^-95 = -\frac{(T - 15)^2}{4} \qquad \text{Add } ^-100 \text{ to both sides.}$$

$$380 = (T - 15)^2 \qquad \text{Multiply both sides by } ^-4.$$
$$380^{1/2} = T - 15 \qquad \text{Raise both sides to the 1/2 power.}$$
$$19.5 \approx T - 15 \qquad \text{Evaluate } 380^{1/2}.$$
$$34.5 \approx T \qquad \text{Add 15 to both sides.} \quad ■$$

Therefore, there is a 5% chance of snow when the temperature is 34.5°F. Examine the graph of the function to see a second solution to the problem. What is it? In a later chapter you will learn some other techniques that will enable you to find multiple solutions to equations.

■ Example 3

a. Given $f(x) = 3.4\, x^{3/2} + 2$, find $f^{-1}(x)$. In other words, solve $x = 3.4y^{3/2} + 2$ for y.

b. Graph $f(x)$, $f^{-1}(x)$, $f(f^{-1}(x))$, and $f^{-1}(f(x))$.

Solution

a.

$$x = 3.4y^{3/2} + 2 \qquad \text{Given equation.}$$

$$x - 2 = 3.4y^{3/2} \qquad \text{Subtract 2 from both sides.}$$

$$\frac{x - 2}{3.4} = y^{3/2} \qquad \text{Divide both sides by 3.4.}$$

$$\left(\frac{x - 2}{3.4}\right)^{2/3} = (y^{3/2})^{2/3} \qquad \begin{array}{l} \text{Raise both sides to the 2/3 power so that the exponent on } y \\ \text{will be 1 when } x \geq 2. \end{array}$$

Therefore, $f^{-1}(x) = \left(\dfrac{x - 2}{3.4}\right)^{2/3}$.

b. Below are the graphs of $f(x)$, $f^{-1}(x)$, $f(f^{-1}(x))$ and $f(x)$, $f^{-1}(x)$, $f^{-1}(f(x))$. Check them with your calculator and try to figure out why they look the way they do. Why does $f(x)$ start at $(0,2)$ and $f^{-1}(x)$ start at $(2,0)$? Why is the graph of $f(f^{-1}(x))$ different from the graph of $f^{-1}(f(x))$?

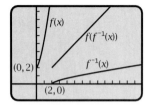
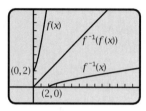

Investigation 7.5.1

Bacterium in a Bottle

For many of the questions in this investigation, there are no "right" answers. Use these questions to guide your discussion. You might want to work with a partner first, and then discuss your ideas and conclusions with your group.

There is a single bacterium in a bottle at 11:00, and this type of bacteria doubles every minute. The bottle will be full of bacteria in one hour.

| 11:01 | There is lots of room in the bottle. |
| 11:02 | There is still lots of room in the bottle. |

. . .

| 12:00 | The bottle is full. |

In your opinion, what percentage of the bottle will be full when the bacteria start to feel crowded? Use the information given to calculate the time at which the bacteria will start to feel crowded. For what percentage of the one-hour time period do you think they will feel uncrowded?

In 1974, it was estimated that the total coal reserves in the United States were about $4.34 \cdot 10^{11}$ tons. Approximately $5.58 \cdot 10^8$ tons were consumed in 1975. If the consumption doubling time was 14 years, how many tons were left in 1988? How many tons will be left in 2002?

Discuss the bacteria's predicament and compare it with the predicament of a nonrenewable resource, such as the United States' coal reserves. Write a paragraph describing a problem that you think exists, and offer some possible solutions. Be prepared to share your results with the class.

Problem Set 7.5

1. Solve each equation for x, where x is a real number.
   a. $x^5 = 50$
   b. $\sqrt[3]{x} = 3.1$
   c. $x^2 = {}^{-}121$
   d. $x^{1/4} - 2 = 3$
   e. $4x^7 - 6 = {}^{-}2$
   f. $3(x^{2/3} + 5) = 207$
   g. $1450 = 800\left(1 + \dfrac{x}{12}\right)^{7.8}$
   h. $14.2 = 222.1 \cdot x^{3.5}$

2. Rewrite each expression without parentheses.
   a. $(27x^6)^{2/3}$
   b. $(16x^8)^{3/4}$
   c. $(36x^{-12})^{3/2}$

3. A 1 mm thick sheet of translucent glass has been designed to reduce the intensity of light. If six sheets are placed together, the outgoing light intensity is 50% of the incoming light intensity. What is the reduction rate of one sheet in this exponential relation?

4. The population of the earth in 1975 was about 4 billion and was doubling every 35 yr.
   a. Write a formula describing the relationship between time and population.
   b. Use the formula to predict the population of the earth today.
   c. Look up the current population of the earth and calculate the percentage error of your prediction.

5. In 1994, the cost of a gallon of milk was $2. At the 1994 rate of inflation, it will cost $4 in the year 2016. What was the rate of inflation in 1994?

6. If $f(x) = x^{2/3}$ and $x \geq 0$, sketch a graph of each function.
   a. $f(x - 4)$
   b. $f(x^2)$
   c. $f(f(x))$
   d. $f^{-1}(x - 4)$

7. **a.** Find the inverse of $f(x) = 2(x^{2/3} - 4)$.
   b. Give a detailed explanation of how you would graph $f(f^{-1}(x))$ on your calculator. (See **Calculator Note 7G**.)
   c. Give a detailed explanation of how you would graph $f(f^{-1}(x + 2))$ on your calculator.

NOTE 7G

8. There is a relationship between the radius of an orbit and the time of one orbit for the moons of Saturn.

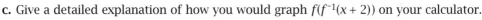

Moon	Radius (100,000 km)	Orbit time (days)	Moon	Radius (100,000 km)	Orbit time (days)
1980S28	1.3767	0.602	Enceladus	2.3804	1.370
1980S27	1.3935	0.613	Tethys	2.9467	1.888
1980S26	1.4170	0.629	Dione	3.7742	2.737
1980S3	1.5142	0.694	1980S6	3.7806	2.739
1980S1	1.5147	0.695	Rhea	5.2710	4.518
Mimas	1.8554	0.942			

Note: The 28th satellite (or moon), discovered in 1980, is 1980S28. Many moons were discovered in 1980 as the *Voyager* spacecraft passed by Saturn on its path through the solar system.

a. Plot the relation (*radius, time*).

b. Find a best-fit line, $y = a + bx$, and write a statement describing how well $y = a + bx$ fits the data. Describe the tools you used to reach this decision.

c. Experiment with different values of a and b in $y = ax^b$ to find the best values for $y = ax^b$. Work with a and b one at a time, first adjusting one and then the other until you have a good fit. Write a statement describing how well $y = ax^b$ fits the data.

9. a. Use your final model from Problem 8 to find the orbit radius for Titan, which has an orbit time of 15.945 days.

    b. Find the orbit time for Phoebe, which has an orbit radius of 1,295,400 km.

10. Create your own problem, one that you think would make a good assessment question for the material in this chapter that you have studied so far. Write out the complete solution to your problem, and explain why you believe it is a good problem. Please make sure that it is a problem or a question, not just an explanation or a description.

Take Another Look 7.5

Take another look at the recursive routine you used in Problem 2 of Problem Set 1.4 to model the population growth of the U.S. each decade since 1790. Write out this recursive routing and then write an explicit exponential model that will provide equivalent (*year, population*) values. Use your explicit exponential model as you complete the following table. What does the variable x represent in your equation $y = ab^x$? Complete the residual column (differences between actual populations and predicted populations) in the table and then graph (*year, residuals*). If you believe it is necessary, describe a process that will improve your explicit model. Using your model, describe the process that will provide the doubling time for these populations and then predict the year when the population will reach 260 million. Write a paragraph summarizing your conclusions and analyzing your assumptions.

Year	Population given by the model	Actual population	Difference
1790	3,929,000	3,929,214	⁻214
1800	–?–	5,308,483	–?–
1810	–?–	7,239,881	–?–
1820	–?–	9,638,453	–?–
1830	–?–	12,866,020	–?–
1840	–?–	17,069,453	–?–
1850	–?–	23,191,876	–?–
1860	–?–	31,443,321	–?–
1870	–?–	39,818,449	–?–
1880	–?–	50,155,783	–?–
1890	–?–	62,947,714	–?–
1900	–?–	75,994,575	–?–
1910	–?–	91,972,266	–?–
1920	–?–	105,713,620	–?–
1930	–?–	122,775,046	–?–
1940	–?–	131,669,275	–?–
1950	–?–	150,697,361	–?–
1960	–?–	179,323,175	–?–
1970	–?–	203,302,031	–?–
1980	–?–	226,545,805	–?–
1990	–?–	248,709,873	–?–

Project

Finding e

In Chapter 2, you looked at discrete growth models; in this chapter, you've extended your study to include continuous models. Sometimes you use a continuous model to model a function that really isn't continuous. Compounding interest is an example of when you might do this. When interest is compounded quarterly, you can model this growth with a continuous function, even though the interest is only added to your account once a quarter. So the continuous function, in this case, is meaningful only for particular domain values. In reality, growth (or decay) does not happen once a year, once a month, or even once a minute; instead it occurs instantaneously and continuously. In the first part of this project, you will find the base for continuous growth. In the second part, you will compare this base with the ones you use for discrete models.

Part 1 Consider $1 invested at 100% annual interest for 1 yr. If the interest is compounded annually, after 1 yr the investment will be worth $2. Write the equation that gives this value. Now find the equation for interest compounded quarterly and determine the value at the end of 1 yr. Repeat this computation, compounding monthly, weekly, daily, hourly, by the minute, and by the second. Write an equation for 100% interest compounded x times each year for 1 yr. What is the limit, or long-run value, of this investment?

Part 2 Find e^1 on your calculator. (Usually e to a power is found above the key marked LN or ln.) In this chapter, you used a base of $(1 + r)$ to indicate $r\%$ growth. In the continuous model, you will use e^r as the base. How do these two numbers compare? Compare the values of a 9% annual decay of 200 g over a 7 yr period with the two models.

$$y = 200(1 - 0.09)^7 = 103.4 \text{ g} \quad \text{and} \quad y = 200e^{-0.09(7)} = 106.5 \text{ g}$$

Look at the graphs of $y_1 = 200(1 - 0.09)^x$ and $y_2 = 200e^{-0.09x}$. When are these graphs the same and when are they different? (Hint: Look at the graph of $y_2 - y_1$.)

Return to any problem involving growth or decay from this chapter. Rework the problem and compare the results you found before with the results you obtain by using this new information. Write a paragraph explaining similarities and differences between the results.

The Logarithmic Function

No one really understood music unless he was a scientist, her father had declared, and not just any scientist, either, oh, no, only the real ones, the theoreticians, whose language was mathematics. She had not understood mathematics until he had explained to her that it was the symbolic language of relationships. "And relationships," he had told her, "contained the essential meaning of life."
—Pearl S. Buck

In the last section, you learned how to solve equations like $x^8 = 32$. The base was represented by a variable and the exponent was a number. In this section, you will investigate solving exponential equations in which the exponent is represented by a variable. You have already solved this kind of equation by graphing, by guess-and-check using substitution, and by changing both sides of an equation to expressions with a common base.

■ ### Example 1

Solve each equation by finding a common base.

a. $49^x = 7$ **b.** $125^x = \sqrt{5}$ **c.** $1000^x = 0.0001$

Solutions

a. $(7^2)^x = 7^1$ **b.** $(5^3)^x = 5^{1/2}$ **c.** $(10^3)^x = 10^{-4}$

$\quad 7^{2x} = 7^1$ $\qquad 5^{3x} = 5^{1/2}$ $\qquad 10^{3x} = 10^{-4}$

$\quad 2x = 1$ $\qquad 3x = \dfrac{1}{2}$ $\qquad 3x = -4$

$\quad x = \dfrac{1}{2}$ $\qquad x = \dfrac{1}{6}$ $\qquad x = \dfrac{-4}{3}$ ■

You could have solved each equation in Example 1 by graphing. In fact, when you can't easily find a common base, you can find the solution by graphing.

The graph of $y = 3^x$ shows that y must be positive. This means, for example, that there is no solution for $3^x = -9$, because the curve doesn't intersect $y = -9$. The graph of $y = 3^x$ never goes below zero; it approaches zero (from above) as the x-values approach negative infinity. This means that $y = 0$ is an **asymptote** of the equation, or a boundary that the curve approaches. If, however, y is any positive number, you can solve the equation by zooming in on the point of intersection between the function and the horizontal line representing the particular y-value.

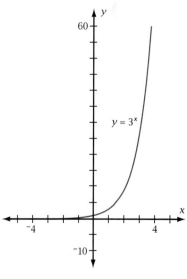

■ Example 2

a. Solve $3^x = 47$.

b. Solve $10^x = 47$.

Solution

a. You can solve the equation $3^x = 47$ by graphing $y = 3^x$ and $y = 47$. This means 47 can be written as a power of 3, even if the exponent is unwieldy. The graph indicates that $x \approx 3.504555375$.

By substitution, $3^x \approx 3^{3.504555375}$.

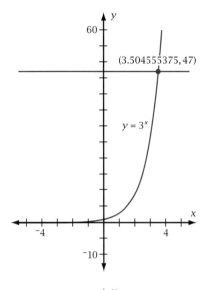

b. You can solve the equation $10^x = 47$ by graphing $y = 10^x$ and $y = 47$. This means 47 can be written as a power of 10. The graph indicates that $x \approx 1.672097858\ldots$.

By substitution, $10x \approx 10^{1.672097858}$. ■

The number 47 isn't special. No matter what positive number replaces 47, you can solve for x. But what if you want to solve the equation $10^x = 47$ without graphing? You'll need an approach, involving inverses, that will "undo" the variable as an exponent. This inverse process will provide an x-value when you have to solve equations like $3^x = 30$, $10^x = 47$, or $6^x = 280$. This means the inverse will provide you with the power (exponent) you can put on a given base to get 30, or 47, or 280. Like all inverses, its graph will be a reflection image of the original function over the line $y = x$, and coordinates of its points will be the reverse of the coordinates of the points of the original function.

Look at the exponential function $y = 4^x$. A table of values for the inverse can be written by simply exchanging the x- and y-values of the original function. See if you can make sense of these values. An input of 1 into the inverse gives a value of 0, because $1 = 4^0$. When you input 16, you get 2, because $16 = 4^2$. In general, the inverse will provide you with *the exponent that you would put on 4 to get x.*

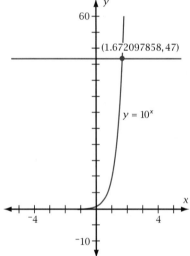

$y = 4^x$		The inverse function, $x = 4^y$	
x	y	x	y
$^-1$	$\frac{1}{4}$	$\frac{1}{4}$	$^-1$
0	1	1	0
1	4	4	1
2	16	16	2
x	4^x	4^x	x

The inverse of the exponential function $y = 4^x$ is called the **logarithm function**. The expression $\log_4 x$ is read "log base 4 of x." The functions $y = 4^x$ and $y = \log_4 x$ are inverses of each other.

You also know that you can name the inverse relation by switching the variables in $y = 4^x$ to get $x = 4^y$. This means $y = \log_4 x$ is equivalent to $x = 4^y$. Stop now and make certain you understand this before going on.

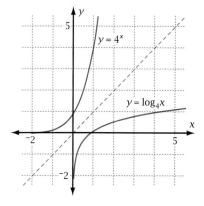

Definition of Logarithm

Given $a = b^x$ and $a, b > 0$, then $\log_b a = x$.

The $\log_b a$ provides the value for x, which is the **exponent** in the defining equation. The logarithm function is an *exponent-producing* function.

The word *logarithm* (from Greek *logos*, ratio, and *arithmos*, number) was invented by the Scot John Napier around 1614. He and Jobst Bürgi, an instrument maker from Liechtenstein, developed logarithms independently of each other during the late 1500s and early 1600s. Their purpose was to make some computations easier. Logarithms became popular very quickly. The mathematician Pierre-Simon de LaPlace said that the invention of logarithms "by shortening the labors, doubled the life of the astronomer." The astronomer Johann Kepler wrote to his friend William Schickard:

John Napier

A Scottish baron has started up, his name I cannot remember, but he has put forth some wonderful mode by which all necessity of multiplications and divisions are commuted to mere additions and subtractions.

■ Example 2 (again)

Solve $10^x = 47$.

Solution

$x = \log_{10} 47$	Using the definition of logs, "the log base 10 of 47" is the exponent you place on 10 to get 47.
$x \approx 1.672097858$	Use the log key on your calculator to get this answer. ■

Ten is the **common base** for logarithms. This means log 47 is understood to be in base 10. The calculator answer for the log of 47 is not an exact answer. The value is actually an **irrational** number—a nonrepeating, nonterminating decimal. You can check your answers by raising 10 to the Ans power, 10^{Ans}. Try working this example on your calculator now.

Example 3

Solve $4^x = 128$.

Solution

The calculator doesn't have a built-in base 4 logarithm function. One way to solve this equation is to convert each side of the equation to a power with a base of ten.

$$4^x = 128$$

$$10^? = 4 \qquad \text{The exponent you put on 10 to get 4 is } \log 4 \approx 0.60206.$$

$$10^? = 128 \qquad \text{The exponent you put on 10 to get 128 is } \log 128 \approx 2.10721.$$

$$(10^{0.60206})^x = 10^{2.10721} \qquad \text{Substitute } 10^{0.60206} \approx 4;\ 10^{2.10721} \approx 128.$$

$$10^{0.60206x} = 10^{2.10721} \qquad \text{Nested power property.}$$

$$0.60206x = 2.10721 \qquad \text{Common base property.}$$

$$x = \frac{2.10721}{0.60206} = 3.5 \qquad \text{Check: } 4^{3.5} = 128. \ \blacksquare$$

This technique always works. Forming a composite of functions that are inverses of each other will produce an output value that is the same as the input. By definition, the equation $10^x = 4$ is equivalent to $x = \log 4$. Substitution from the second equation into the first equation gives you another look at the definition.

$$10^{\log 4} = 4$$

Check this result with your calculator. Is $10^{\log n}$ always equal to n? What two equations can you graph to check this? Is it true for every n? If so, you can use this substitution to help solve equations similar to the one above.

Example 4

A sum of $500 is invested at 8.5% compounded annually. Find how long it will take until the fund grows to $800.

Solution

Let x represent the number of years the investment is held.

$$500(1 + 0.085)^x = 800 \qquad \text{Growth formula for compounding interest.}$$

$$(1.085)^x = 1.6 \qquad \text{Multiply both sides by } 1/500.$$

At this point you could write $x = \log_{1.085} 1.6$, but you don't know base 1.085 logarithms. So you must change to base 10.

$$(10^{\log 1.085})^x = 10^{\log 1.6} \qquad \text{Substitute for 1.085 and 1.6 using the logarithm identity } (10^{\log n} = n).$$

$$10^{x \log 1.085} = 10^{\log 1.6} \qquad \text{Nested power property.}$$

$$x \log 1.085 = \log 1.6 \qquad \text{Common base property.}$$

$$x = \frac{\log 1.6}{\log 1.085}$$

$$x \approx \frac{0.2041199827}{0.03542973818} \approx 5.76126139$$

Therefore, it takes about six years for the fund to grow to $800. ∎

■ Example 5

Solve $\log_6 280 = x$.

Solution

$6^x = 280$ Definition of logarithm.

You could rewrite this as $x = \log_6 280$, but you don't know base 6 logarithms. So you must change the base to ten.

$(10^{\log 6})^x = 10^{\log 280}$ Substitute for 6 and 280 using the logarithm identity.

$10^{x \log 6} = 10^{\log 280}$ Nested power property.

$x \log 6 = \log 280$ Common base property.

$x = \dfrac{\log 280}{\log 6} \approx 3.14483596$ Check this result by calculating $6^{3.14483596}$.

The answer is approximately 280. ∎

Problem Set 7.6

1. Rewrite each logarithm in exponential form using the definition of logarithms.

a. $\log 1000 = x$ **b.** $\log_5 625 = x$ **c.** $\log_7 \sqrt{7} = x$

d. $\log_8 2 = x$ **e.** $\log_5 \dfrac{1}{25} = x$ **f.** $\log_6 1 = x$

2. Use your results from Problem 1 to solve each equation by changing each side of the answer to an expression with a common base of ten.

3. Find the nearest integers, A and B, for each compound inequality.
a. $A < \log 1250 < B$ **b.** $A < \log 125 < B$ **c.** $A < \log 12.5 < B$
d. $A < \log 1.25 < B$ **e.** $A < \log 0.125 < B$ **f.** $A < \log 0.0125 < B$

4. Graph each equation. Write a sentence explaining how it compares to either $y = 10^x$ or $y = \log x$.
a. $y = \log (x + 2)$ **b.** $y = 3 \log (x)$ **c.** $y = {}^-\log (x) - 2$
d. $y = 10^{(x + 2)}$ **e.** $y = 3(10^x)$ **f.** $y = {}^-(10^x) - 2$

5. The function $g(x) = 23(0.94)^x$ gives the Celsius temperature x minutes after a large quantity of ice has been added to a bowl of water. After how many minutes will the water reach 5°C?

6. The United States public debt, in billions of dollars, has been estimated with the model $y = 0.051517(1.1306727)^x$. The exponent represents the number of years since 1900.

   a. According to the model, when did the debt pass $1 trillion ($1000 billion)?

   b. According to the model, what is the annual growth rate of the public debt?

   c. What is the doubling time for this growth model?

7. The relative frequencies of the C notes on a grand piano (C_1, C_2, C_3, C_4, C_5, C_6, C_7, and C_8) are graphed below on the right. These consecutive notes are one octave apart, which means the frequency will double from one C note to the next.

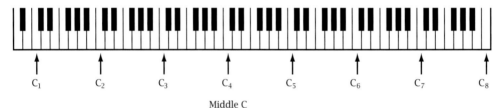

Middle C

   a. If the frequency of middle C (C_4) is 261.6 cycles per second, and the frequency of C_5 is 523.2 cycles per second, find the frequencies of the other C notes.

   b. Even though the frequencies of the C notes form a discrete function, you can model it using a continuous explicit function. Write a function that can be used to generate these notes.

   c. Sketch the general shape of a grand piano and describe how its shape is related to the curve pictured.

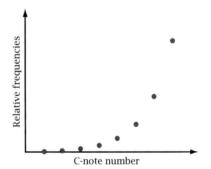

C-note number

8. Carbon-14 is an isotope of carbon that is formed when radiation from the sun strikes ordinary carbon dioxide in the atmosphere. Trees, which get their CO_2 from the air, contain small amounts of carbon-14. Once a tree is cut down, no more carbon-14 is added, and the amount that is present begins to slowly decay. The half-life of the carbon-14 isotope is 5750 yr. That means that if there is 100% at time zero, there is 50% at time 5750 yr.

    a. Find an equation that models the percentage of carbon-14 in a sample of wood.

    b. A piece of wood, supposedly from Noah's Ark, is found to contain 48.37% of its original carbon-14. According to this information, approximately when did the great flood occur? What assumptions are you making, and why is this answer approximate?

9. Crystal has been looking at old radio dials, and she noticed that the numbers are not evenly spaced. She hypothesizes that there is an exponential relationship involved. She turned on the radio at 88.7 FM. After six "clicks" of the tuning knob, she was listening to 92.9 FM.

    a. Write the equation of a general exponential function using a and b.

    b. Name two points that the function must fit. (Use zero clicks for 88.7.)

    c. Write the general form of the equation using the first point, and find a value for a.

    d. Write the general form of the equation using the second point, and solve to find a value for b.

    e. Use the equation you have found to determine how many clicks Crystal should turn to get from 88.7 FM to 106.3 FM.

10. Find a problem in one of the first six sections of this chapter that you cannot solve. Write out the problem and as much of the solution as you can. Then clearly explain what is keeping you from solving the problem. Be as specific and clear as you can.

Section 7.7

Properties of Logarithms

Each problem that I solved became a rule which served afterwards to solve other problems.
—René Descartes

You found out in the last section that your calculator can only calculate with base 10 logarithms. (Actually, it can also use what is called the natural base, *e*, which you may have investigated in the project in Section 7.5.) So what do you do if you have to evaluate an expression like $\log_5 12$, or solve an equation like $y = \log_8 15$? Do you always have to express these logs in terms of a base 10 logarithm? Or is there another way to approach these problems?

Investigation 7.7.1
The Log Function

This investigation will help you to better understand the relationship between a base, an exponent, and a logarithm. It will also help you to learn how you can solve an exponential equation with a base other than ten.

a. Complete the table for the function $x = 4^y$.

x	-?-	-?-	-?-	-?-	-?-	-?-	-?-	-?-	-?-
y	⁻2	⁻1.5	⁻1	⁻0.5	0	0.5	1	1.5	2

b. Enter these data into your calculator, set the appropriate window, and graph the data. Experiment to find the best *a*-value to make the equation $y = a \log x$ fit the data.

c. Repeat steps a and b for the equations $x = 7^y$, $x = 10^y$, and $x = 0.2^y$. Enter your results in a table like the one below. (Have each group member complete one column of the table.)

Base	4	7	10	0.2
a	-?-	-?-	-?-	-?-
Log of the base	-?-	-?-	-?-	-?-

d. As a group, determine the relationship between the base and the *a*-value. (Hint: Look at reciprocals.)

e. Have each group member solve one of the problems below. Be sure that the group agrees with your solution.

Use the relationship you discovered in part d to help you find y in each of the equations below.

i. $4^y = 8$ ii. $5^y = 10$ iii. $7^y = 11$ iv. $3^y = 12$

Look back at Example 5 in Section 7.6. In that example you solved the equation $\log_6 280 = x$ and found that $x = \dfrac{\log 280}{\log 6}$. Therefore, $\log_6 280 = \dfrac{\log 280}{\log 6}$. This is an example of what is called the logarithm change of base property; this property provides a shortcut for solving an exponential equation when the base is a number other than ten.

Logarithm Change of Base Property

$\log_b x = \dfrac{\log x}{\log b}$ for $b, x > 0$

Does this statement agree with your conclusion in Investigation 7.7.1?

■ Example 1

Use the change of base property to solve $5^x = 47$.

Solution

$\log_5 47 = x$ Rewrite in logarithm form.

$\quad x = \dfrac{\log 47}{\log 5}$ Change of base property.

$\quad\quad x \approx 2.39223121$ Check this answer. ■

If a logarithm is an exponent, then it must have properties similar to the properties exponents have. The problems in this section require the use of a special logarithmic ruler, which you will construct in Investigation 7.7.2. Work carefully and accurately so that you can use your ruler to discover additional properties of logarithms.

Investigation 7.7.2
Making a Logarithmic Ruler

To construct your logarithmic ruler, you will need a piece of graph paper and a strip of card stock. Everyone in the class needs to use the same kind of graph paper. Draw two lines in the center of your strip of card stock. (See the dashed lines in the diagram.) Then make a mark every ten units along one of the long edges of your graph paper. Label these marks 0, 1, 2, 3, and so on.

Use your calculator to find log 5, which is approximately 0.699. Find the approximate location of 0.699 units on the graph paper, and draw a line across the width of your card stock ruler. Label this line "5" at both ends of the segment. Use your calculator to find log 10. (You should find that log 10 = 1.) Find the location of one unit on the graph paper and draw another line across your card stock ruler. Label this line "10." Continue to draw lines on your ruler for all of the integers between 1 and 10. Then draw lines for the logs of all the multiples of 10. Next draw lines for the logs of the multiples of 100. Do the same thing for the logs of the multiples of 1000, 10,000, and so on.

Where is zero on your ruler? Why is it difficult to mark the logs of 0.1, 0.01, 0.001, and so on, on your ruler? Where is ⁻1? What is the largest number on your ruler? Note that the distance from 1 to 10 is the same as the distance from 10 to 100. The ruler has no fixed unit length. Can you locate 0.1?

Cut your ruler in half between the dashed lines. Now you have two log rulers, which you will use in the problem set to learn about some other properties of logarithms.

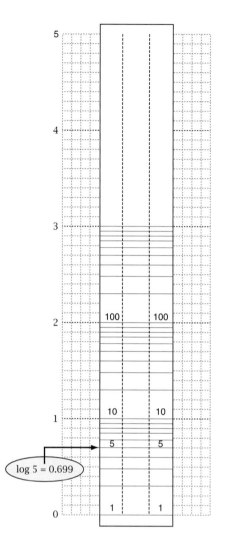

You could use two *ordinary* rulers to find the sum for an addition problem, like 4 + 3 = 7, by sliding one of the rulers along the other ruler as shown in the diagram at the right. Experiment with a few addition and subtraction problems to make sure that you understand the process. Is it possible to model multiplication by using ordinary rulers? Can you model 2 • 4? How? How about 3.5 • 4.7?

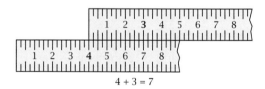

After John Napier published his tables of logarithms in 1614, Henry Briggs, a professor at Gresham College in London, made them easier to use and published a modified version of the tables in 1624. Another professor at Gresham College, Edmund Gunter, was interested in navigation, astronomy, and the construction of sundials (an important method of telling time in those days), all of which required lengthy calculations involving trigonometry. He produced logarithmic tables of sines and of tangents that were published in 1620. These tables helped navigators reduce the number of calculations needed to find their position at sea.

Gunter engraved his logarithms on the wooden shaft of a navigational instrument called a cross-staff and used dividers to measure off various distances. The cross-staff quickly became very popular in England, and later in Europe.

William Oughtred, one of the leading mathematicians of his day, was not particularly interested in computing devices. However, he saw one of Gunter's devices and realized that he could eliminate the dividers by using two lines of numbers and sliding one alongside the other. He didn't think it worth the effort to publish this idea, but was persuaded to do so by one of his students. The slide rule, as Oughtred's device was known, didn't become immediately popular, though certain specialized varieties did—for example, one made for timber merchants. In 1850, Amédée Mannheim, who was a military student in Metz, designed a slide rule with a moving cursor. This was adopted by the French artillery and eventually its use became widespread. Slide rules were used until the 1970s when they were replaced by the electronic calculator.

Problem Set 7.7

1. Use two logarithmic rulers to perform each addition. Look for patterns. Keep a record of both the problem and its answer.
   a. $\log 2 + \log 5$ b. $\log 2 + \log 50$
   c. $\log 30 + \log 30$ d. $\log 40 + \log 5$
   e. Describe any patterns you see.
   f. Use your calculator to confirm the calculations for 1a–d.
   g. Complete the statement, "$\log a + \log b = $ –?–."
      This is called the **logarithm product property**.
   h. Explain why this property works. (Hint: Name another mathematical situation in which you add when multiplying.)

2. Use two logarithmic rulers to perform each subtraction. Look for patterns. Keep a record of both the problem and its answer.
   a. $\log 30 - \log 6$ b. $\log 200 - \log 10$
   c. $\log 600 - \log 20$ d. $\log 600 - \log 15$
   e. Describe any patterns you see.
   f. Use your calculator to confirm the calculations for 2a–d.
   g. Complete the statement, "$\log a - \log b = $ –?–."
      This is called the **logarithm quotient property**.
   h. Explain why this property works. (Hint: Name another mathematical situation in which you subtract when dividing.)

3. Place your log ruler on graph paper to answer these questions. (Be sure to use the same kind of graph paper that you used to construct your log ruler.)

   a. Use your log ruler to find each value.

      i. log 2   ii. log 2^3, or log 8

   b. Compare the two results in 3a. Describe any relationship you see.

   c. Use your log ruler to find each value.

      i. log 50   ii. log 50^2, or log 2500

   d. Compare the two values. Describe any relationship you see.

   e. Use your calculator to confirm the calculations for 3a and 3c.

   f. Complete the statement, "log a^b = -?-."

      This is called the **logarithm power property**.

   g. Is this relationship true for exponents that are not positive integers? Investigate this question with your calculator.

   h. How would you write log $\sqrt{a}$ in terms of log a?

4. Determine whether each equation is true or false. If false, rewrite one side of the equation to make it true.

   a. log 3 + log 7 = log 21   b. log 5 + log 3 = log 8   c. log 16 = 4 log 2

   d. log 5 - log 2 = log 2.5   e. log 9 - log 3 = log 6   f. log $\sqrt{7}$ = log $\frac{7}{2}$

   g. log 35 = 5 log 7   h. log $\frac{1}{4}$ = $^{-}$log 4

   i. $\frac{\log 3}{\log 4}$ = log $\frac{3}{4}$ j. log 64 = 1.5 log 16

5. Rewrite, in your own words, the three properties of logarithms that you discovered in this section.

6. Draw the graph of a function whose inverse is not a function. Carefully describe what must be true about the graph of a function if its inverse is not a function.

7. The table contains consecutive notes of an octave from one C note to the next C note. (C# is called C-sharp.) This *scale of equal temperaments,* complete with semitones, is an exponential sequence, in which the frequency (in cycles per second) of a C note is double that of the previous C note.

	Note	Frequency
Do	C	261.6
	C#	-?-
Re	D	-?-
	D#	-?-
Mi	E	-?-
Fa	F	-?-
	F#	-?-
Sol	G	-?-
	G#	-?-
La	A	-?-
	A#	-?-
Ti	B	-?-
Do	C	523.2

a. Find a function that will generate the semitone frequencies.

b. Fill in the missing table values.

The scale of equal temperaments is also refered to as the well-tempered scale. It is interesting to note that if an instrument is tuned to mathematically exact intervals, it will sound as if it is out of tune. The human ear is needed when tuning instuments.

8. Evaluate the expression $\log_4 9 \cdot \log_9 12 \cdot \log_{12} 16$. (Hint: This might be easier to do without a calculator.)

9. Given that $\log_n 2 = x$, $\log_n 3 = y$, and $\log_n 5 = z$, write each expression in terms of x, y, and z.

   a. $\log_n 6$ **b.** $\log_n 2.5$ **c.** $\log_n 125$ **d.** $\log_n 100$

10. Evaluate each expression using the change of base property.

   a. $\log_2 16$ **b.** $\log_5 8$ **c.** $\log_8 5$ **d.** $\log_3 15$

11. Graph each pair of curves on the same axes. For each pair, graph $f(f^{-1}(x))$ and $f^{-1}(f(x))$. (See **Calculator Note 7H** for help.) You will need to use the change of base property for 11b and 11c.

NOTE

7H

   a. $f(x) = 10^x$ **b.** $f(x) = 2^x$ **c.** $f(x) = 0.5^x$

     $f^{-1}(x) = \log x$ $f^{-1}(x) = \log_2 x$ $f^{-1}(x) = \log_{0.5} x$

   d. Identify the domains of $f(f^{-1}(x))$ and $f^{-1}(f(x))$ for each pair of equations in 11a–c. Why are the domains different?

12. Determine whether each statement is true or false. Feel free to experiment with graphs of logs of other bases.

   a. The log curve is a function.

   b. The log curve has a horizontal asymptote.

   c. The log curve has a vertical asymptote.

   d. The log curve, regardless of its base, contains the point $(1, 0)$.

   e. The log curve has no symmetry.

   f. Log curves of different bases look like vertical stretches (or flips) of the $\log_{10} x$ graph.

13. List as many methods as you can to solve the equation $4^x = 15$. Explain each method completely. Which method do you prefer? Justify your preference.

Applications of Logarithms

It is a mathematical fact that the casting of this pebble from my hand alters the centre of gravity of the universe.
—Thomas Carlyle

In this section you will explore how logarithms are used to solve a wide variety of problems. You can use logarithms to rewrite and solve problems involving exponential and power functions that relate to the natural world as well as to financial situations. You will be better able to make decisions about investing money, borrowing money, disposing of nuclear and toxic waste, interpreting chemical reaction rates, and managing natural resources if you have a good understanding of these functions and problem-solving techniques.

The table below summarizes the properties of exponents and logarithms that you have studied so far in this chapter. Before you go on, be sure that you understand how to apply each of these properties.

Properties of Exponents and Logarithms

$(a^m)(a^n) = a^{(m + n)}$	$\Leftrightarrow$	$\log_a xy = \log_a x + \log_a y$
$\dfrac{a^m}{a^n} = a^{(m - n)}$	$\Leftrightarrow$	$\log_a \dfrac{x}{y} = \log_a x - \log_a y$
$(a^m)^n = a^{mn}$	$\Leftrightarrow$	$\log_a x^n = n \log_a x$
$a^{m/n} = \sqrt[n]{a^m}$		$\log_a x = \dfrac{\log_b x}{\log_b a}$
$(ab)^n = a^n b^n$		Given $x = a^m$, then $\log_a x = m$.
$a^{-n} = \dfrac{1}{a^n}$		
$\left(\dfrac{a}{b}\right)^{-n} = \left(\dfrac{b}{a}\right)^n$		

■ Example 1

More than 800,000 earthquakes are registered by seismographs each year. Most earthquakes are not noticed by anyone. Millions of dollars of damage was caused by a magnitude 7.1 earthquake centered near the San Francisco Bay area in October 1989. In September 1985, a magnitude 8.1 earthquake, which left many people homeless, was recorded in Mexico City. Earthquakes occur without any warning, although scientists hope that by studying the earth's movements they will someday be able to predict earthquakes. A seismograph is an instrument that measures an earthquake's intensity, using what is called the Richter scale. The Richter number is defined as $R = \log\left(\dfrac{I}{I_0}\right)$, where I is the intensity of the quake's vibrations, and I_0 is a standard, low intensity used for comparison. Compare the intensities of the two earthquakes mentioned above.

Damage in Kobe, Japan, as the result of a magnitude 7.2 earthquake on January 18, 1995

Solution

The magnitude $7.1 = \log\left(\dfrac{I}{I_0}\right)$ implies

$\dfrac{I}{I_0} = 10^{7.1}$, or $I = I_0 \cdot 10^{7.1}$ (intensity at San Francisco).

Likewise, $8.1 = \log\left(\dfrac{I}{I_0}\right)$ implies $I = I_0 \cdot 10^{8.1}$ (intensity at Mexico City).

The ratio of the intensities is $\dfrac{I_0 \cdot 10^{8.1}}{I_0 \cdot 10^{7.1}}$.

Therefore, the 1985 Mexico City vibrations were ten times as intense as those during the 1989 San Francisco earthquake. ■

Other natural phenomena whose measurements vary greatly in magnitude (such as sound intensity, star brightness, and chemical acidity) are measured using a **logarithmic scale** like the Richter scale. Logarithmic scales are used because a logarithmic graph increases slowly. On a common log scale (base 10), a measure of 8.1 is *ten times* greater than a measure of 7.1, and 1000 times larger than a measure of 5.1.

$10^{8.1} = 125{,}892{,}541$ $10^{7.1} = 12{,}589{,}254.1$
$10^{5.1} = 125{,}892.541$

What does this mean about an earthquake with magnitude 5.1? How does it compare in intensity to the Mexico City earthquake?

Acid concentrations and star brightness measurements normally have values less than one when measured in common units. Logarithms of these small values are negative. Instead of expressing these measures as negative numbers, it is standard practice to define them as the *opposites* of the logs of the common units. This means that the concentration, *a,* in a solution with a pH value of 2.10 is really $^-\log a = 2.10$, so $a = 10^{-2.1}$. Keep in mind that a pH of 2.10 is *more* concentrated than a pH of 3.70 and that a star of magnitude 2 is *brighter* than a star of magnitude 3.

Example 2

How does the concentration of a nitric acid solution with a pH of 2.10 compare to the concentration of a nitric acid solution with a pH of 3.70?

Solution

The pH of a solution is measured as the negative logarithm of the hydrogen ion concentration, $^-\log[H^+]$. The concentrations of the acids are

$$^-\log a = 2.10 \quad \text{and} \quad ^-\log b = 3.70$$
$$a = 10^{-2.1} \quad \text{and} \quad b = 10^{-3.7}.$$

The ratio of a to b is $\dfrac{a}{b} = \dfrac{10^{-2.1}}{10^{-3.7}} \approx 39.8$.

The first acid is about 40 times as concentrated as the second.

Example 3

A "learning curve" describes the rate at which a task can be learned. Suppose the equation

$$t = ^-144 \log \left(1 - \frac{N}{90}\right)$$

predicts the time t (number of short daily sessions) it will take to achieve a goal of N words per minute on a word processor.

a. Using this equation, how long should it take someone to learn to type 40 words per minute on a word processor?

b. Interpret the shape of the graph as it relates to learning time.

Solution

a. Substitute $N = 40$ in the equation

$$t = ^-144 \log \left(1 - \frac{N}{90}\right)$$

to get $t \approx 37$ short sessions.

b. Many interpretations are possible. It takes much longer to improve your typing speed as you reach higher levels. What limit is involved? ■

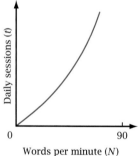

Example 4

The "rate" of a chemical reaction is the speed at which the reaction progresses toward completion. It is dependent on the exponential power of the concentration of one or more of the reactants. The rate at which iron dissolves is dependent on the concentration of acid according to the formula

$$R = k[H^+]^p.$$

The rate R is in grams per hour, k is a constant that depends on the temperature of the solution, and [H+] is the Normal concentration (represented by the abbreviation N) of the acid. The following data were collected from solutions at a temperature of 25°C.

	Concentration	Rate
Solution 1	0.20N	0.56 g/hr
Solution 2	0.60N	15.12 g/hr

What is the rate if the concentration of acid is 0.80N?

Solution

Substitute the data in $R = k\,[H^+]^p$ to get

$$0.56 = k(0.20)^p \quad \text{and} \quad 15.12 = k(0.60)^p.$$

From the first equation, you get $k = \dfrac{0.56}{0.20^p}$, which can be substituted into the second equation to get

$$15.12 = \frac{0.56}{0.20^p}(0.60)^p.$$

$15.12 = 0.56\left(\dfrac{0.60}{0.20}\right)^p$ Power of a product property.

$\dfrac{15.12}{0.56} = 3.0^p$ Multiply by $\dfrac{1}{0.56}$.

$27 = 3.0^p$ Arithmetic.

$p = \log_3 27$ Definition of logarithm.

$p = 3$

Therefore, the value of the constant is $k = \dfrac{0.56}{0.20^3} = 70.0$, and the rate is $R = k\,[H^+]^p = 70.0\,(0.80)^3 = 35.84$ g/hr. So, at a concentration of 0.80N, the rate is 35.84 g/hr. ■

Investigation 7.8.1
A Cup of Hot Water

In this investigation, you will find a relationship between the cooling time of hot water and the temperature of the water as it cools. Be sure to make a note of the room temperature before you begin the experiment.

a. Before collecting any data, draw a sketch of what you would expect the graph of (*time, temperature*) to look like as the water cools. Label the axes and mark the scale on your graph. Did everyone in your group draw the same graph? Discuss any differences of opinion.

b. Heat the water and a container together. (If you can't do this, wait two or three minutes after the hot water is poured into your container before collecting data.) Suspend a thermometer in the water away from the sides and bottom of the container. Collect data by measuring the temperature as the water cools. Do this at one-minute intervals for a while, and then at longer time intervals as the water cools. Record the time and temperature for each measurement. Collect data for as long as possible (at least a half hour).

Time	°C	°F
-?-	-?-	-?-
-?-	-?-	-?-
-?-	-?-	-?-
-?-	-?-	-?-

c. Plot (*time, temperature*) data on an appropriately scaled graph.

You will find a model for this data later on in the unit.

Problem Set 7.8

1. Suppose you invest $3,000 at 6.75% annual interest compounded monthly. How long will it take to triple your money?

2. a. Solve this equation for x: $12.85 = 4.2^x$.
b. Explain how and why this equation can be solved by *taking the log* of both sides.

3. Solve each equation by taking the base 10 logarithm of each side. Store the resulting x-values and use them to check your answers.
a. $800 = 10^x$ **b.** $2048 = 2^x$ **c.** $16 = 0.5^x$
d. $478 = 18.5(10^x)$ **e.** $155 = 24.0(1.89^x)$ **f.** $0.0047 = 19.1(0.21^x)$

4. Many formulas in biology involve rational exponents. One such formula, $A = 0.657(W^{0.425})(h^{0.725})$, relates the surface area of a human being (in square feet) to the person's weight (in pounds) and height (in feet).

a. If someone weighs 120 lb and is 5 ft 6 in. tall, what is that person's surface area?

b. If someone has 17.49 ft² of surface area and is 5 ft 8 in. tall, what is that person's weight?

c. Describe a method you could use to actually measure the surface area of a person in order to verify the given formula.

5. The length of time that milk (and many other perishable substances) will stay fresh varies with the storage temperature. Suppose that milk will keep for 192 hr in a refrigerator at 0°C. Milk that is left out in the kitchen at 22°C will keep for only 42 hr.

a. Assume that this is an exponential relationship, and write an equation that expresses the number of hours, *h*, that milk will keep in terms of the temperature, *T*.

b. Use your equation to predict how long milk will keep at 30°C and at 16°C.

c. If a container of milk kept for 147 hr, what was the temperature?

d. Using all of these data points, graph the relationship between hours and temperature.

e. What is a realistic domain for this relationship? Why?

6. The intensity of sound, *D*, measured in decibels (dB) is given by the formula

$$D = 10 \log \left(\frac{I}{10^{-16}} \right)$$

where *I* is the power of the sound in watts per square centimeter (W/cm²) and 10⁻¹⁶ W/cm² is the power of sound just below the threshold of hearing.

a. Find the number of decibels of a 10^{-13} W/cm² whisper.

b. Find the number of decibels in a normal conversation of $3.16 \cdot 10^{-10}$ W/cm².

c. Find the power of the sound (W/cm²) experienced by the orchestra members seated in front of the brass section, measured at 107 dB.

d. How many times more powerful is a sound of 47 dB than a sound of 42 dB?

7. The altitude of a plane is calculated by measuring atmospheric pressure. This pressure is exponentially related to the plane's height above the earth's surface. At ground level, the pressure is 14.7 psi (pounds per square inch). At a height of 2 mi, the pressure is reduced to 9.46 psi.

a. Use the information about pressure at ground level to find the coefficient of the exponential equation.

b. Use the information about pressure at a height of 2 mi to find the base of the exponential function.

c. What is the pressure at a height of 12,000 ft? (1 mi = 5280 ft.)

d. What is the altitude of an airplane if the atmospheric pressure is 3.65 psi?

8. The half-life of carbon-14, which is used in dating archaeological finds, is 5750 yr.

   a. Assume that 100% of the carbon-14 is present at a time of 0 yr, and 50% is present at a time of 5750 yr. Write the equation that expresses the percentage of carbon-14 remaining as a function of time. (This should be the same equation you found in Problem 8, Problem Set 7.6.)

   b. Some bone pieces with 25% of their carbon-14 remaining were found in Colorado. What is the probable age of the bones?

   c. A piece of the Ark of the Covenant found by Indiana Jones contained 62.45% of its carbon-14. When does this indicate the ark was constructed?

   d. Coal is formed from trees that lived about 100 million years ago. Could carbon-14 dating be used to determine the age of a lump of coal? Explain your answer.

9. Carbon-11 decays at a rate of 3.5% per minute. Assume that 100% is present at time 0 min.

   a. What percent remains after 1 min?

   b. Write the equation that expresses the percent of carbon-11 remaining as a function of time.

   c. What is the half-life of carbon-11?

   d. Explain why carbon-11 is not used for dating archaeological finds.

10. a. Find the average current cost (the last column) for each item listed in the table below.

   b. What average annual inflation rate provides the growth in prices from the 1975 costs to today's costs?

   c. Write an equation and use it to complete the table of values for 1980, 1985, and 1990.

   d. Find the current prices of two goods or services that are of interest to you, and use your equation from 10c to complete the values in the table.

Item	1975 cost ($)	1980 cost ($)	1985 cost ($)	1990 cost ($)	Current cost ($)
Can of Coke	0.25	–?–	–?–	–?–	–?–
Movie ticket	3.00	–?–	–?–	–?–	–?–
Haircut	5.00	–?–	–?–	–?–	–?–
Compact auto	4,000.00	–?–	–?–	–?–	–?–
Big Mac	1.00	–?–	–?–	–?–	–?–
–?–	–?–	–?–	–?–	–?–	–?–
–?–	–?–	–?–	–?–	–?–	–?–

Section 7.9

Curve Straightening and More Data Analysis

Few things are commonplace in themselves. It's our reaction to them that grows dull, as we move forward through the years.
—Arthur Gordon

Tables of data, graphs, sums of residuals, residual plots, correlation coefficients, and experimentation are useful tools in the search for a good model to explain data. You know how to find and use median-median and least-squares linear models of best-fit lines. However, a line is not always a good model for data.

The pendulum experiment in Chapter 5 provides data that are not linear. Many students have tried to model the data they collected in this experiment with a line. A linear model often seems like a good model if there is not much variation in the string lengths. In order to see the curvature of the graph, you need a wide variety of string lengths for your pendulum.

Experimental results from one group of students are listed in the following table. Below on the left is a scatter plot of data and the graph of an equation that the students found by guess-and-check to model their data.

Length (cm)	100	85	75	30	15	5	43	60	89	140	180	195
Period (sec)	2.0	1.9	1.8	1.4	0.9	0.6	1.4	1.6	2.0	2.4	2.6	2.9

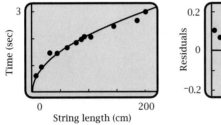
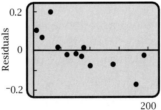

The graph of their equation, $y = 0.21\sqrt{x}$, looks like a pretty good fit. The residual plot shows that the curve should be higher for smaller values of x and lower for higher values of x. The residual sum is $^-0.2074$ and the sum of the squared residuals is 0.1322. (You will be asked to come up with a better model in the problems.)

By doing the investigations and working the examples that follow, you will learn how to find nonlinear models for data. The methods presented in Investigation 7.9.1 and the examples that follow take advantage of everything you have learned about lines. In other words, the strategy is to linearize data, which means you will alter or transform the data to fit a line. You will accomplish this by choosing from possible combinations of (x, y), $(x, \log y)$, $(\log x, \log y)$, and $(\log x, y)$ to find a plot that is nearly linear.

Investigation 7.9.1

Linearizing Data

Work with a partner on this activity. You will summarize the results with your group.

Part 1 The viewing window shown in the graph at the right is a good one to use for the graph of the exponential equation $y_1 = 47(1.61)^x$ over the domain $0 \le x \le 5$.

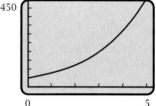

    a. Find the best viewing window to see the graph of $y_2 = \log y_1$. Describe the graph of y_2.

    b. Trace y_2 to find the coordinates of two different points. Store the x- and y-values for each point, keeping all the digits the calculator gives you.

    c. Find a different equation for y_2 in $a + bx$ form. Do not round off the values for a and b.

    d. Find a relationship between the slope of y_2 and the base of y_1. (Hint: Remember, you are learning about logarithms in this chapter.)

    e. Find a relationship between the y-intercept of y_2 and the coefficient, 47, of y_1.

    f. Discuss with your group how the exponential curve $y_1 = ab^x$ was "linearized" (transformed into a line). Write a paragraph that describes the process.

Part 2 The viewing window shown in the graph at the right is a good one to use for the graph of the power equation $y_1 = \pi x^2$ over the domain $0 \le x \le 5$. (This is the equation for the area of a circle with a radius of x.) How can you linearize this curve?

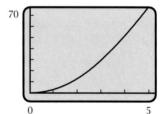

    a. Turn off y_1. Make a table of $(x, \log y_1)$ using the domain $0 < x \le 5$. Because $\log 0$ is not defined, zero has been removed from the domain.

    b. Find the best viewing window to see the graph of $y_2 = \log y_1$. Verify that this graph is not linear.

NOTE
7I

    c. Make a table that shows values of $\log x$ and $\log y$. (If you can't view this table on your calculator, then make a table like the one on the right.) Find a good viewing window and plot the graph of $(\log x, \log y)$. (See **Calculator Note 7I**.) Describe this scatter plot.

x	$y = \pi x^2$	$\log x$	$\log y$
0.5	$0.5^2\pi$	–?–	–?–
1.0	π	–?–	–?–
1.5	$1.5^2\pi$	–?–	–?–
. . .	. . .	. . .	. . .
5	$5^2\pi$	–?–	–?–

d. Use nonrounded values of log x and log y to find a linear equation for y_2. Write this new equation for y_2 in $a + bx$ form.

e. Find a relationship between the slope of y_2 and the exponent of y_1.

f. Find a relationship between the *y*-intercept of y_2 and the coefficient, π, of y_1.

g. Discuss with your group how the power curve $y_1 = ax^b$ was linearized. Write a paragraph that describes the process.

The reason you want to alter functions and data to produce a line is that it is possible to evaluate a degree of "best fit" for a line. You linearized the exponential function $y = ab^x$ by graphing $(x, \log y)$, and you linearized a power function $y = ax^b$ by graphing $(\log x, \log y)$. Here is an explanation of why these linearization methods work.

$y = ab^x$ (exponential function)

$\log y = \log (ab^x)$ Take the log of both sides.

$\log y = \log a + \log b^x$ Log product property.

$\log y = \log a + x \log b$ Log power property.

$y = ax^b$ (power function)

$\log y = \log (ax^b)$

$\log y = \log a + \log x^b$

$\log y = \log a + b \log x$

A substitution of A for log a and B for log b produces the linear forms

$\log y = A + Bx$ and $\log y = A + b \log x.$

Thus, the graphs are of the form

$(x, \log y)$ and $(\log x, \log y).$

■ **Example 1**

The table shows the number of coho salmon in Lake Michigan since their introduction into the lake in 1965. Find a model for this data relating (*time, number of salmon*).

Year	65	70	72	75	78	80	83	86	90
Population (thousands)	25	45	59	83	122	151	219	315	500

Solution

Your first guess might be that this graph has the "look" of a simple exponential curve $y = ab^x$. This is often the case when the only variable controlling the population of a species is the number of that species when food and space are ample and no predators are present.

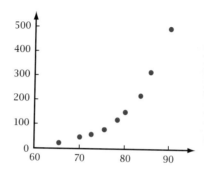

You will want to convert this curve to a line. One way to do this is to mark the *x*-axis of your graph paper from 60 to 90. Then line up your log ruler with each point on the graph to find log *y*. Plot the points (*x*, log *y*) and find the equation of the line. There is a graph paper made that is already marked off in the logarithms of numbers. It is called semilog paper and is used to graph data that grow exponentially, such as data relating to a fish population or to the value of an investment. With the use of semilog paper, a large range of *y*-values can be represented in less space.

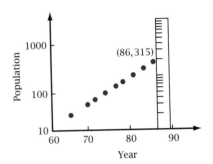

A least-squares line on the new points (*x*, log *y*) gives the equation

$$y \approx {}^{-}1.994 + 0.0522x.$$

Remember that the values of the intercept and the slope, *A* and *B*, are the logs of the constants in your exponential equation. You must raise 10 to the power of each of these to find the actual values. This is called finding the **antilog**.

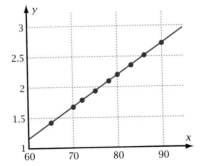

$\log a \approx {}^{-}1.9943$ $\log b \approx 0.0522$
$a = 10^{-1.9943} \approx 0.0101$ $b = 10^{0.0522} \approx 1.1277$
so $y \approx 0.0101(1.1277)^x$

What is the real-world meaning of these two new values? The 1.1277, or (1 + 0.1277), means that the population is growing at a rate of 12.77% annually. The 0.0101 is the salmon population (in thousands) in 1900, your base year. However, in this problem this value has no real meaning, because salmon were not introduced into Lake Michigan until the 1960s. ∎

Example 2

Earlier in the course you looked at the data for the relation (*radius, orbital time*) for the moons of Saturn. Now you will return to the data and find a more analytic solution to the problem.

Moon	Radius (100,000 km)	Orbit time (days)	Moon	Radius (100,000 km)	Orbit time (days)
1980S28	1.3767	0.602	Tethys	2.9467	1.888
1980S27	1.3935	0.613	Dione	3.7742	2.737
1980S26	1.4170	0.629	1980S6	3.7806	2.739
1980S3	1.5142	0.694	Rhea	5.2710	4.518
1980S1	1.5147	0.695	Titan	12.223	15.945
Mimas	1.8554	0.942	Phoebe	12.954	17.395
Enceladus	2.3804	1.370			

Solution

Begin by verifying that the relation isn't linear. A residual plot of (x, y) with a least-squares line should convince you. Next, verify that the graph isn't exponential. Convince yourself that a graph of $(x, \log y)$ does not linearize the data. Your next assumption might be that the data is best related by a power function. Plot $(\log x, \log y)$. (You could draw this graph on graph paper with x- and y-axes that are both marked in logarithmic scales. This kind of graph paper is called double-log paper or log-log paper.)

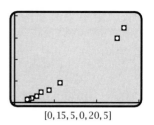

[0, 15, 5, 0, 20, 5]

The data

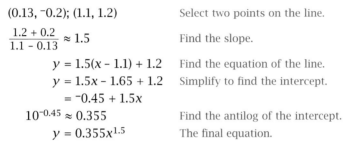

$(0.13, {}^-0.2); (1.1, 1.2)$	Select two points on the line.
$\dfrac{1.2 + 0.2}{1.1 - 0.13} \approx 1.5$	Find the slope.
$y = 1.5(x - 1.1) + 1.2$	Find the equation of the line.
$y = 1.5x - 1.65 + 1.2$	Simplify to find the intercept.
$= {}^-0.45 + 1.5x$	
$10^{-0.45} \approx 0.355$	Find the antilog of the intercept.
$y = 0.355x^{1.5}$	The final equation.

Test this equation by graphing it over the original data. ■

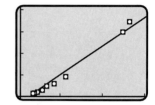

[0, 15, 5, 0, 20, 5]

The best-fit line

How can you decide whether to graph $(x, \log y)$ or $(\log x, \log y)$? Begin by plotting the original data using a good scale. Next, look at the graph and decide what needs to be done to "straighten" the data. Taking the logarithm of only the y-values will "pull" the high end of the curve down. Taking the logarithm of only the x-values will "pull" the rightmost data to the left. Taking the logarithms of both x- and y-values will do a combination of both. You may need to graph more than one possibility to find the best choice. Most of the data in these problems can be linearized by choosing from possible combinations of (x, y), $(x, \log y)$, $(\log x, \log y)$, and $(\log x, y)$.

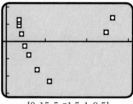

[0, 15, 5, ${}^-1.5$, 1, 0.5]

The residuals

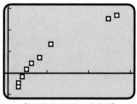

[0, 15, 5, ${}^-0.5$, 1.5, 0.5]

$(x, \log y)$

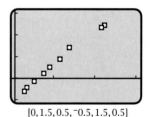

[0, 1.5, 0.5, ${}^-0.5$, 1.5, 0.5]

$(\log x, \log y)$

Problem Set 7.9

1. Find a better model than $y = 0.21\sqrt{x}$ for the pendulum data listed in this section. Graph (x, y), $(x, \log y)$, $(\log x, \log y)$, and $(\log x, y)$. Which one appears to be most linear? Write an equation for this line.

2. Find an equation relating the loudness of spoken words, measured at the source, and the maximum distance at which another person can recognize the speech.

Loudness (dB)	Distance (m)
0.5	0.1
3.2	16.0
5.3	20.4
16.8	30.5
35.8	37.0
84.2	44.5
120.0	47.6
170.0	50.6

   a. Plot the data on your calculator and make a rough sketch on your paper.
   b. Experiment by plotting different combinations of x, y, $\log x$, and $\log y$, until you have found the graph that best linearizes the data.
   c. Find the equation of a line that fits the plot you chose in 2b.
   d. Draw the line from 2c on your graph.
   e. Use the slope and the y-intercept of the equation in 2c to find the function for the original data.
   f. Graph this curve over the original data.

3. Start with a cup of M&Ms.
   a. Put the M&Ms into a large, flat, empty box and mix them. Remove all M&Ms with the M showing. Record the number of M&Ms remaining in the box, mix them up, and repeat the process six or seven times.
   b. Plot the data and find a relationship between (*time, number of M&Ms remaining*).
   c. Count the M&Ms that have no M on either side. How do these affect your data and model? If necessary, correct your model.

4. A cup of hot water is placed in the refrigerator, and the temperature is read at the time intervals listed in the table. Find a relationship between time and temperature.
   a. Plot the data using an appropriate window. Make a rough sketch of this graph.
   b. The graph of the data will resemble an exponential decay curve, except that the x-axis is not the asymptote of the curve. Sketch a horizontal asymptote on your graph of the data. If you shift the curve (the data) down 40 units, the asymptote would lie on the x-axis (approximately). Create a new set of data by subtracting 40

NOTE
7I

from each temperature. (See **Calcu-lator Note 7I**.) Replot the new data in a new window, and make a rough sketch of this graph.

c. Next, graph $(x, \log y)$. Reset the window, plot the new data, and make a rough sketch.

d. Use your calculator to find the equation of the least-squares line for these data.

e. In your equation for 4d, replace y with $\log (y - 40)$, and solve for y. Use the definition of logarithm to find an equation for the original data.

f. Graph this final equation over the original data.

Time (min)	Temp. (°F)	Time (min)	Temp. (°F)
0	159.5	65	62.3
5	143.3	80	55.6
10	125.3	95	51.3
15	111.8	115	46.5
20	102.0	135	44.3
30	88.4	150	42.5
40	78.5	180	40.7
50	70.9		

Note: Overnight temperature is 40°F.

5. Recall that earlier in the course you considered a problem involving the radius of a planet's orbit and the time needed for one orbit of the sun. At that time you found a best-fit line, even though you may not have thought the data were exactly linear.

Planet	Radius (in 10^6 mi)	Period (yr)
Mercury	36.0	0.24
Venus	67.2	0.62
Earth	92.9	1.00
Mars	141.5	1.88
Ceres	257.1	4.60
Jupiter	483.3	11.86
Saturn	886.0	29.46
Uranus	1781.9	84.02
Neptune	2791.6	164.78

Note: Ceres is a large asteroid in the asteroid belt, which has an orbit between Mars and Jupiter.

a. Enter the data into the calculator and graph them in an appropriate window. Make a rough sketch of this graph.

b. Select a linear regression on your calculator, and record the coefficient of correlation.

NOTE
7J

c. Now select an exponential regression (see **Calculator Note 7J**), and record the coefficient of correlation. Then select a power regression, and record the coefficient of correlation. At this point do you agree that the power regression is the best fit?

d. Place the three regression equations in the function menu, and graph these equations over the data.

e. Graph the three residual plots. Record the largest and smallest residuals, and describe any patterns that you recognize.

f. Do you still think the power regression is the best model? Explain why or why not.

6. Experiment with the different types of regression built into your calculator to find the function that best models your results from Investigation 7.8.1.

a. Find a best-fit equation and justify your choice.

b. Name the coefficient of correlation.

c. Sketch a graph of the residuals on your paper.

7. In clear weather, the distance you can see from a window on a plane depends on the curvature of the earth and your height above the earth.

Height (m)	Viewing distance (km)
305	62
610	88
914	108
1,524	139
3,048	197
4,572	241
6,096	278
7,620	311
9,144	340
10,668	368
12,192	393

a. Find a best-fit equation for (*height, view*) using the data in this table.

b. Describe the process (step by step) that you used to find this equation.

8. When A. Quatic starts treating her pool for the season, she begins with a shock treatment of 4 gal of chlorine. Every 24 hr, 15% of the chlorine evaporates. The next morning, she adds 1 quart ($\frac{1}{4}$ gal) of chlorine to the pool, and she continues to do so each morning.

a. How much chlorine is there in the pool after one day (after she adds the first daily quart of chlorine)? After two days? After three days?

b. Use recursive notation to write a formula for this pattern.

c. Use the formula from 8b to build a table of values and sketch a graph of 20 terms.

d. Find an explicit model that fits the data.

Project

Income by Gender

The median annual incomes of year-round full-time workers, ages 25 and above, are listed in this table.

a. Examine different relationships, such as (*time, men*), (*time, women*), (*women, men*), (*time, men – women*), (*time, men/women*), and so on.

b. Find best-fit models for those relationships that seem meaningful.

c. Write an article for your school newspaper in which you interpret some of your models and make predictions about what you expect to happen in the future.

Year	Men (wages in $)	Women (wages in $)
1970	9,521	5,616
1971	10,038	5,872
1972	11,148	6,331
1973	12,088	6,791
1974	12,786	7,370
1975	13,821	8,117
1976	14,732	8,728
1977	15,726	9,257
1978	16,882	10,121
1979	18,711	11,071
1980	20,297	12,156
1981	21,689	13,259
1982	22,857	14,477
1983	23,891	15,292
1984	25,497	16,169
1985	26,365	17,124
1986	27,335	17,675
1987	28,313	18,531

Source: 1990 Statistical Abstract of the United States.

Section 7.10

Chapter Review

Skill is the ability to perform a difficult action correctly, not by virtue of consciously held precepts, but by the unconscious knowledge of innumerable earlier performances and attempts.
—Hodgkin

Exponential functions are a continuous extension of geometric sequences. They can be used to model the growth of populations, the decay of radioactive substances, and other phenomena. The basic form of an exponential function is $y = ab^x$, where a is the initial amount of the quantity and b is the base that represents the rate of growth or decay. Because the exponent can take on all real number values, including negative numbers and fractions, it is important that you understand the meaning of these exponents.

   Until you read this chapter, you had no way to solve an exponential equation, other than guess-and-check. Once you defined the inverse of the exponential function—the logarithmic function—you were able to solve exponential functions algebraically. The basic definition of a logarithm is that given $a = b^x$, then $\log_b a = x$. You learned that the properties of logarithms parallel those of exponents: the logarithm of a product is the sum of the logarithms, the logarithm of a quotient is the difference of the logarithms, and the logarithm of a number raised to a power is the product of the logarithm and that number. Of all these properties, the last one is used most when solving exponential equations and analyzing nonlinear data. By looking at the logarithms of either the x-value, the y-value, or both values in a set of data, you can determine whether a relationship is an exponential function, a power function, or a logarithmic function. You can also use the built-in regressions in your calculator to examine these possibilities.

Problem Set 7.10

1. Evaluate each expression without using a calculator. Then check your work with a calculator.

   a. 4^{-2}

   b. $(-3)^{-1}$

   c. $\left(\dfrac{1}{5}\right)^{-3}$

   d. $49^{1/2}$

   e. $64^{-1/3}$

   f. $\left(\dfrac{9}{16}\right)^{3/2}$

   g. -7^0

   h. $(3)(2)^2$

   i. $(0.6^{-2})^{-1/2}$

2. Rewrite each expression in another form.

   a. $\log x + \log y$

   b. $\log \dfrac{z}{v}$

   c. $(7x^{2.1})(0.3x^{4.7})$

   d. $\log w^k$

   e. $\sqrt[5]{x}$

   f. $\log_5 t$

3. First, solve each equation by using the properties in this chapter to evaluate the expressions. Second, solve each equation by using a graphing approximation.

   a. $4.7^x = 28$

   b. $4.7^{x^2} = 2209$

   c. $\log_x 2.9 = 1.25$

   d. $\log_{3.1} x = 47$

   e. $7x^{2.4} = 101$

   f. $9000 = 500(1.065)^x$

   g. $\log x = 3.771$

   h. $\sqrt[5]{x^3} = 47$

4. A new incentive plan for the Talk Alot long distance phone company varies the cost of a call according to the formula $cost = a + b \log (time)$. When calling long distance, the cost for the first minute is $0.50. The charge for 15 min is $3.44.

   a. Find the a-value of the model.

   b. Find the b-value of the model.

   c. What is the x-intercept of the graph of this model? What is the real-world meaning of the x-intercept?

   d. Use your model to predict the cost of a 30 min call.

   e. If you decide you can only afford to make a $2.00 call, how long can you talk?

5. The data are the number of AIDS cases reported by the state health departments in the United States between 1982 and 1986.

Year	Number of cases
1982	434
1983	1,416
1984	3,196
1985	6,242
1986	10,620

   a. Sketch a picture of the original data on graph paper, and label the axes.

   b. Sketch a picture of the linearized data on graph paper.

   c. Find the equation of the linearized data.

   d. Use your equation to estimate the number of cases reported in 1990 and 1995, and predict the number of cases in 2000.

   e. If the trend continues, when will there be 1 million cases?

   f. Find the latest statistics to see if this model is still true today. If it isn't, try to explain why.

6. The federal minimum hourly wage was increased 13 times from 1955 to 1991.

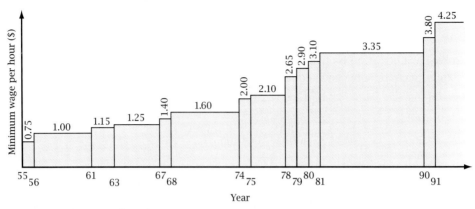

Source: Milwaukee Journal, March 14, 1993.

   a. Find a function that models the data as pictured.
   b. Use your model to predict minimum wages in the years 2000, 2010, and 2020. Include an evaluation of how reasonable these predictions might be.
   c. Use your model to estimate the minimum wage in 1938, when it was first established by the Fair Labor Standards Act. How does your answer compare with the actual 1938 minimum wage of 25¢/hr.

7. If you had to choose a favorite problem from this unit, which would it be? Why?

Take Another Look 7.10

For this investigation you will need at least one sheet of semilogarithmic (semilog) graph paper and one sheet of logarithmic (log-log) graph paper. (You can find this paper at engineering supply stores and university campus bookstores if it's not available from your teacher.)

Take a few minutes to look at the vertical scale on semi-log graph paper. This graph pictured here is from Example 1 in Section 7.9. It shows two cycles on the vertical axis. The labels 10, 100, 1000, . . . form a geometric sequence but log 10, log 100, log 1000, . . . represent the arithmetic sequence 1, 2, 3, ... The horizontal axis is labeled with an arithmetic scale representing equal distances.

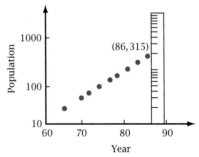

Plot the coho salmon data from Example 1 on your semilog graph paper. Do the points lie on a straight line? Use your graph to find the slope and *y*-intercept of these points (*x*, log *y*), and then follow through to find the exponential model for the original data.

Now take a look at your log-log graph paper. Both the horizontal and vertical scales are logarithm scales. Choose data from an example, previous investigation, problem set, or from Problem Set 7.9 that you think will be linearized by using log-log graph paper. Use this graph paper to find the related algebraic model.

Assessing What You've Learned—Self-Assessment Overview

In each chapter you have been introduced to a new method for assessing what you've learned. Each of these methods will provide you with a part of the picture, but to do an overall assessment you have to consider everything that you do. From now on you should use a variety of methods to assess your learning while you work on the investigations and problems as well as after you complete a chapter.

Although assessment is certainly more than the grade you receive at the end of a quarter or semester, it is usually a fact of life that assessment is reduced to an A, B, C, D, or F. If you had to reduce your assessment of your work in this chapter to one grade, what grade would you give yourself? What are your strengths and weaknesses? How would you justify your grade? Think about all of the ways you can assess what you've learned.

Organizing Your Notebook

- Is your notebook in good shape? Could someone else find something in it if they needed to?

Keeping a Journal

- Look at Problem Sets 7.5, 7.6, and 7.7 for journal prompts.
- Give yourself a grade for this chapter and justify it.

Portfolio

- Have you done any work in this chapter that you would like to include in your portfolio? If so, document it, and put it in.

Performance Assessment

- Demonstrate to someone that you know how to linearize an exponential, logarithmic, or power function by using the list functions in your calculator.

Open-ended Investigations

- Choose one of the Take Another Look investigations or a project, or design your own investigation. Share your results with a classmate, your group, or your teacher.

Constructing Test Questions

- Write several test questions that you think would be useful in determining whether or not a student understands the concepts presented in this chapter.

Group Presentations and Tests

- Review your role (or roles) in any group work you did in this chapter. Do you feel that you contributed to the group's effort? How can you improve your function in a group?

8 Topics in Discrete Mathematics

These four sisters are taking part in the Fiesta Parade in San Antonio, Texas. What are the chances of identical quadruplets being born? Determining the probability of an event occurring is part of a broader topic in mathematics called *discrete mathematics.* You will use matrices and a variety of vertex-edge graphs to solve some of the discrete mathematics problems in this chapter.

Section 8.1

Using Random Numbers

It is the perennial youthfulness of mathematics itself which marks it off with a disconcerting immortality from the other sciences.
—Eric Temple Bell

"It isn't fair," complains Noah. "My car insurance rates are much higher than yours." Feeling very smug, Rita replies, "Well, Noah, that's because insurance companies know the chances are good that I'm a better driver than you, so it will cost them less to insure me." Even though insurance companies can't predict what kind of driving record you might have, they know, based on experience, the driving records for people in your age group, and they use this information to determine what your rates will be. This is just one example of how probability theory and the concept of randomness affect your life.

Many games are based on random outcomes, or chance. Games of chance have existed for a long time. Paintings and excavated material from Egyptian tombs show that games using astragali were established by the time of the First Dynasty, around 3500 B.C. An astragalus is a small bone immediately under the heel-bone, and these bones were used in dice-like games. Later, in the Ptolemaic dynasty (300 to 30 B.C.), games with six-sided dice seem to have become common in Egypt. The ancient Greeks made icosahedral (20-sided) and other polyhedral dice. The ancient Romans were extremely enthusiastic dice players (so enthusiastic, in fact, that laws were passed to forbid gambling except in certain seasons). Gambling casinos and lotteries continue to thrive today, in part because so many people remain more or less ignorant of the idea of randomness. Although probability theory actually began evolving in the seventeenth century as a means of determining the fairness of games, it wasn't until years later that mathematicians and scientists began to realize that probability theory affects the study of sociological and natural phenomena as well.

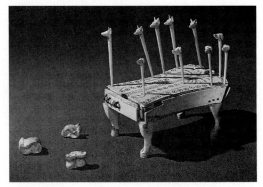

Ancient Egyptian game of Hounds and Jackals with astragali

In this section, you will begin to learn about the concept of randomness. Randomness means that individual outcomes aren't predictable. But the long-range pattern of *many* individual outcomes often *is* predictable, even for random processes. You will probably find that many of the ideas and concepts introduced in this section seem contrary to intuition. This is natural. As you work through this chapter and gain more experience, you will become more comfortable with these concepts.

Statisticians frequently simulate real situations and use summaries of the results to make approximate predictions about what they expect will happen. Many problems can be solved by using random numbers to simulate or model a situation. When you are generating **random numbers**, each number should be equally likely to occur and there should not be a pattern in the sequence of numbers generated. The next investigation will help you to understand what is meant by a random selection.

Investigation 8.1.1

Random Selection

You will need ten chips (or small pieces of paper) and a container to hold them. Write a digit from 0 to 9 on each chip. Be sure to use each digit only once. Place all the chips in the container and mix them thoroughly. Remove the chips one at a time until all are selected. Record the sequence of digits in the order they are selected. After all the chips have been selected, put them back into the container, and repeat this process until you have recorded 30 digits. (For example, you may have the digits

    5 2 8 0 4 7 3 1 6 9 3 8 4 2 5

after emptying the container once, replacing the chips, and removing five more.)

a. After completing the experiment described above, discuss each of the following questions with your group members. Then summarize your conclusions in a paragraph.

- How many 7's are in *your* list of 30 digits? How many 2's? Agree or disagree with this statement and defend your position: *This list of 30 digits is random because there are equal numbers of each digit.*
- Is it ever possible for a digit to appear twice in a row? Three (or more) times in a row? Is it ever possible to predict the next digit? Is it ever possible to name a digit that cannot be next in the list? Describe the implications (if any) that these questions suggest about the randomness of your list of digits.

b. With your group, design a method that would make this selection process more random.

NOTE
8A

The calculator is similar to other electronic computers because it produces pseudorandom numbers calculated by complex formulas. This means the random functions of some calculators can be set to produce exactly the same sequence over and over again. (See **Calculator Note 8A** to find out how to select a unique random number with your calculator.) To see what is meant by pseudorandom, seed your calculator's random number generator with the number 1. You will probably get the same sequence of numbers as someone else with the same kind of calculator, and your sequence might be the same as the list in Example 1.

■ Example 1

Generate a list of 20 random numbers on a calculator. What common characteristic do all random numbers in this list share? What long-range patterns do you observe?

Solution

.7455607728	.8559005971	.2253600617	**.469229188**
.6866902136	.0849241336	.0800630669	.6219079175
.1272157551	.2646513087	**.792829631**	.9489592829
.1176398942	.3445273552	.0031305767	.4990898873
.6666386115	.0598118664	.8057656643	.0963471417

Each random number is a decimal number between 0 and 1. Actually, by calculator design, all numbers generated will be in the interval $0 < x < 1$. This calculator displays ten digits, unless the last digit is 0, as it is in the two boldface numbers in the above list. These numbers are 0.4692291880 and 0.7928296310. You can't predict what the next number will be, but you can see some long-range patterns if you make a histogram of the results.

NOTE
8B

A histogram of these 20 random numbers using a window of [0, 1, 0.1, 0, 8, 1] would look like the graph at the right. The number 0.469229188 is included in the bar between 0.4 and 0.5. What would the histogram look like if you generated many random numbers? If you combined the tallies from thousands of such experiments, what do you think the distribution would look like? Experiment with the random number generator routine in **Calculator Note 8B**. ■

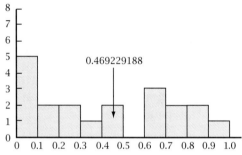

Each possibility for a random number should be equally likely. Ideally, over the long run, any number should occur equally as often as any other. This means histograms will level off as the number of experiments increases.

■ Example 2

How can you use the calculator to simulate rolling a six-sided die with 1, 2, 3, 4, 5, and 6 as equally likely outcomes?

Solution

The *random* command can be used in different ways to model this simulation. You could look at only the first digit. For example, 0.5246891697 would mean a 5, whereas 0.8395459099 would be ignored because the first digit is not a number from 1 through 6. You can also alter the random function so that the only random choices that appear are the numbers 1 through 6. Consider the following exercise, in which x is the random number that is generated.

$0 < x < 1$	By calculator design.
$6 \cdot 0 < 6 \cdot x < 6 \cdot 1$	Multiply each member by 6.
$0 < 6x < 6$	Result gives numbers between 0 and 6.
$0 \leq \text{int } 6x \leq 5$	The integer part, which gives just the numbers 0, 1, 2, 3, 4, and 5.
$1 \leq \text{int } 6x + 1 \leq 6$	Possible outcomes are 1, 2, 3, 4, 5, and 6.

If the random number is 0.7278813624, multiplying by 6 will give you 4.367288174, and int(4.367288174) gives you 4. Adding 1 gives you 5, which is one of the face choices on a six-sided die. (See **Calculator Note 8A**.) ■

NOTE 8A

Investigation 8.1.2
Medical Testing

Hi and Pocon Driack both go to the doctor with the same symptoms. The doctor tests them for *Rarus Diseasus.* Statistics show that 20% of the people with these symptoms actually have the disease. The test the doctor uses is correct 90% of the time.

To simulate this situation, you will generate random digits from 0 through 9. You can use your calculator, make a spinner, draw chips from a bag, or use a random number table.

a. Choose two digits, such as 4 and 7, to represent the 20% chance of having the disease. Then choose one digit, such as 9, to represent the 10% chance of the test failing.

b. Generate two numbers for each trial. The first number indicates whether or not a person has the disease. The second number indicates whether the test results are accurate or inaccurate. If you use the numbers as assigned above, a 5 followed by a 7 would mean the person *does not have the disease* and the test gave *accurate* results. A 7 followed by a 9 means the person *has the disease* and the test gave *inaccurate* results.

c. Work with your partner and randomly generate 50 pairs of numbers. Make a tally of your results. The first pair (5, 7) represents *doesn't have the disease, accurate*. The second pair (7, 9) represents *has the disease, inaccurate*. Combine the group results in one table.

	Test results	
Patient's condition	Accurate	Inaccurate
Doesn't have the disease	–?–	–?–
Has the disease	–?–	–?–

d. A positive test result indicates that a person has the disease, while a negative test result indicates that a person doesn't have the disease. What test results, positive or negative, would be reported for each of the cells in the table in part c?

e. Hi tests positive for the disease and Pocon tests negative. What are the chances that each one has the illness? Use the results in the chart to predict the chance that Hi has the disease and the chance that Pocon has the disease.

f. Write a paragraph summarizing what you learned about medical testing by doing this investigation.

Were you surprised by the results of the investigation? People in many occupations use random numbers to test theories and make predictions. You can use tables of random numbers, or you can generate random numbers with spinners, chips, dice, shuffled decks of numbered cards, or the random function on your calculator. When you get consistent results using randomly generated values, you know that these results are meaningful. It is like using chaos to find order.

Problem Set 8.1

1. Fay Silitator wants to collect homework from only six of her 30 students by using a random selection process. Devise a method she can use to randomly select six students. (Use chips, spinners, cards, or dice in your method.) Remember that her students will insist on fairness.

2. Suppose your job is to randomly assign 100 members of the marching band to ride in five buses that hold 40 passengers each. (The back of each bus will be used to store instruments and equipment.)
a. Describe a method for randomizing the selection process that uses a die.
b. Simulate your selection process. How many of the students are assigned to the first bus? Theoretically, how many students should be assigned to the first bus?
c. Write a random number routine for your calculator that you can use to simulate this selection process.
d. Use your calculator random number routine from 2c to simulate the selection process. How many of the students are assigned to the first bus?
e. How does your answer to 2d compare to your answers to 2b?

3. Rank 3a, 3b, and 3c according to which method will best produce a random integer between 0 and 9, inclusive. Support your reasoning with complete statements.
a. The number of heads when nine pennies are dropped.
b. The length, to the nearest inch, of a standard 9 in. pencil belonging to the next person you meet who has a pencil.
c. The last digit of the page number on your left after an open book is spun and dropped from 4 ft.
d. Write your own method for producing random numbers between 0 and 9.

4. Suppose you have been talked into playing a board game where you need to roll a 6 before you can start playing.

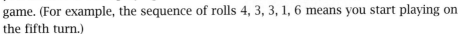

   a. Predict the average number of turns a player should expect to wait before starting to play.

   b. Describe a simulation, using random numbers, that you could use to model this problem.

   c. Do the simulation ten times and record the number of turns, or rolls, you needed to start playing in each game. (For example, the sequence of rolls 4, 3, 3, 1, 6 means you start playing on the fifth turn.)

   d. Find the average number of turns needed to start during these ten games.

   e. Combine your results from 4d with those of three other classmates, and determine the average number of turns a player should expect to wait.

5. Suppose each box of Wheaties® contains one letter from the word CHAMPION. The letters have been equally distributed in the boxes. The grand prize is awarded when you send in all eight letters.

   a. Predict the number of boxes you would expect to buy to get all eight letters.

   b. Describe a method of modeling this problem using a random number table.

   c. Use your method to simulate winning the grand prize. Do this five times. Record your results.

   d. What is the average number of boxes you will have to buy to win the grand prize?

   e. Combine your results with those of several classmates. What is the overall average number of boxes needed to win the grand prize?

6. Simulate rolling a fair die by altering the random number generator routine. (See Part 2 of **Calculator Note 8B**.) This routine will simulate rolling a die many times. Then you can display the results in a histogram. Do the simulation 12 times.

NOTE
8B

   a. Make a table storing the results of each simulation for your 1188 rolls. (List how many 1's, 2's, 3's, and so on.)

Trial number	1's	2's	3's	4's	5's	6's	Proportion of 3's	Cumulative proportion of 3's
1	-?-	-?-	-?-	-?-	-?-	-?-	-?-	-?-/99 = -?-
2	-?-	-?-	-?-	-?-	-?-	-?-	-?-	-?-/198 = -?-
. . .	-?-	-?-	-?-	-?-	-?-	-?-	-?-	-?-/-?- = -?-

   b. What do you think the long-range pattern will be?

c. Make a graph of the *cumulative* proportion of 3's versus the number of tosses. Plot the points (*cumulative number of tosses, cumulative proportion of 3's*). Then plot four more points as you extend the domain of the graph to 2376, 3564, and 4752 trials by *adding* the data from three classmates. Would it make any difference if you were considering 5's instead of 3's? Explain.

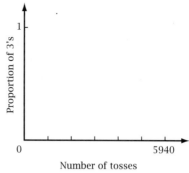

d. The *experimental probability of rolling a 3*, P(3), is the proportion of trials in which the 3 occurs after a very long run of trials, what is the P(3) for the die-roll experiment?

e. Ideally, what do you think P(3) should be? Explain.

7. a. Set your calculator for *dot* mode graphing. (See **Calculator Note 8C.**) What are the range and the possible outcomes of the *y*-values generated by each equation?

NOTE
8C

 i. $y = 6 \text{ rand} - 2$ ii. $y = \text{int } 3 \text{ rand} + 1$

b. Write a calculator routine using random numbers to generate graphs similar to those shown below.

i. 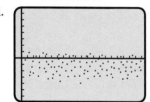   ii. 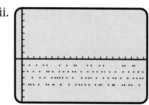   iii.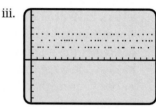

8. Suppose a country permits families to have children until they have exactly one son.

a. Devise and describe a simulation for this problem. Use your simulation to determine the long-run average number of children in a family.

b. What is the long-run average number of girls in a family?

Section 8.2

Random Numbers in Two Dimensions

There are many questions which fools can ask that wise men cannot answer.
—George Polya

Maria can reach 1 meter from her position at the corner of a table that measures 1 meter by 1 meter. Her sister Teresa teases her by dropping small candies randomly on the table. In this drawing, 12 of the 18 candies are within Maria's reach because they are inside the quarter circle pictured. (They are under the curve.) What happens if Teresa teases her with 200 candies? What happens in the long run?

Sometimes you can model a probability situation geometrically. In this section, you will be using some ideas from geometry to calculate probabilities.

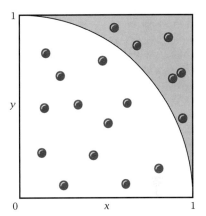

Investigation 8.2.1

Calculator Candy Simulation

Many of you probably have a sister or brother with whom you could play the candy game, but instead you will simulate this game on your calculator and keep track of the results.

NOTE
8D

a. Set a graphing window of [0, 1.5, 0, 0, 1, 0]. Enter and execute the program in **Calculator Note 8D**. Use $n = 200$ for the number of candies. The decimal answer you get is the ratio of $\dfrac{\text{number of points under the curve}}{200}$, and it will probably change every time you run the program because the candies land at random locations on the table.

It makes sense that this answer should have something to do with the area of the table and the area of the quarter circle. In other words, as the number of points increases, the ratio

$\dfrac{\text{area under the curve}}{\text{area of the square}}$ should be near the ratio $\dfrac{\text{number of points under the curve}}{\text{total number of points in the square}}$.

Or, $\dfrac{0.25\pi(1)^2}{1 \cdot 1} = \dfrac{\text{number of points under the curve}}{200}$.

Number of candies within reach $= 200 \cdot \dfrac{0.25\pi(1)^2}{1} = 157$.

If you divide the "target" area by the total area, you can predict the percentage of candies that land under the curve.

b. Simulate the game with 500 candies. How many of them land under the curve?

c. Theoretically, how many should land under the curve?

In the problem set, you will reverse the process and find areas by using this same program.

■ Example 1

Many games use the sum of two dice to determine the next action. Suppose the first die rolled is green and the second one is white. What are the possible outcomes, or sums, when two dice are rolled?

Solution

This two-dimensional graph pictures all possible outcomes when two dice are rolled. The five possible outcomes with a sum of 6 are identified. Point *A*, for example, represents the outcome with 4 on the first die and 2 on the second die. What does point *B* represent? How many different points would represent a sum of 11? ■

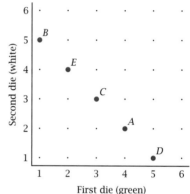

Problem Set 8.2

1. Consider rolling a green and a white die.
   a. How many different outcomes are possible for this two-dice experiment?
   b. How many different outcomes are possible in which there is a 4 on the green die? Draw a diagram to show the location of these points.
   c. How many different outcomes are possible in which there is a 2 or 3 on the white die? Describe the location of all of these points.
   d. How many different outcomes are possible in which there is an even number on the green die and a 5 on the white die?

2. Draw a graph on a grid like the one in Example 1 modeling the two-dice sums, and write equations in terms of x and y for each event.
   a. The dice sum to 9.
   b. The dice sum to 6.
   c. The dice have a difference of 1.
   d. Green + white = 6, and green – white = 2.
   e. Green + white ≤ 5.

3. Find the number of outcomes in each event, and write the fraction that represents the ratio of this number to the 36 total possible outcomes.
  a. The dice sum to 9.
  b. The dice sum to 6.
  c. The dice have a difference of 1.
  d. Green + white = 6, and green − white = 2.
  e. Green + white ≤ 5.

4. At the right is a graph showing the results of a simulation after many trials.
  a. Interpret the meaning of this graph.
  b. What is the long-range probability of success for this simulation?
  c. What would it mean if this proportion graph tended toward 1?
  d. What would it mean if this proportion graph tended toward 0?
  e. What is the range of values possible for numbers representing probabilities?

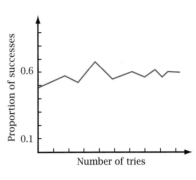

5. a. What is the total area of the square?
  b. What is the area of the shaded region?
  c. Over the long run, what portion of random points will land in the shaded area if both the x- and y-coordinates are determined by $0 < \text{rand} < 12$?
  d. What is the probability that any given random point will land in the shaded area?
  e. What is the probability that any given random point will not land in the shaded area?
  f. What is the probability that any given random point will land on another specific random point? On a specific line?

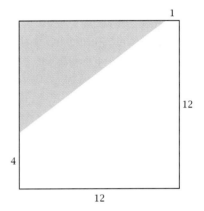

6. The square root curve for all x between 0 and 10 is pictured at the right.
  a. Use the average value of the function to find the area under the curve. (Look back at Problem 14 in Problem Set 5.7.)
  b. What is the area of the rectangle?
  c. What part of the rectangle should be under the curve?
  d. Use the program in **Calculator Note 8E** to approximate the area under the curve.
  e. Compare your answers to 6a, c, and d.

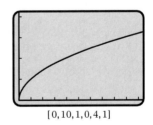

[0, 10, 1, 0, 4, 1]

NOTE
8E

7. Suppose x is a random number between 0 and 8, and y is a random number between 0 and 8. (The variables x and y are not necessarily integers.)

    a. Write a symbolic statement showing the event that the *sum of x and $y \le 6$.*

    b. Draw a two-dimensional picture of all possible outcomes and shade the event that the *sum of x and $y \le 6$.*

    c. Use a picture to determine the probability that the *sum of x and $y \le 6$.*

8. You and your best friend agree to meet between 3:00 and 4:00 this afternoon in the computer room. The first one to arrive will wait 10 min for the other and then leave. Arrival times are random within the hour.

    a. Draw a two-dimensional picture of all possible outcomes and shade the event that you will meet.

    b. What is the probability that the two of you will meet?

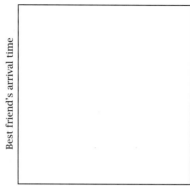

Best friend's arrival time

Your arrival time

9. Suppose your mom and dad have a joint checking account with a total of $400, and you have talked with both of them about the need for cash. Tomorrow, unbeknownst to each other, they each write a check for a random amount less than $400. Find the probability for each event described below.

    a. More than $80 remains in the account.

    b. The account is overdrawn.

    c. The account is overdrawn, but by less than $100.

Take Another Look 8.2

Set your calculator in *parametric* and *dot* graphing modes so that points are plotted but not connected.

    a. What are the minimum and maximum x- and y-values for the equations $x =$ rand and $y =$ rand? Use these values to help set your graphing window. Use your calculator to help you figure out how to control the number of points that are plotted. Explain how you would plot 200 points.

    b. What parametric equations and window values would you use to plot 500 random points on a square bounded by $(0, 0)$, $(6, 0)$, $(6, 6)$, and $(0, 6)$?

    c. What parametric equations would you use to plot only integer x- and y-values so that $1 \le x \le 6$ and $1 \le y \le 6$? Confirm that your equations work and explain why they work.

    d. Now plot one point on the calculator screen with integer x- and y-values so that $1 \le x \le 6$ and $1 \le y \le 6$. Trace the graph and explain what occurs.

    e. Write parametric equations and define window values that you would use to fill in the horizontal segment between points $(2, 3)$ and $(6, 3)$ with random points.

Geometer's Sketchpad Investigation

Random Points and Objects

Step 1 Create point *A* and translate it 10 cm horizontally. Construct a segment *AA'*.

Step 2 Open a new script and click Record.

Step 3 Construct point *B* on *AA'* and translate this point 1 cm vertically.

Step 4 Select point *B* and then point *B'*. Construct a circle with point *B* as the center.

Step 5 Repeat Steps 3 and 4 with a new point *C*.

Step 6 Click Stop on your script.

Step 7 Record if the circles overlap or not. Undo until only the segment remains.

Step 8 Select the segment and play the script.

Step 9 Repeat Steps 7 and 8 until you have done this 50 times. (Or do this ten times, and combine your data with the data collected by four other students.)

Questions

1. What is the experimental probability of two real numbers between 0 and 10 being within two units of each other?
2. Design an experiment to find the experimental probability that a circle of radius 2 cm, whose center is located within a square with a side length of 4 cm, will land totally within the square.

Section 8.3

Some Counting Techniques

I was gratified to be able to answer promptly. I said I don't know.
—Mark Twain

When the outcome of an event cannot be completely determined in advance, you use probability to describe the likelihood that the event will occur. Until now you have defined probability by looking at long-range results of simulations. Probabilities that are based on trials and observations are called **experimental probabilities**. Sometimes, however, it is possible to determine the **theoretical probability** of an event by counting the number of ways a success can happen and comparing this number to the total number of equally likely outcomes. But in order to do this you need to be able to count the number of equally likely outcomes.

Theoretical Probability

If $P(E)$ represents the probability of an event, then

$$P(E) = \frac{\text{the number of different ways an event can occur}}{\text{the total number of possible equally likely outcomes}}.$$

In this section, you will develop some strategies for counting without actually counting. You will also develop strategies to calculate the different ways particular outcomes of random selections can occur.

As people grow and develop, their counting methods become more sophisticated.

Example 1

These are the results of a student survey regarding an important issue in the school.

Reaction	9th grade	10th grade	11th grade	12th grade	Totals
In favor	65	55	79	56	255
Not sure	25	34	17	13	89
Opposed	58	42	88	91	279
Totals	148	131	184	160	623

a. What is the probability that a student is a senior?

b. What is the probability that a student is opposed to the issue?

c. What is the probability that a senior is opposed to the issue?

d. What is the probability that a student is not sure about the issue?

e. What is the probability that a student favoring the issue will be in the ninth grade?

Solution

a. $\dfrac{\text{number of seniors}}{\text{number of students}} = \dfrac{160}{623} \approx 0.257$

b. $\dfrac{\text{number of students opposed}}{\text{number of students}} = \dfrac{279}{623} \approx 0.448$

c. $\dfrac{\text{number of seniors opposed}}{\text{number of seniors}} = \dfrac{91}{160} \approx 0.569$

d. $\dfrac{\text{number of students not sure}}{\text{number of students}} = \dfrac{89}{623} \approx 0.143$

e. $\dfrac{\text{number of ninth grade students in favor}}{\text{number of students in favor}} = \dfrac{65}{255} \approx 0.255$ ■

Example 2

Suppose a red chip, a green chip, and a blue chip are in a bag. One chip at a time is drawn and recorded, and *not* placed back in the bag. How many different arrangements (**permutations**) are possible for the final outcome? (You will learn more about permutations in Chapter 11.)

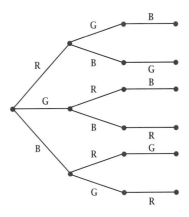

Solution

A tree diagram will help you keep track of all the possible outcomes. If you follow the top branch, the result is RGB, which means red, then green, and then blue have been selected. The six different branches give you all six possible permutations:

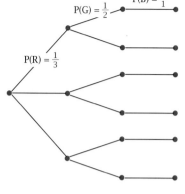

RGB	RBG	GRB
GBR	BRG	BGR

Because all branches are equally likely, the probability of any one branch occurring is $\frac{1}{6}$. This means the top branch (RGB) will occur $\frac{1}{6}$ of the time. Notice the three probabilities listed on the top branch. What is the meaning of $P(R) = \frac{1}{3}$, $P(G) = \frac{1}{2}$, and $P(B) = \frac{1}{1}$? Find a connection between these individual probabilities and the probability of the entire branch. ∎

Investigation 8.3.1

Loops

This investigation works best with a group of four students. You will need three strings, each 24 inches long. One group member needs to be the holder, and the other three group members are takers.

a. The holder holds the three pieces of string in the middle so that the other group members can't see which ends are from the same string.

b. Have each of the other group members grasp the end of a string coming from the left side of the holder's hand in his or her left hand and the end of a string coming from the right side of the holder's hand in his or her right hand.

c. Count the number of loops formed after you untangle the arrangement as well as you can without letting go of the ends of the strings.

d. Repeat a–c several times. Each time count the number of loops that have formed.

e. Make a guess at the probabilities for each outcome.

f. Find a method to calculate the probabilities associated with each possible outcome.

g. Compare your calculated probabilities with those from other groups.

Problem Set 8.3

1. A recipe calls for four ingredients: flour, baking powder, shortening, and milk (F, B, S, M), but there are no directions as to the order in which they should be combined. Chris has never followed a recipe like this before and has no idea which order is best, so he chooses the order at random.

   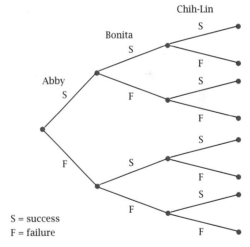

   a. How many different arrangements are there?
   b. What is the probability that milk is first?
   c. What is the probability that flour is first and shortening is second?
   d. What is the probability that the order is FBSM?
   e. What is the probability that the order isn't FBSM?
   f. What is the probability that flour and milk are next to each other?

2. Draw a tree diagram that pictures all possible equally likely outcomes if a coin is flipped as specified.
   a. Twice   b. Three times   c. Four times

3. How many different equally likely outcomes are possible if a coin is flipped as specified?
   a. Twice   b. Three times   c. Four times
   d. Five times   e. Ten times   f. n times

4. Three students are auditioning for different parts in a play. Each student has a 50% chance of success. Use the tree at the right to answer 4a and 4b.
   a. Find the probability that all three students will be successful.
   b. Find the probability that exactly two students will be successful.
   c. If you know that exactly two students have been successful, but do not know which pair, what is the probability that Chih-Lin was successful?

5. You are totally unprepared for a true-or-false quiz and you decide to randomly guess at the answers without reading the problems. There are four questions. Make a tree diagram and use it to find the probabilities in 5a–e.

    a. P(none correct)

    b. P(just one correct)

    c. P(exactly two correct)

    d. P(exactly three correct)

    e. P(all four correct)

    f. What should the sum of the five probabilities in 5a–e be?

    g. If a passing grade means you get at least three correct answers, what is the probability that you passed the quiz?

6. Use the histogram pictured at the right for 6a–d.

    a. Find the frequency of the group scoring from 80 to 90.

    b. Find the sum of all the frequencies.

    c. Find P(a score between 80 and 90).

    d. Find P(a score that is not between 80 and 90).

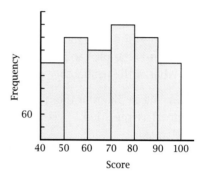

7. The registered voters represented in the table below have been interviewed and rated. Assume that this sample represents the voting public. Find each probability.

    a. P(a randomly chosen voter will be over 45 yr old and liberal)

    b. P(a randomly chosen voter will be conservative)

    c. P(a randomly chosen voter will be conservative if under 30 yr old)

    d. P(a randomly chosen voter will be under 30 yr old if conservative)

	Liberal	Conservative	Totals
Age under 30	210	145	–?–
Age 30–45	235	220	–?–
Age over 45	280	410	–?–
Totals	–?–	–?–	–?–

8. The proportion of phones manufactured at each of three sites, M1, M2, and M3, are 0.2, 0.35, and 0.45, respectively. The diagram also shows some of the proportions of defective (D) and good (G) phones. The top branch indicates that 0.2, or 20%, of the phones are manufactured at plant M1. The proportion of these phones that are defective is 0.05, or 5%. Therefore, 0.95, or 95%, of these phones are good. The probability that a randomly selected phone is both from site M1 and defective is (0.20)(0.05) = 0.01, or 1%.

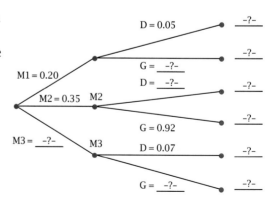

a. Draw the diagram and fill in the blanks.

b. Find P(a site M2 phone is defective).

c. Find P(a randomly chosen phone is defective).

d. Find P(a phone is manufactured at site M2 if you already know it is defective).

9. Two basketball teams, the Port City Parameters and the Eastville Exponents, are tied, and time has run out in the game. However, the Exponents' star player is at the free-throw line with two shots. He makes 83% of the free-throw shots he attempts. Make a tree diagram and use it to find each probability.

   a. P(he misses both shots)

   b. P(he makes at least one of the shots)

   c. P(he makes both shots)

10. Draw a tree diagram to represent the gender of the children in a family with four children. Label the outcome at the end of each branch, for example, FMMF. (There will be 16 branches.) Locate all branches that represent a family with exactly two girls. What is the probability that there are exactly two girls in a family with four children? You may assume that girls and boys are equally likely.

11. A 6 in. cube painted on the outside is cut into 27 smaller congruent cubes. Find the probability that one of the smaller cubes, if picked at random, will have the specified number of painted faces.

    a. Exactly one

    b. Exactly two

    c. Exactly three

    d. No painted face

Permutations and Combinations

In order to compute probabilities, you must first be able to count. There are three functions on your calculator that are very useful for counting things. They are the factorial (!), permutation (nPr), and combination (nCr) functions. Do some research and find out which function you would use to solve each problem below. Explain how the function works and why you chose the one you did to solve the problem. Make up a problem that is similar to those given below, but doesn't involve letters or words.

a. How many ways are there to arrange the six letters in RANDOM? What is the probability that the letters could be randomly arranged to make DROMAN?

b. How many three-letter arrangements (permutations) can you make using the letters of RANDOM? What is the probability that the letters could be randomly arranged and make ARM?

c. How many three-letter collections (combinations) can you make using the letters of RANDOM? What is the probability that the letters D, N, and A could be randomly selected?

Section 8.4

Waiting and Expected Value

Chance favors prepared minds.
—*Louis Pasteur*

Imagine that you are sitting near the rapids on the bank of a rushing river. Salmon are attempting to swim upstream. They must jump out of the water to pass the rapids. While you are sitting on the bank, you observe 100 attempts at passing the rapids and, of those, 35 are successful. Having no other information, you can estimate that the probability of success is 35%.

What is the probability that a salmon will make it on its second attempt? Note that this probability requires that two conditions be met: that the salmon fails on the first jump and that it succeeds on the second. In the diagram, you see that this probability is (0.65)(0.35) = 0.2275, or 22.75%. To determine the probability that the salmon makes it on the first or second jump, you would sum the probability of making it on the first jump and the probability of making it on the second jump. The sum is 0.35 + 0.2275 = 0.5775, or about 58%.

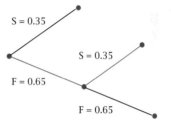

■ Example 1

"Last Minute" Larry has a half-hour lunch break before his afternoon classes. He has neither studied for his vocabulary quiz nor completed his mathematics homework. If he doesn't study his vocabulary, he will likely score only 13 out of 20 points. But if he spends the half hour studying, he could boost his score to 16 points. His mathematics teacher randomly collects homework from 1/3 of the class each day. If the assignment is complete, he will score 10 points. Otherwise, he will get a zero. It will take Larry the entire lunch

period to complete his mathematics homework, so he must choose to do one or the other. Should he study for his vocabulary quiz or do his mathematics homework?

Solution

If Larry studies for the vocabulary quiz, he will get the 16 points in English, but he will score nothing in mathematics if his homework is collected. On the other hand, if he chooses to complete his mathematics homework, he will score 13 points in English and he will have a 1/3 chance of scoring 10 points in mathematics.

	English points	+	Mathematics points	=	Total points	
Study English	16	+	0	=	16 points	
Do mathematics	13	+	0	=	13 points	or
	13	+	10	=	23 points	

To evaluate the mathematics homework options, multiply the probability of each event by the value of the event and find the sum. The result is (2/3)(13) + (1/3)(23) = 16.33 points. Larry could never actually get this number of points, but it serves as an indicator that in this case time spent on mathematics has a slightly higher value (16.33) than time spent on vocabulary (16). ■

Example 2

Pablo really likes purple gumballs. He approaches a nearly empty gumball machine in which there are eight gumballs remaining and only two of them are purple. At worst, Pablo may have to buy seven gumballs before he gets a purple one. Assuming they come in a random order, how many should he *expect* to buy?

Solution

NOTE
8F

A simulation of this situation will give you a value for the experimental probability. You could do this with eight pennies or eight pieces of paper, but it may take quite a while to get an accurate estimate. A programmed simulation on the calculator is much faster. (See **Calculator Note 8F** for a gumball simulation program.)

You can also find the theoretical probability for this simulation. Copy the tree diagram below showing some of the probabilities of success and failure, and determine the probability of each segment.

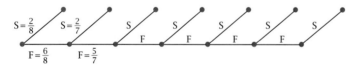

Find the probability of each of the seven branches. Do they sum to one?

Pablo would expect to buy one gumball 25% of the time, and exactly two gumballs about 21% of the time. (Find this on your tree diagram.) That is, if there were 100 different gumball machines, each with their own eight gumballs, he would expect to get a purple gumball on the first try with 25 of the machines. He would expect it to take two tries on 21 of the machines, and three tries on 18 of them. ■

To find the **expected value**, give each branch a value, which is the number of gumballs Pablo would need to purchase in order to get a purple one, and multiply this value by the probability of the branch. Then find the sum of all the branches. What is the expected value of the average number of gumballs purchased?

$$(0.25)(1) + (0.21)(2) + (0.18)(3) + \cdots = -?-$$

Expected Value

The **expected value** is an average value found by multiplying the value of each event by its probability and then summing all of the products.

Investigation 8.4.1

Pennies on a Grid

Darken some lines on graph paper to form one-inch squares. Throw a handful of pennies on the paper. Record the number of coins that land on the paper. Also record the number of coins that do not cover a darkened line. (The example shows two such coins.) Repeat these actions several times to find the experimental probability of landing completely within a square.

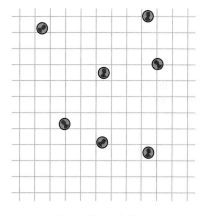

Now imagine a game where you must toss a penny on the paper until one falls within a square. Determine the average number of single pennies tossed until you would be successful (to the nearest 0.1). Write an argument to convince someone that you have found the correct value.

Problem Set 8.4

1. Sly Gamer offers to play a game with Les Mathhe. They will each roll a die. If the sum is greater than seven, Les scores five points. If the sum is less than eight, Sly scores four points.

NOTE
8G

   a. Find a friend and play the game ten times. (See **Calculator Note 8G** if you have no dice.) Record the final score.

   b. What is the experimental probability that Les will win?

   c. Draw a simple tree diagram of this situation showing the theoretical probabilities.

   d. If you consider this game from Les's point of view, his winning value is *positive five* and his losing value is *negative four*. What is the expected value of the game from his point of view?

   e. Suggest a different distribution of points that would favor neither player.

2. Dr. Will Sayphly works quite often with patients who are highly contagious. He has chosen a method of protection that research has claimed "is 98% effective when used correctly."

    a. What is the probability of no failure in 10 correct uses? In 20 uses?

    b. What is the expected number of uses before one failure?

    c. Enter and execute the program in **Calculator Note 8H** and give the expected value after 99 failures.

    d. According to your data what is the greatest number of uses before failure and the smallest number of uses before failure? (You may want to sort the data first.)

    e. Sketch a histogram of the data and summarize the information in the graph in one or two sentences.

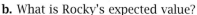

NOTE
8H

3. Rocky Role has organized an outdoor concert. If the weather is good, Rocky will make $400,000. If the weather is bad, he will have to pay the bands and refund all the tickets. This means that he will lose $1 million. According to the weather report, there is a 40% chance of rain.

    a. Make a tree diagram of the outcomes and label the value of each branch.

    b. What is Rocky's expected value?

    c. If Rocky cancels the concert right now, he will only lose $100,000. What should he do? Write an argument to convince Rocky that you are giving him good advice.

4. Research has shown that a blue-footed booby has a 47% chance of surviving from egg to adulthood. You have found a nest of four eggs.

    a. What is the probability that all four will survive to adulthood?

    b. What is the probability that none of the four will survive to adulthood?

    c. How many birds would you expect to survive?

5. You are given the following information about the algebra enrollment in a local high school: 16% sophomore male, 24% sophomore female, 32% junior male, and 28% junior female.

    a. What is the probability that the algebra book you found under the tree belongs to a junior?

    b. If you know that an algebra book belongs to a male, what is the probability that it belongs to a junior?

    c. If there are 100 algebra students, how many of them are male?

    d. If there are 100 algebra students, how many are male juniors?

    e. Do these last two pieces of information agree with your answer to 5b? Why or why not?

6. Return to the data collected in Investigation 8.1.2.

    a. Use the collected data to find each percentage.

        i. People who don't have the disease for whom the test is inaccurate.

        ii. People who don't have the disease for whom the test is accurate.

        iii. People who have the disease for whom the test is accurate.

        iv. People who have the disease for whom the test is inaccurate.

b. What is the probability that the test will indicate a person has the disease?

c. If the test indicates a person has the disease, what is the probability that this person actually has the disease?

d. Draw a tree diagram that shows a 20% probability of having the disease and a 10% probability of the test results being inaccurate.

e. How do the theoretical probabilities you calculated by using the tree diagram compare with experimental probabilities from your data?

7. The tree diagram shows a game played by two players.

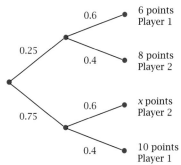

a. Find an *x*-value that gives nearly equal value to each player.

b. Interpret the information in the graph and design a game that would match these probabilities. (You may use coins, dice, spinners, whatever.) Be detailed about the rules of the game and the scoring of points.

8. Create your own problem, which you think would make a good assessment question. It should cover the material you have studied so far in this chapter. Write out the complete solution to your problem and explain why you believe it to be a good problem. Note: Please make sure that it is a problem or a question, not just an explanation or a description.

Project

Coin Toss Game

Return to Investigation 8.4.1.

a. Explain how to use geometric probability to calculate the theoretical probability of a penny landing within a one-inch square. Assume the "lines" on the graph are infinitely thin.

b. Extend the calculation in part a to the probability of a penny landing in a square measuring *a* inches on a side.

c. Extend the problem again to find the probability of a coin of radius *r* inches landing in a square of a^2 square inches.

d. Extend the problem once more to find the probability of a coin of radius *r* inches landing in a square of a^2 square inches drawn with lines that are *t* inches thick.

e. Use your formula to design a game, played with a quarter, that has a probability of success equal to 0.1. Describe your game. Build a game board.

Section 8.5

Chromatic Numbering

Learning is the only thing the mind never exhausts, never fears, and never regrets.
—Leonardo da Vinci

Diagrams with vertices and edges originally were used to solve puzzles, and later to represent electronic circuits and molecules. In 1877, the British mathematician James Joseph Sylvester (1814–1897) gave the name "graph" to these kinds of diagrams in his article "Chemistry and Algebra." The study of these graphs is called **graph theory**. It is a relatively new field of study compared to geometry or algebra. Graph theory principles can be applied to many different types of problems, from sixteenth-century puzzles to the design of transcontinental computer networks. The diagram helps you find a mathematical solution. A probability tree diagram is an application of graph theory. In the rest of this chapter you will be introduced to a few of the basic techniques and many uses of graph theory.

In scientific or medical research, it is often important to classify and identify according to linked or shared attributes. One process of grouping the vertices of a graph is called **chromatic numbering**.

Investigation 8.5.1
Conflict Resolution

Part 1   Fay Silitator is assigning new groups in her class, and she has gathered some information about the students.

- Art and Bao fight when they are put together.
- Carlos and Dan joke all the time and never get any work done when they are together.
- Eyota and Fadil just don't like each other.
- Greg doesn't get along with anybody in the band, which includes Art, Dan, Eyota, Hisa, Isa, and Jill.
- Kono and Lusita always get A's and shouldn't be in the same group.
- Masud, Nam, Oto, and Panya are the class leaders, and no two of them should be in the same group.
- Quincy can't concentrate if he is in the same group with Lusita, Panya, or Ursala.

- Rudo, Sue, and Tai talk only about sports if any two of them are together.
- Vick and Winona just stare at each other if they are in the same group.
- Zahur doesn't like anyone whose first name begins with a vowel.
- Fadil, Hisa, and Quincy haven't worked together since that incident in science class last year.
- Sue and Lusita both like the same guy, so they can't work together; nor can you put either one with Dan.
- Everybody knows why Winona shouldn't work with Ursala.

Can you make four groups of six students and satisfy all the restrictions listed above? Try to do this before reading any further.

Below is a graph of the information. Each person (vertex) is connected by a line (called an **edge**) to every other person with whom he or she should *not* be assigned. For example, you can see that Eyota (located in about the center of the graph) should not be with Greg, Fadil, or Zahur. To use this diagram, you want to look at the information one piece at a time in order to make each connection. Sometimes edges will cross over each other, but this is not a problem. Don't be concerned about the beauty of your graph, and keep in mind that there can be many different correct answers.

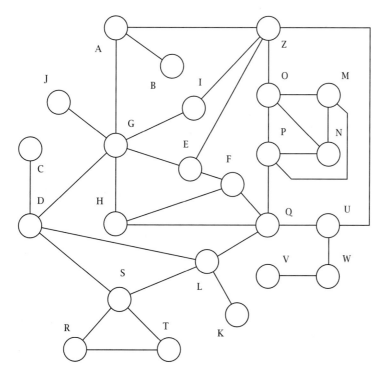

Part 2   To begin, assign a number or color to a person. Each point (vertex) connected to the point representing this person must have a different number. Vertices can have the same number provided they are not connected with an edge. It may help to start with the most complicated part of the graph. You will find a possible solution on page 402, but do not look at it until you have come up with your own grouping solution.

There are many solutions. It is unlikely that your solution is the same as the one shown below. The objective is to find a solution that satisfies all of the restrictions.

Group 1

Bao
Carlos
Greg
Masud
Quincy
Zahur

Group 2

Art
Eyota
Hisa
Jill
Sue
Oto

Group 3

Dan
Kono
Panya
Rudo
Ursala
Vick

Group 4

Isa
Fadil
Nam
Tim
Lusita
Winona

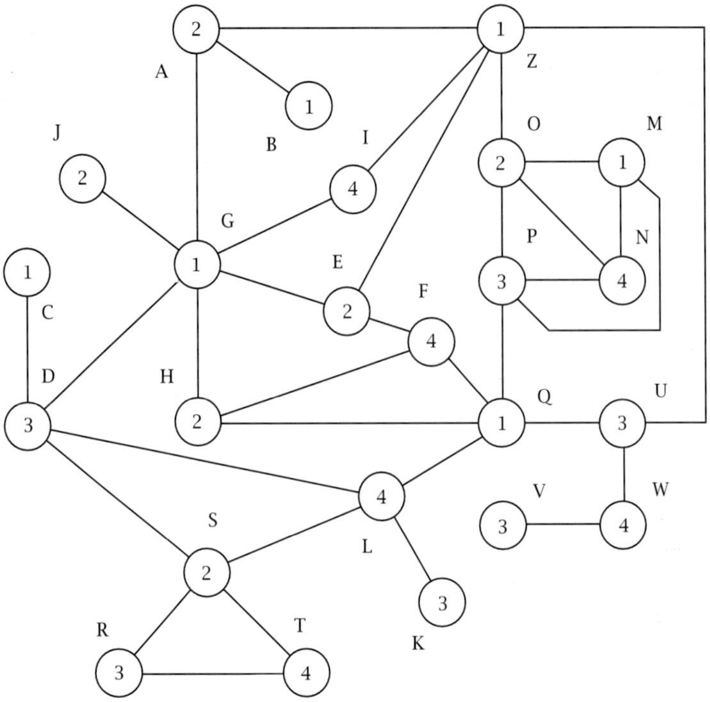

Investigation 8.5.2

Visiting Colleges

Rhoda S. Say is planning to visit several colleges while on spring break. She gathers the following flight information. What is the cheapest fare that allows Rhoda to fly from her home, visit every school, and return to her home?

	USC	Oberlin	Yale	U of M	SMU
Home	$250	$140	$128	$158	$212
SMU	$176	$130	$132	$175	
U of M	$250	$108	$112		
Yale	$315	$150			
Oberlin	$235				

Draw a graph showing the flight path and find the total cost of the trip. Explain why you are convinced there is no cheaper path.

Problem Set 8.5

1. Trace each map below, and color it using the smallest number of colors possible. If two regions share a border, they cannot be the same color. Two regions may be the same color, however, if they only meet at a corner.

   a.

   b.

2. For 2a–d below, design a map with ten regions that can be colored using the same restrictions that were stated in Problem 1.
   a. Use only two colors.
   b. Requires three colors.
   c. Requires four colors.
   d. Requires five colors.
   e. Do you think there is a limit to the number of colors needed to color a very complex map? Give an argument to support your reasoning.

   Problems 1 and 2 are related to the four-color conjecture: Not more than four colors are necessary in order to color a map of a country (divided into regions) in such a way that no two contiguous regions are of the same color. This conjecture was first investigated around 1853 when Francis Guthrie, a graduate student at University College, London, was drawing a map of England. Guthrie noticed that four colors seemed to be sufficient to distinguish the counties and wondered if there was a general theorem that applied to the situation. He discussed it with his brother Frederick, who asked the mathematician Augustus De Morgan, who mentioned it in a letter to the mathematician Sir William Hamilton. Over the years, many mathematicians have devoted much effort to the four-color conjecture. Out of this work has grown much of what is now known as graph theory. In 1976, Kenneth Appel

(1932–) and Wolfgang Haken (1928–), mathematicians at the University of Illinois, said they had a computer-generated "proof" of the conjecture. Their method involved reducing the theorem to a large number of special cases and having the computer check each case. This took six months of computer time. Many mathematicians do not consider Appel and Haken's work to be an adequate proof; for them the four-color conjecture is still a conjecture, not a theorem.

3. The chromatic number of a graph is the smallest number of colors needed so that no connected vertices share the same color. Copy the graphs below on your paper. Find the chromatic number for each graph.

   a. 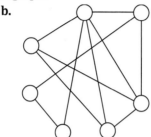   b. 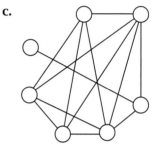   c.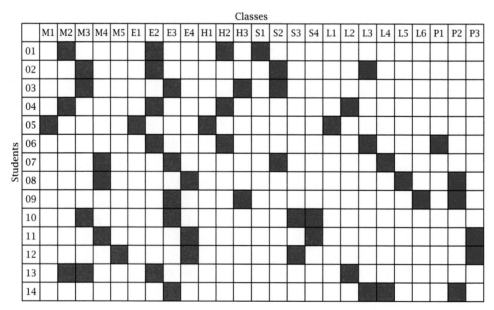

4. Design an exam schedule for spring semester. Assume that the 14 students listed in the grid below are representative of the entire student body. If you can avoid all conflicts within this group, the schedule will work for the entire school. What is the smallest number of time blocks needed to make an exam schedule with no conflicts? (According to this table, student 01 is currently enrolled in classes M2, E2, H2, and S1.) (Hint: Arrange the points on your paper as shown in the diagram on page 405.)

Classes

Students	M1	M2	M3	M4	M5	E1	E2	E3	E4	H1	H2	H3	S1	S2	S3	S4	L1	L2	L3	L4	L5	L6	P1	P2	P3
01		■					■				■		■												
02			■				■							■					■						
03												■	■							■					
04		■				■				■				■											
05	■				■			■							■										
06						■		■										■		■	■		■		
07	■			■			■											■							
08				■			■		■									■		■					
09							■				■													■	
10				■											■	■									
11			■	■		■								■											■
12					■		■							■											
13		■	■			■										■			■						
14							■												■			■			■

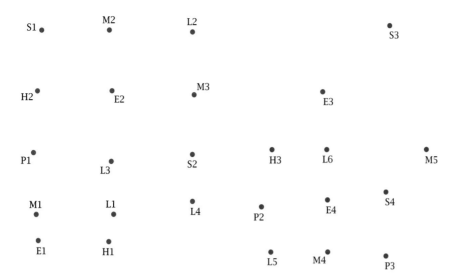

5. Twelve chemicals are stored in 12 tanks. If two tanks contain two chemicals that are dangerous if mixed together, then they must be kept apart in separate storage areas. The table indicates which chemicals are relatively safe and which are dangerously unsafe if mixed. Find the smallest number of storage areas required for this situation. Explain your solution strategy.

	1	2	3	4	5	6	7	8	9	10	11	12
1		S	S	U	S	S	S	U	U	S	U	U
2	S		U	U	U	U	U	U	U	S	U	U
3	S	U		S	U	U	U	S	S	S	S	S
4	U	U	S		U	U	U	S	S	S	U	S
5	S	U	U	U		S	S	U	U	S	U	U
6	S	U	U	U	S		S	U	U	S	U	S
7	S	U	U	U	S	S		U	U	S	U	U
8	U	U	S	S	U	U	U		U	S	U	U
9	U	U	S	S	U	U	U	U		S	U	S
10	S	S	S	S	S	S	S	S	S		S	S
11	U	U	S	U	U	U	U	U	U	S		U
12	U	U	S	S	U	S	U	U	S	S	U	

Take Another Look 8.5

Your task in Investigation 8.5.1 was to find groups of students who could work together. You did this by investigating and highlighting individual conflicts between students. Problems of this type have historically been solved by labeling or coloring vertices of a related graph. Your first step, however, is to decide what your graph's vertices and edges represent.

During this activity you will continue to use vertices, edges, and grouping (or coloring) schemes to systematically assign the smallest number of groupings.

The Federal Communications Commission (FCC) assigns different transmitting frequencies to radio stations whose broadcasts might interfere with each other. The distance between the stations is a factor to be considered. Suppose the FCC decides that stations within 150 miles of each other must be assigned different frequencies. The table lists distances (in miles) between the six radio stations. The problem is to determine the minimum number of different frequencies needed.

	A	B	C	D	E	F
A		88	170	215	60	100
B	88		130	185	95	170
C	170	130		105	220	300
D	215	185	105		220	210
E	60	95	220	220		140
F	100	170	300	210	140	

a. As you model this problem, what should the vertices represent?

b. How will you decide which vertices will be connected with edges?

c. Draw your graph and name two stations that you connected with an edge. Explain why they are connected.

d. The next step is to determine a color assignment so that two connected vertices have different colors. Use as few colors as possible. Explain your system. In terms of FCC frequencies, explain what it means if two vertices have the same color. What does it mean if they have different colors?

e. What is the minimum number of different frequencies needed? Is your solution unique? Explain.

Section 8.6

The Transition Matrix

I regard it as the foremost task of education to insure the survival of these qualities: an enterprising curiosity, an undefeatable spirit, tenacity in pursuit, readiness for sensible self-denial, and above all, compassion.
—Kurt Hahn

Imagine that you attend a meeting and each person there shakes hands with everyone else in the room. This situation lends itself to a number of interesting problem-solving strategies including applications of graph theory. You can draw a diagram of the handshakes made by using a graph made up of a finite collection of edges and vertices. Because each vertex is connected by an edge to every other vertex (everyone shakes hands with everyone else), the handshake graphs are **complete graphs**. Find the chromatic number of each graph pictured at the right, and make a conjecture about the chromatic number of a complete graph.

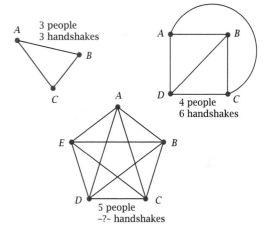

The graphs pictured above that represent three people and four people are called **planar** graphs. The graph that represents five people is a **nonplanar** graph because you cannot draw all the edges without forming intersections at points other than the vertices *A, B, C, D,* and *E.* This is true even though in graph theory you may move vertices to different positions and draw a connecting edge as a curve. To demonstrate planarity of a graph, you only need one two-dimensional picture where the edges do not intersect.

Linda Valdés

Linda Valdés, who is a professor of mathematics at San Jose State University and does research in graph theory, says that graphs may represent a number of situations. One application of graph theory that is important in the computer industries is network design. Network hardware designers consider both cost and efficiency. One aspect of efficiency is making sure that all vertices are reachable from one another. The vertices of a complete graph are always reachable from each other, but if a minimal amount of wiring is to be used in a network, a complete graph is not cost-effective. Part of Valdés's work involves finding graphs with the smallest number of subgraphs whose vertices are all reachable from each other.

Graph theory is also demonstrated by graph games like Dot to Dot or Sprouts, which you may have played. Sprouts was invented on the afternoon of Tuesday,

February 21, 1967, when mathematician John Conway and graduate student Michael Stewart Paterson finished tea in the mathematics department's common room and began doodling on paper in an effort to devise a new pencil-and-paper game.

Investigation 8.6.1

Sprouts

This game is for two players. Start by drawing three points. The first player draws an edge between any two of the points (vertices) and places

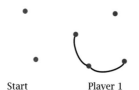

Start   Player 1   Player 2   Player 1

another point somewhere on this edge. The second player then draws another edge between any two points and adds another point somewhere on the new edge. The game also allows a player to add a point somewhere on a new edge that is drawn from a vertex and loops back to the same vertex. Play continues in this manner with the two players alternating turns. The two rules are (1) no edges can intersect, and (2) a vertex cannot have more than three edges connecting to it. A player loses by not being able to make a play. Mark each game you play with an "F" if the first player wins or an "S" if the second player wins.

After playing several games, consider the following questions.

a. Count the number of vertices in each completed game and record this number next to the game. Form a conjecture about the number of vertices and whether the first or second player wins. What is the smallest number of vertices possible in a completed game? What is the greatest number of vertices possible?

b. Is this a fair game? If not, does the advantage lie with the player who moves first or with the player who moves second? Explain your reasoning.

Two vertices are **adjacent** if they are joined by an edge. For example, each vertex in Graph 1 is adjacent to every other vertex.

Graph 2 is a multigraph because it contains two vertices (V_1 and V_2) that are connected by more than one edge. As graphs get more and more complicated, it is difficult to keep track of which vertices are connected. One simple device to keep track of this information is the **adjacency matrix**. (A matrix is an array of numbers, which means the numbers are arranged in rows and columns.)

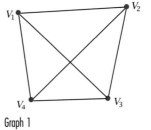 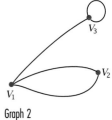

Graph 1   Graph 2

The entry 1 in the matrix for Graph 1 means V_2 and V_3 are joined. In the matrix for Graph 2, the entry 0 means V_2 and V_3 are not joined. Given a graph, you can complete an adjacency matrix, and with an adjacency matrix you can draw a graph.

Notice that the number of vertices in Graph 3 is defined by the dimensions of the matrix associated with the graph. This matrix has four rows and four columns, therefore the graph has four vertices. Each 1 indicates an edge between the vertices, and each 0 indicates no edge between the vertices. The entry 1 in row two and column four indicates an edge between V_2 and V_4.

In 1850, James Joseph Sylvester invented the term *matrix* to denote "an oblong arrangement of terms consisting, suppose, of m lines and n columns." Though he didn't use the idea, his friend Arthur Cayley (1821–1895), another British mathematician, did in his 1855 and 1858 papers.

	Vertex			
	1	2	3	4
1	0	1	1	1
2	1	0	1	1
3	1	1	0	1
4	1	1	1	0

Matrix for Graph 1

	Vertex		
	1	2	3
1	0	2	1
2	2	0	0
3	1	0	1

Matrix for Graph 2

	Vertex			
	1	2	3	4
1	0	0	0	0
2	0	0	1	1
3	0	1	0	1
4	0	1	1	0

Matrix for Graph 3

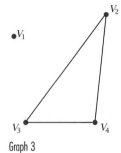

Graph 3

Investigation 8.6.2

Graphs and Matrices

Part 1 Work with a partner to create a graph and an adjacency matrix that represent the following information:

A collection of converters is used to change documents from one word processor format to another. You do not have a universal translator, but rather a set of four translators. Translator 1 will convert documents to and from formats A, B, and F. Translator 2 converts documents between formats B and D. Translator 3 can change documents to and from formats D, E, and F. Finally, translator 4 will convert documents between formats C and E.

Part 2 Have each group member create a graph and a story using all the information in the adjacency matrix below. Then exchange stories and graphs with another group member. Determine whether the story and graph accurately reflect the information given in the adjacency matrix.

	Abe	Blake	Carl	Donna	Eula
Abe	0	1	0	0	1
Blake	1	0	1	0	0
Carl	0	1	0	1	0
Donna	0	0	1	0	1
Eula	1	0	0	1	0

All tables of information can be considered matrices, and they can be used to hold different kinds of information. The entries in the following matrix indicate distances between Washington, D.C., St. Louis, Seattle, New Orleans, and Las Vegas.

	DC	SL	S	NO	LV
DC	0	862	2721	1099	2420
SL	862	0	2135	698	1620
S	2721	2135	0	2590	1180
NO	1099	698	2590	0	1732
LV	2420	1620	1180	1732	0

If you draw a map with the distances indicated, you will have the graph associated with this matrix.

■ Example 1

Draw a directed graph (the edges will have direction) and complete a corresponding matrix that pictures this transition: Each year 10% of the California population moves to another state and 5% of the outsiders move to California.

Solution

The edges of the directed graph indicate this transition. For instance, 0.90 of the Californians stay in the state from one year to the next.

The matrix shows the same situation. The vertical identifier (now) to the left of the matrix indicates the present condition and the horizontal identifier (next year) above the matrix indicates the next condition after the transition. ■

Next year

		C	O
Now	C	0.90	0.10
	O	0.05	0.95

Problem Set 8.6

1. Trace this map of the continental United States and put vertices at the following five cities: Washington, D.C., St. Louis, Seattle, New Orleans, and Las Vegas. Draw the network of edges that connects the cities and has the shortest total length. Refer to the matrix at the top of this page.

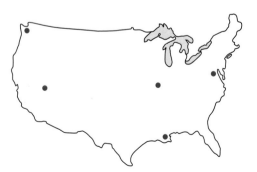

2. Draw planar versions of these solid figures, *ABCD* and *EFGHIJKL,* using the named vertices and edges.

a.

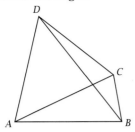

b.

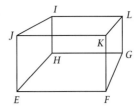

3. A route through a graph that passes through each vertex exactly once and returns to the beginning vertex is called a Hamilton cycle after the Irish mathematician Sir William Rowan Hamilton (1805–1864). The problem of finding an algorithm that would give a Hamilton cycle for any graph is called the Traveling Salesperson Problem.

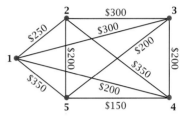

a. How many edges are there in the graph at the right?

b. Create a matrix that shows the cost of one-way airline tickets between each pair of cities.

c. How many different routes through each city start with city 1 and end with city 1? (No segment is used more than once in a route.)

d. Which route is cheapest for a salesperson who wants to start at city 1, visit every other city, and return to where he started?

4. Suppose that in the United States 20 million people live in California and 220 million live outside of California. If the total population remains at 240 million and the year-to-year transition stays the same as in Example 1, find the number of people who live [in CA   outside CA].

a. next year   **b.** 2 yr from now   **c.** 3 yr from now

5. Developing countries have a problem; too many people are moving to the cities. A study of a developing country shows that in a given year 10% of the rural population moves to the city, but only 1% of the urban population goes back to the country.

a. Draw a transition graph that represents this study.

b. Develop a transition matrix for this study.

c. If 16 million of the country's 25 million people live in the city initially, find values for [urban dwellers   rural dwellers].

   i. next year   ii. in 2 yr   iii. in 3 yr

6. A mouse enters a maze at position 1 and proceeds through the maze as shown in the directed graph. At each decision point the mouse is equally likely to choose either path. Find the probability that the mouse will get to the cheese.

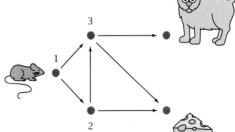

Sensitive Survey

There are some questions that are difficult to survey, because the person being asked may or may not wish their answer to be publicly known. "Have you ever plagiarized on a major paper?" or "Do you believe in space aliens?" are examples of questions that some people may be reluctant to answer. One means of collecting such information is to use random selection and couple the question with a benign and predictable question. Consider the following scenario.

Eric: "Excuse me, Jerry, would you take part in a survey?"

Jerry: "I guess so."

Eric: "You will answer one of two questions, but I will not know which question you are answering. It is important to the results of this survey that you are truthful; can you do that?"

Jerry: "Yes, how does this work?"

Eric: "Look, I have ten cards here; six are black and four are red. You will pick one card, and if it is red, you will answer question one. If it is black, you will answer question two."

Then Eric hands Jerry a page with the following questions on it.

> Q1: (if a red card) Does your social security number end in an even digit?
>
> Q2: (if a black card) Have you ever cheated on a test?

Eric: "Answer only yes or no. Do not tell me which question you are answering."

Next, Eric mixes the cards and holds them out to Jerry. Jerry takes a card, looks again at the paper and responds yes . Then he returns the card to the deck and mixes them again. Eric simply records the yes and goes to the next person.

At the end of the survey, Eric has gathered 47 yeses and 23 noes. Because he knows the probability of the red cards and the probability of an even social security number, he can use this to predict the distribution on his sensitive question. Here are his calculations:

Of 70 people answering the question, 42 will likely have taken black cards and 28 will likely have taken red cards. Of 28 red-card takers, 14 should have answered yes and 14 should have said no. This means that 33 of the 42 black-card takers said yes and 9 said no. This would mean that 78.6% responded yes to the sensitive question.

Part 1   Explain the logic behind Eric's calculations.

Part 2   Conduct your own sensitive question survey with your own questions and calculate your results. Write a summary describing what you did and reporting your results.

Section 8.7

Matrix Operations

It is not once nor twice but times without number that the same ideas make their appearance in the world.
—Aristotle

You have solved this next problem in previous sections by using several different strategies. Now you will see how you can use matrices to solve it.

This look at the solution to the California population problem will help you to understand matrix multiplication. Assume that in the United States there are 20 million people that live in California and 220 million

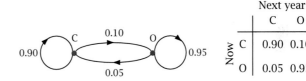

	Next year	
	C	O
C	0.90	0.10
O	0.05	0.95

(Now)

that live outside California. Also assume that the total population of the United States stays at 240 million and the year-to-year transition rates remain the same. Find matrix values for the number of people

[in CA   outside CA]

next year. How many people will be in either place two years from now? Three years from now? You can use the following matrix equation to find the answers to these questions.

$$[\ 20 \quad 220\ ] \begin{bmatrix} 0.90 & 0.10 \\ 0.05 & 0.95 \end{bmatrix} = [\ \text{in CA} \quad \text{outside CA}\ ]$$

The initial matrix, [20   220],

has one row and two columns and is called a 1×2 matrix ("one-by-two matrix"). Call this matrix, matrix A.

The transition matrix, $\begin{bmatrix} 0.90 & 0.10 \\ 0.05 & 0.95 \end{bmatrix}$,

has two rows and two columns and is called a 2×2 matrix. The four individual entries can be identified by their row and column numbers. For example, 0.10 is in row one and column two. If you label the transition matrix as matrix B, 0.10 can be identified as entry B_{12}, indicating 0.10 is in the first row and the second column of matrix B. The top row of matrix B represents the transitions in the present California population, and the bottom row represents the transitions in the present non-California population. See how this matrix relates to the directed graph above.

You can define matrix multiplication by looking at how you calculate the next year's population numbers. The next year's California population will be $20 \cdot 0.90 + 220 \cdot 0.05$, or 29 million people, because 90% of the 20 million Californians stay and 5% of the 220 million non-Californians move in. In effect, you are multiplying the two entries in matrix $A = [\ 20\quad 220\ ]$ by the two entries in the first column of B and adding the two products together. The answer, 29, is entry C_{11} in the answer matrix C.

initial matrix transition matrix   answer matrix

     A B C

$$[\ 20\quad 220\ ] \begin{bmatrix} \mathbf{0.90} & 0.10 \\ \mathbf{0.05} & 0.95 \end{bmatrix} = [\ \mathbf{29}\quad \text{outside CA}\ ]$$

Likewise, next year's population outside California will be $20 \cdot 0.10 + 220 \cdot 0.95$, or 211 million people, because 10% of the Californians move out and 95% of the non-Californians stay out. Again, this is the sum of the products of the row entries in matrix A and the second-column entries of B. The answer, 211, is entry C_{12} in the answer matrix C.

$$[\ 20\quad 220\ ] \begin{bmatrix} 0.90 & \mathbf{0.10} \\ 0.05 & \mathbf{0.95} \end{bmatrix} = [\ 29\quad \mathbf{211}\ ]$$

The equation below gives you the populations in the year following.

$$[\ 29\quad 211\ ] \begin{bmatrix} 0.90 & 0.10 \\ 0.05 & 0.95 \end{bmatrix} = [\ 36.65\quad 203.35\ ]$$

Entry C_{11} of the answer matrix is the sum of the products of the entries in row 1 of matrix A and the entries in the first column of B. Entry C_{12} of the answer matrix is found by multiplying the entries in the first row of matrix A by the entries in the second column of B.

You can continue this process and find the populations three years from now by using the *answer* in another matrix multiplication.

$$[\ 36.65\quad 203.35\ ] \begin{bmatrix} 0.90 & 0.10 \\ 0.05 & 0.95 \end{bmatrix} = [\ C_{11}\quad C_{12}\ ]$$

The entry C_{ij} represents the sum of the products of each entry in row i of the first matrix and the entry in the corresponding position in column j of the second matrix.

To find the value for entry C_{11}, you sum the products of the entries in the first row of the first matrix and the entries in the first column of the second matrix. To find the value for entry C_{12}, you sum the products of the entries in the first row of the first matrix and the entries in the second column of the second matrix.

Investigation 8.7.1

Word to Word

In this investigation you will use the adjacency matrix you created in Part 1 of Investigation 8.6.2. Once again, here is the problem.

A collection of converters is used to change documents from one word processor format to another. You do not have a universal translator; instead, you have a set of four translators that each handle some conversions. Translator 1 will convert documents to and from formats A, B, and F. Translator 2 converts documents between formats B and D. Translator 3 can change documents to and from formats D, E, and F. Finally, translator 4 will convert documents between formats C and E.

Your matrix should look like this:

	A	B	C	D	E	F
A	0	1	0	0	0	1
B	1	0	0	1	0	1
C	0	0	0	0	1	0
D	0	1	0	0	1	1
E	0	0	1	1	0	1
F	1	1	0	1	1	0

Call this transition matrix M. What does the 1 at position M_{24} mean? Consider an initial condition matrix that shows one document from word processor A, [1 0 0 0 0 0]. Multiply this matrix by M and you get the answer matrix shown on the right below. What is the meaning of the 1 in the second column of the answer matrix?

$$[1\ 0\ 0\ 0\ 0\ 0] \begin{bmatrix} 0 & 1 & 0 & 0 & 0 & 1 \\ 1 & 0 & 0 & 1 & 0 & 1 \\ 0 & 0 & 0 & 0 & 1 & 0 \\ 0 & 1 & 0 & 0 & 1 & 1 \\ 0 & 0 & 1 & 1 & 0 & 1 \\ 1 & 1 & 0 & 1 & 1 & 0 \end{bmatrix} = [0\ 1\ 0\ 0\ 0\ 1]$$

Multiply the answer matrix by the same translation matrix. Repeat this process until you get a 1 in the third column of the answer matrix. What does it mean that it took three multiplications to get a 1 in column three?

Problem Set 8.7

1. Find the next year's populations in the California problem by multiplying these matrices.

$$[36.65\quad 203.35] \begin{bmatrix} 0.90 & 0.10 \\ 0.05 & 0.95 \end{bmatrix} = [\text{ CA}\quad \text{non-CA }]$$

2. Suppose the following trends continue for a few years. Of two-car families, 88% remain two-car families in the following year and 12% become one-car families in the following year. Of one-car families, 72% remain one-car families and 28% become two-car families. Currently 4800 families have one car and 4200 have two cars.

  a. Draw a directed graph of this situation.

  b. What 1×2 matrix pictures the present situation? (A_{11} should represent one-car families.)

  c. What 2×2 transition matrix can be used to solve this problem?

  d. Write a matrix equation for this transition.

  e. Find the [one-car   two-car] distribution for one year from now.

  f. Find the [one-car   two-car] distribution for two years from now.

3. Invent a story for the equation below.

$$[\ 20 \quad 220\ ] + [\ 2 \quad 11\ ] = [\ 22 \quad 231\ ]$$

4. Find the value of each missing variable.

  a. $[\ 13 \quad 23\ ] + [\ {}^-6 \quad 31\ ] = [\ x \quad y\ ]$

  b. $\begin{bmatrix} 0.90 & 0.10 \\ 0.05 & 0.95 \end{bmatrix} \cdot \begin{bmatrix} 0.90 & 0.10 \\ 0.05 & 0.95 \end{bmatrix} = \begin{bmatrix} C_{11} & C_{12} \\ C_{21} & C_{22} \end{bmatrix}$

  c. $\begin{bmatrix} 18 & {}^-23 \\ 5.4 & 32.2 \end{bmatrix} + \begin{bmatrix} {}^-2.4 & 12.2 \\ 5.3 & 10 \end{bmatrix} = \begin{bmatrix} a & b \\ c & d \end{bmatrix}$

  d. $10 \cdot \begin{bmatrix} 18 & {}^-23 \\ 5.4 & 32.2 \end{bmatrix} = \begin{bmatrix} a & b \\ c & d \end{bmatrix}$

NOTE
8I

5. Use matrices to find each pair of values for the California population problem. (See Calculator Note 8I.)

  a. The populations after 1 yr

  b. The populations after 2 yr

  c. The populations after 3 yr

  d. The populations in the long run

6. Find each product.

  a. $\begin{bmatrix} 0.90 & 0.10 \\ 0.05 & 0.95 \end{bmatrix} \begin{bmatrix} 0.90 & 0.10 \\ 0.05 & 0.95 \end{bmatrix}$

  b. $\begin{bmatrix} 1 & 0 & 1 \\ 0 & 2 & 0 \\ 1 & 0 & 1 \end{bmatrix} \begin{bmatrix} 1 & 0 & {}^-1 \\ 0 & 2 & 0 \\ {}^-1 & 0 & 1 \end{bmatrix}$

7. A recent study compares the birth weights of English women and their daughters. The weights were split into three categories: low (below 6 lb), average (between 6 and 8 lb), and high (above 8 lb).

	Low	Average	High
Low	-?-	-?-	-?-
Average	-?-	-?-	-?-
High	-?-	-?-	-?-

a. Complete the transition matrix using the information in the graph.

b. If, in the initial generation of women, 25% had birth weights in the low category, 60% in the average category, and 15% in the high category, what was the distribution after one generation? After two generations? After three generations? In the long run?

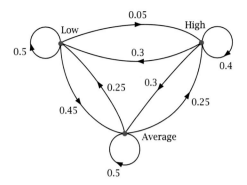

8. Suppose a spider is in a building with three rooms. The spider moves from room to room by choosing a door at random. If the spider starts in Room 1 initially, what is the probability that it will be in Room 1 again after four room changes?

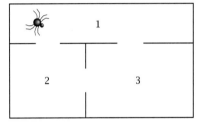

9. Complete the following matrix arithmetic problems. If a problem is impossible, explain why.

a. $\begin{bmatrix} 1 & 2 \\ 3 & -2 \\ 0 & 1 \end{bmatrix} \begin{bmatrix} -3 & -1 & 2 \\ 5 & 2 & -1 \end{bmatrix}$

b. $\begin{bmatrix} 1 & -2 \\ 6 & 3 \end{bmatrix} + \begin{bmatrix} -3 & 7 \\ 2 & 4 \end{bmatrix}$

c. $\begin{bmatrix} 5 & -2 & 7 \end{bmatrix} \begin{bmatrix} -2 & 3 \\ -1 & 0 \\ 3 & 2 \end{bmatrix}$

d. $\begin{bmatrix} 3 & -8 & 10 & 2 \\ -1 & 2 & 3 & 4 \end{bmatrix} \begin{bmatrix} 2 & -5 & 3 & 12 \\ 8 & -4 & 0 & 2 \end{bmatrix}$

e. $\begin{bmatrix} 3 & 6 \\ -4 & 1 \end{bmatrix} - \begin{bmatrix} -1 & 7 \\ -8 & 3 \end{bmatrix}$

f. $\begin{bmatrix} 4 & 11 \\ 7 & 3 \\ 4 & 2 \end{bmatrix} + \begin{bmatrix} 3 & -2 & 7 \\ 5 & 0 & 2 \end{bmatrix}$

10. Find a problem in this chapter that you cannot solve. Write out the problem and as much of the solution as you can. Then clearly explain what is keeping you from solving the problem. Be as specific as you can.

Take Another Look 8.7

Matrix T defines a directed communication network among the five computers. The boldface **1** in row 1, column 2 means that computer A can send messages to computer B.

T	A	B	C	D	E
A	0	**1**	1	0	1
B	0	0	0	1	1
C	0	0	0	1	0
D	0	0	1	0	1
E	1	1	0	1	0

a. Draw a diagram corresponding to matrix T.

b. Use your diagram or matrix T to construct a communication network matrix M that models the communication from one computer to another computer via exactly one relay. The 2 in matrix M indicates that there are two ways computer E can send messages to computer C via exactly one other computer (E to A to C and E to D to C).

M	A	B	C	D	E
A					
B					
C					
D					
E			2		

c. Fill in the missing entries in matrix M.

d. Find the matrix T^2 and compare it to your matrix in part c.

e. Find the sum of corresponding entries of matrix T and matrix T^2. What is the meaning of the entry in row 1, column 4 of the new matrix? What does this new matrix tell you about the communication network among the five computers?

f. What information does matrix T^3 give you?

g. Take another look at the transition matrix $\begin{bmatrix} 0.90 & 0.10 \\ 0.05 & 0.95 \end{bmatrix}$.

What information does the following product give you?

$$\begin{bmatrix} 0.90 & 0.10 \\ 0.05 & 0.95 \end{bmatrix} \cdot \begin{bmatrix} 0.90 & 0.10 \\ 0.05 & 0.95 \end{bmatrix}$$

Why is this true?

Chapter Review

If you ask mathematicians what they do, you always get the same answer. They think. They think about difficult and unusual problems. They do not think about ordinary problems: they just write down the answers.
—M. Egrafov

Discrete mathematics includes a wide variety of topics; many are associated with probability, and others include graph theory and matrices. In this chapter you were introduced to the concept of randomness and you learned how to generate random numbers on your calculator. In addition to using a calculator, you can generate random numbers by using a spinner, dice, or a random number table, or by drawing numbers out of a hat. Random numbers should all have an equal chance of occurring and should, in the long run, occur equally frequently. Using a random number procedure you can simulate many activities and situations to determine the experimental probability of an event. You learned about experimental probability by doing simulations and theoretical probability by comparing the number of successful trials to the total number of possible outcomes. You used tree diagrams to help you count possibilities, and you learned that sometimes probability situations can be represented geometrically. Using what you learned about theoretical probability, you were able to calculate expected value, which is calculated by multiplying the value of each event by its probability and then summing all the products.

Graph theory, and chromatic numbering in particular, can be used to help organize groups and to solve scheduling problems. Use of a directed graph can help you to organize information and can provide you with the needed numbers to create a transition matrix. Multiplication of the initial condition matrix by the transition matrix gives the status after one time period. Repeated multiplication shows the long-run trend of a situation.

Problem Set 8.8

1. Name two different ways to generate random numbers from 0 to 10.

2. Critique each method that might be used to generate random numbers from 1 to 12.
   a. Draw a card from a shuffled deck. The number is equal to the card number (jacks = 11, queens = 12, aces = 1, kings don't count).
   b. Call someone and ask her the number of eggs left in the last carton she bought.
   c. Roll two dice onto a table, close to the table's edge. Add up the number of spots rolled on the dice. If one die falls off, only count the spots on the die that remains on the table. If both fall off, roll again.

3. Write a calculator command that will generate random numbers belonging to each set below.

  a. {3, 4, 5, . . . , 12}
  b. {⁻7, ⁻6, ⁻5, . . . , 2}
  c. ⁻2 < x < 3

4. a. What is the probability that a randomly plotted point will land in the shaded trapezoidal region pictured at the right?

  b. One thousand points are randomly plotted in the rectangular region below at the right. Suppose that 374 of the points land in the shaded portion of the region. What is your best approximation of the area of the shaded portion?

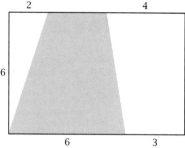

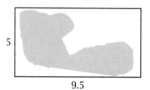

5. Suppose you roll two octahedral (eight-sided) dice.

  a. Draw a diagram that shows all possible outcomes of this experiment.
  b. Indicate on your diagram all the possible outcomes for which the sum of the dice is less than six.
  c. What is the probability that the sum is less than six?
  d. What is the probability that the sum is more than six?

6. a. Draw a tree diagram representing all of the possible results when answering five questions on a true-or-false test.

  b. How many possible ways are there of getting three True and two False answers?
  c. Suppose you knew that the answers to the first two questions on the test were True, and you wrote these answers down. Then you randomly guessed the answers to the remaining three questions. What is the probability that there will be three True and two False answers on the test?

7. The local outlet of Frankfurter Franchise sells three types of hot dogs: plain, with chili, and with sauerkraut. The owners know that 47% of their sales are chili dogs, 36% are plain, and the rest are sauerkraut dogs. They also offer three types of buns: plain, rye, and multigrain. Sixty-two percent of their sales are plain buns, 27% are multigrain, and the rest are rye.

  a. Make a tree diagram showing this information.
  b. What is the probability that the next customer will order a chili dog on rye?
  c. What is the probability that the next customer will *not* order a sauerkraut dog on a plain bun?
  d. What is the probability that the next customer will order either a plain hot dog on a plain bun or a chili dog on a multigrain bun?

8. A survey was taken regarding students' preference for whipped cream or ice cream to be served with chocolate cake. The results tabulated by grade level are reported in the following table.

	9th grade	10th grade	11th grade	12th grade	Total
Ice cream	18	37	85	114	–?–
Whipped cream	5	18	37	58	–?–
Total	–?–	–?–	–?–	–?–	–?–

a. Complete the table.
b. What is the probability that a sophomore will prefer ice cream?
c. What is the probability that a junior will prefer whipped cream?
d. What is the probability that someone who prefers ice cream is a freshman?
e. What is the probability that a student will prefer whipped cream?

9. Rita is playing a friendly game of darts with Noah. On this particular dart board she can score 20 points for a bull's-eye and 10 points, 5 points, or 1 point for the other regions. Although Rita doesn't know exactly where her five darts will land, she has been a fairly consistent dart player over the years. She figures that she hits the bull's-eye 30% of the time, the 10-point circle 40% of the time, the 5-point circle 20% of the time, and the 1-point circle 5% of the time. What is her expected score? Write a paragraph explaining how you calculated your answer.

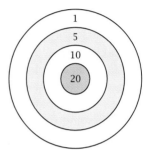

10. A Detroit car rental business has a second outlet in Chicago. The company allows patrons to make local rentals or one-way rentals to the other location. At the end of each month, one-eighth of the cars that start the month in Detroit end up in Chicago, and one-twelfth of the cars that start the month in Chicago end up in Detroit. If at the start of operations there are 500 cars in each city, what would you expect the distribution to be 4 mo later? After many months?

11. In Chapter 8, you explored topics in discrete mathematics. Students in your friend's mathematics class are not studying discrete mathematics, yet your friend is curious about what it is. Explain to her what discrete mathematics is and give reasons for studying it.

12. If you had to choose a favorite problem from this chapter, what would it be? Why?

Assessing What You've Learned

Organizing Your Notebook
- Have you updated the calculator techniques section of your notebook? Be sure that your work is complete and that everything is in order.

Keeping a Journal
- Look in Problem Sets 8.4, 8.7, and 8.8 for journal prompts.

Portfolio
- You may want to organize your portfolio. Be sure that it contains a variety of different kinds of work and problems to demonstrate the breadth of what you've learned to do in this course.

Performance Assessment
- You learned about many different discrete mathematics concepts in this chapter—randomness, counting, tree diagrams, geometric probability, chromatic numbering, network graphs, and transition matrices. Many of these topics might have been new to you. Choose two of these concepts and demonstrate to someone that you understand them.

Open-ended Investigations
- Choose one of the Take Another Look investigations or a project, or design your own investigation. Share your results with a classmate, your group, or your teacher.

Constructing Test Questions
- Write several test questions that you think would be useful in determining whether or not a student understands the concepts presented in this chapter.

Group Presentations and Tests
- Review your role (or roles) in any group work you did in this chapter. Are you becoming a more effective group member? What could you do to be a better group member?

Overall Self-Assessment
- How would you describe your overall understanding of the concepts presented in this chapter? Look at everything you've done. Make use of any of the self-assessment methods you've been introduced to and assess what you've learned in this chapter.

Systems of Equations

Different crops form a patchwork of textures and patterns in the Amish farmland in Lancaster County, Pennsylvania. Farmers have to make decisions about which crops to plant. They have to consider restrictions like the number of acres available, the type of machinery they have, and the cost of growing different crops. A mathematical procedure called *linear programming* can help the farmer make these decisions.

Section 9.1

Zooming In on Systems

The cure for boredom is curiosity. There is no cure for curiosity.
—Ellen Parr

The number of tickets sold for a school activity, such as a spaghetti dinner, helps determine the success of the event. Ticket sales income can be less than, equal to, or greater than expenses. The break-even value is pictured at the intersection of the expense function and the line $y = x$. This graph shows when expenses are equal to income. In this chapter, you will focus on mathematical situations involving multiple equations or conditions that must be satisfied at the same time.

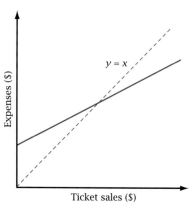

System of Equations

Two or more equations that are solved or studied simultaneously are called a **system of equations**.

■ **Example 1**

Connie Soomer wants to buy a $750 trail bike. At the present time she has only $650 in a savings investment earning 5.9% annual interest compounded monthly. Because of inflation, the cost of the bike will probably increase at a rate of 0.19% per month. Will she ever have enough money saved to buy the bike? If so, when? And how much will it cost at that time?

Solution

One approach to the problem is to write two equations, one that represents the cost of the bike and one that represents the amount of money saved. The increasing bike cost can be modeled with $y_1 = 750(1 + 0.0019)^x$, while $y_2 = 650\left(1 + \frac{0.059}{12}\right)^x$ models the growing value of Connie's account.

If you graph both equations on the same coordinate axis, the solution will be found at the point of intersection.

NOTE

9A

Zooming in on this point you can see that $(47.598, 820.92)$ is a close approximation for the intersection coordinates. (See **Calculator Note 9A.**) This means that after 47.598 months the cost of the bike and the amount saved will be about equal.

Further zooming will produce a better approximation but, because the interest is paid out monthly, the best answer to the question is actually 48 months. At 48 months the cost equation predicts that the bike will cost \$821.54 and the savings equation predicts a balance of \$822.54. ■

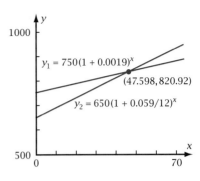

X	Y₁	Y₂
45	816.88	810.52
46	818.43	814.51
47	819.99	818.51
48	821.54	822.54
49	823.11	826.58
50	824.67	830.65
51	826.24	834.73

X=48

■ **Example 2**

Ms. Pham is starting a small business and she needs to decide between long distance phone carriers. One company offers the Phrequent Phoner plan that will cost 20¢ for the first minute and 17¢ for each minute after that. A competing company offers the Pals and Buddies plan that costs 50¢ for the first minute and 11¢ for each additional minute. Under which circumstances is each plan the most desirable?

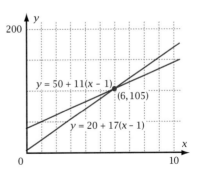

Solution

Because the Phrequent Phoner plan (PP) costs less for the first minute, it is obviously better for very short calls. However, the Pals and Buddies plan (P & B) will probably be cheaper for longer calls because the cost is less for additional minutes. There should be a phone conversation length when both plans cost the same.

A cost equation that models the PP plan is

$$Cost = 20 + 17(\textit{length of call} - 1 \text{ min}) \quad \text{or} \quad y = 20 + 17(x - 1).$$

A cost equation for the P & B plan is

$$Cost = 50 + 11(\textit{length of call} - 1 \text{ min}) \quad \text{or}$$
$$y = 50 + 11(x - 1).$$

In each equation, x represents the call length in minutes and y represents the cost.

A graph of these equations shows the PP plan cost is below the P & B plan cost until the lines intersect. The point of intersection at $(6, 105)$ tells

you that a six-minute call using either plan will cost $1.05. If Ms. Pham believes her average call will last less than six minutes, she should choose the PP plan. But if most of her calls last more than six minutes, the P & B plan is the better option. ■

Investigation 9.1.1

Intersecting Graphs

a. Work with a partner and graph $y_1 = 2^x$ and $y_2 = x^2$. Locate all intersection points of the two curves. How many intersection points are there? How do you know that there aren't any more? Name a graphing window that pictures all of the intersection points. Sketch the graphs, and find the coordinates of each intersection point to the nearest thousandth. Compare your answers to those of other members of your group.

b. With your partner, sketch the graph of $y_3 = 2^x - x^2$. What does it mean when y_3 is zero? When y_3 is positive? When y_3 is negative? Find the missing table values. How do these values relate to the answers from part a? Compare your answers to those of other members in your group.

x	-?-	-?-	-?-
y	0	0	0

c. Have each group member graph one pair of equations listed below. Determine how many intersection points there are for each pair. Compare your results with those of other group members. Describe any patterns you discover.

i. $y = 3^x$ and $y = x^3$ ii. $y = 4^x$ and $y = x^4$

iii. $y = 5^x$ and $y = x^5$ iv. $y = 6^x$ and $y = x^6$

d. Describe what you would do if asked to find all of the intersection points of $y = 10^x$ and $y = x^{10}$.

Problem Set 9.1

1. a. Locate all points of intersection of the two curves $y_1 = x^3 - 5x^2 + 5x + 1$ and $y_2 = x^2 + 1$. Find each point's coordinates to the nearest thousandth.
   b. Describe the x-values that make $y_1 < y_2$. Describe the x-values that make $y_1 > y_2$.

2. Graph the equations $y_1 = 2.5(0.5)^x$ and $y_2 = \dfrac{4 - 2x}{1.7}$.
   a. How many points of intersection are there?
   b. Enter the equation $y_3 = y_1 - y_2$. Evaluate all three equations when $x = 1$. How does the value for y_3 compare to the values for y_1 and y_2?

c. At any point of intersection, the y-values for a pair of intersecting equations will be equal. What does this mean about the y-value for y_3 at such a point? Where will this point appear on the graph of y_3?

d. Graph y_3 and zoom in to find the x-coordinates of each point where the graph crosses the x-axis.

e. What can you conclude about each point where y_1 and y_2 intersect?

3. Find the x-coordinate of each point of intersection of $y_1 = 2(1.02)^x$ and $y_2 = 2.5 \log x$ to the nearest thousandth.

4. The equations $y = 18 + 0.4x$ and $y = 11.2 + 0.54x$ give the lengths of two different springs as mass amounts are separately added to each. The x-value represents the mass amounts.

a. When are the springs the same length?

b. When is one spring at least 10 cm longer than the other?

c. Write a statement comparing the two springs.

5. Write a system of equations that has $(2, 7.5)$ as its solution.

6. The graph below shows the Kangaroo Company's production costs and sales income, or revenue, for its pogo sticks. Use the graph to estimate the answers to the questions below.

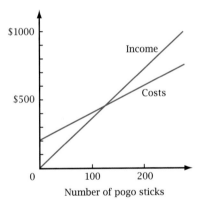

A gasoline-powered pogo stick called a "Hop Rod" was manufactured in 1973. This pogo stick travels at 2.1 miles per hour and gets 565,000 hops per gallon.

a. If 25 pogo sticks are sold, will the company earn a profit? Describe how you would use the graph to answer this question.

b. If the company sells 200 pogo sticks, will it earn a profit? If so, approximately how much?

c. How many pogo sticks must the company sell to break even (that is, to have income equal to costs)?

d. What is the approximate profit if 150 pogo sticks are produced and sold?

7. Winning times in minutes for men and women in the 1500 m Olympic speedskating event are given below.

Year	1964	1968	1972	1976	1980	1984	1988	1992
Men	2:10.3	2:03.4	2:02.96	1:59.38	1:55.44	1:58.36	1:52.06	1:54.81
Women	2:22.6	2:22.4	2:20.85	2:16.58	2:10.95	2:03.42	2:00.68	2:05.87

a. Analyze the data and predict when the winning times for men and women will be the same if the current trends continue.

b. Show each equation that you used to make this prediction.

c. How reasonable do you think your prediction is? Explain your reasoning.

d. The winning times in the 1994 Olympics were 1:51.29 for the men and 2:02.19 for the women. Do these times fit the pattern of your model? Find the residuals for the 1994 entries based on your model.

8. Suppose the long distance phone carriers in Example 2 calculate their charges so that a call of exactly 3 min will cost the same as a call of 3.25 or 3.9 min, and there is no increase in cost until you have been connected for 4 min. Increases are calculated after each additional minute. A calculator function that models this situation is **int** x. This function removes the fractional part of the number and outputs only the integer part.

a. Model this interpretation of phone billings by using the int function to rewrite the cost equations in Example 2.

b. Graph the two new equations representing the Phrequent Phoner plan and the Pals and Buddies plan.

c. Now determine when each plan is the most desirable. Explain your reasoning.

Take Another Look 9.1

Which is larger, π^{10} or 10^{π}? How do the logarithms of the two numbers compare? Is $\log \pi^{10}$ larger than $\log 10^{\pi}$?

Compare 100^{100} and 1000^{10}. Explain why your calculator may not be able to calculate these numbers. Can your calculator compare $\log 100^{100}$ and $\log 1000^{10}$? Explain how you can use the logarithm property $\log_a x^n = n \log_a x$ to make the comparison.

Explore and compare the two functions 100^x and x^{100}. Do they intersect? If so, where? Describe the x-values for which $100^x \geq x^{100}$.

Section 9.2

Substitution and Elimination

Truth will come sooner out of error than from confusion.
—Francis Bacon

You and your friends may have taken, or will soon take, some college entrance examinations, perhaps the PSAT, SAT, or ACT exams. Very often on these exams, or on other standardized tests, you must select from multiple choice answers to questions like these:

i. If $4x + y = 6$, then what is $(4x + y - 3)^2$?
ii. If $4x + 3y = 14$ and $3x - 3y = 13$, what is $7x$?

When answering traditional questions like these, you need to look for creative ways of choosing the answers or figuring them out. Here are some possible strategies you might consider.

i. You can find this value by substituting 6 for $4x + y$ in the expression $(4x + y - 3)^2$. Then $(6 - 3)^2$ gives 9 as the answer. Substitution is a powerful mathematical tool that allows you to rewrite expressions and equations in forms that are easier to use or to solve.
ii. You can solve the second question without actually knowing the x- or y-value by just adding the two equations.

$$\begin{array}{r} 4x + 3y = 14 \\ 3x - 3y = 13 \\ \hline 7x \quad\;\;\; = 27 \end{array}$$

Notice that both $3y$ and ^-3y dropped out. In fact, the y-variable is eliminated when you add the two equations.

In many situations, you can use substitution and elimination to solve problems in a very efficient manner. Another advantage to using these algebraic methods is that you can find an exact solution with them, whereas you will almost always find only an approximate solution by zooming.

■ Example 1

The school football team scored a total of 21 touchdowns and field goals during the season, and they kicked successfully for the extra point on all but two of the touchdowns. Determine the number of touchdowns and field goals if you know the team scored a total of 129 points. Note: Remember, a team scores 6 points for a touchdown and 3 points for a field goal.

Solution

The number of touchdowns (x) plus the number of field goals (y) equals 21. So $x + y = 21$. The 129-point total is the sum of $6x + 3y + (x - 2)$. Why? How many points for a touchdown? For a field goal? Now you need to find the point (x, y) that is common to both equations. The y-value of the first equation is equal to the y-value of the second equation for some x-value. You can find this x-value by solving for y in both situations.

$$x + y = 21 \quad \text{and} \quad 6x + 3y + (x - 2) = 129$$
$$\text{or} \quad y_1 = 21 - x \quad \text{and} \quad y_2 = \frac{129 - 6x - (x - 2)}{3} \quad \text{or} \quad \frac{^-7x + 131}{3}$$

Set $y_1 = y_2$.

$$21 - x = \frac{^-7x + 131}{3}$$
$$63 - 3x = {^-7x} + 131$$
$$4x = 68$$
$$x = 17$$

Then find y by substituting the x-value into either one of the original equations.

$$y_1 = 21 - (17) \quad \text{or} \quad y_2 = \frac{^-7(17) + 131}{3}$$
$$y_1 = 4 \qquad\qquad y_2 = 4$$

The point common to both functions, or the solution to this system, is $(17, 4)$. What do the numbers 17 and 4 represent? This method of solving a system is called **substitution** because you are substituting or replacing something, a variable or an expression, in one equation with an equivalent expression from the other equation. A solution to a system of equations in two variables is a pair

X	Y₁	Y₂
16.7	4.3	4.7
16.8	4.2	4.4667
16.9	4.1	4.2333
17	4	4
17.1	3.9	3.7667
17.2	3.8	3.5333
17.3	3.7	3.3

X=17

of values that satisfies both equations. The table function available on some calculators is a quick method to check that $x = 17$ and $y = 4$ satisfy both of the original equations. ■

■ Example 2

Walter Heether must make a decision about spending $100 to fix his old water heater. It is an electric unit, and he estimates that it costs him $125 a year to provide his home with hot water. His other option is to buy a new gas water heater for $350 (including installation). Because the new unit will be more efficient, he should save 40% on the yearly operating costs. How long will it take until the new unit pays for itself?

CHAPTER 9 SYSTEMS OF EQUATIONS

Solution

If Walter keeps the old electric heater, it will *cost* him $100 plus $125 in operating costs for each *year* he keeps it. If he makes the switch, it will *cost* him $350 plus $125(1 − 0.40), or 350 + 125(0.60) each *year*.

Old Heater

cost = 100 + 125 · *number of years*
$$y = 100 + 125x$$

New Heater

cost = 350 + 75 · *number of years*
$$y = 350 + 75x$$

Use substitution to find *x*.

$$100 + 125x = 350 + 75x$$
$$50x = 250$$
$$x = 5$$

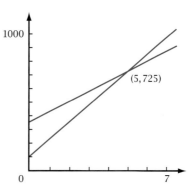

In five years, he will have paid the same amount, $725, for either unit. If he plans to sell the house three years from now, how might this affect his decision about buying the new heater? ■

Investigation 9.2.1

Pick a Number—Get the Point

In this investigation you may discover something very surprising that happens when you multiply both sides of an equation by the same number. Work with a partner and follow the steps below.

Step 1 Graph each equation on graph paper on the same coordinate axis.

Equation One: $7x + 2y = {}^-3$ Equation Two: $3x + 4y = 5$

Where do the lines intersect?

Step 2 **a.** Each partner needs to select a different number.

b. One partner multiplies Equation One by the number he or she chose while the other partner multiplies Equation Two by the number he or she chose.

c. Add the two new equations to form Equation Three.

d. Graph Equation Three on the same coordinate axis as the two original lines, and describe the location of this new line in relation to the original lines.

Step 3 **a.** One partner multiplies the original Equation One by $^-3$ while the other partner multiplies the original Equation Two by 7.

b. Add these two new equations to form Equation Four.

(continued on next page)

c. Graph Equation Four and describe the location of the line representing Equation Four in relation to the two original lines.

d. How does Equation Four differ from the other equations?

Step 4 If necessary, repeat this process with another system (for example, $9y - 5x = 26$ and $4y - 3x = 17$) until you get the point of this investigation. Summarize in your own words what the point of the investigation is.

A standard method that is used to solve a system of linear equations is to combine two given linear equations to create a third new equation. Multiplying both sides of an equation by the same value does not change its solutions or its graph. For example, $2x + y = 6$ and $(^-5)2x + (^-5)y = (^-5)6$ are the same function and have the same graph.

■ Example 3

Solve the system.

$$^-3x + 5y = 6$$
$$2x + y = 6$$

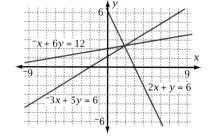

$^-x + 6y = 12$

$2x + y = 6$

$^-3x + 5y = 6$

Solution

Both equations could be multiplied by 1 and added to form the third line in the graph. Notice that all three lines intersect at the same point.

A smarter choice is to multiply the second equation by $^-5$, and then add it to the first equation.

$^-3x + 5y = 6$	Multiply both sides by 1. $\Rightarrow$	$^-3x + 5y = 6$
$2x + y = 6$	Multiply both sides by $^-5$. $\Rightarrow$	$^-10x - 5y = ^-30$
		$^-13x = ^-24$

This eliminates the y-variable and gives $x = \frac{24}{13}$. Verify that this is a vertical line that intersects the graphs of the two original lines at their point of intersection. Substituting this x-value back into either of the original equations gives the y-value. Or, you can use the same process again to eliminate the x-variable.

$^-3x + 5y = 6$	Multiply both sides by 2. $\Rightarrow$	$^-6x + 10y = 12$
$2x + y = 6$	Multiply both sides by 3. $\Rightarrow$	$6x + 3y = 18$
		$13y = 30$
		$y = \frac{30}{13}$

```
-3(24/13)+5(30/1
3)
              6
2(24/13)+(30/13)
              6
```

The calculator display verifies that the solution to this system is $\left(\frac{24}{13}, \frac{30}{13}\right)$. To check the solution, substitute the values in each of the original equations. ■

The **elimination** method is useful because it produces a new equation that eliminates one of the variables. Solving for the variable that remains gives you the *x*- or *y*-coordinate of the point of intersection. It would take a lot of effort to solve this last problem using the graph-and-zoom method if you wanted to obtain the same degree of accuracy. If you had used the substitution method for this problem, you would have had to work with fractions or else maintain a lot of decimal accuracy. To solve this system, the best method to use is the elimination method.

Problem Set 9.2

1. Without zooming in, find an approximate solution to each system by graphing the equations. Then find the exact solution by using the substitution method. List each solution as an ordered pair.

   a. $y = 3.2x + 44.61$ **b.** $y = \frac{2}{3}x - 3$ **c.** $y = 4.7x + 25.1$

   $y = {}^-5.1x + 5.60$ $y = \frac{-5}{6}x + 7$ $3.1x + 2y = 8.2$

2. Without zooming in, find approximate solutions to each system by graphing the equations. Then find the exact solutions by using the substitution method. List each solution as an ordered pair.

   a.

   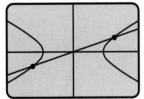

   $\frac{x^2}{4} - y^2 = 25$

   $y = \frac{x}{3}$

   b.

   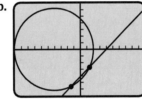

   $(x + 4)^2 + y^2 = 36$

   $y = x - 4$

3. Foe Tagrafer has narrowed her choice to two cameras. The first camera costs $47.00 and uses two alkaline AA batteries. The second camera costs $59.00 and uses one $4.95 lithium battery. She plans to use the camera frequently enough that she would probably replace the AA batteries six times a year at a cost of $11.50. The lithium battery, however, will last an entire year.

   a. Write an equation to represent the expenses for each camera.

   b. How long will it take until the total cost of the less expensive camera is equal to the total cost of the other camera?

   c. Carefully describe three different ways to verify your solution.

4. Use the elimination method to solve for one variable. Then use substitution to find the value of the other variable. List each solution as an ordered pair.

a. $5.2x + 3.6y = 7$

$\quad\;\; {}^-5.2x + 2y = 8.2$

b. $\frac{1}{4}x - \frac{2}{5}y = 3$

$\quad\;\; \frac{3}{8}x + \frac{2}{5}y = 2$

5. a. Find a good graphing window to see the intersection of $y_1 = 4.7x - 4$ and $y_2 = {}^-1.8x + 7$. Sketch the graph and show the dimensions of your graphing window.

b. Make $y_3 = \dfrac{1.8y_1 + 4.7y_2}{6.5}$ and graph all three equations in the same window.

c. Write the equations obtained by multiplying y_1 by 1.8 and y_2 by 4.7. Do not solve.

d. Now solve for y by adding the new equations from 5c.

e. Explain why y_3 intersects at the solution to the problem.

6. In each system, find a multiplier for the first equation so that the sum of this new equation and the original second equation will eliminate x. Then find the y-value. Write each solution as an ordered pair.

a. $2.1x + 3.6y = 7$

$\quad\;\; {}^-6.3x + y = 8.2$

b. $\frac{1}{4}x - \frac{4}{5}y = 7$

$\quad\;\; \frac{3}{4}x + \frac{2}{5}y = 2$

7. Solve each system in Problem 6 by finding a multiplier for the second equation so that the sum of this new equation and the original first equation will eliminate y. Then find the x-value. Write each solution as an ordered pair.

8. Find the ordered pair solution(s) for each system by first finding multipliers that will eliminate one of the variables from the sum of the resulting equations.

a. $3x + 2y = 7$

$\quad\;\; {}^-5x + 4y = 6$

b. $y = x^2 - 4$

$\quad\;\; y = {}^-2x^2 + 2$

9. What temperature on the Fahrenheit scale is three times the equivalent temperature on the Celsius scale?

10. Write a system of two equations that has a solution of $({}^-1.4, 3.6)$.

11. The two sequences below have one term that is the same. Determine which term this is and find its value.

$$u_n = \begin{cases} 12 & \text{if } n = 1 \\ u_{(n-1)} + 0.3 & \text{if } n > 1 \end{cases} \qquad u_n = \begin{cases} 15 & \text{if } n = 1 \\ u_{(n-1)} + 0.2 & \text{if } n > 1 \end{cases}$$

Take Another Look 9.2

In the California problem, the populations reach a steady state over the long run. (See Problem Set 8.7.) This means there is a stage when

$$[\ C \ \ N \ ] \begin{bmatrix} 0.90 & 0.10 \\ 0.05 & 0.95 \end{bmatrix} = [\ C \ \ N \ ],$$

where C represents the California population and N represents the non-California population. If you multiply the two matrices on the left side of the equation, you will get

$$[\ 0.90C + 0.05N \ \ 0.10C + 0.95N \ ] = [\ C \ \ N \ ].$$

(Confirm this result.) If these two matrices are equivalent, then the two components must be equal or

$$
\begin{array}{lll}
0.90C + 0.05N = C & \Rightarrow & 0.05N = 0.10C \\
0.10C + 0.95N = N & \Rightarrow & 0.10C = 0.05N.
\end{array}
$$

Notice that the two resulting equations are the same. Confirm that both are equivalent to $N = 2C$.

Since the total population is always 240 million people, $C + N = 240$ and $N = 2C$ lead to the steady-state or long-run populations of [80   160]. (Check that this answer is correct.)

Now use this same kind of strategy with the long-run populations of urban dwellers and rural dwellers in Problem 5 of Problem Set 8.6.

Section 9.3

Number of Solutions

*If you would be a real seeker after truth, you must at least once in your life doubt,
as far as possible, all things.*
—René Descartes

Consider a function like $y = 4.35x - 6.78$. An infinite
number of (x, y) pairs satisfy the function because every
point on the line is a solution. If you consider a system of
two linear equations, how many solutions might there be?
What generalized statements can you make? Do you have to
consider every problem a unique case? What if you consider
nonlinear functions or parametric functions? In many cases,

X	Y₁
⁻4	⁻24.18
⁻1	⁻11.13
2	1.92
5	14.97
8	28.02
11	41.07
14	54.12

Y₁■4.35X–6.78

you can give a range for the number of solutions if you know the types of equations in
the system. But you will need specific information about the equations in order to
determine the exact number of solutions.

Investigation 9.3.1

Intersecting Lines

In this investigation you will look at what can happen
when you graph a pair of lines. You will also learn the
vocabulary that is used when referring to the possible
relationships between two lines.

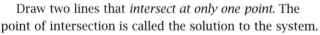

Draw two lines that *intersect at only one point.* The
point of intersection is called the solution to the system.

Now draw a pair of lines that represents a system with *no solutions.* Compare your
drawing with those of others around you. How can you describe a system with no
solution? What relationship exists between the lines? When a system has no solutions,
the equations are said to be **inconsistent**.

Next draw a pair of lines that represents a system with *more than one solution.*
Compare your drawing with those of others around you. How can you describe a
system with more than one solution? What relationship is there between the lines?
When a system of linear equations has more than one solution, the equations are
called **dependent**.

Investigation 9.3.2

Systems of Parametric Equations

If you want to determine whether or not a system of parametric equations has a point
of intersection, you must consider the parameter *t*. In this investigation you will see

how this parameter affects whether or not the graphs actually intersect. Consider the following system of parametric equations.

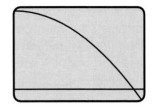

$$x_1 = 3t \quad \text{and} \quad y_1 = 0$$
$$x_2 = 3t \quad \text{and} \quad y_2 = 7 - 4.9t^2$$

Each pair of equations models a pair of marbles rolling horizontally at 3 m/sec. One marble is rolling on the floor and the other marble rolls off a ledge that is 7 m high. The graph pictures the paths of the two marbles. The paths clearly intersect because the second marble falls to the floor when it reaches the edge of the ledge. Do the marbles hit each other? Would they hit each other if the ledge was 5 m high? If the ledge was 2 m high? Discuss your answers with your group.

The equations describe the motion of two objects, with t indicating the time. The question of intersection means "Do the two objects actually hit each other, or do their paths merely cross?" Name the t-coordinate, x-coordinate, and y-coordinate of the point of intersection for each of the three given heights. Compare your answers with those of other group members.

Write a paragraph describing what it means if a system of parametric equations has a point or points of intersection.

■ Example 1

Solve the system of equations $x_{1t} = 3t - 4$, $y_{1t} = t + 2$ and $x_{2t} = 1.5t - 0.6$, $y_{2t} = 4t - 4.6$.

Solution

The equations appear to intersect. Use the substitution technique to check that there is a t-value that produces the same point on each line. Equate either the x-equations or the y-equations and solve for t.

$$y_{1t} = y_{2t}$$
$$t + 2 = 4t - 4.6$$
$$6.6 = 3t$$
$$t = \frac{6.6}{3} = 2.2$$

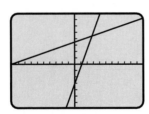

Then substitute this t-value into both sets of x- and y-equations to find the location at that time.

$x = 3t - 4$	$y = t + 2$	$x = 1.5t - 0.6$	$y = 4t - 4.6$
$x = 3(2.2) - 4$	$y = (2.2) + 2$	$x = 1.5(2.2) - 0.6$	$y = 4(2.2) - 4.6$
$x = 2.6$	$y = 4.2$	$x = 2.7$	$y = 4.2$

When $t = 2.2$ sec, the x-values are different, so even though the paths cross each other, the lines do not intersect. ■

Throughout this course you have been asked to find models that correctly interpret various situations. The solutions you find when using your models should make sense. Problem 4 in Problem Set 5.1 asked you to draw a reasonable graph to picture the amount of money you have in an account that is compounded annually. You probably drew a graph very similar to the one pictured here, which shows the value of the account increasing to the larger amount at the instant the money is compounded.

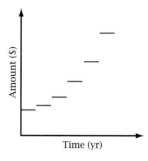

The Forever Green Nursery (Chapter 1) owns 7000 white pine trees. Every year the nursery sells 12% of the remaining trees and plants 600 new trees. The recursive solution you wrote to provide the yearly totals might have been similar to

$$u_0 = 7000 \quad \text{and} \quad u_n = (1 - 0.12)u_{(n-1)} + 600.$$

Did it bother you that some answers reflected fractions of trees? Can you find a better model, so that each answer shows a whole number of trees? One way to do this is to use the **int** function on your calculator. If you assume no fraction of a tree will be harvested, then a reasonable model is

n	Un
0	7000
1	6760
2	6548.8
3	6362.9
4	6199.4
5	6055.5
6	5928.8

n=2

$$u_n = \text{int}\,((1 - 0.12)u_{(n-1)} + 600).$$

Try it. (Be sure your calculator is in *dot* mode.)

The function **int** x ignores the decimal part of a number and outputs only the integer part.

What does the graph of $y = \text{int}\,x$ look like? The table values and graph of $(x, \text{int}\,x)$ both indicate that $y = \text{int}\,x$ rounds a number *down* to the next integer less than or equal to x. This is the function a company uses if they bill to the integer minute at or below the actual time used.

X	Y₁
3.6	3
3.8	3
4	4
4.2	4
4.4	4
4.6	4
4.8	4

Y₁ ≣ int (X)

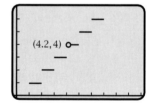

(4.2, 4) o—

The function, $^-\text{int}\,(^-x)$, rounds a number *up* to the next integer greater than or equal to x. If the phone company charges 30¢ a minute for a call, which function gives the cost for a call of 4 min and 12 sec (or 4.2 min): $y = 0.30\,\text{int}\,x$ or $y = ^-0.30\,\text{int}\,(^-x)$? The answer is $y = ^-0.30\,\text{int}\,(^-x)$ because the phone company charges the next minute's fee.

X	Y₂
3.6	4
3.8	4
4	4
4.2	5
4.4	5
4.6	5
4.8	5

Y₂ ≣ ⁻int (⁻X)

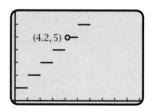

(4.2, 5) o—

Problem Set 9.3

1. **a.** Determine which of the following systems are inconsistent (have no solutions) by graphing.

   i. $y = 0.7x + 8$

   $y = 1.1x - 7$

   iii. $4x + 6y = 9$

   $1.2x + 1.8y = 4.7$

   ii. $y = \frac{3}{4}x - 4$

   $y = 0.75x + 3$

   iv. $\frac{3}{4}x - \frac{1}{2}y = 4$

   $0.75x + 0.5y = 3$

   b. Describe the graphs of the equations of the inconsistent systems.
   c. Try to solve each inconsistent system either by substitution or by elimination. Show your steps. Describe the outcome of these solutions.
   d. Describe how can you recognize an inconsistent linear system without graphing it.

2. For each equation, write a second linear equation that would create an inconsistent system.

   a. $y = 2x + 4$

   c. $2x + 5y = 10$

   b. $y = \frac{-1}{3}x - 3$

   d. $x - 2y = -6$

3. **a.** Which of the following are dependent linear systems? (They have multiple solutions.)

   i. $y = 1.2x + 3$

   $y = 1.2x - 1$

   iii. $4x + 6y = 9$

   $1.2x + 1.8y = 2.7$

   ii. $y = \frac{1}{4}(2x - 1)$

   $y = 0.5x - 0.25$

   iv. $\frac{3}{5}x - \frac{2}{5}y = 3$

   $0.6x + 0.4y = 3$

   b. Describe the graphs of equations of dependent systems.
   c. Solve each dependent system by substitution or elimination. Show your steps. Describe the outcome of each solution.
   d. Describe how can you recognize a dependent linear system without graphing it.

4. Write a second linear equation that would create a dependent system for each given equation.

   a. $y = 2x + 4$

   c. $2x + 5y = 10$

   b. $y = \frac{-1}{3}x - 3$

   d. $x - 2y = -6$

5. For each system of parametric equations, determine when and where they intersect, or whether they have no solution.

   a. $x = 3t + 1$ $x = 2 - 4t^2$

   $y = 8t^2 - 2$ $y = 6t - 3$

   b. $x = 3t + 1$ $x = 2 - 3t$

   $y = 4t + 2$ $y = 4 - 2t$

6. A plane takes off from Detroit at noon flying 200 mi/hr on a heading of 45°. There is no wind. At the same time, a plane takes off from Cleveland, 200 mi directly east. It is flying at 180 mi/hr on a heading of 300°. Should the air traffic controllers make sure that the planes are at different altitudes, or will the planes be in no danger of crashing even if they fly at the same altitude? How close do the planes get to each other?

7. These data were collected from a bouncing ball experiment. Recall that the height is exponentially related to the number of the bounce, $height = a \cdot b^{bounce}$. Find the values of a and b for this function.

Bounce number	Height (cm)
3	34.3
7	8.2

8. The Mother Goose Company ships educational materials to day care providers. One mail service charges a flat rate of $.06 per package plus $.23 per ounce. Another charges $5.50 per package and $1.75 for each pound. Both mailing services bill any fraction of a unit at the rate for the next higher unit. Use the int function and find a breakdown of weights so that the Mother Goose Company uses the most cost-efficient mailer.

9. The angles of elevation to the top of a tower are 40° and 50°, as shown in the picture at the right. Points A and B are 10 m apart. Write two equations involving the distance x and tower height h, and solve for the missing values.

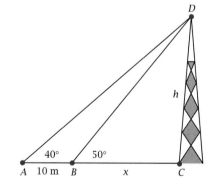

10. The table below gives the populations of San Jose and Detroit.

Year	1950	1960	1970	1980	1990
San Jose	92,280	204,196	459,913	629,442	782,248
Detroit	1,849,568	1,670,144	1,514,063	1,203,339	1,027,974

a. If the current trends continue, when will the population of San Jose surpass the population of Detroit?

b. What will the two populations be at that time?

c. Show the equations you used to make this prediction.

11. Sometimes a system of equations does not have a unique solution. Here is a problem from Mahāvīra, a ninth-century mathematician from Mysore, in southern India. Find at least one solution for Mahāvīra's problem, and explain why your solution is not unique.

> If 3 peacocks cost 2 coins, 4 pigeons cost 3 coins, 5 swans cost 4 coins, and 6 *sārasa* birds cost 5 coins, and if you buy 72 birds for 56 coins, how many of each type bird do you have?

Project

Bifurcation and Systems

A sequence defined by the recursive notation $x_n = 3.2x_{(n-1)}(1 - x_{(n-1)})$ can be looked at in different ways. Start the sequence at any value, for example 0.1, and watch what happens with 3.2Ans(1 − Ans). After about 50 or so iterations you will notice that the answers have fallen into a pattern. Start with another value and you will probably get the same result. But there is one starting value that is quite different. Start with 0.6875 and describe what happens.

If you set up a system of equations, you can find the two-value pattern you saw with the first iteration. Explain how to solve a system when the input of one iteration becomes the output of the next iteration, or when $y = 3.2x(1 - x)$ and $x = 3.2y(1 - y)$. Explain why the value of 0.6875 doesn't lead to the same pattern by showing that it is the solution to $x = 3.2x(1 - x)$.

The formula $x_n = 3.83x_{(n-1)}(1 - x_{(n-1)})$ exhibits slightly different behavior. Start with any value, for example 0.1, and find out what happens after a large number of iterations. Set up a system to solve for this pattern of numbers directly. Find the one number that leads to a constant cycle. Find a pair of numbers that leads to a two-cycle bifurcation like the one you saw in the first example. Explain why this equation would have a different behavior than the first equation.

Section 9.4

Matrix Solutions of Systems

> *When you have eliminated the impossible, whatever remains, however improbable, must be the truth.*
> —*Sir Arthur Conan Doyle*, Sherlock Holmes

One of the earliest known methods for solving systems of linear equations relied on using a calculation device called a counting board. These boards seem to have been developed in China and were later adopted in Japan and Korea. Medieval Europeans used similar devices called line abacuses, counting tables, or reckoning boards. In all of these devices, counters or rods representing numbers were placed in columns and each column represented a place value.

In about 100 B.C. during the Han Dynasty, the Chinese used their counting boards and a method called *fangcheng* to solve systems of linear equations. To do this, they let each column represent a different variable and the coefficients of the variables were placed in the column representing that variable. They placed the constants in another column. Then by doing successive multiplications and divisions they reduced the number of elements in the columns, which led them to the solution for the system of equations. Much later, a similar method, now known as Gaussian elimination, was developed by Karl Gauss.

So far in this chapter you have looked at substitution, elimination, and graphing techniques to solve systems of two equations and two variables, but these methods become more involved and confusing when you are working with systems of more than two variables. In this section you will learn about a solution process involving matrices that is direct and simple for 2×2 systems, as well as for systems with more than two variables, provided all the equations involved are linear.

The system

$$2x + 3y = 7$$
$$x + 4y = 6$$

can be written as a matrix equation,

$$\begin{bmatrix} 2 & 3 \\ 1 & 4 \end{bmatrix} \begin{bmatrix} x \\ y \end{bmatrix} = \begin{bmatrix} 7 \\ 6 \end{bmatrix},$$

and to solve this equation you can use techniques similar to those you use to solve a simple linear equation. But first you must learn how to find an identity matrix and an inverse matrix for a given matrix.

Consider the equation $ax = b$. To solve for x, multiply both sides of the equation by $\frac{1}{a}$, which is the **multiplicative inverse** of a. What is the multiplicative inverse of a real number? The inverse of 2.5, for example, is the number that you can multiply by 2.5 to get 1.

$$2.5a = 1$$

$$a = \frac{1}{2.5} = 0.4 \qquad \text{(Check: } 2.5 \cdot 0.4 = 1\text{)}$$

To solve a system by using matrices, you must find what is called an **inverse matrix**. If an inverse matrix exists, then when you multiply it by your matrix you will get the matrix equivalent of one, which is called the **identity matrix**. Any matrix multiplied by the identity matrix remains unchanged.

Identity Matrix

An **identity matrix**, symbolized by I, is one of a set of matrices that do not alter or transform the elements of any matrix A under multiplication.

$$AI = A \quad \text{and} \quad IA = A$$

Though the dimensions of one identity matrix may differ from another, the property holds true.

In Example 1 you will learn how to find a 2×2 identity matrix, and once you recognize the pattern in an identity matrix, you will not need to find one every time you solve a system using matrices.

■ Example 1

Find an *identity matrix* for $\begin{bmatrix} 2 & 1 \\ 4 & 3 \end{bmatrix}$.

Solution

You want to find a matrix $\begin{bmatrix} a & b \\ c & d \end{bmatrix}$ that satisfies the definition of the identity matrix.

$$\begin{bmatrix} 2 & 1 \\ 4 & 3 \end{bmatrix} \begin{bmatrix} a & b \\ c & d \end{bmatrix} = \begin{bmatrix} 2 & 1 \\ 4 & 3 \end{bmatrix}$$

$$\begin{bmatrix} 2a + c & 2b + d \\ 4a + 3c & 4b + 3d \end{bmatrix} = \begin{bmatrix} 2 & 1 \\ 4 & 3 \end{bmatrix}$$

Because the two matrices are equal, you get the following systems:

$$2a + c = 2 \qquad\qquad 2b + d = 1$$
$$4a + 3c = 4 \qquad\qquad 4b + 3d = 3$$

Use either substitution or elimination to find the answers $a = 1$, $b = 0$, $c = 0$, and $d = 1$. Do this now. This means the 2×2 identity matrix is

$$\begin{bmatrix} 1 & 0 \\ 0 & 1 \end{bmatrix}.$$

There are corresponding identity matrices for matrices with greater dimensions. Will an identity matrix always be square? Why or why not? ■

Now that you know what the identity matrix looks like for a 2 ×2 matrix, you can return to the problem of finding the inverse of a matrix.

Inverse Matrix

The **inverse matrix** of A, symbolized by A^{-1}, is the matrix that will produce an identity matrix when multiplied by A.

$$AA^{-1} = I \quad \text{and} \quad A^{-1}A = I$$

Not every square matrix has an inverse. Can a nonsquare matrix have an inverse? Why or why not?

■ Example 2

Find the inverse of $\begin{bmatrix} 2 & 1 \\ 4 & 3 \end{bmatrix}$.

Solution

Set up a matrix equation.

$$\begin{bmatrix} 2 & 1 \\ 4 & 3 \end{bmatrix} \begin{bmatrix} a & b \\ c & d \end{bmatrix} = \begin{bmatrix} 1 & 0 \\ 0 & 1 \end{bmatrix}$$

Matrix multiplication on the left side of the equation provides the following systems:

$$2a + c = 1 \qquad 2b + d = 0$$
$$4a + 3c = 0 \qquad 4b + 3d = 1$$

Solving these systems, you find the answers $a = 1.5$, $b = {}^-0.5$, $c = {}^-2$, and $d = 1$. The inverse matrix is $\begin{bmatrix} 1.5 & {}^-0.5 \\ {}^-2 & 1 \end{bmatrix}$. Your calculator also provides the inverse of a

NOTE 9B

matrix A, A^{-1}. (See **Calculator Note 9B** for specific instructions.) ■

Return to the system shown at the beginning of this section.

$$2x + 3y = 7$$
$$x + 4y = 6$$

Verify that the system can be written as the matrix equation.

$$\begin{bmatrix} 2 & 3 \\ 1 & 4 \end{bmatrix} \begin{bmatrix} x \\ y \end{bmatrix} = \begin{bmatrix} 7 \\ 6 \end{bmatrix}$$

Let the coefficient matrix be A so that $A = \begin{bmatrix} 2 & 3 \\ 1 & 4 \end{bmatrix}$. Let the variable matrix be X so that $X = \begin{bmatrix} x \\ y \end{bmatrix}$. If the constant matrix is B, then $B = \begin{bmatrix} 7 \\ 6 \end{bmatrix}$, and the equation can

---

be written $AX = B$. The calculator inverse to A is $A^{-1} = \begin{bmatrix} 0.8 & ^-0.6 \\ ^-0.2 & 0.4 \end{bmatrix}$.

Check this result on your calculator.

Multiply both sides of the equation by this inverse to produce the solution to the original system.

$$\begin{bmatrix} 2 & 3 \\ 1 & 4 \end{bmatrix} \begin{bmatrix} x \\ y \end{bmatrix} = \begin{bmatrix} 7 \\ 6 \end{bmatrix} \qquad\qquad AX = B \qquad\qquad \text{Rewrite in matrix form.}$$

$$\begin{bmatrix} 0.8 & ^-0.6 \\ ^-0.2 & 0.4 \end{bmatrix} \begin{bmatrix} 2 & 3 \\ 1 & 4 \end{bmatrix} \begin{bmatrix} x \\ y \end{bmatrix} =$$

$$\qquad\qquad \begin{bmatrix} 0.8 & ^-0.6 \\ ^-0.2 & 0.4 \end{bmatrix} \begin{bmatrix} 7 \\ 6 \end{bmatrix} \qquad A^{-1}AX = A^{-1}B \quad \text{Multiply by the inverse.}$$

$$\begin{bmatrix} 1 & 0 \\ 0 & 1 \end{bmatrix} \begin{bmatrix} x \\ y \end{bmatrix} = \begin{bmatrix} 0.8 & ^-0.6 \\ ^-0.2 & 0.4 \end{bmatrix} \begin{bmatrix} 7 \\ 6 \end{bmatrix} \qquad IX = A^{-1}B \qquad \begin{array}{l}\text{The definition of} \\ \text{inverse.}\end{array}$$

$$\begin{bmatrix} x \\ y \end{bmatrix} = \begin{bmatrix} 0.8 & ^-0.6 \\ ^-0.2 & 0.4 \end{bmatrix} \begin{bmatrix} 7 \\ 6 \end{bmatrix} \qquad\qquad X = A^{-1}B \qquad \begin{array}{l}\text{The definition of} \\ \text{identity.}\end{array}$$

$$\begin{bmatrix} x \\ y \end{bmatrix} = \begin{bmatrix} 2 \\ 1 \end{bmatrix} \qquad\qquad\qquad\qquad \text{Matrix multiplication.}$$

$$2(2) + 3(1) = 7 \quad \text{and} \quad (2) + 4(1) = 6 \qquad \text{Check the solution.}$$

■ Example 3

On a recent trip to the movies, three students— Noah, Carey, and Rita—each spent some money at the concession counter. Noah bought two candy bars, a small drink, and two bags of popcorn for a total of $5.35. Carey spent $4.16 on a candy bar, two small drinks, and a bag of popcorn. Meanwhile, Rita spent $5.85. She didn't buy any candy, but she bought two small drinks and three bags of popcorn. If all the purchases included tax, what was the purchase price for each item?

Solution

Let C = price of a candy bar, D = price of a small drink, and P = price of a bag of popcorn. The purchases may be represented by the following system. What is the meaning of row two?

$$\begin{bmatrix} 2C + 1D + 2P \\ 1C + 2D + 1P \\ 0C + 2D + 3P \end{bmatrix} = \begin{bmatrix} 5.35 \\ 4.16 \\ 5.85 \end{bmatrix}$$

These equations can be translated into the matrix equation

$$\begin{bmatrix} 2 & 1 & 2 \\ 1 & 2 & 1 \\ 0 & 2 & 3 \end{bmatrix} \begin{bmatrix} C \\ D \\ P \end{bmatrix} = \begin{bmatrix} 5.35 \\ 4.16 \\ 5.85 \end{bmatrix} \text{ in the form of } AX = B.$$

Store the coefficient matrix as A and the constant matrix as B.

The solution to the system is $A^{-1}B$, which is $\begin{bmatrix} 0.89 \\ 0.99 \\ 1.29 \end{bmatrix}$.

This means that a candy bar costs \$.89, a small drink costs \$.99, and a bag of popcorn costs \$1.29. Substituting these answers into the original system shows that they are correct.

$2(0.89) + 1(0.99) + 2(1.29) = 5.35$
$1(0.89) + 2(0.99) + 1(1.29) = 4.16$
$2(.99) + 3(1.29) = 5.85$

Another way to check the answers is to store them in the calculator and evaluate the expressions.

Checking the solutions is important! ■

```
0.89→C
            .89
0.99→D
            .99
1.29→P
            1.29
```

```
2C+D+2P
            5.35
C+2D+P
            4.16
2D+3P
            5.85
```

■ Example 4

Solve the following system.

$$x + \tfrac{1}{2}y + \tfrac{1}{3}z = 1$$

$$\tfrac{1}{2}x + \tfrac{1}{3}y + \tfrac{1}{4}z = 2$$

$$\tfrac{1}{3}x + \tfrac{1}{4}y + \tfrac{1}{5}z = 3$$

Solution

NOTE
9B

The difficulty involved in using decimal approximations is illustrated in the table below. There is no problem entering the fractions $\tfrac{1}{2}, \tfrac{1}{4}$, or $\tfrac{1}{5}$ because you can enter exact values for them. But $\tfrac{1}{3}$ is a repeating decimal, and when you enter 0.3333..., you are entering only an approximation of $\tfrac{1}{3}$. Below are the results for various approximation choices. (See **Calculator Note 9B** for help with entering fractions as matrix elements. Not all calculators can do this.)

Approximation	x	y	z
0.333	30.505	−209.990	226.697
0.33333	27.03207	−192.16442	210.15253
1/3	27	−192	210 ■

The lesson to be learned here is that answers must be checked. If they don't work, then adjust for more accuracy in your matrix or look for another technique. If you get 4 E ⁻13 for an answer, this is probably meant to be zero. Likewise, 3.99999992 is probably meant to be 4. The calculator introduces round-off inaccuracies when it finds the inverse matrix and during matrix multiplication. Don't expect your calculator to give you answers that are precise. Check them yourself and adjust for rounding.

Problem Set 9.4

1. Multiply each pair of matrices. If multiplication is not possible, explain why.

   a. $\begin{bmatrix} 5 & 2 \\ 7 & 3 \end{bmatrix}\begin{bmatrix} 1 & -3 \\ 5 & -2 \end{bmatrix}$
   b. $\begin{bmatrix} 4 & -1 \\ 3 & 6 \\ 2 & -3 \end{bmatrix}\begin{bmatrix} 2 & -5 & 0 \\ 1 & -2 & 7 \end{bmatrix}$
   c. $[\ 9\ -3\ ]\begin{bmatrix} 4 & -6 \\ 0 & -2 \\ -1 & 3 \end{bmatrix}$

2. Use matrix multiplication to expand each system. Then solve for each variable by using substitution, elimination, or matrix multiplication.

   a. $\begin{bmatrix} 1 & 5 \\ 6 & 2 \end{bmatrix}\begin{bmatrix} a & b \\ c & d \end{bmatrix} = \begin{bmatrix} -7 & 33 \\ 14 & -26 \end{bmatrix}$
   b. $\begin{bmatrix} 1 & 5 \\ 6 & 2 \end{bmatrix}\begin{bmatrix} a & b \\ c & d \end{bmatrix} = \begin{bmatrix} 1 & 0 \\ 0 & 1 \end{bmatrix}$

3. The calculator gives the second matrix as the inverse of the first. Multiply the two matrices together to verify that they are inverses.

   a. $\begin{bmatrix} 5 & 2 \\ 7 & 3 \end{bmatrix}\begin{bmatrix} 3 & -2 \\ -7 & 5 \end{bmatrix}$
   b. $\begin{bmatrix} 1 & 5 & 4 \\ 6 & 2 & -2 \\ 0 & 3 & 1 \end{bmatrix}\begin{bmatrix} 0.16 & 0.14 & -0.36 \\ -0.12 & 0.02 & 0.52 \\ 0.36 & -0.06 & -0.56 \end{bmatrix}$

   c. In your own words, describe how you know when two matrices are inverses of each other.

4. Find the inverse of each matrix.

   a. $\begin{bmatrix} 4 & 3 \\ 5 & 4 \end{bmatrix}$
   b. $\begin{bmatrix} 6 & 4 & -2 \\ 3 & 1 & -1 \\ 0 & 7 & 3 \end{bmatrix}$

   c. $\begin{bmatrix} 5 & 3 \\ 10 & 7 \end{bmatrix}$
   d. $\begin{bmatrix} -1 & 2 & -3 \\ 2 & 3 & -1 \\ 3 & -2 & -1 \end{bmatrix}$

5. Rewrite each system as a matrix equation.

   a. $5.2x + 3.6y = 7$
   b. $\frac{1}{4}x - \frac{2}{5}y = 3$

   $-5.2x + 2y = 8.2$
   $\frac{3}{8}x + \frac{2}{5}y = 2$

6. Rewrite each system in matrix form and solve by using matrix multiplication. Check your solutions.
   a. $8x + 3y = 41$
   b. $11x - 5y = -38$
   $6x + 5y = 39$
   $9x + 2y = -25$

c. $2x + y - 2z = 1$
$6x + 2y - 4z = 3$
$4x - y + 3z = 5$

d. $4w + x + 2y - 3z = {}^-16$
${}^-3w + 3x - y + 4z = 20$
$5w + 4x + 3y - z = {}^-10$
${}^-w + 2x + 5y + z = {}^-4$

7. Write a system of equations to model each situation, and solve for the appropriate values of the variables.

    a. The perimeter of a rectangle is 44 cm. Its length is 2 cm more than twice its width.

    b. The perimeter of an isosceles triangle is 40 cm. The base length is 2 cm less than the length of a leg of the triangle.

    c. The Fahrenheit reading on a dual thermometer is 0.4 less than three times the Celsius reading.

8. At the High Flying Amusement Park there are three kinds of rides: rides for the timid, rides for the adventurous, and rides for the thrill seekers. You can buy a book that includes the admission fee and ten tickets for each type of ride for the price of just the tickets, or you can pay $5.00 for admission and then buy tickets for each of the rides individually. Noah, Rita, and Carey went to the park. They each decided not to buy the admission book and instead to pay for each ride individually. Noah rode on seven of the rides for the timid, three of the rides for the adventurous, and nine of the rides for the thrill seekers, for a cost of $19.55 for the rides only. Rita rode on nine of the rides for the timid, ten of the rides for the adventurous, and none of the rides for the thrill seekers, for a cost of $13.00 for the rides. Carey paid $24.95 for eight rides for the timid, seven rides for the adventurous, and ten rides for the thrill seekers.

    a. How much did each type of ride cost?

    b. What is the total cost of a 30-ride ticket book?

    c. Would any of the three have been better off purchasing a ticket book, or did they all make the right decision in paying for the admission and the rides separately?

9. The Fan C. Feate Dance Company is given two choices in how they will be paid for their next series of performances. The first option is to receive $12,500 for the series plus 5% of all ticket sales. The second option is $6,800 for the series plus 15% of ticket sales. The company will perform three consecutive nights in a hall that seats 2,200 persons. All tickets will cost $12.

    a. How much will the company receive under each plan if a total of 3,500 tickets are sold for all three performances?

    b. Write an equation that gives the amount the company will receive under the first plan for any number of tickets sold.

    c. Write an equation that gives the amount the company will receive under the second plan for any number of tickets sold.

d. How many tickets must be sold for the second plan to be the better choice?

e. What would your advice be to the company regarding which plan to choose? Justify your choice.

10. During the last semester one-half of the students in Fay Silitator's second-hour class worked on projects about fractals. One-fourth of the class collected and analyzed data, and the rest conducted a survey and analyzed their results. In her third-hour class, one-third worked on projects about fractals, one-half collected and analyzed data, and the rest conducted a survey and analyzed their results. In the seventh-hour class, one-fourth of the students worked on projects about fractals, one-sixth of them collected and analyzed data, and the others conducted a survey and analyzed their results. Overall, there were 18 students who completed projects on fractals, 16 students who collected and analyzed data, and 20 students who conducted surveys and analyzed their results. How many students are in each of Fay Silitator's classes?

11. Being able to solve a system of equations is definitely not "new" mathematics. Mahāvīra, the best-known Indian mathematician of the ninth century, worked the following problem. See if you can solve it.

> The mixed price of 9 citrons and 7 fragrant wood apples is 107; again the mixture price of 7 citrons and 9 fragrant wood apples is 101. O you arithmetician, tell me quickly the price of a citron and of a wood apple here, having distinctly separated those prices well.

Project

Nonlinear Systems with Three Variables

In Section 9.1 you explored how you might solve nonlinear systems in two variables by using graphing techniques. You have also solved linear systems with three variables by using matrices. Using all that you have learned, and some creativity, find the solutions for each system below. Show that the solutions you find satisfy the respective system. Then find a way to convince others that you have found all possible solutions.

a. $z = 9x^2 + 4y^2 - 36$
$z = 3x - 2y$
$z = 6xy + 12$

b. $z = 5(1.02)^x + 7(1.05)^y$
$z = 40(0.97)^x + 50(0.95)^y$
$z = 12x + 15y$

Linear Inequations and Systems

An expert problem solver must be endowed with two incompatible qualities, a restless imagination and a patient pertinacity.
—Howard W. Eves

Frequently, real-world situations involve ranges of values. "Do not spend more than $10"; "Write an essay between two and five pages in length"; "Practice more than an hour each day"; "Be home before ten o'clock"; "The post office is open from nine o'clock until noon"; "Stu Dent has to spend three hours in his room with his homework each evening." From this last statement, you don't know how much time Stu actually spends working on mathematics, or studying chemistry, or even daydreaming about Rachel. The time spent thinking about Rachel is not a concern to you,

except that you cannot say that *mathematics time + chemistry time* = 3 hr. The third variable, daydreaming time, changes your equation to *mathematics time + chemistry time* ≤ 3 hr.

Investigation 9.5.1

Mathematics Time versus Chemistry Time

Part 1   Let *x* hours represent *mathematics time* and *y* hours represent *chemistry time* and graph the equation *mathematics time + chemistry time* = 3 hr.

x (mathematics time)	*y* (chemistry time)	*x + y*
–?–	–?–	–?–
–?–	–?–	–?–
–?–	–?–	–?–
–?–	–?–	–?–

a. The first group member collects at least five pairs of *x*- and *y*-values with a sum of less than 3 hr.

b. The second group member collects at least five pairs of *x*- and *y*-values with a sum more than 3 hr.

c. The third group member collects at least five pairs of *x*- and *y*-values that sum to exactly 3 hr.

d. The fourth group member collects the data from the other group members and fills in the third column of the table.

Part 2   Circle the points on the graph that fit the actual condition *mathematics time + chemistry time* ≤ 3 hr and answer the questions below.

a. Describe where these points are located on the graph.

b. Describe some points that fit the condition but do not make sense for the situation.

c. Describe where all possible solutions to the inequation $x + y \le 3$ are located.

d. Describe where all possible solutions to $x + y > 3$ are located.

When there are one or two variables, you can model the solution of an inequation as a set of ordered pairs graphed on a coordinate plane. The region that contains the solution is shaded. Frequently there are additional commonsense conditions, such as not having negative amounts of time. In the investigation above, there were three conditions: *mathematics time + chemistry time* ≤ 3 hr, *mathematics time* ≥ 0, and *chemistry time* ≥ 0. Because these conditions must be satisfied simultaneously, they form a system.

■ **Example 1**

Stu Dent spent 3 hr in his room with his homework last night. He spent more time working on mathematics than on chemistry. Stu spent at least a half-hour working on chemistry. Restate the conditions of the system algebraically in terms of *x* hours and *y* hours for *mathematics time* and *chemistry time,* respectively. Then graph the inequations and all solutions on the same coordinate axis.

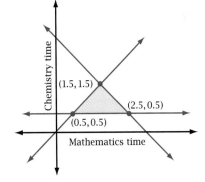

Solution

$$x + y \le 3$$
$$x > y$$
$$y \ge 0.5$$

Convert each inequation to an equation by replacing the inequality sign with an equal sign. Find the points of intersection by using previously learned techniques.

Equations	Intersections
$x + y = 3$ and $x = y$	$(1.5, 1.5)$
$x + y = 3$ and $y = 0.5$	$(2.5, 0.5)$
$x = y$ and $y = 0.5$	$(0.5, 0.5)$

Select one of the lines. Choose a sample point on either side of the line. Test the coordinates of this point in the inequation to see if it makes a true statement. If it does, shade on the side of the line where the point lies. If it doesn't, shade on the other side of the line. Repeat this process for each line. The solution to the entire system is the area that represents the overlap of all the shaded regions. This region is called the **feasible region**, and every point in this region is a possible (feasible) solution to the system. ■

NOTE
9C

See **Calculator Note 9C** for help in graphing systems of inequations on your calculator screen. The appendix suggests that you shade the nonfeasible region. This alternative allows you to see individual points as you move the cursor within the feasible region on your calculator screen.

■ Example 2

Maria is planning a snack of graham crackers and blueberry yogurt. Because she is concerned about nutrition, she wants to make sure that she eats less than 700 calories and no more than 20 g of fat with this snack. She would like to eat at least 17 g of protein and at least 30% of the daily requirement of iron. Use this information to show the choices Maria can make.

Solution

	Serving	Calories	Fat	Protein	Iron
Graham crackers	1 cracker	60	2 g	2 g	6%
Blueberry yogurt	4.5 oz	130	2 g	5 g	1%

Using x as the number of crackers and y as the number of servings of yogurt, you get the following set of condition inequations.

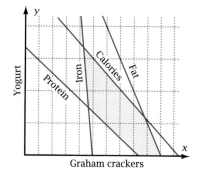

Calories	$60x + 130y \leq 700$
Fat	$2x + 2y \leq 20$
Protein	$2x + 5y \geq 17$
Iron	$6x + 1y \geq 30$
Common sense	$x \geq 0$
Common sense	$y \geq 0$

Here are the vertex points of the feasible region (clockwise from top left).

Calories and iron = $(4.44, 3.33)$
Calories and fat = $(8.57, 1.43)$
Fat and common sense = $(10, 0)$

Common sense and protein = $(8.5, 0)$

Protein and iron = $(4.75, 1.5)$

You are not interested in the intersection points of every pair of lines. In this example, the intersection of the line representing the fat inequation with the line representing the iron inequation occurs outside the feasible region, so you don't list it as a vertex point. The line representing the inequation $y \geq 0$ does not form any part of the actual border of the region even though $y \geq 0$ is satisfied by all points in the feasible region. Frequently, only points in the feasible region that have integer coefficients make sense. So having integer coordinates is another commonsense restriction that you will have to consider. If whole crackers and full yogurt servings are the only possibilities, then points having integer coordinates are the only possible solution points. ■

Problem Set 9.5

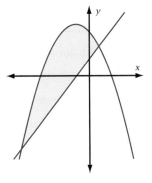

1. The graphs of $y = 2.4x + 2$ and $y = {}^{-}x^2 - 2x + 6.4$ serve as the boundaries of the shaded region. What two inequations identify this region?

Sketch a graph of the feasible region described by each system of inequations in Problems 2–5. Label each vertex point and find its coordinates.

2. $y \leq {}^{-}0.51x + 5$
   $y \leq {}^{-}1.6x + 8$
   $y \geq 0.1x + 2$
   $y \geq 0$
   $x \geq 0$

3. $y \geq 1.6x - 3$
   $y \leq {}^{-}(x - 2)^2 + 4$
   $y \geq 1 - x$
   $y \geq 0$
   $x \geq 0$

4. $4x + 3y \leq 12$
   $1.6x + 2y \leq 8$
   $2x + y \geq 2$
   $y \geq 0$
   $x \geq 0$

5. $y \geq |x - 1|$
   $y \leq \sqrt{9 - x^2}$
   $y \leq 2.5$
   $y \geq 0$
   $x \geq 0$

6. In the Lux Art Gallery, rectangular paintings must satisfy the following restrictions: $200 \leq$ area (in square inches) ≤ 300 and $66 \leq$ perimeter (in inches) ≤ 80.
   a. Write four inequations involving *length* and *width* that represent these conditions.
   b. Graph this system of inequations and identify the feasible region.
   c. Will they hang a picture that measures 12.4 in. by 16.3 in.? A 16 in. by 17.5 in. picture? A 14.3 in. by 17.5 in. picture?

Katchina, by Georgia O'Keeffe (1936).

7. Al Geebra just gave away or sold 40 of his dad's old records. He sold each classical record for $5 and each jazz record for $2. The rest of the records were worthless and he gave them away. Al knows that he sold fewer than 30 records, and that he collected more than $100.

   a. If he sold x classical records and y jazz records, how can you represent the number of records he gave away? (Write this as an expression involving x and y.)

   b. In terms of x, how many dollars did he receive from selling the classical records?

   c. Write the inequation to show that he earned more than $100.

   d. List three commonsense inequations.

   e. Graph this system of inequations.

   f. Name all of the vertices of the feasible region.

8. A parabola $y = ax^2 + bx + c$ passes through the points $(^-2, ^-32)$, $(1, 7)$, and $(3, 63)$.

   a. Describe how you can use matrices and systems to find the values of a, b, and c in this parabola.

   b. Write the equation of this parabola.

   c. Describe how to verify that your answer is correct.

9. How many different methods do you know to solve a system of equations? What are they? Which one do you prefer? Why?

Section 9.6

Linear Programming

Do the things you fear the most, and the death of fear is certain.
—*Ralph Waldo Emerson*

In the last section, you looked at an example about Maria's dietary requirements. The modeling inequations are reprinted below.

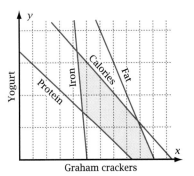

Calories	$60x + 130y \leq 700$
Fat	$2x + 2y \leq 20$
Protein	$2x + 5y \geq 17$
Iron	$6x + y \geq 30$
Common sense	$x \geq 0$
Common sense	$y \geq 0$

The variable x represents the number of graham crackers, and the variable y represents the number of servings of blueberry yogurt.

Suppose each cracker costs \$.06 and each serving of yogurt costs \$.30. Now you can determine the cost of Maria's meals with the equation $cost = 0.06x + 0.30y$. By choosing points in the shaded area, or feasible region, you can list the costs of several different meal combinations. Verify the costs of the following meals that meet her dietary requirements.

$Cost = 0.06x + 0.30y$

Number of crackers (x)	Servings of yogurt (y)	Cost of meal (\$)
5	2	0.90
7	2	1.02
7	1	0.72

What is Maria's least-expensive snack combination? Suppose you assume that the only solutions that make sense are those that are whole numbers (whole crackers and whole servings of yogurt). Identify all of the integer points that are in the feasible region and list the cost for each combination of crackers and yogurt.

x	y	Cost	x	y	Cost	x	y	Cost
5	3	1.20	7	2	1.02	9	0	0.54
5	2	0.90	7	1	0.72	10	0	0.60
6	2	0.96	8	1	0.78			
6	1	0.66	9	1	0.84			

From this listing you can see that the least-expensive combination is *nine crackers and no yogurt*. Cheap, but not very exciting.

This process of finding a feasible region and determining the point that gives the maximum or minimum value to a specific expression, is called **linear programming**.

George Dantzig, who was employed by the United States Air Force in World War II, was asked to develop a method for planning and scheduling. He came up with the method of linear programming and found that it works not only for planning, but also for other problems that can be formulated as a system of linear equations and inequations. In fact, one of the first problems on which Dantzig's method was used wasn't a planning problem at all; it was a diet problem formulated by the economist George Stigler. The problem was: What is the least-expensive combination of foods containing the minimum daily requirement of certain nutrients? Stigler's system had 9 inequalities and used 77 unknowns because only 77 foods and 9 nutrients (calories, protein, calcium, iron, niacin, and vitamins A, B_1, B_2, and C) were considered. In 1948, the system was solved in approximately 120 person-days using hand-operated desk calculators. In 1953, it was solved in approximately 12 minutes on a computer. Dantzig wrote in 1963 that solving it on a post-1960 computer would take less than a minute.

Investigation 9.6.1

Nutritional Elements

Choose two food items. Record information about calories, fat, protein, iron (or other appropriate ingredients) for your two food items. Either use Maria's restrictions or alter the dietary constraints. Using the information and constraints your group has selected, describe and solve a problem similar to the cracker-and-yogurt snack combination problem in this section.

Problem Set 9.6

1. a. Carefully graph each system of inequations.
   b. Determine the coordinates of each vertex of the feasible region.
   c. Find the coordinates of each point in the region with integer coordinates. Then find the point with integer coordinates that gives the highest or lowest value for the final expression. (Do not evaluate each integer point in the feasible region. Evaluate only those that you feel may yield the desired maximum or minimum values.)

   i. $3y \leq {}^-2x + 6$
   $y \leq 6 - 4x$
   $x \geq 0, y \geq 0$
   maximize $5x + 2y$

   ii. $x + y \leq 10$
   $5x + 2y \geq 20$
   ${}^-x + 2y \geq 0$
   minimize $x + 3y$

iii. $3x - y \leq 12$
$x + y \leq 15$
$x \geq 2,\ y \geq 5$
maximize $2x + y$

iv. $x + 2y \geq 10$
$2x + y \geq 12$
$x - y \leq 8$
minimize $3x + 2y$

d. For each system in part c, i–iv, evaluate the maximum or minimum expression at each vertex. What generalizations can you make about the location of the point that provides the maximum or minimum value?

2. a. Graph the system $x \geq 5500$, $y \geq 5000$, $y \leq 3x$, and $x + y = 40{,}000$.

b. Name the integer point that provides the maximum value in the expression $P = 0.08x + 0.10y$. What is this maximum value of P?

3. During the nesting seasons two different bird species inhabit a region 180,000 m² in area. Mr. Chamberlin estimates that this ecological region can provide 72,000 kg of food during the season. Each nesting pair of species X needs 39.6 kg of food during a specified time period and 120 m² of area. Each nesting pair of species Y needs 69.6 kg of food and 90 m² of area. Let x be the number of pairs of species X and y be the number of pairs of species Y.

a. Carefully describe the meaning of $x \geq 0$ and $y \geq 0$.

b. Carefully describe the meaning of $120x + 90y \leq 180{,}000$.

c. Carefully describe the meaning of $39.6x + 69.6y \leq 72{,}000$.

d. Graph the inequations (constraints) listed, and identify each vertex of the feasible region.

e. Maximize the total number of nesting pairs, N, by considering the function $N = x + y$.

4. Draw upon what you've learned in this chapter to create three interesting questions about the graph at the right.

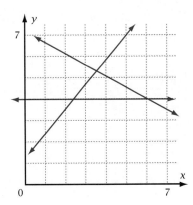

Geometer's Sketchpad Investigation

Linear Programming

You can use Sketchpad to create a very visual solution to a linear programming problem. Follow the steps below to find the solution for the given linear programming problem. (You may want to select the Snap To Grid option for this investigation.)

Constraint inequations
$y \leq {}^-1.5x + 7.5$
$y \leq 2x + 3$
$y \geq {}^-0.3x + 3$

Optimizing expression
$5x + 2y$

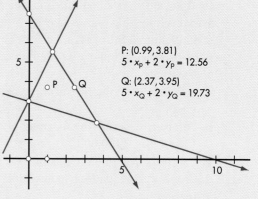

P: (0.99, 3.81)
$5 \cdot x_P + 2 \cdot y_P = 12.56$

Q: (2.37, 3.95)
$5 \cdot x_Q + 2 \cdot y_Q = 19.73$

Step 1 In a new sketch, choose Create Axes from the Graph menu.

Step 2 Graph the boundary line for each inequation. To do this, plot two points on the boundary line and construct the line that contains these points. If necessary, you can scale the axes by moving the point (1, 0).

Step 3 Create all of the points of intersection of the boundary lines. These points are called the **border points** of the feasible region.

Step 4 Create and shade the feasible region.

Step 5 Construct a point P inside the feasible region and measure its coordinates.

Step 6 Use the coordinates of point P to calculate the value of the optimizing expression.

Step 7 Move point P to see how the value of the expression changes. Be sure to keep point P within the feasible region. You may wish to turn off the Snap To Grid option at this point.

Step 8 Construct another point, Q, on the boundary of the feasible region.

Step 9 Use the coordinates of point Q to calculate the value of the optimizing expression.

Step 10 Move point Q to see how the value of the expression changes.

Questions

1. What conclusions can you draw about when the optimizing expression will be at its maximum value? At its minimum value?

2. Create a generic polygon in the first quadrant. Construct point P inside the polygon and point Q on the boundary of the polygon. Define an optimizing expression and calculate its values using the coordinates of P and the coordinates of Q. Determine where the maximum and minimum values occur. Change the shape of your polygon to see how this affects the maximum and minimum values of the optimizing expression. Summarize your conclusions.

3. Do one of the problems given in Problem Set 9.6, Problem 1.

Section 9.7

Applications of Linear Programming

It is not certain that everything is uncertain.
—Blaise Pascal

Noah and Rita are members of the mathematics club, which has the opportunity to sell popcorn at the weekly basketball games. Their job is to figure out whether the club can make money doing this. There are a number of questions they need to answer. How can they maximize profit? What are the expenses, guidelines, and restrictions involved, and what is the break-even point for the amount of popcorn sold? How many members are needed for the most efficient operation? These kinds of questions can be answered by applying linear programming techniques to a situation.

Business or industrial managers often investigate more economical ways of doing something. They must consider physical limitations, standards of quality, customer demand, availability of materials, and manufacturing expenses as restrictions, or constraints. Problems that can be modeled with linear programming may involve anywhere from two variables to hundreds of variables. Computerized modeling programs that analyze up to 200 constraints and 400 variables are regularly used to help businesses choose their best plan of action. In this section, you will look at problems that involve two variables because you are relying on the visual assistance of a two-dimensional graph to help you find the feasible region.

Once you have identified the variables, you must write the constraints, or inequations. You will have to find some way to organize the information. The text of the problem must be broken down, and the mathematical facts extracted. The following example shows one way to carry out this process. As you study this example, be aware that not every problem can be organized in the same way.

■ **Example 1**

The Elite Tweet Pottery Shoppe makes two kinds of birdbaths: glazed and unglazed. The unglazed birdbath requires 1/2 hr to throw on the pottery wheel and 1 hr in the kiln. The glazed birdbath takes 1 hr on the wheel and 6 hr in the kiln. The wheel is available for at most 8 hr/day, and the kiln is available for at most 20 hr/day. The pottery shop's profit on each unglazed birdbath is $10, while its profit on each glazed birdbath is $15. How many of each kind of birdbath should be produced in order to maximize profit?

Solution

The variables in this problem are the number of each type of birdbath. The choice of x and y is arbitrary because neither is dependent on the other. Organize the information into a table.

	Number of unglazed birdbaths (x)	Number of glazed birdbaths (y)	Constraining value
Throwing hours	1/2	1	≤ 8
Firing hours	1	6	≤ 20
Profit	$10	$15	none

Once you have organized the data in a table, the inequations, or constraints, can be written.

Throwing hours constraint: $0.5x + y \leq 8$
Kiln hours constraint: $x + 6y \leq 20$
Commonsense constraints: $x \geq 0; y \geq 0$
The profit expression to be optimized is: $profit = 10x + 15y$

Graph all of the constraint inequations to locate the feasible region. (Note: The nonfeasible region is shaded, allowing you to more easily identify points that are in the feasible region.) You are looking for integer solutions because you will not sell part of a birdbath. Determine the integer points at or closest to each vertex of the region, and calculate the profit for each point.

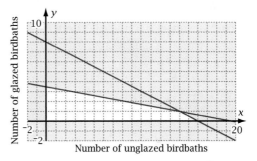

The vertices, or nearest points with integer coordinates, are $(0, 0)$, $(0, 3)$, $(14, 1)$, and $(16, 0)$.

Here are the profits corresponding to each vertex.

$(0, 0)$	$10(0) + 15(0) = \$0$
$(0, 3)$	$10(0) + 15(3) = \$45$
$(14, 1)$	$10(14) + 15(1) = \$155$
$(16, 0)$	$10(16) + 15(0) = \$160$

The profit for each vertex is found by putting the coordinates of the point into the profit equation, $10x + 15y = profit$. Producing no glazed birdbaths and 16 unglazed birdbaths maximizes the profit. However, if you were aware that customers are happier when given a choice of products, would you settle for $155 profit and offer your customers a choice? ∎

Investigation 9.7.1
Paying for College

Marti's parents are about to invest up to $40,000 to save for her college education. The stock fund has been paying 10% per year and the bond fund has been paying 8% per year. Both funds require $5,000 as a minimum investment. Because of recent economic conditions and the advice of their financial advisor, Marti's parents have decided that the amount invested in stocks should be no more than three times the size of their bond investment. The problem is to find the amount they should invest in each fund to maximize their investment.

a. Identify the variables.

b. Translate the limitations or constraints provided into a system of inequations. A table might help you to organize this information.

c. Graph the system of inequations and determine the feasible region. Find each vertex of this region. (If integer solutions are required and a vertex doesn't have integer coefficients, identify integer points near the vertex.)

d. Write a linear function that will maximize the parents' investment.

e. Find the answer to the question.

Problem Set 9.7

1. Xavier, Yolanda, and Zeus have a small business producing handmade shawls and afghans for the Mathematics Teachers Retirement Home. They spin the yarn, dye it, and weave it. A shawl requires 1 hr of spinning, 1 hr of dyeing, and 1 hr of weaving. An afghan needs 2 hr of spinning, 1 hr of dyeing, and 4 hr of weaving. They make a $16 profit per shawl and a $20 profit per afghan. Xavier does the spinning on his day off, when he can spend at most 8 hr spinning.  Yolanda does the dyeing on her day off, when she can spend up to 6 hr dyeing. Zeus does all the weaving on Friday and Saturday, when he has at most 14 hr available. How many of each item should they make each week to maximize their profit?

2. The International Canine Academy raises and trains Siberian sled dogs and dancing French poodles. Breeders can supply ICA with at most 20 poodles and 15 huskies each year. Each poodle eats 2 lb of food a day and each sled dog will eat 6 lb a day.

ICA food supplies are restricted to at most 100 lb of food each day. Poodles require 1000 hr of training per year, while a sled dog requires 250 hr/yr. The academy restricts training time to no more than 10,000 hr each year. How many of each kind of dog should the ICA breed in order to maximize their profit? Find the maximum yearly ICA profit if each poodle will sell for a profit of $200 and each sled dog will sell for a profit of $80.

3. The Elite Tweet Pottery Shoppe budgets a maximum of $1,000/mo for newspaper and radio advertising. The newspaper charges $50 per ad and requires at least four ads per month. The radio station charges $100/min and requires a minimum of 5 min of advertising per month. It is estimated that each newspaper ad reaches 8,000 people and that each minute of radio advertising reaches 15,000 people. What combination of newspaper and radio advertising should the business use in order to reach the maximum number of people? What assumptions did you make in solving this problem? How realistic do you think they are?

4. A small South American country grows coffee and cocoa for export. The country has 500,000 hectares of land available for the crops. It has contracts that require at least 100,000 hectares be devoted to coffee and at least 200,000 hectares to cocoa. Available equipment and labor limit cocoa production to 270,000 hectares. Coffee requires two workers per hectare while cocoa requires five workers per hectare. No more than 1,750,000 workers are available. Coffee provides a profit of $220 per hectare and cocoa provides a profit of $310 per hectare. How many hectares should the country devote to each crop in order to maximize profit? Find the maximum profit.

5. A small electric generating plant is making a decision involving a mixture of low-sulfur (2%) and high-sulfur (6%) oil. The final mixture must have a sulfur content of not more than 4%. At least 1200 barrels of oil are needed. Low-sulfur oil costs $18.50 per barrel and high-sulfur oil costs $14.70 per barrel. How much of each type of oil should be used to keep the cost of oil at a minimum? What is the minimum cost?

Take Another Look 9.7

Have you wondered why so much attention has been given to the vertices (corner points) of feasible regions? For example, the vertex points were specifically identified in the solution to Maria's dietary dilemma in Section 9.6. In fact, the least-expensive cost in the equation $Cost = 0.06x + 0.30y$ was located at one of the five corners.

According to the corner-point principle, if a maximum value or minimum value of a linear expression $P = Ax + By$ exists, it will occur at a corner point of the feasible region. The following investigation will help you understand why this is true. Take some time to graph the six constraint inequations that outline the feasible region pictured at the beginning of Section 9.6.

Now your task is to identify the smallest cost, or smallest value, of $Cost$ in the equation $Cost = 0.06x + 0.30y$. Start by substituting $Cost = \$1.20$ and graph the equation $1.20 = 0.06x + 0.30y$. Then substitute $Cost = \$1.02$ and graph the equation

$1.02 = 0.06x + 0.30y$. You should repeat these steps with each value of *Cost* that was calculated during the solution. What discovery have you made concerning the graphs of this series of equations *Cost* $= 0.06x + 0.30y$?

The graphs of a series of equations $P = Ax + By$ will always be parallel regardless of the value you use for *P*. What is the slope of the lines in these graphs? Solutions for (x, y) must be points within the feasible region. Now can you see why the maximum or minimum value will occur at a corner point? In you own words, explain why you think this will be true.

It is possible that a maximum or minimum value will occur at more than one point. Explain how this can happen.

Project

Nonlinear Programming

Make a complete and accurate graph of the following system of inequations. Locate and label all vertices of the feasible region.

$$3x + 4y \leq 72$$
$$x^2 - 3y \geq 9$$
$$5x + 2y^2 \geq 50$$
$$0.5x - 10^y \leq 4$$

Graph $(x - 10)^2 + (y - 5)^2 = k$ for $k = 25, 50, 75$ on top of the feasible region. What is the largest possible value for *k* for which the graph of this equation still contains a point in the feasible region? Where is this point?

Describe any differences you found between optimizing this system of inequations containing nonlinear inequations and the linear programming problems in the chapter.

Section 9.8

Determinants and System Classification

The chief object of education is not to learn things, but to unlearn things.
—G. K. Chesterton

Inconsistent systems have no solutions. Dependent systems have an infinite number of solutions. In these two special situations, the coefficient matrix will not have an inverse. If you get an error message when trying to solve a system by using matrices and their inverses, you'll know that the system is either dependent or inconsistent.

If the coefficient matrix, A, has no inverse and you ask for A^{-1}, you will get an error message on your calculator. This error message means you must then determine if the system is dependent or inconsistent. In a 2×2 system, you will have to check to see if a point selected from one equation will or will not work in the other equation. If it works, the system is dependent.

■ Example 1

Examine the system

$$3.2x + 2.4y = 9.6$$
$$2x + 1.5y = 6.$$

Solution

$$\begin{bmatrix} 3.2 & 2.4 \\ 2.0 & 1.5 \end{bmatrix} \begin{bmatrix} x \\ y \end{bmatrix} = \begin{bmatrix} 9.6 \\ 6.0 \end{bmatrix}$$

$$\begin{bmatrix} x \\ y \end{bmatrix} = \begin{bmatrix} 3.2 & 2.4 \\ 2.0 & 1.5 \end{bmatrix}^{-1} \begin{bmatrix} 9.6 \\ 6.0 \end{bmatrix} \Rightarrow \text{ERROR}$$

The next step is to find a point that satisfies the first equation. If $x = 1$, then

$3.2(1) + 2.4y = 9.6$, so $y = \frac{9.6 - 3.2}{2.4} = \frac{8}{3}$ and $\left(1, \frac{8}{3}\right)$ is on the first line.

The point $\left(1, \frac{8}{3}\right)$ also works in the second equation because $2(1) + 1.5\left(\frac{8}{3}\right) = 6$. Therefore, the system is dependent. ■

An inverse matrix is found by a long process (the larger the matrix, the longer the process). In this process, small errors tend to magnify themselves. The calculator, even though it may have 12 or more digits of accuracy, sometimes gives an inverse to a matrix when the inverse should not exist.

NOTE

9B

The det *A*, **determinant of matrix *A*,** is a single value or measure associated with a square matrix that you can use to determine whether a matrix has an inverse. (See **Calculator Note 9B.**) Use your calculator to verify that det $\begin{bmatrix} 2 & 1 \\ 4 & 3 \end{bmatrix}$ = 2. What is the determinant, det *B*, for *B* = $\begin{bmatrix} 2 & 6 \\ 3 & 5 \end{bmatrix}$?

Investigation 9.8.1

A Matrix Without an Inverse

Part 1 Assign each group member two of the problems below. When you've finished working the problems, share your results.

Find the inverse and determinant for each 2 × 2 matrix. Some matrices will not have an inverse. Determine a connection between the value of det *A* and the existence of an inverse, A^{-1}.

a. $A = \begin{bmatrix} 2 & 6 \\ 3 & 5 \end{bmatrix}$ **b.** $A = \begin{bmatrix} 7 & 2 \\ 3 & 4 \end{bmatrix}$ **c.** $A = \begin{bmatrix} 3 & 1 \\ 5 & 1 \end{bmatrix}$ **d.** $A = \begin{bmatrix} 2 & 6 \\ 4 & 12 \end{bmatrix}$

e. $A = \begin{bmatrix} 2 & 3 \\ 1 & 4 \end{bmatrix}$ **f.** $A = \begin{bmatrix} \frac{3}{4} & \frac{-1}{2} \\ 3 & -2 \end{bmatrix}$ **g.** $A = \begin{bmatrix} 8 & -3.5 \\ -2 & 1 \end{bmatrix}$ **h.** $A = \begin{bmatrix} 0.6 & -0.4 \\ 0.6 & -0.4 \end{bmatrix}$

Part 2 **a.** Find values for *e* and *f* so that the 2 × 2 matrix $\begin{bmatrix} 2 & 6 \\ e & f \end{bmatrix}$ doesn't have an inverse.

b. What do you notice about the entries in the matrix?

c. Write a hypothesis concerning 2 × 2 matrices that have no inverses.

d. Test your hypothesis by completing the missing elements in the matrix $\begin{bmatrix} 8 & -3.5 \\ -?- & -?- \end{bmatrix}$ so that it has no inverse.

e. What is the determinant, det *A*, for *A* = $\begin{bmatrix} a & b \\ c & d \end{bmatrix}$?

In the seventeenth century, several Chinese mathematics textbooks were imported into Japan by way of Korea allowing Japanese mathematicians to study Chinese algebra and develop it further. In 1683, Takakazu Seki (1642-1708), a Japanese mathematician, discussed determinants for higher degree equations in his book *Kaifukudai no hō (Method of Solving the Dissimulated Problems)*. Ten years later in Europe, the German mathematician, philosopher, and diplomat Gottfried Wilhelm Leibniz (1646-1716) wrote about a similar idea. But no work on determinants was published in Europe until around 1729 when the Scottish mathematician Colin Maclaurin (1678-1746) produced his *A Treatise of Algebra in Three Parts,* in which he discussed determinants for systems of four equations in four unknowns. Leibniz's work on determinants wasn't published until 1850.

Gottfried Wilhelm Leibniz

■ Example 2

Governor Lyle Lott has made some promises to his constituents. He promised the upper class that 20% of their taxes would be spent on the environment, 11% on increasing jobs, and 31% on education. He promised the middle class that 25% of their taxes would be spent on the environment, 8% on creating new jobs, and 33% on education. He promised the poor that 5% of their tax dollars would go to the environment, 31% on increased jobs, and 36% on education. Now he must raise taxes to cover the budget. He needs $18 billion for the environment, $34 billion for new jobs, and $74 billion for education. Explain to the governor the difficulties his promises will cause him.

Solution

The governor sets the taxes at x dollars from the upper class, y dollars from the middle class, and z dollars from the poor.

$$0.20x + 0.25y + 0.05z = 18$$
$$0.11x + 0.08y + 0.31z = 34$$
$$0.31x + 0.33y + 0.36z = 74$$

or

$$\begin{bmatrix} 0.20 & 0.25 & 0.05 \\ 0.11 & 0.08 & 0.31 \\ 0.31 & 0.33 & 0.36 \end{bmatrix} \begin{bmatrix} x \\ y \\ z \end{bmatrix} = \begin{bmatrix} 18 \\ 34 \\ 74 \end{bmatrix}$$

$$\det \begin{bmatrix} 0.20 & 0.25 & 0.05 \\ 0.11 & 0.08 & 0.31 \\ 0.31 & 0.33 & 0.36 \end{bmatrix} = 0 \quad \text{(It may read } 4.6 \cdot 10^{-15} \text{ on your calculator.)}$$

This means (1) there are an infinite number of solutions and the governor has no problems, or (2) there are no solutions, and he again must break a promise. You need three dimensions to visualize this situation because each equation involves three variables, and a three-variable equation determines a plane. If the system is dependent, then the planes intersect in either a line or a plane. If they intersect in a plane, then all three equations must represent the same plane. If they intersect in a line, they resemble three pages of an open book that all intersect in the binding.

If the equations are inconsistent, then the three planes do not have a common point. There are several ways in which you could have an inconsistent system given these equations in three unknowns. The three planes could intersect in three lines, any two of which are parallel; or two of the planes could be parallel, with the third

intersecting them in two parallel lines; or all three planes could be parallel, with at least one of them distinct from the other two.

Start by assuming that the planes intersect in a line. Any two of the planes determine this line and the third is redundant. You need to find the coordinates of one point on this line. To do this, edit the coefficient matrix so that the first row is [1 0 0]. This creates a new system, equivalent to asking where the line meets the plane $x = 0$ (the y-z plane). The solution to this new system gives you the coordinates of one point on the line of intersection of the two planes. Test this point that is on the line of intersection by substituting into the original first equation. If the point satisfies the original first equation, your system is dependent; otherwise, it is inconsistent.

Show that the new coefficient matrix has an inverse by finding its determinant value.

$$\det \begin{bmatrix} 1 & 0 & 0 \\ 0.11 & 0.08 & 0.31 \\ 0.31 & 0.33 & 0.36 \end{bmatrix} = {}^{-}0.0735$$

Find the solution point for the following system:

$$\begin{bmatrix} 1 & 0 & 0 \\ 0.11 & 0.08 & 0.31 \\ 0.31 & 0.33 & 0.36 \end{bmatrix}^{-1} \begin{bmatrix} 18 \\ 34 \\ 74 \end{bmatrix} = \begin{bmatrix} 18 \\ 131.7415 \\ 69.2925 \end{bmatrix}.$$

Substitute the coordinates of this point (18, 131.7415, 69.2925) into the original first equation.

$$0.20(\mathbf{18}) + 0.25(\mathbf{131.7415}) + 0.05(\mathbf{69.2925}) = 40 \neq 18$$

Because this point is not a solution of the original first equation, you know that the governor lied and broke a promise.

Unfortunately, the process described in this example will not work if the line is parallel to the y-z plane, or if the remaining two equations do not intersect in a line (they represent the same plane, or parallel planes). If the determinant is still zero after replacing the first equation, then replace the second row of the matrix with [0 1 0], leaving only the third row intact. When you have produced a point, then test the point in both equations to find if the system is dependent (all equations work) or inconsistent (at least one equation does not work). ■

The ideas presented in this section are true for all linear systems whether they have two variables, ten variables, or more. With more than three variables, the visual or geometric meaning breaks down, but the algebraic meaning remains the same. The method is not 100% foolproof and will still give false results if you end up with a column of zeros.

Problem Set 9.8

1. Use the determinant of the coefficient matrix to determine whether or not each system has a unique solution.

   a. $2x + 3y = 16$
   $5x + 7.5y = 40$

   b. $12.75x - 18.21y = 45.32$
   $3.25x + 5.12y = 9.71$

   c. $2x + y - 4z = 21$
   $7x + 5y + z = 63$
   $3x + 2y - z = 28$

   d. $7.13x - 2.14y + 11.6z = 15.2$
   $9.12x + 5.7y - 8.25z = 21.7$
   $13.7x + 7.12y + 4.41z = 18.11$

   e. $2.5x + 7.1z = 16$
   $3.1x - 2.4y = 12$
   $6y + 22.01z = 9$

   f. $5w + 4x - 3y + 2z = 1$
   $7w - 4x + 5y + z = 8$
   $3w + 2x + y - 6z = 5$
   $4w + 3x - y - 2z = 6$

2. Classify each system in Problem 1 that does not have a unique solution as inconsistent or dependent. Explain your reasoning.

3. Your social studies teacher has decided that the next test will contain questions that will fall into one of four categories: true/false, fill-in-the-blank, matching, or short essay. Each true/false question will be worth 2 points, fill-in-the-blank questions will be worth 4 points each, matching questions will be worth 6 points each, and essays will be worth 10 points each. The test will total 100 points. True/false questions will be designed to take 1 min each, fill-in-the-blank questions will take 2 min each, matching questions will take 5 min each, and essay questions will take 6 min each. The test will last 1 hr. The true/false questions will each use 4 lines of a page, the fill-in-the-blank questions will each use 3 lines, matching questions will each use 15 lines, and the essays will each use 9 lines. The test will fill two pages. There are 110 lines available. Give the teacher as much help as you can so she can plan the test.

4. **a.** Create your own linear system of three unknowns that is dependent.
   b. Create your own linear system of three unknowns that is inconsistent.

5. The title of this chapter is *Systems of Equations*. Although this title is appropriate, suggest another title that is more interesting yet still conveys what the chapter is about. Explain your title and justify why you think it is a good choice.

6. If you had to choose a favorite problem from this chapter, which one would it be? Why?

Take Another Look 9.8

Every day when Penny Wise comes home, she places the dimes and quarters she has collected that day in a glass jar. When she emptied the jar and counted the money one day, she found that she had collected $38.80. How many of each type of coin does she have?

Investigate this problem and write your conclusions. Your solution strategy can be as simple or as complicated as you choose. In fact, one elegant strategy could use two parametric equations to represent the number of dimes and quarters. But your conclusions should contain a response to each of the following.

a. What are the maximum and minimum number of coins she could have?

b. What combinations of coins are possible? How many different solutions are there?

c. Is it possible for the number of dimes to equal the number of quarters?

d. How many of each does she have if she has 250 coins?

e. Clearly explain your solution strategy for this problem.

Project

Inverse by Hand

There are several different methods for finding the inverse of a 3×3 matrix that were used before calculators were available in the mathematics classroom. Find out about two different methods. Use one method to find the inverse of the first matrix, and use the other method to find the inverse of the second matrix. Show that your new matrix is the inverse of the original matrix by multiplying the original matrix by its inverse without using a calculator.

a. $\begin{bmatrix} 4 & 3 & 2 \\ 2 & 1 & 3 \\ 2 & 2 & 4 \end{bmatrix}$
 b. $\begin{bmatrix} -1 & 4 & 3 \\ -0.5 & -3 & 2 \\ -2 & 6 & 7 \end{bmatrix}$

Chapter Review

Any path is only a path . . . look at every path closely and deliberately. Try it as many times as you think is necessary. Then ask yourself, and yourself alone, one question. . . . Does this path have a heart? If it does, the path is good; if it doesn't it is of no use.
—Carlos Castaneda

To solve a system of two equations means you must find the point (or points) where the graphs intersect. If the two equations are lines, then there will be either one solution (intersecting lines), no solutions (parallel lines), or an infinite number of solutions (two equations of the same line). There are several methods to find points of intersection. One is to graphically zoom in on the point until you can determine its coordinates with the desired accuracy. You can also zoom in numerically by using a table. In addition to these methods, there are algebraic techniques. One such technique is substitution. Another, called elimination, involves multiplying either one or both of the equations by specially selected values so that when the resulting equations are added together, one variable is eliminated. A third algebraic method involves the use of matrices. For systems that involve more than three equations and three variables, the matrix method is by far the simplest.

When the system is made up of inequations, the solution is a region in the plane. One important use of systems of inequations is in linear programming. In linear programming problems once the feasible region is determined, an equation for a quantity that is to be optimized is evaluated at the vertices of this region. If only integer points in the region are acceptable and the vertices are not at points with integer coordinates, then points near each vertex need to be investigated. In solving systems with matrices, you may sometimes get an error message on your calculator. This happens because not every matrix has an inverse. The determinant of a matrix is a measure associated with the matrix that can tell you if an inverse exists. The value of the determinant is zero for a matrix without an inverse.

Problem Set 9.9

1. Locate each point of intersection of the two curves $y = {}^-(x - 3)^2 + 5$ and $y = x^2 - 1$. Give all answers to the nearest thousandth.

2. When two lines have very similar slopes it is difficult to graphically find the point of intersection.

a. Find the best graphing window to see the intersection of $y_1 = 3.2x - 4$ and $y_2 = 3.1x - 3$.

b. Graph $y_3 = y_1 - y_2$. What is a good window setting for viewing the intersection of y_3 with $y = 0$ (the x-axis)?

c. Write the equation obtained by substituting the y-value from y_1 into y_2.

d. Solve the equation from 2c for x.

e. Explain why this solution is the same as the x-intercept for y_3.

3. Use substitution to solve each system.

a. $y = 6.2x + 18.4$

$y = {}^-2.1x + 7.40$

b. $y = \frac{3}{4}x - 1$

$\frac{7}{10}x + \frac{2}{5}y = 8$

4. Use elimination to solve each system.

a. $3x + 2y = 4$
$^-3x + 5y = 3$

b. $5x - 4y = 5$
$2x + 10y = 2$

5. Identify each system as dependent or inconsistent.

a. $y = {}^-1.5x + 7$

$y = {}^-3x + 14$

b. $y = \frac{1}{4}(x - 8) + 5$

$y = 0.25x + 3$

c. $2x + 3y = 4$

$1.2x + 1.8y = 2.6$

d. $\frac{3}{5}x - \frac{2}{5}y = 3$

$0.6x - 0.4y = {}^-3$

6. Find the inverse, if it exists, of each matrix.

a. $\begin{bmatrix} 2 & {}^-3 \\ 1 & {}^-4 \end{bmatrix}$

b. $\begin{bmatrix} 5 & 2 & {}^-2 \\ 6 & 1 & {}^-0 \\ {}^-2 & 5 & 3 \end{bmatrix}$

c. $\begin{bmatrix} {}^-2 & 3 \\ 8 & {}^-12 \end{bmatrix}$

d. $\begin{bmatrix} 5 & 2 & {}^-3 \\ 4 & 3 & {}^-1 \\ 7 & {}^-2 & {}^-1 \end{bmatrix}$

7. Solve each system by using matrix multiplication.

a. $8x - 5y = 17$
$6x + 4y = 33$

b. $4w + x + 2y - 3z = {}^-11$
$^-3w + 2x - y + 4z = 20$
$5w + 4x + 6y - z = {}^-10$
$^-2w + 3x + 5y + 7z = {}^-45$

8. Sketch a graph of the region described by each system of inequations. Find the coordinates of each vertex. Then find the point with integer coordinates that gives the maximum value for the final expression.

a. $2x + 3y \le 12$
$6x + y \le 18$
$x + 2y \ge 2$
$x \ge 0, y \ge 0$
maximize $1.65x + 5.2y$

b. $x + y < 50$
$10x + 5y < 440$
$40x + 60y < 2400$
maximize $6x + 7y$

9. Heather (Walter Heether's neighbor) has an electric water heater in need of repair. The repairman says it will cost $300 to fix the unit. She could buy a new gas water heater for $500 including installation, and the new heater would save her 60% of her annual $75 operating costs. How long would it take for the new unit to pay for itself?

10. Art Easte needs a particular color that is five parts red, six parts yellow, and two parts black. Not having the pure colors at his disposal, he finds three color mixtures that he can use. The first is two parts red and four parts yellow, the second is one part red and two parts black, and the last is three parts red, one part yellow, and one part black.

   a. Write an equation that gives the correct portion of red by using the three available color mixtures.

   b. Write an equation that gives the correct portion of yellow and another equation that gives the correct portion of black.

   c. Solve the system.

   d. Find an integer that can be used as a multiplier for your solutions in 10c to provide integer solution values.

   e. Explain your solutions in real-world terms.

11. In this chapter, you looked at ways to solve systems of equations for both two and three variables. Explain the similarities and differences between the graphs of two-variable systems of equations and those of three-variable systems of equations.

12. How has your ability to do mathematics changed through the year? Do you feel that your abilities have improved? Explain.

Assessing What You've Learned

Organizing Your Notebook
   • By now you should have mastered notebook organization. All it takes is a few minutes of maintenance each day.

Keeping a Journal
   • Look in Problem Sets 9.5, 9.8, and 9.9 for journal prompts.

Portfolio
   • How would you assess your portfolio? Are you happy with the work you've chosen? Does your portfolio really reflect your mathematical growth this year? Start thinking about what you would like your final portfolio to look like.

Performance Assessment
   • Choose a problem involving a system of equations. Demonstrate to someone that you know how to solve it using several different methods.

Open-ended Investigations

- Choose one of the Take Another Look investigations or a project, or design your own investigation. Share your results with a classmate, your group, or your teacher.

Constructing Test Questions

- Write several test questions that you think would be useful in determining whether or not a student understands the concepts presented in this chapter.

Group Presentations and Tests

- Did your group function well when working on investigations and problems in this chapter? What were the strengths of your group? What could your group have done differently to improve how they functioned?

Overall Self-Assessment

- Are you pleased with your efforts in this chapter? Do you feel that you were a good learner? How would you assess your overall performance?
- Give yourself a grade for this chapter and justify it.

10

Polynomials

The multiflash records the action of a ping-pong ball during a 1.5-second rally. Using a process called *finite differences*, you can sometimes find a polynomial model to fit a set of data. The family of polynomial functions includes the familiar quadratic function, which can be expressed in a variety of different forms. You can also use polynomial functions to model many different situations including bank balances, absorption of medications, and area and volume relationships.

Finite Differences

Experience is a comb that life gives you after you lose your hair.
—Judith Stern

What would happen if you deposited $100 in a savings account on your fourteenth birthday and continued to deposit $60 on each birthday thereafter? If r is the annual interest rate, then the annual balances of your account would be

100	at 14 years old,
$100(1 + r) + 60$	at 15 years old,
$100(1 + r)^2 + 60(1 + r) + 60$	at 16 years old,

and so on.

The money in your account would grow as the bank compounded interest and you deposited more money. If the interest rate was 6.5%, then immediately after your sixteenth birthday the account value could be represented by the equation below.

Value of first deposit	+	value of second deposit	+	new deposit	=	Total
$100(1 + 0.065)^2$	+	$60(1 + 0.065)$	+	60	=	$237.32
or						
$100(1.065)^2$	+	$60(1.065)$	+	60	=	$237.32

■ Example 1

What similar bank deposit situation does $50(1.08)^2 + 70(1.08) + 90$ represent?

Solution

The expression can model the value of an account that earns 8% interest, beginning immediately after an original birthday deposit of $50, and two more birthday deposits of $70 and $90. ■

■ Example 2

Your friend Penny had a similar account worth $193.84 when she was 16. What interest rate did her three $60 deposits earn?

Solution

You need to find an x-value that satisfies the equation $60x^2 + 60x + 60 = 193.84$. What choice of x works? You can find out by graphing and locating the intersection of $y_1 = 60x^2 + 60x + 60$ and $y_2 = 193.84$. You can see from looking at the table that the *x*-value is between 1 and 1.1. Zoom in on the table values or on the graph. (See the graph on the left below.) You can also find the *x*-value by graphing $y_1 - y_2$ and locating the positive *x*-intercept. (See the graph on the right below.)

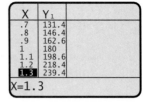

Method 1:

$y_1 = y_2$

$60x^2 + 60x + 60 = 193.84$

Method 2:

$y_1 - y_2 = 0$

$60x^2 + 60x + 60 - 193.84 = 0$

$60x^2 + 60x - 133.84 = 0$

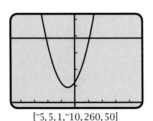

$[^-5, 5, 1, ^-10, 260, 50]$

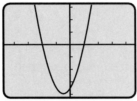

$[^-5, 5, 1, ^-160, 120, 50]$

Only the positive *x*-value has any real meaning in this problem. Repeated zooming gives $x = 1.075$. (Check this result on your calculator.) Therefore, the annual interest rate that provides \$193.84 during this time span is 7.5%. ∎

The equations for your account and Penny's considered only three years of deposits. They also had three **terms**. If the deposits continued for five years, the equation would look like $y = 60x^4 + 60x^3 + 60x^2 + 60x + 60$. This equation is called a **polynomial** equation because it is the sum of terms whose variables have only positive whole-number powers. The highest power of *x* in this equation is 4, so it is called a fourth-**degree** polynomial equation.

Investigation 10.1.1

Falling Objects

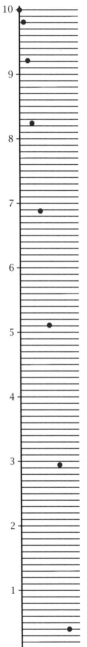

The picture at the right is based on a photograph taken of an object dropped from a height of 10 meters. The photograph was taken in a dark room with a flash that fired every 0.2 second. Carefully determine and record the heights of the ball at each flash, measuring to the nearest 0.01 meter. Record this information in a table like the one below. Read your measurements carefully and check them with others in your group. Accurate measurements are very important.

Time (sec)	0.0	0.2	0.4	0.6	...	...
Height (m)	10.00	-?-	-?-	-?-	-?-	-?-
D_1		-?-	-?-	-?-	-?-	-?-
D_2			-?-	-?-	-?-	-?-

Subtract each pair of consecutive heights (second height minus first height, third height minus second height, and so on) and record the differences in the row labeled D_1. These are called the **first differences**. Do a similar subtraction process on pairs of entries from row D_1 and record the differences in row D_2. These are called the **second differences**. This process is called finding the **finite differences.** You will use this table of information in the next section.

You can predict the degree of a polynomial that fits a set of data whose x-values are in an arithmetic sequence if you follow the steps below.

Step 1 Find the finite differences of the y-values by subtracting consecutive values.

Step 2 Check to see if the first differences, D_1, are all equal nonzero numbers. If the differences are all equal nonzero numbers, then the polynomial that fits the data is linear.

Step 3 If the first differences are not all equal nonzero numbers, then calculate D_2, the finite differences of the D_1 values.

Step 4 Check the second differences, D_2. If they are all equal nonzero numbers, then the polynomial that fits the data points is second degree.

Step 5 If the second differences are not all equal nonzero numbers, continue the subtraction process. If row n is the first row in which the differences D_n are equal nonzero numbers, the polynomial has degree n.

Sometimes an approximate fit is the best you can do with measured data, and you will have to be content with finite differences of *approximately* equal nonzero numbers in D_n.

Investigation 10.1.2
Diagonals of Polygons

In this investigation you will find an equation that expresses the relationship between the number of sides and the number of diagonals of a polygon.

a. First you need to collect the data. Draw a four-sided polygon, a five-sided polygon, a six-sided polygon, and so on. Connect the nonconsecutive vertices of each polygon to form all of the diagonals. Copy and complete the table below. Compare your results with the results of other members in your group.

Number of sides (s)	4	5	6	7	8	9
Number of diagonals (d)	2	–?–	–?–	–?–	–?–	–?–

b. Calculate the finite differences and use them to predict the degree of the relationship. Because these data are not measured, but exact, you will find the differences in one of the levels of finite differences to be exactly equal.

c. Enter the data into your calculator and graph them. Choose one of the data points and call it (s, d).

d. Substitute the coordinates of point (s, d) from part c into the equation $d = as^2 + bs + c$ to get an equation in terms of a, b, and c.

e. Choose two other points and repeat the process from part d. You now have a system of three equations and three unknowns. Solve the system to find values for a, b, and c.

f. Use the values for a, b, and c from part e to write an equation. Graph this equation to verify that it fits your data points.

g. Use your model to predict the number of diagonals in an octagon and the number in a dodecagon (12 sides).

h. How many sides will a polygon with 230 diagonals have?

When using the process developed in Investigation 10.1.2 to find a best-fit equation for measured data, you must choose your points carefully. When the data are measured, as they are in Investigation 10.1.1, your equation will most likely not fit all of the data points exactly. You will find a better-fitting model for all of the data points by choosing three representative points that are not close together.

The method of finite differences was used by the Chinese astronomer Li Chunfeng in the seventh century to find a quadratic equation to express the sun's apparent motion across the sky as a function of time. The Iranian astronomer Ghiyāth al-Dīn Jamshīd Mas'ūd al-Khashī, who worked at the Samarkand observatory of Sultan Ulugh Beg in the fifteenth century, also used finite difference methods when calculating the celestial longitudes of planets.

Finite difference methods were further developed in seventeenth- and eighteenth-century Europe. They were used to eliminate calculations involving multiplication and division when constructing tables of polynomial values. Some functions, such as logarithms and trigonometric functions, are not given by polynomials. These function values could be calculated, however, by approximating the function with a polynomial and then evaluating that polynomial. Before electronic calculators became available in 1972, tables of functions were extremely important. It was not uncommon for a late-eighteenth-century European scientist to have over 125 volumes of various kinds of tables.

The method of finite differences was also used in the design of nineteenth-century automatic calculating machines called difference engines. Some were built in Sweden by Martin Wiberg and by the father-and-son team Georg and Edvard Scheutz. These machines were used to produce the values for mathematical tables to be published.

Problem Set 10.1

1. Meg Abux opens a savings account by depositing $10,000. The annual interest, i, is compounded monthly. At the end of the second month, $5,000 is added. At the end of the fourth month, $2,000 is added. (Nothing is added at the end of the first or third month.)

   a. Write an expression for the balance in the account at the end of the fourth month, using x to represent the multiplier $(1 + i/12)$.

   b. Name x-values that will provide a good graphing window. (Use common sense to estimate values for i, the interest rate.)

   c. Use your calculator to trace the graph of the curve and find the x-value needed to give a balance of $17,300 at the end of the fourth month.

   d. What is the annual interest rate, i?

2. Dr. Jeck L. Hyde takes 30 mg of a medication that will disappear from his blood at a rate of p percent per day.

   a. In writing an expression to represent the amount of the medication remaining in his blood, will you use $\left(1 + \dfrac{p}{100}\right)$ or $\left(1 - \dfrac{p}{100}\right)$ as your multiplier? Give a reason for your choice.

   b. Write an expression (using x as the multiplier) that gives the amount in Dr. Hyde's blood after three full days have passed.

   c. What x-value leaves 5 mg of the medication in his blood after three days?

   d. What percentage of the medication, p, is removed each day?

3. Dr. Hyde takes 50 mg of a medication on day 1, 70 mg on day 2, and 90 mg on day 3. This medication disappears at a rate of q percent per day.

   a. Write an expression, using x as the multiplier $\left(1 - \dfrac{q}{100}\right)$, that gives the amount of medication in Dr. Hyde's blood after three days.

   b. What x-value leaves 50 mg of the medication in his blood?

   c. What percentage of the medication is removed each day?

4. **a.** The equation $s = 0.5n^2 + 0.5n$ generates triangular numbers. Copy the table below and enter the triangular numbers in the row labeled s.

   b. Find the finite differences D_1 and D_2 between the consecutive values of s.

n	1	2	3	4	5	6	7
s	-?-	-?-	-?-	-?-	-?-	-?-	-?-
D_1		-?-	-?-	-?-	-?-	-?-	-?-
D_2			-?-	-?-	-?-	-?-	-?-

c. What is the degree of the polynomial function in 4a? How is this degree related to the finite differences?

d. Why do you think triangular numbers (the *s* row above) are called triangular? Answer in complete sentences. (Hint: You might want to create a geometric dot pattern.)

5. The data in 5a and 5b represent the heights of separate objects at different times during their falls. Compute the finite differences until one of D_1, D_2, and so on, consists of all *nonzero constants*.

a.

Time in sec (*t*)	0	1	2	3	4	5	6
Height in m (*h*)	80	95.1	100.4	95.9	81.6	57.5	23.6

b.

Time in sec (*t*)	0	1	2	3	4	5	6
Height in m (*h*)	4	63.1	112.4	151.9	181.6	201.5	211.6

c. Use what you know about the finite differences to predict the degree of the equation that you would use to model each data set.

d. Find the equation that will fit the data in 5a.

6. You can use blocks to build pyramids such as those shown below. All of the pyramids are solid with no empty space inside.

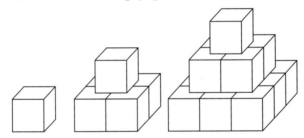

a. Copy and complete the table to show the number of layers in each pyramid and the number of blocks needed to build it.

Layers (*n*)	1	2	3	4	5	6
Blocks (*b*)	-?-	-?-	-?-	-?-	-?-	-?-

b. Use finite differences to find the degree of the relationship.

c. Write an equation for this relationship. (Hint: You will need to use four points to build your equation.)

d. Use your model to predict the number of blocks needed to build a pyramid eight layers high.

e. Graph and trace the curve to find the number of layers in a pyramid built with 650 blocks.

Section 10.2

Different Quadratic Forms

It is hard to fight an enemy who has outposts in your head.
—Sally Kempton

You have seen how polynomial equations can be used to represent bank balances, the levels of medication in the bloodstream, geometric patterns, and other applications. Often you are able to use finite differences to find the polynomial equation that models a set of data. And you've learned that one way to solve a polynomial equation is to graph and trace. However, a polynomial equation can be written in a variety of different forms, and each form is useful depending on what you want to do with the equation. In this section and the next, you will learn about three different forms in which you can express a polynomial equation.

Investigation 10.2.1

Patterns of Squares

Determine the number of 1-centimeter segments used to create each figure and complete the table below.

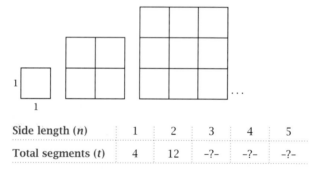

Side length (n)	1	2	3	4	5
Total segments (t)	4	12	-?-	-?-	-?-

Calculate the finite differences until you have a common value. Find the equation (in terms of n and t) to fit these data. When you have found the equation, test its graph to see that it contains the data.

You might recognize the graph of the equation in Investigation 10.2.1 as a parabola. You can write the equation of this parabola as $t = 2(n + 0.5)^2 - 0.5$, although this probably doesn't look like the equation you found. Are the two equations equivalent? How can you tell? Are there other forms for quadratic equations? When is one form better than another? These are questions that you will explore in this section and the next.

One way to determine whether
$t = 2(n + 0.5)^2 - 0.5$ and $t = 2n^2 + 2n$ are
equivalent equations is to see if their graphs are
the same. You may have to trace both graphs
and check the coordinates. Another way to
determine if the equations are equivalent is to
use some algebra to remove the parentheses in
the first expression.

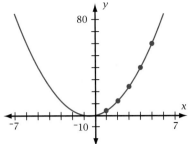

$2(n + 0.5)^2 - 0.5$	Original expression.
$2(n^2 + 0.5n + 0.5n + 0.25) - 0.5$	Multiply $(n + 0.5)(n + 0.5)$.
$2(n^2 + n + 0.25) - 0.5$	Add like terms.
$2n^2 + 2n + 0.5 - 0.5$	Multiply $2(n^2 + n + 0.25)$.
$2n^2 + 2n$	Add like terms.

This final expression is the same one that you found in Investigation 10.2.1.

In Section 10.3, you will explore a third popular form for the quadratic equation, $2n(n + 1)$. Here is a summary of the forms in which you can write a quadratic equation.

Polynomial form	$y = ax^2 + bx + c$	$2n^2 + 2n$
Vertex form	$y = A(x - H)^2 + K$	$2(n + 0.5)^2 - 0.5$
Factored form	$y = A(x - R_1)(x - R_2)$	$2(n - 0)(n + 1)$

Problem Set 10.2

Use a "friendly" graphing window for most of the graphs in this problem set. A background grid may also be helpful.

1. Each quadratic equation below is written in vertex form. Graph each function. Then remove the parentheses to write each equation in polynomial form. Graph the new form of the quadratic equation to check that you removed the parentheses correctly.
   a. $y = (x - 2)^2 + 3$
   b. $y = (x + 4)^2 - 2$
   c. $y = 2(x - 5)^2 - 4$
   d. $y = -0.5(x + 1)^2 + 4$
   e. $y = -3(x - 4)^2$
   f. $y = 1.5(x - 0)^2 - 3$

2. Write each equation without parentheses.
   a. $y = -0.5(x + H)^2 + 4$
   b. $y = A(x - 4)^2$
   c. $y = A(x - H)^2 + K$

3. Write an equation in vertex form that describes each *transformation* of $y = x^2$. Next, use algebra to remove the parentheses and rewrite the equation in polynomial form. Finally, graph both forms of the equation to make certain your new equation is correct.
   a. Slide the graph 3 units left and then 2 units down.
   b. Reflect the graph over the x-axis, slide it 4 units right, and move it 3 units up.
   c. Stretch the graph so that the y-values double, slide it 2 units right, and move it 4 units down.
   d. Multiply the y-values by -0.5, slide the graph 1.5 units left, and move it up 3 units.

e. Stretch the graph by a factor of *A* vertically, slide it *H* units right, and slide it *K* units up. (You won't be able to graph this equation without assigning values to *A*, *H*, and *K*.)

4. Find the values of *a*, *b*, and *c* for each equation.
   a. $ax^2 + bx + c = 3x^2 + 2x - 5$
   b. $ax^2 + bx + c = 3x^2 + (2 + d)x + 14s^2$
   c. $ax^2 + bx + c = 2(x + 3)^2 + 4$
   d. $ax^2 + bx + c = {}^-3(x - 5)^2 - 1$

5. Suppose $ax^2 + bx + c = A(x - H)^2 + K$. (Use the answer to Problem 2c to find the coefficients of x^2, *x*, and the constant.)
   a. $ax^2 + bx + c = \underline{-?-}\, x^2 + \underline{-?-}\, x + \underline{-?-}$
   b. What is the relationship between *a* and *A*?
   c. Set the coefficients of the *x*-terms equal to each other, and solve for *H*. Substitute *a* for *A*, and find *H* in terms of *a* and *b*.
   d. Set the two constants equal to each other, and solve for *K*. Substitute your answers from 5b and 5c, and find an expression for *K* in terms of *a*, *b*, and *c*.
   e. Explain how you can check that your values give the same equation.

6. Use the results from Problem 5 to find the vertex of each parabola. Write each equation in vertex form. Check your work by graphing.
   a. $y = 3x^2 - 13x + 12$ **b.** $y = x^2 + 6x + 11$ **c.** $y = x^2 + 2x - 8$
   d. $h(t) = {}^-16t^2 + 44t + 5$ **e.** $y = {}^-2x^2 + 5x + 9$

7. The temperature you perceive often depends on the wind speed. This phenomenon is called the wind-chill factor. The following information is collected at a temperature reading of 30°F. At 5 mi/hr, the wind chill is 27°F; at 20 mi/hr, it is 4°F; and at 40 mi/hr, it is ⁻5°F. Find a quadratic model for these data and locate the vertex.

8. The local outlet store charges $2 for a pack of AAA batteries. On the average, 200 packs are sold each day. A survey indicates that the sales will decrease by an average of five packs per day for each $0.10 increase in price.
   a. Use the information given to complete the row labeled "number sold."

Selling price	2.00	2.10	2.20	2.30	2.40
Number sold	200	-?-	-?-	-?-	-?-
Revenue	-?-	-?-	-?-	-?-	-?-
D_1		-?-	-?-	-?-	-?-
D_2			-?-	-?-	-?-

b. Calculate the revenue using the selling price and the number sold. Then calculate the first and second differences.

c. Write an equation that describes the relationship between the revenue, y, and the selling price, x, charged per pack.

d. Graph the equation and find the maximum revenue. What selling price provides maximum revenue?

9. You are designing a rectangular garden and you need a fence to keep the varmints out. You have 80 m of fence and are trying to determine the largest possible area for your garden.

a. Complete the following table for the widths provided.

Width	5	10	15	20	25
Length	–?–	–?–	–?–	–?–	–?–
Area	–?–	–?–	–?–	–?–	–?–

b. Find an equation relating the area and the width of the garden.

c. Which width provides the largest possible area? What is that area?

d. Describe a situation that produces no area.

e. Describe a situation that produces a negative area.

10. a. Use three points from your (*time, height*) data in Investigation 10.1.1 to find an equation that will fit the curve.

b. Enter your equation in y_1 and set an appropriate graphing window. Record the window settings.

c. Trace the curve and match the points in the illustration for Investigation 10.1.1 to the points on your graph. Give the differences (residuals) for each point. Use the residuals to help you modify your equation to get the best fit that you can.

Section 10.3

Factored Polynomials

Men occasionally stumble over the truth, but most of them pick themselves up and hurry off as if nothing happened.
—*Winston Churchill*

You discovered that the formula for the number of diagonals in a polygon of n sides is $d = 0.5n^2 - 1.5n$. How can you find the number of sides if you are told there are 230 diagonals? You can graph and trace the curve until you find the point where the y-value is 230. Or you can make a table and look up the correct value there. Another technique is to write a new equation, $0.5n^2 - 1.5n = 230$. Then subtract 230 from each side to get $0.5n^2 - 1.5n - 230 = 0$. Graph this new equation. The solutions to this equation will be the x-values where the new graph crosses the x-axis. These values are called the **roots** of the equation. In this section, you will learn how to write equations of polynomials when you know the roots. You will also learn about one more form of a polynomial equation, the factored form, and how it relates to the roots of the equation.

Investigation 10.3.1

Open-Top Boxes

You will need graph paper and scissors for this activity.

a. Have each group member cut several 16-unit by 20-unit rectangles out of graph paper.

b. By cutting a square with sides of length x from each corner of the rectangle, as shown at right, your group will construct open-top boxes. Use *all* possible integer values of x.

c. Record the dimensions of each box and calculate the box's volume. Prepare a table showing the x-values and volumes of the boxes. Collect the data from other group members and complete the table.

d. Use finite differences to find the degree of the relation. Write an equation that gives the volume, V, in terms of x, the side length of the removed square.

e. Graph the equation and determine the x-intercepts. (There are three.) Call these three values r_1, r_2, and r_3. What happens if you try to make boxes by using these values as x? What x-values make sense in this context?

f. Graph the equation $y = (x - r_1)(x - r_2)(x - r_3)$, as well as the equation you found in part d. What are the similarities and differences between the graphs? How can you alter the second equation to make the graphs of the two equations identical?

g. In general, if the side length of the removed square is x, what will be the length and width of the finished box? What will be its height? Use this information to write an expression for the volume of the box. How does this expression relate to the equation you found in part d?

Consider each graph pictured below. The x-intercepts have been marked.

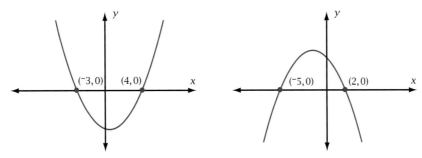

It should be no surprise that the y-coordinate is zero at each x-intercept. In fact, every point on the x-axis has a y-coordinate of zero. You will use this information and the **zero-factor property** to find the x-intercepts.

Think of numbers that multiply to zero: $a \cdot b = 0$. Whatever numbers you substitute to make this statement true will have the following characteristic: *At least one of the factors must be zero.* Complete each statement below so that it is true. Compare your answers with those of others in your group.

$$\underline{?} \cdot 16.2 = 0 \qquad 3(\underline{?} - 4)(\underline{?} - 9) = 0 \qquad {}^-1.4(x - 5.6)(x + 3.1) = 0$$

■ Example 1

Suppose $y = {}^-1.4(x - 5.6)(x + 3.1)$. Look at the graph and the equation and name the x-intercepts. What are the coordinates of the vertex?

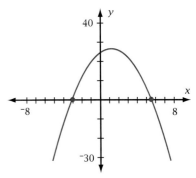

Solution

The x-intercepts will be the two x-values that make $y = 0$.

$$0 = {}^-1.4(x - 5.6)(x + 3.1)$$

5.6 works because ${}^-1.4(\mathbf{5.6 - 5.6})(5.6 + 3.1) = 0$.

${}^-3.1$ works because ${}^-1.4({}^-3.1 - 5.6)(\mathbf{{}^-3.1 + 3.1}) = 0$.

Because parabolas have reflection symmetry, the x-coordinate of the vertex is halfway between the x-coordinates of the intercepts (it is the average of the two x-coordinates at the intercepts). Therefore, the vertex has as its x-coordinate

$$\frac{(-3.1 + 5.6)}{2} = 1.25.$$

You can substitute this value into the original equation to find the y-coordinate of the vertex: $y = -1.4(1.25 - 5.6)(1.25 + 3.1) = 26.4915$. Therefore, the vertex is at $(1.25, 26.4915)$.

So $H = 1.25$, $K = 26.4915$, and $A = -1.4$.

Vertex form $\qquad y = A(x - H)^2 + K \qquad y = -1.4(x - 1.25)^2 + 26.4915$

Expanding either the factored form or vertex form gives you

Polynomial form $\qquad y = ax^2 + bx + c \qquad y = -1.4x^2 + 3.5x + 24.304.$ ■

■ Example 2

Build an equation for a graph with x-intercepts at -2.5, 7.5, and 3.2.

Solution

The x-intercept of -2.5 means $(x + 2.5)$ is a factor because $(-2.5 + 2.5) = 0$. Likewise, 7.5 means $(x - 7.5)$ is a factor, and 3.2 means $(x - 3.2)$ is a factor. So the **factored form** $y = A(x - r_1)(x - r_2)(x - r_3)$ is $y = A(x + 2.5)(x - 7.5)(x - 3.2)$.

You can choose different values for A and experiment to see what effect each choice will have on the graph. You will soon be able to predict the effect produced by different positive or negative values of A.

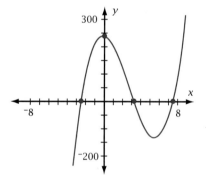 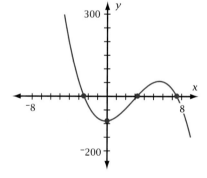

The equation of the graph on the left is $y = 4(x - 7.5)(x + 2.5)(x - 3.2)$. Notice that the x-intercepts are correct. The y-intercept has 0 as an x-value. Substituting $x = 0$ into the equation gives 240 as the y-intercept. The equation of the graph on the right has the same x-intercepts. The equation is $y = -1.5(x - 7.5)(x + 2.5)(x - 3.2)$. Substituting $x = 0$, you find the y-intercept is -90. ■

Problem Set 10.3

1. **a.** Find the *x*-intercepts and *y*-intercept of $y = 2.5(x - 7.5)(x + 2.5)(x - 3.2)$.
   b. Remove the parentheses and write the equation in polynomial form.
   c. Graph the polynomial form to check your work.

2. A projectile is shot from the bottom of a well. It comes
   up to ground level after 0.7 sec and falls back to ground
   level again at 2.8 sec.
   a. Complete the equation of this graph using the points
   $(0.7, 0)$ and $(2.8, 0)$: $y = {}^-4.9(\, -?- \,)(\, -?- \,)$. The height
   (in meters) is given by *y*, and the time is represented
   by *x*.
   b. Find the vertex. What is the real-world meaning of
   this value?
   c. Find the *y*-intercept. What is the real-world meaning
   of this value?
   d. If $^-4.9$ is changed to a different nonzero number,
   what varies in the graph? What stays the same?

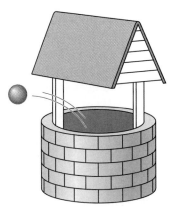

3. Find the *x*-intercepts and *y*-intercept for the graph of each equation, without actually
   graphing. If the equation represents a parabola, find the vertex. Check each answer by
   graphing.
   a. $y = {}^-0.25(x + 1.5)(x + 6)$ **b.** $y = 3(x - 4)(x - 4)$
   c. $y = {}^-2(x - 3)(x + 2)(x + 5)$ **d.** $y = 5(x + 3)(x + 3)(x - 3)$

4. Sketch a graph for each description.
   a. A quadratic equation with one *x*-intercept
   b. A quadratic equation with no *x*-intercepts
   c. A cubic equation with one *x*-intercept
   d. A cubic equation with two *x*-intercepts

5. **a.** Write the factored form of the equation for each graph. Make certain the graph
   passes through the points indicated.

   i.
   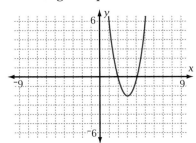

   ii.
   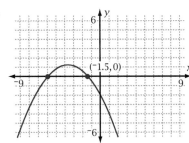

   b. Write the polynomial form of the equation for each graph.
   c. Write the vertex form of the equation for each graph.

6. Let $y_1 = x + 2$ and $y_2 = x - 3$. Graph y_1, y_2, and $y_3 = y_1y_2$. How does the graph of y_3 compare to the graphs of y_1 and y_2?

7. a. Write the equation of the polynomial of least degree that contains the x-intercepts pictured.

    b. Adjust the leading factor A so that it contains the y-intercept $(0, 180)$. You may need to do some exploring to find an A-value that works.

    c. Write the equation that contains points that are exactly 100 units up from the graph pictured.

    d. Write the equation that contains points that are exactly four units left of the points pictured.

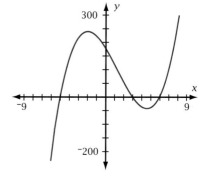

8. The area of each figure below can be expressed as a quadratic expression. Express the area of each figure in (i) factored form and (ii) polynomial form.

a.

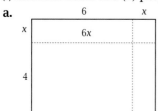

b.

9. a. Fill in the blanks for each figure.

    i.

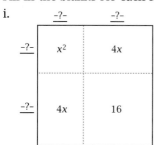

    ii.

    b. Express the area of each figure above in factored form and polynomial form.

10. Write each polynomial in factored form. (Use area models if you wish, or graph the polynomials and look for x-intercepts.)

    a. $x^2 - 10x + 24$ **b.** $x^2 - 6x + 9$ **c.** $x^2 - 64$

    d. $x^2 - 2x - 120$ **e.** $4x^2 - 88x + 480$ **f.** $6x^2 - 7x - 5$

    g. $x^2 - (R_1 + R_2)x + R_1R_2$ **h.** $a^2 + 2ab + b^2$

11. a. Is it possible to find a quadratic polynomial that contains the points $(-4, -2)$, $(-1, 7)$, and $(2, 16)$? Explain why or why not.

    b. Find a quadratic polynomial that has vertex $(-2, 3)$ and contains the point $(4, 12)$.

Section 10.4

The Quadratic Formula

Knowledge is of two kinds. We know a subject ourselves, or we know where we can find information upon it.
—*Samuel Johnson*

Algebra came to Europe through Latin translations of Arabic texts. Most of these translations were done in Spain. One of the most influential of these texts was *Hisab al-jabr wa'l-muqabala* (*The Book of Restoration and Confrontation*), written around A.D. 825 by Muhammad ibn Musa al-Khwārizmī and first translated into Latin in 1145. Al-Khwārizmī, who extended the Babylonians' geometric representation of algebraic concepts, was interested in finding roots of polynomial equations whereas the Babylonians wanted to find expressions to represent side lengths. The ideas expressed by these early mathematicians led to a process called factoring.

Very few quadratic functions can be solved by factoring. Although you can always graph the function and trace to find the x-intercepts, you are often not able to find exact solutions. In this section, you will learn about an algebraic formula that you can always use to find the exact solutions to a quadratic function.

The polynomial $x^2 - 6x + 9$ is a perfect square because both factors are the same: $x^2 - 6x + 9 = (x - 3)^2$. Another perfect-square polynomial is $x^2 + 16x + 64$, because $x^2 + 16x + 64 = (x + 8)^2$.

Each large rectangle below is a pictorial representation of a perfect square. The areas of the smaller rectangles represent the terms of the polynomial, and the side lengths represent the factors.

$$(x + 5)(x + 5) = (x + 5)^2$$
$$= x^2 + 5x + 5x + 25$$
$$= x^2 + 10x + 25$$

	x	5
x	x^2	$5x$
5	$5x$	25

$$(a + b)(a + b) = (a + b)^2$$
$$= a^2 + ab + ab + b^2$$
$$= a^2 + 2ab + b^2$$

	a	b
a	a^2	ab
b	ab	b^2

■ **Example 1**

Suppose you start with an equation and want to find the x-values, or the roots, that satisfy the equation. If you already have a perfect square like $(x + 3)^2 = 16$, it's easy.

Solution

$$x + 3 = \pm\sqrt{16}$$
$$x + 3 = \pm 4$$
$$x = \pm 4 - 3$$
$$x = 1 \quad \text{or} \quad x = {}^-7$$

Check this result by calculating $(\mathbf{1} + 3)^2$ and $({}^-\mathbf{7} + 3)^2$. ■

■ **Example 2**

Find the x-intercepts (also called zeros) of an unstretched parabola that opens upward with a vertex at $({}^-3, {}^-16)$.

Solution

The graph $y = (x + 3)^2 - 16$ crosses the x-axis when

$$(x + 3)^2 - 16 = 0 \quad \text{or}$$
$$(x + 3)^2 = 16.$$

So the x-intercepts are at 1 and $^-7$. Check this result by graphing. ■

Solving quadratic equations is routine when the expression is already written as a perfect square or in *vertex form*. In general, when $y = A(x - H)^2 + K$, you can find the zeros, or roots, by using this process.

Start with $A(x - H)^2 + K = 0$.	Replace y with zero.
$A(x - H)^2 = {}^-K$	Add ^-K to both sides.
$(x - H)^2 = \dfrac{{}^-K}{A}$	Multiply both sides by $\dfrac{1}{A}$.
$(x - H) = \pm\sqrt{\dfrac{{}^-K}{A}}$	Take the square root of both sides.
$x = H \pm \sqrt{\dfrac{{}^-K}{A}}$	Add H to both sides.

Notice that there are two zeros, $x = H + \sqrt{\dfrac{{}^-K}{A}}$ and $x = H - \sqrt{\dfrac{{}^-K}{A}}$.

Because all parabolas have a vertex and can be written in vertex form, you can use the formula given above for x to find the zeros of any parabola.

■ **Example 3**

Find the zeros, or x-intercepts, of $y = {}^-3(x - 2)^2 + 5$.

Solution

$$x = H \pm \sqrt{\frac{-K}{A}} = 2 \pm \sqrt{\frac{-5}{-3}} \approx 2 \pm 1.291 = 3.291, \; -0.709 \quad \blacksquare$$

Suppose you want to find the *x*-intercepts and the equation is in polynomial form, $y = ax^2 + bx + c$. You must either rewrite the equation in vertex form or create a modified formula that uses *a*, *b*, and *c* instead of *A*, *H*, and *K*. You have already made the connection between the coefficients of $ax^2 + bx + c$ and $A(x - H)^2 + K$ (Problem Set 10.2, Problem 5).

$$A = a, \quad H = \frac{-b}{2a}, \quad \text{and} \quad K = c - \frac{b^2}{4a}.$$

Start with $\qquad x = H \pm \sqrt{\dfrac{-K}{A}}$.   The zeros in vertex form.

$$x = \frac{-b}{2a} \pm \sqrt{\frac{-\left(c - \frac{b^2}{4a}\right)}{a}} \qquad \text{Substitute for } H, K, \text{ and } A.$$

$$x = \frac{-b}{2a} \pm \sqrt{\frac{\frac{b^2}{4a} - c}{a}} \qquad \text{Remove the parentheses.}$$

$$x = \frac{-b}{2a} \pm \sqrt{\frac{\frac{b^2}{4a} - \frac{4ac}{4a}}{a}} \qquad \text{Rewrite with a common denominator.}$$

$$x = \frac{-b}{2a} \pm \sqrt{\frac{b^2 - 4ac}{4a^2}} \qquad \text{Rewrite as a simple fraction.}$$

$$x = \frac{-b}{2a} \pm \frac{\sqrt{b^2 - 4ac}}{\sqrt{4a^2}} \qquad \text{Simplify again.}$$

$$x = \frac{-b}{2a} \pm \frac{\sqrt{b^2 - 4ac}}{2a} \qquad \text{Simplify the radical in the denominator.}$$

$$x = \frac{-b \pm \sqrt{b^2 - 4ac}}{2a} \qquad \text{Rewrite using the common denominator.}$$

The Quadratic Formula

Vertex form

If $A(x - H)^2 + K = 0$, then the solutions are $x = H \pm \sqrt{\dfrac{-K}{A}}$.

Polynomial form

If $ax^2 + bx + c = 0$, then the solutions are $x = \dfrac{-b \pm \sqrt{b^2 - 4ac}}{2a}$.

■ **Example 4**

Find the *x*-intercepts of $y = x^2 - 14x - 26$.

Solution

$x^2 - 14x - 26 = 0$ $a = 1$, $b = {}^-14$, and $c = {}^-26$.

$x = \dfrac{{}^-({}^-14) \pm \sqrt{({}^-14)^2 - 4(1)({}^-26)}}{2(1)}$ (Be careful with the parentheses.)

$x = \dfrac{14 \pm \sqrt{300}}{2(1)}$

$x = 7 \pm 0.5\sqrt{300}$ (The **exact** answers.)

The x-intercepts are at $7 + 0.5\sqrt{300} \approx 15.66$ and $7 - 0.5\sqrt{300} \approx {}^-1.66$. Do these values agree with the values found by tracing the graph? ■

Many problems that involve objects under the influence of the earth's gravity can be modeled using polynomial equations. The distance measurements for projectile motion problems are normally in either meters or feet. The initial coefficient of the polynomial used to model this motion is related to the acceleration due to gravity, g, for which the numerical value depends on whether you're using the English or metric system of measurement. In the metric system, g is 9.8 m/sec². In the English system, it is 32 ft/sec². The initial coefficient of the polynomial is $({}^-1/2)g$. You can write equations representing projectile motion in $y=$ form using the variable x or in parametric form using t.

■ ### Example 5

Ovida Fentz hits a baseball so that it travels at a speed of 120 ft/sec and at an angle of 30° to the ground (horizontal). If his bat contacts the ball at a height of 3 ft above the ground, how far does the ball travel before it hits the ground?

Solution

You can best model this situation by viewing the ball's motion as a parametric curve and breaking the motion into its horizontal and vertical components. This situation resembles problems you have done before, except that the ball leaves the bat at an angle. Draw a picture and write equations for the x- and y-components of the motion.

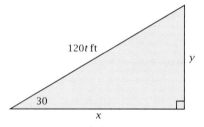

$\cos 30° = \dfrac{x}{120t}$ $\sin 30° = \dfrac{y}{120t}$

$x = 120t \cos 30°$ $y = 120t \sin 30°$

Because the x-direction of the motion is affected only by Ovida hitting the ball, the horizontal distance will be given by $x = 120t \cos 30°$. The vertical motion is affected by Ovida hitting the ball and also by the force of gravity pulling the ball down. In this case, the equation becomes $y = {}^-16t^2 + 120t \sin 30° + 3$. Notice that this equation is a second-degree polynomial. What is the meaning of the 3 in the equation? What is the meaning of the $^-16t^2$? If you want to find out when the ball hits the ground, you need to know when the y-value is 0. You can trace the graph, but now you also have the algebraic tools to solve the equation.

$^-16t^2 + 120t(0.5) + 3 = 0$	Evaluate sin 30°.
$^-16t^2 + 60t + 3 = 0$	Multiply.
$a = {}^-16, b = 60, c = 3$	Identify values of a, b, and c for the quadratic formula.
$t = \dfrac{^-60 \pm \sqrt{60^2 - 4(^-16)(3)}}{2(^-16)}$	Substitute into the quadratic formula.
$t \approx {}^-0.049, 3.799$	Evaluate the quadratic formula and take the positive root. (Why do you ignore the negative root?)

The t-value of 3.799 means the ball reaches the ground 3.799 sec after being hit. To determine how far the ball has traveled, substitute this t-value into the x-equation.

$x = 120(3.799) \cos 30° \approx 394.84$ ft ■

When an object is projected straight upward (like a rocket, or like a ball thrown straight up), the situation can be modeled with one equation for y in terms of t.

■ **Example 6**

An object is projected upward with a velocity of 40 ft/sec from a starting height of 4 ft. When will the object hit the ground?

Solution

The height of the object at time t is represented by the equation $y = {}^-16t^2 + v_0 t + s_0$ because the heights are in feet. The initial velocity, v_0, is 40 ft/sec and the initial height, s_0, is 4 ft. Because the distance is measured in feet, the initial coefficient is $^-16$. Thus, the equation is $y = {}^-16t^2 + 40t + 4$. To find the time when the object will hit the ground, set $y = 0$. So $^-16t^2 + 40t + 4 = 0$, $a = {}^-16$, $b = 40$, and $c = 4$.

$$x = \frac{^-b \pm \sqrt{b^2 - 4ac}}{2a} \quad \text{will become} \quad t = \frac{^-40 \pm \sqrt{(40)^2 - 4(^-16)(4)}}{2(^-16)}, \quad \text{or}$$

$$t = \frac{^-40 \pm \sqrt{1856}}{^-32}.$$

Therefore, $t \approx {}^-0.096$ or $t \approx 2.596$.

Because negative solutions make no sense in this problem, the time must be 2.596 sec. Check this result by graphing the equation. ■

The methods used in Examples 5 and 6 for writing equations to model projectile motion problems are summarized in the box below.

Projectile Motion Equations

Parametric model

$x = v_0 t \cos A + x_0$; $y = at^2 + v_0 t \sin A + y_0$, where x = horizontal motion, y = vertical motion, x_0 = horizontal start, y_0 = vertical start, $a = {}^-4.9$ or ${}^-16$, v_0 = initial velocity, and A = initial angle.

Function model

$y = ax^2 + v_0 x + s_0$, where y = height in meters or feet, $a = {}^-4.9 \text{ m/sec}^2$ or ${}^-16 \text{ ft/sec}^2$, x = time in seconds, v_0 = initial velocity in m/sec or ft/sec, and s_0 = initial height in meters or feet.

Investigation 10.4.1

Getting Sunburned

The data in the table below were published in the *Mesa* (Arizona) *Tribune* on August 8, 1993. It gives the number of minutes needed to redden untanned Caucasian skin at different times of the day based on the predicted weather for that day.

Time	9 a.m.	10 a.m.	11 a.m.	Noon	1 p.m.	2 p.m.	3 p.m.	4 p.m.
Minutes	34	20	15	13	14	18	32	60

Plot the data and find an equation to fit the curve. Explain why you think the equation you found is the best-fit equation. What is an appropriate domain for your equation? Use your equation to determine at what times of the day skin will burn in 30 min. Do you think the equation would be different for a different part of the country? Explain your reasoning.

Problem Set 10.4

1. Factor each polynomial.
   a. $4x^2 - 12x + 9$
   b. $x^2 + 5x + \dfrac{25}{4}$
   c. $x^2 - 2xy + y^2$

2. Solve for x.

a. $(x - 2.3)^2 = 25$ **b.** $(x + 4.45)^2 = 12.25$ **c.** $\left(x - \dfrac{3}{4}\right)^2 = \dfrac{25}{16}$

3. Rewrite each equation in polynomial form. Identify a, b, and c, and solve for x using the quadratic formula. Express each solution in exact form and as a decimal approximation to the nearest 0.001.

a. $3x^2 - 13x = 10$ **b.** $x^2 - 13 = 5x$ **c.** $3x^2 + 5x = {}^{-}1$

d. $3x^2 - 2 - 3x = 0$ **e.** $14(x - 4) - (x + 2) = (x + 2)(x - 4)$

4. Find the time and position when the projectile described by each pair of equations reaches the ground.

a. $x = 5t - 3$
$y = {}^{-}4.9t^2 + 5t + 7$

b. $x = 7t + 2$
$y = {}^{-}16t^2 + 2t + 100$

c. $x = 9$
$y = {}^{-}4.9t^2 - 3.17t + 470$

5. Write a quadratic polynomial for each situation described.

a. Solutions 3 and $^{-}3$ **b.** Solutions 4 and $\dfrac{{}^{-}2}{5}$ **c.** Solutions R_1 and R_2

d. A projectile shot from the bottom of a well that reaches ground level at 1.1 sec and 4.7 sec.

6. Use the quadratic formula to find the x-intercepts (to the nearest 0.01) for $y = 2x^2 + 2x + 5$. Explain your dilemma. Is there a way to recognize this situation without using the formula? Write another quadratic equation that has no x-intercepts.

7. Assume that the table below gives the minimum stopping distance (in feet) required to stop a car traveling at the given speed on dry pavement.

Speed (mi/hr)	10	20	30	40	50	60	70
Stopping distance (ft)	19	42	73	116	173	248	343

a. Write a quadratic equation that contains any three points in the data.
b. Compare your equation to those of others in your group. Did everyone get the same equation? Why or why not?
c. Describe a method for selecting data points that builds the most accurate model of the given information.

8. In Example 4, you found $7 + 0.5\sqrt{300}$ and $7 - 0.5\sqrt{300}$ as the solutions to $x^2 - 14x - 26 = 0$. Substitute these exact answers for x to verify that they work.

9. A 20 ft ladder is leaning against a building.
a. Write an equation for y in terms of x.
b. Find the height of the building if the foot of the ladder is 10 ft from the building.
c. Find the distance of the foot of the ladder from the building if the ladder must reach 18 ft up the wall.
d. Write both the *name* and *statement of the formula* you used to write the equation in 9a.

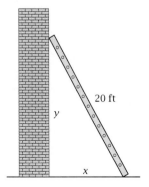

10. Write a calculator program that uses the quadratic formula to solve equations. The program should prompt the user to *input* values for *a*, *b*, and *c* for equations in the form $ax^2 + bx + c = 0$, and it should *calculate* and *display* the two solutions. Your program can be quite elaborate or very simple.

11. Great Gonzo, the human cannonball, is fired out of a cannon at a speed of 40 ft/sec. The cannon is tilted at an angle of 60°. A 10 ft diameter net is hung 10 ft above the floor at a distance of 30 ft from the cannon. Does Gonzo land in the net? Record the equations you used to model this motion.

12. So far in this chapter you have looked at three different forms for a quadratic expression or equation. Discuss each of the forms, explaining why and in what situation you might prefer to use that form.

Take Another Look 10.4

Take another look at the quadratic function $y = ax^2 + bx + c$. Is the graph of (x, y) predictable as *c* varies? A quick look should indicate that the graph just slides up or down for different *c*-values, which are actually the *y*-intercepts. In fact, the vertex of the parabola also moves up and down along a vertical line.

1. This activity will help you discover what happens to the vertex location of a series of parabolas when *b* and *c* are held constant but *a* varies. The equation $h(t) = -\frac{1}{2}gt^2 + v_0t + h_0$ models the height of a ball when thrown straight up in the air. For example, $h(t) = -4.9t^2 + 23t + 2$ models the height of a ball when thrown straight up in the air at 23 m/sec from an initial height of 2 m. The initial coefficient, -4.9, is $-\frac{1}{2}g$, where *g* is the acceleration due to the earth's gravity in meters per second per second, or m/sec². This simplified model ignores many factors, including the effect of air resistance.

   a. Graph the (*time, height*) relationship expressed in the equation $h(t) = -4.9t^2 + 23t + 2$. Then find and explain the meaning of the coordinates at the vertex of the parabola.

   b. Consider what would happen if you were on the surface of another planet. Imagine tossing a ball upward at 23 m/sec from an initial height of 2 m on the surface of each planet (or moon) listed in the table. Ignore the physical or practical restrictions involved. Use the generic form of the projectile motion equation, $h(t) = -\frac{1}{2}gt^2 + v_0t + h_0$, to write a specific equation for each planet not marked with an asterisk. For each equation you write, use $v_0 = 23$ as the initial velocity, $h_0 = 2$ as the initial height, and the value of *g* provided in the table.

Planet	Acceleration due to gravity	Time to maximum height (sec)	Maximum height (m)
Mercury	3.92	-?-	-?-
Venus	8.82	-?-	-?-
Earth	9.80	-?-	-?-
Mars*	3.92	-?-	-?-
Jupiter	26.46	-?-	-?-
Saturn	11.76	-?-	-?-
Uranus*	9.80	-?-	-?-
Neptune*	9.80	-?-	-?-
Pluto*	not available	-?-	-?-
Our moon	1.67	-?-	-?-
Our sun	274.4	-?-	-?-

c. When you graph these equations on the same coordinate axis, you will see a pattern in the location of the vertices. Locate the maximum height, and the corresponding time, for a ball thrown from each celestial surface. Find a least-squares regression model, $y = ax + b$, that fits these vertex data values, (*time, maximum height*).

2. In this part of the activity, you will look at the pattern formed by the vertices of the parabolas when a and c are held constant and b varies. Graph a family of equations based on $h(t) = {}^-4.9t^2 + v_0 t + 2$ for a variety of different initial velocities (perhaps $5 \leq v_0 \leq 50$ in increments of 5 m/sec^2). These equations represent the height of a ball that is thrown upward from the surface of the earth. Locate the vertex for each graph. As the initial velocity changes, the maximum point, or vertex, appears to be located on a parabola. Find a quadratic model that fits these vertex points (*time, maximum height*) for the Earth data.

Section 10.5

Applications and Algebraic Solutions

Information's pretty thin stuff unless mixed with experience.
—Clarence Day

So far in this chapter you have explored a variety of methods for solving quadratic equations. You have used graph-and-zoom techniques as well as several algebraic methods. In this section you will explore a variety of real-world applications for these techniques. Keep in mind that often there is more than one way to solve a problem. As you work the problems, share, compare, and discuss your methods with others.

■ Example 1

What interest rate provides a total value of $193.84 after three $60 deposits on Nick's fourteenth, fifteenth, and sixteenth birthdays?

Solution

In Section 10.1, you graphed and located the intersection of $y_1 = 60x^2 + 60x + 60$ and $y_2 = 193.84$ by tracing and zooming. (See the graph on the left below.) You also obtained the same solution for x by graphing $y_1 - y_2$ and locating the positive x-intercept. (See the graph on the right below.)

$y_1 = y_2$ or $y_1 - y_2 = 0$
$60x^2 + 60x + 60 = 193.84$ $60x^2 + 60x + 60 - 193.84 = 0$
                                                    $60x^2 + 60x - 133.84 = 0$

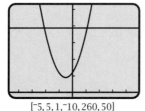

$[\text{-}5, 5, 1, \text{-}10, 260, 50]$

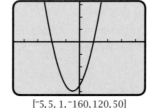

$[\text{-}5, 5, 1, \text{-}160, 120, 50]$

Instead of tracing and zooming, you could also find the solution by using the quadratic formula.

$60x^2 + 60x - 133.84 = 0$ $a = 60, b = 60, c = \text{-}133.84$

$x = \dfrac{\text{-}60 \pm \sqrt{60^2 - 4(60)(\text{-}133.84)}}{2(60)} \approx 1.07501 \text{ or } \text{-}2.07501$

Because you are looking for growth, the negative solution is **extraneous**, which means it has no meaning in this situation. Therefore, the annual interest rate is approximately 7.5%. ■

■ Example 2

An object is thrown vertically upward at 38 m/sec from a height of 55 m. Give the equation for the object's height. How high does it get? When does it hit the ground?

Solution

The equation describing the height from the ground at any time t is

$$H(t) = {}^-4.9t^2 + 38t + 55.$$

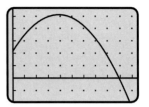

Ground level is the x-intercept, so use the quadratic formula to solve the equation when $H(t) = 0$.

$$t = \frac{{}^-b \pm \sqrt{b^2 - 4ac}}{2a} = \frac{{}^-38 \pm \sqrt{(38)^2 - 4({}^-4.9)(55)}}{2({}^-4.9)} = 9.002 \quad \text{or} \quad {}^-1.247$$

Again, the negative answer is extraneous, so the time in the air is approximately 9.002 sec. The maximum height of the parabola is at the vertex (H, K). Because the vertex is located on the line of symmetry, the roots will be equally distant from that vertex on opposite sides. The average of these two roots will give the x-value of the point halfway between.

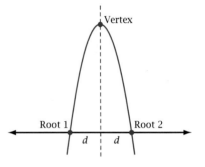

$$H = \frac{{}^-1.247 + 9.002}{2} \approx 3.88$$

Substitute this x-value into the original equation to find the y-value of the vertex: $K = {}^-4.9(3.88)^2 + 38(3.88) + 55 \approx 128.67$. ■

Investigation 10.5.1

Making a Suitcase

You will need graph paper and scissors for this activity.

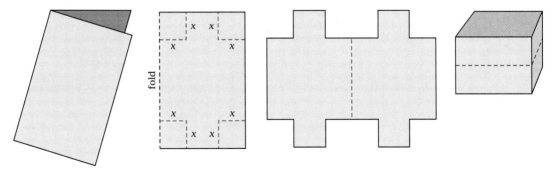

a. Fold a piece of paper in half as shown above. (Each member of the group should choose a different x-value.) Then, using your x-value for the length of the side of the square, cut four equal-sized squares from the corners and fold your paper to form a box with a top. Determine the volume of your box.

b. Write an equation in factored form (in terms of x) for the volume of the box.

c. What x-values make sense in this context?

d. What x-value will give the box with the greatest volume? What is the maximum volume?

e. Did anyone in your group construct the box with maximum volume? If not, construct this maximum-volume box. Compare this box to other boxes that your group constructed. Does it look like it has the greatest volume? Explain.

Problem Set 10.5

Solve each problem using algebraic manipulation and formulas. When appropriate, you can check your solutions with a graph.

1. An object is dropped from the top of a building into a pool of water at ground level. The splash occurs 6.8 sec after the object is dropped. How high is the building in meters? In feet?

2. An object was projected upward and the following data were collected.

Time in sec (t)	1	2	3	4	5	6
Height in m (h)	120.1	205.4	280.9	346.6	402.4	448.4

a. Write the specific equation relating time and height for this object.
b. What was the initial height? The initial velocity?
c. At what time did the object reach its maximum height?
d. What was the maximum height?
e. At what time was the object 300 m high?
f. At what time did the object hit the ground?

3. The local discount store charges $6.60 for a flashlight. On the average, 200 of them are sold each day. A survey indicates that the sales will decrease by an average of ten flashlights per day for each $.50 increase in price.
a. Write an equation that describes the relationship between the revenue, y, and the selling price, x, charged per flashlight. (A table might help.)
b. What selling price provides maximum revenue?

4. You are enclosing a rectangular area to create a dog run. You have 80 ft of fence and want to build a pen with the largest possible area for your dog, so you build the dog run using an existing building as one side. Find the areas for some selected values of x.

a. Write an equation relating the area, y, and width, x.

b. What width provides the largest possible area? What is that area?

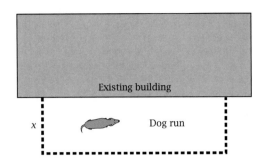

Existing building

x Dog run

5. a. Write a formula relating the greatest number of pizza pieces, y, you can obtain from x cuts.

b. Use the formula to find the maximum number of pieces with five cuts and with ten cuts. Is there a greatest number of pieces? Explain why or why not.

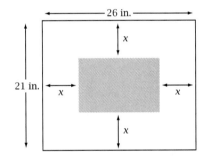

One cut   Two cuts   Three cuts

6. This 26 in. by 21 in. rectangle has been divided into two regions. The width of the unshaded border region is x inches.

a. Express the area (A) of the shaded part as a function of x and graph it.

b. Determine what x-values and A-values make sense.

c. Find the x-value that makes the two regions (shaded and unshaded) equal in area.

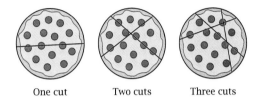

7. A new $11,000 car is financed at 7.5% annual interest. Interest is charged on the unpaid monthly balance. Let $x = 1 + \dfrac{0.075}{12}$. Write a quadratic equation that provides the balance after two payments of M dollars each.

8. The Mathematics Club plans to sell mathematical T-shirts. They can purchase the shirts for $6.50 each. They surveyed 400 students to determine the highest price each would be willing to pay for a T-shirt. These data are summarized in the following table.

Price ($)	8.00	8.50	9.00	9.50	10.00	10.50	11.00
Number of students	400	373	344	313	280	245	208
Profit	–?–	–?–	–?–	–?–	–?–	–?–	–?–

a. Write an equation relating price charged and profit.

b. Determine the price that will result in the maximum possible total profit.

c. What price would result in a profit of $0.00?

9. The data in the table represent the amount of water in a draining bathtub and the amount of time since the plug was pulled.

Amount of water (L)	38.4	30.0	19.6	7.2
Time (min)	1	1.5	2	2.5

a. Write an equation expressing liters (L) in terms of time (t).

b. How much water was in the tub when the plug was pulled?

c. How long did it take the tub to empty?

Higher-Degree Polynomials

*Everybody gets so much information all day long that they lose their
common sense.*
—Gertrude Stein

Earlier in the chapter you looked at equations like $60x^2 + 60x + 60 = 149.544$. There
are many interpretations of this equation. Consider a regular daily dose of
medication, and let x represent the rate at which the medication is absorbed by the
body. (If x represents the absorption rate and the elimination rate is 18% per day,
then $x = (1 - 0.18)$.) In this case, the first term, $60x^2$, represents the amount of a
60 mg dose remaining after two days. The second term, $60x$, represents the amount
of a 60 mg dose remaining after one day. The third term, 60 mg, represents the
dose taken at the beginning of the third day. The sum, 149.544 mg, represents the
total amount remaining in the body after two days plus the dose taken at the
beginning of the third day.

■ Example 1

Suppose 60 mg of a medication is taken daily for
three days. Then the dose is reduced to 40 mg on
the fourth day and 25 mg on the fifth day.
Allowing for different elimination rates (a%) for
different people, let $x = 1 - a/100$. What is the
expression that gives the amount of medication in
the system?

Solution

60	at day 1
$60x + \mathbf{60}$	at day 2
$60x^2 + 60x + \mathbf{60}$	at day 3
$60x^3 + 60x^2 + 60x + \mathbf{40}$	at day 4
$60x^4 + 60x^3 + 60x^2 + 40x + \mathbf{25}$	at day 5

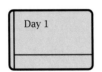   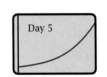

The first term, $60x^4$, gives the amount of the first day's dose that remains after four
days. The second term, $60x^3$, gives the amount of the second day's dose that remains
after three days, and so on. Five different types of polynomials are used in this
example.

$$y = 60$$ constant polynomial (zero degree)
$$y = 60x + 60$$ linear polynomial (first degree)
$$y = 60x^2 + 60x + 60$$ quadratic polynomial (second degree)
$$y = 60x^3 + 60x^2 + 60x + 40$$ cubic polynomial (third degree)
$$y = 60x^4 + 60x^3 + 60x^2 + 40x + 25$$ fourth-degree polynomial ■

Polynomials with degree 3 or more are called higher-degree polynomials. Instead of continuing with $a, b, c, \ldots$, as coefficients, you can use subscripted variables.

Polynomial Equations of Degree *n*

A polynomial equation of degree n can be expressed as

$$y = a_n x^n + a_{n-1}x^{n-1} + a_{n-2}x^{n-2} + \cdots + a_2 x^2 + a_1 x + a_0 \,,$$

where the leading coefficient $a_n \neq 0$, and exponents, n, $n-1$, and so on, are positive integers.

Investigation 10.6.1

The Largest Triangle

Take a sheet of paper and fold the upper left corner so that it touches some point on the bottom edge. Find the area of triangle A formed in the lower left corner of the paper. The objective of this investigation is to find the distance (x) along the 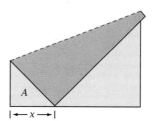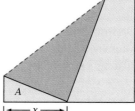 bottom of the paper that produces the triangle with the greatest area. Work with your group and devise a method for collecting and sharing data. Explain in some detail your group's strategy for finding the largest triangle.

Polynomials with real coefficients have graphs that have a y-intercept, possibly one or more x-intercepts, and other features like turning points (local maxima or minima). In this section you will discover the connection between a polynomial and its graph, which will allow you to predict when certain features will occur in the graph.

■ Example 2

Find a polynomial that contains the x-intercepts $(3, 0)$, $(5, 0)$, and $(-4, 0)$. Find a connection between the factors of a polynomial and the x-intercepts. (Zeros and roots are other names for the values at x-intercepts.)

Solution

The polynomial with *x*-intercepts at (3, 0), (5, 0), and (⁻4, 0) isn't quadratic because it has too many *x*-intercepts. It could be a third-, fourth-, fifth-, or higher-degree polynomial. Consider a cubic equation, because that is the lowest possible degree you can have with three roots. The expression (*x* – 3) is equal to zero when *x* is 3, (*x* – 5) is equal to zero when *x* is 5, and (*x* + 4) is equal to zero when *x* is ⁻4. Therefore, $y = A(x - 3)(x - 5)(x + 4)$ will work as the equation for different nonzero choices of *A*.

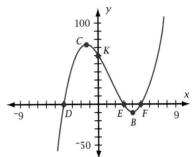

This is the graph of $y = A(x - 3)(x - 5)(x + 4)$ with *A* equal to 1.

Notice that points *D*, *E*, and *F* are the three required *x*-intercepts and point *K* is the *y*-intercept (0, 60). Do you see why it is 60? ■

Point *B* is a **local minimum point** because it is the lowest point in its immediate neighborhood of *x*-values. Point *C* is a **local maximum point** because it is the highest point in its immediate neighborhood of *x*-values.

In the problems, you will have the opportunity to substitute other values for *A* in the equation $y = A(x - 3)(x - 5)(x + 4)$ to see the effect on the graph. You will also explore what happens with different exponents on the three factors. For example, what is different and what is the same for $y = A(x - 3)(x - 5)(x + 4)^2$?

You can identify the degree of many polynomial graphs by looking at their shapes. Every third-degree polynomial has essentially one of the shapes shown below. The graph on the left is $y = x^3$. It can be translated horizontally or vertically, stretched, or flipped. The graph on the right shows one possible transformation.

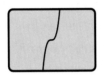 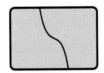

The next two graphs are of the general cubic equation $y = ax^3 + bx^2 + cx + d$. In the graph on the left, *a* is positive. It is negative in the graph on the right.

Take time to graph several cubic equations. What you see will depend on your graphing window. You get a global view by selecting a large viewing screen. The global view gives you the end behavior information about the graph at the right and left extremes of the *x*-axis, but tends to diminish individual features of the graph. Switching from a small to a large viewing screen is like stepping back from an object that you are looking at.

Problem Set 10.6

1. **a.** Write a linear equation with x-intercept at $(4, 0)$.
   b. Write a quadratic equation with its only x-intercept at $(4, 0)$.
   c. Write a cubic equation with its only x-intercept at $(4, 0)$.

2. The graph for $y = 2(x - 3)(x - 5)(x + 4)^2$ has zeros at 3, 5, and $^-4$ because they are the only possible x-values that make $y = 0$. This is a fourth-degree polynomial, but it has only three different x-intercepts. Graph each equation below, and name a graphing window that provides a **complete graph**. Complete graphs display all of the relevant features, including local extrema.
   a. $y = 2(x - 3)(x - 5)(x + 4)^2$ **b.** $y = 2(x - 3)^2(x - 5)(x + 4)$
   c. $y = 2(x - 3)(x - 5)^2(x + 4)$ **d.** $y = 2(x - 3)^2(x - 5)(x + 4)^2$
   e. Describe a connection between the exponent on a factor and what happens at that x-intercept.

3. Both graphs below are of the same polynomial function. The one on the left is not a complete graph.

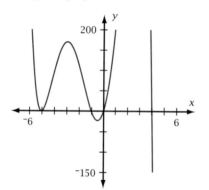 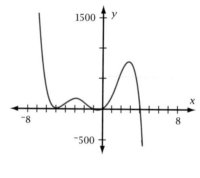

   a. How many x-intercepts are there?
   b. What is the smallest possible degree for this polynomial?
   c. Write an equation of the graph pictured that includes the points $(0, 0)$, $(^-5, 0)$, $(4, 0)$, $(^-1, 0)$, and $(1, 216)$. You may have to use an exponent on a factor to get it right.

4. In this problem, you will investigate the graph of $y = A(x - 3)^n$ with different values of A and n.
   a. Suppose $n = 2$. Try different values of A and describe the effect of each A-value on the graph.
   b. Suppose $A = ^-2$. Try different values of n and describe the effect of each n-value on the graph.
   c. What is the same about the graphs of $y = (x - 3)^2$ and $y = (x - 3)^4$? What is different?
   d. What is the same about the graphs of $y = (x - 3)^1$ and $y = (x - 3)^3$? What is different?
   e. Predict what the graph of $y = (x - 3)^2(x - 5)^3(x + 1)(x + 4)^2$ will look like. Verify your guess. This is an eighth-degree polynomial with zeros $\{3, 3, 5, 5, 5, ^-1, ^-4, ^-4\}$.

5. A fourth-degree polynomial has the equation $y = ax^4 + bx^3 + cx^2 + dx + e$ for real values of a, b, c, d, and e. Try different values for each coefficient. Be sure to include positive, negative, and zero values. Make a sketch of each different type of curve you get. Concentrate on the shape of the curve. You do not need to include the x-axis in your sketches. Compare your graphs with others in the class and come up with six or more different shapes that describe all fourth-degree functions.

6. True or false: Every polynomial equation has at least one solution. Explain your answer. Modify the statement, if necessary, to make it true.

7. In each graph, $A = 1$ or $^-1$. Write equations in factored form that will produce each graph.

a.

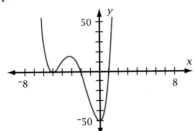

b.

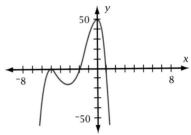

c.

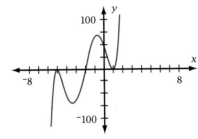

d.

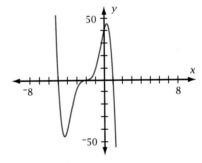

e. Name the zeros of each polynomial in 7a–d above. If a factor has degree n, list the zero n times.

8. The paper-folding investigation in this section relates the area of a triangle to the length of its base, x. Explore the problem further by answering the following questions.

a. Use very careful measurements to find the area when the x-value is 3. Then find the area for an x-value of 6.

b. Name two x-values that produce an area of zero.

c. Given the equation $area = A(x - R_1)(x - R_2)(x - R_3)$, what do the results of 8b tell you about the problem?

d. Use the values from 8a and the equation from 8c to write two equations. Solve this system, and give the equation in factored form.

e. Graph your equation and find the maximum value for the area.

Geometer's Sketchpad Investigation

The Largest Triangle

Use Sketchpad to simulate Investigation 10.6.1. Before looking at the steps below, try to make this drawing yourself.

Step 1   Open a new sketch and create point *A* in the lower left corner of the window.

Step 2   Translate *A* horizontally by 8.5 cm to create point *D*. Similarly, translate *A* vertically by 8.5 cm to create point *C*.

Step 3   Construct segment *AD* and segment *AC*.

Step 4   Construct Point on Object on segment *AD*. Label the point *E*. This is the point that the folded-down corner of the triangle touches.

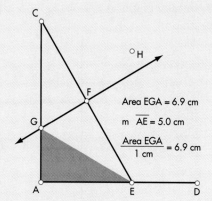

Area EGA = 6.9 cm

m $\overline{AE}$ = 5.0 cm

$\dfrac{\text{Area EGA}}{1 \text{ cm}}$ = 6.9 cm

Step 5   Construct segment *EC* and construct its midpoint, *F*.

Step 6   Construct line *l* perpendicular to segment *EC* through midpoint *F*. This is the fold line. Construct point of intersection *G* of line *l* and segment *AC*.

Step 7   Select points *E*, *G*, and *A*, and construct the polygon interior. Measure the area of triangle *EGA*. Construct segment *AE* and measure its length.

Step 8   Translate *E* vertically by the area of the triangle. Label this point *H*. (To translate a point by an "area" measurement, you must first change the area measurement to a length measurement. You can do this by dividing the area of triangle *EGA* by 1 unit.)

Step 9   Select point *H* and choose Trace Point.

Questions

1. Move point *E* along segment *AD* and observe the path of point *H*. Record and plot (*length, area*). (You can create this table of values using the values calculated by Sketchpad.) Derive an equation for this curve. The curve should fit the data you collected very accurately. Find the maximum area for the triangle algebraically.

2. Use Sketchpad to model Investigation 10.5.1.

Project
Coefficient of Fit

The coefficient of correlation, *r*, which you learned about earlier in this course, is a measure of the data, and not of the model used to fit the data. The coefficient of correlation measures how well the data fit a linear model. You can use another coefficient, called the coefficient of fit, with any model, linear or not. The coefficient of fit is "model dependent" and is based on the residuals. You can use this measure for any data set after you find a model, and it is useful when making comparisons between different models.

NOTE
10A

The Greek letter rho, ρ, is used to represent the coefficient of fit. The first person to use this notation was Francis Ysidro Edgeworth (1845–1926), an Irishman, who was interested in using mathematics in economics and other social sciences. As with the coefficient of correlation, it is the coefficient of fit *squared* that is a meaningful measure. The formula for the coefficient of fit (see the box below) has been coded into a calculator program found in **Calculator Note 10A.** The variables used in the formula are σ_y for the standard deviation of the *y*-data and σ_r for the root mean square of the residuals. The standard deviation is the square root of the average of the squares of the differences between the values and the mean value. The root mean square is the square root of the average of the squares of the residuals. (See the Standard Deviation Project following Section 3.2 if you aren't familiar with this term.) The symbol σ is the Greek letter sigma.

Coefficient of Fit
The formula for the **coefficient of fit** (ρ) uses the standard deviation of the *y*-data, σ_y, and the root mean square of the residuals, σ_r.

$$\sigma_y^2 = \frac{\sum\limits_{i=1}^{n}(y_i - \bar{y})^2}{n} \qquad \sigma_r^2 = \frac{\sum\limits_{i=1}^{n}(y_i - f(x_i))^2}{n} \qquad \rho = \sqrt{\frac{\sigma_y^2 - \sigma_r^2}{\sigma_y^2}}$$

The ρ value is always between zero and one. A ρ value of one is a perfect fit and a ρ value of zero indicates no fit at all.

Try applying this formula to Problem 5 in Problem Set 7.9.

No Real Solutions

To navigate by a landmark tied to your own ship's head is ultimately impossible.
—Paul Ramsey

You have explored several ways to solve quadratic equations. You can graph and zoom in to find the *x*-intercepts, you can make a table of values and zoom in numerically, or you can use the quadratic formula. But what happens if you try to use the quadratic formula on an equation whose graph has no *x*-intercepts?

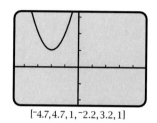

$[\text{-}4.7, 4.7, 1, \text{-}2.2, 3.2, 1]$

Graph $y = x^2 + 4x + 5$. It has no *x*-intercepts. Using the quadratic formula you will get

$$x = \frac{\text{-}4 \pm \sqrt{16 - 4(1)(5)}}{2} = \frac{\text{-}4 \pm \sqrt{\text{-}4}}{2}.$$

How do you take the square root of a negative number? This problem has bothered people for a long time. Mathematicians invented a new kind of number to deal with situations like this. Since the 1500s, the square root of a negative number has been called an **imaginary number**. In the late 1700s, Leonhard Euler introduced the symbol *i* to represent $\sqrt{\text{-}1}$. He wrote:

> Since all numbers which it is possible to conceive are either greater or less than 0, or are 0 itself, it is evident that we cannot rank the square root of a negative number amongst possible numbers, and we must therefore say that it is an impossible quantity. In this manner we are led to the idea of numbers, which from their nature are impossible; and therefore they are usually called *imaginary quantities,* because they exist merely in the imagination. All such expressions as $\sqrt{\text{-}1}$, $\sqrt{\text{-}2}$ . . . are consequently impossible, or imaginary numbers, since they represent roots of negative quantities; . . . . But notwithstanding this these numbers present themselves to the mind; they exist in our imagination, and we still have a sufficient idea of them; since we know that by $\sqrt{\text{-}4}$ is meant a number which, multiplied by itself, produces $\text{-}4$; for this reason also, nothing prevents us from making use of these imaginary numbers, and employing them in calculation.

If you rewrite $\sqrt{\text{-}4}$ in its imaginary form, it is $\sqrt{4}\,\sqrt{\text{-}1} = 2i$. Therefore, the two solutions of the given equation are

$\frac{\text{-}4 + 2i}{2}$ and $\frac{\text{-}4 - 2i}{2}$, or $\text{-}2 + i$ and $\text{-}2 - i$.

Numbers such as $\sqrt{\text{-}3}$ are usually rewritten as $i\sqrt{3}$ before performing any computations. Don't write $\sqrt{3}i$ because others can't tell whether *i* is or isn't under the radical.

Imagine a tank of water with a motorized device that creates waves that are 5 centimeters high from crest to trough. What happens to the waves when you add another similar device right next to it? Will the waves created be 10 centimeters? They may be, or there may be no waves at all, or they could be any height in between, like 2.5 centimeters or 7.5 centimeters. If the motors are synchronized, the waves will be 10 centimeters high. If they are running one quarter-cycle out of phase, then the waves will be about 7 centimeters high. Something similar happens when you combine a real number and an imaginary number.

Wave pool and swimmers at Mt. Tom Summerside Recreation Area in Massachusetts.

The combination of a real number and an imaginary number creates a new type of number called a complex number. These are different from the numbers you have used before. They are numbers with a phase or a direction. You know that 5 + 5 = 10, but 5 + 5*i* is not 10, any more than a place 5 kilometers north and 5 kilometers east of you is 10 kilometers away. It is about 7 kilometers to the northeast—a new direction altogether. Complex numbers help describe many applications involving waves, including electrical systems, displacement of objects, the flow of air over and below an aircraft wing, and the flow of fluids around barriers. Using complex numbers actually enables you to model these situations more realistically.

The definition of an imaginary number can be extended a little by considering the meaning of square root. You know that $\sqrt{81} = 9$ because $9^2 = 81$, and likewise $\sqrt{-1} = i$ means $i^2 = {}^-1$.

■ **Example 1**

Simplify the following numerical expressions, and write each as one complex number, using the same properties you have used for real numbers.

a. $3(2 - 4i)$ **b.** $2 - 4i + 3 + 5i$

c. $(2 - 4i) - (3 + 5i)$ **d.** $(2 - 4i)^2$

e. $(2 - 4i)(3 + 5i)$

Solution

a. $3(2 - 4i) = \mathbf{6 - 12\textit{i}}$ **b.** $2 - 4i + 3 + 5i = \mathbf{5 + \textit{i}}$

c. $(2 - 4i) - (3 + 5i) = \mathbf{{}^-1 - 9\textit{i}}$

d. $(2 - 4i)^2 = 4 - 16i + 16i^2$ **e.** $(2 - 4i)(3 + 5i) = 6 + 10i - 12i - 20i^2$
$$= 4 - 16i + 16(-1)$$
$$ = 6 - 2i + 20$$
$$= \mathbf{{}^-12 - 16\textit{i}}$$
$$ = \mathbf{26 - 2\textit{i}} \ \blacksquare$$

Did you notice that each of the answers is in the form $a + bi$? If b is zero, the answer is a real number. If a is zero, and b is a nonzero number, then the answer is a pure imaginary number. In general, numbers of the form $a + bi$ are called **complex numbers**.

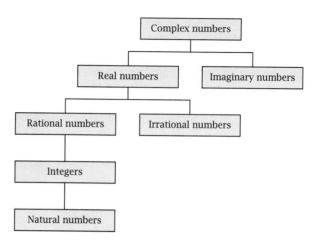

Problem Set 10.7

1. Solve each equation. Label each solution as real or nonreal (complex). (Note: The nonreal answers always occur in pairs: $a + bi$ and $a - bi$. These are called **complex conjugate pairs**.)

a. $x^2 - 4x + 6 = 0$ **b.** $x^2 + 1 = 0$ **c.** $x^2 + x = {}^-1$

2. Write a quadratic equation that has the given solutions.

a. $^-3$ and 5 **b.** $^-3.5$ and $^-3.5$
c. $5i$ and ^-5i **d.** $2 + i$ and $2 - i$

3. Write the lowest-degree equation with integer coefficients that has at least the given set of zeros and the given y-intercept.

a. $^-4, 5, ^-2, ^-2$ and y-intercept at $^-80$.
b. $^-4, 5, ^-2, ^-2$ and y-intercept at 160.
c. $\frac{1}{3}, \frac{-5}{2}, 0$ and y-intercept at 0.
d. $^-5i, ^-1, ^-1, ^-1, 4$ and y-intercept at 100.

4. Solve for x.

a. $x^2 - 10ix - 9i^2 = 0$ **b.** $x^2 - 3ix = 2$
c. Why don't the solutions to 4a and 4b come in conjugate pairs?

5. The quadratic formula $x = \dfrac{^-b \pm \sqrt{b^2 - 4ac}}{2a}$ provides solutions to $ax^2 + bx + c = 0$. Make up some rules involving a, b, and c that determine each of the conditions specified below.

a. The solutions (roots or zeros) are nonreal.
b. The solutions are real.
c. The solutions are equal.

6. Without using your calculator, sketch a graph of $y = {}^-3(x + 2)^2(x - 3)(x - 6) + 50$. (Hint: What happens when $x = {}^-2$ or 3 or 6?) Verify your sketch with your calculator.

7. For x-values near 1 you can use the polynomial equation
$y = 0.0723[6(x - 1) - 3(x - 1)^2 + 2(x - 1)^3]$ as an approximation for $\log x$.

a. Sketch a graph of both $y = \log x$ and the polynomial equation above for $0 \le x \le 2$.

b. What is the most obvious root of the polynomial?

c. Show algebraically that
$$0.0723[6(x - 1) - 3(x - 1)^2 + 2(x - 1)^3] = 0.0723[(x - 1)(6 - 3(x - 1) + 2(x - 1)^2)].$$

d. Find the roots of $6 - 3(x - 1) + 2(x - 1)^2 = 0$.

8. For 8a and 8b, graph each equation as y_1. Then let $y_2 = |y_1|$. For 8c, you are given the graph of y_1. Predict what the graph of y_2 will look like. Check your work.

a. $y_1 = 3x - 2$　　　　**b.** $y_1 = (x - 4)^2 - 2$

c.

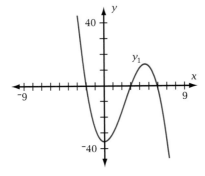

NOTE
10B

9. Write a calculator program or adapt an existing program that will provide solutions to *any* quadratic equation with real-number coefficients. (See **Calculator Note 10B**.)

Take Another Look 10.7

In this section you have solved equations with nonreal or complex solutions in the form $a + bi$. Nonreal complex numbers, like $3 + 4i$, cannot be graphed on the real number line, but they can be located on the coordinate plane. In the graph at the right, $3 + 4i$ is located at the point with rectangular coordinates (3, 4). In general, a complex number $a + bi$ has (a, b) as its rectangular coordinates. The horizontal axis is called the **real axis**, and the vertical axis is called the **imaginary axis**.

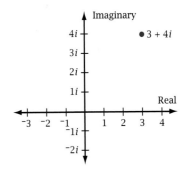

Now that you see what $3 + 4i$ means geometrically, take some time to explore the meaning of multiplying by i.

$$i \cdot (3 + 4i) = 3i + 4i^2 = {}^-4 + 3i.$$

Plot both $3 + 4i$ and $^-4 + 3i$ on your graph paper.

Plot the complex number associated with point B. Multiply this complex number by i and plot the point associated with the result. Do the same thing for point C. What happens to $\triangle ABC$ when the complex number associated with each vertex is multiplied by i and the

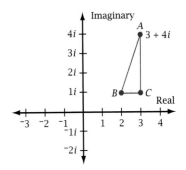

points representing these new numbers are plotted? Make a general statement about the geometric meaning of $i \cdot (a + bi)$. Show that this conjecture is also true for $i \cdot 5$.

Explore the geometric meaning for $i^2 \cdot (a + bi)$. One possible way to do this is to multiply each complex number associated with the vertices of $\triangle ABC$ by i^2. Plot the points resulting from each multiplication. Make a conjecture for $i^n \cdot (a + bi)$. Confirm your conjecture.

Project

Least-Squares Polynomial Fit

In this chapter you have fit polynomials to data by selecting certain points to represent the set. Using this kind of selective approach, you can choose those points that you feel are important and ignore some others. When finding the quadratic fit model, each point is as significant as any other and the sum of the squares of the residuals is minimized. (You will learn more about the derivations of the formulas in calculus.)

The quadratic fit involves finding three constants a, b, and c for $y = ax^2 + bx + c$. This means you must find three equations. Set the sum of the residuals equal to zero. Then x times the residuals is also equal to zero, and finally x^2 times the residuals is also equal to zero.

$$\left. \begin{array}{l} \sum_{i=1}^{n}(y_i - f(x_i)) = 0 \\[2ex] \sum_{i=1}^{n}(x_i y_i - x_i f(x_i)) = 0 \\[2ex] \sum_{i=1}^{n}(x_i^2 y_i - x_i^2 f(x_i)) = 0 \end{array} \right\} \Rightarrow \left\{ \begin{array}{l} \sum_{i=1}^{n} y_i = a\sum x_i^2 + b\sum x_i + cn \\[2ex] \sum_{i=1}^{n} x_i y_i = a\sum x_i^3 + b\sum x_i^2 + c\sum x_i \\[2ex] \sum_{i=1}^{n} x_i^2 y_i = a\sum x_i^4 + b\sum x_i^3 + c\sum x_i^2 \end{array} \right.$$

A chemical is added to make varnish smoother and easier to apply, but it also affects the drying time of the varnish. The following data were collected by adding the chemical to equal amounts of varnish, then recording how long it took before the varnish was dry to the touch. The amount of the additive, in grams, is recorded as x and the drying time, in hours, is recorded as y. Complete the table on page 517 and find each sum.

NOTE 10C

Use the sums from the table to write the systems of equations listed on the right above. Use matrices to find values of a, b, and c that give the best-fit quadratic equation for the data. Some calculators have polynomial fits as a statistical calculation. (See **Calculator Note 10C** for instructions on how to use your calculator to check the results. If your calculator does not have the functions built in, then you will have to enter the program.)

Sample number	x	x^2	x^3	x^4	y	xy	x^2y
1	1.0	–?–	–?–	–?–	8.5	–?–	–?–
2	2.0	–?–	–?–	–?–	8.0	–?–	–?–
3	3.0	–?–	–?–	–?–	6.0	–?–	–?–
4	4.0	–?–	–?–	–?–	5.0	–?–	–?–
5	5.0	–?–	–?–	–?–	6.0	–?–	–?–
6	6.0	–?–	–?–	–?–	5.5	–?–	–?–
7	7.0	–?–	–?–	–?–	6.5	–?–	–?–
8	8.0	–?–	–?–	–?–	7.0	–?–	–?–
Σ	–?–	–?–	–?–	–?–	–?–	–?–	–?–

More About Finding Solutions

Things don't turn up in the world until somebody turns them up.
—James A. Garfield

This is the graph of $y = x^3 - 6x^2 + 11x - 6$. The graph indicates zeros at 1, 2, and 3. This brings up the question, how can you find the zeros when the equation is given as a polynomial, but the x-intercepts aren't as obvious?

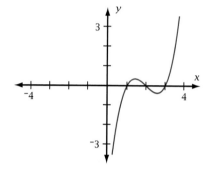

Can you use the graph and the information in the polynomial to help find the zeros?

Even without referring to the graph, you have evidence that a factored form of $x^3 - 6x^2 + 11x - 6$ is $(x - 1)(x - 2)(x - 3)$, because $(x)(x)(x) = x^3$ and $(^-1)(^-2)(^-3) = ^-6$.

■ **Example 1**

What are the zeros of
$P(x) = x^5 - 6x^4 + 20x^3 - 60x^2 + 99x - 54$?

Solution

The graph has a cubic look and shows x-intercepts at 1, 2, and 3. This means that
$(x - 1)(x - 2)(x - 3) = x^3 - 6x^2 + 11x - 6$ is a factor.
The task is to find another factor so that
$(x^3 - 6x^2 + 11x - 6)(\text{factor}) =$
$x^5 - 6x^4 + 20x^3 - 60x^2 + 99x - 54$. ■

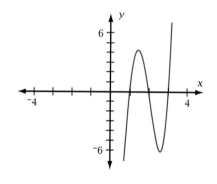

You can find another factor by using division.

$$
\begin{array}{r}
x^2 + 9 \\
x^3 - 6x^2 + 11x - 6 \overline{\smash)\,x^5 - 6x^4 + 20x^3 - 60x^2 + 99x - 54} \\
x^5 - 6x^4 + 11x^3 - 6x^2 \\
\hline
9x^3 - 54x^2 + 99x - 54 \\
9x^3 - 54x^2 + 99x - 54 \\
\hline
0
\end{array}
$$

Divide x^3 into x^5 to get x^2.

Multiply the divisor by x^2.

Subtract and divide x^3 into $9x^3$.

Multiply the divisor by 9.

The remainder is zero.

Division of polynomials is similar to the long division process you learned in grade school, and it is equally difficult. Both the original polynomial and the divisor are written in descending order of the powers of x. If any degree is missing, insert a term with 0 as coefficient as a place holder. For example, you can write the polynomial expression $x^4 + 3x^2 - 5x + 8$ as $x^4 + 0x^3 + 3x^2 - 5x + 8$.

The remainder of zero means the divisor, $D(x)$, and the quotient, $Q(x)$, are both factors of the polynomial, $P(x)$. Thus, $P(x) = D(x) \cdot Q(x)$.

$$x^5 - 6x^4 + 20x^3 - 60x^2 + 99x - 54 = (x^3 - 6x^2 + 11x - 6)(x^2 + 9)$$
$$= (x - 1)(x - 2)(x - 3)(x^2 + 9)$$

Another way to find this missing factor is to have the calculator do the division for you, and graph the result. Graph

$$y = (x^5 - 6x^4 + 20x^3 - 60x^2 + 99x - 54)/(x^3 - 6x^2 + 11x - 6).$$

The result should look familiar. It is the parabola $y = x^2 + 9$. This means that the missing factor is $x^2 + 9$. Now that the polynomial is in factored form, you can easily find the zeros. You knew three of them from the graph. There are two more zeros to find because this is a fifth-degree polynomial. They are contained in $x^2 + 9$. What values of x make $x^2 + 9$ equal zero?

$$x^2 + 9 = 0$$
$$x^2 = {}^-9$$
$$x = \pm\sqrt{-9} = \pm 3i$$

Therefore, the five solutions are 1, 2, 3, $3i$, and ${}^-3i$. Notice that the complex solutions are a conjugate pair. This means that if the coefficients of a polynomial are real numbers, and the polynomial has one complex root, then the conjugate of that complex root must also be a root.

■ Example 2

Find the zeros of $y = 6x^3 + 11x^2 - 17x - 30$.

Solution

All three zeros are real because the graph has three x-intercepts. By tracing or making a table you can find that both ${}^-2$ and $-\frac{3}{2}$ are solutions. The other root is somewhere between 1 and 2. How can you find the exact solution without zooming?

Instead of using guess-and-check, you can divide by the associated factors $(x + 2)$ and $\left(x + \frac{3}{2}\right)$ using polynomial division, and reduce the expression

$$\frac{6x^3 + 11x^2 - 17x - 30}{(x + 2)(x + 1.5)} \, .$$

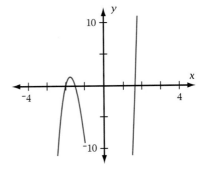

Another choice is a shortcut called **synthetic division**. Synthetic division is based on using a **nested form** of the polynomial to evaluate the polynomial at particular x-values. This evaluation only involves multiplication and addition. As you can see below, ⁻2 is a solution because it makes the remainder equal to zero.

Long Division

$$6x^2 - 1x - 15$$

$$x + 2 \overline{\smash{\big)}\ 6x^3 + 11x^2 - 17x - 30}$$

$$\underline{⁻6x^3 - 12x^2}$$

$$⁻1x^2 - 17x - 30$$

$$\underline{1x^2 + 2x}$$

$$⁻15x - 30$$

$$\underline{15x + 30}$$

$$0$$

Synthetic Division

$$P(x) = 6x^3 + 11x^2 - 17x - 30$$

⁻2	6	11	⁻17	⁻30
		⁻12	2	30
	6	⁻1	⁻15	0

Synthetic division is a shortcut to the long division process. See if you can figure out the individual steps by studying the example. (Hint: The synthetic division process uses only multiplication and addition.)

The number furthest to the right in the last row of a synthetic division is the remainder, which in this case is 0. When the remainder in a division problem is zero, you know that the divisor is a factor. This means ⁻2 is a solution and the polynomial $6x^3 + 11x^2 - 17x - 30$ factors into the divisor $(x + 2)$ and the quotient $6x^2 - x - 15$. You could use any of the methods you've learned—simple factoring, quadratic formula, synthetic division, or graphing—to reduce the quotient even further. Study the synthetic division process with the other root, ⁻1.5.

⁻1.5	6	⁻1	⁻15
		⁻9	15
	6	⁻10	0

You know that ⁻1.5 or $-\frac{3}{2}$ is a solution because the remainder is again zero. The quotient is the remaining factor $(6x - 10)$. Therefore, the three zeros are ⁻2, $-\frac{3}{2}$, and $\frac{5}{3}$. ∎

The quotient, $6x - 10$, is the remaining factor, which implies $x = \frac{5}{3}$. *Every polynomial function with degree n has exactly n complex zeros.* This means that all cubic equations have three roots and three factors. They may be repeated roots, such as the roots of $x^3 - 15x^2 + 75x - 125 = 0$, whose three roots are 5, 5, and 5. (See what this situation looks like by graphing $y = x^3 - 15x^2 + 75x - 125$.) Or two of the roots may be imaginary or complex, such as the roots of $x^3 + 5x^2 - 24x - 130 = 0$, whose three roots are 5, ⁻5 + i, and ⁻5 - i. (Graph $y = x^3 + 5x^2 - 24x - 130$ to see what this situation looks like.)

Investigation 10.8.1

A Leaky Bottle Experiment

For this investigation you will need a translucent plastic water container with a hole in the bottom (a 1-liter plastic bleach bottle or soda bottle works well), a metric ruler, a marker, some tape, and a timing device.

Assignment of Tasks

Assign a task to each group member. One team member holds the bottle. The second team member keeps track of the time, the third team member reads the water-level heights, and the fourth team member records the data.

Procedure

Make a mark on the side of the container at a height of 15 cm. (Be sure this mark is on the vertical part of the container and not the rounded part of the bottle neck.) The bottle holder fills the container with water to this mark, keeping a finger on the hole and adjusting the water level with his or her finger if necessary. The water-level reader needs to attach the ruler to the container with tape.

When the timekeeper says go, the person holding the bottle removes his or her finger from the hole and lets the water run out freely. The timekeeper, who has the timing device, will call out the time every 10 sec. When the timekeeper does this, the water-level reader reads aloud the water level to the nearest millimeter. The recorder records the data. Stop measuring the water level before it reaches the rounded portion at the bottom of the bottle.

Data Analysis

a. Sketch a graph of the data. Look at the graph and make a conjecture as to the type of function represented by the data.

b. Explain what physical properties or laws might predict this type of behavior.

c. Use the method of finite differences to investigate your conjecture in part a. Find the equation that you believe best fits the data.

d. Add the graph of the equation you found in part c to your data plot.

e. On a separate graph, show the residuals related to your equation.

f. From your work, predict when the container would be empty. How long would it take to drain if you started with the container filled to a height of 20 cm?

Problem Set 10.8

1. Division produces a quotient and often a remainder. Rewrite $P(x)$ in the form $P(x) = D(x) \cdot Q(x) + R$, where $D(x)$ is the given divisor, $Q(x)$ is the quotient, and R is the remainder. For example, $x^3 + 2x^2 + 3x - 4 = (x - 1)(x^2 + 3x + 6) + 2$. Remember that you must use zero coefficients for missing terms when doing long division or synthetic division.

   a. $P(x) = 47$ and $D(x) = 11$

   b. $P(x) = 6x^4 - 5x^3 + 7x^2 - 12x + 15$ and $D(x) = x - 1$

   c. $P(x) = x^3 - x^2 - 10x + 16$ and $D(x) = x - 2$

2. Consider $y = x^5 - 6x^4 + 20x^3 - 60x^2 + 99x - 54$.

   a. Find $P(1)$ by using synthetic division, and name the quotient polynomial, $Q_1(x)$, so that $(x - 1) \, Q_1(x) = 0$.

   b. Use synthetic division on the quotient polynomial, $Q_1(x)$, and name a new quotient polynomial, $Q_2(x)$, so that $(x - 1)(x - 2) \, Q_2(x) = 0$.

   c. Use synthetic division on the quotient polynomial, $Q_2(x)$, and name a new quotient polynomial, $Q_3(x)$, so that $(x - 1)(x - 2)(x - 3) \, Q_3(x) = 0$.

NOTE
10D

   d. Find the two solutions of the quadratic quotient polynomial remaining by using the quadratic formula.

   e. Synthetic division can be done with your calculator by entering the program in **Calculator Note 10D**. Use this program to check your answers to 2a–c.

3. **a.** How many zeros does $y = x^4 + 3x^3 - 11x^2 - 3x + 10$ have?

   b. Name the x-intercepts.

   c. Name the y-intercept.

   d. Write the polynomial in factored form.

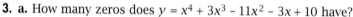

4. As you trace to find the value of an x-intercept on a graph, you see the y-values jump from positive to negative when you pass over the root. By zooming in between these values, you find more and more accurate approximations for x. These actions can be automated once the low and high boundaries for x have been entered. The automation uses successive midpoints and is called the **bisection method**. Find the x-intercepts for each equation by using the program in **Calculator Note 10E**.

NOTE
10E

   a. $y = x^5 - x^4 - 16x + 16$ **b.** $y = 2x^3 + 15x^2 + 6x - 6$

   c. $y = 0.2(x - 12)^5 - 6(x - 12)^3 - (x - 12)^2 + 1$ **d.** $y = 2x^4 + 2x^3 - 14x^2 - 9x - 12$

5. Consider $y = x - \dfrac{x^3}{3!} + \dfrac{x^5}{5!} - \dfrac{x^7}{7!} + \cdots$. (The pattern continues.)

   a. Graph $y = x - \dfrac{x^3}{3!} + \dfrac{x^5}{5!} - \dfrac{x^7}{7!}$ and find the zeros.

   b. Graph $y = x - \dfrac{x^3}{3!} + \dfrac{x^5}{5!} - \dfrac{x^7}{7!} + \dfrac{x^9}{9!} - \dfrac{x^{11}}{11!}$ and find the zeros.

   c. Continue the pattern in part b and describe what is happening.

6. As you move closer and closer to the end of the school year, think about how you felt at the start of the year about your mathematics class, working in groups, and your ability to learn. Has your perspective changed? Explain.

7. In this chapter you looked at a number of different ways to solve polynomial equations. Discuss at least three of the methods. What are the advantages and disadvantages of each method? Which method do you prefer? Why?

Take Another Look 10.8

You have looked at monthly installments, auto loans, and mortgage payments several different times during the course. Take another look at these kinds of problems by using an explicit formula to find the monthly payment size, P (in dollars), for an initial loan or mortgage of A (in dollars) over a period of n months at an annual interest rate of $R\%$. To make the work easier, the formula will use the monthly interest rate r (as a decimal), which is equal to $R/12$.

Begin with a recursive definition: $A_{n+1} = A_n(1 + r) - P$. This should be familiar because you have used it frequently. The new unpaid balance, A_{n+1}, is the old unpaid balance, A_n, increased by the interest and reduced by a monthly payment. This means

$$A_1 = A_0(1 + r) - P$$
$$A_2 = A_1(1 + r) - P$$
$$A_3 = A_2(1 + r) - P \quad \text{and so on.}$$

a. Use substitution to explain why $A_2 = A_1(1 + r) - P$ is equivalent to
$A_2 = A_0(1 + r)^2 - P(1 + r) - P$.

b. Use substitution to explain why $A_3 = A_2(1 + r) - P$ is equivalent to
$A_3 = A_0(1 + r)^3 - P(1 + r)^2 - P(1 + r) - P$.

c. Write similar polynomial equations for A_4 and A_n.

d. Explain why the equation you found for A_n in part c is equivalent to
$A_n = A_0(1 + r)^n - P[(1 + r)^{n-1} + (1 + r)^{n-2} + (1 + r)^{n-3} + \cdots + (1 + r)^1 + 1]$.
(If it isn't, you will need to revise your response to part c.)

e. The bracketed expression in part d contains a geometric series. If you work backwards and look at the last term in the brackets as the first term of a series, then the first term is 1 and the common ratio is $(1 + r)$. How many terms are in $1 + (1 + r)^1 + \cdots + (1 + r)^{n-3} + (1 + r)^{n-2} + (1 + r)^{n-1}$? Explain how you would substitute into the explicit geometric series formula $S_n = \dfrac{u_1[1 - r^n]}{1 - r}$ you used in Chapter 2 to find the sum of the series.

f. Verify that the equation in part d is equivalent to $A_n = A_0(1 + r)^n - \dfrac{P[(1 + r)^n - 1]}{r}$.

g. If the loan is paid off after n payments, then $A_n = 0$. Now explain why $P = \dfrac{A_0 r(1 + r)^n}{(1 + r)^n - 1}$. Remember that r is the monthly interest rate.

h. Use the formula in part g to find the monthly payment size for a 60 mo auto loan of $11,000 at 11%.

i. Use the formula in part g to find the size of the mortgage you can get with an annual interest rate of 7.5% if you can afford a monthly payment of $620.

Mandelbrot Set

Benoit Mandelbrot wrote of the term *fractal*:

> I coined *fractal* from the Latin adjective *fractus*. The corresponding Latin verb *frangere* means "to break": to create irregular fragments. It is therefore sensible—and how appropriate for our needs!—that, in addition to "fragmented" (as in *fraction* or *refraction*), *fractus* should also mean "irregular," both meanings being preserved in *fragment*. . . .

Mandelbrot at age 5

In his book *The Fractal Geometry of Nature*, Mandelbrot discusses such fractals as the Cantor set, the Sierpiński triangle, and the Koch snowflake.

The most famous of all fractal images is created using a recursively defined quadratic expression. Choose some value, z, square it, and add a constant, c. This becomes the new z-value. Repeat the process. One of two things will happen: either the value will "explode" up to infinity, or it will not. Look at two patterns, one for $z_1 = 0$ and $c = 0.5$, and one for $z_1 = 0$ and $c = {}^-0.5$.

$$z_2 = z_1^2 + 0.5 = 0.5 \qquad z_2 = z_1^2 - 0.5 = {}^-0.5$$
$$z_3 = z_2^2 + 0.5 = 0.75 \qquad z_3 = z_2^2 - 0.5 = {}^-0.25$$
$$z_4 = z_3^2 + 0.5 = 1.0625 \qquad z_4 = z_3^2 - 0.5 = {}^-0.4375$$
$$z_5 = z_4^2 + 0.5 = 1.6289 \ldots \qquad z_5 = z_4^2 - 0.5 = {}^-0.3085 \ldots$$
$$z_6 = z_5^2 + 0.5 = 3.1533 \ldots \qquad z_6 = z_5^2 - 0.5 = {}^-0.4048 \ldots$$
$$z_{10} = z_9^2 + 0.5 = 144{,}131{,}442 \qquad z_{10} = z_9^2 - 0.5 = {}^-0.3773 \ldots$$
$$z_{\text{big}} = \text{very big} \qquad z_{\text{big}} = {}^-0.3660254038 \ldots$$

Check this result by using a recursion routine on your calculator. What will happen if $z_1 = 0$ and $c = 0.25$? What will happen if c or z is a complex number, for example, if $z_1 = 0$ and $c = {}^-0.4 + 0.5i$?

Note: If your calculator does not work with complex numbers, use a matrix for $a + bi$, such as

```
[A]
     [[-.4  -.5]
      [.5   -.4]]
Ans²+[A]
     [[-.49  -.1]
      [.1   -.49]]
```

$$[A] = \begin{bmatrix} a & -b \\ b & a \end{bmatrix}.$$

Then enter [A] and use a recursive routine to calculate the expression $\text{Ans}^2 + [A]$.

Give an argument that explains why $\begin{bmatrix} a & -b \\ b & a \end{bmatrix}^2$ works like $(a + bi)^2$.

What will happen if you choose to color a point black if it does not explode and white if it does? The result will be a coloring of a complex plane into a pattern that looks like the graph shown. Your project is to choose a small section on the boundary of the black area of this graph and create a graph of that section.

Zooming in on the Mandelbrot set

You will find a program in

NOTE

10F

Calculator Note 10F that will analyze every point in the window to determine if it is to be black or white. The program uses the fact that if a point gets more than two units from the origin, it will never come back. If it remains within two units of the origin after 50 iterations, then it will likely stay in that range. Look at this graph, and select a good window. Then run the program. Make a sketch of your result. Note any similarities between your graph and the original graph. Zoom in as many times as you wish and form a conclusion from your results.

Benoit Mandelbrot first saw what is now called the Mandelbrot set in 1979. In 1992 he said:

It starts with a formula so simple that that no one could possibly have expected so much from it. You program this silly little formula into your trusty personal computer or workstation, and suddenly everything breaks loose. . . . Fractal geometry has revealed simple rules and complicated effects. The complication one sees is not only most extraordinary but is also spontaneously attractive, and often breathtakingly beautiful. Besides, you may change the formula by what seems a tiny amount, and the complication is replaced by something altogether different, but equally beautiful.

Benoit Mandelbrot

If you would like to find out more about this remarkable set, read Arthur Clarke's book entitled *The Mandelbrot Set.*

Chapter Review

If you want a man to keep his head when the crisis comes, you must give him some training before it comes.
—Lucius Seneca

Polynomials can be used to represent the balance in a savings account when annual deposits are made, the areas of regions, and the volumes of boxes. When examining a set of data whose *x*-values form an arithmetic sequence, you can calculate the differences between successive *y*-values to find the degree of a polynomial that will fit the data. Oftentimes this process does not work well with measured data because of the errors involved in measuring. When you know the degree of the polynomial, you can define a system of equations to solve for the coefficients. Polynomial equations can be written in several forms. The form $a_n x^n + a_{n-1} x^{n-1} + \cdots + a_0 x^0$ is called polynomial form. Quadratic equations, which are second-degree polynomial equations, can also be written in vertex form. Another alternative form for a polynomial equation is called factored form, with each factor corresponding to a root of the equation. There are the same number of roots as the degree of the polynomial, although some roots may occur more than once. In some cases these roots may include imaginary or complex numbers. If the coefficients of a polynomial are real, then any complex roots will come in complex conjugate pairs. In a quadratic equation the roots can be found by using the quadratic formula. The degree of a polynomial function determines the shape of its graph. The graphs may have bumps and valleys where you will find local minimums and maximums. By varying the coefficients you can change the relative sizes of these bumps, and in some cases these bumps flatten out and disappear.

Problem Set 10.9

Some of the problems below are simple and straightforward, but most of them require investigation, thought, and checking your solutions along the way. You will need to use root-finding techniques, such as graphing, the quadratic formula, and synthetic division. Share, compare, and work with others until you are sure that you understand the problem and have found the solution.

1. Given three noncollinear points, how many triangles can you draw? Given four points, no three of which are collinear, how many triangles can you draw? Given five points, no three of which are collinear, how many triangles can you draw? How many triangles can be drawn from *n* points, no three of which are collinear?

2. Each equation is written in polynomial form, vertex form, or factored form. Write each equation in the other two forms if possible.

a. $y = 2(x - 2)^2 - 16$ **b.** $y = {}^{-}3(x - 5)(x + 1)$

c. $y = x^2 + 3x + 2$ **d.** $y = (x + 1)(x - 3)(x + 4)$

e. $y = 2x^2 + 5x - 6$ **f.** $y = {}^{-}(x + 7)^2 - 2$

3. Sketch a graph and label the coordinates of all zeros and of local maxima and minima. (Each coordinate should be accurate to the nearest 0.001.)

a. $y = 2(x - 2)^2 - 16$ **b.** $y = {}^{-}3(x - 5)(x + 1)$

c. $y = x^2 - 3x + 2$ **d.** $y = (x + 1)(x - 3)(x + 4)$

e. $y = x^3 + 2x^2 - 19x + 20$ **f.** $y = 5x^5 + 38x^4 + 79x^3 - 8x^2 - 102x + 36$

4. Write the equation of each graph.

a.

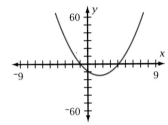

b.

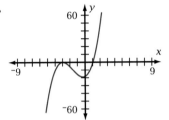

c.

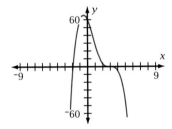

d.

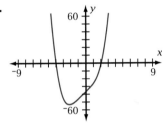

(Hint: One of the zeros occurs at $x = 3i$.)

5. A rectangular package must have a maximum combined girth and length of 108 in. (by postal regulations). This means $4x + y \leq 108$. Find the dimensions of the package with maximum volume. (Assume the cross-section is always a square with side length x.) Making a table might be helpful.

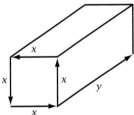

6. What ideas or topics were introduced in this chapter that you feel you do not quite understand or see the purpose of? Give examples.

7. Find three problems in the chapter that you feel are representative of the chapter. Write out each problem and its solution. For each problem, explain why you feel it is representative of the chapter. Please use complete sentences.

Assessing What You've Learned

As you work through the rest of the book continue to assess what you've learned. You may not be using all of the methods of self-assessment, but you will probably want to use at least three of them. Perhaps you'd like to try a method you haven't been using. Below is a list of all the methods that have been described. You may want to refer back to the chapter where they were originally introduced.

- Organizing Your Notebook (Chapter 0)
- Keeping a Journal (Chapter 1)
- Portfolio (Chapter 2)
- Performance Assessment (Chapter 3)
- Open-ended Investigations (Chapter 4)
- Constructing Test Questions (Chapter 5)
- Group Presentations and Tests (Chapter 6)
- Overall Self-Assessment (Chapter 7)

Probability and Statistics

This American is an "outlier" amongst the Indian sightseers at the historic temple in Halebid, Kamataka, India. By looking at the normal distribution curve, you can see which data values do not fit the overall trend. The height of the American is probably more than two standard deviations from the mean of the heights of the Indians.

Permutations and Probability

A small error in the beginning is a great one in the end.
—Saint Thomas Aquinas

How many different outfits—consisting of a sweater, pants, and shoes—could you wear if you were to select from four different sweaters, six different pairs of pants, and two pairs of shoes?

Visualize a tree with four choices of sweaters and six different pants for each sweater. This extended tree has a sweater-pants-shoe sequence along each of the 48 paths that represent the 48 different outfits. Each of the 24 sweater and pants outfits can be matched with two pairs of shoes.

Each different outfit can be represented by a path through a tree diagram. How many outfits or paths are there? Each path is a sequence of three segments representing a sweater *and* a pair of pants *and* a pair of shoes. This partial tree diagram pictures six pairs of pants for each sweater, followed by two pairs of shoes for each sweater and pants outfit. (Drawing all 48 paths would be difficult and messy.)

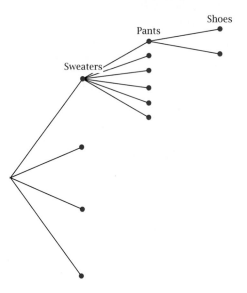

The total number of outfits with four choices, then six choices, and then two choices can be found by drawing a tree diagram or by using the **counting principle** (4 • 6 • 2 = 48 choices).

The Egyptian scribe Ahmes asked and answered a similar problem in about 1650 B.C.

> In each of seven houses there are seven cats, each cat kills seven mice, each mouse would have eaten seven ears of wheat, each ear of wheat will produce seven *hekat* of grain; how many items altogether?

In 1202, the Italian mathematician Leonardo of Pisa, also known as Fibonacci, included a similar problem in his book, *Liber Abacci*.

Seven old women are going to Rome; each of them has seven mules; each mule carries seven sacks; each sack contains seven loaves; each loaf has seven knives; and each knife has seven sheaths. What is the total number of things?

You might also know the old English nursery rhyme:

As I was going to St. Ives,
I met a man with seven wives,
Each wife had seven sacks,
Each sack had seven cats,
Each cat had seven kits,
Kits, cats, sacks, and wives,
How many were going to St. Ives?

Each of these problems can be illustrated by a tree diagram. One historian suggests that the purpose of all these rather silly problems was to illustrate the counting principle.

Counting Principle

Suppose there are n_1 ways to make the first choice, n_2 ways to make the second choice, n_3 ways to make the third choice, and so on. The product $n_1 \cdot n_2 \cdot n_3 \cdot \ldots$ represents the total number of different ways (outcomes) in which the entire sequence of choices can be made.

The counting principle provides a method for finding the total number of outcomes. However, the solutions will be more meaningful if you look for patterns, and sketch or visualize a representative tree diagram.

■ Example 1

You have been asked to arrange five different pictures along a wall.

a. How many different ways can you arrange the five pictures along a wall?

b. If you select the arrangements at random, what is the probability of any one of these outcomes?

c. How many different ways can you select and arrange any three of the five pictures in a row?

d. What is the probability of randomly selecting one of the outcomes in part c?

Solution

a. The pictures are labeled A, B, C, D, and E. Choose one of the pictures, then choose one of the remaining four pictures, then choose one of the remaining three pictures, then choose one of the remaining two pictures, and then choose the remaining picture. The pictures can be arranged in $\underline{5} \cdot \underline{4} \cdot \underline{3} \cdot \underline{2} \cdot \underline{1} = 120$ ways.

b. Visualize a tree diagram with 120 different paths, each containing five branch segments. Because the arrangement of the paths was made at random, all paths are equally likely, so the probability of any single path, such as CABED, occurring is $\frac{1}{120}$, or one path out of 120 total paths. You can also get this answer by multiplying the probabilities of each branch along the path:
$$\frac{1}{5} \cdot \frac{1}{4} \cdot \frac{1}{3} \cdot \frac{1}{2} \cdot \frac{1}{1} = \frac{1}{120}.$$

c. What if you only need to hang three of the pictures? Begin by choosing one of the original five pictures. Then choose one of the remaining four pictures, and then choose one of the remaining three pictures. The three pictures can be arranged in $\underline{5} \cdot \underline{4} \cdot \underline{3} = 60$ ways.

d. The probability of randomly selecting one of the arrangements, such as DAB, is $\frac{1}{60}$ (one of the 60 paths, or $\frac{1}{5} \cdot \frac{1}{4} \cdot \frac{1}{3} = \frac{1}{60}$). ■

Probability of a Path

If n_1, n_2, n_3, . . . represent choice 1, choice 2, choice 3, . . . along a path, the probability of this sequence of choices occurring can be found by multiplying the probabilities for each choice (branch segment) along the path.

$$P(n_1 \text{ and } n_2 \text{ and } n_3 \text{ and } . . .) = P(n_1) \cdot P(n_2) \cdot P(n_3) \cdot . . .$$

In Example 1, the order in each sequence is significant, and once a choice is made, that choice cannot be used again in the same sequence. Arrangements like those in Example 1 were first called permutations by the Swiss mathematician Jacob Bernoulli (1654-1705) in his book *Ars Conjectandi* (*The Art of Conjecture*). Jacob Bernoulli came from a family of mathematicians—at least eleven members of this family made significant contributions to the development of mathematics.

Jacob Bernoulli's brothers, Jacques and Jean, were also mathematicians.

Permutation

A **permutation** is an arrangement or selection of objects from a set when order is important.

Investigation 11.1.1

The Factorial Function

In this investigation you will explore how the ! function works on your calculator. (The expression $n!$ is read "n factorial.")

a. Have each group member find the value of $n!$ for each choice of n and complete a table like the one below.

n	1	2	3	4	5	6	7
$n!$	-?-	-?-	-?-	-?-	-?-	-?-	-?-

b. Discuss the following questions in your group.
  i. What can you do to the value of 6! to get 7!?
  ii. What can you do to the value of 6! to get 5!?
  iii. What does 8! mean?
  iv. Describe a real-life situation involving 8!.

c. Have each group member choose one of the questions below. Then share your results with other group members.
  i. What happens when you try to compute 1.5! on your calculator?
  ii. What happens when you try to compute (⁻3)! on your calculator?
  iii. What is the largest value of n for which you can find $n!$ on your calculator? Explain why you think the calculator can't calculate $n!$ for larger values of n.
  iv. What is the smallest value of n for which you can find $n!$?

d. Use your results for parts b and c to create and write a definition for $n!$ that seems to match the design of your calculator's factorial function.

e. Define $n!$ recursively.

f. Describe what a graph of $y = n!$ should look like. Can you display this graph on your calculator. Why or why not?

NOTE
11A

In Example 1a, you permuted or arranged all five of the five pictures, $_5P_5 = 120$, and in Example 1c you permuted three of the five pictures, $_5P_3 = 60$, to obtain the total number of arrangements. The notation $_nP_r$ is read "n things permuted r at a time." See **Calculator Note 11A** for an explanation of how to compute permutations on your calculator.

▣ Example 2

Suppose there are seven flute players in an ensemble. How many different arrangements of these players can be made for each situation specified below?

a. All seven players are seated in a row.

b. Any four players are selected to sit in a row.

c. All seven players are seated, but Fiona must be first and Steven must be seventh.

d. All seven players are seated, but Donald and Elizabeth must be next to each other.

Solution

a. $_7P_7 = \underline{7} \cdot \underline{6} \cdot \underline{5} \cdot \underline{4} \cdot \underline{3} \cdot \underline{2} \cdot \underline{1} = 5040$. There are seven choices for the first chair, six choices remaining for the second chair, five for the third chair, and so on.

b. $_7P_4 = \underline{7} \cdot \underline{6} \cdot \underline{5} \cdot \underline{4} = 840$. There are only four slots or chairs to fill. There are seven choices for the first chair, six choices remaining for the second chair, five for the third chair, and, finally, four for the fourth chair.

c. <u>Fiona</u> _____ _____ _____ _____ _____ <u>Steven</u>.
This arrangement means there is one choice for the first chair and one choice for the seventh chair. The other chairs can be filled in $_5P_5$ ways. Therefore, the counting principle suggests $\underline{1} \cdot \underline{5} \cdot \underline{4} \cdot \underline{3} \cdot \underline{2} \cdot \underline{1} \cdot \underline{1} = 120$ different arrangements. It is important that Fiona's and Steven's positions be established first. In general, take care of any special circumstances before you establish your counting scheme. *Don't start multiplying before thinking about the meaning of the numbers in the sequence, or before drawing or visualizing a tree diagram.*

d. One way of thinking through this arrangement is to consider Donald and Elizabeth as a unit or element. Imagine them actually tied together somewhere in the sequence $\underline{\text{-?-}} \cdot \underline{\text{-?-}} \cdot \underline{\text{-?-}} \cdot \underline{\text{DE}} \cdot \underline{\text{-?-}} \cdot \underline{\text{-?-}}$. Now there are six elements to be arranged in $_6P_6 = 720$ different arrangements. Multiply this number (720) by 2 because the unit could be either DE or ED in each of the 720 arrangements. Therefore, there are 1440 different arrangements with Donald and Elizabeth seated next to each other. ▪

Sometimes the challenge is to decide how to apply the counting strategy in a particular problem. You must think carefully about each problem. In the previous examples, you have used tree diagrams, the counting principle, and your calculator to find the number of permutations. Be sure to think about each problem, and avoid the temptation to blindly apply formulas.

■ Example 3

a. How many different license plates are available if any three letters from the alphabet are followed by any three digits?

b. How many different license plates are available if three letters are followed by three digits or three digits are followed by three letters?

Solution

a. License plates allow multiple use of letters and digits, so $\underline{26} \cdot \underline{26} \cdot \underline{26} \cdot \underline{10} \cdot \underline{10} \cdot \underline{10}$ = 17,576,000 represents the number of license plates available.

b. You could have either $\underline{26} \cdot \underline{26} \cdot \underline{26} \cdot \underline{10} \cdot \underline{10} \cdot \underline{10}$ plates if the letters are first, or $\underline{10} \cdot \underline{10} \cdot \underline{10} \cdot \underline{26} \cdot \underline{26} \cdot \underline{26}$ license plates if the digits are first. Therefore, there are 35,152,000 such plates. ■

An arrangement is not considered a permutation if a letter or digit is used more than once. The definition of a permutation states that it is an arrangement without replacement or, in this case, duplication. The license plate *MTM 351* is not a permutation.

Problem Set 11.1

1. a. In how many ways can the eight different mathematics books for grades 1 through 8 be arranged on a shelf?

b. How many ways can the books be arranged so that the Grade 5 book will be the rightmost book?

c. Use the answers from 1a and 1b to to find the probability that the Grade 5 book will be the rightmost book if the books are arranged at random.

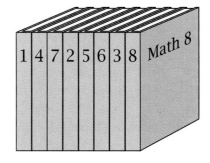

d. Explain how to compute the probability in 1c by using another method.

e. If the books are arranged randomly, what is the probability that the last book on the right is an even number? Explain how you determined this probability.

f. How many ways can the books be arranged so that the books are in increasing order from left to right?

g. How many ways can the books be arranged so that the books are out of sequence (not in strictly increasing order)?

h. What is the probability that the books are out of sequence?

2. Evaluate each factorial expression in a–f. (Some answers will contain n.)

a. $\dfrac{12!}{11!}$ **b.** $\dfrac{7!}{6!}$ **c.** $\dfrac{(n+1)!}{n!}$ **d.** $\dfrac{n!}{(n-1)!}$

e. $\dfrac{120!}{118!}$ **f.** $\dfrac{n!}{(n-2)!}$ **g.** Find n if $\dfrac{(n+1)!}{n!} = 15$.

3. a. Describe a real-life situation involving $_7P_3$.

  b. Explain the relationship between $_7P_3$ and $\dfrac{7!}{4!}$.

  c. Describe several different ways to find the value of $_nP_r$.

4. The ten digits 0, 1, 2, 3, . . . , 9 are arranged randomly with no repetition of digits.

  a. How many different arrangements are possible?

  b. What is the probability that the number formed is greater than or equal to 7 billion?

  c. What is the probability that the number formed is divisible by 5?

  d. What is the probability that the numbers 4, 5, and 6 are next to each other (in this order) in the number formed?

5. How many different 800 telephone numbers (1-800- -?- -?- -?- - -?- -?- -?- -?-) are available? (The numbers 0 or 1 are not allowed in the first slot.)

6. A computer is programmed to list all of the permutations for N items. Compute $N!$. Figure out how long it will take for the computer to list all of the possibilities. Use an appropriate time unit for each answer (minutes, hours, days, or years).

N	Permutation ($N!$)	Time (sec)
5	120	0.00012
10	3,628,800	3.6288
12	-?-	-?-
13	-?-	-?-
15	-?-	-?-
20	-?-	-?-

7. You have purchased four tickets to a charity raffle in which only 50 tickets were sold. Three prizes will be awarded. Assume that the prizes are drawn in reverse order: that is, third prize is drawn first, second prize is drawn second, and first prize is drawn last. Also assume that once a ticket is drawn it cannot be drawn again.

  a. What is the probability that you will win *only* the first prize?

  b. What is the probability that you will win both the first and second prizes, but not third prize?

  c. What is the probability that you will win the second or third prize?

  d. If the prizes are gift certificates for $25, $10, and $5, respectively, what is your expected value? Recall from Chapter 8 that the expected value is the sum of the products of the probability of each possible event multiplied by the value of that event.

Take Another Look 11.1

Recently a new prefix had to be defined for toll-free numbers because of increased demand. A related problem is that of assigning area codes. Area codes have had to be reconfigured to allow phone companies to keep up with the increased demand for telephone service. Read the article below. Then determine how many new area codes will result from this "new look" for area codes. You may have to do some research to find out if there are any restrictions for the first digit or last digit in an area code.

A New Look For Area Codes

In 1995, new area codes began to have a different look. The middle number of the area code isn't a zero or a one anymore.

California's first area code with the new look, 562, will be coming to Southern California no later than February 1, 1997.

We've already upgraded our equipment to accept the new area codes, and we've notified customers with PBX equipment to make similar changes. If you have programmable phones or other equipment, you may need to make changes so these new codes can be reached.

Why is This Happening?

There simply aren't any more area codes available with zero or one as the middle number.

New area codes:

Chicago, Il.	630	Atlanta, Ga.	770
Alabama	334	Connecticut	860
Washington	360	Tennessee	423
Houston, Tx.	281	Bermuda	441
Arizona	520	Oregon	541
Colorado	970	Miami, Fl.	954
Tampa, Fl.	941	South Carolina	864
Virginia	540	Florida (No.)	352

So, all new area codes will have a number from two through nine as the middle number. This allows for 640 new area codes.

The new number combinations won't affect the way you dial your calls.

Section 11.2

Combinations and Probability

Science moves, but slowly, slowly, creeping on from point to point.
—Alfred Tennyson

This tree diagram pictures the possible outcomes when a coin is tossed three times.

3 Hs	one path
2 Hs and 1 T	three paths
1 H and 2 Ts	three paths
3 Ts	one path

H — •1 HHH
T — •2 HHT
H — •3 HTH
T — •4 HTT
H — •5 THH
T — •6 THT
H — •7 TTH
T — •8 TTT

If you are not concerned about what order the heads and tails occur, then paths 2, 3, and 5 can be lumped together as (2 heads and 1 tail) and paths 4, 6, and 7 can be lumped together as (1 head and 2 tails).

The diagram and the counting principle both indicate $\underline{2} \cdot \underline{2} \cdot \underline{2} = 8$ equally likely outcomes: 2 choices, then 2 choices, then 2 choices.

The probabilities of the four different outcomes are as follows:

$P \text{ (three heads)} = \dfrac{1}{8}$ $\qquad$ $P \text{ (exactly two heads)} = \dfrac{3}{8}$

$P \text{ (exactly two tails)} = \dfrac{3}{8}$ $\qquad$ $P \text{ (three tails)} = \dfrac{1}{8}$

In this section you will develop a counting formula that you will use throughout the chapter. Understanding the connection between a tree diagram and the formula will help you to understand the more complicated ideas to come. Think visually, and draw one or more representations for each problem you investigate.

■ **Example 1**

At the first meeting of the International Club, the members are getting acquainted by introducing themselves and shaking hands. Each member shakes hands with every other member. How many handshakes are there in each of the situations listed below?

a. Three people are in the room.

b. Four people are in the room.

c. Five people are in the room.

d. Fifteen people are in the room.

Solution

The points (**vertices**) pictured can represent the three, four, or five people in a room, and the lines (**edges**) can represent the handshakes. You can find the answer by counting, but as you add more people to the group it will become more difficult to draw and count the number of handshakes.

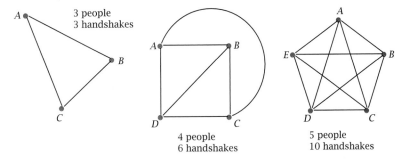

The four edges at each vertex in the five-person handshake solution might suggest that there are 4 · 5 edges. However, if you use this method to count edges, then an edge like *DB* will be counted at vertex *D* and again at vertex *B*. Because *DB* is the same as *BD*, you are counting twice as many edges as the actual total. The handshake problem is an example of "a combination of five things taken two at a time," $_5C_2$. (Sometimes this notation is read as "five choose two.") The order in which two vertices are taken doesn't matter and, because there are $_5P_2 = 20$ permutations of five vertices taken two at a time, you have

$$2 \cdot {_5C_2} = {_5P_2} \quad \text{or} \quad {_5C_2} = \frac{_5P_2}{2} = \frac{20}{2} = 10.$$

The same pattern continues for 15 people (vertices). The edge between any two vertices represents a handshake. Each person shakes hands with 14 others. The value 15 · 14 = 210 = $_{15}P_2$ is twice as large as the number you want, so there are $_{15}C_2 = 105$ handshakes. ∎

Combination

A **combination** is a selection of objects from a set in which order is not important.

■ Example 2

Ann, Ben, Chang, and Dena are members of the International Club, and they have volunteered to be on a committee that will arrange a reception for foreign exchange students. Usually there are only three students on the committee. How many different three-member committees can be formed with these four students?

Solution

Note that order isn't important in this case. ABD and BDA are the same committee and shouldn't be counted more than once. The number of different committee combinations will be fewer than the $_4P_3 = 24$ arrangements listed below. The number of combinations for a committee will always be fewer that the number of permutations.

ABC	**ABD**	**ACD**	**BCD**
ACB	ADB	ADC	BDC
BAC	BAD	CAD	CBD
BCA	BDA	CDA	CDB
CAB	DAB	DAC	DBC
CBA	DBA	DCA	DCB

Each of the four committees in the top row can represent all of the arrangements listed in its column. Therefore, the permutation total, $_4P_3$, is equal to 24 and is six times the number of distinct combinations. There are always fewer combinations of a set of elements than there are permutations of that set. Because the combination number $_4C_3$ represents a collection of three elements from a set of four, without regard to order, and $_4P_3 = 24 = 6 \cdot {}_4C_3$, you can see that $_4C_3 = 4$. What is the relationship between 3! and the 6 in this example? ■

Example 3

Les Luhk seems to have the worst luck getting Saturday night dates. On the average he has a 10% success rate; that is, only 10% of the girls he asks to go out with him will accept. On a particular Saturday, he faxes requests to seven potential dates. (Are you beginning to understand part of his problem?) What is the probability that he will end up with *two* dates?

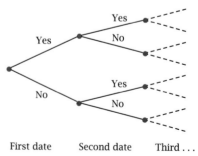

Solution

The tree diagram for this problem has seven stages (one for each potential date), and splits into two possibilities (success or failure) at each point on the path. Therefore, there are $2 \cdot 2 \cdot 2 \cdot 2 \cdot 2 \cdot 2 \cdot 2 = 2^7 = 128$ possibilities. The question is, how many of the 128 separate paths contain 2 successes and 5 failures? Because order is not important, you can find the number of paths that fit this description by finding a combination number. There are $_7C_2$ or 21 branches. (Could you also compute $_7C_5$? Why or why not?) For any one of these paths, the probability is

First date   Second date   Third . . .

$$0.1 \cdot 0.1 \cdot 0.9 \cdot 0.9 \cdot 0.9 \cdot 0.9 \cdot 0.9 = 0.0059049.$$

Multiply the number of paths representing two dates by the probability of each path occurring to find the probability that Les will end up with exactly two dates.

$$21 \cdot 0.0059 = 0.124$$

Therefore, the probability is 12.4% that he will end up with two dates. ∎

Investigation 11.2.1

Winning the Lottery

You will do Part 1 of this investigation with the whole class. Then, in Part 2, you will work with your group to discuss and analyze the results.

The game: Consider a state lottery called Lotto 47. Twice a week, players select six different numbers between 1 and 47, inclusive. The state lottery commission also selects six numbers from 1 through 47. Selection order doesn't matter, but a player needs to match all six numbers to win the Lotto.

Part 1

Step 1　For five minutes, write down as many different sets of six numbers as you can. Write only numbers between 1 and 47, inclusive.

Step 2　As a class, determine a **random number routine** that generates numbers in the list $\{1, 2, 3, \ldots, 47\}$.

Step 3　Next, everyone stands up.

Step 4　The teacher will generate a set of six random numbers. After the first number is generated, any person who does *not* have that number written anywhere in any set sits down.

Step 5　The second number is generated. Any person who does not have the first and second number in the *same* set sits down.

Step 6　Repeat Step 5 until no one is standing or until you have generated six numbers. (If a number repeats itself, simply skip it, and generate another number.)

Part 2　Work together with your group to answer the questions below.

    a. What does it mean if someone is still standing after all six numbers have been called?

    b. What is the probability that any one set of six numbers wins?

    c. At $1 for each set of six numbers, how much did each group member invest during the five minutes? What was the total group investment?

    d. Estimate the total amount invested by the entire class in the five minutes. Explain how you determined this estimate.

e. Estimate the probability that someone in your class wins. Explain how you determined this estimate.

f. Estimate the probability that someone in your school would win if everyone in the school participated in this activity. Explain how you determined this estimate.

g. If each of the possible sets of six numbers are written on 1-inch chips, and all the chips are laid end to end, how long will the line of chips be? (Use appropriate units, not inches.) Be sure to explain how you determined this length.

h. Have each group member write a paragraph or story that compares his or her chances of winning Lotto 47 with some other remote possibility whose probability is approximately the same.

Problem Set 11.2

1. a. What is the relationship between $_7P_2$ and $_7C_2$?
  b. What is the relationship between $_7P_3$ and $_7C_3$?
  c. What is the relationship between $_7P_4$ and $_7C_4$?
  d. What is the relationship between $_7P_7$ and $_7C_7$?
  e. Describe how you can find $_nC_r$ if you know $_nP_r$.

2. Evaluate each factorial expression.

  a. $\dfrac{10!}{3!7!}$ **b.** $\dfrac{7!}{4!3!}$ **c.** $\dfrac{15!}{13!2!}$ **d.** $\dfrac{7!}{7!0!}$

3. Find each combination number.

  a. $_{10}C_7$ **b.** $_7C_3$ **c.** $_{15}C_2$ **d.** $_7C_0$

4. Compare each answer in Problem 3 with the corresponding answer in Problem 2.
  a. Explain how $_{10}C_4$ is related to the factorial expression $\dfrac{10!}{4!6!}$.
  b. Find a different number r so that $_{10}C_r$ has the same answer as $_{10}C_4$.
  c. Explain why the two combination numbers in 4b are the same.
  d. Write a factorial expression that is equivalent to $_nC_r$.

5. Express the relationship between each pair of permutations or combinations below. You may use tree diagrams, formulas, written statements, or another method of your choice.

  a. $_nP_r$ and $_{n+1}P_r$ **b.** $_nP_r$ and $_nP_{r+1}$ **c.** $_nC_r$ and $_{n+1}C_r$ **d.** $_nC_r$ and $_nC_{r+1}$

6. Imagine there are 20 students in the class, and the teacher will randomly select six students to give an oral report on "Using Probability in the Work Place." Noah and Rita are considering the possibility of working together on one report and hoping that the teacher will not call on both of them.
  a. How many different ways are there of selecting groups of six students?
  b. How many of these groups include both Noah and Rita?

    c. What is the probability that Noah and Rita will both be called upon to give their reports?

    d. What would you advise Noah and Rita to do, given the probability you determined in 6c?

7. Suppose you are to answer any four of the seven essay questions on the history test and the teacher doesn't care in which order you answer them.

    a. How many different question combinations are possible?

    b. What is the probability that you include Essay Question 5 if you randomly select your combination?

8. A coin is tossed five times and it comes up heads four out of five times. In your opinion, is this event a rare occurrence? Defend your position.

9. Data collected over the last ten years show that it will rain sometime during 30% of the days in the spring.

    a. How likely is it that there will be a week with exactly five rainy days?

    b. How likely is it that there will be a week with exactly six rainy days?

    c. How likely is it that there will be a week with exactly seven rainy days?

    d. How likely is it that there will be a week with at least five rainy days? (To answer this question, you must add several paths.)

10. Write a short letter to Pika Lock Company and explain why their "combination locks" should be called "permutation locks." Be sure to tell them how a true "combination lock" would work.

Binomial Theorem

Life forms illogical patterns. It is haphazard and full of beauties which I try to catch as they fly by, for who knows whether any of them will ever return?
—*Margot Fonteyn*

Probability is an area of mathematics that is rich with patterns. Long-range patterns are used by insurance companies when computing rates, by lottery commissioners when predicting prizes and revenue, by casino owners when determining odds, by meteorologists when predicting the weather, and by pollsters when reporting survey results. You can describe random phenomena outcomes, in which there are two possible choices, using the laws of counting and probability. In this section you will learn about the binomial theorem and how it can be used to compute probabilities.

A tree diagram can show the different results that occur when you flip a coin three times. In this situation there are eight outcomes that are usually counted as four different possibilities—three heads, two heads, one head, and no heads (or no tails, one tail, two tails, and three tails).

You can also use a binomial expansion to give you these counting numbers. At first glance, the expansion of the binomial

$$(H + T)^3 \quad \text{or} \quad (H + T)(H + T)(H + T)$$

may not seem to be related to counting possible outcomes. To begin expanding this binomial, you multiply the H and the T in the first pair with the H and the T in the second pair.

$$(H + T)(H + T) = (HH + HT + TH + TT)$$

Then multiply each term of that result with the H and the T in the third pair.

$$(HH + HT + TH + TT)(H + T) = HHH + HHT + HTH + HTT + THH + THT + TTH + TTT$$

Write the result using exponents.

$$H^3 + H^2T + H^2T + HT^2 + H^2T + HT^2 + HT^2 + T^3$$

A meteorologist studying weather data charts so that he can make long-range predictions

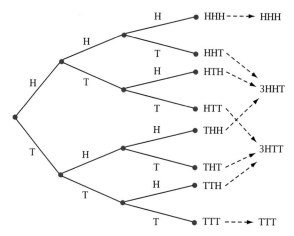

Combine similar terms and you will have $1H^3 + 3H^2T + 3HT^2 + 1T^3$

How is this last expression related to the outcome shown in the tree diagram above?

This four-term polynomial is the result of expanding the binomial $(H + T)^3$. **Binomials**, or two-term expressions, like $(H + T)$ or $(1 + r)$ appear frequently in mathematics, and combination numbers show up in the expansion of binomials. The numbers 1, 3, 3, 1 from the expansion of $(H + T)^3 = 1H^3 + 3H^2T + 3HT^2 + 1T^3$ represent the coefficients of the expanded binomial, as well as totals for the different outcomes for three coins. The one path with no tails is represented by $_3C_0$; the three paths with one tail are represented by $_3C_1$; the three paths with two tails are represented by $_3C_2$; and the one path with three tails is represented by $_3C_3$. The 3 before the C represents the number of coins, which in this case is three.

Investigation 11.3.1

The Binomial Expansion

There are many connections between a binomial expansion and combination numbers. In this investigation, you will explore some of these connections. Work with your group or with a partner. When possible, share the tasks.

a. Verify and complete the binomial expansions below. The easiest way to complete the expansion is to multiply the previous result by $(H + T)$. For example, to expand $(H + T)^3$, first find $(H + T)^2$. Then multiply that result by $(H + T)$ to get the final result.

$$(H + T)^0 = \quad\quad\quad 1$$
$$(H + T)^1 = \quad\quad\quad 1H + 1T$$
$$(H + T)^2 = \quad\quad 1H^2 + 2HT + 1T^2$$
$$(H + T)^3 = 1H^3 + 3H^2T + 3HT^2 + 1T^3$$
$$(H + T)^4 = \text{complete this one}$$
$$(H + T)^5 = \text{complete this one}$$

b. The paths of a tree diagram for $(H + T)^5$ produce the combination numbers for five objects chosen one at a time, five objects chosen two at a time, and so on. Compute the combination numbers on your calculator.

The number of paths with 0 tails = $_5C_0$ = -?-.
The number of paths with 1 tail = $_5C_1$ = -?-.
The number of paths with 2 tails = $_5C_2$ = -?-.
The number of paths with 3 tails = $_5C_3$ = -?-.
The number of paths with 4 tails = $_5C_4$ = -?-.
The number of paths with 5 tails = $_5C_5$ = -?-.

c. **i.** Find the sum of the combination numbers (the coefficients) in each expansion in part a.

ii. What is the sum for $(H + T)^6$?

(continued on next page)

iii. What is the sum for $(H + T)^7$?

iv. What is the sum for $(H + T)^n$?

d. Arrange the combination numbers that appear in the expansions of $(H + T)^0$ through $(H + T)^7$ in part a in a triangular pattern as shown below. Keep the rows and columns organized. Copy the first five rows as shown and continue adding rows until you have a total of ten rows. This triangle is called **Pascal's triangle**. (Hint: You may find a connection between a combination number in a given row and two combination numbers in the previous row.)

```
        1
      1   1
    1   2   1
  1   3   3   1
1   4   6   4   1
. . .
```

e. Use the combination numbers from Pascal's triangle to write out the expansion of $(a + b)^{10}$.

f. Use the combination numbers from Pascal's triangle to name the first five terms of $(p + q)^{12}$.

g. Write the first three terms of the expansion $(a + b)^n$. What is the sixth term? What is the xth term where $0 < x \le n$? List the last three terms.

Pascal's triangle and its properties were known for a long time before Blaise Pascal ever wrote about it. The triangle was first described in China around 1100 by Jia Xian. Its properties were used to calculate the roots of numbers. In 1303, Zhu Shijie discussed the triangle's connection with binomial coefficients. Abū Bakr ibn Muhammad ibn al Husayn al-Karajī, who lived in Baghdad around A.D. 1029, is said to have been the first Islamic mathematician to discover the connection between the triangle and binomial coefficients. The Indian mathematician Bhāskara described the triangle's connection with combinations in 1150 in his book *Lilavātī*. Niccolò Tartaglia used the triangle in 1556 to enumerate all possible dice throws. (The triangle is still known in Italy as Tartaglia's triangle.) Other European authors as well discussed the triangle and its properties.

Interesting patterns occur when you use different colors for odd and even numbers in Pascal's triangle.

Étienne Pascal introduced his 14-year-old son Blaise to Marin Mersenne, another French mathematician, at about the same time that Mersenne's books discussing the triangle were being published. The young Pascal continued to visit Mersenne and it is very likely that he was familiar with Mersenne's work on the triangle. Ten years later, Blaise Pascal wrote his *Traité du Triangle Arithmétique* (*Treatise on the Arithmetical Triangle*). The *Traité*, published in 1665, gives a synthesis and proof of the triangle's main properties (all of which were known before that time) and describes its use in solving expected value problems in games of chance. Pierre de Montmort referred to the triangle as Pascal's triangle in 1708 and Abraham de Moivre christened it Pascal's arithmetical triangle in 1730. It is now generally known as Pascal's triangle.

In the following example you will see how combination numbers can be used to describe a natural phenomenon.

■ Example 1

A hatching yellow-bellied sapsucker has a 0.58 probability of surviving to adulthood. Given a nest of six eggs, what are the respective probabilities for $0, 1, \ldots, 6$ birds to survive?

Solution

The probability of survival or success is 0.58 for each hatching bird, so the probability of not surviving until adulthood is $1 - 0.58 = 0.42$. First, you will need to expand the binomial $(0.58 + 0.42)^6$. Look for patterns as you study the expansion.

$$_6C_0 \cdot 0.58^6 + {_6}C_1 \cdot 0.58^5 \cdot 0.42 + {_6}C_2 \cdot 0.58^4 \cdot 0.42^2 + {_6}C_3 \cdot 0.58^3 \cdot 0.42^3$$
$$+ {_6}C_4 \cdot 0.58^2 \cdot 0.42^4 + {_6}C_5 \cdot 0.58 \cdot 0.42^5 + {_6}C_6 \cdot 0.42^6$$
$$= 1 \cdot 0.58^6 + 6 \cdot 0.58^5 \cdot 0.42 + 15 \cdot 0.58^4 \cdot 0.42^2 + 20 \cdot 0.58^3 \cdot 0.42^3$$
$$+ 15 \cdot 0.58^2 \cdot 0.42^4 + 6 \cdot 0.58 \cdot 0.42^5 + 1 \cdot 0.42^6$$
$$= 0.038 + 0.165 + 0.299 + 0.289 + 0.157 + 0.045 + 0.005$$

Survival	0 birds	1 bird	2 birds	3 birds	4 birds	5 birds	6 birds
Exactly	0.5%	4.5%	15.7%	28.9%	–?–	16.5%	3.8%
At most	3.8%	20.3%	–?–	–?–	94.9%	99.5%	100%
At least	100%	–?–	–?–	–?–	20.7%	5%	0.5%

The information in the row labeled "exactly" comes directly from the terms of the expansion and gives you the percentages of *exactly* $0, 1, \ldots, 6$ birds surviving. Find the missing percentage in the "exactly" row.

Find the two missing percentages in the "at most" row. To find the probability that *at most* two birds survive, find the sum of the probabilities of zero, one, and two birds surviving.

To find the *at least* probabilities, you will need to add the probabilities from the right in the "exactly" row. Find the three missing percentages in the "at least" row. Why don't the "at most" and "at least" values for each number of birds add up to 100%? Make a statement about birds that incorporates the 20.3% entry located in the "at most" row. ■

Investigation 11.3.2

Free Throw

NOTE
11B

Using what resources you have available, attempt ten free-throw shots. If you don't have access to a real basketball and hoop, be creative with what you have. If you make all ten (or zero) baskets, continue to shoot until you miss (or make) one. Use this information to calculate the experimental probability of your success on any given shot. Enter the program in **Calculator Note 11B** into your calculator. When you run the program, you will be asked to enter p as your personal probability of success. The program will use p and the corresponding probability of failure $(1 - p)$ as it simulates 250 trials of this ten-shot experiment. Then it will display a histogram of the results.

Next, calculate the 11 theoretical probabilities for making each of zero to ten baskets based on your experimental probability. For example, if your probability of success is 30%, then the probability that you will make six out of ten shots is

$$_{10}C_6(0.3)(0.3)(0.3)(0.3)(0.3)(0.3)(0.7)(0.7)(0.7)(0.7) = 210(0.3)^6(0.7)^4 \approx 0.037.$$

Why? Now multiply each of these 11 values by 250 and create a frequency histogram of the theoretical values. Sketch the calculator histogram next to the theoretical histogram. Then write a paragraph summarizing what this information tells you.

Problem Set 11.3

1. a. List the equally likely outcomes if a coin is tossed twice.
   b. List the equally likely outcomes if two coins are tossed once.
   c. Draw a tree diagram that pictures the answers to 1a and 1b.
   d. Describe the connection between the combination numbers $_2C_0 = 1$, $_2C_1 = 2$, and $_2C_2 = 1$, and the results of your answers to 1a, 1b, and 1c.
   e. Give a real-world meaning to the equation

   $(H + T)^2 = 1 \cdot H^2 + 2 \cdot HT + 1 \cdot T^2$.

2. Expand each binomial, combining similar terms when possible.
   a. $(x + y)^4$ **b.** $(p + q)^5$ **c.** $(2x + 3)^3$ **d.** $(3x - 4)^4$

3. Enter the equation $y_1 = (8\ _nC_r\ x)\ p^{(8-x)}(1-p)^x$ into your calculator.

    a. Find y_1 as x takes on the values $\{0, 1, 2, 3, \ldots, 8\}$ when $p = 0.50$. What is the sum of these nine values?

    b. Describe a method, using your calculator's statistics capabilities, that makes 3a easier to answer. Make a scatter plot of (x, y).

    c. Find y_1 as x takes on the values $\{0, 1, 2, 3, \ldots, 8\}$ when $p = 0.55$. What is the sum of these nine values? Make a scatter plot of (x, y).

    d. Compare and describe the scatter plots of (x, y) created by y_1 as p increases in increments of 0.05.

4. Dr. Zeus is using a method of treatment that is 97% effective.

    a. What is the probability that there will be no failure in 30 treatments?

    b. What is the probability that there will be three failures in 30 treatments?

    c. Let x represent the number of failures in 30 treatments. Enter an equation in y_1 that will provide a table of values representing the probability $P(x)$ for any value of x.

    d. Use the equation and table from 4c to find the probability that there will be less than three failures in 30 treatments.

NOTE
11C

5. The university medical research team has developed a new test that is 88% effective at detecting a disease in its early stages. What is the probability that there will be more than 20 false readings in 100 applications of the test? (You may wish to enter and use the program in **Calculator Note 11C**.)

6. Suppose the probability is 0.12 that a penny chosen at random was minted before 1975.

    a. What is the probability that you will find 25 or more such coins in a bag containing 100 pennies?

    b. What is the probability that you will find 25 or more such coins in two bags containing 100 pennies each?

    c. What is the probability that you will find 25 or more such coins in three bags containing 100 pennies each?

7. In the Vedic period (1000 to 400 B.C.) in India, Sushruta's great work on medicine, written in about the sixth century B.C., contained the statement that 63 combinations may be made out of six different tastes (*rasa*)—bitter, sour, saltish, astringent, sweet, hot—by taking the *rasa* one at a time, two at a time, three at a time, and so on. Explain how Sushruta obtained the 63 combinations. (In 1150, the Indian mathematician Bhāskara used Sushruta's problem of combining tastes as an example in his book *Lilavātī* to describe the connection between combinations and what is today called Pascal's triangle.)

8. The solution to the following problem will be used in Problem 8, Problem Set 11.4.

NOTE
11D

   a. Take the last two digits of your phone number, divide by 200 and add 0.25. Use this result as your probability of success, p, on one trial. Graph the binomial distribution showing the distribution of successes in 90 trials, $y = {}_{90}C_x \cdot p^x (1 - p)^{90 - x}$, in the window given in **Calculator Note 11D**.

   b. The exponential equation (as you well know) is $y = ab^x$. The curve $y = ab^{x^2}$ can be used to approximate the binomial curve if you apply a horizontal shift to this equation so that it is not centered on the y-axis. Experiment with values of a and b until you can best match the binomial distribution graph. (Hint: The value of b will be slightly less than 1, and a can be found by looking at the maximum value for the first function.)

Take Another Look 11.3

Take another look at combination numbers by using *parametric* mode on your calculator.

t	${}_5C_t$	${}_5P_t$	${}_5P_t \div {}_5C_t$
0	1	-?-	-?-
1	5	-?-	-?-
2	10	-?-	-?-
3	10	-?-	-?-
4	5	-?-	-?-
5	1	-?-	-?-

In Investigation 11.3.1, you considered all of the combination numbers for five objects. You can find the same combination numbers by using the parametric equations $x = t$ and $y = {}_5C_t$. Check your calculator's table to confirm the values listed in the table above. Describe what your calculator shows for values of $t < 0$ or $t > 5$. Does this result make sense to you? Now find a good viewing window and graph the parametric equations given above. Remember, these are discrete values, so be sure your calculator is in *dot* (not *connected*) mode.

Now write a second and third pair of parametric equations that will allow you to complete the table. What alternative heading could you use for the last column?

Repeat this entire activity to explore combination numbers for twelve objects. Consider generalizing your functions by using ${}_nC_t$, ${}_nP_t$, and ${}_nP_t \div {}_nC_t$ and storing the value 12 in n.

Look again at Problem 3c in Problem Set 11.3, but this time model the problem in *parametric* mode. Name the window values you used. Be sure your calculator is in *dot* mode.

Project

Trinomial Distribution

In this chapter you have been introduced to binomial distributions. When there are three options instead of two, the situation is similar. Begin this project by expanding each trinomial given below. Note that the first answer will have 6 terms, the second will have 10 terms, and the third will have 15 terms.

$$(x + y + z)^2 \qquad (x + y + z)^3 \qquad (x + y + z)^4$$

Make some generalizations about $(x + y + z)^n$. Include a formula for $(x + y + z)^n$ involving factorials for the coefficients of the terms.

Use what you have learned about trinomial distributions to solve the problem below.

The probability of a passenger buying a first-class airline ticket is 0.05, and the probability that she will buy a business-class ticket is 0.08. If 81 seats are sold, then what is the probability that there are exactly 4 seats in first class, 6 in business class, and 71 in coach? A plane has 100 seats, 10 in first class, 10 in business class, and 80 in coach. Explain how to find the probability that any of the three sections will be overfilled if 81 seats are sold. What is the probability that both first class and business are overfilled?

Section 11.4

Standard Deviation

The eye—it cannot choose but see;
We cannot bid the ear be still;
Our bodies feel, where'er they be,
Against or with our will.
—William Wordsworth

Pulse rates are measured in beats per minute. A distribution of the pulse rates of 50 cross-country runners might be quite different from that of 50 senior citizens, or 50 of your classmates. What is your pulse rate and how does it compare with the pulse rates of others? What different statistical tools might be useful to describe similarities and differences in these distributions? Certainly measures of central tendency like the mean, median, and mode would be useful.

Deviations from an average pulse rate, the total range of rates, the amount of variability, and any measures that help to describe the overall shape of a distribution are also valuable tools. To be useful, a measure of variability should be both universally acceptable and capable of measuring some dimension of the data. The standard deviation is the natural measure of spread (or dispersion) for certain types of distributions.

Data values	Pulse rates	Deviations $x_i - \overline{x}$	Squared deviations
x_1	64	$64 - 72 = {}^-8$	64
x_2	65	$65 - 72 = {}^-7$	49
x_3	70	$70 - 72 = {}^-2$	4
x_4	71	$71 - 72 = {}^-1$	1
x_5	73	$73 - 72 = 1$	1
x_6	79	$79 - 72 = 7$	49
x_7	82	$82 - 72 = 10$	100
		Total	268

Suppose the mean of several pulse rates is 72. Individual deviations, $x_i - \overline{x}$, for each data value, x_i, are listed in the table. The last column contains the squares of these individual deviations, or $(x_i - \overline{x})^2$. The standard deviation is the square root of the average entry in the last column, or $\sqrt{\frac{268}{7}}$. If all the pulse rates were 72 beats per minute, the standard deviation would be zero. Can you explain why the standard deviation would be zero? Usually the data values will differ from the mean value. Standard deviation is a way of averaging the amount of deviation from the mean.

Investigation 11.4.1
Measuring a Cord Length

Part 1

A cord measuring somewhere between 1.5 m and 2 m in length will be passed about the class. Use a meterstick to measure the length of this cord as accurately as you can. Don't share this measurement with your classmates, but instead record it on a scrap of paper. Place the record of your measurement in the envelope that came with the cord.

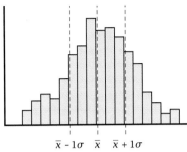

$\bar{x} - 1\sigma$　$\bar{x}$　$\bar{x} + 1\sigma$

Part 2

a. When all the students have recorded their measurements, enter the list of cord measurements into your calculator. Have each group member create several histograms with different bar widths. As a group, determine the bar width that gives the best picture of the data, and make a sketch of this histogram. Find the mean value of the data and draw a vertical line at the mean.

b. Work individually to find the deviation of each measurement from the mean and then square each deviation.

The mean value of the sum of the squares of the deviations is called the **variance** of the data. The units of this variance are centimeters squared, which is a little confusing because your cord measurements had nothing to do with area, so a number involving squared measures of length doesn't make much sense. However, the measurement that you want to find is the square root of the variance, which is called the standard deviation of the data. The units of the standard deviation of the measured cords are centimeters.

c. Now find the standard deviation of the data, and add two more vertical lines to your sketch: one that is one standard deviation above the mean, and another that is one standard deviation below the mean.

d. Write a paragraph describing how well you think people can measure. Include a discussion about the meaning of the standard deviation as it relates to the data in this investigation.

NOTE

11E

The term *standard deviation* was used for the first time by Karl Pearson in 1893, although he sometimes used the words "standard divergence" instead. The first to use the term *variance* was Ronald Aymler Fisher (1890-1962), an English scientist who laid the foundations of modern mathematical statistics and experimental method, including the design and analysis of experiments. He defined variance as the square of the standard deviation in an article he wrote in 1918. The standard deviation is a widely used measure of spread that you can use in much the same way you have used the mean absolute deviation (MAD) in Chapter 3. One advantage of the standard deviation is that it is a built-in function on most calculators, computer spreadsheets, and analysis tools. See **Calculator Note 11E** for instructions on how to calculate standard deviation with your calculator so that you can concentrate on the meaning of this measure rather than on calculating the number. The lowercase Greek letter sigma (σ) is used to represent standard deviation.

Variance and Standard Deviation

The **variance** of a data set is the mean of the sum of the squares of the deviations from the mean of the data.

$$\sigma^2 = \frac{\sum_{i=1}^{n}(x_i - \bar{x})^2}{n}$$

The **standard deviation** is a measure of spread used for data sets. It is equal to the square root of the variance.

$$\sigma = \sqrt{\frac{\sum_{i=1}^{n}(x_i - \bar{x})^2}{n}}$$

■ Example 1

Five hundred pennies were weighed, and the individual penny masses varied from 2.7 g to 3.4 g. The following table gives the frequencies of each different mass in the set of 500 pennies.

Mass (g)	2.7	2.8	2.9	3.0	3.1	3.2	3.3	3.4
Frequency	2	15	57	111	138	109	54	14

Find the mean and the standard deviation of the data. How far from the mean is a weight of 2.7 g?

Solution

NOTE 11E

Enter the data in the calculator as described in **Calculator Note 11E**. The mean is 3.0962 g, and the standard deviation is 0.1383 g. Take a moment to verify these values. A penny with a mass of 2.7 g is $\frac{3.0692 - 2.7}{0.1383} = 2.86$ standard deviations below the mean. ■

To say that a penny's weight is *0.4 g less than the mean* does not tell you if this measurement is a rare event or a common event. But to say that the weight is *2.86 standard deviations less than the mean* indicates this measurement is a rare event because most values in a normal distribution should be within one standard deviation of the mean, and almost all are within two standard deviations of the mean.

Any penny mass, x_i, can be converted to this standardized score for a comparative analysis. The calculation $\frac{x_i - \bar{x}}{\sigma}$ tells you how many standard deviations x_i is from the mean, providing a relative measure that allows you to compare one data set with another.

■ Example 2

Rita scored 670 on the mathematics portion and 740 on the verbal portion of a standardized test. The mean mathematics score for all students was 550, with $\sigma = 80$. The mean verbal score was 610, with $\sigma = 95$. Did Rita do better on the mathematics portion or on the verbal portion of the test?

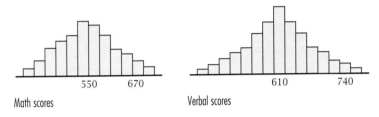

Math scores Verbal scores

Solution

Rita scored 670 – 550 = 120 points above the mean in the mathematics portion of the test and 740 – 610 = 130 points above the mean in the verbal portion. Based on these numbers, you might say the verbal score is the better score. On the other hand, the mathematics score is $\frac{670 - 550}{80} = \frac{120}{80} = 1.5$ standard deviations above the mean and the verbal score is only $\frac{740 - 610}{95} = \frac{130}{95} = 1.37$ standard deviations above the mean. This comparative measure indicates she did slightly better on the mathematics portion of the test. ■

The mean is probably the most commonly used measure of center, and the standard deviation is a measure of a distribution's spread about the mean. These two measures go together. The units of this measure of spread are the same as the units of the data. The standard deviation, like the mean, involves every value in the set, so it is strongly influenced by outliers. Therefore, this measure is very sensitive when the distribution of data is skewed. The strongest argument for using standard deviation is its close ties to a common type of distribution, the normal distribution. Because the spread of the data in such a distribution is quite predictable, you can use standard deviation to determine probabilities. You will soon learn, for example, that in a large set of cord length measurements, two-thirds of the data will be within one standard deviation of the mean, which means you could predict that the probability that the next measurement is within one standard deviation will be about 67%.

■ Example 3

Dee Visor created an adapter that will plug into the lighter socket of a car to recharge a video camera. She plans to sell 10,000 adapters in the first year. Dee needs several top-quality resistors for each unit. She purchased a package of one hundred 4.7-ohm resistors from Impedance Inc. and a package of one hundred 4.7-ohm resistors from Electrical Obstructions. She tested all of the resistors and recorded the results in a table.

Resistance (ohms)	4.697	4.698	4.699	4.700	4.701	4.702	4.703	4.704
Impedance Inc. (100 count)	5	9	17	27	21	13	3	5
Electrical Obstructions (100 count)	2	4	23	32	21	5	7	6

The first 5 in the table indicates that five of the Impedance Inc. resistors were found to be 4.697 ohms. Her specifications require that each resistor be no more than 0.002 ohms from its labeled value of 4.7 ohms. Which resistors should she order?

Solution

She can only use resistors between 4.698 and 4.702 ohms, inclusive. *Be certain you understand why this range is chosen before continuing.* This means that out of the first package she must discard $5 + 3 + 5 = 13$ resistors. The package from Electrical Obstructions contains $2 + 7 + 6 = 15$ rejects. Looking at this information, you might recommend that she buy from Impedance Inc. But further calculations show the first set has a standard deviation of 0.00165 ohms, while the second set has a standard deviation of 0.00155 ohms. The larger standard deviation for the Impedance Inc. resistors implies that the data for these resistors are more spread out, and that over the long run, Dee would end up discarding more resistors from Impedance Inc. ■

Problem Set 11.4

1. a. Which of these sets of data would you expect to have the larger standard deviation? Explain your reasoning.

  5 23 36 48 63   or   112 115 118 119 121

b. Calculate the mean and the standard deviation of each set by using the definitions, rather than by using the built-in function keys on your calculator.

c. Multiply the data values in each of the two given sets by 10. Then find the mean and the standard deviation of the new sets. How do these measures compare to those you found in 1b?

d. Add 10 to the data values in each of the two given sets. Then find the mean and the standard deviation of the new sets. How do these measures compare to those you found in 1b?

2. a. Select a set of four numbers from the whole numbers 1 to 8 inclusive (repeats are allowed) that has the smallest possible standard deviation. Explain your thinking as you make these selections.

b. This time select four numbers that have the largest possible standard deviation. Explain your thinking.

3. Pierre, Hans, and Juanita have taken national language exams in French, German, and Spanish, respectively. Pierre scored 88, Hans scored 84, and Juanita scored 91. The national means and standard deviations for the tests are: French, $\bar{x} = 72$, $\sigma = 8.5$; German, $\bar{x} = 72$, $\sigma = 5.8$; and Spanish, $\bar{x} = 85$, $\sigma = 6.1$.

a. From the information given, can you determine which test is most difficult? Why or why not?

b. Which test do you suspect had the widest range of scores nationally? Explain your reasoning.

c. Which of the three friends did *best* when compared to the national norms? Explain your reasoning.

NOTE
11F

4. Collect data from the sum of two 6-sided dice rolled 99 times. (See **Calculator Note 11F** for a calculator simulation.)

a. Find the mean and the standard deviation of the sums.

b. How many of the 99 sums are within one standard deviation of the mean?

c. What percentage of the data are within one standard deviation of the mean?

d. What percentage of the data are within two standard deviations of the mean?

5. Describe the standard deviation for each histogram and compare the standard deviations. The domain of the horizontal axis is 50 to 100 in each diagram.

a.   **b.**   **c.**

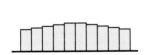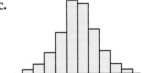

6. The tables on the next page list the ages of American presidents and vice-presidents when they first took office.

a. Predict the mean ages of the presidents and of the vice-presidents when they first took office. Which should have the larger standard deviation?

b. Enter the two separate lists of data into your calculator and calculate the mean and the standard deviation for each list.

c. Use your calculator to graph a histogram for each data set. Use the same scale for each graph.

d. Create two new lists by converting the ages in each list to a standardized scale by calculating $\frac{x_i - \bar{x}}{\sigma}$.

e. Describe the range of values in the new distributions.
f. Graph a histogram for each of these standardized distributions. Use an Xmin of ⁻3.5, an Xmax of 3.5, and an Xscl of 1.
g. Compare and describe the graphs from 6f.

President	Age	President	Age	President	Age
Washington	57	Buchanan	65	Hoover	54
J. Adams	61	Lincoln	52	F. D. Roosevelt	51
Jefferson	57	Grant	46	Truman	60
Madison	57	Hayes	54	Eisenhower	62
Monroe	58	Garfield	49	Kennedy	43
J. Q. Adams	57	Arthur	50	L. B. Johnson	55
Jackson	61	Cleveland	47	Nixon	56
Van Buren	54	B. Harrison	55	Ford	61
W. Harrison	68	McKinley	54	Carter	52
Tyler	51	T. Roosevelt	46	Reagan	69
Polk	49	Taft	51	Bush	64
Taylor	64	Wilson	56	W. Clinton	46
Fillmore	50	Harding	55		
Pierce	48	Coolidge	51		

Vice-president	Age	Vice-president	Age	Vice-president	Age
J. Adams	53	A. Johnson	56	Curtis	69
Jefferson	53	Colfax	45	Garner	64
Burr	45	Wilson	61	Wallace	52
G. H. Clinton	65	Wheeler	57	Truman	60
Gerry	68	Arthur	50	Barkley	71
Tompkins	42	Hendricks	65	Nixon	40
Calhoun	42	Stevenson	57	L. B. Johnson	52
Van Buren	50	Morton	64	Humphrey	53
R. M. Johnson	55	Hobart	52	Agnew	50
Tyler	50	T. Roosevelt	42	Ford	60
Dallas	52	Fairbanks	52	Rockefeller	66
Fillmore	49	Sherman	53	Mondale	49
King	66	Marshall	58	Bush	56
Breckinridge	36	Coolidge	48	Quayle	41
Hamlin	51	Dawes	59	Gore	44

7. Consider the number of heads when 15 fair coins are all tossed at once.

    a. Use the binomial probability distribution, $P(x) = {}_{15}C_x\, p^x(1-p)^{15-x}$, to complete a table of theoretical results for 500 trials of this experiment. (The entries in the second row, lableled $P(x)$, indicate the results of one trial.) Round off the frequencies (in row 3) to whole-number values.

Heads (x)	0	1	2	...	14	15	Total
$P(x)$	(0.5^{15})	–?–	–?–		–?–	–?–	= 1
Frequency	$500(0.5^{15})$	–?–	–?–	...	–?–	–?–	= 500

    b. Create a histogram showing the total number of heads.

    c. Find the mean and the standard deviation of the number of heads.

    d. How many of the 500 trials are within one standard deviation of the mean?

    e. What percentage of the data are within one standard deviation of the mean?

    f. What percentage of the data are within two standard deviations of the mean?

    g. What percentage of the data are within three standard deviations of the mean?

8. Enter the equation for the binomial distribution $y_1 = {}_{90}C_x\, p^x(1-p)^{90-x}$ using the window given in **Calculator Note 11D** and the same probability of success that you used in Problem 8, Problem Set 11.3. Place the values from 0 to 90 into the data set. Your goal is to find the mean and the standard deviation of the function values by using the probabilities as frequencies. The calculator uses only integer values of frequency to compute the values needed. To approximate the frequencies, round off 1000 times each probability to a whole-number value. (See **Calculator Note 11G**.) Now find the mean and the standard deviation of the data.

NOTE
11D

NOTE
11G

Take Another Look 11.4

For positive integers n, when the expression $(a + b)^n$ is expanded into the sum of $n + 1$ terms, the result is

$$(a + b)^n = \sum_{k=0}^{n} {}_nC_k\, a^{(n-k)}\, b^k.$$

This relationship is known as the binomial theorem. For values of n that are not too large, Pascal's triangle can be used to determine the binomial coefficients, or you can find the coefficients with your calculator.

As you make sense of the expression

$$\sum_{k=0}^{n} {}_{n}C_{k} \, a^{(n-k)} b^{k},$$

you can use it directly to expand the binomial $(a + b)^n$. Carefully describe how you can use it to expand $(a + b)^9$.

Write out the first four terms and the last two terms of $\sum_{k=0}^{n} {}_{n}C_{k} \, a^{(n-k)} b^{k}$.

Project

Helping Out

Go to the counseling, administrative, or food services department in your school and offer to gather some information on a topic or an issue of their choosing. Formulate your question in terms of a yes or no response. Collect the data, then provide graphs and an interpretation of the data you collected. Be sure to indicate in your written report how the data were collected and why you chose that particular method of data collection.

An important part of collecting information is designing the question so that it is unbiased. Have several people read your question and judge if it has a bias. For example, here are two biased questions: "Do you believe we should have capital punishment and that the government should devalue human life and kill prisoners for some crimes?" and "Do you believe we should have capital punishment and save taxpayers the thousands of dollars each year that it costs to confine a prisoner who has no chance of parole?" These questions are phrased in such a way as to lead people to favor one side or the other of an issue. Modify your question until there is no bias present.

Normal Distributions

Life is either a daring adventure or nothing at all. Security is mostly a superstition. It does not exist in nature.
—Helen Keller

Penny Punkuall has worked for many years as an actuary in the same office. It takes her an average of 23 minutes to get to work every day, with a standard deviation of 4.1 minutes. As she leaves her home, she notes that she must be at the office in 25 minutes. Because Penny uses public transportation, she cannot control the time it takes her to get to work. What is the probability that she will be late?

With no other information available, you will have to make some assumptions. What does this distribution of times look like? Is the distribution symmetric, as it is in Figures 1 and 2, or are Penny's travel times somewhat erratic, as it is in Figure 3? Figure 2 implies that some travel times are less than the average of 23 minutes and some travel times are more. In fact, Figure 2 suggests that the times are divided quite equally about the mean, and that generally Penny's travel times are near the average of 23 minutes. What information does the histogram in Figure 1 give you?

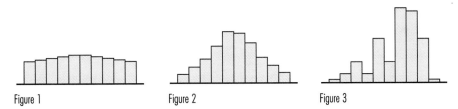

Figure 1   Figure 2   Figure 3

The **normal distribution** can be used to determine probabilities. How this distribution got to be called "normal" is unclear. The curve associated with this distribution has also been called the curve of error, the curve of facility of error, das Fehlerkurve, the Gaussian curve, the Laplace-Gaussian curve, and the probability curve. Francis Galton (1822–1911) was probably the first to call it the normal curve. It is both symmetric and bell-shaped, like a binomial distribution. In fact, the binomial distribution, $(p + q)^n$, becomes a normal distribution as the values of n grow increasingly large. Normal distributions and normal curves are used in many types of studies, some of which describe biological and psychological measurements. Gauss developed the idea of a normal distribution to describe the variation in the measurements made by surveyors and astronomers as they remeasured the same quantities (or what they thought were the same quantities). In this section, you will be introduced to some properties of the normal distribution and the related normal curve.

In the last section, you found that the mean penny mass was 3.1 grams and that the standard deviation was 0.1383 grams for the following distribution of 500 penny masses varying from 2.7 grams to 3.4 grams.

Mass (g)	2.7	2.8	2.9	3.0	3.1	3.2	3.3	3.4
Frequency	2	15	57	111	138	109	54	14

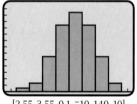 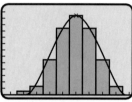

[2.55, 3.55, 0.1, ‾10, 140, 10]   (min=3.05 max=3.15 n=138)

The equation $y = ab^{x^2}$ can be used to approximate or model this distribution. It requires a horizontal shift because the curve pictured is symmetric about the mean mass of 3.1 grams. In the equation $y = ab^{(x - 3.1)^2}$, the 3.1 shifts the graph 3.1 grams to the right. How do these shifts relate to the transformations you studied in Chapter 5?

The calculations below show how the values for a and b can be found. To find a, substitute the x- and y-values that correspond to the mean value (3.1, 138) into the equation.

$$138 = ab^{(3.1 - 3.1)^2} = ab^0 \quad \text{means} \quad a = 138 \text{ or } y = 138b^{(x - 3.1)^2}$$

Then substitute the x- and y-values for any other table entry to find the value of b. In this case, the entry (2.8, 15) was used.

$$15 = 138b^{(2.8 - 3.1)^2}$$
$$15 = 138b^{0.09}$$

Solve for b:

$$b = \sqrt[0.09]{\frac{15}{138}} \approx 2 \cdot 10^{-11}$$

Now substitute the values for a and b into the original equation resulting in the equation

$$y = 138(2 \cdot 10^{-11})^{(x - 3.1)^2}.$$

In a normal distribution, the variable values are actually continuous rather than discrete, because it is just as likely that a penny will weigh 3.2147883 grams as 3.2 grams.

Investigation 11.5.1

Areas and Distributions

NOTE
11H

Work with your group on this investigation, sharing tasks and comparing answers whenever possible.

The curve $y = 138(2 \cdot 10^{-11})^{(x - 3.1)^2}$ models the distribution of penny masses. Find the area under this curve by using the area program in **Calculator Note 11H**. When you run this program you must input a value for the left endpoint (or starting value), a value for the right endpoint (or ending value), and the number of subdivisions. The greater the number of subdivisions, the more accuracy in the answer (and the longer it takes to complete the calculation). For left endpoint 1, right endpoint 5, and 500 subdivisions, you should get an area of approximately 49.18. Do this calculation on your calculator now.

A relative frequency distribution of this collection of pennies corresponds to the approximations given by $y = 2.8(2 \cdot 10^{-11})^{(x - 3.1)^2}$. The smaller coefficient 2.8 is the number that provides an area of 1 between the curve and the x-axis (138 divided by 49.18). Normal curves approximate histograms of probabilities. Because a probability distribution sums to 1, the area under a normal curve is 1, allowing you to answer probability questions.

Graph the equation

$$y = 2.8(2 \cdot 10^{-11})^{(x - 3.1)^2}$$

NOTE
11H

on your calculator. What is the maximum value of this function? Run the area program in **Calculator Note 11H** using the starting point, endpoint, and number of subdivisions given in the table to verify the area values.

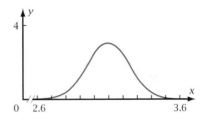

Starting point	2.6	2.6	2.6	2.6	1	0
Endpoint	3.6	3.6	3.6	3.6	5	6
Number of subdivisions	10	100	1,000	10,000	1,000	1,000
Area	0.9089	0.9896	0.9985	0.9993	0.9989	0.9989

The pattern and information pictured in the table show that by choosing a larger interval, or by using more subdivisions, the area increases toward 1. Now use the same program to find the area under the curve when x is greater than 3.3. You will have to decide how much accuracy is needed for the solution and then choose your values accordingly. As a general rule of thumb, you will need about 10^n divisions to get *n* digits of accuracy. How close is the estimate using 100 subdivisions? For the graph pictured, the approximate area is 0.08. This means the probability is 0.08, or 8%, which means that about 1 out of 13 of the pennies will weigh more than 3.3 grams. Describe how you can use this answer to determine the probability of a penny weighing less than or equal to 3.3 grams.

In a histogram, the sum of the column heights is the total number in the distribution. Similarly, the area under the distribution curve represents all of the numbers involved in the distribution. In the last investigation, you found the area under the curve by using the area program. You were faced with the problem that this curve has no endpoints because it approaches zero asymptotically. Because the curve seems to drop so quickly toward zero, you may have assumed that the area beyond a certain point was minimal.

■ Example 1

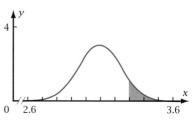

Professor Ty Tration at Whatts Amatta U recently gave a chemistry test. He found that the distribution of test scores fit the curve $y = 21(0.991)^{(x - 82)^2}$. Use his model to find frequencies for some of the test scores. What is the mean and the standard deviation of all scores from 62 to 102, inclusive?

Solution

NOTE
11I

Enter *all* scores and frequencies from 62 to 102 (inclusive) by using the equation to reconstruct the data set. Some of the frequency values predicted by the model are listed below. (See **Calculator Note 11I** for one way to enter the data quickly and accurately.) It is very unlikely that these are the actual scores and frequencies in the distribution, but they must be close to the actual data if the curve fits the distribution.

Score	65	70	75	80	82	85	90	95	100
Frequency	2	6	13	20	21	19	12	5	1

Check with your calculator to see that the table is correct, that the standard deviation is 7.4 points, and that the mean is 82. ■

In a symmetric data set the mean is always in the middle. In general, 99.99% of the area is within four standard deviations (in each direction) from the mean. Look at the area under the curve $y = 21(0.991)^{(x - 82)^2}$ from $82 - 4(7.4) \approx 52$ to $82 + 4(7.4) \approx 112$.

You should find that the area is about 391. (Check this result on your own.) You will continue working with this example in the problem set.

The mean determines the symmetrical center of the curve or the distribution, but it does not control the steepness of the curve. The slope, which is determined by the standard deviation of the distribution, controls the width, or spread, of the curve. If two normal curves have the same mean, the taller and more narrow graph is the one with the smaller standard deviation. Below are three normal distributions with a mean of 50. The vertical scales are adjusted so that the curves are all the same height. (Looking at the *y*-scales, you can see that the graph on the left would be the tallest graph if the same *y*-scales were used for each graph.) Note that at a distance of one standard deviation from the mean the graphs all have the same relative height.

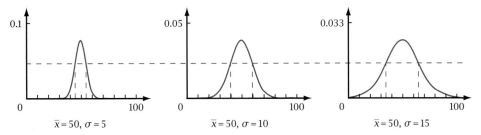

All normal curves are symmetric about their means and bell-shaped, as in the curves above. Their tail values fall off very rapidly. The two points where the curvature changes are each located one standard deviation away from the mean. In general, 68% of all data described by a normal distribution fall within one standard deviation of the mean, 95% of the data fall within two standard deviations, and 99.7% fall within three standard deviations of the mean. The information given by the standard deviation determines the shape, height, and width of any normal distribution curve.

Problem Set 11.5

1. Assume that the mean height of an adult male gorilla is 5 ft 8 in., with a standard deviation of 2.8 in.
   a. Sketch the graph of the normal distribution of gorilla heights. Shade the portion of this graph that indicates heights that are greater than 6 ft.
   b. Sketch the graph of the normal distribution of gorilla heights if instead the standard deviation is 3.2 in.
   c. Compare your sketches and explain your reasoning.

2. The life span of a tribble has a mean value of 28 days, with a standard deviation of 4 days. Sketch the normal curve for a life span distribution. Shade the portion of the curve showing that tribbles live 24 to 28 days.

3. Chocolate Frosted Sugar Bombs are packaged in 16 oz boxes. The filling machine is set to put 16.8 oz in the box, with a standard deviation of 0.7 oz. Sketch a graph of the normal distribution curve and shade the portion of boxes that are under the required weight.

4. Water collected from several different locations and depths of a lake will likely have a normal distribution of pH values. The pH of a solution measures the strength of the acidity of that solution. The mean value plus or minus one standard deviation is defined to be the pH range of the lake. Lake Fishbegon has a pH range of 5.8 to 7.2. Shade those portions of the normal curve that are outside this range.

5. Professor Ty Tration's distribution of test scores fit the curve $y = 21(0.991)^{(x - 82)^2}$. This distribution has a mean of 82 and a standard deviation of 7.4. Following Example 1, you found the area under the curve to be 391. Use the area program to find the percentages of the total area as specified in 5a–c.
   a. Within one standard deviation of the mean
   b. Within two standard deviations of the mean
   c. Within three standard deviations of the mean

6. a. Convert the equation $y = 21(0.991)^{(x - 82)^2}$ to a normal curve by finding the value of a in $y = a(0.991)^{(x - 82)^2}$ that provides an area of 1 under the curve.
   b. Use your new equation to find the percentage of the data that fall within one standard deviation of the mean.
   c. Use your new equation to find the percentage of the data that fall within two standard deviations of the mean.
   d. Use your new equation to find the percentage of the data that fall within three standard deviations of the mean.

7. The following data were collected from 493 college women.

Height (cm)	148–50	150–52	152–54	154–56	156–58	158–60	160–62	162–64
Frequency	2	5	9	15	27	40	52	63

Height (cm)	164–66	166–68	168–70	170–72	172–74	174–76	176–78	178–80
Frequency	66	64	53	39	28	16	9	5

   a. Find the mean and the standard deviation of the heights.
   b. Sketch the histogram of the given data.
   c. Write an equation based on the model $y = ab^{x^2}$ that approximates the histogram.
   d. Find the equation for a normal curve using the height data.

8. a. Find the mean and the standard deviation of the data below that represent the pulse rates of 50 people.

66	75	83	73	87	94	79	93	87	64
80	72	84	82	80	73	74	80	83	68
86	70	73	62	77	90	82	85	84	80
80	79	81	82	76	95	76	82	79	91
82	66	78	73	72	77	71	79	82	88

b. Sketch a histogram of the data.

c. Sketch a normal distribution curve that approximates the histogram. Write the equation of this curve.

d. Find the equation for a normal curve using the pulse rate data.

e. Would you say that these pulse rates are normally distributed? Why or why not?

NOTE
11H

9. Give a line-by-line explanation of how the area-under-a-curve program works. (See **Calculator Note 11H.**)

Take Another Look 11.5

Samuel Johnson has been quoted as saying, "You don't have to eat the whole ox to know that the meat is tough." The existence and use of public opinion polls, surveys, the census, and market research sampling to find out what people like to watch, do, drive, eat, or wear provide ample evidence that information about an entire population can be obtained from a subset of that population.

Sample variability should be expected. Candidates for public office expect that two samples using different sets of voters will provide slightly different results. But if the results of different samples are too scattered or spread out, they demonstrate a lack of sampling precision that means the results are not repeatable, predictable, or useful.

A common type of sample error is biased sampling. With biased sampling, the results of a particular statistic consistently underestimate or overestimate what is actually true within the entire population. On the other hand, unbiased sampling, over the long run, will provide a correct estimate of the particular parameter of interest within the population. In fact, the sample averages will be useful to predict the population averages. Your goal is to have a representative sample of the population you are studying.

Consider asking the students in your school this question: "How many years of school mathematics do you expect to complete by the time you have finished high school?"

a. Describe the complete procedure you would use to gather this information including how you would select students to be questioned.

b. Will the significance of your results change depending on whether you surveyed 10, 100, or 1000 students? Explain your thinking.

c. Does it matter who is surveyed or how or what they are asked? Explain your response completely.

d. What other important factors should be considered when collecting information for this survey?

A survey doesn't need to sample a large portion of the population in order to accurately represent an entire population. An important step in collecting accurate data is to use a random selection process. Two important keys for accurate survey results are (1) the way you phrase the questions and (2) how you select the sample of people to be surveyed. A question can be worded in such a way that it will make one response more likely than another. Or you might be asking a question that someone will be reluctant to answer honestly if he or she knows you will know who the responder is. Designing a survey that elicits meaningful responses is a difficult process.

Geometer's Sketchpad Investigation

Normal Curves

In Section 11.5, you learned that the general equation for a normal curve is $y = ab^{x^2}$. The steps below show one way that you can use Sketchpad to graph this function. The dynamic properties of Sketchpad will enable you to play with the curve and to look at the family of normal curves generated by the general equation.

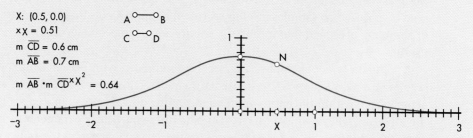

X: (0.5, 0.0)
$x_X = 0.51$
m $\overline{CD}$ = 0.6 cm
m $\overline{AB}$ = 0.7 cm

m $\overline{AB} \cdot$ m $\overline{CD}^{x_X^2}$ = 0.64

Step 1 Open a new sketch and choose Create Axes. Construct point *X* on the *x*-axis, and measure the coordinates for that point. Choose Calculate from the Measure menu, and double-click on the coordinates to get the value of the *x*-coordinate.

Step 2 Create two segments, *AB* and *CD*, that are each less than 1 cm long. Measure the length of each segment.

Step 3 Use the calculator to evaluate the equation for a normal curve $y = ab^{x^2}$. (The length of segment AB will represent the a-value. Similarly, the length of segment CD will represent the b-value. The x-coordinate of point X will represent the x-value.)

Step 4 Select, in the following order, the x-coordinate value for point X (the x-value) and the result from Step 3 (the y-value). Then select Plot as (x, y) from the Graph menu. Label the point N.

Step 5 Select point N and point X, in that order. Construct the locus.

If the value for $b < 1$, then you should get a normal curve, as shown above. If the value for $b > 1$, play with the scale of your graph until you see a normal curve.

Questions

1. Play with your curve. Change the scale of the graph, the value of a, and the value of b. What happens when the value of $b > 1$? What happens as the value of a increases? What happens to the shape of the curve as b goes from 0 to 1?

2. Draw a new curve based on the value of standard deviation, σ, and sample size n. (Create two segments and let their lengths represent the values of σ and n.) Calculate the values of a and b using a formula that will be formally introduced in Section 11.6:

$$a = \frac{n}{\sigma\sqrt{2\pi}} \quad \text{and} \quad b = 1 - \frac{1}{2(\sigma)^2}.$$

Vary the values of σ and n and look at how the shape of the curve varies. Describe the shape for large values of σ. Describe the shape for small values of σ.

Using the Normal Curve

Knowledge is the knowing that we can not know.
—*Ralph Waldo Emerson*

Mayor Polly Tishon just learned that there are 4700 unemployed working-age adults in her town. Should she be concerned? Her level of concern will depend on a number of variables, such as the size of her town and how many people are usually unemployed at any given time. If data over the last five-year interval indicate a mean of 4000 unemployed working-age adults, with a standard deviation of 500, she may have a legitimate concern. The current unemployment, however, may be just part of other normal changes in the community, or it may be the result of a new trend. How unusual is the unemployment figure of 4700? Even though the data may not be a perfect normal distribution, Mayor Polly Tishon can still use a normal distribution curve as a good model to make predictions and decisions about this situation.

You already know that the normal curve equation with a total area of 1 can be modeled by $y = ab^{x^2}$. In Problem 6 of Problem Set 11.5, you were asked to find the coefficient a in $y = a(0.991)^{(x-82)^2}$. The coefficient a, the value of the base, and the shift of the mean provide the particular model to fit the data. How is the value of a determined for this function? How is the value of the base, 0.991, determined for this function? The standard deviation must be involved because this measure determines the shape of the curve.

Investigation 11.6.1

The Normal Curve Equation

Do you recognize the mean and the standard deviation of the unemployment statistics in the equation

$$y_1 = \left(\frac{1}{500\sqrt{2\pi}} \right)\left(1 - \frac{1}{2(500)^2} \right)^{(x-4000)^2}?$$

Enter this equation into your calculator and graph the normal curve in the window pictured. Now calculate the values of

$$a = \frac{1}{\sigma\sqrt{2\pi}} \quad \text{and} \quad b = 1 - \frac{1}{2(\sigma)^2} \quad \text{where } \sigma = 500.$$

Confirm the equation and then graph
$y_2 = 0.0007979(0.999998)^{(x - 4000)^2}$.

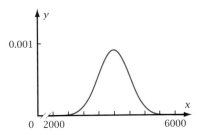

Check that the two graphs (y_1 and y_2) and the table entries for $2000 \le x \le 6000$ are the same. Use the program in **Calculator Note 11H** with a starting value of 2000, an ending value of 6000, and 500 divisions. Where did 2000 and 6000 come from? In a normal distribution there will be hardly any area beyond four standard deviations from the mean. In fact, you should find that the area under this curve is 0.9979, or approximately 1, as expected.

If the number of unemployed people is distributed normally, the area under this curve to the right of 4700 will provide the probability that more than 4700 people will be unemployed. To find this probability, use the program with a starting value of 4700, an ending value of 6000, and 500 divisions.

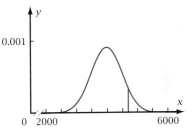

When you complete these calculations, you will find that under normal conditions, the probability of this event happening is 8%. Write an explanation for Mayor Polly Tishon that she can use to help her address this situation when talking to the media.

Finding the probability, or likelihood, of an event takes a good understanding of the normal curve and its geometric properties. Observe the different approaches as you work on the examples and problems in this section. Sometimes the information is reversed in a problem—the probability is given and you need to find the interval of values that should represent the event. To solve these problems you will use a program to find endpoints of the interval. The program is designed to match the given area (probability) with the interval at the left end of the normal curve. You will need to reinterpret some problems before using the program to solve them.

■ **Example 1**

Chuck O'Latt wishes to advertise the abundance of chips in his cookies. The research division at his factory has calculated that the mean number of chips in a cookie is 22.5, with a standard deviation of 4.5 chips. Chuck wants to advertise a number that will accurately represent 95% of the cookies sold. What should he advertise as the number of chips in a cookie?

Solution

NOTE
11J

The program Chuck is using (reprinted for you in **Calculator Note 11J**) will always find the right end of an interval, so Chuck should consider the unshaded portion of the graph pictured here. When he runs the program, he will give 0.05 as the percent. Do you see why? Remember, the probability of an event being true and the probability of it not being true must always add up to one. The program gives a value of 15.12 chips. (Check this result!) He can probably advertise that "all cookies have at least 15 chips," but you know that only 95% or more of all his cookies have at least 15 chips. ■

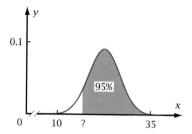

In Example 1, you were given the area (probability) to the right of a line, but you adjusted and worked with the region left of that line. Frequently you will need to use the symmetry of the curve to find the values that you are looking for.

■ Example 2

Inventor Cray Z. Eyedea invented an apparatus for cold sufferers to wear when trying to get a good night's sleep. The unit must fit tightly about the nose. Because noses come in such a wide range of sizes, Cray knows it is probably only feasible to produce units to fit 80% of the population. Medical research shows that the mean adult nose is 2.41 cm long, with a standard deviation of 0.34 cm. What range of sizes will Cray's apparatus fit?

Solution

The fairest way to fit 80% of the targeted population is to choose a range that is centered on the mean. Because of the symmetry of the curve, Cray knows that the area left of the shaded region must be the same as the area to the right of the shaded region. The three areas are 0.10, 0.80, and 0.10 because $0.10 + 0.80 + 0.10 = 1.00$. Try using the program with the value $\bar{x} = 2.41$,

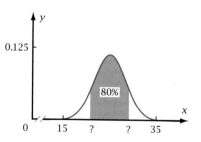

$\sigma = 0.34$, and a probability of 0.1. Remember, the program requires you to furnish the probability of the leftmost region. When you run the program you will get an error message because the program formula is limited. The program requires *that the standard deviation entered be greater than two.*

Cray thinks quickly and converts all measurements to millimeters. He finds that the mean length is 24.1 mm and the standard deviation is 3.4 mm. He enters the values $\bar{x} = 24.1$, $\sigma = 3.4$, and the probability of 0.1, and the program provides him with an answer of 19.9 mm. This result represents the nose measurement at the right end of the leftmost region. The lower deviation from the mean is 24.1 − 19.9 = 4.2 mm and, because of the curve's symmetry, he finds the upper deviation value by adding to the mean: 24.1 + 4.2 = 28.3 mm. So, to fit 80% of the population he must make his device adjust to fit noses between 1.99 cm and 2.83 cm. Gesundheit! ■

Problem Set 11.6

1. Penny Punkuall has worked for many years as an actuary in the same office. By her calculations, it takes her an average of 23 min to get to work every day, with a standard deviation of 4.1 min. As she leaves her home one day, she notes that she must be at the office in 25 min. What is the probability that she will be late?

2. The "You Gotta Be Nuts" candy bar has an average weight of 75.3 g, with a standard deviation of 4.7 g.
   a. What weight should the company advertise to be truthful 80% of the time? (Write a complete sentence using your numerical answer.)
   b. What weight should the company advertise to be truthful 90% of the time? (Write a complete sentence using your numerical answer.)
   c. What weight should the company advertise to be truthful 95% of the time? (Write a complete sentence using your numerical answer.)

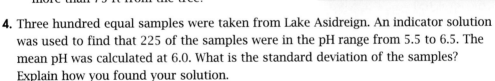

3. Acorns will fall around the base of a tree in a somewhat normal distribution with a standard deviation of 20 ft away from the base.
   a. What is the probability that an acorn will land more than 50 ft from the tree?
   b. What is the probability that an acorn will land more than 75 ft from the tree?

4. Three hundred equal samples were taken from Lake Asidreign. An indicator solution was used to find that 225 of the samples were in the pH range from 5.5 to 6.5. The mean pH was calculated at 6.0. What is the standard deviation of the samples? Explain how you found your solution.

5. Makers of "Sweet Swallows" 100% fruit drink have found that their filling machine will fill a bottle with a standard deviation of 0.75 oz. The control on the machine will change the mean value, but will not affect the standard deviation.
   a. Where should they set the mean so that 90% of the bottles have at least 12 oz in them?
   b. If a fruit drink bottle can hold 13.5 oz before overflowing, what percentage of the bottles will overflow at the setting suggested in 5a?

6. Assume that the probability of high school students needing corrective lenses is 28%.

NOTE

11F

   a. What is the probability that exactly 25 out of 95 students will need corrective lenses?

   b. In how many of 1000 groups of 95 students would you expect to find exactly 25 students needing corrective lenses?

   c. Repeat this calculation for all values from 0 to 95. Create a data set with x-values between 0 and 95 inclusive and y-values as the frequency of the event. (See **Calculator Note 11F** to automate this calculation.)

   d. Find the standard deviation of this data set.

   e. Compare this number to $\sqrt{95(0.28)(0.72)}$.

7. Enter the two functions below into your calculator. The first function represents the binomial distributions and the second function represents the normal curve. Use the variables N, P, S, and M in your equations. The variable N is the number of trials, P is the probability of success, S is the standard deviation, and M is the mean.

$$y_1 = (N_nC_r\, x)P^x(1 - P)^{(N - x)} \qquad y_2 = \left(\frac{1}{S\sqrt{2\pi}}\right)\left(1 - \frac{1}{2S^2}\right)^{(x - M)^2}$$

   a. Complete the table below by calculating $M = NP$ and $S = \sqrt{NP(1 - P)}$.

N	47	64	150	Your choice	Your choice
P	0.3	0.8	0.18	0.61	Your choice
M	–?–	–?–	–?–	–?–	–?–
S	–?–	–?–	–?–	–?–	–?–

   b. Store the first column of values in the proper variables, and graph both equations using a range that will give integer values along the x-axis.

   c. Repeat 7b for the other four columns. Make a statement about your observations.

Take Another Look 11.6

1. Problem 5 in Problem Set 10.8 introduces an extension of the concept of polynomial to an expression with an infinite number of terms. A power series has the form $f(x) = a_0 + a_1 x + a_2 x^2 + a_3 x^3 + \cdots + a_{n-1} x^{n-1} + a_n x^n + \cdots$ with the a's as coefficients. Power series provide approximations for several important functions that are built into calculators. Better approximations are obtained by using more terms. The ! function is frequently involved in a power series.

   Now investigate the value of the power series $f(x) = 1 + \frac{x}{1} + \frac{x^2}{2!} + \frac{x^3}{3!} + \frac{x^4}{4!} + \cdots$. You can do this by finding the value (when $x = 1$) for the first five terms, the first six terms, and so on. Explain what you have discovered. What is achieved by considering more terms of the power series?

   The limit of this power series is Euler's number e. Now investigate the values of more and more terms of the power series when $x = 2$ and when $x = 3$. Locate the e^x function on your calculator and explain what you have discovered.

2. In Take Another Look 11.4, you discovered that for positive integers n, when the expression $(a + b)^n$ is expanded into the sum of $n + 1$ terms, the result is

$$(a + b)^n = \sum_{k=0}^{n} {}_nC_k\, a^{(n-k)} b^k.$$

Use this binomial theorem to investigate the expansion of $\left(1 + \frac{1}{n}\right)^n$ for several positive integer choices of n. Write out and evaluate the expansions for $\left(1 + \frac{1}{2}\right)^2$, $\left(1 + \frac{1}{3}\right)^3$, $\left(1 + \frac{1}{4}\right)^4$, and $\left(1 + \frac{1}{5}\right)^5$. Then predict the long-run value of $\left(1 + \frac{1}{n}\right)^n$ as n approaches infinity. What is this long-run limit of $\left(1 + \frac{1}{n}\right)^n$? Describe how to duplicate this value by using a calculator function key.

Project

Normal Curves and e

NOTE
11J

The program in **Calculator Note 11J** for a normal distribution comes with the stipulation that you should only use it with a standard deviation greater than two. This is a rather unusual condition that is necessary because the formula is only approximate. The actual formula for continuous exponential growth is

$$y = \frac{1}{\sigma\sqrt{2\pi}}\, e^{-(x-\bar{x})^2/2\sigma^2},$$

which uses the constant e. (If you do not know what e is, then see Take Another Look 11.6 or the project titled Finding e in Chapter 7.) Compare the graph of this new equation with the graph generated by the program in **Calculator Note 11J**. Make sketches of the graphs of both equations using $\bar{x} = 50$ for three different standard deviations, $\sigma = 10$, $\sigma = 3$, and $\sigma = 0.5$. (You can see what the equation in the program is by looking at the equation in y_4 after you've run the program.)

Select a problem from Problem Set 11.6 and solve it again by using the new formula. How much error resulted from using the formula given in the chapter?

Chapter Review

. . . so little stress is laid on the pleasure of becoming an educated person, the enormous interest it adds to life. To be able to be caught up in the world of thought—that is to be educated.
—Edith Hamilton

In this chapter you reviewed some of the informal counting strategies from Chapter 8, and you were introduced to more formal counting techniques. The counting principle states that when there are n_1 ways to make the first choice, n_2 ways to make the second choice, n_3 ways to make the third choice, and so on, the product $n_1 \cdot n_2 \cdot n_3 \cdot \ldots$ represents the total number of different ways in which the entire sequence of choices can be made. These arrangements of choices, in which the order is important, are called permutations. The notation $_nP_r$ indicates the number of ways of choosing r things out of n possible choices. If the order is unimportant, then arrangements are called combinations and are written $_nC_r$, the number of combinations of r things from a set of n choices. Your calculator can automatically calculate permutation numbers and combination numbers, but before you use the calculator, you should be sure that you understand the situation and can visualize the possibilities. Combination numbers also appear as coefficients in binomial expansions that can be used to help calculate probabilities when there are only two possible outcomes.

In this chapter you were also introduced to some additional statistical tools. The standard deviation is similar to the mean absolute deviation discussed in Chapter 3. It gives information about the spread of data on either side of the mean value. Many biological and psychological measurements are distributed in a "bell-shaped" fashion, similar to the binomial distribution. This "bell" is called a normal distribution. The normal curve can be used to calculate probabilities. The area under the entire normal curve is equal to one. The area between two specific x-values is the probability of a value in that range occurring. When using the normal curve, you do not find the probability of a single exact value, but the probability of a range of values. To create a normal curve for a set of data, you need to know the mean and the standard deviation of the data.

Problem Set 11.7

1. Twelve candidates for a job (seven males and five females) are to be called into a room one at a time.
   a. How many different interview orders are possible?
   b. If the interview order is generated randomly, what is the probability that the first five candidates will be female?

2. Stamin Blackwood just picked up his bridge hand of 13 cards. He has ten red cards and three black cards. How unusual is it for the first ten cards he picks up to be red? Explain in detail so that Stamin will understand your answer.

3. Anna Chovey can take exactly 20 more pizza orders before closing. She has enough pepperoni for 16 more pizzas. On a typical night, 65% of her orders are for pepperoni pizzas. What is the probability that she will run short if she doesn't apply the pepperoni conservatively? (Hint: You will need to add four calculations for this answer.)

4. Rewrite each expression without parentheses.
   a. $100(1 - x)^8$ **b.** $600(1 + x/12)^5$

5. The height of each adult in Normalville was measured to the nearest inch. Find the mean and the standard deviation of the heights. Make a statement about the meaning of the standard deviation in this problem.

Height (in.)	60	61	62	63	64	65	66	67
Frequency	1	1	4	6	8	10	9	8

Height (in.)	68	69	70	71	72	73	74	75
Frequency	13	10	5	6	6	3	6	3

6. The heights of all adults in Bigtown are normally distributed with a mean of 167 cm and a standard deviation of 8.5 cm. Sketch a graph of the distribution curve of these heights, and shade the portion of that graph showing the percentage of people shorter than 155 cm.

7. Find the probability of guessing exactly six right answers out of ten true-or-false questions. Describe your solution process.

8. Write expressions involving x, n, and $!$ that are equivalent to $_nC_r$ and $_nP_r$.

9. Find the probability of guessing seven or more correct answers on a ten-question multiple choice quiz if each question has five choices.

10. Assume that United States males who are 6 ft tall and between the ages of 18 and 24 have a mean weight of 175 lb and that their weights are normally distributed with a standard deviation of 14 lb.
   a. Find the equation of a normal curve that will provide a probability distribution representing this information.
   b. What percentage of these males weigh less than 160 lb?
   c. Find two weights that will include between them 90% of all these males.
   d. What percentage of these males weigh between 180 lb and 200 lb?

Assessing What You've Learned

Be sure to choose at least three different ways to assess what you've learned. Which method or methods seem to work best for you?

- Organizing Your Notebook (Chapter 0)
- Keeping a Journal (Chapter 1)
- Portfolio (Chapter 2)
- Performance Assessment (Chapter 3)
- Open-ended Investigations (Chapter 4)
- Constructing Test Questions (Chapter 5)
- Group Presentations and Tests (Chapter 6)
- Overall Self-Assessment (Chapter 7)

12 Functions and Relations

These Arctic hares on Ellesmere Island in Canada live in very large groups. A realistic population growth model will have to take into account different factors that affect the rate of growth, such as food availability and predator-prey situations.

The Inverse Variation Function

Besides learning to see, there is another art to be learned—not to see what is not.
—Maria Mitchell

You probably know from experience that a lighter tree climber can crawl farther out on a limb than a heavier climber can.

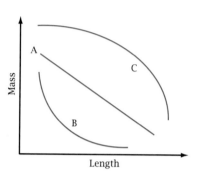

If a stick or a pole is held so that some of it hangs over the edge of a table, the amount hanging over the edge will control the amount of force or mass that can be applied to the end of the pole. What do you think the graph of (*length, mass*) will look like when the mass amount is applied to a length of pole until it breaks? Is the relationship linear, like that pictured in graph A, or does it resemble one of the curves, B or C? The next investigation will give you a chance to collect data and experiment with this relationship.

Investigation 12.1.1

The Breaking-Point Experiment

Equipment Needed
You will need several pieces of spaghetti, a small film canister, some string or thread, some weights (M&Ms, pennies, or other *small* measures of mass), and tape.

Procedure
Lay a piece of spaghetti on a desk or table so that its length is perpendicular to one of the sides of the table and one end extends over the edge of the table. (See the diagram on the next page.) Attach the string to the film canister so that you can suspend the canister from one end of the spaghetti. (You may need to tape the string or thread to the spaghetti.)

Then place your mass weights into the container one at a time until the spaghetti breaks. Record the number of mass weights and the distance from the table edge to the end of the spaghetti. Repeat the experiment several times, each time changing the length of the extension.

Data Analysis

Work with a partner, then share your results with other group members.

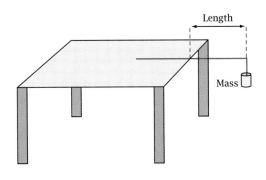

Length

Mass

a. Make a graph of (*length, number of mass weights*).

b. Does the relationship appear to be linear? If not, describe the appearance of the graph.

c. Use guess-and-check to write an equation that is a good fit with the plotted data.

Corey Ekt and Misty Ake were each asked to enter equations on the classroom view screen that would graph $y = \frac{2}{3}x - 4$. Corey entered $y = (2/3)x - 4$ and Misty entered $y = 2/3x - 4$. The graphs are pictured below. Which is correct? Misty Ake entered the equation incorrectly for her calculator, so her result is an unusual graph. Misty's calculator interprets $y = 2/3x - 4$ as $y = \frac{2}{3x} - 4$. Your calculator may not make this same interpretation. Misty's result is an example of a **rational function**.

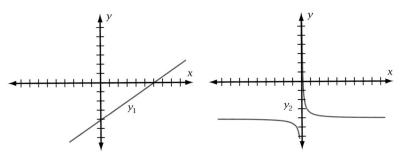

Rational Function

A **rational function** is one that can be written as the quotient of two polynomials, $f(x) = \frac{p(x)}{q(x)}$. The denominator polynomial must be of degree one or more.

Misty's rational function is $f(x) = \frac{2}{3x} - 4$, which can be written as

$\frac{2}{3x} - \frac{4 \cdot 3x}{3x} = \frac{2 - 12x}{3x}$. In this example, $p(x) = 2 - 12x$ and $q(x) = 3x$.

The parent rational function $f(x) = \frac{1}{x}$ demonstrates features that are characteristic of more complicated examples. Graph this function on your calculator, and verify the discussion that follows. The graph is made up of two pieces. One part occurs where x is negative and the other where x is positive. Notice that there is *no value* for this function when $x = 0$.

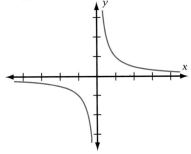

Complete a table similar to the one below for x-values close to zero. A vertical line at $x = 0$ is called a **vertical asymptote** because the function approaches this line as x gets closer to zero.

x	⁻1	⁻0.1	⁻0.01	⁻0.001	0.001	0.01	0.1	1
y	⁻1	-?-	-?-	-?-	-?-	-?-	-?-	1

Now complete a table for x-values toward the extreme ends of the axis. As x approaches the extreme values at the left and right ends of the x-axis, the graph approaches the horizontal axis. The horizontal line $y = 0$ is called a **horizontal asymptote** because the function approaches the line as x takes on extreme values. This asymptote is an end behavior model of the function. In general, the **end behavior** of a function is its behavior for x-values that are large in absolute value.

x	⁻10,000	⁻1,000	⁻100	⁻10	10	100	1,000	10,000
y	-?-	-?-	-?-	⁻0.1	0.1	-?-	-?-	-?-

If you think of $y = \dfrac{1}{x}$ as a parent function, then $y = \dfrac{1}{x} + 1$, $y = \dfrac{1}{x - 2}$, and $y = 3\left(\dfrac{1}{x}\right)$ are typical examples of transformed rational functions. Do you remember what happens to a function when x is replaced with (x – 2)? Both graphs below are of the function $y = \dfrac{1}{x - 2}$. Frequently, rational function graphs on the calculator may include a vertical-like drag line that *is not part of the graph*. However, it will look much like the graph of the vertical asymptote. See if you can figure out how, why, or when the calculator will draw in a drag line. Try experimenting with "friendly" and "nonfriendly" domains.

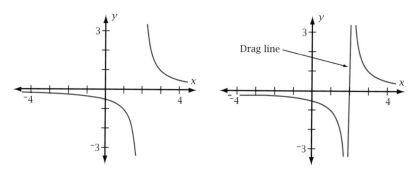

Investigation 12.1.2

Increase the Percentage

Your group will need about 200 tokens (chips, markers, or beans) in two colors; for example, dark beans and light beans.

Part 1 **a.** Start by making a pile containing 70 dark beans and 30 light beans. Calculate the percentage of light beans by computing the fraction

$$\frac{\text{number of light beans}}{\text{total number of beans}}.$$

Record your results in a table like the one below as you continue adding ten more light beans to the pile and recalculating the percentage each time.

Number of light beans added (x)	0	10	20	30	. . .	x
Total number of light beans	30	–?–	–?–	–?–	. . .	–?–
Total number of beans	100	–?–	–?–	–?–	. . .	–?–
Percentage of the total that are light (y)	30%	–?–	–?–	–?–	. . .	–?–

b. Write a paragraph that responds to the following questions: How many light beans must you add so that the percentage of light beans is 60%? So that the percentage is 75%? So that the percentage is 90%? Will the percentage of light beans ever reach 100%? Why or why not?

Part 2 **a.** Start over with 70 dark beans and 30 light beans. Record your results as you continue to remove five light beans from the pile, recalculating the percentage each time.

Number of light beans removed (x)	0	5	10	15	. . .	x
Total number of light beans	30	–?–	–?–	–?–	. . .	–?–
Total number of beans	100	–?–	–?–	–?–	. . .	–?–
Percentage of the total that are light (y)	30%	–?–	–?–	–?–	. . .	–?–

b. Plot the data from both tables on the same coordinate axes. Plot (*total number of light beans added [or removed], percent of light beans*). Use negative values for x in the second table, and enter the percentages in decimal form. The domain should include $-30 \le x \le 60$, and the range should include $0 \le y \le 1$ (decimal versions of the percentage values). Do the data appear to be linear?

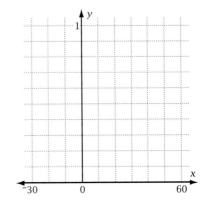

c. Write an equation involving x that describes the data values.

d. Add to the paragraph you wrote in Part 1 by describing any conclusions you were able to make based on your graphs and the equation you wrote.

Problem Set 12.1

1. Use $f(x) = \frac{1}{x}$ as the parent function. Sketch a graph and write an equation for each transformation of $f(x)$.
   a. Slide the graph two units up.
   b. Slide it three units to the right.
   c. Slide it one unit down and four units to the left.
   d. Stretch it to twice its present vertical height.
   e. Stretch it to three times its horizontal width, and shift it up one unit.

2. Write an altered form of the equation $y = \frac{1}{x}$ so that its graph will satisfy each set of criteria below.
   a. A horizontal asymptote at $y = 2$ and a vertical asymptote at $x = 0$
   b. A horizontal asymptote at $y = {}^-4$ and a vertical asymptote at $x = 2$
   c. A horizontal asymptote at $y = 3$ and a vertical asymptote at $x = {}^-4$

3. Write a rational equation to describe each graph. Some equations will need stretch factors. Assume that the distance between two grid marks represents one unit.

   a.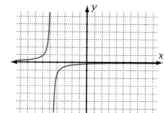

   b.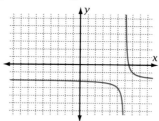

   c.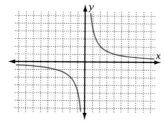

   d.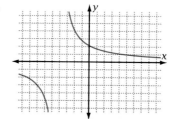

4. Police air patrols help monitor the flow of traffic on busy expressways. Explain how an air patrol officer with a stopwatch and a calculator can determine the speed of a vehicle on a highway with marks placed every 0.25 mi.

5. This graph pictures the number of milliliters of a pure acid that must be added to 55 mL of a 38% acid solution to raise the acid level of the solution to 64%.

    a. How many milliliters of pure acid were in the original solution?

    b. Write an equation for $f(x)$ and $g(x)$, letting x represent the number of added milliliters of pure acid.

    c. Find x when the solution is at 64%.

    d. Describe the end behavior of $f(x)$.

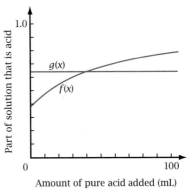

6. If a basketball team's present record is 42 wins and 36 losses, how many consecutive games must it win so that its winning record reaches 60%?

7. In a 1 gal container of 2% milk, 2% of the liquid is fat. How much of the liquid would need to be emptied and replaced with pure fat so that the container could be labeled as whole (4%) milk?

8. a. Graph $y = \dfrac{2x - 13}{x - 5}$.

    b. Graph $y = \dfrac{3x + 11}{x + 3}$.

    c. Use synthetic or long division and rewrite each fraction above. The result will be an equation in the form $y = a \pm \dfrac{b}{q(x)}$ for some values of a, b, and $q(x)$. Graph each new equation.

    d. Compare the graphs in 8a and 8b with the results of 8c. Describe any differences.

    e. Describe the graphs in 8a and 8b in terms of translations and stretches of the parent function.

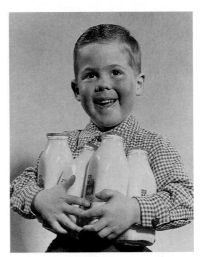

Rational Functions

War is the unfolding of miscalculations.
—Barbara Tuchman

Rational functions create interesting and very different kinds of graphs from those you have studied previously. Although it is difficult to find real-world applications for some of these functions, their graphs are fun to explore and may give you new insights into algebraic concepts. The graphs of these functions are often in two or more parts if you look at a nonrestricted domain. This is because the denominator, a polynomial function, may be equal to zero at some point, so the function will be undefined at that point. Sometimes it may be difficult to see the different parts of the graph because they may be separated by only one missing point. At other times you will see two parts that look very similar—one part may look like a reflection or rotation of the other part. Or you may get multiple parts that each look totally different.

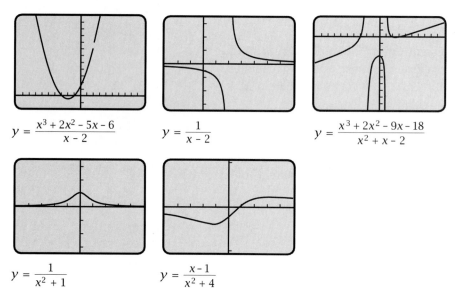

$$y = \frac{x^3 + 2x^2 - 5x - 6}{x - 2}$$

$$y = \frac{1}{x - 2}$$

$$y = \frac{x^3 + 2x^2 - 9x - 18}{x^2 + x - 2}$$

$$y = \frac{1}{x^2 + 1}$$

$$y = \frac{x - 1}{x^2 + 4}$$

In this section you will explore local and end (or global) behavior of rational functions, and you will learn how to predict some of the features of a rational function's graph by studying the equation. By definition, a rational function can always be written as a quotient of two polynomials, and the polynomial in the denominator must contain the variable. When closely examining a rational function, you will often find that it is helpful to look at the equation in factored form.

Investigation 12.2.1

Predicting Asymptotes and Holes

In this investigation you will consider the graphs of four rational functions and the local behavior of each at, and near, $x = 2$.

Part 1 Have each group member investigate each of the graphs below. Share your discoveries and conclusions with other group members.

Find a match between the graphs and the rational functions listed below. Use a "friendly" window as you graph and trace your equations. Describe the unusual occurrences at and near $x = 2$, and try to explain the equation feature that makes the graph look the way it does. (You will not actually see the hole pictured in the last graph unless you turn off the coordinate axes.)

a.
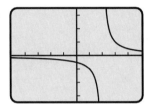

b.
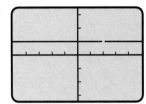

c.
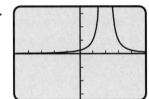

d.
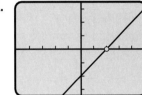

i. $y = \dfrac{1}{(x - 2)^2}$ ii. $y = \dfrac{1}{x - 2}$ iii. $y = \dfrac{(x - 2)^2}{x - 2}$ iv. $y = \dfrac{x - 2}{x - 2}$

Part 2 Have each group member choose one of the graphs below. Name a rational function equation for your graph, and write a few sentences that explain the appearance of your graph.

a.
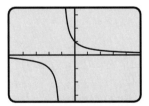

b.

c.
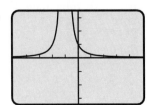

d.
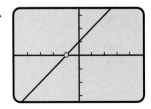

(continued on next page)

Part 3 Write a summary of what your group learned in this investigation about holes and asymptotes.

You have already considered $y = \frac{1}{x}$, some transformations of this function, and some of the peculiarities involving graphs of more complicated rational functions. You know that $y = \frac{1}{x}$ has both horizontal and vertical asymptotes. What do you think the graph would look like if you added x to $\frac{1}{x}$? Reflect on this question for a minute. Then graph $y = x + \frac{1}{x}$.

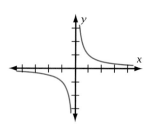

■ Example 1

Describe the graph of $y = x + \frac{1}{x}$.

Solution

The values of $\frac{1}{x}$ are added to the values of x rather than being added to zero. This means the graph has an asymptote at the line $y = x$ instead of at the x-axis. The graph of $y = x + \frac{1}{x}$ has a **slant asymptote** whose equation is $y = x$.

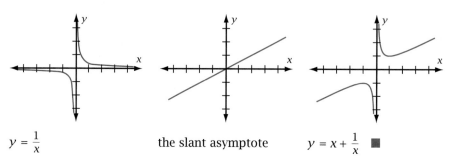

$y = \frac{1}{x}$ the slant asymptote $y = x + \frac{1}{x}$ ■

Investigation 12.2.2
Constant Volume

For this investigation you will need several different cylindrical containers, each with a different radius. You will also need water, salt, sand, or some other substance that can be poured into the containers.

a. Pour your substance into one of the containers. Measure the inside radius and filled height, and record these values in a table.

---

b. Then carefully pour the entire contents from the original container into another cylindrical container with a different radius. (The volume of the contents of the containers will remain constant throughout the investigation, but the radii and corresponding heights of the containers will vary.)

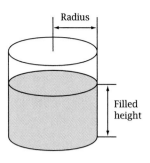

Radius

Filled height

c. Repeat this process for several different cylindrical containers and record the data pair (*radius, height*) for each container, using the table from Step a.

d. Plot the data on your calculator and confirm that this is not a linear relation.

e. Find a regression model that is a good fit for your data. (Remember that correlation coefficients, residual plots, and sums of squares of residuals are tools that help you make this decision.) Justify why you think your model is a good one.

f. Compare your model with $y = \frac{k}{x}$, $y = \frac{k}{x^2}$, $y = \frac{k}{x^3}$, and so on, and, if possible, write your equation in one of these forms. Explain why you think your (*radius, height*) data is an inverse, inverse square, or inverse cube relationship.

Problem Set 12.2

1. Predict what each graph will look like. Then use your calculator with a "friendly" graphing window to confirm your thinking. Make a sketch of each graph.

   a. $y = x - 2 + \frac{1}{x}$ **b.** $y = {}^-2x + 3 + \frac{2}{x}$ **c.** $y = 3 + \frac{x-2}{x-2}$

   d. Describe any asymptotes or holes in the graphs in 1a–c. Explain why each asymptote or hole occurs.

2. Graph each equation on your calculator, and make a sketch of the graph on your paper. Use a "friendly" graphing window. Indicate any asymptotes or holes on your sketches.

   a. $y = \frac{(5-x)}{(x-5)}$ **b.** $y = \frac{3x+6}{x+2}$ **c.** $y = \frac{(x+3)(x-4)}{x-4}$

   d. Describe any asymptotes or holes in the graphs in 2a–c. Explain why each asymptote or hole occurs.

3. Write an equation for each graph. Assume the distance between two grid marks represents one unit. Note the position of each **hole**.

   a.   **b.**   **c.**

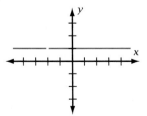
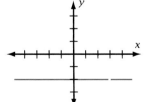
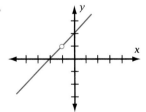

4. a. Predict what the graph of $y = {}^-x + \dfrac{4}{x-3}$ will look like. Confirm your prediction by graphing.

  b. Describe the global behavior of the graph. (Use a large graphing window.)

  c. Describe the behavior of the graph near $x = 3$. (Use a small graphing window.)

  d. Show the algebraic manipulations needed to rewrite the expression ${}^-x + \dfrac{4}{x-3}$ as $\dfrac{{}^-x^2 + 3x + 4}{x-3}$.

  e. What are the roots of ${}^-x^2 + 3x + 4 = 0$? Of $\dfrac{{}^-x^2 + 3x + 4}{x-3} = 0$?

5. The two graphs pictured below show the same function. The left graph is a global look at the function, and the right graph is a local look.

  a. List all the important facts you can about the function from its graphs.

  b. Find the equation of the apparent line in the first graph.

  c. Give an example of an equation with an asymptote at $x = {}^-2$.

  d. Name a polynomial with roots at $x = {}^-3$ and $x = 1$.

  e. Write an equation for the function shown in the graphs. Graph the function to check your answer.

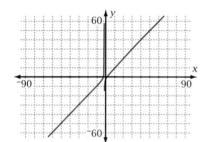 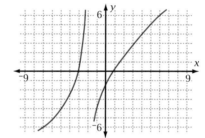

6. The two graphs pictured below are of the same function. Write an equation for this function.

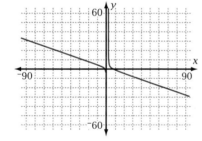 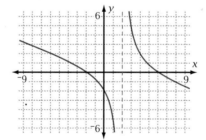

7. Consider the graph of $y = \dfrac{(x-1)(x+4)}{(x-2)(x+3)}$.

  a. Describe local-behavior oddities of the graph.

  b. Describe the global behavior of the graph.

  c. Sketch the graph.

8. Solve each equation or inequation for x and describe your solution process.

   a. $\dfrac{2}{x-1} + x = 5$ **b.** $\dfrac{2}{x-1} + x = 2$ **c.** $\dfrac{x-3}{x+2} \geq 2$

9. A machine drill removes a 2 in. radius core from a cylinder. Suppose you want the amount of material left after the core is removed to remain constant. The table below compares the height (h) and radius (x) needed if the volume of the hollow cylinder is to remain the same.

Radius (x)	2.5	3.0	3.5	4.0	4.5	5.0	5.5	6.0	6.5
Height (h)	56.6	25.5	15.4	10.6	7.8	6.1	4.9	4.0	3.3

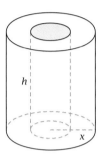

   a. Plot the points (x, h) and draw a smooth curve through them.

   b. Explain what happens to the height of the figure as the radius gets smaller. How small can x be?

   c. Write a formula for volume in terms of x and h.

   d. Solve the formula in 9c for h. What function describes the height in terms of x?

   e. What is the fixed volume?

Project

Going Downhill Fast

Design an investigation to determine a relationship between the tilt (or degree of slant) of a long tube and the time it takes a ball to travel the length of the tube. Use the following questions as a guide as you write up the project, collect the data, and complete the investigation. What will a graph of the relation (*angle, time*) look like? As the tube angle becomes steeper, what is the effect on the time it takes a ball to roll through the tube? What angle values make sense? Will the graph have an *x*-intercept? A *y*-intercept? What meaning can be attached to the intercepts? To the slope?

Refining the Growth Model

Responsibility is the one thing people dread most of all. Yet it is the one thing in the world that develops us.
—Frank Crain

You have studied growth recursively and explicitly since the beginning of the course. Until now you have assumed that the rate of growth, *r*, remained constant over time, which meant you used the recursive equations

$$u_n = u_{(n-1)} + r \cdot u_{(n-1)} \quad \text{or} \quad (1+r) \cdot u_{(n-1)}$$

and the explicit formula

$$u_n = u_0(1+r)^n$$

to model the growth of populations or money, or the decay of radioactive elements. As you have seen, the long-term result either increased to infinity or decreased to zero, as pictured below.

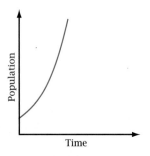 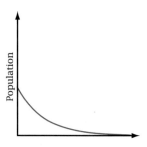

Ecosystems are complicated and generally require sophisticated assumptions regarding population growth. Environmental situations rarely support unlimited growth. Because of space and resource limitations, or competition between individuals or species, certain environments may only support a population up to a limiting value, *L*. For example, a large field may provide enough food to feed 500 healthy rabbits. If presently there are no rabbits living in the field, what would you expect to happen if you introduced 100 rabbits into the field? What would happen if you introduced 700 rabbits? Any representative model should include both the growth rate of the rabbits and the survival rate, which is partially dependent on the total food supply. As the population approaches or exceeds the limiting value, the growth rate of the rabbit population may slow because the rabbits are no longer healthy or because some rabbits will simply leave the area in search of more food.

When you sketch a (*time, population*) graph, it might show slower growth (or decay) as the population approaches the limiting number. This means the actual growth rate isn't a constant value, for example, *r* = 6%, but rather is a function related to the present population. You have seen graphs with a limiting value or horizontal asymptote, such as the graphs of the pine tree population, of medicine levels in the bloodstream, and of chlorine levels in a pool. Each of these recursively defined functions involve both adding to, and subtracting from, the preceding value.

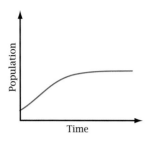

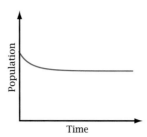

Net growth is affected by births, deaths, immigration, and emigration. If you assume that the next population u_n will have a net growth that depends on the present population size $u_{(n-1)}$, then the net growth rate will be a function of the population, written $f(u_{(n-1)})$. This changes the simple growth model of $u_n = u_{(n-1)} + r \cdot u_{(n-1)}$, in which the rate, r, is a constant, to a growth model with a variable rate.

Investigation 12.3.1
Variable Rates

Work with a partner on this investigation, then share your results with other group members.

Part 1   Consider the rabbits discussed above. When food and space are unlimited, the population growth rate of the rabbits is 20%, or 0.20. The population that can be supported is 500 rabbits. Complete each statement and write a sentence explaining the statement.

   a. When the population is less than 500, the growth rate will be –?–.

   b. When the population is more than 500, the growth rate will be –?–.

   c. When the population is very small, the rate will have a value near –?–.

   d. When the population is 500, the rate will have a value of . . .

   Write an equation of a line that contains the points (*population, rate*) by using $(0, 0.20)$ and $(500, 0)$. If this is a model of the rate based on population, what is the rate when the population is 100? What is the rate when the population is 700? (Answer each question using complete sentences.)

Part 2 Extend this investigation by finding the line that gives the variable rate for each situation below. Test some values in your model to find the rates and check that the values make sense.

   a. An unrestricted growth rate of 0.20 and a population limit of 1000.

   b. An unrestricted growth rate of 0.30 and a population limit of 500.

   c. An unrestricted growth rate of 0.20 and a population limit of L.

   d. An unrestricted growth rate of r and a population limit of L.

   Show that your solution to the situation described in d is equivalent to the model
   $$y = r\left(1 - \frac{x}{L}\right).$$

   If you use more formal sequence notation, the variable rate function can be written as

   $$f(u_{(n-1)}) = r\left(1 - \frac{u_{(n-1)}}{L}\right).$$

This growth rate function was used in the population model formulated in the nineteenth century by Pierre François Verhulst (1804–1849), who was a professor at the Université Libre (Free University) of Brussels. He worked with social statistician and astronomer Adolphe Quételet. At that time social scientists generally assumed that Malthus's belief that a population increased exponentially was correct, because data on population growth that might contradict Malthus's ideas were not available then. But Quételet believed that checks on population growth needed to be accounted for in a more systematic manner than Malthus described. Verhulst was able to incorporate the changes in growth rate in a mathematical model. This population model with a variable growth rate is

   new population = old population + net growth rate • old population.

   $$u_n \quad = \quad u_{(n-1)} \quad + \quad r\left(1 - \frac{u_{(n-1)}}{L}\right) \quad u_{(n-1)}.$$

■ Example 1

Suppose the unrestricted growth rate, r, of a deer population on a small island is 12% annually, and the island limit, L, is 2000 deer. Find the net growth rate for 1 yr for each of the following initial populations. Use the net rate function

   $$f(u_{(n-1)}) = r\left(1 - \frac{u_{(n-1)}}{L}\right).$$

   a. 0   **b.** 300   **c.** 1000

   d. 1500   **e.** 3000

Solution

The function for the rate will be $0.12\left(1 - \dfrac{u_{(n-1)}}{2000}\right)$.

For each of the given populations, the growth rate will be as follows:

a. $0.12\left(1 - \dfrac{0}{2000}\right) = 0.12$, or 12%

b. $0.12\left(1 - \dfrac{300}{2000}\right) = 0.102$, or 10.2%

c. $0.12\left(1 - \dfrac{1000}{2000}\right) = 0.06$, or 6%

d. $0.12\left(1 - \dfrac{1500}{2000}\right) = 0.03$, or 3%

e. $0.12\left(1 - \dfrac{3000}{2000}\right) = {}^-0.06$, or ⁻6%

In the example the population grew at the unrestricted rate of 12% when the population was very small. As the population became larger, the rate decreased, and the population grew at a slower rate. When you examine a population that exceeds the limit, the rate is a decay rate rather than a growth rate. ■

■ Example 2

Because *new population = old population + net growth rate • old population*, the equation

$$u_n = u_{(n-1)} + r\left(1 - \frac{u_{(n-1)}}{L}\right)u_{(n-1)}$$

implies that the net growth rate is variable. Use this equation to find the next year's deer population with the values for r, L, and $u_{(n-1)}$ from Example 1.

Solution

The population function and the values from Example 1 give

$$u_n = u_{(n-1)} + 0.12\left(1 - \frac{u_{(n-1)}}{2000}\right)u_{(n-1)}.$$

For each of the given populations, the next year's population will be as follows:

a. $u_n = 0 + 0.12\left(1 - \dfrac{0}{2000}\right)0 = 0$ deer

b. $u_n = 300 + 0.12\left(1 - \dfrac{300}{2000}\right)300 = 330.6$, or 331 deer

c. $u_n = 1000 + 0.12\left(1 - \dfrac{1000}{2000}\right)1000 = 1060$ deer

d. $u_n = 1500 + 0.12\left(1 - \dfrac{1500}{2000}\right)1500 = 1545$ deer

e. $u_n = 3000 + 0.12\left(1 - \dfrac{3000}{2000}\right)3000 = 2820$ deer ■

■ **Example 3**

Suppose the present deer population is 300. Use a 12% unrestricted growth rate and a carrying capacity, or maximum population, of 2000 deer to find the population after 50 yr. Make a graph showing (*time, population*) over the next 50 yr.

Solution

The recursive function used to predict deer population is

$$u_n = u_{(n-1)} + 0.12\left(1 - \frac{u_{(n-1)}}{2000}\right)u_{(n-1)}.$$

A seed value, or start value, of 300 for $n = 0$ gives $u_{50} \approx 1976$. The graph shows the population as it grows toward the horizontal asymptote or capacity of 2000 deer. ■

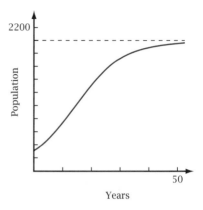

Problem Set 12.3

1. Suppose that a population of size P grows by the amount $0.08\left(1 - \frac{P}{500}\right)P$ each year.
   a. What is the real-world meaning of the 0.08 and the 500?
   b. If the initial population is 50, what will the population be next year?
   c. Find the populations at 5, 15, 25, . . . , 65 yr.
   d. What is the long-run population?
   e. Sketch a graph of this population model.

2. Bacteria grown in a culture dish are provided with plenty of food, but a limited amount of growing space. Eventually the population will become overcrowded, even though there is plenty of food. The bacteria grow at a rate of 125% each week. The initial population is 50 and the capacity of the dish is 5000. Give the net rate and population after 20 weeks.

3. Suppose the expression $d + 0.35\left(1 - \frac{d}{750}\right)d$ will give the number of daisies growing in the median strip of a highway. Presently there are about 100 daisies. Write a paragraph or two explaining what will happen. Explain and support your reasoning.

4. Suppose the information in the following table was gathered on the number of grasshoppers in a vacant lot. Experiment with different unrestricted growth rates and limiting populations to best model the population of grasshoppers.

Year	1984	1985	1986	1987	1988	1989
Population	3,283	4,365	5,603	6,895	8,104	9,107

Year	1990	1991	1992	1993	1994
Population	9,843	10,330	10,626	10,796	10,890

5. Suppose next year's state deer population in millions is generated by

$$u_n = u_{(n-1)} + 0.60\left(1 - \frac{u_{(n-1)}}{5}\right)u_{(n-1)} - 0.8$$

where u_0 represents the present deer population of 7 million. Assume the annual harvest rate is 0.8 million.

a. What happens in the long run?

b. Change the harvest rate several times and look at the resulting long-run population values and how the population approaches these values. Explain how the number harvested affects the growth rate and the long-run values.

6. Suppose the weeds in Dan D. Lyon's yard have an unrestricted annual growth rate of 210%, with a limit of 10,000 weeds. This year he has calculated that there are 100 weeds in his yard.

a. Find the population 6 yr from now.

b. Find the population for 34, 35, 36, 37, 38, and 39 yr from now.

c. Sketch a graph of the first 10 yr.

d. Provide and describe a theory about this situation.

7. The population in Kermit T. F.'s backyard frog pond began with only two frogs. The population limit of the pond is 470 frogs. The annual rate of unrestricted frog population growth is 295%. Study the population numbers for the first 20 yr. Using these values, can you predict the population for year 21? Why or why not?

8. A mathematical study of ecology would not be complete without considering predator and prey relationships. The two equations below represent a possible model in which the population of the prey (rabbits) and the population of the predator (foxes) partially depend on each other.

new rabbit = rabbit (1 + 0.04 - 0.002*fox*)
new fox = fox (1 + 0.001*rabbit* - 0.03)

- The growth rate of rabbits if there are no foxes is 4%.
- The death rate of foxes if there are no rabbits is 3%.
- The expressions $^-0.002fox$ and $^+0.001rabbit$ represent a proportional decline in rabbits and increase in foxes because of the "encounters" between the two species.

a. Suppose that initially there are 38 rabbits and 15 foxes, and that each time period is 1 mo. Graph the populations over a 40 yr period.

b. Study this model by using different initial values. Keep a record of your values, your observations, and any peaks and valleys in the two populations. Try to explain the population patterns. Does a steady state exist under the proper conditions?

This is an example of the Lotka–Volterra predator-prey model developed independently by American statistician Alfred Lotka in 1925 and Italian professor Vito Volterra in 1928. Further variations on this model have been developed that reflect additional assumptions about the situation; for instance, that predators can only handle a finite number of prey in a unit of time.

Take Another Look 12.3

A small island has a population of 10,000,000 that has been growing at the rate of 3 percent a year. However, the recursive population prediction model,

$$u_{(n + 1)} = \begin{cases} 10000000 & \text{if } n = 0 \\ u_n + 0.03 \cdot u_n & \text{if } n > 0, \end{cases}$$

has seemed less effective as the population nears a projected ceiling or maximum of 25,000,000 people. The growth rate is slowing more and more noticeably; it seems to vary according to the actual population. Some have forecasted the growth rate will be 0 percent a year when the population reaches 25,000,000 people. Create an improved population model reflecting this situation, which you could use as a replacement for the current ineffective model. Explain why your model is better, no matter what size the population. Use your model to project the island population during the next several decades. Sketch a population projection graph for the next 200 years.

Section 12.4

Functions Involving Distance

The most dangerous thing in the world is to leap a chasm in two jumps.
—David Lloyd George

Imagine a timed competition in which you carry an empty pail from point *A* to point *C,* which is located somewhere along the edge of a pool. Your task is to fill the pail, and then quickly move to point *B* and empty it. Luck, physical fitness, common sense, a calm attitude, and a little mathematics will make a difference. Finding the path of shortest length will help to minimize the effort, distance, and time involved. It's difficult to imagine that anyone would travel 5 m straight down from *A,* then 20 m along the edge of the pool, and finally 7 m up to *B.* What is the shortest distance from point *A* to the pool edge and then to point *B*?

Investigation 12.4.1

Water Bucket

Work on this investigation with your group. Share tasks when possible and compare your results.

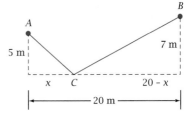

Part 1　Refer to the shortest-distance problem described above. The objective is to find the location of point *C,* which is *x* meters from the end of the pool, so that *AC* + *CB* is the shortest path possible.

    a. Make a scale drawing of the situation on graph paper. Use 5 cm, 7 cm, 20 cm, and *x* cm as the distances.

    b. Find the total length of *AC* + *CB* for several different values of *x* and record your data.

    c. What is the best location for *C* so that the total length is as short as possible? Is there more than one best location?

    d. Describe at least two alternative methods for finding this solution. For one of your methods use the Pythagorean theorem to find an equation.

    e. Make a scale drawing of your solution.

Part 2   You can move faster with an empty pail than you can with a pail full of water. Certainly this might have implications for winning the contest if the amount of water you empty out at point *B* is important enough to be recorded. This means you must move carefully so as not to spill water. Suppose that you can carry an empty pail at a rate of 1.2 m/sec and that you can carefully carry a full pail at a rate of 0.4 m/sec.

a. Go back to the data collected in Part 1 and find the time needed for each *x*-value.

b. Now find a solution so that you minimize the time from point *A* to the pool edge, then to point *B*. What is your minimum time? Describe your solution process.

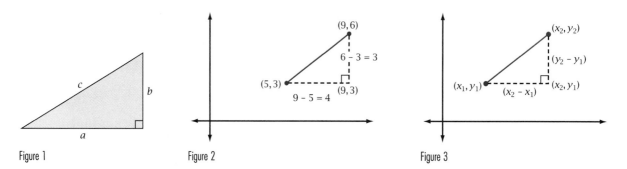

Figure 1   Figure 2   Figure 3

Here is a quick review of some distance and parametric concepts. Figure 1 represents the usual statement of the Pythagorean theorem, $a^2 + b^2 = c^2$, where the legs of the right triangle are of lengths *a* and *b*, and the hypotenuse has length *c*. Figure 2 shows how to calculate the distance between two points that are located at $(5, 3)$ and $(9, 6)$. The horizontal distance between the points is 4 and the vertical distance between them is 3. Using the Pythagorean theorem, the distance between the two points is $\sqrt{4^2 + 3^2}$, or 5, so the points are five units apart. Figure 3 shows the general case. If two points are located at (x_1, y_1) and (x_2, y_2), then $a^2 + b^2 = c^2$ is equivalent to

$$(x_2 - x_1)^2 + (y_2 - y_1)^2 = (distance\ between\ the\ two\ points)^2.$$

Distance on the Coordinate Plane

The distance between two points located at (x_1, y_1) and (x_2, y_2) is $\sqrt{(x_2 - x_1)^2 + (y_2 - y_1)^2}$.

If (x, y) is any point located on the circumference of a circle, its distance from the center $(0, 0)$ is $\sqrt{(x - 0)^2 + (y - 0)^2}$, or the *radius* $= \sqrt{x^2 + y^2}$. Previously you have used this information to write the equation of a unit circle, $x^2 + y^2 = 1$ or $y = \pm\sqrt{1 - x^2}$.

Because $\cos A = \frac{x}{1}$ and $\sin A = \frac{y}{1}$, you can use the parametric equations $x = \cos t$ and $y = \sin t$ to graph a unit circle. The parameter *t* represents degree measure, and if the range of *t*-values is $0° \le t \le 360°$, you will get one complete rotation, or the graph of a circle. The parameter *t* can also represent time. The range $0° \le t \le 360°$ could represent one revolution occurring in 360 seconds. What would the range of *t*-values be if one revolution occurs in 36 seconds? In 20 seconds?

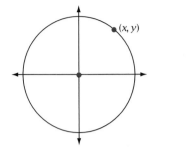 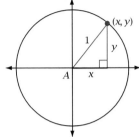

■ Example 1

Simulate the motion of an object as it completes one 5 ft radius circle in 20 sec.

Solution

The parametric equations $x = 5 \cos Bt$ and $y = 5 \sin Bt$ provide the correct radius. Now you need to find a value for B that changes 20 sec to degrees. This means you want $Bt = 360°$ when $t = 20$ sec.

$$B \cdot 20 \text{ sec} = 360°$$
$$B = 18°/\text{sec}$$

Time (sec)	Angle (deg)	x (ft)	y (ft)
0	0	5	0
5	90	0	5
10	180	⁻5	0
15	270	0	⁻5
20	360	5	0

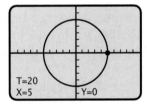

When $B = 18°/\text{sec}$, the graph of the two equations shows one complete rotation in 20 sec. Test this by setting $0 \le t \le 20$ in your graphing window. Remember, the parameter t now represents time in seconds. ■

Trace the above graph and notice the beginning point of the circle. Then replace t with $(t - 2.5)$ in each equation. Again trace and identify the beginning point of the circle. What would you substitute for t if you want the circle to begin at the bottommost point?

Problem Set 12.4

1. A patient must be rushed from an off-shore oil rig to a doctor in the nearest town.

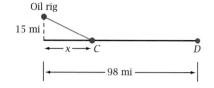

    a. Where should the boat meet the ambulance so that the trip to the doctor is the shortest possible distance?

    b. How far must the boat travel? How far must the ambulance travel?

    c. Suppose the boat can move at 23 mi/hr and the ambulance can travel at 70 mi/hr. Where should the boat meet the ambulance so that the trip time is as short as possible? How far does the boat travel at this speed? How far does the ambulance travel?

2. A 10 m pole and a 13 m pole are 20 m apart at their bases. A wire connects the top of each pole with a point on the ground between them.

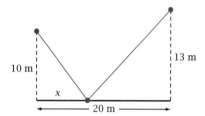

    a. Make a table of values for (*x*, *wire length*) and graph the relationship.

    b. What values of *x* and *wire length* make sense in this situation?

    c. Where should a wire be fastened to the ground so that a minimum length of wire is used to connect the tops of two poles to the same point on the ground?

3. A 24 ft ladder is held upright against a wall. The top of the ladder slides down the wall while the foot of the ladder is dragged outward along the ground at a steady rate of 2 ft/sec.

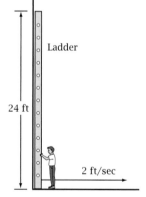

    a. How long will it take before the entire ladder is lying on the ground?

    b. Find the height of the ladder top at 1 sec intervals while the ladder slides down the wall.

Time (sec)	0	1	2	. . .
Height (ft)	24	–?–	–?–	. . .

    c. Does the ladder slide down the wall at a steady rate of 2 ft/sec? Explain.

    d. Write parametric equations that model each variable specified below.

        i. The location of the foot of the ladder.

        ii. The location of the top of the ladder.

    e. Write a complete explanation of the rate at which the ladder slides down the wall.

4. You are standing on the ground and spot an airplane flying in your direction at 450 mi/hr. (You will need to change this rate to mi/sec.) The plane flies at a constant height of 7 mi.

a. How long before the plane flies 8 mi and is directly overhead?

b. Write an equation that gives the actual distance between you and the plane. (Ignore your height.)

c. Use the equation from 4b to complete the following table.

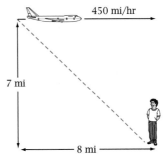

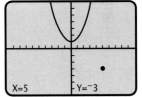

Time (sec)	0	1	5	10	20	30	-?-
Ground distance (mi)	8	-?-	-?-	-?-	-?-	-?-	0
Actual distance (mi)	-?-	-?-	-?-	-?-	-?-	-?-	7

d. Graph (*time, actual distance*).

5. a. Write an equation that provides a graph of the distance between the point $(5, ^-3)$ and any point (x, y) on the parabola $y = 0.5x^2 + 1$.

b. What is the minimum distance and at what point (x, y) does it occur?

6. Sandra Noi is riding on a 100 ft diameter Ferris wheel that can complete one revolution every 30 sec. The wheel is 5 ft from the ground at its lowest point. Her little sister, Ann, who is standing 90 ft away from the base of the Ferris wheel, is screaming at her.

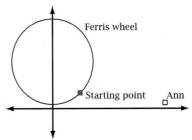

a. Write parametric equations and find a graphing window that will simulate Sandra's Ferris wheel ride and the location of her sister, Ann Noi. Sandra's ride starts at a point one-fourth of the distance from the bottom to the top of the wheel, and the entire Ferris wheel moves in a counterclockwise circular motion.

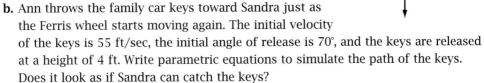

b. Ann throws the family car keys toward Sandra just as the Ferris wheel starts moving again. The initial velocity of the keys is 55 ft/sec, the initial angle of release is 70°, and the keys are released at a height of 4 ft. Write parametric equations to simulate the path of the keys. Does it look as if Sandra can catch the keys?

c. Write an equation picturing (*time, distance between keys and Sandra*). Will the keys be close enough for Sandra to catch them? How close do they get? At what time are they the closest?

7. A tack is embedded in a tire with a 30 in. (2.5 ft) radius. The vehicle is moving forward at 25 ft/sec.

a. If the tack starts at the ground, how long does it take before it makes one full revolution and is on the ground again?

b. Write parametric equations that simulate the position of the tack relative to the ground during the time 0 sec ≤ t ≤ 5 sec.

c. Sketch the graph of the tack position (*horizontal distance, height of tack*) over a time period of 5 sec.

Take Another Look 12.4

Take a minute or so to refer back to web graphs in Example 3 of Section 5.9, Investigation 5.9.1, Take Another Look 7.4, and the Bifurcation and Systems Project in Section 9.3. Web graphs give you an interesting perspective on sequence values and long-run patterns.

Consider again Problems 5 and 6 in Problem Set 12.3, but this time analyze and solve them by using web graphs. Then write an explanation that describes how to make and analyze web graphs. Finally, explain the connection between web graphs and nonweb graphs.

Project

Basketball

Sketch a graph of (*time, height*) for a typical free-throw attempt. Your graph should show what is happening over a period of ten seconds. Then sketch the typical path of a successful free throw. Do some research. What are the distances involved? How high is the rim? What is the floor distance from the free-throw line to the front rim? What is the diameter of the basket? What is the length of the bracket that fastens the basket to the backboard? Collect some data for a shooter (perhaps yourself) that provides the height of the ball at release, the angle at release, typical maximum height, and the time from release until the ball reaches the basket.

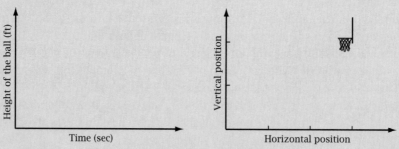

Using your data, write parametric equations that will simulate a successful free throw. Write a report on this project that includes the information collected, your data, equations, and graphs. Also indicate how you collected the information, list some of the problems involved, and describe how you solved them.

Source: Based on an activity developed by Arne Engebretsen.

The Circle and the Ellipse

*Every habit and faculty is maintained and increased by the corresponding actions:
the habit of walking by walking, the habit of running by running. If you would be
a good reader, read; if a writer, write.*
—*Epictetus*

The orbital paths of the earth around the sun, the moon around the earth, and satellites around the earth are examples of an important mathematical curve—the ellipse. The path of a stream of water forced into the air from a pressurized hose, the path of a kicked football, and the pattern of cables hanging between the towers of the Golden Gate Bridge are all examples of the parabola. The design of nuclear cooling towers, transmission gears, and the long-range navigational system known as LORAN all depend on the hyperbola.

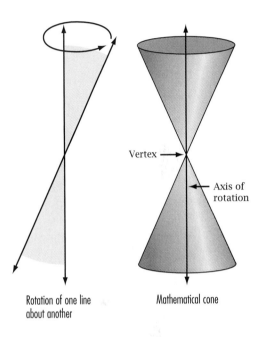

Rotation of one line
about another

Mathematical cone

Students of mathematics have studied **conic sections** since the early Greeks. These interesting planar mathematical curves—the circle, the ellipse, the parabola, and the hyperbola—are classified as conic sections because each can be created by slicing a cone. Menaechmus, a Greek mathematician who lived in the fourth century B.C., thought of conic sections as coming from different kinds of cones: Parabolas came from right-angled cones, ellipses from acute-angled cones, and hyperbolas from obtuse-angled cones. Three centuries later, Apollonius of Perga showed how all three kinds of curves could be obtained from the same cone. He also gave the curves the names we use today.

A mathematical cone is formed when two lines meet at an acute angle and one of the lines is rotated around the other (the axis).

In this section you will investigate two conic sections—the circle and the ellipse.

Definition of a Circle

A **circle** is a set of points, *P*, located a constant distance, *r*, from a fixed point, *C*. The fixed point is called the **center** and the constant distance is called the **radius**. Two equivalent symbolic descriptions of a circle are $|P - C| = r$ and $PC = r$.

Definition of an Ellipse

An **ellipse** is a set of points, P, the sum of whose distances from two fixed points, F_1 and F_2, is always a constant length, d. That is, $F_1P + F_2P = d$. The two fixed points are called **foci**.

Investigation 12.5.1

Constructing a Circle and an Ellipse

Part 1 **The Circle**

You will need a ruler for this part of the investigation. Draw a point near the center of a paper. Choose a distance that is less than 10 cm. (Have each group member choose a different distance.) Use your ruler to locate 12 or more points at that distance from your fixed point. Connect the points with a smooth curve. Explain the symbolic description $PC = r$ in terms of your drawing.

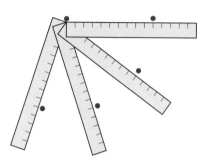

Compare your drawing with drawings made by others in your group. Describe any differences that you notice.

Part 2 **The Ellipse**

You will need two rulers for this part of the investigation. Fold a paper in half along its length. Locate the center of the crease and label this point C. Draw two points in the crease on either side of C so that they are equal distances from C. Label these points F_1 and F_2. Now choose a length, d, which is greater than the distance between F_1 and F_2 and less than 25 cm. Think of two numbers, a and b, that add up to your selected distance. Using both rulers, find a point that is a units from F_1 and b units from F_2. Repeat this process with other choices of a and b until you have enough points to define the shape. Connect the points with a smooth curve. Explain $F_1P + F_2P = d$ in terms of your drawing.

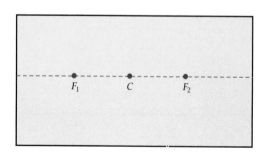

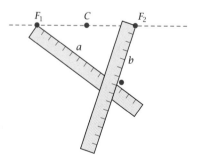

The method you used to construct an ellipse in Investigation 12.5.1 was discovered by Abū Alī al-Hasan ibn al-Haytham, who lived from about A.D. 965 to 1041 in Basra, Iraq, and Alexandria, Egypt. Several centuries later his work on optics was translated into Latin. His name was translated into Latin as well and he is also known as Alhazen.

If a point represented by (x, y) is a generic point anywhere on the circumference of a unit circle, solving $x^2 + y^2 = 1^2$ for y gives

$$x^2 + y^2 = 1^2$$
$$y^2 = 1 - x^2$$
$$y = \pm\sqrt{1 - x^2}.$$

Using the same logic, the equation of a circle centered at the origin with a radius of r units will satisfy the relation $x^2 + y^2 = r^2$. You can enter the two functions $y = \pm\sqrt{r^2 - x^2}$ to produce the graph with your calculator. The equations $x(t) = r \cos t$ and $y(t) = r \sin t$ also produce the same graph in *parametric* mode. Take a moment now to explain to yourself why the parametric equations give the same graph. You can shift the graph horizontally and vertically by replacing x with $x - h$ for some number h and replacing y with $y - k$ for some number k.

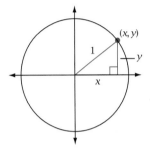

Equation of a Circle

A circle with the center located at point (h, k) with a radius of r has the equation

$$(x - h)^2 + (y - k)^2 = r^2 \quad \text{or} \quad \begin{cases} x(t) = r \cos t + h \\ y(t) = r \sin t + k. \end{cases}$$

■ **Example 1**

Write the equation of a circle that has a center at $(3, {}^-2)$ and that is tangent to the line $y = 2x + 1$.

Solution

If the line is tangent to the circle, then it is perpendicular to a diameter of the circle at the point of tangency. The tangent line has a slope of 2, so a line containing the diameter will have a slope of $^-1/2$, and it will pass through the center of the circle $(3, {}^-2)$. Therefore, one form of its equation is $y = \frac{^-1}{2}(x - 3) - 2$. Confirm that this line intersects the tangent line at $(^-0.6, {}^-0.2)$.

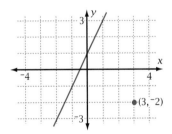

The distance between (⁻0.6, ⁻0.2) and the center is $\sqrt{16.2} \approx 4.025$. Check that this result is true. Therefore, the equation of this circle is

$$(x - 3)^2 + (y + 2)^2 = 16.2 \quad \text{or} \quad \begin{cases} x(t) = 4.025 \cos t + 3 \\ y(t) = 4.025 \sin t - 2. \end{cases} \quad \blacksquare$$

If you stretch a circle horizontally and vertically by the same amount, you will still have a circle. However, if the horizontal stretch is different from the vertical stretch, the resulting figure is an **ellipse**. A circle is to an ellipse as a square is to a rectangle.

■ Example 2

Write the equation of an ellipse that is centered at the origin, is 6 units tall, and is 4 units wide.

Solution

You can start with a unit circle, $x^2 + y^2 = 1$. This circle has a diameter of 2 units and can be stretched vertically by a factor of 3 to make it 6 units tall. To make it 4 units wide you must stretch it horizontally by a factor of 2. You can accomplish these transformations using either strategy shown below.

Function transformation

Replace y with $\frac{y}{3}$ and x with $\frac{x}{2}$.

$$\left(\frac{x}{2}\right)^2 + \left(\frac{y}{3}\right)^2 = 1 \quad \text{or} \quad \frac{x^2}{4} + \frac{y^2}{9} = 1$$

Parametric transformation

$$\begin{cases} x(t) = 2 \cos t \\ y(t) = 3 \sin t \end{cases}$$

Solve the nonparametric form for y, graph both the positive and negative roots, and check that this is the correct ellipse.

$$\left(\frac{x}{2}\right)^2 + \left(\frac{y}{3}\right)^2 = 1$$

$$\left(\frac{y}{3}\right)^2 = 1 - \left(\frac{x}{2}\right)^2$$

$$\frac{y}{3} = \pm\sqrt{1 - \left(\frac{x}{2}\right)^2}$$

$$y = \pm 3\sqrt{1 - \left(\frac{x}{2}\right)^2} \quad \blacksquare$$

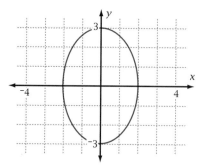

Equation of an Ellipse

An **ellipse** with the center shifted to the point (h, k) with a horizontal stretch of a and a vertical stretch of b has the equation

$$\left(\frac{x - h}{a}\right)^2 + \left(\frac{y - k}{b}\right)^2 = 1 \quad \text{or} \quad \begin{cases} x(t) = a \cos t + h \\ y(t) = b \sin t + k. \end{cases}$$

Investigation 12.5.2

Shine On

For this investigation you will need graph paper, a
pencil, and a flashlight. Work with a partner, then
share the results with your group.

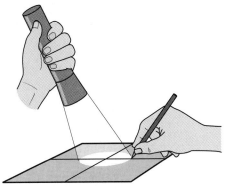

    Draw a pair of coordinate axes at the center of
your graph paper. Shine a flashlight on the graph
paper at an angle. For best results, the room
should be quite dark. Try to align the major axis
of the ellipse formed by the beam with one axis of
the paper. Now carefully trace the edge of the
beam as your partner holds the light steady. (If
you have a ring stand and clamps available, use
them to hold the flashlight steady.) You might start by placing four points on the
paper to help the flashlight holder stay on target. Collect the coordinates of about 20
points, and try to find an equation that fits the data as closely as possible. Name the
lengths of both the major and minor axes. Finally, verify that the coordinates of some
of your collected points do satisfy your equation.

Problem Set 12.5

1. Graph each circle on your calculator. Sketch the graph on your paper and label the
   radius and the center.

   a. $x^2 + y^2 = 4$ **b.** $(x - 3)^2 + y^2 = 1$

   c. $(x + 1)^2 + (y - 2)^2 = 9$ **d.** $x^2 + (y - 1.5)^2 = 0.25$

   e. $\begin{cases} x(t) = 2\cos t + 1 \\ y(t) = 2\sin t + 2 \end{cases}$ **f.** $\begin{cases} x(t) = 4\cos t - 3 \\ y(t) = 4\sin t \end{cases}$

2. Write nonparametric and parametric equations for each graph. (The distance between
   grid marks represents one unit.)

   a.

   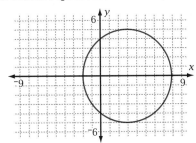

   b.

   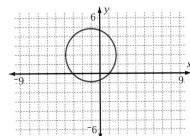

c.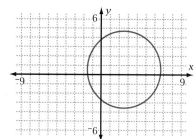

d.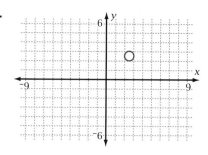

3. Sketch a graph of each equation. Label the four vertices (the extreme points on each axis) of each ellipse.

a. $\left(\dfrac{x}{2}\right)^2 + \left(\dfrac{y}{4}\right)^2 = 1$

b. $\left(\dfrac{x-2}{3}\right)^2 + \left(\dfrac{y+2}{1}\right)^2 = 1$

c. $\left(\dfrac{x-4}{3}\right)^2 + \left(\dfrac{y-1}{3}\right)^2 = 1$

d. $y = \pm 2\sqrt{1 - \left(\dfrac{x+2}{3}\right)^2} - 1$

e. $\begin{cases} x(t) = 4\cos t - 1 \\ y(t) = 2\sin t + 3 \end{cases}$

f. $\begin{cases} x(t) = 3\cos t + 3 \\ y(t) = 5\sin t \end{cases}$

4. Write nonparametric and parametric equations for each graph.

a.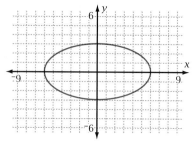

b.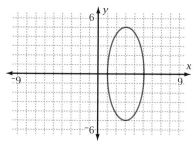

c.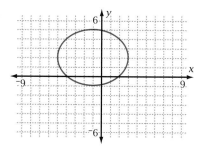

d.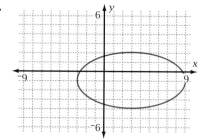

5. Planets, moons, and comets move in orbits around a central object. Johannes Kepler was the first European to think that planets moved in elliptical rather than circular orbits with the sun at one focus. (He also introduced the term *focus*.) Kepler, who worked as an assistant to the astronomer Tycho Brahe, was able to check his hypotheses because he had access to Brahe's astronomical data, considered to be the finest pretelescope data. Without Brahe's data Kepler might have stayed with his first hypothesis—that the planets moved in circular orbits which lay on spheres that could be circumscribed around regular polyhedra that were supposed to lie between the planets.

Suppose a grid is laid down on the solar system in the plane of a comet's orbit, with the origin at the location of the sun and the x-axis running through the longer axis of the orbit, as shown in the diagram below. The table gives the approximate position of a comet circling the sun.

a. Find the best equation to match the data. Both x and y are measured in astronomical units (AU).

Tycho Brahe's observatory, Uraniborg, on the island of Hven. His younger sister, Sophia (1556–1643), was also interested in astronomy.

x	-2.1	12.9	62.6	244.5	579.3	778.1
y	5.5	16.3	31.5	54.6	62.0	51.6

x	900.1	982.4	923.4	663.0	450.0	141.6
y	36.1	10.9	-31.5	-59.2	-62.8	-44.5

b. Find the y-value when the x-value is 493.0 AU.

c. What is the farthest distance of the comet from the sun?

d. If the sun, which is now at the origin, were located near the opposite end of the ellipse, what would its coordinates be?

6. a. Construct an ellipse by using a string, a ruler, two tacks, a pencil, and graph paper that is fastened to a piece of cardboard. Use the tacks to fasten a 16 cm string at F_1 and F_2, the foci of the ellipse.

b. If the midpoint of F_1 and F_2 is $(0, 0)$, what are the coordinates of the leftmost and rightmost points? These points are called the vertices at the ends of the major (longer) axis.

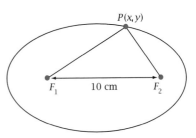

c. What are the coordinates of the topmost and bottommost points? These points are called the vertices at the ends of the minor (shorter) axis.

d. Write an equation that represents this ellipse.

e. Use your equation from 6d to graph the distance relation $PF_1 + PF_2 = d$. Describe the values of $PF_1 + PF_2$.

7. Visualize constructing the ellipse pictured on the right with two tacks and a string.

a. How long will the string be?

b. Where will you place the tacks?

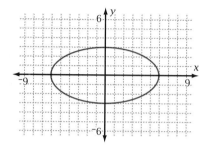

8. The moon's greatest distance from the earth is 252,710 mi and its smallest distance is 221,643 mi. Write an equation that describes the moon's orbit around the earth.

9. A point moves in the plane so that the sum of its distances from $(-2, 1)$ and $(4, 1)$ is always ten units. What is the equation of the path of this point?

Section 12.6

The Parabola

You may drive out nature with a fork, yet still she will return.
—Horace

The designs of telescope lenses, spotlights, and other paraboloid reflecting surfaces are based on a remarkable property of parabolas—a ray that travels parallel to the axis will strike the surface of the parabola or paraboloid and reflect toward the **focus**. Likewise, when a ray from the focus strikes the curve, it will reflect in a ray that is parallel to the axis of symmetry.

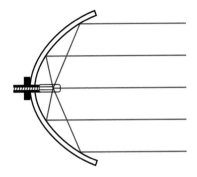

Definition of a Parabola

A **parabola** is a set of points, *P*, that are equally distant from a fixed point, *F*, and a fixed line, *l*. The fixed point is called a **focus** and the line is called a **directrix**.

Investigation 12.6.1

Constructing the Parabola

You will need two rulers for this activity. Fold a paper in half along its length. Draw line *l* in the lower half of the paper so that it is perpendicular to the crease. Draw point *F* above this line and on the crease. (Have each group member place point *F* at a different distance from the line.) To locate point *P*, place one of the rulers so that its 0 mark is on line *l* and it is perpendicular to line *l*. Place the 0 mark of the other ruler on point *F*. The intersection of the two rulers will represent point *P*. Adjust the position of the second ruler so that the distance from *F* to *P* is the same as the distance from *P* to line *l*. Mark the location of point *P*. Move the first ruler to a new position that is parallel to the original

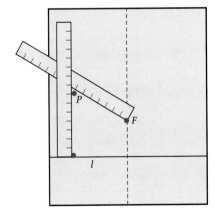

one. Repeat this point-location process until you have plotted enough points to define the shape. Draw a smooth curve to connect the points. Can you see that the distance from point *P* to point *F* is the same as the distance from point *P* to line *l*?

Compare your drawing with drawings made by others in your group. Describe any differences that you notice.

You have studied the parabola on several different occasions, and you have applied parabolic equations to a variety of situations. However, in this section you will study the parabola from a different perspective and learn about two of its important features—the **focus** and the **directrix**. Remember, from the definition of a parabola, the distance from a point *P* on the curve to the focus *F* is always the same as the perpendicular distance from that point *P* to the directrix line *l*.

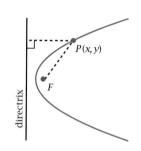

How can you locate the focus of a parabola? Suppose the parabola is horizontal and located with its vertex at the origin. It has a focus inside the curve at a point $(f, 0)$. The vertex is on the curve and should be the same distance from the focus as it is from the directrix. This means the equation of the directrix is $x = {}^{-}f$. Supply the reasons for each step in the following derivation.

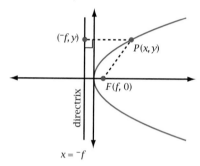

$$\sqrt{(x - f)^2 + (y - 0)^2} = \sqrt{(x + f)^2 + (y - y)^2}$$
$$\sqrt{(x - f)^2 + y^2} = \sqrt{(x + f)^2 + 0^2}$$
$$(x - f)^2 + y^2 = (x + f)^2$$
$$x^2 - 2fx + f^2 + y^2 = x^2 + 2fx + f^2$$
$$y^2 = 4fx$$

This result means that the coefficient of the linear variable *x* is $4f$ where *f* is the directed distance from the vertex to the focus.

■ Example 1

Consider the equation $y^2 = x$.

a. Draw the graph, and write the equation of this graph after each transformation has been performed.

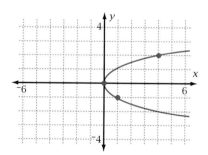

   i. Stretched vertically by a factor of 3.

   ii. Then shifted horizontally 2 units.

   iii. Then shifted vertically ⁻4 units.

b. Where is the focus of $y^2 = x$?

c. What is the equation of the directrix of $y^2 = x$?

The final graph will look like the one pictured on the right.

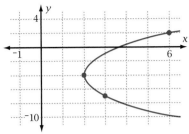

Solution

The original function contains the points $(0, 0)$, $(4, 2)$, and $(1, {}^-1)$. When stretched vertically, the points become $(0, 0)$, $(4, 6)$, and $(1, {}^-3)$. When translated horizontally, the points become $(2, 0)$, $(6, 6)$, and $(3, {}^-3)$. Finally, the last shift moves the points to $(2, {}^-4)$, $(6, 2)$, and $(3, {}^-7)$.

$$y^2 = x$$

$$\left(\frac{y}{3}\right)^2 = x \qquad\qquad \text{Vertical stretch.}$$

$$\left(\frac{y}{3}\right)^2 = (x - 2) \qquad\qquad \text{Horizontal translation.}$$

$$\left(\frac{y + 4}{3}\right)^2 = x - 2 \qquad\qquad \text{Vertical translation.}$$

When you look at this same process parametrically, begin with $\begin{cases} x(t) = t^2 \\ y(t) = t. \end{cases}$

Stretch 3 units vertically, $\begin{cases} x(t) = t^2 \\ y(t) = 3t, \end{cases}$ then 2 units right, $\begin{cases} x(t) = t^2 + 2 \\ y(t) = 3t, \end{cases}$

and finally 4 units down, $\begin{cases} x(t) = t^2 + 2 \\ y(t) = 3t - 4 \end{cases}$. ∎

Equation of a Parabola

A **vertical parabola** with the vertex shifted to the point (h, k) with a horizontal stretch of a and a vertical stretch of b has the equation

$$\frac{y - k}{b} = \left(\frac{x - h}{a}\right)^2 \quad \text{or} \quad \begin{cases} x(t) = at + h \\ y(t) = bt^2 + k. \end{cases}$$

A **horizontal parabola** under the same conditions has the equation

$$\left(\frac{y - k}{b}\right)^2 = \frac{x - h}{a} \quad \text{or} \quad \begin{cases} x(t) = at^2 + h \\ y(t) = bt + k. \end{cases}$$

You can use the general form $y^2 = 4fx$ to locate the focus and the directrix of the equation $y^2 = x$. The coefficient of the linear variable x is $4f$. This means $4f = 1$, the focus is at $\left(\frac{1}{4}, 0\right)$, and the directrix has the equation $x = \frac{-1}{4}$.

Now locate the focus and the directrix of the image $\left(\frac{y + 4}{3}\right)^2 = x - 2$ or $(y + 4)^2 = 9(x - 2)$. This means $4f = 9$ or $f = 2.25$ and both the focus and the directrix will be 2.25 units from the vertex $(2, ^-4)$. Therefore, the directrix of the image is at $x = ^-0.25$ and the focus is $(4.25, ^-4)$.

Investigation 12.6.2

A Rolling Ball

For this investigation your group will need a clipboard or board, some tape, graph paper, carbon paper, and a large ball bearing.

Tape the graph paper to a board or clipboard. Lay the board on a table and prop one end up with two books. Practice rolling a large ball bearing from the lower left corner of the board so that it rolls up the board and back down, rolling off the board at the lower right. When you can do this consistently, tape a sheet of carbon paper (black side down) over the graph paper. Roll the ball bearing one more time. Then remove the carbon paper and draw coordinate axes on the graph paper wherever you believe they belong. Carefully locate several points on the curve left by the carbon paper trace.

With your partner, find the equation that best fits the data. Did you assume that the curve was a parabola or half an ellipse? Give a reason for your choice. Make a plot of the residuals. Now test the other curve option and plot its residuals. Using your residual plots, describe which model is the better choice.

Share your results with your group and make a group decision as to whether the path is elliptical or parabolic.

Problem Set 12.6

1. Sketch a graph of each equation. Label the vertex, the focus, and the directrix.

a. $\left(\dfrac{x}{2}\right)^2 + 5 = y$

b. $(y + 2)^2 - 2 = x$

c. $^-(x + 3)^2 + 1 = 2y$

d. $2y^2 = ^-x + 4$

e. $\begin{cases} x(t) = 4t - 1 \\ y(t) = 2t^2 + 3 \end{cases}$

f. $\begin{cases} x(t) = 3t^2 + 3 \\ y(t) = 5t \end{cases}$

2. Write the equation of each parabola. Name the focus and the directrix. (For the four problems, write at least one of the equations in nonparametric form, and at least one equation in parametric form.)

a.

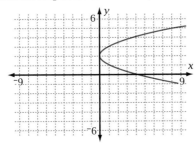

b.

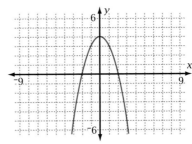

c.

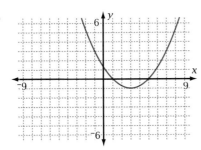

d.

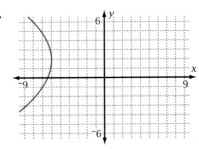

3. The pilot of a small boat charted a course so that the path of the boat would be the same distance from an upcoming rock as it was from the shoreline. Describe and explain the path of the boat.

4. a. Describe the graph represented by $\sqrt{(x-0)^2 + (y-3)^2} = \sqrt{(x-x)^2 + (y+1)^2}$.
   b. Rewrite the equation by solving for y.
   c. Graph the equation.

5. a. Describe the graph represented by $\sqrt{(x-2.5)^2 + (y-y)^2} = \sqrt{(x-3.5)^2 + (y-4)^2}$.
   b. Rewrite the equation by solving for y.
   c. Graph the equation.

6. Find the function that describes a parabola containing the points $(3.6, 0.764)$, $(5, 1.436)$, and $(5.8, {}^-2.404)$.

7. Find the equation of a circle that contains the points $(2, 4)$, $({}^-5, 5)$, and $({}^-6, {}^-2)$. (There are several ways to solve this problem. None of them are very easy.)

The Hyperbola

The empire of man over things is founded on the arts and sciences alone, for nature is only to be commanded by obeying her.
—Sir Francis Bacon

The last conic section that you will learn about is the hyperbola. Comets travel in orbits that are either parabolic, elliptical, or hyperbolic. Halley's comet, which can be seen from earth approximately every 76 years, has an elliptical orbit. Comets that come close to another object, but never return, are on a hyperbolic path. The two light shadows on a wall next to a cylindrical lampshade form two branches of a hyperbola. Similarly, a sonic-boom shock curve formed along the ground by a plane traveling faster than sound is actually one branch of a hyperbola.

Edmund Halley

Definition of a Hyperbola

A **hyperbola** is a set of points, *P*, so located that the difference of the distances from two fixed points, F_1 and F_2, remains constant: $|F_1P - F_2P| = d$. The two fixed points are called **foci**.

Investigation 12.7.1

Constructing a Hyperbola

Fold a paper in half along its length. Locate the center of the crease and label this point *C*. Draw two points in the crease on either side of *C* so that they are equal distances from *C*. Have each group member select a different length—one that is less than the distance between the points. Think of two numbers, *a* and *b*, whose difference is your selected length. Using two rulers, find a point that is *a* units from F_1 and *b* units from F_2. Repeat this process with other choices of *a* and *b* until you

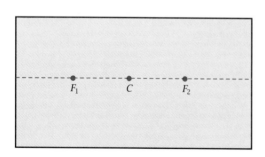

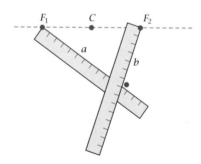

have located enough points to define the shape. Connect the points with a smooth curve. Be sure the difference between a and b remains constant. Explain $|F_1P - F_2P| = d$ in terms of your drawing.

Compare your drawing with the drawings made by others in your group. Describe any differences that you notice.

■ **Example 1**

Graph the **unit hyperbola**, $x^2 - y^2 = 1$.

Solution

To graph this as a function of y, you must first solve for y.

$$x^2 - y^2 = 1$$
$$-y^2 = 1 - x^2 \quad \text{or} \quad y^2 = x^2 - 1$$
$$y = \pm\sqrt{x^2 - 1} \quad ■$$

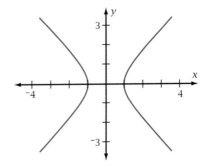

If you include the graphs of $y = x$ and $y = -x$ on the same coordinate axes, you will notice that they pass through the vertices of a square with corners at $(1, 1)$, $(1, -1)$, $(-1, -1)$, and $(-1, 1)$. As you zoom out, the hyperbola approaches the two lines, which are called asymptotes of the hyperbola.

Before you move on, consider the graph and features of $y^2 - x^2 = 1$. Look at the similarities to, and the differences from, the graph of $x^2 - y^2 = 1$.

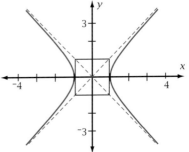

The equation of a hyperbola looks much like the equation of the ellipse except that the terms are not both positive. For example, the equation $\left(\frac{y}{4}\right)^2 - \left(\frac{x}{3}\right)^2 = 1$ is a hyperbola, while $\left(\frac{y}{4}\right)^2 + \left(\frac{x}{3}\right)^2 = 1$ is an ellipse.

■ **Example 2**

Graph $\left(\frac{y}{4}\right)^2 - \left(\frac{x}{3}\right)^2 = 1$.

Solution

To graph this as a function of y, you must first solve for y.

$$\left(\frac{y}{4}\right)^2 - \left(\frac{x}{3}\right)^2 = 1$$

$$\left(\frac{y}{4}\right)^2 = 1 + \left(\frac{x}{3}\right)^2$$

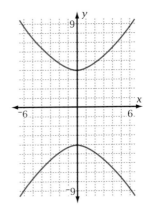

$$\frac{y}{4} = \pm\sqrt{1 + \left(\frac{x}{3}\right)^2}$$

$$y = \pm 4\sqrt{1 + \left(\frac{x}{3}\right)^2} \quad \blacksquare$$

When you sketch a hyperbola by hand, you will find it easier if you sketch the asymptotes first. Begin by drawing a rectangle centered at the origin that measures 6 units across and 8 units high (See Figure 1). Look at the original equations in Example 2 and you will recognize where these dimensions came from. Do you see how the square contained in the unit hyperbola has been stretched? Draw the diagonals of this rectangle, and extend them outside the rectangle. (See Figure 2). These lines are the asymptotes of the curve. Now add two curves so that each one touches the center of one of the sides of the rectangle and the ends swing out, asymptotically approaching the diagonal lines (see Figure 3). If

Comets travel in elliptical or hyperbolic orbits. Comet Ikeya-Seki was first observed by two amateur comet hunters, Kaori Ikeya and Tsumotu Seki, in late September 1965. Some scientists think this comet may be the same as one that appeared in 1106.

you write the equations of these two asymptotes and graph them on your calculator, you will see that the hyperbola does approach them asymptotically. The asymptotes provide you with an end behavior model of the hyperbola.

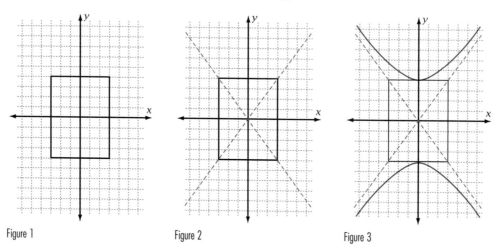

Figure 1   Figure 2   Figure 3

When you create parametric equations from a two-variable relation, your first choice is critical because you must begin by defining one of the two variables as a function of t. The other variable is defined by the original relation. Sometimes the geometry of the situation helps you to make this first assignment—as it does with circles. Sometimes logic helps—as is the case with parabolas. With the hyperbola, start with the equation of the **unit hyperbola**, $x^2 - y^2 = 1$.

$$x^2 - y^2 = 1$$ Unit hyperbola

$$x^2 = 1 + y^2$$ Add y^2 to both sides.

$$\frac{x^2}{x^2} = \frac{1}{x^2} + \frac{y^2}{x^2}$$ Divide by x^2.

$$1 = \left(\frac{1}{x}\right)^2 + \left(\frac{y}{x}\right)^2$$ Re-express

Also, $1 = \cos^2 t + \sin^2 t$

Substitute $\frac{1}{x} = \cos t$ and $\frac{y}{x} = \sin t$

or $x = \dfrac{1}{\cos t}$ $\quad y = \dfrac{\sin t}{\cos t} = \tan t.$

Equation of a Hyperbola

An equation of a **hyperbola** that opens horizontally with the center shifted to the point (h, k), a horizontal stretch of a, and a vertical stretch of b will have the equation

$$\left(\frac{x-h}{a}\right)^2 - \left(\frac{y-k}{b}\right)^2 = 1 \quad \text{or} \quad \begin{cases} x(t) = \dfrac{a}{\cos t} + h \\ y(t) = b \tan t + k. \end{cases}$$

If the hyperbola opens vertically, then the equation will be

$$\left(\frac{y-k}{b}\right)^2 - \left(\frac{x-h}{a}\right)^2 = 1 \quad \text{or} \quad \begin{cases} x(t) = a \tan t + h \\ y(t) = \dfrac{b}{\cos t} + k. \end{cases}$$

■ Example 3

Write the equation for the graph.

Solution

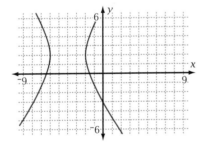

The center is between the vertices at the point $(^-4, 2)$. The horizontal radius, $a = 2$, is the distance between the center and a vertex. The value of b is more difficult to find. Here are several options.

- You can choose to work backwards by first sketching the asymptotes and then drawing the rectangle to find the value of b.
- You can experiment with your calculator to find the best value.
- You can choose a point and solve for b algebraically.

Whatever your choice (go ahead and try them all), you will find b to be 3. Now the proper form of the equation is either of the following.

$$\left(\frac{x+4}{2}\right)^2 - \left(\frac{y-2}{3}\right)^2 = 1 \quad \text{or} \quad \begin{cases} x(t) = \dfrac{2}{\cos t} - 4 \\ y(t) = 3 \tan t + 2. \end{cases} \quad ■$$

Either equation will provide the graph of the pictured hyperbola.

Problem Set 12.7

1. Sketch a graph of each hyperbola. Label each vertex and write the equation of each asymptote.

a. $\left(\dfrac{x}{2}\right)^2 - \left(\dfrac{y}{4}\right)^2 = 1$

b. $\left(\dfrac{y+2}{1}\right)^2 - \left(\dfrac{x-2}{3}\right)^2 = 1$

c. $\left(\dfrac{x-4}{3}\right)^2 - \left(\dfrac{y-1}{3}\right)^2 = 1$

d. $y = \pm 2\sqrt{1 + \left(\dfrac{x+2}{3}\right)^2} - 1$

e. $\begin{cases} x(t) = \dfrac{4}{\cos t} - 1 \\ y(t) = 2\tan t + 3 \end{cases}$

f. $\begin{cases} x(t) = 3\tan t + 1 \\ y(t) = \dfrac{5}{\cos t} \end{cases}$

2. Write the equation of each hyperbola in both nonparametric and parametric form. Write the equation of each asymptote.

a.

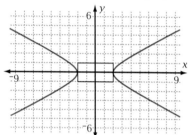

b.

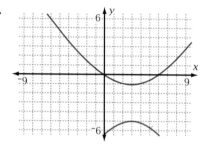

c.

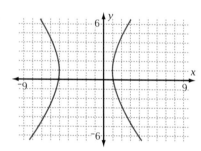

d.

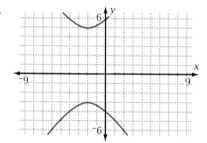

3. Each branch of a hyperbola has a focus. You can locate these foci by rotating the rectangle about its center so that opposite corners lie on the line of symmetry that contains the vertices of the hyperbola. From the diagrams at the top of the next page, you can see that the distance from the origin to a focus is one-half the length of the diagonal of the rectangle.

a. Find the coordinates of the foci for $x^2 - y^2 = 1$.

b. Find the coordinates of the foci for $\left(\dfrac{y+2}{1}\right)^2 - \left(\dfrac{x-2}{3}\right)^2 = 1$.

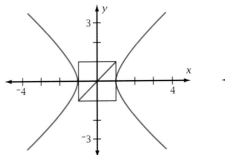 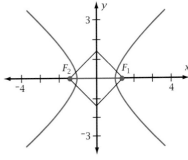

4. A point moves in the plane so that the difference of its distances from (⁻2, 1) and (4, 1) is always ten units. What is the equation of the path of this point?

5. Graph and write the equation of a hyperbola that has an upper vertex at (⁻2.35, 1.46) and is asymptotic to the line $y = 1.5x + 1.035$.

6. Find the smallest vertical distance between $y = \pm 2\sqrt{1 + \left(\frac{x+2}{3}\right)^2} - 1$ and its asymptote for each of the following x-values.

x-value	5	10	20	40
Distance	-?-	-?-	-?-	-?-

7. A receiver can determine the distance to a homing transmitter by its signal strength, but it cannot determine the direction. The following distances (in miles) were gathered as the car receiver traveled due north.

Distance (mi)	0.0	2.0	4.0	6.0	8.0	10.0	12.0	14.0	16.0
Signal strength	9.82	7.91	6.04	4.30	2.92	2.55	3.54	5.15	6.96

a. Find the equation of the hyperbola that best fits the data.
b. Name the center of this hyperbola.
c. What does this point tell you?

8. Find a problem that you have encountered in this chapter that you cannot solve. Write out the problem and as much of the solution as you can. Then, clearly explain what is keeping you from solving the problem. Be as specific as you can.

Take Another Look 12.7

1. Take another look at the hyperbola definition in this section. The expression $|F_1P - F_2P| = d$ identifies F_1 and F_2 as the two fixed points (the foci) and P as any point on the curve. The expression $F_1P - F_2P$ represents the constant difference, d, between the distances from P to each focus. The absolute value means the difference will be either $+d$ or $-d$, depending on the particular branch that P is located on.

Identify the foci and explain the meaning of the 2 on the right side of the equation below.

$$\left| \sqrt{(x+2)^2 + y^2} - \sqrt{(x-2)^2 + y^2} \right| = 2$$

Is the origin at the center of the segment joining your foci? It should be. If it is, the hyperbola can be written in the form $\left(\dfrac{x}{a}\right)^2 - \left(\dfrac{y}{b}\right)^2 = 1$. Rewriting the equation in this vertex form requires a lot of algebraic manipulation. Provide a reason for every step below.

McDonnell Planetarium at the St. Louis Science Center

$$\sqrt{(x+2)^2 + y^2} - \sqrt{(x-2)^2 + y^2} = 2 \qquad \text{(Assuming the difference is positive.)}$$

$$\sqrt{(x+2)^2 + y^2} = 2 + \sqrt{(x-2)^2 + y^2}$$

$$\left(\sqrt{(x+2)^2 + y^2}\right)^2 = \left(2 + \sqrt{(x-2)^2 + y^2}\right)^2$$

$$(x+2)^2 + y^2 = 4 + 4\sqrt{(x-2)^2 + y^2} + (x-2)^2 + y^2$$

$$x^2 + 4x + 4 + y^2 = 4 + x^2 - 4x + 4 + y^2 + 4\sqrt{(x-2)^2 + y^2}$$

$$8x - 4 = 4\sqrt{(x-2)^2 + y^2}$$

$$2x - 1 = \sqrt{(x-2)^2 + y^2}$$

$$(2x-1)^2 = \left(\sqrt{(x-2)^2 + y^2}\right)^2$$

$$4x^2 - 4x + 1 = (x-2)^2 + y^2$$

$$4x^2 - 4x + 1 = x^2 - 4x + 4 + y^2$$

$$3x^2 = 3 + y^2$$

$$3x^2 - y^2 = 3$$

$$\frac{x^2}{1} - \frac{y^2}{3} = 1 \qquad \text{Done!}$$

The resulting equation identifies a hyperbola with foci at $(2, 0)$ and $(^-2, 0)$ and vertices at $(1, 0)$ and $(^-1, 0)$. Graph this hyperbola. Sketch the asymptotes and the rectangle. Finally, refer to the explanation provided in Problem 3 of Problem Set 12.7, and describe the connection between the rectangle in your sketch and the foci locations.

2. Start with the equation $\left| \sqrt{(x+3)^2 + y^2} + \sqrt{(x-3)^2 + y^2} \right| = 10$ and do a derivation similar to the one for the hyperbola in part 1 and show that this equation is equivalent to $\left(\dfrac{x}{5}\right)^2 + \left(\dfrac{y}{4}\right)^2 = 1$. What does the graph of this equation look like?

Piston Pressure

In this project you will investigate the relationship between the volume of air in a piston and the amount of pressure on the trapped column of air. Use a set of masses and a large (60 cc) medical syringe with one end sealed (closed). Dangle a heavy thread into the syringe so that you can more easily push the piston down to somewhere between the 25 cc and 50 cc marks. (The thread breaks the seal allowing trapped air to escape.) Then remove the thread and let the piston rise back up until it stops moving. Record this ending volume and pair it with a mass of zero. Continue by carefully adding various mass amounts to the top of the piston, pushing down, and letting the piston rise. Record (*mass, volume*) for 12 to 20 data points. To increase the accuracy of your experiment, repeat the process and record a new list of volume readings as you use the same mass amounts.

Mass (kg)	0	0.5	1	. . .
Volume 1	–?–	–?–	–?–	. . .
Volume 2	–?–	–?–	–?–	. . .
Pressure	–?–	–?–	–?–	. . .
Average volume	–?–	–?–	–?–	. . .

At this point you could plot the data and try to write a best-fit equation for the (*mass, volume*) data. But this relationship might be quite difficult to determine. An easier alternative would be to convert mass to pressure, then plot calculated points involving (*pressure, volume*), and, finally, write a best-fit equation for this (*pressure, volume*) relationship. The conversion calculations will seem messy, but the function might be easier to determine after you make the conversions.

1. Convert the mass placed on the syringe into force (pressure) by multiplying the mass (in kg) by 9.8 m/sec^2.
2. Divide the result by the cross-sectional area of the syringe (in cm^2). Use πr^2 to find the area of the opening of the cylinder.

(continued on next page)

3. Now add the air pressure in the room. Use 10 N/cm² for the air pressure if you do not know the actual barometric pressure in the room. The symbol N represents Newtons. If you have a barometer, find the mercury height (in mm) and multiply it by 0.01333 to find the air pressure in the room.

Example calculation: $0.5 \text{ kg} \cdot 9.8 \dfrac{\text{m}}{\text{sec}^2} \div 4.9 \text{ cm}^2 + 10 \dfrac{\text{N}}{\text{cm}^2} = 11 \dfrac{\text{N}}{\text{cm}^2}$

Make a graph by plotting the (*pressure, volume*) data and write a short paragraph responding to the following questions: Based on your graph, what pressure would be needed to reduce the volume to zero? What would the volume be if the pressure was zero? Write an equation that fits the (*pressure, volume*) data you collected in this project. Explain the process you used to discover this equation.

The General Quadratic

The rules of the game: learn everything, read everything, inquire into everything.
—*Marguerite Yourcenar, from her novel Memoirs of Hadrian*

Circles, parabolas, ellipses, and hyperbolas are called quadratic curves (or second-degree curves) because two is the highest power on either of the variables. One general equation form can be used to generate all of the quadratic curves you have studied in this chapter.

General Quadratic Equation

The **general quadratic equation** has the form

$$Ax^2 + Bxy + Cy^2 + Dx + Ey + F = 0,$$

where A, B, and C are not all zero; that is, they are not *all* zero, but one or two of these coefficients could be zero.

In this section you will solve the general quadratic equation for y so that you can use your calculator to graph it. You will also learn how to convert the general quadratic form of a graph into the center-vertex form and the center-vertex form into the general quadratic form.

■ Example 1

Solve for y and sketch the curve $4x^2 - 9y^2 + 144 = 0$. Then put the equation in center-vertex form.

Solution

Solve for y.

$$-9y^2 = -4x^2 - 144$$

$$y^2 = \frac{4}{9}x^2 + 16$$

$$y = \pm\sqrt{\frac{4}{9}x^2 + 16}$$

Rewrite the equation in center-vertex form.

$$4x^2 - 9y^2 = -144$$

$$\frac{4x^2 - 9y^2}{-144} = 1$$

$$\frac{y^2}{16} - \frac{x^2}{36} = 1 \quad ■$$

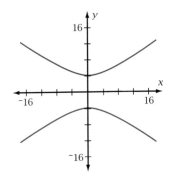

Now you can use your calculator to graph the $y=$ form of the equation, or you can use sketching techniques you learned in previous sections to graph the equation in center-vertex form. When Dx or Ey terms are present in the general quadratic equation $Ax^2 + Bxy + Cy^2 + Dx + Ey + F = 0$, the process of writing a center-vertex form is a little more complex.

The general form $x^2 + y^2 - 14x + 33 = 0$ does not tell you much about its graph. But the same equation written in its center-vertex form, $(x - 7)^2 + y^2 = 16$, indicates a circle with center at $(7, 0)$ and a radius of 4 units. One way to show that the two equations are equivalent is to expand the binomial in $(x - 7)^2 + y^2 = 16$.

Do you think this spider knows about parabolas?

$(x - 7)(x - 7) + y^2 = 16$ Definition of squaring.

$x^2 - 7x - 7x + 49 + y^2 = 16$ Expand the binomial.

$x^2 - 14x + 49 + y^2 = 16$ Combine terms.

$x^2 + y^2 - 14x + 33 = 0$ Equation in general form.

Reversing the process is called **completing the square**. It involves "discovering" the number (49 in this example) that will make the trinomial a perfect square. By using $(x \pm h)^2 = x^2 \pm 2hx + h^2$, you can find the numbers needed to complete the squares and convert equations to the center-vertex form. The key is to recognize that the coefficient of the linear term, $-14x$, is twice the value of h. This means h must be -7.

$x^2 + y^2 - 14x + 33 = 0$

$x^2 - 14x + y^2 = -33$ Separate the variables.

$x^2 - 14x + 49 + y^2 = -33 + 49$ Add 49 to both sides of the equation.

$(x - 7)^2 + y^2 = 16$ Write the trinomial in perfect-square form.

The procedure for completing the square uses the familiar expansion for perfect-square binomials, $(x \pm h)^2 = x^2 \pm 2hx + h^2$.

■ Example 2

Rewrite each quadratic equation so that the expression involving the variable x is a perfect square.

a. $x^2 - 10x + 25 = y$ **b.** $x^2 - 10x = y$ **c.** $x^2 - 10x + 14 = y$

Solution

a. This one is easy because $x^2 - 10x + 25$ is already the same as $(x - 5)^2$. The $(x \pm h)^2 = x^2 \pm 2hx + h^2$ pattern is expressed as $(x - 5)^2 = x^2 - 2(5)x + 5^2$. Therefore, an equivalent equation is $(x - 5)^2 = y$.

b. The expression on the left needs the additional term "25" so that it is equivalent to $(x - 5)^2$.

$$x^2 - 10x + 25 = y + 25 \qquad \text{Add 25 to both sides of the equation.}$$

Note that the square of half the coefficient of x, or $\left(\dfrac{-10}{2}\right)^2$, is the same as 25.

Therefore, an equivalent equation written as a perfect square is $(x - 5)^2 = y + 25$.

c.

$x^2 - 10x + 14 = y$	Start with the given equation.
$x^2 - 10x = y - 14$	Subtract the constant from both sides.
$x^2 - 10x + 25 = y - 14 + 25$	Add $\left(\dfrac{-10}{2}\right)^2$ to both sides.
$(x - 5)^2 = y + 11$	An equivalent equation. ∎

At least one of the expressions $A(x - h)^2$ or $B(y - k)^2$ is always present in the familiar center-vertex form for a quadratic equation.

■ Example 3

Graph the equation $y^2 - 4x + 6y + 1 = 0$.

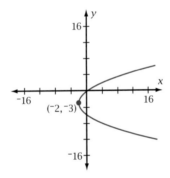

Solution

$y^2 + 6y = 4x - 1$	Separate the variables.
$y^2 + 6y + 9 = 4x - 1 + 9$	Add 9 to both sides $\left(\dfrac{6}{2} = 3 \text{ and } 3^2 = 9\right)$.
$(y + 3)^2 = 4x + 8$	Simplify.
$(y + 3)^2 = 4(x + 2)$	Factor the expression on the right (**center-vertex form**).
$y + 3 = \pm\sqrt{4(x + 2)}$	Take the square root of both sides.
$y = \pm 2\sqrt{x + 2} - 3$	Subtract 3 from both sides ($y=$ **form**). ∎

The final two steps in this example show you how to change the equation into $y=$ form once you have obtained the center-vertex form. However, if you only want to graph a relation and find intercepts, and you don't need information about the center or focus, you can obtain the $y=$ form more directly by using the quadratic formula.

The Quadratic Formula

Vertex form

If $A(x - H)^2 + K = 0$, then the solutions are $x = H \pm \sqrt{\dfrac{-K}{A}}$.

Polynomial form

If $ax^2 + bx + c = 0$, then the solutions are $x = \dfrac{-b \pm \sqrt{b^2 - 4ac}}{2a}$.

■ Example 3 revisited

Solve the equation $y^2 - 4x + 6y + 1 = 0$ by using the quadratic formula.

Solution

$y^2 - 4x + 6y + 1 = 0$ The original equation (a quadratic in the variable y).

$y^2 + 6y - 4x + 1 = 0$ Identify the formula constants as $a = 1$, $b = 6$, and $c = {}^-4x + 1$.

$y = \dfrac{-b \pm \sqrt{b^2 - 4ac}}{2a} = \dfrac{{}^-6 \pm \sqrt{6^2 - 4(1)({}^-4x + 1)}}{(2)(1)}$ ■

Check that this equation is the same as $y = {}^\pm\sqrt{4(x + 2)} - 3$. Do you see why the two equations are equivalent?

■ Example 4

Graph $x^2 + 4y^2 - 10x + 16y + 37 = 0$.

Solution

In this equation you must complete the square for both variables.

$$x^2 - 10x + 4y^2 + 16y = {}^-37$$

$$(x^2 - 10x) + 4(y^2 + 4y) = {}^-37$$

$$(x^2 - 10x + 25) + 4(y^2 + 4y + 4) = {}^-37 + 25 + 16$$

$$(x - 5)^2 + 4(y + 2)^2 = 4$$

$$\frac{(x - 5)^2}{4} + \frac{(y + 2)^2}{1} = 1 \qquad \text{center-vertex form}$$

$$\frac{(y + 2)^2}{1} = 1 - \frac{(x - 5)^2}{4}$$

$$(y + 2) = {}^\pm\sqrt{1 - \frac{(x - 5)^2}{4}}$$

$$y = {}^\pm\sqrt{1 - \frac{(x - 5)^2}{4}} - 2 \qquad y\text{= form} \quad ■$$

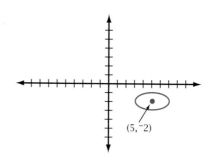

(5, ̄2)

The problems in the problem set will help you understand the examples, let you practice the process of completing the square, and give you the opportunity to use the quadratic formula.

Problem Set 12.8

1. Rewrite each equation in the general quadratic form as defined in the beginning of this section.

a. $(x + 7)^2 = 9(y - 11)$

b. $\dfrac{(x - 7)^2}{9} + \dfrac{(y + 11)^2}{1} = 1$

2. Find the values for a, b, c, d, and e as you complete the square for $15x^2 + 21x$.

a. $15x^2 + 21x = 15(x^2 + ax)$ $(15a = 21)$

b. $15(x^2 + ax) = 15(x^2 + 2bx)$ $(2b = a)$

c. $15(x^2 + 2bx) = 15(x^2 + 2bx + c) - 15c$ $(b^2 = c)$

d. $15(x^2 + 2bx + c) - 15c = 15(x^2 + 2bx + c) - d$ $(15c = d)$

e. $15(x^2 + 2bx + c) - d = 15(x + e)^2 - d$ $(\sqrt{c} = e)$

3. Identify each equation as true or false. If it is false, correct it to make it true.

a. $y^2 + 11y + 121 = (y + 11)^2$

b. $x^2 - 18x + 81 = (x - 9)^2$

c. $5y^2 + 10y + 5 = 5(y + 1)^2$

d. $4x^2 + 24x + 36 = 4(x + 6)^2$

4. Match each equation to one of the graphs. Assume that the distance between two grid marks represents one unit.

a. $9x^2 + 4y^2 - 36 = 0$

b. $x^2 - 4y^2 - 8x = 0$

c. $3x^2 - 30x + 5y + 55 = 0$

d. $x^2 + y^2 + 2x - 6y - 15 = 0$

i.
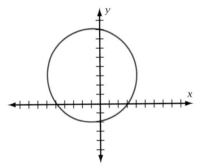

ii.
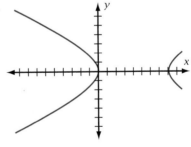

iii.
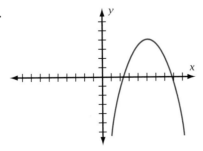

iv.
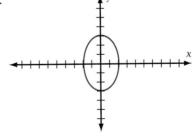

5. Rewrite each equation in center-vertex form, and identify the curve.

   a. $25x^2 - 4y^2 + 100 = 0$ **b.** $4y^2 - 10x + 16y + 36 = 0$

   c. $4x^2 + 4y^2 + 24x - 8y + 39 = 0$ **d.** $3x^2 + 5y^2 - 12x + 20y + 8 = 0$

6. Rewrite each equation in $y=$ form by solving for y with the quadratic formula. Graph each curve.

   a. $25x^2 - 4y^2 + 100 = 0$ **b.** $4y^2 - 10x + 16y + 36 = 0$

   c. $4x^2 + 4y^2 + 24x - 8y + 39 = 0$ **d.** $3x^2 + 5y^2 - 12x + 20y + 8 = 0$

7. The towers of this parabolic suspension bridge are 400 m apart and 50 m above the suspended roadway. The cable is 4 m above the roadway at the halfway point. Write an equation that models the parabolic shape of the cable.

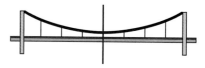

8. Explain in your own words the difference between the center-vertex form and the $y=$ form of a quadratic equation. Under what circumstances would you want to use each of these forms?

Take Another Look 12.8

During this chapter you have frequently been asked to recognize or graph an ellipse of the form

$$\left(\frac{x}{a}\right)^2 + \left(\frac{y}{b}\right)^2 = 1.$$

You have not considered equations like

$$\left(\frac{x}{a}\right)^3 + \left(\frac{y}{b}\right)^3 = 1, \text{ or } \left(\frac{x}{a}\right)^4 + \left(\frac{y}{b}\right)^4 = 1, \text{ or more generally } \left(\frac{x}{a}\right)^n + \left(\frac{y}{b}\right)^n = 1.$$

The Lamé curve is a generalized ellipse (or superellipse) when $n > 2$. Investigate several Lamé curve graphs in a "friendly" graphing window. In this investigation, assume that $a > 0$ and $b > 0$. You already know what effect the values of a and b have on an ellipse. Do they have the same effect on a Lamé curve? For fixed values of a and b try different n values, including positive, negative, whole-number, and fraction values. Explore the graph shapes and properties for different values of n. Summarize your discoveries.

Source: Based on a workshop given by Chuck Vander Embse.

Geometer's Sketchpad Investigation

Constructing an Ellipse

The steps below show you one way to construct an ellipse by using Sketchpad.

Step 1 Construct a segment and label the endpoints A and B.

Step 2 Construct a point on segment AB. Label this point C.

Step 3 Construct line segments AC and CB.

Step 4 Construct and label points F_1 and F_2 to represent the foci of your ellipse.

Step 5 Construct a circle with center F_1 and radius AC. Construct another circle with center F_2 and radius CB.

Step 6 If necessary, adjust your model so that the circles intersect. Construct the two intersection points of the circles. Select the intersection points and choose Trace Point from the Display menu.

Step 7 Drag point C back and forth along segment AB. The trace of the two points should be an ellipse.

Questions

1. Explain why the intersection points of the two circles satisfy the distance definition of an ellipse.
2. Experiment with different locations of the focal points to see how the shape of the ellipse changes. (One way to do this is to first select one of the points of intersection of the two circles, then select point C and construct a locus. Repeat this process for the other point of intersection. Then move F_1 or F_2 and observe what happens to the loci.) Describe your findings.
3. How far apart can the two focal points be before you can no longer draw an ellipse?
4. Use Sketchpad to create a parabola based on its distance definition.
5. Use Sketchpad to create a hyperbola based on its distance definition.

The Rotation Matrix

What is the hardest task in the world? To think.
—Ralph Waldo Emerson

Without some kind of graphing utility, you would find it very difficult to graph a conic section that is rotated off the horizontal and vertical axes like the one shown at the right. The graph comes from the equation

$$Ax^2 + Bxy + Cy^2 + Dx + Ey + F = 0.$$

The rotation indicates the presence of an xy-term in the general equation.

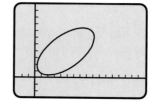

■ Example 1

Solve for y and graph the conic section determined by
$16x^2 - 24xy + 25y^2 - 60x - 80y + 100 = 0$.

Solution

You can solve for y by using the quadratic formula. The first step is to identify the coefficients a, b, and c in the equation $ay^2 + by + c = 0$.

Arches National Park, Utah

$$\boxed{25} \, y^2 + \boxed{(-80 - 24x)} \, y + \boxed{16x^2 - 60x + 100} = 0$$

$$y = \frac{-b \pm \sqrt{b^2 - 4ac}}{2a}; \ a = 25, \ b = -80 - 24x, \ c = 16x^2 - 60x + 100$$

Graph $y = \dfrac{-(-80 - 24x) \pm \sqrt{(-80 - 24x)^2 - 4 \cdot 25(16x^2 - 60x + 100)}}{(2 \cdot 25)}$.

Be sure your graph matches the ellipse pictured and described above. ■

Investigation 12.9.1

Transformations and Matrices

a. Draw coordinate axes so that its origin is near the center of your graph paper. Mark two points, A and B, which are close to each other and located in the first quadrant. (You will increase your accuracy if you don't place A and B too close to the origin.) Use a straightedge to connect each point to the origin.

Have each person in the group select a different arbitrary angle of rotation, θ. Do not choose θ equal to 45° or 90°. Use a compass or a ruler and protractor to locate points C and D. Points C and D should be the images of points A and B after they are rotated $\theta°$ counterclockwise about the origin. Find the coordinates of points C and D as accurately as you can.

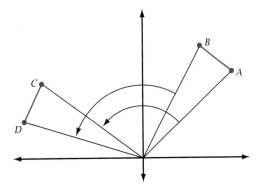

b. Find the matrix that will transform segment AB to segment CD by placing the coordinates of the points A, B, C, and D into the second and third matrices shown below. Then use an inverse matrix to find the entries of the first (transformation) matrix. Multiply to check your answer.

$$\begin{bmatrix} e & f \\ g & h \end{bmatrix} \begin{bmatrix} A_x & B_x \\ A_y & B_y \end{bmatrix} = \begin{bmatrix} C_x & D_x \\ C_y & D_y \end{bmatrix}$$

c. Find the sine and cosine of the rotation angle θ that you used to locate points C and D. Determine a connection between the entries of the first (transformation) matrix in the above equation and your sine and cosine values. Form a conjecture about a matrix that will rotate a graph $\theta°$ counterclockwise about the origin. Compare your results with those of others.

The drawing shows the images after rotating points $(1, 0)$ and $(0, 1)$ $\theta°$ counterclockwise about the origin. Do you see why the point $(1, 0)$ rotates into $(\cos \theta, \sin \theta)$? The point $(0, 1)$ rotates into (a, b) because the two triangles (drawn to the x-axis) are congruent. Rename a and b in terms of $\cos \theta$ and $\sin \theta$. Then substitute your expressions for a and b in the matrix

$$\begin{bmatrix} \cos \theta & a \\ \sin \theta & b \end{bmatrix}.$$

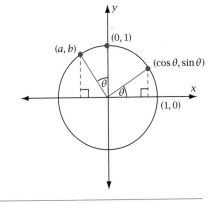

General Rotation Matrix

The **general rotation** matrix for a counterclockwise rotation through an angle of $\theta°$ is

$$\begin{bmatrix} \cos \theta & -\sin \theta \\ \sin \theta & \cos \theta \end{bmatrix}.$$

Example 2

Rotate the point $(5, 2)$ counterclockwise $60°$ with respect to the origin.

Solution

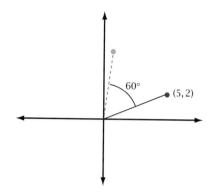

$$\begin{bmatrix} \cos 60° & -\sin 60° \\ \sin 60° & \cos 60° \end{bmatrix} = \begin{bmatrix} 0.5 & -0.866 \\ 0.866 & 0.5 \end{bmatrix}$$

$$\begin{bmatrix} 0.5 & -0.866 \\ 0.866 & 0.5 \end{bmatrix} \begin{bmatrix} 5 \\ 2 \end{bmatrix} = \begin{bmatrix} 0.768 \\ 5.33 \end{bmatrix}$$

Check to see if you can enter and calculate this solution more directly in your calculator by using

$$\begin{bmatrix} \cos 60° & -\sin 60° \\ \sin 60° & \cos 60° \end{bmatrix} \begin{bmatrix} 5 \\ 2 \end{bmatrix} = \begin{bmatrix} 0.768 \\ 5.33 \end{bmatrix}.$$

You can verify your results by finding the distance from each point to the origin and by finding the difference between the two angles that are measured from the positive ray of the x-axis to the rays originating at the origin and passing through the points.

$$\sqrt{5^2 + 2^2} \approx 5.385 \qquad \sqrt{0.768^2 + 5.33^2} \approx 5.385$$

$$\tan^{-1}\left(\frac{2}{5}\right) \approx 21.8° \qquad \tan^{-1}\left(\frac{5.33}{0.768}\right) \approx 81.8°$$

The new point is the same distance from the origin and has been rotated $60°$ further from the x-axis. ■

Example 3

Rotate the parabola $\begin{cases} x(t) = 3t^2 + 3 \\ y(t) = 5t \end{cases}$ counterclockwise $135°$.

Solution

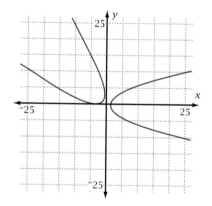

$$\begin{bmatrix} \cos 135° & -\sin 135° \\ \sin 135° & \cos 135° \end{bmatrix} \begin{bmatrix} 3t^2 + 3 \\ 5t \end{bmatrix}$$

$$\approx \begin{bmatrix} -2.1t^2 - 3.5t - 2.1 \\ 2.1t^2 - 3.5t + 2.1 \end{bmatrix}$$

Verify this result by graphing the original parabola $\begin{cases} x_1 = 3t^2 + 3 \\ y_1 = 5t \end{cases}$ and the image parabola

$$\begin{cases} x(t) = -2.1t^2 - 3.5t - 2.1 \\ y(t) = 2.1t^2 - 3.5t + 2.1 \end{cases}. \quad ■$$

In general, the image equations $\begin{bmatrix} x_2 \\ y_2 \end{bmatrix}$ can be directly entered into your calculator because

$$\begin{bmatrix} \cos\theta & -\sin\theta \\ \sin\theta & \cos\theta \end{bmatrix} \begin{bmatrix} x_1 \\ y_1 \end{bmatrix} = \begin{bmatrix} x_1\cos\theta - y_1\sin\theta \\ x_1\sin\theta + y_1\cos\theta \end{bmatrix}.$$

This means that after parametric equations for x_1 and y_1 are entered, you can graph the image by entering

$$x_2 = x_1\cos\theta - y_1\sin\theta \quad \text{and} \quad y_2 = x_1\sin\theta + y_1\cos\theta.$$

However, if you cannot change to parametric form, you must replace each x and y in the equation with the rotated equivalent. This is demonstrated in the following example.

■ Example 4

Rotate the hyperbola $x^2 - y^2 = 1$ counterclockwise $90°$ about the origin.

Solution

Replace each x and y in the equation $x^2 - y^2 = 1$ with the rotated equivalents $x_2 = x_1\cos\theta - y_1\sin\theta$ and $y_2 = x_1\sin\theta + y_1\cos\theta$.

$(x\cos 90° - y\sin 90°)^2 - (x\sin 90° + y\cos 90°)^2 = 1$
$(x \cdot 0 - y \cdot 1)^2 - (x \cdot 1 + y \cdot 0)^2 = 1$
$y^2 - x^2 = 1$ (This is the rotated hyperbola.)   ■

Problem Set 12.9

1. Find the rotation matrix for each angle. Round off decimals to the nearest thousandth.
   a. $30°$ counterclockwise
   b. $147°$ counterclockwise
   c. $270°$ counterclockwise
   d. $213°$ clockwise

2. Rotate the triangle formed by $(1, {}^-2)$, $(4, 5)$, and $(7, {}^-2)$ counterclockwise $90°$. Give the coordinates of the new vertices, and sketch both the original and the rotated triangle on a grid.

3. Rotate the ellipse $x = 3\cos t$ and $y = 2\sin t$ through an angle of $30°$.
   a. Graph both curves.
   b. Write the parametric equations of the image curve.

4. Rotate the triangle pictured at the right $180°$ counterclockwise about the origin.
   a. Name the new vertices.
   b. What composition of reflections gives the same image?

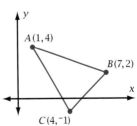

5. Sketch the figure pictured at the right on graph paper, and enter the vertices in

$$[B] = \begin{bmatrix} 3 & 6 & 6 & 3 \\ 1 & 1 & 3 & 3 \end{bmatrix}.$$

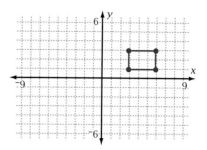

For each choice of [A], find the matrix result after multiplying [A] [B]. Graph the images, and identify the transformation that occurred.

a. $[A] = \begin{bmatrix} 1 & 0 \\ 0 & -1 \end{bmatrix}$ b. $[A] = \begin{bmatrix} -1 & 0 \\ 0 & 1 \end{bmatrix}$

c. $[A] = \begin{bmatrix} 0 & -1 \\ 1 & 0 \end{bmatrix}$ d. $[A] = \begin{bmatrix} -1 & 0 \\ 0 & -1 \end{bmatrix}$ e. $[A] = \begin{bmatrix} 0 & 1 \\ 1 & 0 \end{bmatrix}$

6. a. Predict the graph of $x_1 = \tan t$ and $y_1 = \dfrac{1}{\cos t}$.

   b. Describe what the equations for $x_2 = x_1 \cos \theta - y_1 \sin \theta$ and $y_2 = x_1 \sin \theta + y_1 \cos \theta$ accomplish when $\theta = -50°$.

   c. Draw the graphs.

7. Graph $xy = 4$. Find the equation of its image after a rotation of 45°. (Use the replacements for x and y described in Example 4.)

8. a. Write parametric equations that will draw the larger equilateral triangle pictured at the right on your calculator.

   b. Write parametric equations that will transform the larger triangle into the smaller triangle.

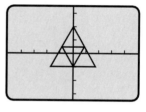

Chapter Review

*I do not know what I may appear to the world, but to myself I seem to have been
only like a boy playing on the seashore, and diverting myself in now and then
finding a smoother pebble or a prettier shell than ordinary, whilst the great ocean
of truth lay all undiscovered before me.*
—Isaac Newton

You were introduced to several new functions and relations in this chapter and you
looked at some old friends in a different way. First you looked at the inverse variation
function, an example of a rational function. You also looked at the recursive model
for exponential growth or decay in a new way. Because the original model assumes
unlimited resources and no limitations to growth, it is not actually a good model for
many populations. A model that incorporates a variable growth rate is much more
appropriate. Variable growth models are more complicated to use, but they provide
more realistic predictions.

    Another set of relations covered in this chapter were defined by a distance between
a fixed point or points and another infinite set of points. They are called conic
sections because these shapes can be formed by slicing a cone at various angles. The
simplest of the conic shapes is the circle, the set of points a fixed distance from a
fixed point called the center. Closely related to the circle is the ellipse. This curve can
be thought of as a circle that has been stretched unevenly in the horizontal and
vertical directions. The ellipse can be defined as the set of points so situated that the
sum of their distances from two fixed points, the foci, is a constant. The parabola is
another conic, which you studied in earlier chapters. It can be defined as the set of
points that are equally distant from a fixed point called the focus and a fixed line
called the directrix. The last of the conics is the hyperbola. The definition of a
hyperbola is similar to the definition of an ellipse, except that the difference between
the distances from the foci remains constant. The equations for these conics can be
written parametrically or in xy-form. Each of these conics can be oriented either
vertically or horizontally. (Of course with a circle, the orientation doesn't make any
difference.) You can also rotate a curve by multiplying the original equation in
parametric form by a rotation matrix, or you can replace each x- and y-value with the
rotated equivalents.

Problem Set 12.10

1. How many ounces of pure sugar must you add to a 20 oz container of a 12% sugar
solution so that the solution is at least 42% sugar?

2. Describe how to section, or slice, a mathematical cone to produce each of the following items.

    a. Circle   **b.** Ellipse   **c.** Parabola   **d.** Hyperbola

    e. Point   **f.** One line   **g.** Two lines

3. a. Write the equation for the graph shown at right in center-vertex form.

    b. Write the parametric equations for this graph.

    c. Name the center and the foci.

    d. Write the general quadratic form of the equation for this graph.

    e. Write the parametric equations of the graph after a counterclockwise rotation through an angle of 75°.

    f. Write the general quadratic for the equation of this rotated graph.

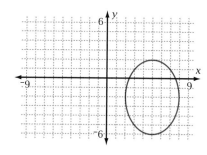

4. a. Write the equations of the asymptotes of the graph pictured.

    b. Write the general quadratic equation for this hyperbola.

    c. Write a function that will give the *vertical distance* between the asymptote with positive slope and the upper part of the right-hand branch of the hyperbola as a point moves to the right from the origin.

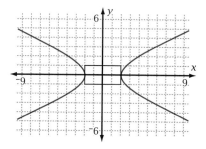

    d. Use the function from 4c to complete the missing table values.

x	0	1	2	10	...	20
Distance	–?–	–?–	–?–	–?–	...	–?–

5. a. Graph $y = \dfrac{2x - 14}{x - 5}$.

    b. What are the horizontal and vertical asymptotes of this function?

    c. Write a distance function that records the vertical distance between a point moving on the graph and the horizontal asymptote.

    d. Use the function from 5c to complete the missing table values.

x	0	3	5	10	...	20
Distance	–?–	–?–	–?–	–?–	...	–?–

6. How can you alter the equation of $y = \dfrac{2x - 14}{x - 5}$ so that the new graph is the same as the original graph except for a hole at $x = {}^-3$? Verify your new equation by graphing it on your calculator.

7. On her way to school Ellen drove at a steady speed for the first 2 mi. After glancing at her watch, she drove 20 mi/hr faster during the remaining 3.5 mi. How fast did she drive during the two portions of this trip if the total time involved was 10 min? Explain your solution process.

8. Eric cycled 34 mi on his bike and then ran the last 13 mi in the "World's Most Common" competition. On a good day he can run fast and bike fast. On a bad day he does them both slowly. Overall, his average bike speed is consistently 11 mi/hr faster than his average running speed.

    a. Write a function relating (*average running speed, total time*).
    b. Draw the graph of this function and describe the features of the graph.
    c. What *x*- and *y*-values make sense?
    d. If Eric's total time for this event was 5 hr, what was his average running speed?

9. What was the most interesting concept you learned about in this chapter? Explain it in a way that would convince someone else that you have learned it.

Assessing What You've Learned

Be sure to choose at least three different ways to assess what you've learned.

- Organizing Your Notebook (Chapter 0)
- Keeping a Journal (Chapter 1)
- Portfolio (Chapter 2)
- Performance Assessment (Chapter 3)
- Open-ended Investigations (Chapter 4)
- Constructing Test Questions (Chapter 5)
- Group Presentations and Tests (Chapter 6)
- Overall Self-Assessment (Chapter 7)

13

Trigonometric Functions

The tribal drummers and a dancer are performing in Ninga, Burundi. The sounds made by musical instruments can be modeled using a combination of trigonometric functions. Usually these equations are very complicated because the sounds themselves are complex. Trigonometric functions are used to model periodic functions—functions that repeat over a period of time.

Defining the Circular Function

Experience isn't interesting till it begins to repeat itself—in fact, till it does that, it hardly is experience.
—Elizabeth Bowen

Have you ever wondered how the exact time of sunrise or sunset is known for each day, even years in advance? Or have you been curious about what gives each musical instrument its unique sound? The water depth caused by the tide at the ocean shoreline, the motion of a young child on a swing, your height as you ride a Ferris wheel, and the number of hours between sunrise and sunset each day are predictable. In this chapter you will study mathematical functions that help to explain these phenomena and other cyclical or repetitive motions.

Investigation 13.1.1

Anne Fibian and the Paddle Wheel

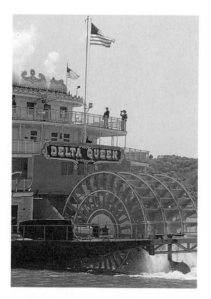

While swimming along, a frog by the name of Anne Fibian reaches out and grabs onto a paddle of a 10 m diameter paddle wheel. The axle of this wheel is at the water level. Anne is immediately lifted from the surface of the river and begins her journey clinging tightly to the paddle. The wheel is slowly spinning at one revolution every 6 min. This means that Anne will be underwater for 3 min during each rotation. Your first task is to cut out a paper model of the wheel, using a 1 cm = 1 m scale, and draw a frog on the edge of your wheel. Then use your wheel and a ruler to collect data to complete the following table. The time is measured in seconds. Note that the wheel is turning through 1° per second, so in 30 sec it turns through 30°. The height from the surface of the water is in meters (centimeters for your model) and may be either positive (above the water) or negative (below the water). Describe the situation when the height is zero.

Time (sec)	0	30	45	60	90	120	135	150	180	240	270
Height (m)	0	-?-	-?-	-?-	-?-	-?-	-?-	-?-	-?-	-?-	-?-

Time (sec)	300	360	420	480	540	600	660	720	780	840	900
Height (m)	-?-	-?-	-?-	-?-	-?-	-?-	-?-	-?-	-?-	-?-	-?-

Enter this data into your calculator and plot a (*time, height*) graph. With the calculator in *degree* mode, find the transformations needed to make the parent curve, $y = \sin x$, best fit the data. Use your model to calculate Anne's height after 315 sec. Use your model to find at least three times when Anne is close to 4 m under water. Write a short report that includes a graph and the answers to the above questions.

The initial definition of the sine function found in Chapter 6 is no longer adequate, because the ratio of the opposite side to the hypotenuse in a right triangle cannot help you find the sines of angles whose measures are greater than 90°. In this section, you will use what you discovered in Investigation 13.1.1 to extend the definition.

■ Example 1

Use your calculator to find the sine of each angle, and explain what each result means in terms of a lily pad stuck on Anne's paddle wheel at a distance of 1 m from the center.

a. $\sin 30°$ **b.** $\sin 150°$

c. $\sin 210°$ **d.** $\sin 330°$

Solution

Using your calculator, you will get $\sin 30° = \sin 150° = 0.5$, and $\sin 210° = \sin 330° = {}^{-}0.5$. How can each of these angles have sines that are either 0.5 or ${}^{-}0.5$?

a. After 30 sec, the wheel has rotated 30°. To find the height of the lily pad above the water, draw a triangle like the one shown.

$$\sin 30° = \frac{y}{1}$$

$$y = \sin 30° = 0.5$$

The distance from the surface of the water to the lily pad is the sine of the angle.

b. After 150 sec, the paddle wheel has rotated 150°. To determine the height of the lily pad above the water, draw a right triangle by

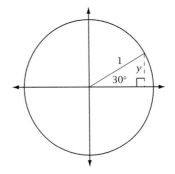

dropping a perpendicular line to the x-axis. Again, the angle you use to find the height is 30°. This acute angle within the triangle is called the **reference angle**.

$$\sin 30° = \frac{y}{1}$$

$$y = \sin 30° = 0.5$$

This angle has the same sine as a 150° angle, and again the sine represents the vertical distance of the lily pad from the surface of the water.

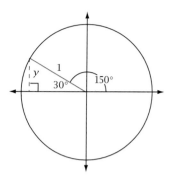

c. After 210 sec, the paddle wheel has rotated 210°. The triangle again has a reference angle of 30°.

$$\sin 30° = \frac{y}{1}$$

$$y = \sin 30° = 0.5$$

Because the lily pad is underwater, the answer must be negative, so $y = {}^{-}0.5$. This means that $\sin 210° = {}^{-}0.5$, which represents the vertical distance below the surface of the water.

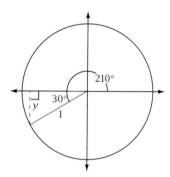

d. After 330 sec, the paddle wheel has rotated 330°. Repeating the previous steps, you again work with a 30° reference angle.

$$\sin 30° = \frac{y}{1}$$

$$y = \sin 30° = 0.5$$

Because the lily pad is underwater, the answer will be negative, so

$$y = {}^{-}0.5 \quad \text{and} \quad \sin 330° = {}^{-}0.5. \quad \blacksquare$$

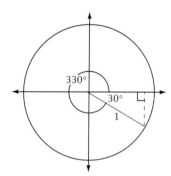

Notice that the sine of the angle through which the paddle wheel has turned, automatically tells you the distance from the surface and whether the lily pad is above or below the water. So the sine of angle A can be defined as the distance from the surface of the water to a lily pad stuck 1 m from the center of a paddle wheel after it has rotated $A°$ counterclockwise from the surface of the water.

A more mathematical definition of the sine of an angle is as follows.

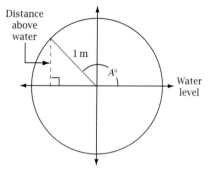

Sine of an Angle

The **sine** of an angle A is the y-coordinate of a point rotated $A°$ counterclockwise about the origin from the positive x-axis on a circle with a radius of 1 unit.

The domain of the function $\sin A$ is measured in degrees and, because the paddle wheel can keep rotating, the measure of the angle can increase beyond $360°$. In the investigation, the time Anne spent on the wheel was directly related to the angle through which the wheel turned. Because the wheel was turning before Anne got on, both the time and the angle can be

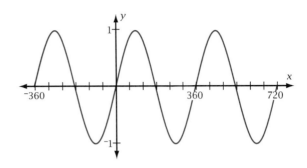

negative values. This means that you can find the sine of any positive or negative angle. If the measure of angle A is negative, for example $A = {}^-30°$, then this point represents the position of the paddle 30 seconds before Anne got onto it. Another way to think of this is that the point has been rotated $30°$ *clockwise* about the origin from the positive x-axis on a circle with a radius of 1 unit.

Also, because the lily pad repeats the exact same journey each time around, the graph of the sine of the angle will repeat itself over and over again. Explain why the graph above shows this endless journey of the lily pad.

Your graph of Anne's distance from the surface of the water in Investigation 13.1.1 had an equation similar to $y = 5 \sin x$. What is the role of the 5 in the equation? How does the graph of Anne's distance from the surface compare to the graph of the lily pad's distance from the surface? Graph both of the equations on the same axis to see.

Because you know that you can find the sine for any angle, it is also reasonable to assume that the cosine and tangent also can be defined for any angle.

■ Example 2

Use a calculator to find the cosine of each angle.

a. $150°$

b. $320°$

Compare each result to the cosine of the reference angle.

Solution

a. According to the calculator, $\cos 150° = {}^-0.866$. The reference angle is $30°$. In the triangle shown, you can see that $\cos 30° = \frac{x}{1}$. Because this x-value will be negative, you must change the sign. This means $\cos 150° = {}^-\cos 30° \approx {}^-0.866$.

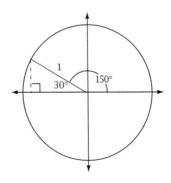

b. According to the calculator, cos 320° = 0.766.

The reference angle is 40° and the triangle suggests the equation $\cos 40° = \frac{x}{1}$. So $x \approx 0.766$. Therefore, cos 320° = cos 40° ≈ 0.766. ■

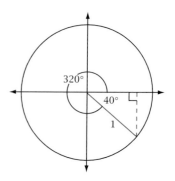

Notice that in each case the cosine of the angle is equal to the x-coordinate of the point on the circle. With respect to the paddle wheel example, this means that when the lily pad, which is located 1 meter from the center of the paddle wheel, has rotated A° counterclockwise, the cosine of the angle gives its horizontal position from the center of the wheel. Positive numbers mean the lily pad is to the right of the center, and negative numbers mean it is to the left of the center.

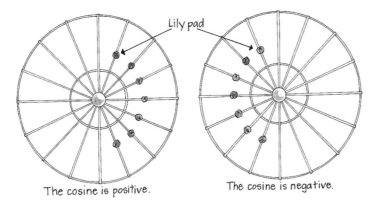

The cosine is positive.   The cosine is negative.

Here is a more mathematical definition of cosine.

Cosine of an Angle

The **cosine** of an angle A is the x-coordinate of a point rotated A° counterclockwise about the origin from the positive x-axis on a circle with a radius of 1 unit.

Again, you can visualize a negative angle, such as ⁻40°, as the position of the point 40 seconds before the lily pad got stuck to it. A rotation of ⁻40° will identify the same point that a rotation of 320° will identify.

Problem Set 13.1

1. Use your calculator to find each value. Then draw paddle-wheel diagrams to show the meaning of the value. Name the reference angle.

a. sin 85°   **b.** cos 147°   **c.** sin 280°   **d.** cos 310°   **e.** sin ⁻47°

2. a. Carefully sketch a graph of $y = \sin x$ for $0° \le x \le 360°$ on your paper.

b. Predict how the graph of $y = \sin x + 2$ will compare to the graph of $y = \sin x$. Verify your prediction with your calculator, and record a sketch of the graph.

c. Predict how the graph of $y = \sin(x - 180°)$ will compare to the graph of $y = \sin x$. Verify your prediction with your calculator, and record a sketch of the graph.

d. Predict how the graph of $y = 2\sin(x - 180°) + 3$ will compare to the graph of $y = \sin x$. Verify your prediction with your calculator, and record a sketch of the graph.

3. As the paddle wheel turns, the slope of a line that joins the lily pad to the center of the wheel changes.

a. Determine the x- and y-coordinates that correspond to each position of the lily pad. Record these values in a table like the one below. (Remember, the coordinates of the lily pad are the cosine and sine of the rotation angle of the wheel.)

Angle A	0°	30°	60°	90°	120°	150°	180°
x-coordinate	-?-	-?-	-?-	-?-	-?-	-?-	-?-
y-coordinate	-?-	-?-	-?-	-?-	-?-	-?-	-?-
Slope	-?-	-?-	-?-	-?-	-?-	-?-	-?-
tan A	-?-	-?-	-?-	-?-	-?-	-?-	-?-

Angle A	210°	240°	270°	300°	315°	330°	360°
x-coordinate	-?-	-?-	-?-	-?-	-?-	-?-	-?-
y-coordinate	-?-	-?-	-?-	-?-	-?-	-?-	-?-
Slope	-?-	-?-	-?-	-?-	-?-	-?-	-?-
tan A	-?-	-?-	-?-	-?-	-?-	-?-	-?-

b. To find the slope of these lines, you can use the coordinates of the lily pad's location and the coordinates of the center of the wheel (the origin). So the slope is equal to the ratio $\frac{y\text{-coordinate}}{x\text{-coordinate}}$. Compute the slope of the line between the lily pad and the center of the wheel for each angle, and record the results in the table.

c. The slope is the same as the ratio of the leg lengths of the reference triangle. Why? What is another name for the ratio of the leg lengths of a right triangle?

d. Find the tangent of each angle in the table. Compare the tangent values to the slopes. What do you notice?

e. Write a definition of the tangent of angle A using the lily-pad-and-paddle-wheel scenario.

4. a. Carefully sketch a graph of $y = \tan x$ for $0° \le x \le 360°$.

b. What happens at $x = 90°$? Explain why this is so.

c. Why are the values of $\tan 40°$ and $\tan 220°$ the same? Explain in terms of your definition of tangent.

When a portion of the graph of a function like sine or tangent repeats over and over again, the function is **periodic**. The **period** of such a function is the length of the *x*-interval required for the graph of one complete cycle before the graph begins to repeat itself.

5. Graph each function and name its period.

    a. $y = \sin x$ **b.** $y = \cos x$ **c.** $y = \tan x$ **d.** $y = \sin 2x$ **e.** $y = \tan 3x$

6. a. On your calculator, graph $y = \sin ax$ with *a*-values of 1, 2, 3, 4, and 5. Write a sentence explaining how the *a*-value affects the period of the sine graph.

    b. What is the period of $y = \sin ax$?

7. a. Using what you discovered in Problem 6, predict the period of $y = \tan 2x$. Use your calculator to verify or revise your answer.

    b. Predict the period of $y = \tan \frac{1}{3}x$. Use your calculator to verify or revise your answer.

    c. How does the change in the period compare to other transformations you have studied?

8. Determine the period for each graph below. Next, find any vertical stretches. Then find the horizontal or vertical shifts, if any. Finally, write an equation for each graph. There may be more than one correct equation. Verify each equation with your calculator.

a.

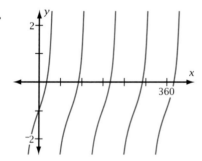

b.

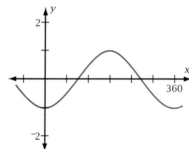

c.

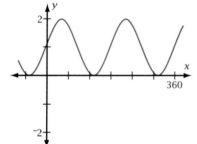

d.

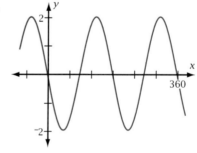

9. A plane flying 300 mi from Detroit to Chicago has been put in a holding pattern above the Chicago airport. The holding pattern is a circle with a diameter of 20 mi that the plane completes every 15 min. Complete the following steps to write an equation that models the distance of the plane from Detroit as a function of time.

  a. What is the period of this motion?
  b. What vertical stretch is needed to show the diameter of 20 mi?
  c. What shift is needed to show the 300 mi distance between the airports?
  d. Write an equation modeling the plane's distance from Detroit while it is flying in this holding pattern.

Project

Design a Picnic Table

Your task is to accurately describe the pieces of lumber needed to build a picnic table like that shown below. Determine the lengths of all pieces, as well as the angles that need to be cut. Make scale drawings of all pieces.

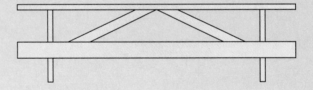
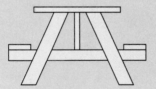

Section 13.2

Other Periodic Functions

Since we cannot be universal and know all that is to be known of everything, we ought to know a little about everything. For it is far better to know something about everything than to know all about one thing. This universality is best. If we can have both, still better; but if we must choose, we ought to choose the former.
—Blaise Pascal

Many situations are accurately and conveniently modeled with the sine, cosine, or tangent functions. However, in some applications the equation or model can be written more concisely if you use variations on these original three functions. These new functions share many common properties with the basic trigonometric functions, but they also have some interesting properties of their own.

■ Example 1

Bill Durr has been hired to construct a collection of ramps for InTune Piano Movers. The ramps must be built with a 7° incline angle. The movers need ramp heights of 20 cm, 35 cm, 47 cm, 75 cm, and 100 cm. Find the length of the boards that Bill will need for the inclined surface of each ramp.

Solution

Bill makes a drawing of a ramp. He labels the height of the ramp h and the length of the board b. For each ramp, the angle is 7°. Bill writes the equation

$$\sin 7° = \frac{h}{b}.$$

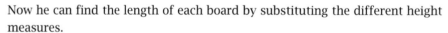

Because he needs to know the length of the board, he solves for b and gets the following result.

$$b = h \cdot \frac{1}{\sin 7°}$$

Now he can find the length of each board by substituting the different height measures.

$$20 \cdot \frac{1}{\sin 7°} \approx 164.1 \text{ cm} \qquad 35 \cdot \frac{1}{\sin 7°} \approx 287.2 \text{ cm} \qquad 47 \cdot \frac{1}{\sin 7°} \approx 385.7 \text{ cm}$$

$$75 \cdot \frac{1}{\sin 7°} \approx 615.4 \text{ cm} \qquad 100 \cdot \frac{1}{\sin 7°} \approx 820.6 \text{ cm} \quad ■$$

As you can see, each equation involves the reciprocal of the sine function. This reciprocal is called the **cosecant** function, abbreviated **csc**. So another way to write Bill's final equation is $b = h \cdot \csc 7°$.

The reciprocal of the cosine also has a special name, **secant**, abbreviated **sec**. And the reciprocal of the tangent is the **cotangent**, or **cot**.

Secant, Cosecant, and Cotangent

secant $A° = \sec A° = \dfrac{1}{\cos A°}$ cosecant $A° = \csc A° = \dfrac{1}{\sin A°}$

cotangent $A° = \cot A° = \dfrac{1}{\tan A°}$

Your calculator does not have special keys for these reciprocal functions. So you must convert them to sin, cos, or tan in order to enter them into your calculator. One way to do this is to use the reciprocal key $\boxed{x^{-1}}$. To enter csc x, you can enter $(\sin x)\boxed{x^{-1}}$, but it's probably easier to enter 1/sin x.

The reciprocal trigonometric functions were developed during the ninth century by astronomers, mostly Islamic, who lived and traveled in a region stretching from India to Spain. Though these functions are interrelated and it is now easy to compute one if you know its relationship to another, before calculating machines became available astronomers had to use tables of values for all of these functions.

Investigation 13.2.1

Reciprocal Function Graphs

In this investigation, you will explore the graphs of the reciprocal trigonometric functions. Choose Part 1, Part 2, or Part 3 of the investigation. Be prepared as a group to report your findings to the rest of the class.

(Note: Some of these graphs will have vertical asymptotes that are not actually part of the graph. The function breaks at these values and starts up again on the other side. However, it may appear that the asymptotes are drawn on your screen. These "fake asymptotes," or "drag lines," occur when the calculator connects a point from the top to the bottom of the screen. If your window is set so that a pixel has the exact value of the asymptote, then there will be no drag line drawn. Otherwise, the calculator will connect the pieces of the graph.)

Part 1   **a.** Graph $y = \sin x$ and $y = \csc x$ in the same graphing window, and carefully sketch the graph of both functions on the same coordinate axes.

         b. Compare the y-values of sin x and csc x for several different x-values. How does the range for sin x compare to the range for csc x? What is the period of the cosecant curve?

c. Where are the asymptotes located for $y = \csc x$? How can you explain these with reference to the ramp-building example above?

Part 2 **a.** Graph $y = \cos x$ and $y = \sec x$ in the same graphing window, and carefully sketch the graph of both functions on the same coordinate axes.

b. Compare the y-values of $\cos x$ and $\sec x$ for several different x-values. How does the range for $\cos x$ compare to the range for $\sec x$? What is the period of the secant curve?

c. Where are the vertical asymptotes located for $y = \sec x$?

Part 3 **a.** Graph $y = \tan x$ and $y = \cot x$ in the same graphing window, and carefully sketch the graph of each function on your paper.

b. Compare the y-values of $\tan x$ and $\cot x$ for several different x-values. How does the range for $\tan x$ compare to the range for $\cot x$? What is the period for the cotangent curve?

c. Where are the vertical asymptotes for $y = \cot x$? How does the graph of the cotangent compare to the graph of the tangent?

Part 4 **a.** Based on the presentations given by other groups, answer the questions for the parts of the investigation your group did not do.

b. Write a paragraph describing the similarities and differences between the secant graph and the cosecant graph. (Hint: Look at the similarities and differences of the sine and cosine graphs.) ,

c. One way to define $\cot x$ is to say that it is the ratio of $\cos x/\sin x$. Using this definition of $\cot x$, explain how you could use your knowledge of the graphs of $\sin x$ and $\cos x$ to sketch a graph of $\cot x$.

In Investigation 13.2.1, you found that the graphs of the secant and the cosecant were transformations of each other. This was also true for the sine and cosine graphs. This means that you can always write the equation of a sine curve in at least two different ways.

■ **Example 2**

Write three different equations of the graph shown.

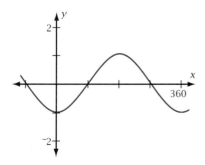

Solution

a. You can think of this graph as a sine curve that has been shifted to the right by 90°. This gives an equation of $y = \sin(x - 90°)$.

b. You can also think of this graph as a sine curve that has been flipped over the x-axis and shifted to the left by 90°. This gives an equation of $y = {}^-\!\sin(x + 90°)$.

c. This graph is also a cosine curve that has been flipped over the x-axis, $y = {}^-\!\cos x$.

Because the sine and cosine functions are periodic, you can shift their graphs either left or right to get the same image. Find three more correct answers. Be sure to graph them on your calculator to verify that each equation gives the same graph. ■

Problem Set 13.2

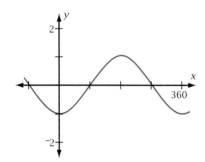

1. a. Sketch the function shown and label it $f(x)$. Then sketch a graph of $\dfrac{1}{f(x)}$ on the same coordinate axes.

b. Enter the equation for $f(x)$ into y_1 and $\dfrac{1}{f(x)}$ into y_2 and confirm that your sketches in part a are correct.

2. Find at least two different equations for each graph.

a.

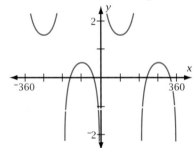

b.

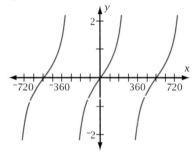

c.

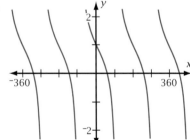

d.

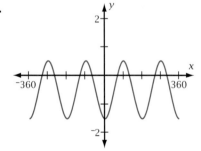

3. a. What effect does the d-value have on the graph of $y = \sin x + d$? Be specific.
   b. What effect does the a-value have on the graph of $y = a \sin x$? Be specific.
   c. What effect does the b-value have on the graph of $y = \sin bx$? Be specific.
   d. What effect does the c-value have on the graph of $y = \sin(x - c)$? Be specific.
   e. Use what you have discovered to sketch a graph of $y = 2 \sin 3x + 4$. Verify your sketch on your calculator.

4. a. A small bug is crawling counterclockwise around the rim of a 24 in. diameter tire. The rim is 15 in. in diameter. The slow-moving bug is now at its maximum height and is crawling at a constant rate of one-fourth of a revolution per minute. Write an equation and sketch a graph modeling the bug's height from the ground over the next 20 min.

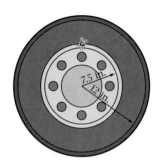

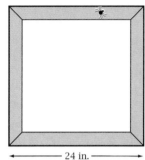

b. Suppose instead that the bug is crawling counterclockwise around this square picture frame. The square has side lengths of 24 in. and the bug is crawling at a constant rate of one-fourth of a revolution per minute. If the bug is now 6 ft from the floor, sketch a graph of its (*time, height from floor*) over the next 20 min.

← 24 in. →

5. Annie Thropologist is standing 20 m from the base of a cliff. Looking through her binoculars, she sees the remains of ancient cliff dwellings in the cliff face. To map the area, she must know the height of the dwellings above the canyon floor. Annie holds her binoculars at eye level, 1.5 m above the ground.

a. Write an equation that relates the angle at which she holds the binoculars to the height of the object she sees.

b. The top of the cliff is at an angle of 58° from the horizontal when viewed from where Annie is standing. How high is the cliff?

c. From where Annie is standing, she sees ruins at angles of 36° and 40° from the horizontal. How high are the ruins?

d. If cliff swallows built a nest in the cliff face 10 m above the canyon floor, at what angle should Annie focus her binoculars to observe the birds?

6. The chart below shows the number of hours between sunrise and sunset for the period between December 21, 1995, and July 23, 1996, in New Orleans, Louisiana, which is located at W 90°05′ N 29°58′.

Date	Hours	Date	Hours	Date	Hours	Date	Hours
21 Dec	10.217	14 Feb	11.100	9 Apr	12.733	3 Jun	13.983
26 Dec	10.233	19 Feb	11.250	14 Apr	12.833	8 Jun	14.017
31 Dec	10.250	24 Feb	11.400	19 Apr	13.017	13 Jun	14.050
5 Jan	10.283	29 Feb	11.533	24 Apr	13.150	18 Jun	14.083
10 Jan	10.350	5 Mar	11.683	29 Apr	13.300	23 Jun	14.083
15 Jan	10.417	10 Mar	11.833	4 May	13.417	28 Jun	14.050
20 Jan	10.517	15 Mar	11.983	9 May	13.533	3 Jul	14.017
25 Jan	10.617	20 Mar	12.133	14 May	13.650	8 Jul	13.983
30 Jan	10.717	25 Mar	12.283	19 May	13.750	13 Jul	13.900
4 Feb	10.850	30 Mar	12.433	24 May	13.833	18 Jul	13.833
9 Feb	10.967	4 Apr	12.583	29 May	13.917	23 Jul	13.750

a. Graph (*day, hours of daylight*) and find an equation of a best-fit curve. Use December 31 as day zero.

b. Use your model to determine the date in 1996 on which there was the least amount of daylight. How many hours of daylight was this?

c. Describe what you think a graph for Homer, Alaska, at 60° N latitude would look like compared to this graph.

7. The table below shows the maximum safe speed for a vehicle traveling around a curve and the angle of "banking" on the curve.

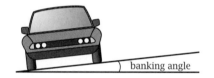

banking angle

Angle	1°	2°	3°	4°	5°	6°	7°
Speed (mi/hr)	26.2	37.0	45.4	52.4	58.6	64.2	69.4

a. Plot a graph of (*banking angle, speed squared*).

b. Try to fit the data with a sine curve. Check the residuals for your curve. What do the residuals imply?

c. Try to fit the data with a tangent curve. Check the residuals for your curve. What do the residuals imply?

d. What do your best-fit equation and its graph imply about a road banked at an angle of 90°?

8. Parametric equations $x = 5 \cos Bt$ and $y = 5 \sin Bt$ can be used to simulate a circular motion on a circle with a radius of 5 ft. The circle starts at $(^-5, 0)$ and finishes at the same point 20 sec later, where $B = 18°/\text{sec}$ and t is replaced with $(t - 10)$.

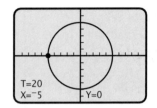

  a. Graph this simulation in a "friendly" window with a factor of 2.

  b. Write a function that models the distance of the cursor from the left margin of the window during the interval $0 \le t \le 20$.

  c. Draw a graph of the function you wrote in 8b.

  d. Write a function that models the distance of the cursor from the bottom margin of the window during the interval $0 \le t \le 20$.

  e. Draw a graph of the function you wrote in 8d.

9. Find another function that has the same graph as each function named below.

  a. $y = \cos(90° - x)$ **b.** $y = \sin(90° - x)$

  c. $y = \tan(90° - x)$ **d.** $y = \cos(^-x)$

  e. $y = \sin(^-x)$ **f.** $y = \tan(^-x)$

  g. $y = \sin(x + 360°)$ **h.** $y = \cos(90° + x)$

Take Another Look 13.2

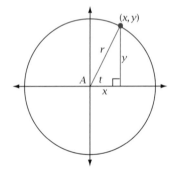

You have been graphing circles with radius r and t degrees at the central angle A by using the parametric equations $x = r \cos t$ and $y = r \sin t$. A friendly and "squared-up" window with $0° \le t \le 360°$ in steps of 15° works beautifully if your calculator is in *degree* and *parametric* modes.

Consider the alternative to *degree* mode. What is *radian* mode? What are radians? Where do they come from and why are they important? How many does it take to complete one revolution of a circle? (Hint: It has something to do with the circumference of your circle.) Do some exploring by using your calculator and parametric equations (in *radian* mode) to draw the graph of a circle of radius 1 centered at $(0, 0)$.

Geometer's Sketchpad Investigation

Constructing Trigonometric Curves

You can use Sketchpad to animate the basic trigonometric functions. Use the following steps to plot the sine function.

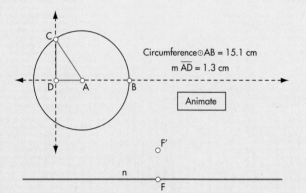

Circumference⊙AB = 15.1 cm

m $\overline{AD}$ = 1.3 cm

Animate

Step 1 Construct horizontal line AB.

Step 2 Construct a circle with center A and radius endpoint B.

Step 3 Construct point C on the circle.

Step 4 Construct a perpendicular to line AB through point C. Mark the point where both lines intersect as D. Hide the lines.

Step 5 Construct segments AD, CD, and AC.

Step 6 Select the circle and measure its circumference. Select the circumference and mark this distance. Create point E below the circle and translate this point horizontally by the marked distance. Construct the segment EE′ and label it n. Hide the endpoints.

Step 7 Select points D and C, in that order, and mark the vector. Construct point F on line n, and translate point F by the vector.

Step 8 Select point F′ and choose Trace Point from the Display menu.

Step 9 In the following order, select point F, segment n, point C, and the circle.

Step 10 Make an action button that animates point F on segment n one-way, and animates point C on the circle one-way. Double-click on the Animate button and observe the action.

Questions

1. Make a similar construction to animate the cosine curve. Because the cosine is a horizontal distance, you could rotate point C 90° around the center, A, and form another triangle, AC′E, by using a method similar to the one you used to construct triangle CAB. Translate point F by the marked vector distance from point E to point C. Redefine the Animate button, and trace both the sine and the cosine curves on one sketch. Explain how your sketch demonstrates that the cosine curve is a translation of the sine curve by 90°.

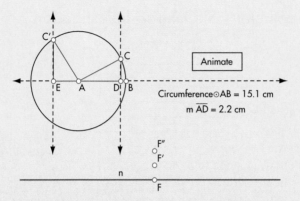

Animate

Circumference⊙AB = 15.1 cm

m $\overline{AD}$ = 2.2 cm

2. Use Sketchpad to animate the action of the tangent curve. You may wish to construct a line perpendicular to line *AD* at *B*, and then mark where line *AC* intersects this line. Why does the value of the tangent become undefined?

3. Use Sketchpad to demonstrate the secant, cosecant, and cotangent curves. What happens at the points where these curves are undefined?

4. Examine your sketch from Question 1 carefully. How can you use it to demonstrate the following trigonometric identities: $^-\sin A = \sin (^-A)$ and $\cos A = \cos (^-A)$? Devise a good method to demonstrate these identities clearly.

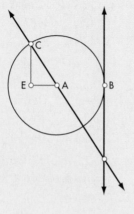

Section 13.3

Combinations of Functions

Genius is the gold in the mine; talent is the miner that works and brings it out.
—Lady Marguerite Blessington

Some applications require a combination of more than one function to make a realistic model. The sound produced by a musical instrument is actually the combination of several different sounds. To accurately reproduce an instrumental sound on an electronic synthesizer, you must specify the relative strengths of each of the individual component sounds and pitches. Each of these individual pitches can be represented by a sine function, and these sine functions are literally added together to create the desired effect.

Each band or orchestra instrument has its own characteristic sound. Flutes and violins sound very different even if they are playing the same note. One reason for this is that as each instrument plays a note, like an A, it also plays the next higher A and E, and several other notes that form its overtone series. The individual notes and overtones are difficult to hear and are present in varying degrees of loudness for different instruments. The graphs and equations below show a flute and a violin playing the same A above middle C.

The fundamental period for both graphs is the same. This period is determined by the term $A \sin 440x$, which represents the basic tone. The "bumps" in the graphs are caused by the overtones, which correspond to the remaining terms in the equations. The coefficients of these terms indicate the loudness of each overtone and, because the coefficients differ, the heights of these bumps also differ. Both equations are composed of several different sine functions. The numbers 440, 880, 1320, 1760, and so on, are the frequencies of the tones (measured in cycles per second). All of the frequencies are multiples of the basic frequency, 440. One cycle is completed when $\sin 440x = \sin 360°$, and this occurs when the period is $\frac{360}{440}$, or when $x \approx 0.82$ seconds. The variable x is a measure of time, and y represents the loudness or amplitude of the sound.

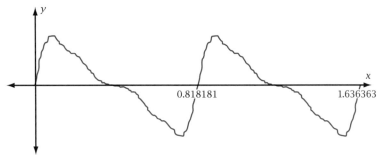

Flute: $y = 16 \sin 440x + 9 \sin 880x + 3 \sin 1320x + 2.5 \sin 1760x + 1.0 \sin 2200x$

The flute equation contains five different terms. The first term, 16 sin 440x, is the fundamental tone—and the loudest tone, because its coefficient, 16, is the largest coefficient. Notice that, by comparison, the coefficients of the other terms are much smaller. This gives the flute its characteristic clear sound.

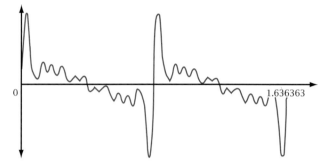

Violin: $y = 19 \sin 440x + 9 \sin 880x + 8 \sin 1320x$
$+ 9 \sin 1760x + 12.5 \sin 2200x + 10.5 \sin 2640x$
$+ 14 \sin 3080x + 11 \sin 3520x + 8 \sin 3960x$
$+ 7 \sin 4400x + 5.5 \sin 4840x + 1.0 \sin 5280x$
$+ 4.5 \sin 5720x + 4.0 \sin 6160x + 3 \sin 6600x$

The violin sound for the same note is much more complicated, containing 15 different pitches. The coefficients of some of the other tones are quite large compared to the initial term. This makes the sound of a violin more complex. Each musical instrument will have its own typical sound and graph. Different musicians will slightly affect the sound of the note as well as the shape of the graph, but the basic graph shape will remain the same. You might try entering these equations in your calculator and reproducing the graphs. Then modify the coefficients of some of the terms and observe how the graph is affected.

Investigation 13.3.1
Period Search

What is the period of a function created by adding two sine functions together? How can you predict the graph of the sum of two different sine functions? In this investigation you will explore how the period of a function depends on the periods of each part of the equation. For parts a and c, divide the tasks among group members. Work together with your group to answer the questions in parts b, d, and e.

a	b	Period
1	2	–?–
2	3	–?–
3	6	–?–
2	4	–?–
4	12	–?–

a. Set your graphing window to $0° \le x \le 720°$ and $^-2 \le y \le 2$. Mark the x-axis in units of 180°. You will graph equations of the form $y = \sin ax + \sin bx$. Use the pairs of a- and b-values listed in the preceding table. Then record the period for each pair.

b. Write a statement that explains how to find the period of a function $y = \sin ax + \sin bx$ where a and b are whole numbers.

c. Set your graphing window to $0° \le x \le 3600°$ and $^-2 \le y \le 2$. Mark the x-axis in units of 360°. Graph equations of the form $y = \sin ax + \sin bx$. This time the values of a and b are fractions. Record the period for each (a, b) pair. To see one complete cycle of the function, you may need to increase the Xmax value.

a	b	Period
$\frac{1}{2}$	$\frac{1}{4}$	-?-
$\frac{1}{2}$	$\frac{1}{3}$	-?-
$\frac{1}{2}$	$\frac{1}{5}$	-?-
$\frac{5}{6}$	$\frac{3}{4}$	-?-
$\frac{5}{8}$	$\frac{3}{10}$	-?-

d. Write a statement that explains how to find the period of a function $y = \sin ax + \sin bx$ when a and b are fractions. It may be helpful to rewrite each period as a multiple of 360°. For example, if the period is 720°, write it as $2 \cdot 360°$.

e. Predict the period for $y = \sin \frac{2}{3}x + \sin 4x + \sin \frac{1}{8}x$. Explain your reasoning.

Problem Set 13.3

1. Find an equation and a graphing window that provide exactly one cycle of a sine wave during a span of 45 days. (Hint: Find B in $y = \sin Bx$ so that one cycle is completed at $x = 45$ days.)

2. Some people believe that three aspects of their lives are governed by rhythmic cycles. These are the physical cycle of 23 days, the emotional cycle of 28 days, and the intellectual cycle of 33 days. These biorhythm cycles supposedly begin on the day you are born and continue throughout your life.

a. Determine your age in days.

b. Write equations for each of the three cycles. In these equations, the period will be measured in days and x will represent the number of days since your birth. Use an amplitude, or maximum height, of 1 for each cycle.

c. Plot the three cycles for one month starting with today. Write a paragraph describing what these cycles predict for you during the next month.

d. What is the period of the graph of the sum of the cycles? In other words, what is the length of time before all three cycles have the same y-value as they do at your starting time?

3. a. Carefully graph $y_1 = \cos^2 x$ and $y_2 = \sin^2 x$ on your calculator.

b. Complete a table of values for the sum of y_1 and y_2.

x	0°	30°	60°	90°	120°	150°	...
$\cos^2 x + \sin^2 x$	-?-	-?-	-?-	-?-	-?-	-?-	...

Describe what a plot of all possible pairs from the table would look like. Explain what it means if you connect these points with a smooth curve.

c. Graph $y = \cos^2 x + \sin^2 x$ on your calculator. Look at the graph, or a table generated from this equation, and complete the following statement: $\cos^2 x + \sin^2 x = $ –?– for all x. A statement, such as this one, that is always true is called an **identity**.

d. Use the definitions of $\sin x$ and $\cos x$ given in this chapter and the equation of a circle to show algebraically why this identity is true.

4. A popular amusement park ride is the double Ferris wheel. Sandra Noi is on the ride. Each small wheel takes 20 sec to make a single rotation. The two-wheel set takes 30 sec to revolve once. The dimensions of the ride are as given at the right.

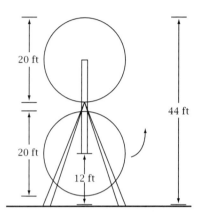

a. Sandra gets on at the foot of the bottom wheel. Write an equation that will model her position as this wheel spins around.

b. The entire ride (the two-wheel set) starts rotating at the same time that the two smaller wheels begin to rotate. Write an equation that models the height of the center of Sandra's wheel as the entire ride revolves.

c. Because the two motions occur simultaneously, you can sum the two equations to write a final equation for Sandra's position. Write this equation.

d. During a 5 min ride, how many times is Sandra within 6 ft of the ground?

5. a. Graph $y_1 = \cos^2 x$ and $y_2 = \sin^2 x$ on your calculator screen.

b. Complete a table of values for the difference between y_1 and y_2.

x	0°	30°	60°	90°	120°	150°	...
$\cos^2 x - \sin^2 x$	–?–	–?–	–?–	–?–	–?–	–?–	...

Describe what a plot of all possible pairs from the above table would look like. Explain what it means if you connect these points with a smooth curve.

c. Graph $y = \cos^2 x - \sin^2 x$. What other equation would give the same graph?

d. State what you discovered in 5c as an identity.

6. Graph $y = 2 \sin x \cos x$ on your calculator. What other equation would give the same graph? State your results as an identity.

7. a. Graph $y = (\sin x - \cos x)^2$ on your calculator. What other equation, without a horizontal shift, would give the same graph?

b. Expand the right side of the equation and use the identities you discovered in Problems 3 and 6 to write an equivalent expression.

8. Do the following tasks for each equation in a–d.
   i. Carefully sketch a graph on your paper.
   ii. Write another equation that would provide the same graph.
   iii. Show algebraically why each pair forms an identity.

a. $y = 1 - \cos^2 x$
(Hint: Problem 3c should help.)

b. $y = \tan^2 x + 1$

(Hint: Substitute $\dfrac{\sin^2 x}{\cos^2 x} + 1$ for $\tan^2 x + 1$ and find a common denominator.)

c. $y = \sec x - \sin x \tan x$

d. $y = \dfrac{1}{\sin^2 x} - \dfrac{1}{\tan^2 x}$

9. If two musicians are playing tones that differ slightly in frequency, they create a sometimes annoying pulsing pattern of loud and soft sounds called beats. At times the two tones cancel each other out, and at times they combine to make a louder sound. The number of beats (or pulses) per second is called the **beat frequency**, and good musicians know how to use this beat frequency to tune their instruments. Create a graph of the combined tones 440 cycles/sec and 442 cycles/sec and use it to find the beat frequency.

Take Another Look 13.3

If you use x to represent the number of days since January 1, you can use the equation

$$H(x) = 12 + 2.4 \cdot \sin\left(\frac{360°(x - 80)}{365}\right)$$

to find the number of hours of daylight on any day of the year in Philadelphia.

a. Find the number of hours of daylight for today's date in Philadelphia.

b. Explain the real-world meaning of every number, variable, operation, and expression involved in this equation.

c. Find the number of hours of daylight in Philadelphia on the dates given below. On two days during the year the length of night and day are approximately the same everywhere on earth. Although the dates vary, they occur close to March 21 and September 22. The term solstice refers to the time when the sun is furthest from the celestial equator. The solstice occurs twice during the year—about June 21 and December 21.

   i. March 21—the vernal equinox

   ii. June 21—the summer solstice

   iii. September 22—the autumnal equinox

   iv. December 21—the winter solstice

d. Write a function for (*date, number of hours of darkness*) in Philadelphia.

e. Find an equation for the number of hours of daylight that would work for your own location.

The Law of Sines and the Law of Cosines

Education is a private matter between the person and the world of knowledge and experience, and has little to do with school or college.
—Lillian Smith

Two pilots fly over Chicago at the same time. One is cruising at 400 mi/hr on a heading of 105° and the other is cruising at 450 mi/hr on a heading of 260°. How far apart will they be after two hours? This question involves familiar rate-time relationships, but the triangle

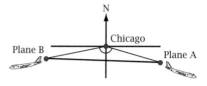

formed by the paths is not a right triangle. In this section you will discover useful relationships involving the sides and angles of nonright, or **oblique**, triangles and apply those relationships to situations much like the distance problem presented here.

Investigation 13.4.1

Oblique Triangles

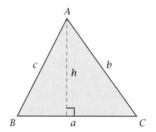

Have each group member draw a different acute triangle. Label the angles *A*, *B*, and *C*. Label the side opposite angle *A* as *a*, the side opposite angle *B* as *b*, and the side opposite angle *C* as *c*. Draw the altitude from the vertex of angle *A* to side *a*. Label the altitude *h*.

a. The altitude *h* separates the original triangle into two right triangles, one containing angle *B* and the other containing angle *C*. Use your knowledge of right triangle trigonometry to write an expression involving sin *B* and *h*, and an expression with sin *C* and *h*. Now combine the two expressions by eliminating *h*. Write this new expression as a proportion in the following form: $\frac{\sin B}{?} = \frac{\sin C}{?}$.

b. Now draw the altitude from angle *B* to side *b* and label it *j*. Repeat part a using trigonometric expressions involving *j*, sin *C*, and sin *A*. The result will be a proportion in the following form: $\frac{\sin C}{?} = \frac{?}{?}$.

c. Compare the proportions that you have written. They can be combined into one extended proportion, $\frac{?}{?} = \frac{?}{?} = \frac{?}{?}$. Fill in the numerators and denominators of this expression.

d. Check the results of other members of your group. Did everyone get the same extended proportion in part c?

e. Have each group member draw a different obtuse triangle and measure all of the angles and side lengths and verify that the expression from part c is still true.

■ Example 1

The Daredevil Cliffs rise vertically from the beach. The beach slopes gently down to the water at an angle of 3° from the horizontal. Lying at the water's edge, 50 ft from the base of the cliff, Cliff Scaylor determines that from where he is lying, the line to the top of the cliff makes an angle of 70° with the line to the base of the cliff. How high is the cliff?

Solution

Make a diagram of the situation. Do you see where the 93° and 17° angles come from? This is not a right triangle, but you can make two right triangles by drawing in the altitude from the vertex of the 93° angle to the opposite side. Label the length of this altitude h.

The height of the cliff is the hypotenuse of one of the two right triangles. Using the 17° and 70° angles, you can write

$$\sin 17° = \frac{h}{c} \qquad \text{and} \quad \sin 70° = \frac{h}{50}$$
$$\text{or} \qquad h = c \sin 17° \quad \text{and} \qquad h = 50 \sin 70°.$$

Substituting for h gives $c \sin 17° = 50 \sin 70°$.

Solving for c gives $c = \dfrac{50 \sin 70°}{\sin 17°}$, or 160.7 ft. ■

The length of the altitude that you added to the diagram was not involved in the final calculations. The final equation can be written as $\dfrac{\sin 17°}{50} = \dfrac{\sin 17°}{c}$.

This relationship, the ratio of the sine of an angle to the length of the opposite side, is constant throughout the triangle. This means that you can draw the altitude to any side and get the same relationship for the other sides and angles in the triangle. This relationship is called the **Law of Sines**. You can use the **Law of Sines** to find missing parts of triangles.

The Law of Sines

For any triangle ABC,

$$\frac{\sin A}{a} = \frac{\sin B}{b} = \frac{\sin C}{c}.$$

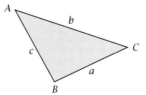

■ Example 2

Find the length of side a.

Solution

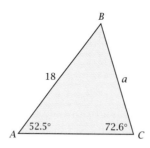

Use the Law of Sines.

$$\frac{\sin 52.5°}{a} = \frac{\sin 72.6°}{18}$$

$$18 \sin 52.5° = a \sin 72.6°$$

$$a = \frac{18 \sin 52.5°}{\sin 72.6°}$$

$$a \approx 15.0 \quad ■$$

■ Example 3

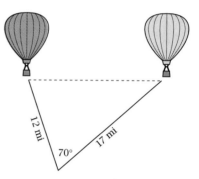

The air traffic controller at Plainfield Airport observes that two hot air balloons are at the same altitude. One is 12 mi from the airport and the other is 17 mi away. If the observed angle between the balloons is 70°, how far apart are they?

Solution

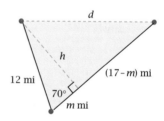

In this case the Law of Sines does not help. You only know one angle, and if you try to set up an equation using the Law of Sines, you will have more than one variable. (Take a minute to write an equation using the Law of Sines to convince yourself that the equation will have more than one variable.) So you must try something else. Again, draw an altitude to form two right triangles. This time draw it from the balloon on the left to the opposite side of the triangle so that one of the right triangles formed contains the 70° angle. (You could also draw the altitude from the balloon on the right to the opposite side.) The 17 mi side has been split into two parts. Label one part m and the other part $17 - m$. Label the altitude h. You can now write two equations using the Pythagorean theorem.

$$m^2 + h^2 = 12^2 \quad \text{and} \quad (17 - m)^2 + h^2 = d^2$$
$$m^2 + h^2 = 144$$

and $\quad 289 - 34m + m^2 + h^2 = d^2$	Multiply and expand.
$h^2 = 144 - m^2$	Solve the first equation for h^2.
$289 - 34m + m^2 + 144 - m^2 = d^2$	Substitute for h^2 in the second equation.
$289 + 144 - 34m = d^2$	Combine like terms.

Using the right triangles, you can write $\cos 70° = \frac{m}{12}$ or $m = 12 \cos 70°$. Substitute the m-value into the equation to get

$d^2 = 289 + 144 - 34(12 \cos 70°).$

$d \approx 17.1$ mi   Take the square root of both sides. ∎

The procedure followed in Example 3 is lengthy and complicated, but it can be repeated any time you know two sides and the included angle in a triangle and wish to find the length of the third side. Notice that the expression for d^2 could also be written as $17^2 + 12^2 - 2(17)(12)\cos 70°$, which looks a lot like the Pythagorean theorem (with the exception of the last term). This extra term is twice the product of the sides and the cosine of the angle between them. In general form, this modified Pythagorean relationship is called the **Law of Cosines**.

The Law of Cosines

For any triangle ABC,

$c^2 = a^2 + b^2 - 2ab \cos C.$

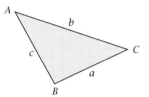

■ **Example 4**

a. Use the Law of Cosines to find the length of the unknown side.

b. Use the Law of Sines to find the measure of angle A.

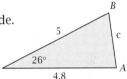

Solution

a. Use the Law of Cosines.

$c^2 = 5^2 + 4.8^2 - 2(5)(4.8) \cos 26°$

$c^2 = 25 + 23.04 - 48 \cos 26°$

$c^2 \approx 4.90$, so $c \approx 2.21$.

b. Use the Law of Sines.

$\dfrac{\sin 26°}{2.21} = \dfrac{\sin A}{5}$

$2.21 \sin A = 5 \sin 26°$

$\sin A = \dfrac{5 \sin 26°}{2.21} \approx 0.9917$

$A = \sin^{-1}(0.9917) \approx 83°$

To find the measure of the last angle, use the fact that the three angles sum to 180°.

$B = 180° - 26° - 83° = 71°$ ∎

You may have noticed that as you completed the calculations in Example 4 with a rounded approximation for c (1.42), you did not get precisely the same values that were given for sin A and the measure of angle A. In general, you should use all of the numbers following the decimal point that are displayed on the calculator and only round at the end. An easy way to retain the calculator accuracy is to use the Ans function to recall the previous answer for the next calculation. That way, the accuracy will be preserved for further calculations. Round your final answer to the desired number of decimal places.

In deciding which law to use first, consider the triangle parts whose measurements you know and their relationships to each other. Then use the law that involves those given parts and the missing part that you want to find. In all cases, you need to verify that the answers you get make sense in the context of the problem or in a sketch of the triangle.

Problem Set 13.4

1. Find the measure of each unknown angle and the length of each unknown side.

   a.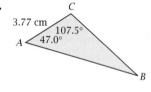

   b.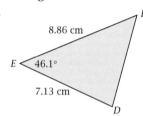

   c.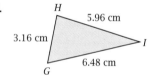

   d.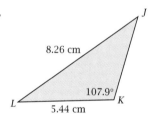

2. Refer to your work in Problem 1 and describe how you know whether to use the Law of Sines or the Law of Cosines to solve for an unknown part of a triangle. What situations are most appropriate for each law?

3. Two pilots are flying over Chicago. One is cruising at 400 mi/hr on a heading of 105°, and the other is cruising at 450 mi/hr on a heading of 260°. How far apart are they 2 hr later?

4. The Thumper is a truck used to find underground deposits. The entire body of the truck can raise itself off the ground, and then, at the press of a button, the truck crashes down to the ground. Sonic sensing equipment times the echo of the vibration to determine the distance to any underground phenomenon, such as a cave, an oil

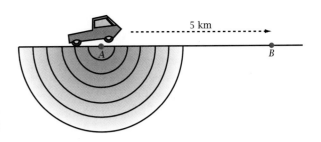

pocket, a different density of rock, and so on. From a sounding at point *A*, the truck locates an underground chamber 7 km away. Moving to point *B*, 5 km from point *A*, the truck takes a second sounding and finds the chamber is 3 km away from that point. Assuming that the underground chamber lies in the same vertical plane as *A* and *B*, what more can you say about its location?

5. The Pinched Finger Folding Chair Company is considering changing the angle where the chair legs meet to 50° to improve stability. The rear leg is 55 cm long and is attached to the front leg at a point 75 cm from the front leg's foot. How far apart will the legs be spread at the floor?

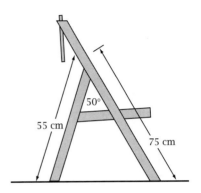

6. The SS *Minnow* was lost at sea in a deep fog. Moving at a heading of 107° degrees, the skipper sighted a light at a heading of 60°. The same light reappeared through the fog after the skipper had sailed 1.5 km on his initial course. The second sighting of the light was at a heading of 34°. What is the position of the boat relative to the light at the time of the second sighting? Find both the heading and the distance.

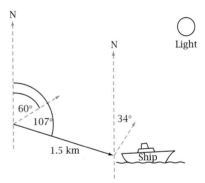

7. Triangulation can be used to locate airplanes, boats, or vehicles that transmit a signal from a radio or a cellular phone. By measuring the strength of the signal at three fixed receiving locations, the distances can be found and the direction calculated. Receiver B is located 18 km from receiver A in a direction of 122° from north. Receiver C is located 26 km from receiver A in a direction of 80° from north. The signal from source D to receiver A indicates a range of 15 km. The distance from source D to receiver B is 8 km, and the distance from source D to receiver C is 25 km. What is the direction from A to the source? (Hint: You might try making a scale drawing of

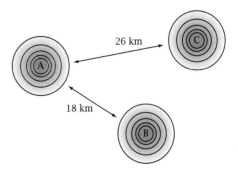

this situation. Then use your compass to get a general idea of the location of D before starting the calculations.)

8. One way to calculate distances to nearby stars is to measure the angle to the star at 6 mo intervals. A star is measured at a 42.13204° angle from the ecliptic (the plane of the earth's orbit). The angle is 42.13226° from the ecliptic 6 mo later. The diameter of the earth's orbit is 296,000,000 km (3.13 • 10^{-5} light years). What is the distance to the star?

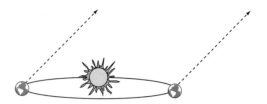

Project

Sum and Difference Identities

Write an expression for the length of d using the distance formula. Write another expression for d using the Law of Cosines on the isosceles triangle with vertex C. Equate these two expressions. Expand and look for ways to use the identity $\sin^2 x + \cos^2 x = 1$ to reduce the equation as much as possible. Solve this equation for $\cos C$ in terms of $\sin A$, $\cos A$, $\sin B$, and $\cos B$. Because the measure of angle C is equal to the measure of angle A minus the measure of angle B, complete the following identity: $\cos (A - B) = $ -?-. Test your new formula by finding $\cos (110° - 30°)$.

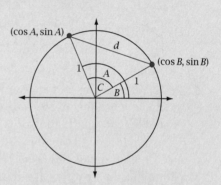

a. In your formula for $\cos (A - B)$, replace B with ^-B and rewrite the identity, this time for $\cos (A + B)$. Look at the graphs of $\cos (^-x)$ and $\sin (^-x)$ from 0° to 360°. How can you rewrite $\cos (^-B)$ without using a negative angle? How can you rewrite $\sin (^-B)$ without using a negative angle? What is your new formula for $\cos (A + B)$ without using negative angles?

b. Study the two statements below.

$\sin x = \cos (90° - x)$. (Graph both sides of the equation to see that this is true.)
$\sin (A - B) = \cos (90° - (A + B)) = \cos ((90° - A) - B)$

Use the identity from part a to write an identity for $\sin (A - B)$.

c. Use the identity from part b to help you to discover an identity for $\sin (A + B)$.

d. Use your identities to find exact values for $\cos 75°$ and $\sin 15°$.

Section 13.5

Trigonometric Equations and Inverse Functions

It is a wholesome and necessary thing for us to turn again to the earth and in the contemplation of her beauties to know the sense of wonder and humility.
—*Rachel Carson*

Tides are caused by gravitational forces, or attractions, between the earth, the moon, and the sun as the moon circles the earth. You can model the height of the ocean in a seaport with a combination of sine functions of different phases, periods, and amplitudes. In the nineteenth century, the result of combining sine functions was computed by using a machine called a tide predicter. The predicter produced a graph from which tide tables were calculated.

Tide predicter

The height of the water at a river mouth varies during the tide cycle. If the height is defined by the equation $h(t) = 7.5 \sin 30t + 15$, where t is measured in hours, when is the height 11.5 feet? How long before the tide will be at that height again? What is the cycle length modeled by this equation? These are important questions if you live near or visit the ocean, or if in your occupation you will be studying tide cycles.

What is the meaning of 11.5 in the equation $11.5 = 7.5 \sin 30t + 15$? How do you solve for t? There are many different times when the water depth is at 11.5 feet, but if you calculate the inverse sine on your calculator you will only get one of these answers. This is because the calculator is a function tool, so it will only give you one output for any input. You will need to interpret the calculator results to find the other solutions. In the next example you will see that the calculator answer for an inverse function is not always the angle that you're looking for.

■ **Example 1**

Find the measure of the indicated angle.

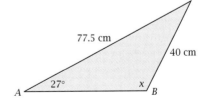

Solution

Use the Law of Sines.

$$\frac{\sin B}{77.5} = \frac{\sin 27°}{40}$$

$$40 \sin B = 77.5 \sin 27°$$

$$\sin B = \frac{77.5 \sin 27°}{40}$$

The calculator answer is $B \approx 61.6°$. But this answer doesn't make sense for the diagram. The angle should be obtuse, not acute. In this case, the calculator has given you the reference angle of the correct answer. The obtuse angle with the same sine as 61.6° is 180 – 61.6, or 118.4°.

It may take some extra time, but by drawing the known triangle parts to scale, you can determine whether the angle you are seeking is acute or obtuse. ■

Suppose a mass is suspended from a spring. The mass is then pulled down slightly, stretching the spring. When released, the mass will move up and down. In reality, the displacement gradually decreases and finally the mass returns to rest. However, if the original displacement is small, then this decrease in the motion of the mass will occur much more slowly and can be ignored during the first seconds of the oscillation. The height of the mass in relation to its resting position is given by a sine or cosine function. In general, the equation $y = A \sin B(x - C)$ or $y = A \cos B(x - C)$ provides this height. The coefficient A is called the amplitude of the oscillation, or the maximum distance from the resting position. The variable B is the frequency of the motion, usually given in cycles per second. For this equation, 360° represents one entire cycle of motion, and C is the phase shift. If the mass starts at a position other than where the parent curve begins, you must shift the curve horizontally to properly model the start of the motion.

■ **Example 2**

A mass is pulled 3 cm from its resting position and then released. It makes ten complete bounces in 8 sec. At what times during the first 2 sec was the mass 1.5 cm above its resting position?

Solution

First write the equation. The amplitude of the vibration is 3 because the mass is pulled down 3 cm. The frequency is ten cycles (or 10(360)°) in 8 sec, or 450°/sec. Because the motion starts at the bottom, the graph could be a standard sine curve that has been shifted one-quarter of a period to the right. (See the graph on page 675.) A better alternative is to use the cosine curve, which starts at its maximum value, because you can simply flip it over the x-axis to get the correct starting position. The alternative equation using

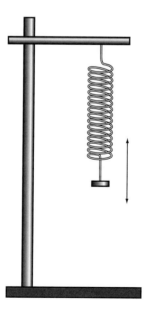

the cosine function is $y = {}^-3 \cos 450x$. Now you can find the time when the height, y, is 1.5 cm.

One method is to graph the equations $y_1 = {}^-3 \cos 450x$ and $y_2 = 1.5$ and look for the points of intersection. From the graph you can see that there are five points of intersection. You have several options for finding them. You can zoom in on the points or use the built-in intersection finder in your calculator. Another method is to solve the equation formed by equating the two y-values.

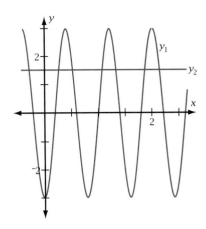

$$ {}^-3 \cos 450x = 1.5 $$

$$ \cos 450x = \frac{1.5}{{}^-3} \qquad \text{Divide by } {}^-3. $$

$$ 450x = \cos^{-1}({}^-0.5) \qquad \text{Calculate the inverse cosine.} $$

$$ 450x = 120° $$

$$ x \approx 0.266667 \text{ sec} \qquad \text{Divide by } 450. $$

This is the answer at the first intersection. The next solution comes at the next angle with cosine equal to $\cos 120°$. That angle is 240°.

$$ 450x = 240°, \text{ so } x \approx 0.533333 \text{ sec.} $$

Because the function is periodic, the other three answers will come at one-period intervals to these two original answers. Adding the period of 0.8 sec gives the next two answers. Adding another period will give the final answer. The complete set of answers is

$$ x \approx 0.266667, 0.533333, 1.066667, 1.333333, 1.866667 \text{ sec.} \quad ■ $$

In many cases, equations involving trigonometric functions can be most easily solved with a calculator graph.

■ Example 3

The first mass is pulled down 3 cm from its resting position and released. A second mass is pulled 4 cm down from its resting position. It is released just as the first mass passes its resting position on its way up. When released, the second mass makes 12 complete bounces in 8 sec. At what times during the first 2 sec of the second mass's motion will the two masses be at the same height?

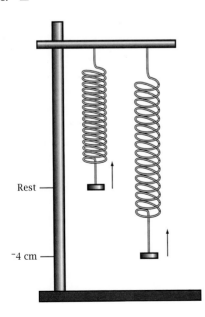

Solution

The equation for the second mass has an amplitude of 4. The frequency is 12(360°) in 8 sec or 540°/sec. The curve is again a cosine graph with a vertical flip. However, the period is 2/3 sec, so the equation is $y = -4 \cos 540x$. The equation for the first mass must be modified because it is now at the resting point when you begin timing. The sine curve is at a height of zero when x is zero, so it will be easier to use a sine equation $y = 3 \sin 450x$ for this mass.

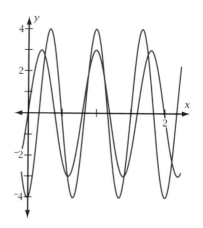

Graph both equations in the same window. You can see that they intersect six times during the first 2 sec. In this case, setting the two equations equal to each other is of no help, because you can't get rid of the sines and cosines or combine the variables. Your best bet is to use your calculator. Instead of looking for the intersections of the curves, you could make a third equation, $y_3 = y_1 - y_2$. Graph only this equation. You can find the solutions where y_3 intersects the x-axis.

NOTE

13A

Now you need to find the roots of y_3. Use the calculator's built-in root finder or solver (see **Calculator Note 13A**) to see if you can get these six answers:

$x \approx 0.248411, 0.589580, 0.884027, 1.115973, 1.410420, 1.751589.$ ∎

Investigation 13.5.1

Inverse Trigonometric Functions

Have you ever graphed the inverse of a sine or cosine graph? Can you visualize what such a graph would look like? You probably recall that (x, y) and (y, x) are inverses of each other. This investigation will help you discover and explain some interesting features of the graphs of trigonometric functions and their inverses.

Work with a partner in this investigation. Have the first pair of partners do parts a–d exactly as written. Have the second pair of partners do parts a–d, but instead of investigating $\sin A$ and its inverse, investigate $\cos A$ and its inverse. After completing parts a–d, share your results with the other members of your group. Have each group member complete parts e and f.

Enter the A-values in this table into a calculator data list and use the list functions to calculate the other table entries.

A	0°	5°	10°	15°	20°	25°	...	90°	95°	100°	...	450°
$\sin A$	-?-	-?-	-?-	-?-	-?-	-?-	...	-?-	-?-	-?-	...	-?-
$\sin^{-1}(\sin A)$	-?-	-?-	-?-	-?-	-?-	-?-	...	-?-	-?-	-?-	...	-?-

a. Plot the points $(A, \sin A)$ on your calculator screen. You will see a familiar graph. Record a sketch of this graph on your paper.

b. Plot the points $(\sin A, \sin^{-1}(\sin A))$ on your calculator screen. (You will need to redefine your window when you do this.) Is this graph a function? Compare the number of points plotted to the number of actual data points in your lists. Trace the graph and look through your data lists and then explain what has happened. Record a sketch of this graph on your paper.

c. Your first point plot, $(A, \sin A)$, was a graph of points from the sine function. Inverse relations are formed by switching the *x*- and *y*-coordinates of the points. Now graph the inverse sine by switching the coordinates. Use window values of $^-1.5 \le x \le 1.5$ and $^-100 \le y \le 360$. Create a plot of $(\sin A, A)$. Use the smallest mark on your calculator to mark these points. Is this graph a function? Explain. Now add a plot of the points $(\sin A, \sin^{-1}(\sin A))$ to your calculator screen using a different mark. Describe the similarities and differences in the two data plots. Why do you suppose the calculator gives only restricted values in the plot of $(\sin A, \sin^{-1}(\sin A))$?

d. In previous work you discovered that $f^{-1}(f(x)) = x$. Is this true for the sine function? Study the values and the graph of $(A, \sin^{-1}(\sin A))$. Describe and explain the relationship between A and $\sin^{-1}(\sin A)$. You may need more angles, including negative angles, to be confident of your conclusions.

e. Explore $\sin(\sin^{-1} x)$ and $\cos(\cos^{-1} x)$ using graphs and tables. Be careful to identify a reasonable domain before graphing.

f. Draw accurate graphs of the $\sin^{-1} x$ and $\cos^{-1} x$ functions. Write a few sentences about each, explaining the domain and range of each function.

Problem Set 13.5

1. Find the measure of the indicated angle in each triangle.

a.
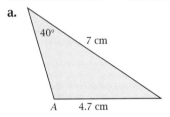
40°
7 cm
A   4.7 cm

b.
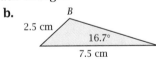
B
2.5 cm
16.7°
7.5 cm

2. Be sure your calculator is in *parametric* mode for this problem. However, do not expect to find one window that will provide you with a good view of all of these functions and their inverses.

   a. Graph $x_{1t} = t$, $y_{1t} = \sin t$ and its inverse relation, $x_{2t} = \sin t$, $y_{2t} = t$. What range of *t*-values will give the same graph for the inverse as $y = \sin^{-1} x$ in *function* mode? Record a sketch of both parametric graphs.

b. Graph $x_{1t} = t$, $y_{1t} = \sin 2t$ and its inverse relation. What range of *t*-values makes the inverse a function? Record a sketch of both parametric graphs.

   c. Graph $x_{1t} = t$, $y_{1t} = \sin \frac{1}{2}t$. What range of *t*-values makes the inverse a function? Record a sketch of both parametric graphs.

   d. In 2b and 2c, the period of the original function was changed. How does this period affect the range of the inverse function?

3. The height of the water (measured in feet) at a river's mouth varies during the tide cycle. The water height is $h(t) = 7.5 \sin 30t + 15$, where *t* is measured in hours. If you use $t = 0$ for the present time, during what time intervals over the next 48 hr is the river depth 11.5 ft or more?

Low tide and high tide in Gloucester, Massachusetts

4. As a pendulum swings, a graph of (*time, its height above its resting position*) follows a sine or cosine curve. Though the height is never below this resting position, it is customary to refer to the heights on one side of the swing as negative values and on the other side as positive values. The pendulum on Mark Tyme's grandfather clock makes 12 complete swings in 10 sec and its height is 1 cm above the resting level at each end of the swing.

   a. Write an equation that models the height of a swinging pendulum relative to its resting position.

   b. How many times during a 1 min interval does the pendulum pass through the resting position? Start the time interval when the pendulum is at the farthest point from its resting position.

5. A mass hanging from a spring is pulled 2 cm down from its resting position and released. It makes 12 complete bounces in 10 sec. At what times during the first 3 sec was it 0.5 cm below its resting position?

6. Two masses are each hanging at rest from different springs. They are each pulled down 2.5 cm and then released. The first mass makes eight complete bounces in 8 sec while the second makes ten bounces in 8 sec.

   a. During the first 3 sec, how many times are the two springs at the same height?

   b. During what percentage of the first 3 sec are the springs within 1 cm of each other?

7. Find the first five positive *x*-values that make each equation true.

    a. sec *x* = ⁻2.5

    b. (csc *x* − cot *x*)(sec *x* + 1) = 0.8

8. Carefully describe similarities and differences between the graphs of (sin *x*, *x*) and $y = \sin^{-1} x$.

9. Household electric appliances plug into wall outlets. In the United States, most electric circuits supply 110 volts at 60 cycles/sec. (Actually, the maximum voltage is $110\sqrt{2}$.)

    a. Use the sine (or cosine) function and write an equation for (*time, voltage*) that models this information.

    b. Sketch and label a graph picturing three complete cycles.

10. a. The time between high and low tide in a river harbor is approximately 7 hr. The high-tide depth of 16 ft occurs at noon and the average river depth is 11 ft. Write an equation modeling this (*time, depth*) relationship.

    b. If a boat requires a water depth of at least 9 ft, find the next two time periods when the boat will not be able to enter the harbor.

Project

A Dampened Sine Curve

In Section 13.5, you modeled the motion of springs and pendulums using sine curves. In each case, the assumption was made that the amplitude of the motion did not decrease over time. This is not actually true. The motion gradually decreases in amplitude until the object comes to rest. In this project you will investigate this phenomenon.

    Set up a pendulum with a protractor at the top. Start the string at a 20° angle from the center. Determine the period of the pendulum. Begin the experiment again and record the angle of the swing after each swing, or at regular intervals of swings, until the pendulum is nearly at rest. Determine the height of the pendulum at each of these angles.

    Plot the data (*time, height*) and draw a smooth sine curve to fit the points. Draw another curve that connects the set of maximum points of the curve. Find an equation that models this last curve drawn. Use this equation as the amplitude for the dampened sine function that will model the entire motion.

Section 13.6

Polar Curves

The only difference between a rut and a grave is their dimensions.
—Ellen Glasgow

It's time to let your hair down, have fun, be creative, and at the same time learn about a very different kind of graphing that's related to trigonometric functions.

In this section you will discover and use a coordinate system where surprisingly simple equations give very interesting graphs. Elegant and complicated-looking graphs, like the one pictured here, are frequently based on very simple relationships. You'll be surprised and intrigued by the variety of graphs and equations you will encounter.

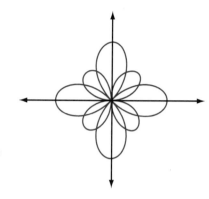

NOTE

13B

Graph the semicircle $y = \sqrt{16 - x^2}$ in a "friendly" window, and then watch the (x, y) coordinates appear as you trace around the semicircle. Follow the procedure given in **Calculator Note 13B** to set your calculator for graphing and displaying coordinates in polar coordinate form. Now, as you trace the graph again, the angle values change but the radius value remains constant. Can you explain why?

This relationship can be expressed with an equation in polar coordinates, using the variables r and θ to describe the graph. Polar equations are usually written as $r = f(\theta)$, where r is a distance from the origin and θ is an angle measured counterclockwise from the positive ray of the horizontal axis. Coordinates of points are given as (r, θ). Remember that a negative angle is measured clockwise from the positive ray of the horizontal axis.

■ **Example 1**

Graph the polar equation $r = 4$.

Solution

NOTE

13C

This is the set of points four units from the origin—a circle with radius 4. There is no θ in this equation, so no matter what your angle measures, the point will be four units from the origin. (See **Calculator Note 13C** for help with graphing polar equations.)

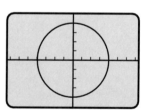

	0°	30°	45°	60°	90°	. . .
r	4	4	4	4	4	. . .

■

CHAPTER 13 TRIGONOMETRIC FUNCTIONS

■ Example 2

Graph the polar equation $r = 3 \cos 2\theta$ with $0 \le \theta \le 360°$.

Solution

θ	r
0°	3.00
10°	2.81
20°	2.30
30°	1.50
40°	0.52
50°	⁻0.52
. . .	. . .

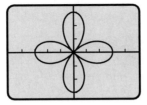

As you graph this equation on your calculator, you will see the four-petal rose that is pictured. To understand how this graph was formed, look at a table of (r, θ). To plot a point given in polar coordinates, imagine standing at the origin. Rotate yourself through the angle (for example, 30° counterclockwise from the positive ray of the horizontal axis). Then imagine walking straight out from the origin and placing a point at distance r. If r is positive, walk forward. If r is negative, walk backward. As θ increases from 0° to 360°, use this technique to locate points (r, θ) on the curve and then connect them with a smooth curve. Try drawing this graph on polar graph paper. What is the role of the coefficient 3 in the equation?

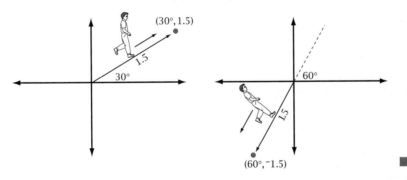

Investigation 13.6.1

Rose Curves

Look at the equation, window, and graph for the four-petal rose in Example 2. Why do you think there are four petals? What creates the rose or flower shape? Concentrate on the connection between the trace numbers displayed on your calculator and the points. This beautiful graph comes from an equation that can be generalized as

$r = a \cos n\theta$. In this investigation, you will explore rose curves, their symmetries, and the relationship between the number of petals and the value of n. Group members will probably enjoy doing this investigation on their own. But be sure to share any discoveries that you make with others.

a. Graph the family of curves $r = 3 \cos n\theta$ with $n = 1, 2, 3, 4, 5$, and 6. Write statements that describe the curves for even n and odd n.

b. Graph the family of curves $r = 3 \sin n\theta$ with $n = 1, 2, 3, 4, 5$, and 6. Write statements that describe the curves for even n-values and odd n-values. How do these curves differ from the curves you graphed in part a?

c. Find a way to graph a rose with only two petals. Explain why your method works.

d. Find a connection between the polar graph $r = a \cos n\theta$ and the associated function graph $y = a \cos n\theta$. Can you look at the graph of $y = a \cos n\theta$ and predict the shape and number of petals in the polar graph? Explain.

Rose curves were named by Guido Grandi (1671–1742) when he was trying to give a geometric definition for curves in the shape of flowers. He called them rhodonea after the Greek word for rose. He also gave a geometric definition for flower-like curves inscribed in a sphere. These he called clelias after the Countess Clelia Borromeo of Genoa, who, because of her proficiency in science, mathematics, mechanics, and languages, was known as *gloria Genuensium* (the glory of the Genoese). Grandi carried on extensive correspondences with the scientists of his day. He wrote about the rhodonea and clelia to Leibnitz in 1713. Later he presented his work in a memoir to the Royal Society of London. He published his complete theory related to these curves in 1728.

If you apply the Pythagorean theorem to the figure at the right, $r^2 = x^2 + y^2$ or $r = \sqrt{x^2 + y^2}$. Also, $\tan \theta = \frac{y}{x}$ or $\theta = \tan^{-1} \frac{y}{x}$. The actual value of θ depends on the quadrant in which the point (x, y) is located. These two equations allow you to convert between polar form and rectangular form. However, because many of the curves are not functions in the rectangular coordinate system, you cannot always easily solve the equations for y. By using the information in the drawing, you can also define two other equations, $x = r \cos \theta$ and $y = r \sin \theta$, which will help you understand the link between parametric and polar equations.

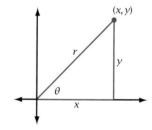

■ Example 3

Convert the polar equations to rectangular form.

a. $r = 4$

b. $r = 2 \cos \theta + 2$ (The graph of this equation is called a **cardioid**. You will explore this curve in the problem set.)

Solution

a. Replace r with $\sqrt{x^2 + y^2}$, which gives you $\sqrt{x^2 + y^2} = 4$, or $x^2 + y^2 = 16$. Do you recognize this as the equation of a circle in rectangular form centered at the origin with radius 4? However, because a circle is not a function, it will take two equations, $y = \pm\sqrt{16 - x^2}$, to graph the entire circle.

b. Replace r with $\sqrt{x^2 + y^2}$ and $\cos\theta$ with $\dfrac{x}{r}$ or $\dfrac{x}{\sqrt{x^2 + y^2}}$ to get

$$\sqrt{x^2 + y^2} = 2\left(\frac{x}{\sqrt{x^2 + y^2}}\right) + 2.$$

$$x^2 + y^2 = 2x + 2\sqrt{x^2 + y^2} \qquad \text{Multiply by } \sqrt{x^2 + y^2}.$$

$$x^2 - 2x + y^2 = 2\sqrt{x^2 + y^2} \qquad \text{Subtract } 2x \text{ from both sides.}$$

$$(x^2 - 2x + y^2)^2 = 4(x^2 + y^2) \qquad \text{Square both sides.}$$

This is as good as it gets. After all this effort, you still haven't solved the equation for y. You might be able to find some points by choosing an x-value and then solving the resulting equation for y, but even that won't be easy. Certainly the polar form of this graph is easier to work with than the rectangular (function) form.

The parametric form, however, is quite manageable. If $r = 2\cos\theta + 2$ is given as the polar equation, you can use the equations $x = r\cos\theta$ and $y = r\sin\theta$. Just substitute $2\cos\theta + 2$ for r and t for θ to get $x = (2\cos t + 2)\cos t$ and $y = (2\cos t + 2)\sin t$. ∎

The spiral is another curve that is easy to graph in polar form. Graph the equation $r = 0.01\theta$. See what happens when you use a larger range of values for θ. You may want to zoom out on your graph to see more. What happens when you change your range of θ-values to include negative values? Can you explain why? You will continue this exploration in the problem set.

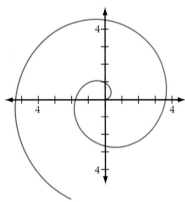

Problem Set 13.6

1. The coordinates $(2, 30°)$ and $(-2, -150°)$ identify the same point. Give two additional sets of polar coordinates that also name this point.

2. Give two additional sets of polar coordinates that locate the same point as $(-3, 60°)$.

3. a. Complete a table, like the one below, for the curve $r = 3 \cos 3\theta$ for $0° \le \theta \le 180°$. Try to find a calculator process that makes this task easier.

θ	0°	5°	10°	15°	20°	25°	30°	35°	40°	45°	50°	55°	60°
r	-?-	-?-	-?-	-?-	-?-	-?-	-?-	-?-	-?-	-?-	-?-	-?-	-?-

θ	65°	70°	75°	80°	85°	90°	95°	100°	105°	110°	115°	...
r	-?-	-?-	-?-	-?-	-?-	-?-	-?-	-?-	-?-	-?-	-?-	...

b. Draw the graph for the data in 3a on polar graph paper. Be sure to connect the dots in a smooth curve as θ grows from 0° to 360°.

4. a. Graph the spiral $r = 0.01\theta$ using $0° \le \theta \le 360°$.
   b. Graph the equation $r = {}^-0.01\theta$ using $^-360° \le \theta \le 0°$. How does this graph compare to the original graph? Explain why this transformation occurs.
   c. Graph the equation $r = {}^-0.01\theta$ using $0° \le \theta \le 360°$. How does this graph compare to the original graph? Explain why this transformation occurs.
   d. Graph the equation $r = 0.02\theta$ using $0° \le \theta \le 360°$. How does this graph compare to the original graph? Explain why this transformation occurs.

5. The family of curves $r = a(\cos \theta \pm 1)$ and $r = a(\sin \theta \pm 1)$ are called cardioids because they somewhat resemble a heart shape. In 1741, Johann Castillon (1708-1791) wrote his first two mathematical articles and in them he gave the cardioid curve its name. Because of its many different properties, the cardioid has been studied by many different people for many different reasons. The curve can be generated by a point on one circle that rolls around another circle of equal size without slipping. (For instance, if you could attach a pencil or a piece of lead to the edge of a penny and then roll that penny around another one, you would trace a cardioid.) Cardioids are also formed when light is reflected by a circle. If you drink tea or coffee in the afternoon sun, you may have seen a cardioid in your cup.
   a. Graph the cardioids $r = \cos \theta + 1$ and $r = \cos \theta - 1$. How do they differ?
   b. Graph the cardioid $r = \sin \theta + 1$. How does it differ from those graphed in 5a?
   c. Graph the cardioids $r = 2(\cos \theta + 1)$, $r = 3(\cos \theta + 1)$, and $r = 0.5(\cos \theta + 1)$ on the same set of axes. How does the value of a affect the graph of $r = a(\cos \theta + 1)$?

6. A special microphone called a cardioid microphone is designed to pick up sound at equal intensity levels from any point on a cardioid around the microphone. The microphone is oriented so that the dimple of the curve is directed toward the audience and the performing ensemble is placed around the large curve of the cardioid shape.
   a. Draw pictures of several cardioids like those in Problem 5c. Explain why a cardioid microphone will not pick up audience noise as well as it picks up sound from the performers, even if the audience is actually closer to the microphone.

b. A quintet of musicians is to perform around a cardioid microphone. After placing the microphone, they decide that they should be evenly spaced on the cardioid. What is the distance from the microphone for each performer?

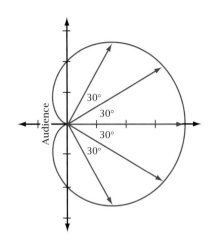

7. Write a polar equation for each graph. It may take more than one equation in some cases. Be sure to indicate the range of θ-values you used.

a.

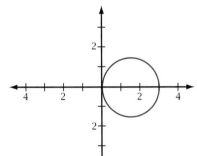

b.

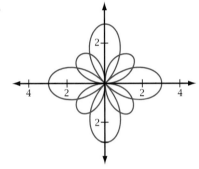

c.

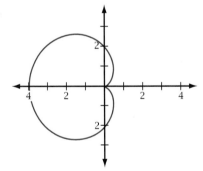

d.

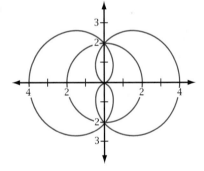

8. Graph each equation and name an interval for θ that provides a complete graph.

a. $r = 3 \cos 2.5\theta$

b. $r^2 = 4 \cos 2.5\theta$

c. $r = 3 \sin 7\theta + 4 \cos 2\theta$

d. $r^2 = \sin \dfrac{5\theta}{8}$

Take Another Look 13.6

Beautiful and interesting Lissajous curves can be created on your calculator. They can be generated parametrically by the equations

$x = a \sin kt$

$y = b \sin m(t + a)$.

For example, graph $x = 2 \cos t$ and $y = 3 \sin 2t$, and then try $x = 2 \cos 3t$ and $y = 3 \sin 2t$. A Lissajous curve can also be produced in a physics lab by combining the motions of two pendulums that are swinging at right angles to each other.

In a "friendly" graphing window, create several Lissajous curves that are interesting to you. Try to predict the graphic results when you alter the equations. What alterations produce rose curves? Share your graphs, equations, and discoveries with your classmates and teacher.

Polar Coordinates and Complex Numbers

Mistakes are part of the dues one pays for a full life.
—Sophia Loren

In Chapter 10, you solved equations with nonreal or complex solutions of the form $a + bi$. Complex numbers, like $3 + 4i$, cannot be graphed on the number line, but they can be graphed on a coordinate plane using either rectangular or polar coordinates. In the graph below, the horizontal axis is called the **real axis**, and the vertical axis is called the **imaginary axis**.

A complex number $a + bi$ has (a, b) as its rectangular coordinates. This means $3 + 4i$ is located at the point with rectangular coordinates $(3, 4)$. The real part of the complex number $3 + 4i$ is 3 and the imaginary part is $4i$. These coordinates can be changed to polar form by using the conversion equations

$$r = \sqrt{a^2 + b^2}, \ \theta = \tan^{-1} \frac{b}{a}.$$

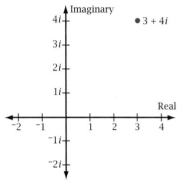

■ **Example 1**

Rewrite each complex number using polar coordinates.

a. $3 + 4i$

b. $^{-}3 - 4i$

Solution

a. The complex number $3 + 4i$ is located in the first quadrant. You can find $\theta = \tan^{-1} \frac{4}{3} \approx 53.13°$, a first quadrant angle, and $r = \sqrt{3^2 + 4^2} = 5$. Therefore, the real part is $5 \cos 53°$ and the imaginary part is $5i \sin 53°$. So the complex number $3 + 4i$ can be written as $5 \cos 53° + 5i \sin 53°$ in polar form.

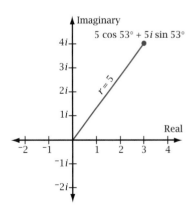

b. The complex number ⁻3 – 4*i* is located in the
third quadrant. Again, calculate the θ-value
using $\tan^{-1} \frac{-4}{-3} \approx 53.13°$. In this case the angle is
a reference angle, and the third quadrant angle
is 233.13°. The *r*-value is the same as in part a,
so the polar form of ⁻3 – 4*i* is
5 cos 233.13° + 5*i* sin 233.13°. ■

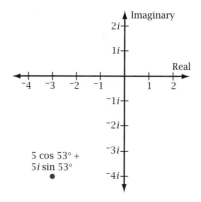

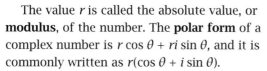

The value *r* is called the absolute value, or
modulus, of the number. The **polar form** of a
complex number is $r \cos \theta + ri \sin \theta$, and it is
commonly written as $r(\cos \theta + i \sin \theta)$.

Several people independently came up with the idea that complex numbers could be
graphed as points on a plane. One of them, Caspar Wessel (1745–1818), born in Vestby,
Norway, was a cartographer and surveyor. He was interested in defining addition and
multiplication for line segments and in the process noticed that *i* could be graphed as
(0, 1). In Investigation 13.7.1, you will use polar coordinates to do the kind of
multiplication that Wessel did using line segments.

Wessel's work remained relatively unknown until 1895. Meanwhile, in 1806, Jean
Argand, a bookkeeper in Paris, privately published his work on the geometric
representation of complex numbers without even putting his name on the title page.
His idea was that $\sqrt{-1}$ was the mean proportional between ⁺1 and ⁻1, so geometrically
it ought to be a line segment that was the mean proportional between two oppositely
directed line segments. Argand was the first to use the term *module* (modulus) for the
length of the line segment corresponding to a complex number and also the first to
use the word *absolute* for the absolute value of a number. Several other people had
thought of graphing complex numbers, but this idea was not really put to use until
1831 when Karl Friedrich Gauss, by then famous for his impressive mathematical
work and his prediction of the position of the planetoid Ceres, published an article on
graphing complex numbers.

Investigation 13.7.1

Multiplication of Complex Numbers

In this investigation you will discover a pattern involving the multiplication of
complex numbers that are written in polar form. Though a bit complicated at first,
this important discovery will allow you to easily multiply and divide complex
numbers, raise them to any power, and graph powers of complex numbers. You might
want to work with a partner on this investigation and compare notes with other group
members as you work.

a. Multiply each pair of complex numbers and write your answer in $a + bi$ form. (Remember, $i^2 = {}^-1$.)

    i. $(2+ 3i)(3 + i)$ ii. $(1 + 4i)(3 - 2i)$ iii. $({}^-1 + 2i)(3 - 4i)$

NOTE

13D

b. Convert $2 + 3i$ and $3 + i$ to polar form. (See **Calculator Note 13D** for assistance.) Convert the product of these numbers to polar form. Do this for each product in part a. Find a relationship between the angles of the two factors and the angle of their product. This relationship will be true for all three problems. Describe the relationship between the r-values (absolute values) of the factors and the r-value of the product.

c. Study the following multiplication of $a(\cos \theta + i \sin \theta)$ and $b(\cos \varPhi + i \sin \varPhi)$.

    $(a \cos \theta + ai \sin \theta)(b \cos \varPhi + bi \sin \varPhi)$
    $= ab \cos \theta \cos \varPhi + abi \cos \theta \sin \varPhi + abi \sin \theta \cos \varPhi + abi^2 \sin \theta \sin \varPhi$
    $= ab(\cos \theta \cos \varPhi - \sin \theta \sin \varPhi) + abi(\cos \theta \sin \varPhi + \sin \theta \cos \varPhi)$

d. Set your calculator in *function* mode. Let $\theta = 45°$ and graph $y_1 = \cos 45° \cos x - \sin 45° \sin x$. This is a graph of the real part of your temporary answer.

    Compare this graph with the graph of $y = \cos x$. Modify the equation $y = \cos x$ so that the graphs match.

    Choose another value for θ and repeat this graph-and-modify process until you can complete the following identity:

    $\cos \theta \cos \varPhi - \sin \theta \sin \varPhi = {-}?{-}.$

e. Let $\theta = 45°$ and graph $y_1 = \cos 45° \sin x + \sin 45° \cos x$. This is a graph of the imaginary part of the temporary answer.

    Compare this graph with the graph of $y = \sin x$. Modify the equation $y = \sin x$ so that the graphs match.

    Choose another value for θ and repeat the graph-and-modify process until you can complete the following identity:

    $\cos \theta \sin \varPhi + \sin \theta \cos \varPhi = {-}?{-}.$

f. Complete the following definition for the multiplication of complex numbers in polar form: $(a \cos \theta + ai \sin \theta)(b \cos \varPhi + bi \sin \varPhi) = {-}?{-}.$

    Now multiply $4.25(\cos 23.4° + i \sin 23.4°)$ and $2.5(\cos 32.5° + i \sin 32.5°)$. Write your answer in polar form and then convert it to $a + bi$ form. Carefully explain your procedure.

Before logarithms were invented, an identity, like the ones you discovered in Investigation 13.7.1, was used in the method of prosthaphaeresis. The word *prosthaphaeresis* comes from the Greek words for addition and subtraction, and the method was designed (as were logarithms) to replace multiplication by addition and subtraction. Prosthaphaeresis was invented by Tycho Brahe and his assistant Paul Wittich to aid them in astronomical calculations. It was further developed by Jobst Bürgi and may have helped inspire his invention of logarithms.

Example 2

a. Use the results of Investigation 13.7.1 to rewrite $(5(\cos 47° + i \sin 47°))^2$ without an exponent.

b. Rewrite $(5(\cos 47° + i \sin 47°))^3$ without an exponent.

Solution

a. $(5(\cos 47° + i \sin 47°))^2$
$= (5(\cos 47° + i \sin 47°))(5(\cos 47° + i \sin 47°))$
$= 25(\cos (47° + 47°) + i \sin (47° + 47°))$
$= 25(\cos 94° + i \sin 94°)$

b. $(5(\cos 47° + i \sin 47°))^3$
$= (5(\cos 47° + i \sin 47°))^2 (5(\cos 47° + i \sin 47°))^1$
$= (25(\cos 2 \cdot 47° + i \sin 2 \cdot 47°))(5(\cos 47° + i \sin 47°))$
$= 125(\cos (2 \cdot 47° + 47°) + i \sin (2 \cdot 47° + 47°))$
$= 5^3(\cos 3 \cdot 47° + i \sin 3 \cdot 47°)$ ∎

This example suggests a generalization for powers and roots of complex numbers.

Powers and Roots of Complex Numbers
$(r(\cos \theta + i \sin \theta))^n = r^n(\cos n\theta + i \sin n\theta)$

You know that $1^3 = 1$, and so 1 itself is a cube root of 1. There are no other real numbers whose cube is 1. Pause for a moment and make sure you are convinced that 1 is the only real-number cube root of 1, and that you could explain why it is so, before you read on. However, there might also be nonreal numbers that are cube roots of 1. Example 3 explains how you can find the other cube roots of 1.

Example 3

Find the three cube roots of 1.

Solution

The number 1 can be expressed as the complex number $1 + 0i$, or $1(\cos 0° + i \sin 0°)$, or $1(\cos 360° + i \sin 360°)$, or $1(\cos 720° + i \sin 720°)$, and so on, with any multiple of 360°.
Raise each of these representations to the 1/3 power (the cube root).

$$1^{1/3} \cos \left(\left(\frac{1}{3} \right) 0° \right) + i \sin \left(\left(\frac{1}{3} \right) 0° \right) = 1(\cos 0° + i \sin 0°) = 1 + 0i$$

$$1^{1/3} \cos \left(\left(\frac{1}{3} \right) 360° \right) + i \sin \left(\left(\frac{1}{3} \right) 360° \right) = 1(\cos 120° + i \sin 120°) = {}^-0.5 + 0.866i$$

$$1^{1/3} \cos \left(\left(\frac{1}{3} \right) 720° \right) + i \sin \left(\left(\frac{1}{3} \right) 720° \right) = 1(\cos 240° + i \sin 240°) \approx {}^-0.5 - 0.866i$$

The next multiple of 360 gives

$$1\left(\cos\left(\frac{1}{3}\right)1080° + i\sin\left(\frac{1}{3}\right)1080°\right)$$

$$= 1(\cos 360° + i\sin 360°)$$
$$= 1(\cos 0° + i\sin 0°)$$

and solutions are repeated for any other multiple of 360. Therefore, there are only the three unique answers. Confirm that these are the only three roots of 1 before you move on. ∎

Graph the three cube roots of 1 on the complex plane. Notice how the roots are evenly distributed around the origin. If you connect each point to the origin, there is 120° between each of these connectors. This symmetry of the roots can help you to predict the location of the complex roots of a number.

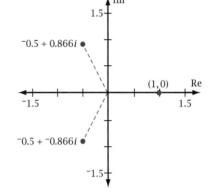

■ Example 4

Find the fifth roots of 32. How many are there? Describe their location on a coordinate axes.

Solution

First write 32 as a complex number, $32 + 0i$, and then convert to polar form: $32(\cos 0° + i\sin 0°)$. Be sure you understand why you can use any multiple of 360° to generate other forms of this same number, for example, $32(\cos 360° + i\sin 360°)$, $32(\cos 720° + i\sin 720°)$, and so on. Now apply the generalization $(r(\cos\theta + i\sin\theta))^n = r^n(\cos n\theta + i\sin n\theta)$ using $n = \frac{1}{5}$ and the first five choices of θ: 0°, 360°, 720°, 1080°, and 1440°. The five roots are given below.

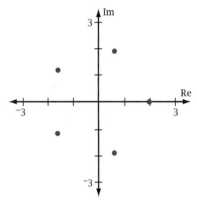

$$32^{1/5}\cos\left(\left(\frac{1}{5}\right)0°\right) + i\sin\left(\left(\frac{1}{5}\right)0°\right) = 2(\cos 0° + i\sin 0°) = 2 + 0i = 2$$

$$32^{1/5}\cos\left(\left(\frac{1}{5}\right)360°\right) + i\sin\left(\left(\frac{1}{5}\right)360°\right) = 2(\cos 72° + i\sin 72°) = 0.618 + 1.902i$$

$$32^{1/5}\cos\left(\left(\frac{1}{5}\right)720°\right) + i\sin\left(\left(\frac{1}{5}\right)720°\right) = 2(\cos 144° + i\sin 144°) = {}^-1.618 + 1.176i$$

$$32^{1/5}\cos\left(\left(\frac{1}{5}\right)1080°\right) + i\sin\left(\left(\frac{1}{5}\right)1080°\right) = 2(\cos 216° + i\sin 216°) = {}^-1.618 - 1.176i$$

$$32^{1/5}\cos\left(\left(\frac{1}{5}\right)1440°\right) + i\sin\left(\left(\frac{1}{5}\right)1440°\right) = 2(\cos 288° + i\sin 288°) = 0.618 - 1.902i$$

Notice that the angles for each root are incremented by 72°. If you plot them on the complex plane using a "friendly" window, the five points will be evenly distributed around the origin. ■

Until now you have only plotted complex numbers as points. Now you will consider an extension for graphing **complex functions**. Complex functions involve variables that represent complex numbers. They are usually written with the variable z to distinguish them from functions of real numbers. It is not possible to graph a complex-valued function (a function that has complex numbers as outputs) in the same way you graph something like $y = x^2$. You would need two dimensions for the independent variable z and two others for the dependent variable $f(z)$. You would need four dimensions to graph $w = z^2$ because w and z each represent a complex number. However, functions related to $w = z^2$ can be graphed. One way is to plot the result of repeated iteration on a point, which you will do in Investigation 13.7.2. The other is to graph the numbers produced at each step of the iteration. You will explore this approach in Example 5.

Investigation 13.7.2

Prisoners and Escapees

You know that many recursive functions involving real numbers approach a long-run limiting value. Other recursive functions seem to grow infinitely large. Both of the above cases are true for functions involving complex variables. In this investigation you will graph the results of iterating $z_n = \left(z_{(n-1)}\right)^2$, using many different seed values.

For this investigation you will need to label a grid, as explained in part a, and to divide the grid into regions. Each group member will be responsible for collecting the data for their region. Or you might decide to work as partners, checking each other's results as you do the calculations.

a. Label a region on your graph paper as shown at the right. Note that the spaces are labeled, not the lines. In other words, each square will have coordinates similar to the pixels on a calculator screen.

b. Choose a point. The coordinates of the point are the real and imaginary parts of the complex number. For example, the point $(0.3, {}^-0.2)$ represents the number $0.3 - 0.2i$. Use this number as the seed for your recursive formula. It will probably be easiest to change to polar form for squaring. (See

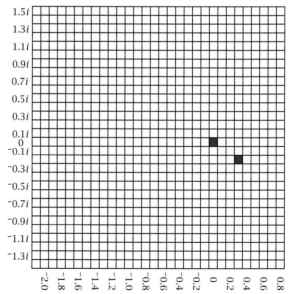

Calculator Note 13D for help in changing forms.) After several squarings you will notice one of two things happening: either the modulus will shrink to nearly zero, or it will become extremely large. If your seed number causes the function to go to zero, then color the associated square black. If your seed number causes the function to grow very large, then color it a different color.

Two sample points have been colored for you in the above grid. The point $(0.3, {}^-0.2)$ becomes $(0.36, {}^-33.6°)$ in polar form. Repeated squaring gives $(0.13, {}^-67°)$, $(0.0169, {}^-134°)$, and then $(0.00028, 90.5°)$. The modulus is headed toward zero, so the point is colored black. Work together with your group to check all of the points. Use any patterns you discover to lessen the number of points you actually have to compute.

c. Describe the location of any point with a modulus that goes to zero. These points make up the **prisoner set**; they will never leave this region, no matter how many times you iterate. Describe the location of any point with a modulus that grows infinitely large. These points make up the **escape set**; they keep moving farther and farther away as the iteration progresses. Describe the boundary of the prisoner and escape sets. These boundary points form a **Julia set**, and they remain on the boundary between prisoners and escapees no matter how many times they are iterated.

The second graphing method that you can use for recursively defined complex functions is to plot each number generated as the function is iterated.

■ **Example 5**

Graph the points generated by $z_n = \begin{cases} 0 & \text{if } n = 0 \\ \pm\sqrt{z_{(n-1)} - i} & \text{if } n > 0. \end{cases}$

Solution

The $\pm$ in the second line of the formula indicates that you can choose either the positive or negative root as you iterate the function. You could flip a coin each time to decide which root to choose. The table on page 694 shows a possible set of the first ten numbers generated. If you try to generate some points for this function, you will probably get a different set, because your coin will indicate the negative root at different steps than the author's did. However, your points should appear to land on the same shape.

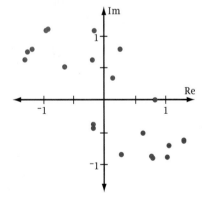

Real	Imaginary	Real	Imaginary
0.7071	⁻0.7071	⁻0.0989	1.1371
⁻1.1302	0.7552	⁻0.1873	⁻0.3660
0.1145	⁻1.0690	0.7718	⁻0.8849
1.0457	⁻0.9894	1.1850	⁻0.7953
⁻1.2832	0.7752	1.2915	⁻0.6950

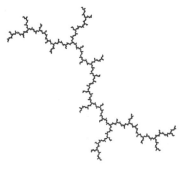

NOTE
13E

Initially, a random set of points appears on the graph. As you continue plotting many more points, a definite shape emerges. This plot shows the result of more than 10,000 iterations. (See **Calculator Note 13E** for a program to generate a plot similar to this one.) ■

Julia sets are named after Gaston Julia (1893–1978), who was a world-famous mathematician in the 1920s. He fought as a soldier during the First World War and lost his nose as a result of his wounds. His work on the properties of Julia sets was difficult to communicate without computer graphics and remained largely unknown until his former student Benoit Mandelbrot called attention to it in his work on fractals.

Gaston Julia

Different views of Julia sets

Problem Set 13.7

1. Plot each complex number.

    a. $2 + 2i$ **b.** $^-1 + i$ **c.** $0 - i$ **d.** $4 - 3i$ **e.** $^-3 - 2i$

2. Convert each number in Problem 1 to polar form.

3. Find and plot all of the cube roots of 8.

4. Find and plot all of the fifth roots of 1.

5. Perform the indicated complex arithmetic. You may want to change some of the numbers to polar form before doing the arithmetic. Write your answers in rectangular form.

a. $(3 - 5i) + (2 + 7i)$ **b.** $(2 + i\sqrt{12})^3$ **c.** $(4(\cos 27° + i \sin 27°))^{-1}$

d. $(4 + 4i)(3 - 3i)^{-1}$ **e.** $\dfrac{1}{^-4 + 4i}$

f. $6(\cos 36° + i \sin 36°) \cdot 2(\cos 54° + i \sin 54°)$

6. a. Plot $(1 + i)$, $(1 + i)^2$, $(1 + i)^3$, $(1 + i)^4$, $(1 + i)^5$, $(1 + i)^6$, and $(1 + i)^7$ on the same complex plane. What will happen to the points as you continue to raise $(1 + i)$ to higher powers?

b. Repeat 6a using $(0.5 + 0.5i)$. What will happen to the points as you continue to raise $(0.5 + 0.5i)$ to higher and higher powers?

c. Explain the differences and similarities in the results of 6a and 6b.

7. Parametric equations and graphs provide easy access and interesting connections to roots and powers of complex numbers. Explore this idea with the complex number $(^-1 - i)$.

a. Find r and θ in the expression $r(\cos \theta + i \sin \theta)$ so that it represents the polar form of $(^-1 - i)$.

b. Write the polar form for $(^-1 - i)^t$. In this situation the parameter represents the power of the complex number.

c. Write parametric equations using $x = r^t \cos t\theta$ and $y = r^t \sin t\theta$ that represent the polar form you found in 7b. Complete a table of values for $0 \le t \le 10$.

t	0	1	2	3	4	5	6	7	8	9	10
x	-?-	-?-	-?-	-?-	-?-	-?-	-?-	-?-	-?-	-?-	-?-
y	-?-	-?-	-?-	-?-	-?-	-?-	-?-	-?-	-?-	-?-	-?-

d. Find a window that includes the points in the table and graph the parametric equations using a Tstep of 0.1. Be sure to square up the window. Trace the graph and locate the points listed in the table. What do these points represent?

8. a. Repeat parts a–d from Problem 7 using the complex number $(0.05 + 0.866i)$. This time use $0 \le t \le 12$.

b. Predict and then verify the point determined by $(0.05 + 0.866i)^{463}$. Explain why this point is the same as one of those listed in the table in Problem 7c.

9. a. In Example 4 of this section you found the fifth roots of 32. Do this again using the parametric equations $x = 2 \cos \left(\dfrac{360t}{5} \right)$ and $y = 2 \sin \left(\dfrac{360t}{5} \right)$. Explain the table values and your graph.

b. Find and graph the sixth roots of 32 by using parametric equations.

10. a. Iterate the function $z_n = \sqrt[3]{z_{(n-1)}}$. Start with $z_0 = 1 + i$ and plot the value of the function at each step of the iteration. Continue until you can confidently describe what will happen to the value of the function in the long run.

b. Repeat 10a using $z_0 = {}^-0.5 + 0.5i$.

c. Repeat 10a using any other point of your choice as z_0.

d. What generalizations can you make about iterating this function?

11. Construct a grid on graph paper like the one in Investigation 13.7.2. Identify the grid locations for the three cube roots of 1 that were found in Example 3. Mark these three points with different colors. Consider grid locations for complex numbers z that lie approximately on a circle containing the three marked points. Iterate these locations

NOTE
13E

through the function $z_n = z_{(n-1)} - \dfrac{z^3 - 1}{3z^2}$. Use the program in **Calculator Note 13E** to do this. Each initial location z will eventually iterate to one of the three roots. Color the initial location with the same color as the corresponding root.

What happens when you continue iterating a new point that is located between two points of different color. Do you get the same result with another point? Explain what you have found to be true as you iterate any point that lies between a pair of different-colored points.

Project

More on Julia Sets

In this project you will do some more investigating of the Julia set.

a. Follow the procedure outlined in Example 5 from Section 13.7 with

$$z_n = \begin{cases} 0 & \text{if } n = 1 \\ \pm\sqrt{z_{(n-1)} - c} & \text{if } n > 1 \end{cases}$$

using $c = {}^-0.5 + 0.5i$. Plot the points by hand.

b. On your graph paper mark off a 30-by-30 grid using a scale of $^-1.5 \le x \le 1.5$ and $^-1.5 \le y \le 1.5$. Iterate each location through the function $z_n = (z_{n-1})^2 + c$. Color each prisoner point black.

c. Repeat parts a and b again using $c = {}^-1 + 0i$.

d. Based on your results for parts a–c, describe the connection between the Julia set and the prisoner set. How are the equations that you used to generate the Julia set and the prisoner set related to each other?

NOTE
13F

e. Use the program in **Calculator Note 13F** to plot more points in the Julia set. Compare your graphs. Experiment with other values of c. If possible print out a copy of your favorite Julia set and record the equation used to graph it.

Section 13.8

Chapter Review

That is what learning is. You suddenly understand something you've understood
all your life, but in a new way.
—Doris Lessing

In this chapter you expanded your understanding of trigonometry to include circular functions, their graphs, and their applications. You can think of the sine and cosine of an angle as the *y*- and *x*-coordinates of a point on the unit circle. The remaining trigonometric functions are also defined either as a ratio of a *y*-coordinate to an *x*-coordinate or as a ratio of one of these coordinates to the distance from the origin to the point. Graphs of the trigonometric functions have domains that extend in both the positive and negative directions. The Law of Sines and the Law of Cosines are used to find the measures of unknown parts of oblique triangles. Oftentimes you will have to use a combination of the two laws. You also learned how to use the inverse of a trigonometric function to solve for the measure of an angle when you knew the value of the function.

You were introduced to a new way to identify the location of a point—polar coordinates. Polar coordinates are expressed in terms of *r*, the distance from the origin, and *θ*, an angle measured from the positive *x*-axis to the ray passing through the origin and the point. This coordinate system is useful for graphing circles and other curves, such as cardioids and rose curves, as well as for visualizing complex numbers. You will find it much easier to multiply complex numbers and to raise them to a power if you first express these complex numbers by using polar coordinates. You can also use polar coordinates to find the real and complex roots of a number.

Problem Set 13.8

1. For each equation, state the period and name one other equation that has the same graph.
   a. $y = 2 \sin 3(x - 30°)$ **b.** $y = {}^{-}3 \cos 4x$ **c.** $y = \sec 2x$ **d.** $y = \tan ({}^{-}2x) + 1$

2. Write an equation for each graph a–d.

   a.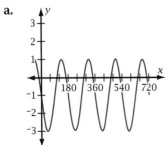

   b.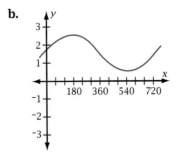

c.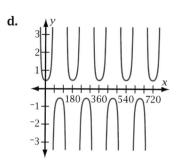

d.

3. The table below shows the number of hours of daylight from December 21, 1995 to July 23, 1996 in Portland, Maine, which is located at W 70° 17′, N 43° 40′.

Date	Hours	Date	Hours	Date	Hours	Date	Hours
21 Dec	8.933	14 Feb	10.450	9 Apr	13.167	3 Jun	15.283
26 Dec	8.950	19 Feb	10.683	14 Apr	13.400	8 Jun	15.350
31 Dec	8.983	24 Feb	10.933	19 Apr	13.650	13 Jun	15.417
5 Jan	9.050	29 Feb	11.167	24 Apr	13.883	18 Jun	15.450
10 Jan	9.150	5 Mar	11.417	29 Apr	14.100	23 Jun	15.450
15 Jan	9.283	10 Mar	11.667	4 May	14.317	28 Jun	15.417
20 Jan	9.433	15 Mar	11.917	9 May	14.500	3 Jul	15.350
25 Jan	9.617	20 Mar	12.167	14 May	14.700	8 Jul	15.267
30 Jan	9.800	25 Mar	12.417	19 May	14.867	13 Jul	15.150
4 Feb	10.017	30 Mar	12.667	24 May	15.033	18 Jul	15.033
9 Feb	10.217	4 Apr	12.917	29 May	15.167	23 Jul	14.867

a. Graph (*date, hours of daylight*) and determine the equation for your best-fit curve.
b. Use your model to determine the date in 1996 on which there was the most amount of daylight. How many hours of daylight was this?
c. On what dates in 1996 were there equal amounts of daylight and darkness?

4. a. Graph $y_1 = \sec^2 x$ and $y_2 = \tan^2 x$ on the same coordinate axes.
b. Alter one of the equations in 4a so that the resulting graphs are identical. What is the trigonometric identity you have discovered?

5. Find the length of each unknown side and the measure of each unknown angle.

a.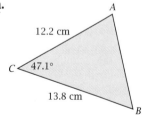

b.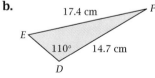

6. Explain how you decide whether to use the Law of Sines or the Law of Cosines when trying to solve for an unknown side or angle of a triangle.

7. When a spaceship is launched into earth orbit, it follows a sinusoidal path around the earth. The axis of this sine curve is the equator. Suppose that ten minutes after noon, a spaceship is at its greatest distance from the equator, 100 mi. It makes a complete revolution of the earth in 105 min. Write an equation to model the path of the spaceship. How far from the equator was the spaceship at noon? How many orbits will the spaceship make during a three-day flight?

8. State two sets of polar coordinates that name the same point as $(5, 40°)$.

9. Graph the equation $r = 2(\cos \theta + 1)$ for $0° \le \theta \le 360°$.
  a. What equation will reflect this graph across the y-axis?
  b. What equation will rotate the graph $90°$ counterclockwise?

10. Plot each complex number.
  a. $3 + 4i$ **b.** $^{-}2 - i$ **c.** $2(\cos 30° + i \sin 30°)$ **d.** $(4 - i)^2$ **e.** i^6
  f. $(4(\cos 48° + i \sin 48°))^{(1/4)}$ (Be sure to plot all four roots.)

11. Iterate the function $z_n = (z_{(n-1)})^3$. What are the possible results for various values of z_0?

Assessing What You've Learned

Be sure to choose at least three different ways to assess what you've learned.

- Organizing Your Notebook (Chapter 0)
- Keeping a Journal (Chapter 1)
- Portfolio (Chapter 2)
- Performance Assessment (Chapter 3)
- Open-ended Investigations (Chapter 4)
- Constructing Test Questions (Chapter 5)
- Group Presentations and Tests (Chapter 6)
- Overall Self-Assessment (Chapter 7)

Selected Answers for Problem Sets

Chapter 0

Problem Set 0.1

1. a. 10.63014581   **b.** 1.95   **c.** 30

2. a. $(-4)^2 = 16, -4^2 = -16$ **d.**

```
17→X
            17
X²
           289
-X²
          -289
```

3. a. i. 8
    ii. 0.8

4. a. Area of a triangle
    i. 268.755   ii. 1.70154
  b. Height of an object in free fall
    i. 87.39   ii. 1358.8416
  c. Slope of a line given two points
    i. -1.221428571 ii. Undefined

Problem Set 0.2

1. a. i. $1.23439632 \cdot 10^7$
    ii. $8.164967851 \cdot 10^{-5}$
  b. i. $6.63466667 \cdot 10^{-34}$
    ii. $1.116 \cdot 10^{-33}$

2. a. 347,895,000   **b.** 0.000 000 000 008 247   **c.** 140,000

4. $2 \cdot 10^{18}$ neurons

6. c. i. 260 km   ii. 253.5 km   iii. Approximately 3%

7. a. 14,496,768 lb or 7,248.384 T   **b.** Yes: answers will vary.

Problem Set 0.3

1. Answers will vary.
  a. Xmin = -2 or less, Xmax = 3 or more, Xscl = 1 or less,
    Ymin = 5 or less, Ymax = 21 or more, Yscl = 1 or more

b. Xmin = 0 or less, Xmax = 4 or more, Xscl = 1 or less,
Ymin = −4 or less, Ymax = 12 or more, Yscl = 1 or more

2. $20 \cdot 1.5^h$

a.

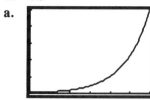

[0, 12, 2, 0, 2500, 500]

b.

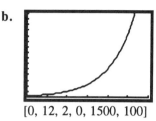

[0, 12, 2, 0, 1500, 100]

c.

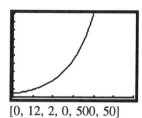

[0, 12, 2, 0, 500, 50]

d.

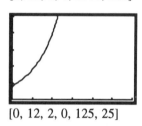

[0, 12, 2, 0, 125, 25]

3. a.

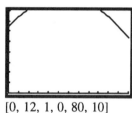

[0, 12, 1, 0, 80, 10]

b.

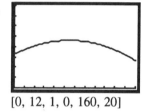

[0, 12, 1, 0, 160, 20]

c.

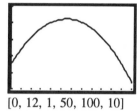

[0, 12, 1, 50, 100, 10]

d. The view window in part c gives the best picture because the graph fills most of the screen and the critical area of the maximum is shown.

4. Answers will vary.
   a. Range of −25 to 35 for y-values is good.
   b. Range of −50 to 300 for y-values is good.
   c. Range of −10 to 50 for y-values is good.

5. a. i. 14.4   ii. 33.76
   b. i. 0.0030448   ii. $3.43232 \cdot 10^{-6}$

Chapter 1

Problem Set 1.1

1. 6, 9, 13.5, . . . ; geometric; $u_{10} = 230.6601563$

2. 6 | ENTER | seeds the sequence. Ans + 3.2 | ENTER | can be repeated to generate the terms; $u_{10} = 34.8$.

3. a. 2 | ENTER | seeds the sequence. Ans • 3 | ENTER | . . . ; $u_{15} = 9,565,938$
   b. 10 | ENTER | Ans • 0.5 | ENTER | . . . ; $u_{12} = 0.004\ 882\ 812\ 5$
   c. 0.4 | ENTER | Ans • 0.1 | ENTER | . . . ; $u_{10} = 4 \cdot 10^{-10}$

4. a. Between 12 and 13 min   **b.** Between 28 and 29 min   **c.** Ans + 2.4 – 3.1

7. a. $60.00   **b.** $33.75   **c.** 9 weeks

Problem Set 1.2

1. a.

Generations back	0	1	2	3	4	17	n
Ancestors in a generation	$u_0 = 1$	$u_1 = 2$	$u_2 = 4$	$u_3 = 8$	$u_4 = 16$	$u_{17} = 131{,}072$	$u_n = 2u_{(n-1)}$

b. Multiply the number in the preceding generation by 2.
c. 4,194,304. About 22 generations back, Jill would have almost 5 million ancestors.
d. 550 yr ago
e. Answers will vary.

3. About 25 time periods or between 24,000 and 25,000 yr; 100 ENTER

Ans • 0.8855 ENTER and so on.

5. a. 25,098   **b.** $\approx 64.07\%$ **c.** 3.2%
d. Using 0.032 as the rate you get a population of 73,553, which is too large. You need to find a smaller rate than 3.2% to compensate for the compounding effect.
e. 0.025
f. 50,147; this is less than half the 1980 population because the relationship is nonlinear.

Problem Set 1.3

1. a. 747.45, 818.04   **c.** The sequence levels out at 840.

2. a. 1, 2, 6, 24, 120, 720

3. a. $u_n = \begin{cases} 49.06 & \text{if } n = 1 \\ 1.18 + u_{(n-1)} & \text{if } n > 1 \end{cases}$

4. a. $u_1 = 24{,}000$ and $u_n = \left(1 + \frac{0.064}{12}\right) \cdot u_{(n-1)} - 100$
b. $24,000; $24,028; $24,056.15; $24,084.45; $24,112.90
c. The balance after 4 mo
d. $24,346.03; $25,108.03

6. $u_1 = 20$ and $u_n = (1 - 0.25) \cdot u_{(n-1)}$; between 10 and 11 days

9. a. $u_1 = 11{,}000$ and $u_n = \left(1 + \frac{0.096}{12}\right) \cdot u_{(n-1)} - 274$
b. $11,000; $10,814; $10,626.51; $10,437.52; $10,247.02
c. 49 mo with a final payment of $167.73
d. $13,319.73

Problem Set 1.4

1. a. (1, 2.5); (2, 4); (3, 5.5); (4, 7); (5, 8.5); (6, 10)
b. Answers will vary. One possible window is [0, 7, 1, 0, 11, 1].

c. 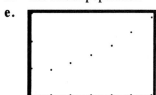   **d.** The sketch will look like the graph for part c.

2. **a.** $(0, 3929000)$; $(1, 4871960)$; $(2, 6041230)$; $(3, 7491126)$; $(4, 9288996)$; $(5, 11518355)$

b. The initial population   **c.** 24%   **d.** Geometric

e.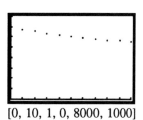

```
WINDOW FORMAT
Xmin=0
Xmax=6
Xscl=1
Ymin=0
Ymax=15000000
Yscl=5000000
```

5.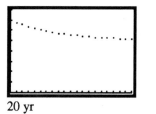

[0, 50, 5, 0, 8000, 1000]

This is a set of discrete points.

6. **a.** The slime takes over during the seventh day.

b. The concentration increases to 3.333333333 ppm. The pool will never be pure chlorine.

Problem Set 1.5

1. $u_{10} = 56$; $u_{20} = 116$; $u_{30} = 176$

2. **a.** $1,905.56   **b.** $3,631.15   **c.** $6,919.38

3. **a.**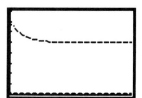

[0, 10, 1, 0, 8000, 1000]

b.

20 yr

30 yr

c. In the long run, the number of trees stabilizes at 5000. $u_{75} = 5000$.

5. **a.** $u_0 = 5000$, $u_n = (1 + 0.085/12)u_{(n-1)}$; $123.98

b.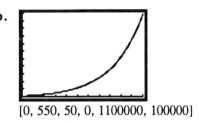

[0, 550, 50, 0, 1100000, 100000]

7. **a.** 2 million   **b.** 11 million   **c.** 29 million

8. **a.** 1, 1, 2, 3, 5, 8, 13, 21, 34, 55
b. The ratios are 1, 2, 1.5, 1.6, 1.625, ... The ratios are approaching 1.618033989.

Problem Set 1.6

1. 2, 8, 18, 32, 50

3. **a.** 0.3333333333
b. 0.333333333333333; the sum is the same as for ten terms because the calculator cannot display more digits.
c. $0.\overline{3}$ or 1/3.

4. **a.** 144   **b.** 400

5. 1200 min (20 hr); 4550 min (75.8 hr)

7. First plan: $38,373,180,000; Second plan: $45,035,996,273,704; The second plan is more profitable by $44,997,623,093,704.

8. 0.3939393939

Chapter Review
Problem Set 1.7

1. **a.** 3, 6, 9, 12, 15, 18, 21, 24, 27, 30   **b.** $u_n = \begin{cases} 3 & \text{if } n = 1 \\ u_{(n-1)} + 3 & \text{if } n > 1 \end{cases}$
c. 3384 cans   **d.** 13 rows

2. **a.** 511   **b.** 40th   **c.** 79   **d.** 820

3. **a.** 34.171875   **b.** Tenth   **c.** 45.5625   **d.** 887.3125

4. **a.** $657.03   **b.** $4,083.21

5. 5299 students; 5208 students

6. 359 payments of $637.96 and one payment of $620.46

7. **a.** −3, −1.5, 0, 1.5, 3   **b.** 2, 4, 10, 28, 82

Chapter 2

Problem Set 2.1

1. a. $\frac{5}{3}$, 7, 18, $36\frac{2}{3}$, 65   **b.** Neither

3. a. 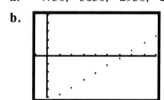   **b.** -3 **c.** -3
d. 21   **e.** $u_n = -3n + 21$
f. $u_{10} = -9$ **g.** $y = -3x + 21$

5. a. (1, 7) and (6, 27)   **b.** $m = 4$ **c.** 3, 7, 11, 15, 19, 23, 27
d. $y = 4x + 3$ **e.** $u_n = 4n + 3$
f. The slope and the common difference are the same.

7. a. 231 mi   **b.** $d = 54x + 15$ **c.**
d. If only distances on the hour are considered, it is arithmetic. Otherwise the distance depends on time—a continuous rather than discrete notion.

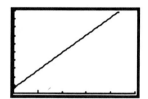

8. a. -4750, -3850, -2950, -2050, -1150, -250, 650, . . .
b.   **c.** \$900 profit per car sold
d. \$900 profit per car sold
e. $-\$4{,}750$ (y-intercept) represents expenses even if no cars are sold; 5.27 (x-intercept) means at least 6 cars must be sold to make any profit.
f. $d = 900c - 4750$

10. a. They are the same and will always be the same.
b. The trick is to look at the total income at the end of each six-month period. Assume that the raise goes into effect at the beginning of the next time period. Although the total earnings are different at the end of the odd-numbered six-month periods, at the end of each year the total income is always the same.

	Case 1	Total earnings	Case 2	Total earnings
First 6 mo	9,200	9,200	8,950	8,950
First yr	9,200	18,400	9,450	18,400
Third 6 mo	10,200	28,600	9,950	28,350
Second yr	10,200	38,800	10,450	38,800
Fifth 6 mo	11,200	50,000	10,950	49,750
Third yr	11,200	61,200	11,450	61,200

Problem Set 2.2

1. 7650

3. a. 149   **b.** 5625

4. a. -6639.7

5. a. 229   **b.** $5n - 1$ **c.** 5359

6. 88 gal

7. A sequence with positive slope (line *a*)
A sequence with negative slope (line *b*)
A sequence with zero slope (line *c*)

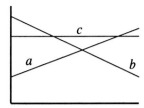

Problem Set 2.3

1. 9,565,938

2. $2,302.03; after 23 yr the balance is $5,139.23.

3. a. The value of $4,000 after 10 yr of compounded interest at 7.2%
   b. The value of $4,000 after 4 yr of interest compounded monthly
   c. $1500(1 + 0.055)^8$

6. a. ii   **b.** i   **c.** iii

7. a. ≈ 10.74 inches   **b.** 21st rebound; 31st rebound

Problem Set 2.4

1. a. 3069   **b.** 22   **c.** 2.8   **d.** 0.95

3. a.

n	1	2	3	4	5	6	7
S_n	5	15	35	75	155	315	635

   b. No
   c. When $r = 0$

4. a. 92.224   **b.** 99.9529815   **c.** 99.9997157

6. a. $1^2 + 2^2 + 3^2 + 4^2 + 5^2 + 6^2 + 7^2 = 140$ **b.** $3^2 + 4^2 + 5^2 + 6^2 + 7^2 = 135$

7. a. $2^{63} \approx 9.22 \cdot 10^{18}$ **b.** $2^{64} - 1 \approx 1.84 \cdot 10^{19}$

   c. $\displaystyle\sum_{n-1}^{64} 2^{(n-1)}$

Problem Set 2.5

1. $S_{10} = 60$; $S_n = 6n$; infinite

2. **a.** $S_{10} \approx 12.96$; $S_{40} \approx 13.33$
   b. $S_{10} \approx 170.48$; $S_{40} \approx 481{,}572$
   c. $S_{10} \approx 40$; $S_{40} \approx 160$
   d. The inequality $r > 1$ gives the top graph; $r = 1$ gives the middle graph; $0 < r < 1$ gives the bottom graph.
   e. When $|r| < 1$

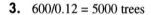

3. $600/0.12 = 5000$ trees

4. **a.** 0.149382716   **b.** ≈ 0.1499974597 **c.** 0.15

8. At age 30, Prudence has \$35,120.59 and Charity has \$2,000; at age 65, Prudence has \$716,950.60 and Charity has \$472,249.45.

9. **a.** 1.414   **b.** 0.125   **c.** P approaches 109.25 and A approaches 128.

Problem Set 2.6

1. Geome tree

		1	2	3	4	n	∞
a.	Length of the last segment	1	0.5	0.25	0.125	$1\left(\frac{1}{2}\right)^{(n-1)}$	0
b.	Length of the path	1	1.5	1.75	1.875	$\dfrac{1\left(1 - \left(\frac{1}{2}\right)^{n}\right)}{1 - \frac{1}{2}}$	2
c.	Total number of segments	1	3	7	15	$2^n - 1$	∞
d.	Sum of the lengths of all segments	1	2	3	4	n	∞
e.	Height of the tree	1	1.354	1.604	1.692		1.8047
f.	Width of the tree	0	0.707	1.207	1.384		1.609

2. Koch snowflake

		1	2	3	4	n	∞
a.	Length of each segment	1	$\frac{1}{3}$	$\frac{1}{9}$	$\frac{1}{27}$	$\left(\frac{1}{3}\right)^{(n-1)}$	0
b.	Total number of segments	3	12	48	192	$3 \cdot 4^{(n-1)}$	∞
c.	Perimeter	3	4	$5\frac{1}{3}$	$\frac{64}{9}$	$\dfrac{3 \cdot 4^{(n-1)}}{3^{(n-1)}}$	∞
d.	Area	0.43301	0.577	0.641	0.67001		

3. Sierpiński triangle

		1	2	3	4	n	∞
a.	Length of last side	1	$\frac{1}{2}$	$\frac{1}{4}$	$\frac{1}{8}$	$\left(\frac{1}{2}\right)^{(n-1)}$	0
b.	Number of triangles	1	3	9	27	$3^{(n-1)}$	∞
c.	Perimeter of each	3	$\frac{3}{2}$	$\frac{3}{4}$	$\frac{3}{8}$	$\frac{3}{2^{n-1}}$	0
d.	Area of each	$\frac{\sqrt{3}}{4}$	$\frac{\sqrt{3}}{16}$	$\frac{\sqrt{3}}{64}$	$\frac{\sqrt{3}}{256}$	$\frac{\sqrt{3}}{4^n}$	0
e.	Sum of perimeters	3	4.5	6.75	10.125	$\frac{3^n}{2^{(n-1)}}$	∞
f.	Sum of areas	$\frac{\sqrt{3}}{4}$	$\frac{3\sqrt{3}}{16}$	$\frac{9\sqrt{3}}{64}$	$\frac{27\sqrt{3}}{256}$	$\frac{3^{(n-1)}\sqrt{3}}{4^n}$	0

Chapter Review

Problem Set 2.7

1. a. 3, 6, 9, . . . , 30

   c. $u_n = 3n$ **d.** 3384 cans

   b. $u_n = \begin{cases} 3 & \text{if } n = 1 \\ u_{(n-1)} + 3 & \text{if } n > 1 \end{cases}$

   e. 13 rows

2. a. 511   **b.** 40th   **c.** 79   **d.** 820

3. a. 144, 1,728, 20,736, $4.3 \cdot 10^8$

   c. $u_n = 12^n$ **d.** $9.7 \cdot 10^{12}$ bugs

   b. $u_n = \begin{cases} 12 & \text{if } n = 1 \\ 12 \cdot u_{(n-1)} & \text{if } n > 1 \end{cases}$

4. a. 34.171875   **b.** tenth term   **c.** 45.5625   **d.** 887.3125

   e. The sum approaches 1024.

5. a. $657.03   **b.** $4,083.21

6. a. 5327 students   **b.** 5208 students

7. a. ≈ 139.67 cm   **b.** ≈ 1206.65 cm   **c.** 4000 cm

8. ≈ 56.488 ft; 60 ft

9. 359 payments of $637.96 and 1 payment of $620.46

10. a. $\left(\frac{2}{3}\right)^0$, $\left(\frac{2}{3}\right)^1$, $\left(\frac{2}{3}\right)^2$, $\left(\frac{2}{3}\right)^3$, and so on.   **b.** $C_n \to 0$

Chapter 3

Problem Set 3.1

1. The median is 84 and the mean is 84 for both Connie and Ozzie. Neither measure separately or combined indicates the larger test score variation for Ozzie's scores.

3. a.

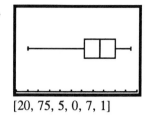

[20, 75, 5, 0, 7, 1]

b. {25, 51, 58, 65, 72}
c. 56.55
d. 98

4. a. Outliers for Connie: below 77.5 or above 89.5; Outliers for Ozzie: below 49 or above 121
   b. Outliers for Homer: below 30 or above 86; one outlier: 25 < 30

6. a. {74,300, 87,050, 105,000, 153,900, 246,900}

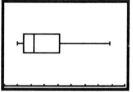

[50000, 275000, 25000, 0, 10, 1]
There are no outliers.

b. {74,300, 84,650, 93,600, 105,750, 116,800}

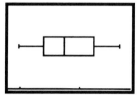

[70000, 120000, 25000, 0, 10, 1]

10. a. The tube price median is $2.01 and the mean is $2.13; the median cleaning rank is 66.5 and the mean rank is 67.25.

   b. Price

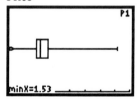

[1.53, 1.96, 2.01, 2.15, 3.29]

Rank

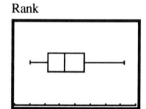

[55, 61, 66.5, 73, 86]

Problem Set 3.2

1. This implies than no CDs can be shipped that measure more than 12.12 cm or less than 11.88 cm.

4. a. 47.1, 45.9, 47.9, 47.4, 45.1, 46.0, 45.7, 45.3
   b. The mean absolute deviation is 0.875 cm.
   c. 47.9, 47.4, 45.1, 45.3

5. a. First period has pulse rates most alike because it has the smallest mean absolute deviation.
   b. You can't really tell which class has the students with the fastest pulse. First period rates are more consistent around the mean of 79.4 because it has the lowest MAD value. Sixth period must have some very high rates and some very low rates to have the highest MAD value.
   c. Answers will vary. Data sets with lower MAD values will have shorter box plots.

8. **b.** Juneau has more consistent temperatures ranging from 24°F to 56°F compared to New York temperatures ranging from 32°F to 77°F. The mean absolute deviation for Juneau is 9.83°F and for New York 14.0°F.

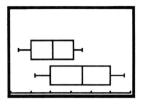

9. **a.** The median is 75 and the interquartile range is 19.

b. The mean is 80.88 and the mean absolute deviation is 15.9.

c. The outliers are below 39 or above 115. Therefore, 147 and 158 are outliers.

d.

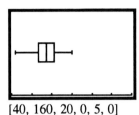

[40, 160, 20, 0, 5, 0]

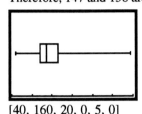

[40, 160, 20, 0, 5, 0]

e. **i.** The mean is 74.65 and the mean absolute deviation is 9.3.

   ii. The median is 74 and the interquartile range is 15.

f. The mean is affected more than the median; the mean absolute deviation is affected more than the interquartile range. This is because the mean absolute deviation involves the mean and the interquartile range involves the median.

Problem Set 3.3

1. **a.** The graph should look exactly like the graph in the problem. [2, 13, 1, 0, 200, 50]

b. It is mound shaped because 7 is the most likely dice total, then 6 and 8, then 5 and 9, and so on.

c. The mean sum can be computed by evaluating $\frac{2(26) + 3(56) + \cdots + 12(21)}{1000}$. The median sum can be found by counting in from the left or right. The median will be the average of the 500th and 501st roll total.

2. **a.** This population of 95 farmers tends to plant two to five acres of sweet corn. The frequencies are on the left.

b.

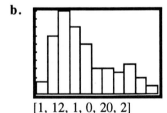

[1, 12, 1, 0, 20, 2]

c.

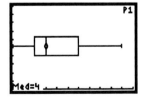

5. **a.** HW {4, 27.5, 40.5, 49, 65}; TV {5, 26, 36.5, 58, 95}; TV has the larger spread. The spread for HW is 61, and the spread for TV is 90.

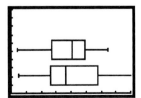

b.

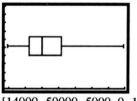

HW [0, 100, 5, 0, 5, 1]   TV [0, 100, 5, 0, 5, 1]

7. a. The MAD of the stadium capacities is 7282. The MAD of the attendance figures is 6254. Attendance MAD is less than stadium capacity MAD. This means the stadium capacity values are more spread out.

c. Capacity

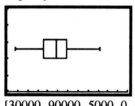

[30000, 90000, 5000, 0, 5, 1]   [30000, 90000, 5000, 0, 10, 1]

Attendance

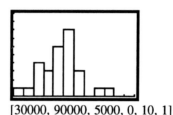

[14000, 50000, 5000, 0, 10, 1]   [10000, 50000, 5000, 0, 10, 1]

Chapter Review
Problem Set 3.4

1. Plot B because the data is much more spread out.

2. a. Answers will vary, but the graph for plot C should be much higher. The shapes should take into account the scale on the horizontal axis and the way values are compacted between the quartiles.

   b. Seven data values are in the lower whisker in plot C. Six data values are in each whisker in plot D.

   c. Plot B has the larger MAD because the box plot is longer and the range of data values is much greater.

4. The mean of the extreme highs is 118°F with a MAD of 17°F. The mean of the extreme lows is ⁻60°F with a MAD of 38°F. Antarctica is two MADs from the mean high and *almost* two MADs from the mean low.

5. a. Answers will vary, but the mean absolute deviation near 0 means a tall, skinny graph.

   b. Answers will vary, but the mean absolute deviation of about 5 means a shorter but longer graph.

7. a.

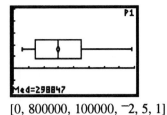

$[0, 800000, 100000, {}^{-}2, 5, 1]$

b.

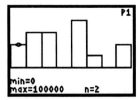

$[0, 800000, 100000, {}^{-}2, 5, 1]$

c.–d. Answers will vary. The shape really depends on how the additional sales are distributed.

Chapter 4

Problem Set 4.1

1. Answers will vary. Here are some examples.
   a. Too many points are above the line.
   b. Most of the points at the left are below the line.
   c. The line doesn't follow the tendency of the data from first to last point.
   d. Points at each end are concentrated on one side of the line.
   e. This is the best of the lot.
   f. There are no points below the line.

2. For Problems 1–6, answers will vary. Possible answers are given.
   a. y-intercept is about 1.7; point (4, 4).
   b. y-intercept is about 1.8; point (3, 4).
   c. y-intercept is about 7.5; point (2, 6).

3. Answers will vary for the best-fit line.

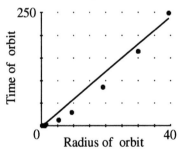

6. a. 6
   b. $[0, 22, 2, 20, 45, 5]$

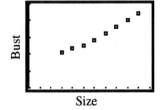 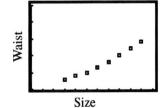 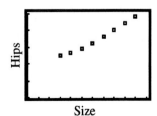

[20, 45, 5, 20, 45, 5]

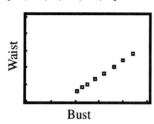
Waist / Bust

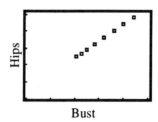
Hips / Bust

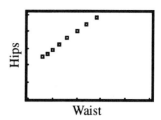
Hips / Waist

Problem Set 4.2

1. a. $\frac{3}{2}$　　　**b.** $\frac{-2}{3}$

2. a. 3　　　**b.** -2.8　　　**d.** $+2.4$

3. a. $y = \frac{3}{2}x - 6$　　　**b.** $y = -1.124x + 2.643$

For Problems 5 and 6, the equation of the line should be close to that of the median-median line, whose equation is given.

5. $y = 5.59x - 8.03$

6. $y = 0.32x - 1820$

Problem Set 4.3

1. a. 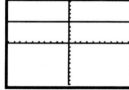　　　**b.** Answers will vary, but the y-coordinate should always be 5.　　　**c.** Slope = 0

3. $x = 3$; Line(3, Ymin, 3, Ymax) or ⎹2nd⎸ [DRAW] ⎹4⎸ (Vertical)

5. a. For each additional story, the building height increases by about 13 ft.
　　b. The stories of a building are often not all the same height, the first floor or two are usually taller. The intercept of about 20 represents this difference in the height of the initial stories.
　　c. Domain $0 \le x \le 80$; range $0 \le y \le 1100$

Note: The equations in the answers for Problems 7–10 may vary depending on the chosen point. Any line that fits the data "by eye" should be considered acceptable as long as the student can justify his or her choice of an equation.

8. a. $y = -1.75x + 582.25$ (using the points (87, 430) and (91, 423))
　　b. Years after 1900
　　c. There has been a 1.75 point decrease per year in the average verbal score.
　　d. 414 points for 1996, 412 for 1997, 411 for 1998, 409 for 1999, 407 for 2000
　　e. 442 points
　　f. There is a limit to the extrapolation in this model. Using it to predict very far beyond the given data is very unreliable.

9. The answers given are based on midrange *x*-values.

a.

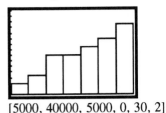

[5000, 40000, 5000, 0, 30, 2]

b. $y = 0.00065x - 1.125$ (using the points for incomes of \$32,500 and \$12,500)

c. As family incomes increase by \$1,000, the percent of students in grades 9–12 using computers at home increases by 0.65%.

d. 38.2%

10. a. (If you choose to draw a histogram, you will have to draw it on paper because the calculator requires you to enter whole numbers for the frequencies.) $y = -5.07x + 181.3$ (using the points $(17, 96.2)$ and $(32, 19.6)$)

b. Percent of men not married

c. About 5.07% of the total male population gets married each year.

d. -31.3%

e. The model does not extrapolate very well, or it becomes nonlinear after age 30.

Problem Set 4.4

1. a. 10, 11, 10   b. 17, 16, 17

2. a. $y = -0.674x + 21.2$ b. $y = 2.47x + 39.6$

3. $y = 0.75x - 9.9$

4. $y = -1.8x + 72.9$

7. a. 5, 5, 5   b. $(30, 58.1), (55, 66.2), (80, 70)$

c. 0.238; each year the life expectancy of a male child increases by 0.238 yr.

d. $y = 0.238x + 50.96$ e. $y = 0.238x + 53.11$

f. $y = 0.238x + 51.68$ g. 70.24

h. 73.34, 64.53   i. The year 2019

10. a. $y = -0.344x + 257.6$ b. A drop of 0.344 sec each year

c. 3:45.95   d. Eventually the record would be 1 mi in 0 sec.

e. Answers may vary. For example, a new world record was set in Italy on September 5, 1993, by Noureddine Morceli of 3:44.39 for the mile. The model would predict the record in 1993 to be $y = -0.344(1993) + 912 = 226.4$ or 3:46.4.

Problem Set 4.5

1. a. -0.2 b. -0.4 c. 0.6

2. a. The residuals are below the *x*-axis on either end and above the *x*-axis in the middle.

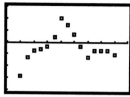

[10, 100, 10, −4, 3, 1]

b. By drawing a line that is parallel to the median-median line but with a smaller *y*-intercept, more points will lie closer to the line.

c. $y = 0.238x + 50.95$

d. 0.7 yr

3. a.

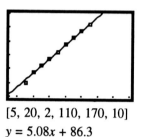

[5, 20, 2, 110, 170, 10]

$y = 5.08x + 86.3$

c. Ages 7 and 15

b.

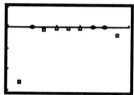

[6, 16, 2, −3, 1, 1]

The range of the residuals is from −2.6 to 0.017.

d. Answers may vary. At age 7, you are at the end of the initial growth of a child, and at age 15, you are at the end of the secondary growth of a child.

4. a.

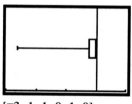

[−3, 1, 1, 0, 1, 0]

b. The residuals are not evenly divided. There are more negative values than positive ones, and the most negative value is an outlier indicating that this point does not fit the model well at all.

7. a. This is not a good model because the residuals form a pattern, which suggests that there is a better model to fit the data.

b. This is a good model because the residuals are close to 0, centered around the *x*-axis, and do not form a pattern.

c. This is a good model, but because there is a definite slope to the residuals, you should adjust the slope of the line.

Problem Set 4.6

1. The three summary points remain the same, so the median-median line will be the same. The outliers could change the summary points if they affect the medians of the groups.

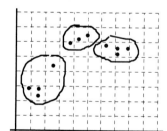

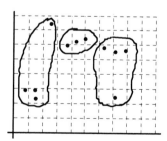

3. The new least-squares equation is $y = 0.4699x - 0.0013$. The new median-median line is $y = 0.4699x - 0.00195$. The outlier has less effect on the median-median line. The median-median line is said to be resistant because an outlier will not have as great an effect on this equation as it does on the least-squares equation.

4. Answers will vary.

5. a. $y = 5.235x + 84.3$ **c.** The median-median line is a better fit.

7. a. $(400, 113{,}394.27)$, $(500, 42{,}201.91)$, $(600, {}^-28{,}990.44)$, $(700, {}^-100{,}182.80)$; 2
    b. $y = 398{,}163.69 - 711.92x$ **c.** $\approx \$559.28$

8. Answers will vary.

Problem Set 4.7

1. 12

2. $y = {}^-1.5x + 6$

4. a. $y = 59.2 - 0.536x$ **b.** $r = {}^-0.9966$
    c. The data has a negative correlation (as the years increase, the percent of dropouts decreases), and about $({}^-0.09966)^2$ or 99.3% of the points lie between narrow bands on either side of the least-squares line.
    d. 20.6%   **e.** About 9 or 10 out of 10.

5. a. Volumes versus cost: $r = 0.60458$, $r^2 = 37\%$; circulation versus cost: $r = 0.5826$, $r^2 = 34\%$
    b. Answers will vary.

8. a. Student to faculty: $f = 0.066s + 55.08$; faculty to student: $s = 5.12f + 631.5$
    b. The correlation coefficient, r, is 0.85 for both equations.

Problem Set 4.8

1. a. First; the points lie more on a curve than on a line.
    b. Second; these points are closest to a line.
    c. Second; the slope is negative, or as x increases, y decreases.

2. a. $y = {}^-5.693 + 7.250x$

x	4	7	11	12.9	16	18.5
y	22	47	74	87	111	128
$y_1(x)$	23.3	45.1	74.1	87.8	110.3	128.4
Residual	-1.31	1.94	-0.06	-0.83	0.69	-0.43
Residual^2	1.710	3.772	0.003	0.695	0.478	0.188

    b. $^-1.3$ to 1.9   **c.** 5.27   **d.** 0.88   **e.** 6.85
    f. The residuals are all close to the line, with the mean absolute residual only 0.88 from the line. If you find the mean of the squares of the residuals, you get 1.14, which again is rather close to the line. The line is a good fit.

5. a. $y = 0.497 + 0.312x$ **b.** 4.55

7. a. 303

b. Schools more than one mean absolute deviation from the mean

Boston University	University of Central Florida
Bowling Green State University	University of Cincinnati
DePauw University	University of Iowa
Florida State University	University of Massachusetts
Howard University	University of Miami
Miami University of Ohio	University of Michigan
Michigan State University	University of Nevada
New Mexico State University	University of South Florida
New York University	University of Utah
Penn State	University of Virginia
Princeton University	Webster University
Stanford University	Western Michigan University

All but two of the schools have enrollments greater than 10,000.

c. Schools more than two mean absolute deviations from the mean

Michigan State University	University of Michigan
New York University	University of South Florida
Penn State	University of Utah
University of Miami	Western Michigan University

All but three schools have enrollments greater than 30,000.

d. As the enrollment gets larger, there is more variation in the student-faculty ratios.

Chapter Review

Problem Set 4.9

1. −51.316

2. 23.45

3. $x = 19.94$

4. Answers will vary.
   a. [1500, 3500, 250, 40, 80, 10]   **b.** [0, 110, 10, 0, 200, 20]   **c.** [0, 110, 10, 0, 110, 10]

5. $m \approx 0.024$

6. $y = 0.024x - 0.699$

7.

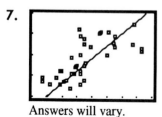

Answers will vary.

8. The domain is nonnegative numbers; that make sense in this situation. ($1667 \le$ daily calorie supply ≤ 3336). The units of the domain are calories.

9. The units of slope are years of life expectancy per number of calories.

10. For each calorie you would expect your life expectancy to increase by 0.024 yr.

11. Answers will vary between 2300 and 2400.

12. Answers will vary between 46 and 52.

13. 55.5 yr

14. (34, 51), (57, 53), (88, 69)

15. $m \approx 0.33$

16. $y = 0.33x + 37.7$

17.

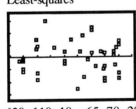

$[0, 110, 10, -20, 15, 5]$

The residuals seem to be evenly distributed above and below the line. There is no pattern in the residuals, which indicates a line is a good model.

18. The residual for Ethiopia is 1.89.

19. Guinea

20. $y = 166.8 - 1.26x$

21. For every 1 percent increase in the availability of health services, the number of infant deaths decreases by 1.26.

22. $y = -1.31x + 176.23$

Least-squares

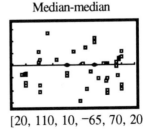

$[20, 110, 10, -65, 70, 20]$
MAD $= 21.03$

Median-median

$[20, 110, 10, -65, 70, 20]$
MAD $= 21.36$

The least-squares line is slightly better than the median-median line if you compare the MADs.

23. Least-squares model: 97.33; median-median model: 104.45

24. $r \approx -0.77$, $r^2 \approx 0.6$; 60% of the points lie in a narrow band on either side of the least-squares line.

25. $y = 165.41 - 1.25x$; $r \approx -0.86$, $r^2 \approx 0.74$

Chapter 5

Problem Set 5.1

1. **a.** Answers will vary. The curve, which appears to be a parabola, might describe the relationship between the amount of time the ball is in the air and how far away from the ground it is.
   b. Answers will vary. Some possible units are seconds and feet.
   c. Answers will vary. One possible answer is a domain of 60 sec and a range of 200 ft.
   d. No, the distance is not measured directly.

There will be many different correct answers for Problems 4–21. The graph and description should match up to justify the choice made. Be sure to consider discrete situations.

4.

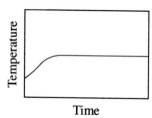

5.

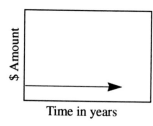

7.

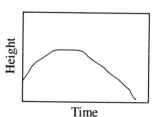

9.

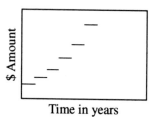

10.

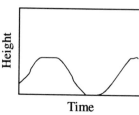

14.

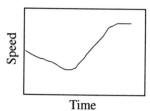

16.

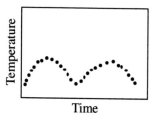

18.

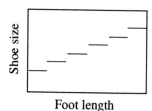

Problem Set 5.2

1. Graph A: (4, 17), (5, 21)
   Graph B: (3, 14.0625), (4, 10.547), (5, 7.910), (6, 5.933), (7, 4.449)
   Graph C: (2, 10), (3, 20), (4, 40), (5, 80), (6, 160)

2. **a.**

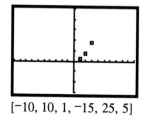

$[-10, 10, 1, -15, 25, 5]$

   b. $f(x) = x^2$

   c.

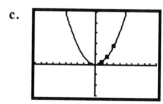

4. a.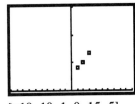

[−10, 10, 1, 0, 15, 5]

b. $4(1.3)^{(x-1)}$

c.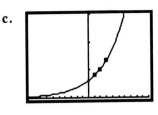

5. a. $(4, f(4))$ is 4 units right of the origin and 8.788 units up from the x-axis.

b. $(7.25, 20.616)$

c. 16.93 is the height of the segment.

d.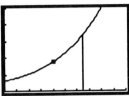

7. a.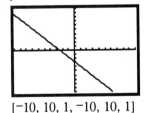

[0, 52, 4, 0, 500, 100]

$y = 100(1 + 0.03)^x$

b. $136.39

c. $465.09

d. Something that starts the year costing $100 will cost $465.09 at the end of the year.

e. 36.6 weeks

Problem Set 5.3

1. a. There are many correct answers including $(4, 0)$, $(2, ^-4)$, $(1, ^-6)$, and $(0, ^-8)$.

b. Each of the points listed works in both forms of the equation.

c. Select another point and demonstrate that it works for both equations.

3. a. The slope is $\frac{^-758}{660} \approx ^-1.1485$;
$y = ^-1.1485x - 2.7921$

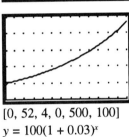

[−10, 10, 1, −10, 10, 1]

b. $y = ^-1.1485x - 0.7921$

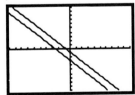

4. a. $y = \frac{^-3}{2}x - 6$

c. $y = \frac{2}{3}x + \frac{8}{3}$

e. Rectangle

b. $y = \frac{2}{3}x - 6$

d. $y = \frac{^-3}{2}x + \frac{27}{2}$

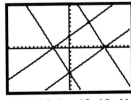

[−15, 15, 1, −10, 10, 1]

5. a. Answers will vary with the calculators. For a TI-82, a window would be $[-4.7, 4.7, 1, -3.1, 3.1, 1]$.
b. Answers will vary with the calculators. For a TI-82, a window would be $[0, 9.4, 1, 0, 6.2, 1]$.

7. a. Answers will vary. Some possible points are $(1, 1.414)$, $(2, 2.828)$ $(3, 4.243)$, $(4, 5.657)$, and so on. The equation of a best-fit line is $y = 1.414x$.
b. $k \approx 1.414$ **c.** 9.05 **d.** 24.25

8. a. \$12,500; this is the original value of the equipment.
b. ø; after 10 yr, the equipment has no value.
c. -1250; each year the value of the equipment decreases by \$1,250.
d. $y = -1{,}250x + 12{,}500$
e. After 4.8 yr

Problem Set 5.4

1. a. $y = x^2 - 6$ **b.** $y = x^2 - 3$ **c.** $y = x^2 + 2$ **d.** $y = x^2 + 4$

2. a. i. $f(x) = x^2 - 6$ ii. $f(x) = x^2 + 2$
b. i. $y = x^2 - 5$, down 5 units   ii. $y = x^2 + 4$, up 4 units
c. $f(x) + c$ is c units up or down from $f(x)$. It goes up if c is positive and down if c is negative.

3. a. $y = (x - 4)^2$ **b.** $y = (x - 7)^2$ **c.** $y = (x + 5)^2$

4. a. The graph moves 3 units to the right.   **b.** The graph moves 3 units to the left.
c. The graph moves 2 units up.   **d.** The graph moves 2 units down.

5. a. $y = (x - 2)^2$ **b.** $y = (x - 2)^2 - 5$ **c.** $y = (x + 6)^2$ **d.** $y = (x + 6)^2 + 2$

7. a. $y = -x^2$ **b.** $y = -x^2 + 2$

8. $y = -(x - 2)^2 + 2$

10. A parabola with an equation of $y = -(x - 25)^2 + 625$

12. a.

Time	0	0.5	1	1.5	2
Height	64	60	48	28	0

Average height = 40 ft

b.

Time	0	0.25	0.5	0.75	1	1.25	1.5	1.75	2
Height	64	63	60	55	48	39	28	15	0

Average height = 41.3 ft

c.

Time	0	0.1	0.2	0.3	0.4	0.5	0.6	0.7	0.8	0.9	1
Height	64	63.8	63.4	62.6	61.4	60	58.2	56.2	53.8	51.0	48

Time	1.1	1.2	1.3	1.4	1.5	1.6	1.7	1.8	1.9	2
Height	44.6	41.0	37.0	32.6	28	23.0	17.8	12.2	6.24	0

Average height = 42.13

d. The ball starts out moving slowly and speeds up as it falls. As you increase the frequency of the measurements, you are adding more large numbers to the list. This makes the average increase.

Problem Set 5.5

1. a. $y = \sqrt{x} + 3$ **b.** $y = \sqrt{x} - 4$ **c.** $y = \sqrt{x} + 1$

   d. $y = \sqrt{x} - 3$ **e.** $y = \sqrt{x + 5}$ **f.** $y = \sqrt{x - 2}$

   g. $y = \sqrt{x + 5} + 2$ **h.** $y = \sqrt{x - 3} + 1$ **i.** $y = \sqrt{x - 1} - 4$

2. a. If x is replaced with $(x - 3)$, the graph moves 3 units to the right; if it is replaced with $(x + 3)$, the graph moves 3 units to the left.

   b. If y is replaced with $(y - 2)$, the graph moves 2 units up; if it is replaced with $(y + 2)$, the graph moves 2 units down.

3. a. $y = -\sqrt{x}$ **b.** $y = -\sqrt{x} - 3$ **c.** $y = -\sqrt{x + 6} + 5$

6. a. There are x-values on each parabola that have more than one y-value.

   b. $y = \pm\sqrt{x + 4}$; $y = \pm\sqrt{x} + 2$ **c.** $y^2 = x + 4$; $(y - 2)^2 = x$

7. First, rewrite the parabola in the form $y = \pm\sqrt{x + 3} + 2$.

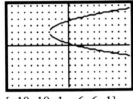

[−10, 10, 1, −6, 6, 1]

Problem Set 5.6

1. a. $y = |x| + 2$ **b.** $y = |x| - 5$

2. a. $y = |x + 4|$ **b.** $y = |x - 3|$

5. a. $y = (x - 5)^2$ **b.** $y = -|x + 4|$ **c.** $y = -|x + 4| + 3$

8. a. The graph will move 5 units to the right.

   b. The graph will flip over the y-axis.

9. $(1, 3)$; $(7, 3)$; 1 and 7

10. $y_1 = |x + 3|$, $y_2 = 5$; the solutions are 2 and −8, the x-coordinates of the intersection points.

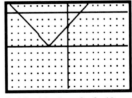

[−10, 10, 1, −6, 6, 1]

12. $|x| = \begin{cases} -x & \text{if } x < 0 \\ x & \text{if } x \geq 0 \end{cases}$

Problem Set 5.7

1. $y = 2\sqrt{1-x^2}$

2. a. $y = 3\sqrt{1-x^2}$ **b.** $y = 0.5\sqrt{1-x^2}$

3. a. 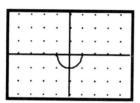   **b.** 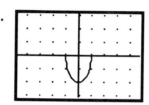   **c.**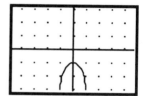

6. Graph 1: $y = -5\sqrt{1-(x+2)^2} + 3$

Graph 2: $y = 4\sqrt{1-(x-3)^2} - 2$

7. a. $y = \sqrt{1-x^2} + 2$ **b.** $y = \sqrt{1-(x+3)^2}$ **c.** $y = 2\sqrt{1-x^2}$

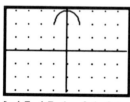   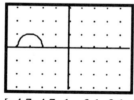 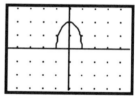

$[-4.7, 4.7, 1, -3.1, 3.1, 1]$ $[-4.7, 4.7, 1, -3.1, 3.1, 1]$ $[-4.7, 4.7, 1, -3.1, 3.1, 1]$

d. $y = \sqrt{1-\left(\frac{x}{2}\right)^2}$

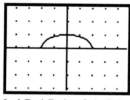

$[-4.7, 4.7, 1, -3.1, 3.1, 1]$

9. a. $y = 2\sqrt{1-\left(\frac{x}{3}\right)^2}$ **b.** $y = -2\sqrt{1-\left(\frac{x}{3}\right)^2}$

11. a. $y = +3\sqrt{1-(2x)^2}$; $y = -3\sqrt{1-(2x)^2}$
   b. $y = \pm3\sqrt{1-(2x)^2}$
   c. $y^2 = 9(1-(2x)^2)$

14. **a.** Average value = 0.546

x	−1	−0.5	0	0.5	1
$f(x)$	0	0.87	1	0.87	0

b. Average value = 0.690

x	−1	−0.8	−0.6	−0.4	−0.2	0	0.2	0.4	0.6	0.8	1
$f(x)$	0	0.6	0.8	0.92	0.98	1	0.98	0.92	0.8	0.6	0

c. For x-values spaced 0.1 units apart, the average value = 0.739.
For x-values spaced 0.01 units apart, the average value = 0.781.

d. The average value will approach 0.785.

Problem Set 5.8

1. **a.** 4 **b.** 2 **c.** −4 and 4
d. −2, 0, and 3.5 **e.** $0 \le y \le 4$ **f.** $-4 \le x \le 4$

2. **a.**

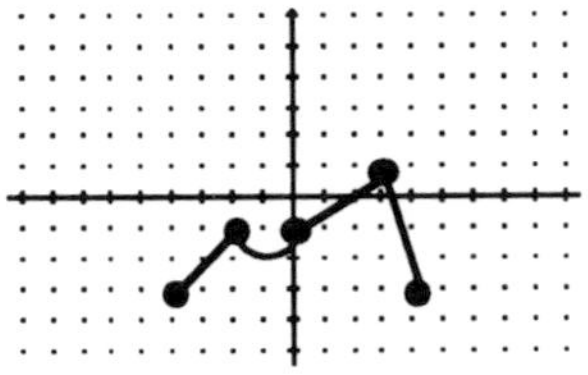

b.

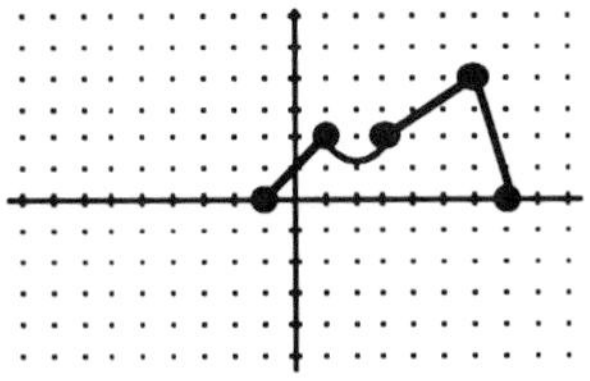

c.

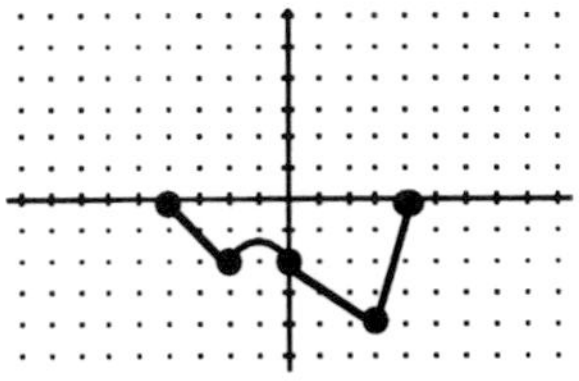

d.

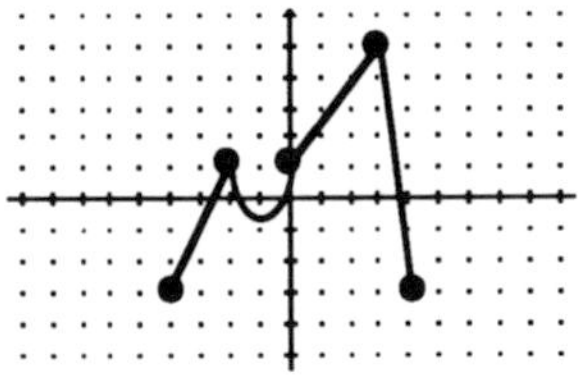

e.

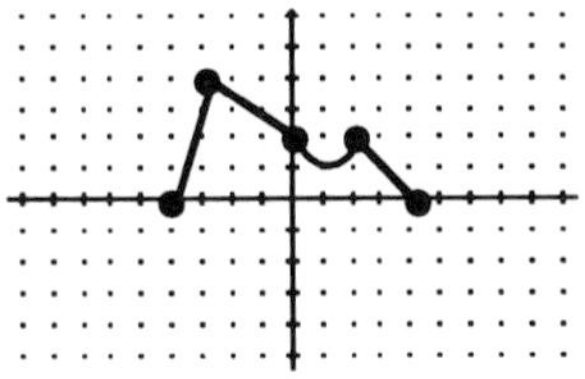

f.

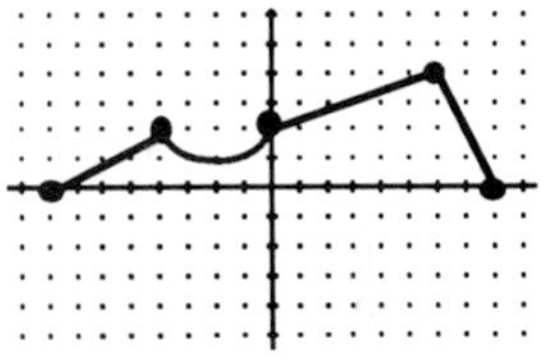

4. **a.** None

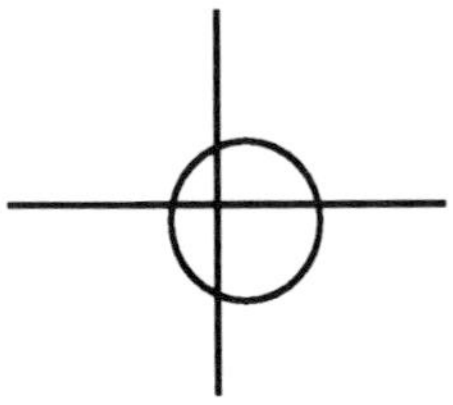

b. Some

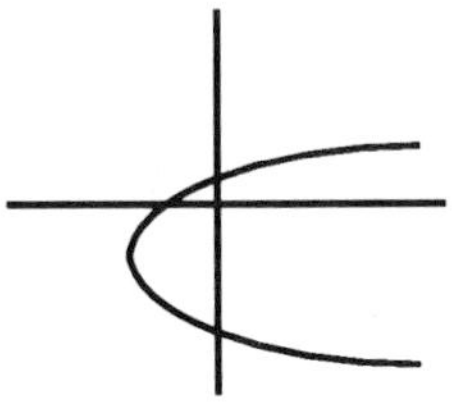

c. Some

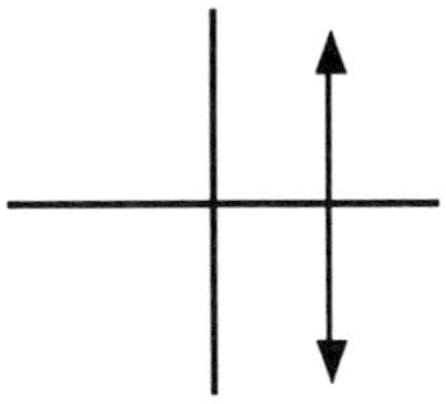

5. **a.** Stretch y-values by 2, and then slide down 3 units.
b. Slide right 4 units, and then slide down 2 units.
c. Flip vertical, slide 3 units left and 1 unit up.
d. Compress y-values by $\frac{1}{2}$, slide 2 units right and 3 units down.

8. Evaluate the function at many points. Then average these to find the average value (2). Multiply this average value by the width of the interval (3) to get the area, which is 6.

11. $y = 2(x - 2) + 6$ or $y = 2x + 2$

Problem Set 5.9

1. **a.** 12 L/min
   c. Between 40 and 45 sec

   b.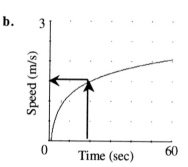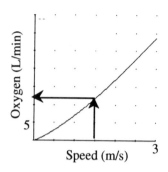

2. **a.** $y = |(x-3)^2 - 1|$
   b. $f(x) = |x|$; $g(x) = (x-3)^2 - 1$

5. **a.** 2
   b. 1

7. **a.** $g(f(2)) = 2$
   b. $f(g(-1)) = -1$
   c. $g(f(x)) = g(2x-1) = x$ for all x
   d. $f(g(x)) = f\left(\frac{1}{2}x + \frac{1}{2}\right) = x$
   e. The two functions "undo" the effects of each other, thus giving back the original starting value.

   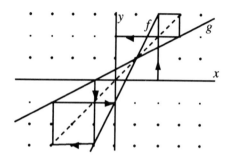

8. **a.** $f(g(3)) = 4$
   b. $f(g(2)) = 3$

   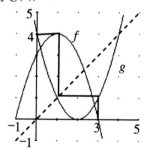 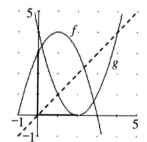

Chapter Review
Problem Set 5.10

1. For a time there are no pops. Then the popping rate begins slowly to increase. When the popping reaches a furious intensity, it seems to nearly level out. Shortly thereafter, it peaks. Then the number of pops per second drops radically to a minimal value and tapers off quickly until the last pop is heard.

   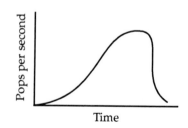

2. a. $^-7$ **b.** $^-1$ **c.** 100   **d.** $^-2x^2 + 11$

    e. $(^-2x + 8)^2$ **f.** $(^-2x + 7)^2 - 2$

3. a. The graph is translated 3 units down.   **b.** The graph is translated 3 units right.

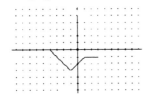   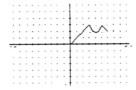

4. a. Slide the graph 2 units left and then 3 units down.

    b. Double all of the x-values. Then reflect the graph over the x-axis and slide the graph up 1 unit.

    c. Shrink the x-values by dividing them by 2, double the y-values, slide the graph 1 unit to the right, and then slide the graph 3 units up.

5. a. $y = \frac{2}{3}x - 2$ **b.** $y = \pm\sqrt{x + 3} - 1$ **c.** $y = \pm\sqrt{\left(1 - (x - 2)^2\right)}$

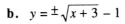

6. a. Slide the graph down 2 units.   **b.** Slide the graph 2 units to the right and then 1 unit up.

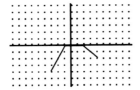   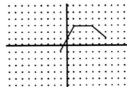

    c. Reflect the graph over the x-axis.   **d.** Double all the y-values. Then slide the graph 1 unit to the left and 3 units down.

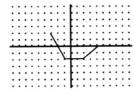   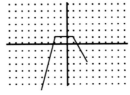

    e. Reflect the graph over the y-axis, and then slide the graph up 1 unit.   **f.** Double all the x-values, and then slide the graph 2 units down.

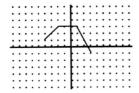   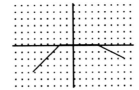

g. Reflect the graph over the *x*-axis, slide the graph 3 units to the right, and then slide the graph 1 unit up.

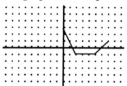

h. Multiply all the *x*-values by 1.5. Then multiple all the *y*-values by $^{-}2$, and slide the graph 1 unit right and 2 units down.

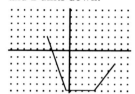

7. a. Parent function: $y = \sqrt{1 - x^2}$; equation is $y = 3\sqrt{(1 - x^2)} - 1$.

b. Parent function: $y = \sqrt{1 - x^2}$; equation is $y = 2\sqrt{1 - \left(\frac{x}{5}\right)^2} + 3$.

c. Parent function: $y = \sqrt{1 - x^2}$; equation is $y = 4\sqrt{1 - \left(\frac{x - 3}{4}\right)^2} - 1$.

d. Parent function: $y = x$; equation is $y = (x - 2)^2 - 4$

e. Parent function: $y = x^2$; equation is $y = ^{-}2(x + 1)^2$

f. Parent function: $y = \sqrt{x}$; equation is $y = ^{-}\sqrt{^{-}(x - 2)} - 3$

g. Parent function: $y = |x|$; equation is $y = 0.5|x + 2| - 2$

h. Parent function: $y = |x|$; equation is $y = ^{-}2|x - 3| + 2$

Chapter 6

Problem Set 6.1

1. a.

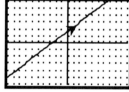

b.

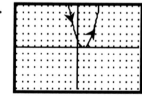

c.

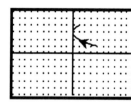

d.

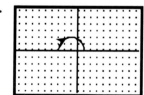

To find the *t*-interval for parts a and b, trace the graph. For part a, $^{-}3 \le t \le 2.5$ works. For part b, $^{-}2.5 \le t \le 2.5$ works.

2. a.

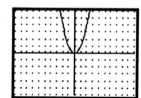

b.

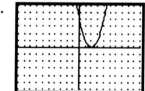

The graph is shifted to the right 2 units.

c.

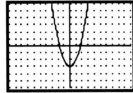

The graph is shifted down 3 units.

d.

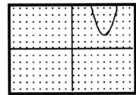

The graph will be shifted to the right 5 units and up 2 units.

e. The graph will be shifted horizontally a units and vertically b units. Answers will vary for the graphs.

4. a. This looks like the family of half-circles from Chapter 5. The parametric equations would be $x = t$ and

$$y = 2\sqrt{1 - \left(\frac{t}{2}\right)^2}.$$

b. Slide the graph 2 units to the right. The parametric equations would be $x = t + 2$ and $y = 2\sqrt{1 - \left(\frac{t}{2}\right)^2}$.

c. Flip the graph over the x-axis and slide up 1 unit. The parametric equations would be $x = t$ and

$$y = -2\sqrt{1 - \left(\frac{t}{2}\right)^2} + 1.$$

d. Stretch the graph horizontally by a factor of 2 and slide up 1 unit. The parametric equations would be

$$x = 2t \text{ and } y = 2\sqrt{1 - \left(\frac{t}{2}\right)^2} + 1.$$

Problem Set 6.2

1. a. $y = (x - 1)^2$

b. $y = \frac{2}{3}x + \frac{5}{3}$

2. a. $y = \frac{x + 7}{2}$

b. $y = \pm\sqrt{x} + 1$

4. $-\sqrt{6.2} \le t \le \sqrt{6.2}$

5. a. The graph is reflected over the x-axis.

b. The graph is reflected over the y-axis.

c. The graph is reflected over the x-axis and then the y-axis (or over the y-axis and then the x-axis).

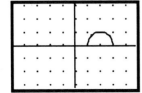 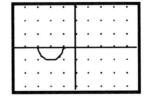

7. a. Tanker A: $x = 18t$ and $y = 1$; Tanker B: $x = 22(t - 5)$ and $y = 2$

   b. [0, 50, .5, 0, 900, 100, −1, 3, 1]

   c. $t = 27.5$ hr, $d = 495$ mi

   d. Tanker A: $x = 18t$ and $y = 1$; Tanker B: $x = 900 - 22t$ and $y = 2$. The time interval is $21.25 \le t \le 23.75$. The distances are between 382.5 and 427.5 mi out from Corpus Christi.

Problem Set 6.3

1. a. 17.334   **b.** 57.577   **c.** 22.780

2. a. 31.19°   **b.** 29.91°   **c.** 49.69°

3. a. 25.3°   **b.** 66.7 cm

4. a. The graph is a line segment at a 39° angle with the horizontal axis. The initial and end points depend on the interval used for t.

   b. Trace and select a point. Find the inverse tangent of the ratio of the x- and y-values of the point. The angle is 39°.

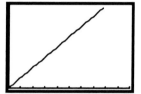

6. $x = t \cos 57°$ and $y = t \sin 57°$; an interval that includes $\dfrac{-3.1}{\sin 57°} \le t \le \dfrac{3.1}{\sin 57°}$

9. a. $x = t \cos 47°$, $y = t \sin 47°$; $\dfrac{-3.1}{\sin 47°} \le t \le \dfrac{3.1}{\sin 47°}$ (The t-interval assumes you are using a "friendly" window on a TI-82 or TI-83 in which the distance between the pixels is 0.1.)

   b. $x = t \cos 115°$, $y = t \sin 115°$; $\dfrac{-3.1}{\sin 115°} \le t \le \dfrac{3.1}{\sin 115°}$

10. a. $x = 10t \cos 30°$, $y = 10t \sin 30°$

   b. $0 \le t \le 10$

   c. The 10 represents 10 mi/hr, t represents time in hours, 30° is the angle with the x axis, x is the horizontal position at any time, and y is the vertical position at any time.

   d. Points on the graph are drawn as a simulation of the actual position of the tanker at any time t.

Problem Set 6.4

2. a. $x = 1 \cos t$, $y = 1 \sin t$

   b.

Angle A	0°	30°	45°	60°	90°	120°	135°
$\cos A$	1	0.866	0.707	0.5	0	−0.5	−0.707
$\sin A$	0	0.5	0.707	0.866	1	0.866	0.707

   c. Cosine A is the x-coordinate of the point where the line extending the central angle A crosses the perimeter of the unit circle.

   d. Sine A is the y-coordinate of the point where the line extending the central angle A crosses the perimeter of the unit circle.

3. a. $x = 2 \cos t + 2$, $y = 2 \sin t$ **b.** $x = 2 \cos t - 3$, $y = 2 \sin t$

4. a. $\cos t = \frac{x}{3}$, $\sin t = \frac{y}{3}$

b. $(\cos t)^2 = \frac{x^2}{9}$, $(\sin t)^2 = \frac{y^2}{9}$

c. $(\cos t)^2 + (\sin t)^2 = \frac{x^2}{9} + \frac{y^2}{9}$

d. $1 = \frac{x^2}{9} + \frac{y^2}{9}$

e. $9 = x^2 + y^2$ or $x^2 + y^2 = 9$

f. 3

6. a. $x = 2 \cos t$
$y = 3 \sin t$

b. $x = 4 \cos t$
$y = \sin t$

c. $x = 2 \cos t$
$y = 4 \sin t$

8. a. For Problem 7a

    a. $\cos t = \frac{x}{2}$, $\sin t = \frac{y}{3}$

    b. $(\cos t)^2 + (\sin t)^2 = \frac{x^2}{4} + \frac{y^2}{9}$

    c. $1 = \frac{x^2}{4} + \frac{y^2}{9}$

b. For Problem 7c

    a. $\cos t = \frac{x}{2.5}$, $\sin t = \frac{y-2}{1.5}$

    b. $(\cos t) + (\sin t) = \frac{x^2}{6.25} + \frac{(y-2)^2}{2.25}$

    c. $1 = \frac{x^2}{6.25} + \frac{(y-2)^2}{2.25}$

Problem Set 6.5

1. Pat moves at a compass heading of 53.1°; the pilot is on a heading of 265.4°.

2. (Assuming the river flows toward the top of the page and the boat is heading from left to right.)

    a. $y = 2t$

    b. $x = 6t$

    d. 0.5 mi downstream

    e. 1.58 mi

    c.

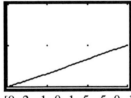

[0, 2, .1, 0, 1 .5, .5, .5, 0, 1, .5]

3. a. $y = 25t$

    b. $x = -120t$

    d. 58.3 mi to the north

    e. Approximately 286 mi

    f. 122.6 mi/hr

    c.

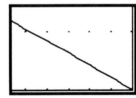

[0, 3, 0.1, −280, 0, 50, 0, 70, 50]

5. a. The plane is 975 mi north and 97.5 mi east of Orlando.

    b. It actually traveled 979.86 mi.

    c. The speed the plane traveled was 251.2 mi/hr.

    e. The heading at which the plane traveled was 5.71°.

6. a. $x = 1.5t$

    b. $y = -16t^2 + 2.75$

    c.

    d. 0.62 ft

    e. 0.41 sec

[0, 1, 0.01, 0, 2, 0.5, 0, 3, 1]

Problem Set 6.6

1. a. $y = -4t \sin A$ **b.** $y = 3t$ **c.** $48.59°$

     d. $x = 4t \cos 48.59°$ (for the boat) and $x = 0$ (for the river)

     e. $x = 4t \cos 48.59°$ and $y = -4t \sin 48.59° + 3t$

2. a.

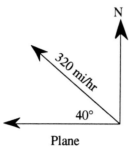

Plane

     b. Plane: $x = -320t \cos 40°$, $y = 320t \sin 40°$

c.

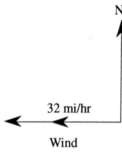

Wind

     d. Wind: $x = -32t$, $y = 0$

     e. $x = -320t \cos 40° -32t$, $y = 320t \sin 40°$

     f. 1385.7 mi west (-1385.7) and 1028.5 mi north

4. a. The plane makes a 20° angle with the axis.
The wind makes a 70° angle with the axis.

     b. Plane: $x = -220t \cos 20°$, $y = -220t \sin 20°$
Wind: $x = 40t \cos 70°$, $y = -40t \sin 70°$

     c. $x = -220t \cos 20° + 40t \cos 70°$,
$y = -220t \sin 20° - 40t \sin 70°$

     d. The plane will be 965.26 mi west and 564.16 mi
south of its starting point.

     e. The actual distance is 1118.04 mi from the start.

     f. The actual heading is 239.70°.

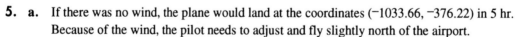

Plane   Wind

5. a. If there was no wind, the plane would land at the coordinates (-1033.66, -376.22) in 5 hr.
Because of the wind, the pilot needs to adjust and fly slightly north of the airport.

     b. Let A be the angle with the horizontal in the equations $x = -220t \cos A + 40t \cos 70°$,
$y = -220t \sin A - 40t \sin 70°$. $A = 9.56°$ gets the plane very close in about 5.08 hr.

     c.

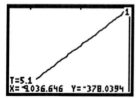

Zoom in and trace to
find (-1033, -377).

[0, 5.5, 0.1, -1200, 0, 500, -400, 0, 500]

7. a.

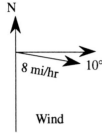

$x = 8t \cos 10°$
$y = {}^-8t \sin 10°$

Wind

b.

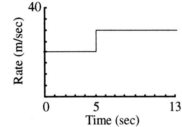

$x = 10t \cos 75°$
$y = 10t \sin 75°$

Bird

c. $x = 8t \cos 10° + 10t \cos 75°$; $y = {}^-8t \sin 10° - 10t \sin 75°$; 83.73 mi east and 88.39 mi south

d. 136.6° heading

Chapter Review

Problem Set 6.7

1. a.

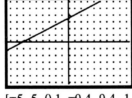

b.

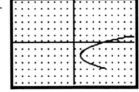

2. a.

t	x	y
3	⁻8	0.5
0	1	2
⁻3	10	⁻1

b. $y = \frac{6}{11}$

c. $x = \frac{5}{2}$

d.

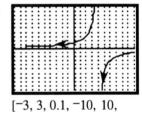

$[{}^-3, 3, 0.1, {}^-10, 10,$
$1, {}^-10, 10, 1]$

When $t = {}^-1$ the
equation is undefined.

3. a. i.

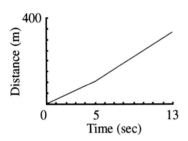

$[{}^-5, 5, 0.1, {}^-9.4, 9.4, 1, {}^-6.2, 6.2, 1]$

ii. $y = \frac{x + 7}{2}$

iii. The graph is the same as in part i.

b. i.

$[{}^-2, 6, 0.1, {}^-9.4, 9.4, 1, {}^-6.2, 6.2, 1]$

ii. $y = \pm \sqrt{x - 1} - 2$

iii. The graph is the same except for restrictions
for t.

c. i.

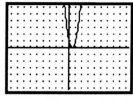

$[{-4}, 3, 0.1, {-9.4}, 9.4, 1, {-6.2}, 6.2, 1]$

ii. $y = (2x - 1)^2$

iii. The graph in this window is the same as in part i.

d. i.

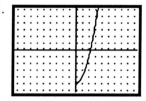

$[{-5}, 10, 0.1, {-9.4}, 9.4, 1, {-6.2}, 6.2, 1]$

ii. $y = x^2 - 5$

iii. The parametric graph shows only one side of the parabola. The equation in ii gives the complete parabola.

4. Problem 3a

i. $\cdot x = {-(2t - 5)}, y = t + 1$

iii. $x = 2t - 5, y = t + 4$

ii. $x = 2t - 5, y = {-(t + 1)}$

iv. $x = 2t - 9, y = t - 1$

Problem 3c

i. $x = -\frac{t+1}{2}, y = t^2$

iii. $x = \frac{t+1}{2}, y = t^2 + 3$

ii. $x = \frac{t+1}{2}, y = {-(t^2)}$

iv. $x = \frac{t+1}{2} - 4, y = t^2 - 2$

5. **a.** 42.83° **b.** 28.30° **c.** 22.98 **d.** 12.86

e. 21.36 **f.** 17.11

6.

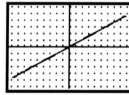

$[{-10}, 10, 0.1, {-9.4}, 9.4, 1, {-6.2}, 6.2, 1]$; angle is 28°.

7. Using the edge of the pool as the point $(0, 0)$, the x-equation would be $x = 4t + 1.5$ and the y-equation would be $y = {-4.9}t^2 + 10$. She hits at a point 7.2 m from the edge.

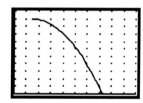

8. 1.43 ft/sec

9. No, he will miss the monkey.

10. He will hit the monkey. Both the monkey and the dart are falling at the same rate.

11. Flying at a heading of 107.77° will take him to his destination if the wind averages 25 mi/hr. If the wind were 30 mi/hr continuously, he could miss his destination by as much as 8 mi.

Chapter 7

Problem Set 7.1

1. a. $y = 1.151(1 + 0.015)^x$
   b.

Year	Population (in billions)
1991	1.151
1992	1.168
1993	1.186
1994	1.204
1995	1.222
1996	1.240
1997	1.259
1998	1.277
1999	1.297
2000	1.316

   c. 2063, 3.364 billion
   d. Answers will vary. (The dangers involved in this long-range prediction are great.)

2. a. $y_n = 2.56(2.5)^x$; fifth day: 250; sixth day: 625   **b.** $7.56(2.5)^{3.5} \approx 63.25$
   c. 728 cm   **d.** 11 days 13 hr; 9 p.m. on day 11

4. Answers will vary between 2000 and 2300. The actual value is approximately 2056.

Problem Set 7.2

1. a. $49^{5/2}$ is the square root of 49 raised to the fifth power = 16,807.
   b. $16^{3/4}$ is the fourth root of 16 raised to the third power = 8.
   c. $64^{5/3}$ is the cube root of 64 raised to the fifth power = 1024.
   d. $32^{2/5}$ is the fifth root of 32 squared = 4.

2. a. 16 kg   **b.** 25 kg   **c.** 91 cm

3. a. $x^{1/4}$ **b.** $x^{3/5}$

4. a. 128   **b.** 81

6. a. $\sqrt[3]{x^2}$ **b.** $\sqrt[4]{x^{11}}$ or $x^2\sqrt[4]{x^3}$

8. a. $b(x) = \begin{cases} 1 & \text{if } x = 0 \\ b(x-1) \cdot 1.04 & \text{if } x > 0 \end{cases}$ **b.** $b(x) = 1.04^x$ **c.** About 100 yr

10. a. 4000 is the initial investment.
   b. You are earning 7.2% interest on your investment.
   c. The interest is compounded monthly.
   d. This is one month after the investment was made.
   e. This is at the time the investment was made.
   f. This is one month before the investment was made.
   g. $x \approx 115.9$

Problem Set 7.3

1. a. $\frac{1}{27} = 0.037037\ldots$
  b. $\frac{1}{5} = 0.2$
  c. -216
  d. $\frac{1}{144} = 0.0069444\ldots$

2. a. $\frac{1}{8x^3}$
  b. $\frac{2}{x^3}$
  c. $x^{7/6}$
  d. $2x^{3/2}$

5. a. -2
  b. -3
  c. -5
  d. 0

6. As the base increases, the graphs become steeper. They all intersect the y-axis at $(0, 1)$. The graph of $y = 6^x$ should be the steepest one. It will contain the points $(0, 1)$ and $(1, 6)$.

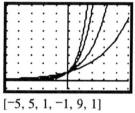

$[-5, 5, 1, -1, 9, 1]$

7. As the base increases, the graphs flatten out. They all intersect the y-axis at $(0, 1)$. All of these equations involve raising a number between 0 and 1 to a power. The graph of the equation $y = 0.1^x$ should be steeper than any of these given. It will contain the points $(0, 1)$ and $(-1, 10)$.

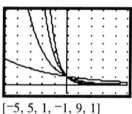

$[-5, 5, 1, -1, 9, 1]$

8. Each equation in Problem 6 involves a base larger than 1. In Problem 7 each base is less than 1.
  a. $y = 2.5^x$
  b. $y = 0.35^x$

Problem Set 7.4

1. a. $x = t + 2, y = 2t - 3$

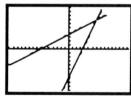

$[-6, 6, 0.1, -15, 15, 1, -10, 10, 1]$

  b. $x = t + 1, y = t^2$

$[-6, 6, 0.1, -15, 15, 1, -10, 10, 1]$

  c. $x = \frac{t-2}{3}, y = \frac{1}{2}t + 1$

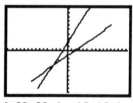

$[-20, 20, 1, -15, 15, 1, -10, 10, 1]$

  d. $x = 2(t - 1)^2, y = t - 3$

$[-10, 10, 1, -15, 15, 1, -10, 10, 1]$

  e. The original graph and its inverse are symmetric with respect to the line $y = x$.
  f. $x = t, y = t$

2. Graph c is the inverse because the x- and y-coordinates have been switched from the original graph and both graphs are symmetric to the line $y = x$.

3. a. $y = 2x - 11$ **b.** $x = 2t - 1, y = t + 5$ **c.** $x = 2y - 11$

    d. The nonparametric equations are exactly the same except that the variables have been switched.

5. Answers will vary; $t \geq 3$ works and so does $t \leq 3$.

7. a. Answers will vary. One possibility: $x = t$ and $y = (t + 1)^2 - 2$.

    b. $x = (t + 1)^2 - 2, y = t$ **c.** $x = (y + 1)^2 - 2$ or $y = \pm\sqrt{x + 2} - 1$

    d. $f(x) = (x + 1)^2 - 2$. The inverse is not a function, so it will take two equations to write it:
    $y = \sqrt{x + 2} - 1$ and $y = -\sqrt{x + 2} - 1$.

8. a. $f(x) = 2x - 3$ and $f^{-1}(x) = \frac{x + 3}{2}$ **b.** $f(x) = \frac{4 - 3x}{2}$ and $f^{-1}(x) = \frac{4 - 2x}{3}$

    c. $f(x) = \frac{-1}{2}x^2 + \frac{3}{2}$; the inverse is not a function, so $f^{-1}(x)$ notation doesn't apply: $y = \pm\sqrt{-2x + 3}$.

Problem Set 7.5

1. a. 2.187   **b.** 29.791   **c.** No solution   **d.** 625   **e.** 1

2. a. $9x^4$ **b.** $8x^6$

3. 0.109 or 10.9%

4. a. $P = 4 \cdot 1.02^t$ where t is number of years since 1975.

    b. Answers will vary.

    c. Answers will vary.

6. a.

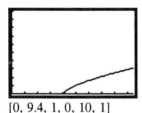

[0, 9.4, 1, 0, 10, 1]

b.

[−4.7, 4.7, 1, −3.1, 3.1, 1]

c.

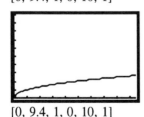

[0, 9.4, 1, 0, 10, 1]

d.

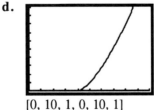

[0, 10, 1, 0, 10, 1]

8. a.

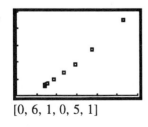

[0, 6, 1, 0, 5, 1]

    b. The least-squares line of best fit is $y = -0.8118 + 9.681x$. The residuals form a definite pattern, which means the line is not a good fit.

    c. Answers will vary but should be close to $y = 0.37x^{1.5}$. For this equation there is no pattern in the residuals.

Problem Set 7.6

1. a. $10^x = 1000$ **b.** $5^x = 625$ **c.** $7^x = \sqrt{7}$ **d.** $8^x = 2$

  e. $5^x = \dfrac{1}{25}$ **f.** $6^x = 1$

4. The window used for all of the graphs is $[^-4.7, 4.7, 1, ^-3.1, 3.1, 1]$.

a.

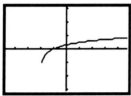

The graph is shifted 2 units to the left of $y = \log x$.

b.

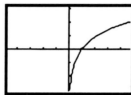

The graph of $y = \log x$ is stretched vertically by a factor of 3.

c.

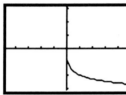

The graph is flipped over the x-axis and then shifted 2 units down from $y = \log x$.

5. In about 25 min

7. a. $C_1 = 32.7$, $C_2 = 65.4$, $C_3 = 130.8$, $C_6 = 1046.4$, $C_7 = 2092.8$, $C_8 = 4185.6$

  b. $y = 16.35(2)^x$

  c. Answers will vary, but string lengths are related to the frequencies. Longer lengths have shorter frequencies.

8. a. $y = 100(0.999879)^x$ **b.** Approximately 6002 yr ago; answers will vary.

Problem Set 7.7

1. a. $\log 10$ **b.** $\log 100$ **c.** $\log 900$ **d.** $\log 200$

  e. To get the answer, multiply the arguments.

  f. Answers are the same as for parts 1a.–1d.

  g. $\log a + \log b = \log ab$

  h. Logs are exponents, and when you multiply exponential expressions with the same base, you add the exponents.

3. a. i. 0.3 ii. 0.9 **b.** $\log 2^3 = 3 \log 2$

  c. i. 1.7 ii. 3.4 **d.** $\log 50^2 = 2 \log 50$

  e. Answers are the same. **f.** $\log a^b = b \log a$

  g. Yes **h.** $\dfrac{1}{2} \log a$

5. Answers will vary. For example, the log of a product is the sum of the logs. The log of a quotient is the difference of the logs. The log of a number raised to a power is the power times the log of the number.

6. Answers will vary. For example, if a horizontal line will intersect f in more than one point, its inverse is not a function.

9. a. $x + y$ **b.** $z - x$

10. a. 4 **b.** 1.292

11. a.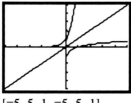

[−5, 5, 1, −5, 5, 1]

b.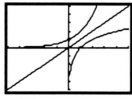

[−5, 5, 1, −5, 5, 1]

c.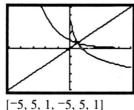

[−5, 5, 1, −5, 5, 1]

d. The domain of $f(f^{-1}(x))$ is all positive real numbers, while the domain of $f^{-1}(f(x))$ is all real numbers. The difference is that the inside function in $f(f^{-1}(x))$ is a logarithm that uses only positive values, while in $f^{-1}(f(x))$ the inside function is an exponential that can accept any real number as an input.

12. a. True **b.** False **c.** True **d.** True
e. True **f.** True

Problem Set 7.8

1. About 195.9 mo

2. a. 1.779

b. By definition, $12.85 = 4.2^x$ is $x = \log_{4.2} 12.85$. Using the change of base property, $x = \frac{\log 12.85}{\log 4.2}$. If you took the log of both sides, you would have $\log 12.85 = \log 4.2^x$; using the logarithm power property, $\log 12.85 = x\log 4.2$; dividing both sides by $\log 4.2, \frac{\log 12.85}{\log 4.2} = x$. Using the definition of logarithms or "taking the log" of both sides results in the same solution.

3. a. 2.903 **b.** 11 **c.** −4

4. a. 17.3 ft² **b.** 114 lb

6. a. 30 dB **b.** 65 dB **c.** $5 \cdot 10^{-6}$ W/cm² **d.** 3.16 times louder

Problem Set 7.9

1. $y = 0.21\sqrt{x}$

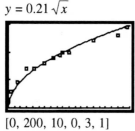

[0, 200, 10, 0, 3, 1]

(x, y)

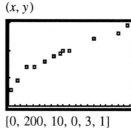

[0, 200, 10, 0, 3, 1]

$(x, \log y)$

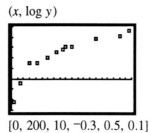

[0, 200, 10, −0.3, 0.5, 0.1]

(log *x*, log *y*) (log *x*, *y*)

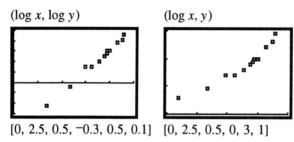

[0, 2.5, 0.5, −0.3, 0.5, 0.1]   [0, 2.5, 0.5, 0, 3, 1]

The graph of (log *x*, log *y*) appears to be the most linear; $y \approx 0.303x^{0.417}$. (Answers will vary depending on the method used to find the equation of the line. Be sure to check your answer graphically to make sure it appears to fit).

2. **a.**

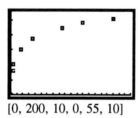

[0, 200, 10, 0, 55, 10]

b. (log *x*, *y*)

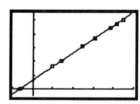

[−0.5, 2.5, 0.5, −5, 55, 10]

c. The equation should be close to $y = 20x + 6$.

d.

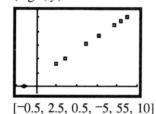

e. $y = 20 \log x + 6$ (Answers will vary depending on the method used to find the equation of the line. Be sure to check your answer graphically to make sure the equation fits.)

f.

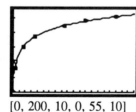

[0, 200, 10, 0, 55, 10]

4. **a.**

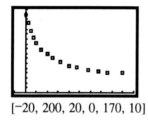

[−20, 200, 20, 0, 170, 10]

b.

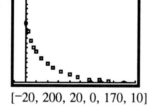

[−20, 200, 20, 0, 170, 10]

c.

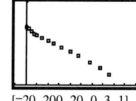

[−20, 200, 20, 0, 3, 1]

d. $y = 2.062 - 0.0113x$ **e.** $y = 115.35(0.9743^x) + 40$ **f.**

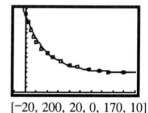

[−20, 200, 20, 0, 170, 10]

5. a.

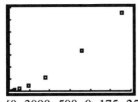

[0, 3000, 500, 0, 175, 25]

b. LinReg($a + bx$): $r = 0.9885$

c. ExpReg: $r = 0.8857$
PwrReg: $r = 0.999999$

d.

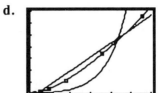

e. Residual plot for the
linear regression

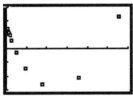

[0, 3000, 500, −15, 15, 5]

Residual plot for the
exponential regression

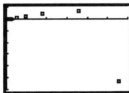

[0, 3000, 500, −300, 50, 50]

Residual plot for the
power regression

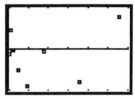

[0, 3000, 500, −0.01, 0.01. 0.01]

Chapter Review

Problem Set 7.10

1. a. $\frac{1}{16}$ **b.** $-\frac{1}{3}$ **c.** 125 **d.** 7 **e.** $\frac{1}{4}$

f. $\frac{27}{64}$ **g.** −1 **h.** 12 **i.** 0.6

2. a. $\log xy$ **b.** $\log z - \log v$ **c.** $2.1x^{6.8}$ **d.** $k \log w$ **e.** $x^{1/5}$

f. $\frac{\log t}{\log 5}$

3. a. 2.153 **b.** 2.231 **c.** 2.344 **d.** $1.242 \cdot 10^{23}$ **e.** 3.041

f. 45.897 **g.** 5902 **h.** 612

4. a. 0.50 **b.** 2.4998 **c.** 0.63; the first 0.63 min is free. **d.** $4.19

e. 3.98 min

5. a.

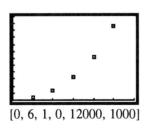

[0, 6, 1, 0, 12000, 1000]

b. $(x, \log y)$ $(\log x, \log y)$ $(\log x, y)$

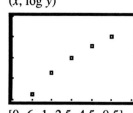 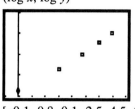 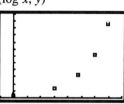

[0, 6, 1, 2.5, 4.5, 0.5]   [−0.1, 0.8, 0.1, 2.5, 4.5, 0.5]   [−0.1, 0.8, 0.1, 0, 12000, 1000]

c. The graphs of $(x, \log y)$ and $(\log x, \log y)$ both look more linear than $(\log x, y)$, indicating that the best fit for the original data is either a power regression or an exponential regression. The exponential regression on the calculator gives you $y = 249.15(2.20)^x$ with $r = 0.988$. The power regression gives you $y = 398.14x^{1.98}$ with $r = 0.997$. To determine which is indeed the best fit for the original data, you need to calculate the residuals. Answers will vary as to which regression provides the better fit.

d. Using the exponential regression: 1990 = 136,046; 1995 = 6,989,589; 2000 = 359,101,100
Using the power regression: 1990 = 24,386; 1995 = 63,737; 2000 = 121,357

e. Using the power regression: 1981 + 52 yr or the year 2033.
Using the exponential regression: 1981 + 11 yr or the year 1992.

6. a. There are many ways to select data points: using midpoints of the intervals, using one point for each year, and other methods. The equations generated will vary depending on the choice of method. However, the answers for parts b and c should be similar. Using (55, 0.75) as the first value, and each time the wage changed as a data point, the power regression equation is $y \approx (1.3592 \cdot 10^{-6})x^{3.3185}$. The exponential regression equation is $y = 0.067(1.05)^x$. Answers will vary as to which is the better model for the data.

b. Power regression: 2000, $5.40; 2010, $7.12; 2020, $9.39; exponential regression: 2000, $8.81; 2010, $14.35; 2020, $23.38

c. Power regression: $0.28; exponential regression: $0.43

Chapter 8

Problem Set 8.1

Many of the questions in this problem set ask the student to devise a method to randomly select an outcome or to generate a set of random numbers. In these answers, one example is given, but it is by no means the only method.

2. a. Answers will vary.

b. Theoretically, $\frac{1}{5}$ of the students or 20 should be assigned to each bus.

c. Alter the Random Number Generator Routine to `seq (int 5rand + 1,x,1,99,1)→L`$_1$. You will need to do one more roll to get 100 rolls.

3. Each one of these procedures for producing random numbers has shortcomings.

a. Middle numbers (3 through 7) occur more commonly than 1, 2, 8, or 9.

b. Very few pencils will be 0 in. or 1 in. in length.

c. Books tend to open to pages that are used more than others.

d. Answers will vary. You could alter the Random Number Generator Routine to `seq (int 9rand + 1,x,1,99,1)→L`$_1$. (See Calculator Note 8B.)

5. e. Answers will vary. Average numbers should be about 22 boxes.

7. a. i. $-2 < x < 4$ ii. $\{1, 2, 3\}$

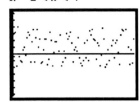

b. i. 5 rand – 4 ii. int 4 rand – 4 iii. int 3 rand + 2

Problem Set 8.2

1. a. 36 different outcomes
   b. 6 different outcomes, all in the column representing green 4
   c. 12 different outcomes, all in the rows representing white 2 and white 3
   d. 3 different outcomes

2. a. $x + y = 9$ (4 different outcomes)
   b. $x + y = 6$ (5 different outcomes)
   c. $x - y = 1$ or $y - x = 1$ (10 different outcomes)
   d. $x + y = 6$ and $x - y = 2$ (1 outcome)
   e. $x + y \le 5$ (10 different outcomes)

3. a. $4; \frac{4}{36}$ **b.** $5; \frac{5}{36}$ **c.** $10; \frac{10}{36}$ **d.** $1; \frac{1}{36}$ **e.** $10; \frac{10}{36}$

5. a. 144 **b.** 44 **c.** 0.306 **d.** $\frac{44}{144} = 0.306$ **e.** 0.694
   f. 0; 0

7. a. $x + y \le 6$ **b.** 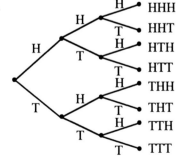 **c.** 0.28

Problem Set 8.3

1. a. 24 **b.** $\frac{1}{4}$ **c.** $\frac{2}{24}$ or $\frac{1}{12}$ **d.** $\frac{1}{24}$ **e.** $\frac{23}{24}$
   f. $\frac{12}{24}$ or $\frac{1}{2}$

2. a.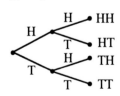

b.

H
  H HHH
  T HHT
  H HTH
H
  T HTT
  H THH
  T
  H TTH
T
  T TTT

3. a. 2^2 **b.** 2^3 **c.** 2^4

5. a. 0.0625 **b.** 0.25 **c.** 0.375 **d.** 0.25 **e.** 0.0625
 f. 1 **g.** 0.313

7.

	Liberal	Conservative	Totals
Age under 30	210	145	355
Age 30–45	235	220	455
Age over 45	280	410	690
Totals	725	775	1500

a. 0.187 **b.** 0.517 **c.** 0.408 **d.** 0.187

8. a.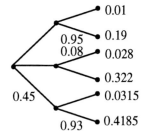

b. 0.08
c. 0.0695
d. 0.4029

9.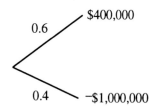

a. 0.0289
b. 0.9711
c. 0.6889

Problem Set 8.4

1. d. ⁻0.25

3. a.

$400,000
0.6

0.4 ⁻$1,000,000

b. ⁻$160,000
c. Answers will vary.

4. a. 4.9% **b.** 7.9% **c.** 1.88 birds

6. b. P(testing positive) = $\dfrac{\text{number of positive tests}}{\text{number of people tested}}$

 c. P(having disease if tested positive) = $\dfrac{\text{number of diseased people testing positive}}{\text{number of people testing positive}}$

d.

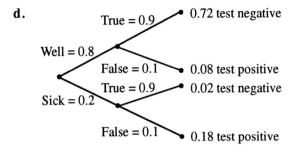

Problem Set 8.5

1. a. 3 colors

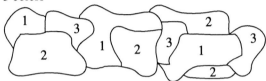

3. a. 3

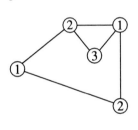

b. 4

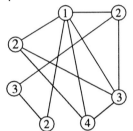

c. 5

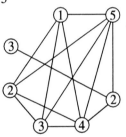

4. Draw the diagram as suggested in the problem. Connect each vertex (class) with an edge to any other class with which they should not be grouped. Any two vertices (classes) that are connected by an edge must be different colors or numbers. The best schedule will have 5 exam periods. The following is one possible solution.

Period 1: L1, L2, L3, L5, H3, P3, S3
Period 2: M1, M2, M4, S2, S4, P1
Period 3: E1, E2, E3, E4
Period 4: H1, H2, M3, M5, P2
Period 5: S1, L4, L6, H3, P3

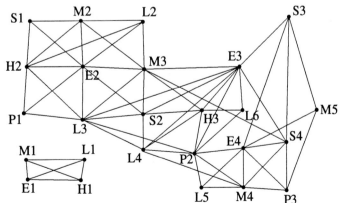

Problem Set 8.6

1.
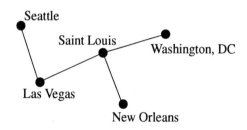

2. a. 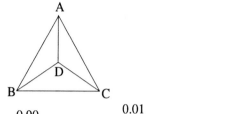   **b.**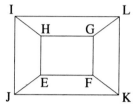

5. a.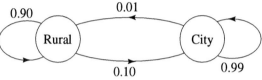

b.

	City	Rural
City	0.99	0.01
Rural	0.10	0.90

c. i. $\begin{bmatrix} 16.74 & 8.26 \end{bmatrix}$

ii. $\begin{bmatrix} 17.3986 & 7.6014 \end{bmatrix}$

iii. $\begin{bmatrix} 17.984754 & 7.015246 \end{bmatrix}$

Problem Set 8.7

1. $\begin{bmatrix} 43.15 & 196.84 \end{bmatrix}$

4. a. $\begin{bmatrix} 7 & 54 \end{bmatrix}$ **b.** $\begin{bmatrix} 0.815 & 0.185 \\ 0.0925 & 0.9075 \end{bmatrix}$ **c.** $\begin{bmatrix} 15.6 & ^-10.8 \\ 10.7 & 42.2 \end{bmatrix}$ **d.** $\begin{bmatrix} 180 & ^-230 \\ 54 & 322 \end{bmatrix}$

5. a. $\begin{bmatrix} 29 & 211 \end{bmatrix}$ **b.** $\begin{bmatrix} 36.65 & 203.35 \end{bmatrix}$ **c.** $\begin{bmatrix} 43.1525 & 196.84751 \end{bmatrix}$ **d.** $\begin{bmatrix} 80 & 160 \end{bmatrix}$

6. a. $\begin{bmatrix} 0.815 & 0.185 \\ 0.0925 & 0.9075 \end{bmatrix}$ **b.** $\begin{bmatrix} 0 & 0 & 0 \\ 0 & 4 & 0 \\ 0 & 0 & 0 \end{bmatrix}$

7. a.

	Low	Average	High
Low	0.5	0.45	0.05
Average	0.25	0.5	0.25
High	0.3	0.3	0.4

b. After one generation $\begin{bmatrix} 0.32 & 0.4575 & 0.2225 \end{bmatrix}$
After two generations
$\begin{bmatrix} 0.341125 & 0.4395 & 0.219375 \end{bmatrix}$
After three generations
$\begin{bmatrix} 0.34625 & 0.43906875 & 0.21468125 \end{bmatrix}$
In the long run
$\begin{bmatrix} 0.3474903475 & 0.4401544402 & 0.2123552124 \end{bmatrix}$

Chapter Review

Problem Set 8.8

2. Answers will vary.
   a. Look for a well shuffled full deck after each draw to ensure a random pick each time.
   b. A painfully slow method if you need many numbers. Will randomness depend on who is called?
   c. This depends on randomness involved in falling off and besides, the numbers 1–12 aren't equally likely.

3. **a.** int 10 rand + 3   **b.** int 10 rand – 7   **c.** 5 rand – 2

4. **a.** $\frac{1}{2}$ **b.** 17.765

5. **a.** 64 possible outcomes   **b.** 10 possible outcomes
   c. $\frac{10}{64} \approx 0.156$ **d.** $\frac{49}{64} \approx 0.766$

6. **a.** There are 32 branches.   **b.** 10 ways   **c.** 0.375

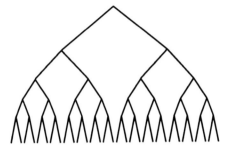

7. **a.**

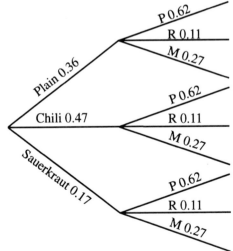

   b. 0.0517
   c. 0.8946
   d. 0.3501

8. **a.**

	9th grade	10th grade	11th grade	12th grade	Total
Ice cream	18	37	85	114	254
Whipped cream	5	18	37	58	118
Total	23	55	122	172	372

b. 0.673

d. 0.071

c. 0.303

e. 0.317

9. 11.05

10. $[479.167 \quad 520.833]; [400 \quad 600]$

Chapter 9

Problem Set 9.1

1. a. $(0, 1), (1, 2), (5, 26)$ **b.** When $x < 0$ or when $1 < x < 5$; when $0 < x < 1$ or $x > 5$

2. b. 1.25, 1.176470588, 0.0735294118; y_3 is the difference between y_1 and y_2.
  c. $y_3 = 0$
  d. The graph never crosses the x-axis.
  e. The equations do not intersect.

4. a. The springs are the same length when 48.57 g of mass are added.
  b. When 120 g have been added, the second spring is 10 cm longer.

7. a. Answers will vary depending on the regression equations used. If least-squares lines are used, they intersect in approximately the year 2022.
  b. Answers will vary. The least-squares lines are $y = 162.04 - 0.54x$ for men and $y = 198.76 - 0.84x$ for women if 1900 is listed as $x = 0$.
  d. For the 1994 Olympics, $x = 94$. Using the men's model, the predicted time would be $y = 162.04 - 0.54(94) = 111.28$ sec $= 1.85$ min or 1:51. The model is off $1:51.29 - 1:51 = 0.29$ sec. Using the women's model, the predicted time would be $y = 198.76 - 0.84(94) = 119.8$ sec $= 2.00$ min. The model is off by $2:02.19 - 2:00 = 2.19$ sec. The actual times are close to the predicted times of the models. The residual for the 1994 mens' time is 0.005 min and for the 1994 women's time is 0.0305 min.

Problem Set 9.2

1. a. $(-4.7, 29.57)$ **b.** $\left(6\frac{2}{3}, 1\frac{4}{9}\right)$ **c.** $(-3.36, 9.308)$

2. a. $(13.42, 4.47)$ and $(-13.42, -4.47)$ **b.** $(1.41, -2.59)$ and $(-1.41, -5.41)$

3. a. $y = 47 + 11.5x$; $y = 59 + 4.95x$ **b.** $x \approx 1.83$ yr **c.** Answers will vary.

4. a. $(-0.53297, 2.71429)$ **b.** $\left(8, -\frac{5}{2}\right)$

5. Graphing windows will vary.

  a.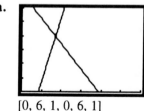

  $[0, 6, 1, 0, 6, 1]$

  b.

  $[0, 6, 1, 0, 6, 1]$

  c. $1.8y = 8.46x - 7.2$
     $4.7y = -8.46x + 32.9$
  d. $y \approx 3.954$

6. a. Multiply by 3; $y \approx 2.475$; $(-0.9088, 2.4746)$
   b. Multiply by -3; $y \approx -6.786$; $(6.286, -6.786)$

11. The 31st term; 21

Problem Set 9.3

1. a. ii, iii
   b. The lines are parallel.
   c. The result is a numerical impossibility.
   d. The lines have the same slope.

2. Answers will vary. Samples are given below.
   a. $y = 2x + b$ where b is any number except 4.
   b. $y = \frac{-1}{3}x + b$ where b is any number except -3.
   c. $2x + 5y = b$ where b is any number except 10.
   d. $x - 2y = b$ where b is any number except -6.

3. a. ii, iii
   b. The lines are the same.
   c. The result is a true statement.
   d. They have the same slope and the same intercept; or they are multiples of each other.

4. Answers will vary. Samples are given below.
   a. $2y = 4x + 8$, or multiply the original equation by any other number.
   b. $3y = -x - 9$, or multiply the original equation by any other number.

5. a. $t = 0.25, x = 1.75, y = -1.5$
   b. No solution

7. $a = 100$ and $b = 0.7$

10. a. Answers will vary. If a least-squares model is used for both populations, the lines intersect approximately in the year 1996.
   b. 903,634 people
   c. The least-squares lines are $y = -830,011.6 + 18,051.82x$ and $y = 293,0012.7 - 21,099.93x$.

Problem Set 9.4

1. a. $\begin{bmatrix} 15 & -19 \\ 22 & -27 \end{bmatrix}$
   b. $\begin{bmatrix} 7 & -18 & -7 \\ 12 & -27 & 42 \\ 1 & -4 & -21 \end{bmatrix}$
   c. This is not possible because you need the same number of rows in the second matrix as you have columns in the first matrix.

2. a. $a = 3, b = -7, c = -2, d = 8$
   b. $a = \frac{-1}{14}, b = \frac{5}{28}, c = \frac{3}{14}, d = \frac{-1}{28}$

3. a. Yes, it's an inverse.
   c. Answers will vary. Two matrices are inverses if when you multiply them together you get the identity matrix as the answer.

4. a. $\begin{bmatrix} 4 & -3 \\ -5 & 4 \end{bmatrix}$
   b. $\begin{bmatrix} -0.5555 & 1.4444 & 0.1111 \\ 0.5 & -1 & 0 \\ -1.6666 & 2.3333 & 0.3333 \end{bmatrix}$

5. a. $\begin{bmatrix} 5.2 & 3.6 \\ -5.2 & 2 \end{bmatrix}\begin{bmatrix} x \\ y \end{bmatrix} = \begin{bmatrix} 7 \\ 8.2 \end{bmatrix}$

6. a. $\begin{bmatrix} 4 \\ 3 \end{bmatrix}$ **b.** $\begin{bmatrix} -3 \\ 1 \end{bmatrix}$

8. a. The three equations are: $7t + 3a + 9s = 19.55$; $9t + 10a = 13$; $8t + 7a + 10s = 24.95$
Rides for the timid cost $0.50. Rides for the adventurous cost $0.85. Rides for the thrill seekers cost $1.50.

   b. $28.50

   c. Carey would have been better off buying a ticket book for $28.50 because it cost her $24.95 + $5.00 or $29.95.

Problem Set 9.5

1. $y \geq 2.4x + 2$ and $y \leq {}^-x^2 - 2x + 6.4$; All inequations are shaded so that the feasible region is not shaded.

2.

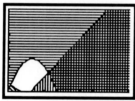

[0, 10, 1, 0, 10, 1]

Vertex points: (0, 2), (0, 5), (2.752, 3.596), (3.529, 2.353)

3.

Vertex points: (1, 0), (1.875, 0), (3.307, 2.291), (0.209, 0.791)

[0, 10, 1, 0, 10, 1]

6. a. $xy \geq 200$, $xy \leq 300$, $x + y \geq 33$, $x + y \leq 40$ or $y \geq \frac{200}{x}$, $y \leq \frac{300}{x}$, $y \geq 33 - x$, $y \leq 40 - x$

   b.

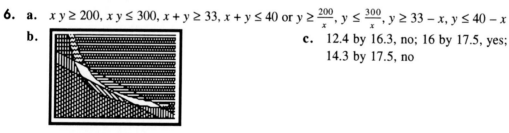

   c. 12.4 by 16.3, no; 16 by 17.5, yes; 14.3 by 17.5, no

8. a. First, substitute the given point values for x and y in the generic equation. There will be three equations in three variables, a, b, and c. Set up a matrix equation in the form [A] [X] = [B] and find [X].

   b. The parabola is $3x^2 + 16x - 12$.

Problem Set 9.6

Change the window format to Grid On in order to see the integer points in the feasible region. All inequations are shaded such that the feasible region is not shaded. Points on the border are part of the interior also because the inequations are not strict inequations.

1. i. **a.** $y \leq \frac{-2x + 6}{3}$, $y \leq 6 - 4x$, $x > 0$, $y > 0$

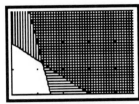

[0, 4.7, 1, 0, 3.2, 1]

b. (0, 0), (1.5, 0), (1.2, 1.2), (0, 2)

c. (0, 0), (0, 1), (0, 2), (1, 0), (1, 1);
The maximum value of 7 occurs at (1, 1).

ii. **a.** $y \leq 10 - x$, $y \geq \frac{20 - 5x}{2}$, $y \geq \frac{x}{2}$,
$x > 0$, $y > 0$

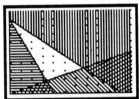

[0, 11, 1, 0, 11, 1]

b. (3.3333, 1.6667), (6.6667, 3.3333), (0, 10)

c. (0, 10), (1, 8), (1, 9), (2, 6), (2, 7), (2, 8), (3, 3),
(3, 4), (3, 5), (3, 6), (3, 7), (4, 2), (4, 3), (4, 4),
(4, 5), (4, 6), (5, 3), (5, 4), (5, 5), (6, 3), (6, 4).
The minimum value of 10 occurs at (4, 2).

iii. **a.** $y \geq 3x - 12$, $y \leq 15 - x$, $x \geq 2$, $y \geq 5$

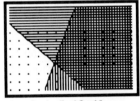

[2, 12, 1, 5, 12, 1]

b. (2, 5), (5.6667, 5), (6.75, 8.25), (2, 13)

c. (2, 5), (2, 6) . . . (2, 13); (3, 5), (3, 6) . . . (3, 12)
(4, 5), (4, 6) . . . (4, 11); (5, 5), (5, 6) . . . (5, 10)
(6, 6), (6, 7) . . . (6, 9)
The maximum value of 21 occurs at (6, 9).

iv. **a.** $y \geq \frac{10 - x}{2}$, $y \geq 12 - 2x$, $y \geq x - 8$

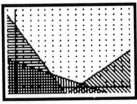

[−1, 15, 1, −1, 15, 1]

b. (4.6667, 2.6667), (8.6667, 0.6667)

c. There are an infinite set of possible interior points.
The minimum value of 20 occurs at (4, 4).

2. a.

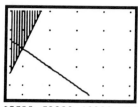

[5500, 50000, 10000, 5000, 50000, 10000]

b. (10,000, 30,000); 3,800

Problem Set 9.7

1.

	Number of shawls (x)	Number of afghans (y)	Constraining value
Spinning (hr)	1	2	≤ 8
Dyeing (hr)	1	1	≤ 6
Weaving (hr)	1	4	≤ 14
Profit	\$16	\$20	

$x + 2y \leq 8$, $x + y \leq 6$, $x + 4y \leq 14$, $x \geq 0$, $y \geq 0$: Profit $= 16x + 20y$

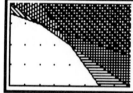

Vertices: (0, 0), (6, 0), (4, 2), (2, 3), (0, 3.5)
The maximum profit occurs at (4, 2) or $16(4) + 20(2) = \$104$.
They should make four shawls and two afghans.

[0, 8, 1, 0, 4, 1]

2.

	Siberians	Poodles	Constraining value
Number of poodles		y	≤ 20
Number of Siberians	x		≤ 15
Food	6	2	≤ 100
Training	250	1000	≤ 10000
Profit	80	200	

$y \leq 20$, $x \leq 15$, $6x + 2y \leq 100$, $250x + 1{,}000y \leq 10{,}000$, $x \geq 0$, $y \geq 0$: Profit $= 80x + 200y$

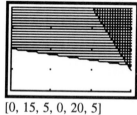

The vertices of the feasible region are (0, 0), (15, 0), (15, 5), (14.5455, 6.3636), and (0, 10).
To maximize profits, they should raise 14 Siberians and 6 poodles: $80(14) + 200(6) = \$2,320$.

[0, 15, 5, 0, 20, 5]

Problem Set 9.8

1. Only parts b and d have solutions; all other coefficient matrices have a determinant of zero.

2. a. Dependent; the point (16, ⁻5.333333) works in both equations.

   c. Dependent; the point (21, ⁻17, 1) works in all equations.

   e. Inconsistent; the point (16,15.667, ⁻3.862) does not work in the first equation, but does work in the other two.

   f. Inconsistent; the point (1, 1.209, 1.116, 0.256) does not work in the first equation, but does work in the other three.

3.

	True/false (w)	Fill in the blank (x)	Matching (y)	Essay (z)	Constraints
Points	$2w$	$4x$	$6y$	$10z$	$= 100$
Time	$1w$	$2x$	$5y$	$6z$	$= 60$
Lines	$4w$	$3x$	$15y$	$9z$	$= 110$

The equations are: $2w + 4x + 6y + 10z = 100$, $1w + 2x + 5y + 6z = 60$, and $4w + 3x + 15y + 9z = 110$. Two integer solutions are (2, 6, 2, 6) and (5, 1, 1, 8).

Chapter Review

Problem Set 9.9

1. (0.634, ⁻0.598) and (2.366, 4.598)

2. a. Answers will vary. No window is really good to see the intersection, but one possible window is [0, 20, 2, 0, 45, 5].

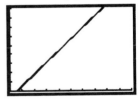

b.

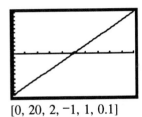

[0, 20, 2, ⁻1, 1, 0.1]

   c. $3.2x - 4 = 3.1x - 3$ **d.** $x = 10$

   e. Equation 1 can be rewritten as $0 = 3.2x - 4 - y$. Now substitute the second equation, which equals y, into the above equation, resulting in $0 = 3.2x - 4 - (3.1x - 3)$. Solving this resulting equation for x will give you the x-intercept for y_3.

3. a. (⁻1.325, 10.183)   **b.** (8.4, 5.3)

4. a. $\left(\frac{2}{3}, 1\right)$ **b.** (1, 0)

5. 5a is consistent; 5c and 5d are inconsistent; 5b is dependent.

6. a. $\begin{bmatrix} 0.8 & ⁻0.6 \\ 0.2 & ⁻0.4 \end{bmatrix}$ **b.** $\begin{bmatrix} ⁻0.0353 & 0.1882 & ⁻0.0235 \\ 0.2118 & ⁻0.1294 & 0.1412 \\ ⁻0.3765 & 0.3412 & 0.0824 \end{bmatrix}$

c. None

d. $\begin{bmatrix} -0.0893 & 0.1429 & 0.125 \\ -0.0536 & 0.2857 & -0.125 \\ -0.5179 & 0.4286 & 0.125 \end{bmatrix} = \begin{bmatrix} -\frac{5}{56} & \frac{1}{7} & \frac{1}{8} \\ -\frac{3}{56} & \frac{2}{7} & -\frac{1}{8} \\ -\frac{29}{56} & \frac{3}{7} & \frac{1}{8} \end{bmatrix}$

7. a. $\begin{bmatrix} 3.758 \\ 2.613 \end{bmatrix}$

b. $\begin{bmatrix} -39.143 \\ 24.592 \\ 8.816 \\ -34.449 \end{bmatrix}$

8. a. $y \le \frac{12 - 2x}{3}, y \le 18 - 6x, y \ge \frac{2 - x}{2}, x > 0, y \ge 0$

[0, 5, 1 ,0, 6, 1]

The vertices are (0, 4), (2.625, 2.25), (3, 0), (2, 0), and (0, 1).
The maximum value occurs at (0, 4): 1.65(0) + 5.2(4) = 20.8.

b. $y \le 50 - x, y \le \frac{440 - 10x}{5}, y \le \frac{2400 - 40x}{60}$

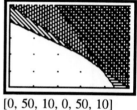

[0, 50, 10, 0, 50, 10]

The vertices are (0, 40), (30, 20), (38, 12), and (44, 0).
The maximum value occurs at (30, 20): 6(30) + 7(20) = 320.

9. A new heater will pay for itself in about 4.4 yr.

10. a. $2x + 1y + 3z = 5$

b. $4x + 0y + 1z = 6; 0x + 2y + 1z = 2$

c. $x = 1.375; y = 0.75; z = 0.5$

d. Change the matrix to fractions. The multiplier is 8; 11, 6, 4.

e. 11 parts of mixture 1, 6 parts of mixture 2, 4 parts of mixture 3

Chapter 10

Problem Set 10.1

1. a. $y = 10{,}000x^4 + 5{,}000x^2 + 2{,}000$ **c.** 1.006 **d.** 7.2%

2. a. $\left(1 - \frac{p}{100}\right)$ **b.** $30x^3$ **c.** 55 **d.** 45%

3. a. $50x^3 + 70x^2 + 90x$ **b.** 0.3976 **c.** 60.24%

5. a. $D_1 = 15.1, 5.3, -4.5, -14.3, -24.1, -33.9; D_2 = -9.8, -9.8, \ldots$

b. $D_1 = 59.1, 49.3, 39.5, 29.7, 19.9, 10.1; D_2 = -9.8, -9.8, \ldots$

c. Second degree

d. $h = {}^-4.9t^2 + 20t + 80$

Problem Set 10.2

1. a. $y = x^2 - 4x + 7$ **b.** $y = x^2 + 8x + 14$ **c.** $y = 2x^2 - 20x + 46$ **d.** $y = {}^-0.5x^2 - x + 3.5$
e. $y = {}^-3x^2 + 24x - 48$ **f.** $y = 1.5x^2 - 3$

2. a. $y = {}^-0.5x^2 - Hx - 0.5H^2 + 4$ **b.** $y = Ax^2 - 8Ax + 16A$
c. $y = Ax^2 - 2AHx + AH^2 + K$

3. a. $y = (x + 3)^2 - 2; y = x^2 + 6x + 7$
b. $y = {}^-(x - 4)^2 + 3; y = {}^-x^2 + 8x - 13$
c. $y = 2(x - 2)^2 - 4; y = 2x^2 - 8x + 4$
d. $y = {}^-0.5(x + 1.5)^2 + 3; y = {}^-0.5x^2 - 1.5x + 1.875$
e. $y = A(x - H)^2 + K; y = Ax^2 - 2AHx + AH^2 + K$

4. a. $3, 2, {}^-5$ **b.** $3, 2 + d, 14s^2$

5. a. $A, {}^-2AH, K + AH^2$ **b.** $a = A$ **c.** $b = {}^-2AH; H = \frac{{}^-b}{2a}$ **d.** $c = K + AH^2; K = c - \frac{b^2}{4a}$

6. a. $(2.17, {}^-2.08); y = 3(x - 2.17)^2 - 2.08$ **b.** $({}^-3, 2); y = (x + 3)^2 + 2$
c. $({}^-1, {}^-9); y = (x + 1)^2 - 9$

8. a. Number sold = 200, 195, 190, 185, 180
b. Revenue = 400, 409.50, 418, 425.50, 432; D_1 = 9.5, 8.5, 7.5, 6.5; D_2 = ${}^-1, {}^-1, {}^-1$
c. $y = {}^-50x^2 + 300x$
d. $450; $3

Problem Set 10.3

1. a. x-intercepts, 7.5, ${}^-2.5$, 3.2; y-intercept, 150 **b.** $y = 2.5x^3 - 20.5x^2 - 6.875x + 150$

c.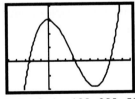
$[{}^-5, 10, 1, {}^-100, 200, 50]$

2. a. $y = {}^-4.9(x - 0.7)(x - 2.8)$
b. $(1.75, 5.4)$; at 1.75 sec, the ball reaches a height of 5.4 m.
c. ${}^-9.604$; the well is 9.6 m deep.
d. The maximum changes, but the roots stay the same.

3. a. x-intercepts, ${}^-1.5$ and ${}^-6$; y-intercept, ${}^-2.25$; vertex, $({}^-3.75, 1.265625)$
b. x-intercept, 4; y-intercept, 48; vertex, $(4, 0)$

5. a. i. $y = 2(x - 2)(x - 4)$ **ii.** $y = {}^-0.25(x + 6)(x + 1.5)$

b. i. $y = 2x^2 - 12x + 16$ ii. $y = -0.25x^2 - 1.875x - 2.25$

c. i. $y = 2(x - 3)^2 - 2$ ii. $y = -0.25(x + 3.75)^2 + 1.265625$

7. a. $y = A(x + 5)(x - 3)(x - 6)$ **b.** $A = 2$

c. $y = 2(x + 5)(x - 3)(x - 6) + 100$ **d.** $y = 2(x + 9)(x + 1)(x - 2)$

9. a. i.

	x	4
x	x^2	$4x$
4	$4x$	16

ii.

	$2x$	6
x	$2x^2$	$6x$
3	$6x$	18

b. For the figure in 9a.i: $A = (x + 4)^2$; $A = x^2 + 8x + 16$; For the figure in 9a.ii: $A = (2x + 6)(x + 3)$; $A = 2x^2 + 12x + 18$

10. a. $(x - 6)(x - 4)$ **b.** $(x - 3)^2$ **c.** $(x + 8)(x - 8)$ **d.** $(x + 10)(x - 12)$

Problem Set 10.4

1. a. $(2x - 3)^2$ **b.** $\left(x + \frac{5}{2}\right)^2$ **c.** $(x - y)^2$

2. a. $-2.7, 7.3$ **b.** $-7.95, -0.95$ **c.** $-\frac{1}{2}, 2$

3. a. $3x^2 - 13x - 10 = 0$ **b.** $x^2 - 5x - 13 = 0$

$a = 3, b = -13, c = -10$ $a = 1, b = -5, c = -13$

$\frac{-2}{3}, 5$ or $-0.667, 5$ $\frac{5 \pm \sqrt{77}}{2}$ or $-1.887, 6.887$

c. $3x^2 + 5x + 1 = 0$

$a = 3, b = 5, c = 1$

$\frac{-5 \pm \sqrt{13}}{6}$ or $-1.434, -0.232$

5. Answers will vary. Those listed below are only examples.

a. $(x - 3)(x + 3) = 0$ **b.** $(x - 4)(5x + 2) = 0$ **c.** $(x - R_1)(x - R_2) = 0$ **d.** $-4.9(x - 1.1)(x - 4.7) = 0$

6. Answers will vary. The calculator will give an error message or produce an answer in complex form. The value under the radical is negative. The graph does not cross the x-axis. Example: $y = x^2 + 1$.

8. $\left(7 + 0.5\sqrt{300}\right)^2 - 14\left(7 + 0.5\sqrt{300}\right) - 26$ $\left(7 - 0.5\sqrt{300}\right)^2 - 14\left(7 - 0.5\sqrt{300}\right) - 26$

$49 + 7\sqrt{300} + 75 - 98 - 7\sqrt{300} - 26$ $49 - 7\sqrt{300} + 75 - 98 + 7\sqrt{300} - 26$

$49 + 75 - 98 - 26 + 7\sqrt{300} - 7\sqrt{300}$ $49 + 75 - 98 - 26 - 7\sqrt{300} + 7\sqrt{300}$

$124 - 124 = 0$ $124 - 124 = 0$

9. a. $y = \sqrt{400 - x^2}$ **b.** 17.3 ft **c.** 8.7 ft **d.** Pythagorean theorem: $a^2 + b^2 = c^2$

Problem Set 10.5

1. $y = -4.9x^2 = 227$ m; $y = -16x^2 = 740$ ft

2. a. $H(t) = -4.9t^2 + 100t + 25$ **b.** Height = 25 m; velocity = 100 m/sec
    c. 10.2 sec   **d.** 535 m
    e. 3.27 sec and 17.1 sec   **f.** 20.7 sec

3. a. $y = -20x^2 + 332x$ **b.** $8.30 each for a total of $1,377.80

7. $y = 11000x^2 - Mx - M$

9. a. $L = -4t^2 - 6.8t + 49.2$ **b.** 49.2 L   **c.** 2.76 min

Problem Set 10.6

1. a. $y = x - 4$ **b.** $y = (x - 4)^2$ **c.** $y = (x - 4)^3$

2. a.

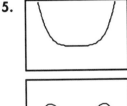

[−6, 6, 1, −150, 500, 100]

b.

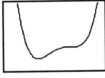

[−6, 6, 1, −700, 100, 100]

c.

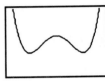

[−6, 6, 1, −1000, 100, 100]

3. a. 4 x-intercepts   **b.** Fifth degree   **c.** $y = -x(x + 5)^2(x + 1)(x - 4)$

5.

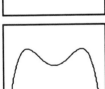

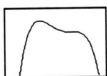
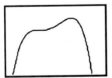

7. a. $y = (x + 5)^2(x + 2)(x - 1)$ **b.** $y = -(x + 5)^2(x + 2)(x - 1)$
    c. $y = (x + 5)^2(x + 2)(x - 1)^2$ **d.** $y = -(x + 5)(x + 2)^3(x - 1)$
    e. $\{-5, -5, -2, 1\}$ $\{-5, -5, -2, 1\}$ $\{-5, -5, -2, 1, 1\}$ $\{-5, -2, -2, -2, 1\}$

Problem Set 10.7

1. a. $2 \pm i\sqrt{2}$ or $2 \pm 1.41i$; complex   **b.** $\pm i$; complex
    c. $\frac{-1 \pm i\sqrt{3}}{2} = -0.5 \pm 0.866i$; complex

2. a. $x^2 - 2x - 15 = 0$ **d.** $x^2 - 4x + 5 = 0$

3. a. $y = (x + 4)(x - 5)(x + 2)^2$ **b.** $y = -2(x + 4)(x - 5)(x + 2)^2$
    c. $y = Ax(3x - 1)(5x + 2)$ **d.** $y = (x^2 + 25)(x + 1)^3(x - 4)$

4. a. $10.83i, -0.83i$ **b.** $2i, i$
    c. The solutions do not come in conjugate pairs because the coefficients of the equation are imaginary.

5. a. $b^2 < 4ac$ **b.** $b^2 \geq 4ac$ **c.** $b^2 = 4ac$

7. a.

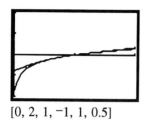

$[0, 2, 1, -1, 1, 0.5]$

b. 1

c. $0.0723\left[6(x-1) - 3(x-1)^2 + 2(x-1)^3\right]$
$= 0.0723\left[(x-1)\left(6 - 3(x-1) + 2(x-1)^2\right)\right]$

d. $1.75 \pm 1.56i$

Problem Set 10.8

1. a. $11(4) + 3 = 47$ **b.** $(x - 1)(6x^3 + x^2 + 8x - 4) + 11$
     c. $(x - 2)(x^2 + x - 8)$

2. a. $x^4 - 5x^3 + 15x^2 - 45x + 54$ **b.** $x^3 - 3x^2 + 9x - 27$
     c. $x^2 + 9$ **d.** $\pm 3i$ **e.** (Calculator check)

4. a. $\pm 2i, \pm 2, \pm 1$ **b.** $-7.011074, -0.942787, 0.45386126$

5. a. $-3.079, 0, 3.079$ **b.** $-3.141, 0, 3.141$ **c.** As the pattern continues, the real roots approach 0 and $\pm \pi$.

Chapter Review
Problem Set 10.9

1. $1; 4; 10; 20; 35; \ldots$; the expression for n points is $\frac{1}{6}n^3 - \frac{1}{2}n^2 + \frac{1}{3}n$.

2. a. $y = 2x^2 - 8x - 8; \; y = 2(x - 4.828)(x + 0.828)$
   b. $y = -3x^2 + 12x + 15; \; y = -3(x - 2)^2 + 27$
   c. $y = (x + 1)(x + 2); \; y = (x + 1.5)^2 - 0.25$
   d. $y = x^3 + 2x^2 - 11x - 12$
   e. $y = 2(x + 3.386)(x - 0.886); \; y = 2(x + 1.25)^2 - 9.125$
   f. $y = -x^2 - 14x - 51; \; y = -(x + 7 + 1.414i)(x + 7 - 1.414i)$

3. 3a.–d., use the information from Problem 2 a.–d.

a.

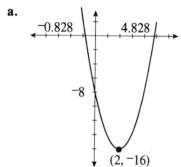

b.

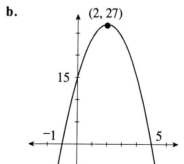

c.

d.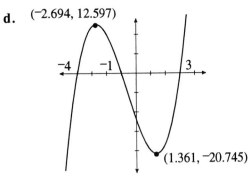

e.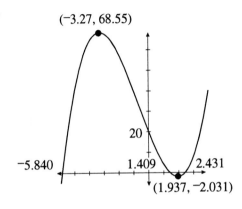

f.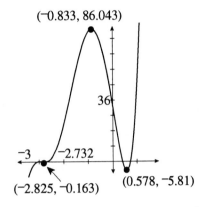

4. a. $y = 2(x + 1)(x - 4)$ **b.** $y = 2(x + 3)^2(x - 1)$ **c.** $y = -(x + 2)(x - 3)^3$
  d. $y = 0.5(x + 4)(x - 2)(x^2 + 9)$

5. 18 in. × 18 in. × 36 in.

Chapter 11

Problem Set 11.1

1. a. $8! = 40{,}320$ **b.** $7! = 5040$ **c.** $\frac{1}{8}$ **e.** 0.5; answers will vary.
  f. 1   **g.** 40,319   **h.** 0.999975

2. a. 12   **b.** 7   **c.** $n + 1$ **d.** n
  e. $120(119) = 14{,}280$ **f.** $n(n - 1)$ **g.** $n + 1 = 15; n = 14$

5. 8,000,000

6.

N	Permutation (N!)	Time
5	120	0.00012 sec
10	3,628,800	3.6288 sec
12	479,001,600	≈ 8 min
13	6,227,020,800	≈ 1.7 hr
15	≈ $1.31 \cdot 10^{12}$	≈ 15 days
20	≈ $2.43 \cdot 10^{18}$	≈ 771 centuries

Problem Set 11.2

1. **a.** $_7P_2 = 2 \cdot {}_7C_2 \ (2 = 2!)$ **b.** $_7P_3 = 6 \cdot {}_7C_3 \ (6 = 3!)$ **c.** $_7P_4 = 24 \cdot {}_7C_4 \ (24 = 4!)$
     d. $_7P_7 = 5040 \cdot {}_7C_7 \ (5040 = 7!)$

2. **a.** 120   **b.** 35   **c.** 105   **d.** 1

3. **a.** 120   **b.** 35   **c.** 105   **d.** 1

4. **a.** $_{10}C_4 = \frac{10!}{6!4!}$ **b.** $_{10}C_4 = {}_{10}C_6$ **c.** $\frac{10!}{6!4!} = \frac{10!}{4!6!}$

6. **a.** 38,760   **b.** 3060   **c.** 0.08

9. **a.** $_7C_5(0.3)^5(0.7)^2 = 0.0250047$ **b.** $_7C_6(0.3)^6(0.7)^1 = 0.0035721$
     c. $_7C_7(0.3)^7(0.7)^0 = 0.0002187$ **d.** $0.0025 + 0.00357 + 0.00022 = 0.2879$

Problem Set 11.3

1. **a.** HH, HT, TH, TT   **b.** HH, HT, TH, TT   **c.**
     d. The combination number $_2C_0$ is the number of
       times you get no tails when two coins are
       tossed; $_2C_1$ is the number of times you get 1
       tail when two coins are tossed; $_2C_2$ is the
       number of times you get 2 tails when two
       coins are tossed.

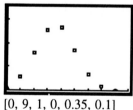

     e. The terms represent the long-range distribution
       of 2 heads, 1 head, and 0 heads.

2. **a.** $x^4 + 4x^3y + 6x^2y^2 + 4xy^3 + y^4$ **b.** $p^5 + 5p^4q + 10p^3q^2 + 10p^2q^3 + 5pq^4 + q^5$
     c. $8x^3 + 36x^2 + 54x + 27$ **d.** $81x^4 - 432x^3 + 864x^2 - 768x + 256$

3. **a.** 1   **b.** Answers will vary.   **c.** 1

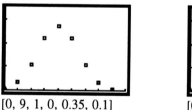   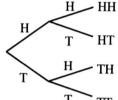

    [0, 9, 1, 0, 0.35, 0.1]   [0, 9, 1, 0, 0.35, 0.1]

4. **a.** 0.40   **b.** ≈ 0.94

7. $_6C_1 + {}_6C_2 \ {}_6C_3 \ {}_6C_4 \ {}_6C_5 \ {}_6C_6 = 63$

Problem Set 11.4

1. **a.** Answers will vary, but the second set has less spread.
    b. First set: mean = 35, standard deviation = 19.99; second set: mean = 117, standard deviation = 3.16
    c. Both the mean and the standard deviations are ten times the original numbers.

3. b. This is clearly the French exam, which has the greatest standard deviation; answers will vary.
   c. Hans; answers will vary.

4. a. Answers will vary, but $\bar{x}$ should be close to 7, and σ should be close to 2.4.
   b. Close to 67 **c.** Close to 68% **d.** Close to 95%

Problem Set 11.5

1. a.

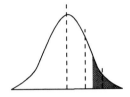

2.

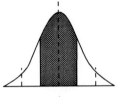

3.

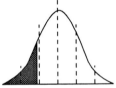

5. a. For $a = 75$, $b = 89$, and $n = 500$, the probability is 65.5%.
   b. For $a = 67$, $b = 97$, and $n = 500$, the probability is 95.65%.
   c. For $a = 60$, $b = 104$, and $n = 500$, the probability is 99.74%

7. a. $\bar{x} = 165$; $\sigma \approx 5.82$

b.

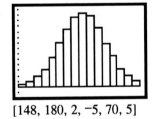

[148, 180, 2, −5, 70, 5]

c. Using the points (66, 165) and (151, 5), the equation is $y = 66(0.99)^{(x - 165)^2}$.

d. For $a = 142$, $b = 188$, and $n = 500$, the normalizing equation is $y = 0.0567(0.99)^{(x - 165)^2}$.

Problem Set 11.6

1. 31%

2. a. 71.4 g **b.** 69.3 g **c.** 66.6 g

3. a. 0.0145 **b.** 0.0025

6. a. 0.08655 **b.** 86 or 87 groups **d.** 4.3634 **e.** 4.3763

Chapter Review
Problem Set 11.7

1. a. $12! = 479{,}001{,}600$ **b.** $\frac{5!7!}{12!} = 0.00126$ or 0.13%

2. 0.0217

3. $\displaystyle\sum_{i=17}^{20} {}_{20}C_i(0.65)^i(0.35)^{20-i} = 0.044$ or 4.4%

4. a. $100 - 800x + 2800x^2 - 5600x^3 + 7000x^4 - 5600x^5 + 2800x^6 - 800x^7 + 100x^8$
    b. $600 + 250x + 41.667x^2 + 3.4722x^3 + 0.14468x^4 + 0.002411x^5$

5. The mean is 67.8 in., and the standard deviation is 3.6 in. Approximately 67% of the adults in Normalville are between 64 in. and 71 in. tall.

6. $y = \dfrac{1}{8.5\sqrt{2\pi}}\left(1 - \dfrac{1}{2(8.5)^2}\right)^{(x-167)^2}$

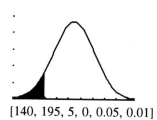

$[140, 195, 5, 0, 0.05, 0.01]$

7. 0.205

8. ${}_nC_r = \dfrac{n!}{r!(n-r)!}$; ${}_nP_r = \dfrac{n!}{(n-r)!}$

9. 0.00086

10. a. $y = \dfrac{1}{14\sqrt{2\pi}}\left(1 - \dfrac{1}{2(14)^2}\right)^{(x-175)^2}$ **b.** 14%
    c. 152 lb to 198 lb

Chapter 12

Problem Set 12.1

1. a. $f(x) = \dfrac{1}{x} + 2$

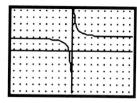

c. $f(x) = \dfrac{1}{x+4} - 1$

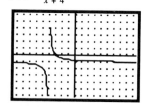

d. $f(x) = \dfrac{1}{x/2}$ or $\dfrac{2}{x}$

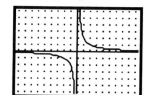

e. $f(x) = \dfrac{1}{x/3} + 1$ or $\dfrac{3}{x} + 1$

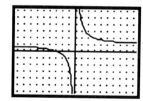

2. a. $y = \frac{1}{x} + 2$ **b.** $y = \frac{1}{x-2} - 4$

3. a. $y = \frac{-1}{x+5}$ **b.** $y = \frac{1}{x-6} - 2$

5. a. 20.9 ml   **b.** $f(x) = \frac{20.9+x}{55+x}$ and $g(x) = 0.64$

   c. ≈ 39.72 **d.** The graph slowly approaches 1.0.

8. a. 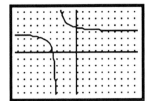   **b.**

Problem Set 12.2

1. a. 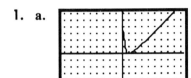   **b.** 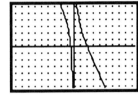   **c.**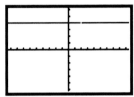

2. a. 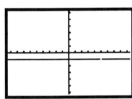   **b.** 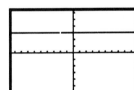   **c.**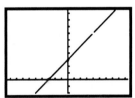

3. a. $y = 0 + \frac{x+2}{x+2}$ **b.** $y = {}^{-}3 + \frac{x-3}{x-3}$ **c.** $y = \frac{(x+2)(x+1)}{x+1}$

5. a. The graph has a slant asymptote of $y = x$, vertical asymptote at $x = {}^{-}2$, and has been vertically stretched by $^{-}3$.

   b. $y = x$

   c. Answers will vary. One possibility is $y = \frac{1}{x+2}$.

   d. Answers will vary. One possibility is $y = (x+3)(x-1)$.

   e. $y = x + \frac{-3}{x+2}$ or $\frac{(x+3)(x-1)}{x+2}$

7. a. The graph has x-intercepts at 1 and $^{-}4$ and vertical asymptotes at $x = 2$ and $x = {}^{-}3$. The y-intercept is $\frac{2}{3}$.

   b. The graph has a horizontal asymptote at $y = 1$.

   c.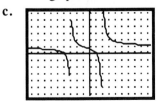

Problem Set 12.3

1. a. The unrestricted growth rate is 8% and the population limit is 500.

    b. 53.6
    c. 70.38, 131.75, 220.44, . . . , 476.99

    d. 500
    e.

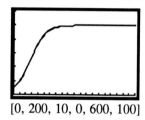

[0, 200, 10, 0, 600, 100]

2. After 20 weeks the bacteria population is at 5000. This is a net rate increase of 26% per week.

6. a. 8074 weeds
    b. 8,237.3; 11,286; 8,237.3; 11,286; 8,237.3; 11,286

    c.

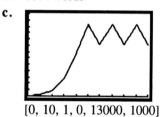

[0, 10, 1, 0, 13000, 1000]

Problem Set 12.4

1. a. The shortest possible distance occurs when the boat travels directly to point D.

    b. The boat would travel approximately 99.1 mi and the ambulance 0 mi.

    c. The shortest time (2.016 hr) occurs when $x \approx 5.218$. Using this point the boat travels approximately 15.88 mi and the ambulance approximately 92.782 mi.

2. a. $y = \sqrt{10^2 + x^2} + \sqrt{(20 - x)^2 + 13^2}$

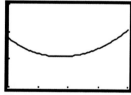

[0, 20, 5, 25, 40, 5]

x	0	1	2	3	4	5	6	7	8	9	10
Wire length	33.85	33.07	32.40	31.84	31.39	31.03	30.77	30.59	30.50	30.48	30.54

    b. $0 \le x \le 20$, $30 \le wire\ length \le 43$

    c. Fasten it at $x \approx 8.696$ m for a minimum wire length of ≈ 30.48 m.

4. a. 64 sec (0.125 mi/sec; distance = 8 mi)

    b. $d = \sqrt{7^2 + (8 - 0.125t)^2}$

c.

Time (sec)	0	1	5	10	20	30	64
Ground distance (mi)	8	7.875	7.375	6.75	5.5	4.25	0
Actual distance (mi)	10.63	10.536	10.168	9.7243	8.9022	8.1892	7

d.

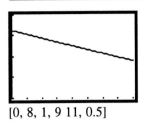

[0, 8, 1, 9 11, 0.5]

Problem Set 12.5

1. a. Center at $(0, 0)$ and radius 2.

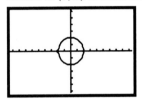

b. Center at $(3, 0)$ and radius 1.

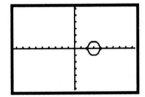

c. Center at $(-1, 2)$ and radius 3.

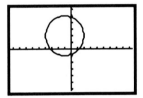

d. Center at $(0, 1.5)$ and radius 0.5.

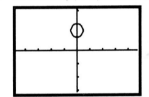

e. Center at $(1, 2)$ and radius 2.

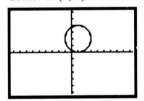

f. Center at $(-3, 0)$ and radius 4.

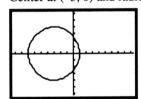

2. a. $x = 5 \cos t + 3$ and $y = 5 \sin t$ or $(x - 3)^2 + y^2 = 25$

b. $x = 3 \cos t - 1$ and $y = 3 \sin t + 2$ or $(x + 1)^2 + (y - 2)^2 = 9$

3. a. $(2, 0), (-2, 0), (0, 4), (0, -4)$

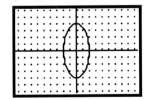

b. $(5, -2), (-1, -2), (2, -1), (2, -3)$

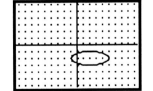

c. $(1, 1), (7, 1), (4, 4), (4, -2)$

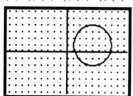

4. a. $x = 6 \cos t$ and $y = 3 \sin t$ or $\left(\frac{x}{6}\right)^2 + \left(\frac{y}{6}\right)^2 = 1$

b. $x = 2 \cos t + 3$ and $y = 5 \sin t$ or $\left(\frac{x-3}{2}\right)^2 + \left(\frac{y}{5}\right)^2 = 1$

5. a. Answers will vary. The equation $\left(\frac{x-493}{497}\right)^2 + \left(\frac{y}{63}\right)^2 = 1$ is a good fit.

b. ± 63 AU   **c.** 990 AU   **d.** $(986, 0)$

7. a. The string will be 12 units long.   **b.** $\left(3\sqrt{3}, 0\right)$ and $\left(-3\sqrt{3}, 0\right)$

Problem Set 12.6

1. a. Vertex $(0, 5)$; focus $(0, 6)$; directrix $y = 4$ **b.** Vertex $(-2, -2)$; focus $(-1.75, -2)$; directrix $x = -2.25$

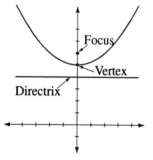

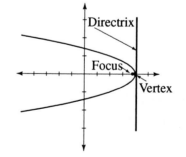

c. Vertex $(-3, 1)$; focus $(-3, 0.5)$; directrix $y = 1$ **d.** Vertex $(4, 0)$; focus $(3.875, 0)$; directrix $x = 4.125$

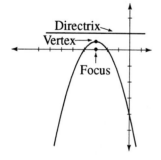

e. Vertex $(-1, 3)$; focus $(-1, 5)$; directrix $y = 1$

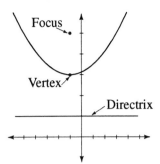

f. Vertex $(3, 0)$; focus $\left(\frac{61}{12}, 0\right)$; directrix $x = \frac{11}{12}$

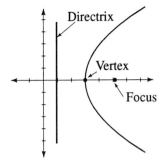

2. **a.** $x = t^2$ and $y = t + 2$ or $x = (y - 2)^2$; vertex $(0, 2)$, focus $(0.25, 2)$, and directrix $x = {}^-0.25$

   b. $x = t$ and $y = {}^-t^2 + 4$ or $y = {}^-x^2 + 4$; vertex $(0, 4)$, focus $(0, 3.75)$, and directrix $y = 4.25$

3. The path will be parabolic. The rock is the focus and the shoreline is the directrix.

4. **a.** The graph is a parabola with vertex $(0, 1)$, focus $(0, 3)$, and directrix $y = -1$.

   b. $y = \frac{x^2}{8} + 1$ or $y = 0.125x^2 + 1$

   c.

6. $y = {}^-2.4x^2 + 21.12x - 44.164$

Problem Set 12.7

1. **a.** The vertices are $(-2, 0)$ and $(2, 0)$. The equations of the asymptotes are $y = {}^\pm 2x$.

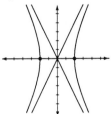

   b. The vertices are $(2, -1)$ and $(2, -5)$. The equations of the asymptotes are $y = {}^\pm 3(x - 2) - 2$.

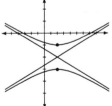

   c. The vertices are $(1, 1)$ and $(7, 1)$. The equations of the asymptotes are $y = {}^\pm(x - 4) + 1$.

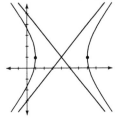

   d. The vertices are $(-2, 1)$ and $(-2, -3)$. The equations of the asymptotes are $y = {}^\pm\frac{2}{3}(x + 2) - 1$.

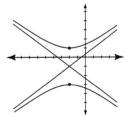

e. The vertices are (−5, 3) and (3, 3). The equations of the asymptotes are $y = {}^\pm0.5(x + 1) + 3$.

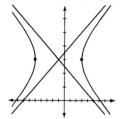

f. The vertices are (3, 5) and (3, −5). The equations of the asymptotes are $y = {}^{\pm}\frac{5}{3}(x - 3)$.

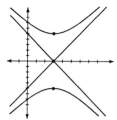

2. a. $x = \frac{2}{\cos t}$ and $y = \tan t$; $\left(\frac{x}{2}\right)^2 - \left(\frac{y}{1}\right)^2 = 1$; $y = {}^\pm0.5x$.

b. $x = 2\tan t + 3$ and $y = \frac{2}{\cos t} - 3$; $\left(\frac{y+3}{2}\right)^2 - \left(\frac{x-3}{2}\right)^2 = 1$ $y = {}^\pm(x - 3) - 3$

3. a. $\left(\pm\sqrt{2}, 0\right)$

b. $\left(2, -2 + \sqrt{10}\right)$ and $\left(2, -2 - \sqrt{10}\right)$

4. $\left|\sqrt{(x+2)^2 + (y-1)^2} - \sqrt{(x-4)^2 + (y-1)^2}\right| = 10$

6.

x-value	5	10	20	40
Distance	0.41	0.25	0.14	0.07

Problem Set 12.8

1. a. $1x^2 + 0xy + 0y^2 + 14x - 9y + 148 = 0$

b. $1x^2 + 0xy + 9y^2 - 14x + 198y + 1129 = 0$

2. a. $a = 1.4$ **b.** $b = 0.7$ **c.** 0.49   **d.** 7.35
   e. 0.7

4. a. iv   **b.** ii   **c.** iii   **d.** i

6. a. $y = \frac{\pm\sqrt{400x^2 + 1600}}{-8}$

b. $y = \frac{-16 \pm \sqrt{160x - 320}}{8}$

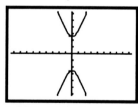

[−18.8, 18.8, 2, −12.4, 12.4, 2]

[−18.8, 18.8, 2, −12.4, 12.4, 2]

7. $y = 0.00115x^2 + 4$

Problem Set 12.9

1. a. $\begin{bmatrix} 0.866 & -0.5 \\ 0.2 & 0.866 \end{bmatrix}$

b. $\begin{bmatrix} -0.839 & -0.545 \\ 0.545 & -0.839 \end{bmatrix}$

c. $\begin{bmatrix} 0 & 1 \\ -1 & 0 \end{bmatrix}$

d. $\begin{bmatrix} -0.839 & -0.545 \\ 0.545 & -0.839 \end{bmatrix}$

2. The vertices of the rotated triangle are (2, 1), (−5, 4), and (2, 7).

4. a. The vertices of the rotated triangle are (−1, −4), (−7, −2), and (−4, 1).
   b. A reflection over the *x*-axis followed by a reflection over the *y*-axis (or vice versa).

6. a. The graph is a unit hyperbola that opens vertically.
   b. The equations for x_2 and y_2 rotate the original hyperbola 50° counterclockwise.
   c.

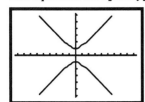 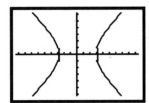

7. $y = \frac{4}{x}$ $x^2 - y^2 = 8$

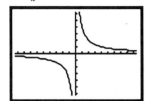

Chapter Review
Problem Set 12.10

1. Approximately 10.34 oz

2. a. The slice is perpendicular to the axis of rotation.
   b. The slice intersects only one branch of the cone. The angle is not perpendicular to the axis of rotation.
   c. The slice intersects only one branch of the cone and is parallel to an edge.
   d. The slice intersects both branches of the cone but does not contain the vertex.
   e. The slice intersects at the vertex.
   f. The slice is along an edge.
   g. The axis of rotation is contained in the slice.

3. a. $\left(\frac{x-5}{3}\right)^2 + \left(\frac{y+2}{4}\right)^2 = 1$
   b. $x = 3\cos t + 5$ and $y = 4\sin t - 2$
   c. The center is (5, −2). The foci are $\left(5, -2 + \sqrt{7}\right)$ and $\left(5, -2 - \sqrt{7}\right)$.
   d. $16x^2 + 9y^2 - 160x + 36y + 292 = 0$
   e. $x = (3\cos t + 5)\cos 75 - (4\sin t - 2)\sin 75$; $y = (3\cos t + 5)\sin 75 + (4\sin t - 2)\cos 75$
   f. $16(x\cos 75 - y\sin 75)^2 + 9(x\sin 75 + y\cos 75)^2 - 160(x\cos 75 - y\sin 75) + 36(x\sin 75 + y\cos 75)$
   $+ 292 = 0.$

4. a. $y = \pm0.5x$ **b.** $x^2 - 4y^2 - 4 = 0$ **c.** Distance $= 0.5x - \sqrt{\frac{x^2}{4} - 1}$
   d.

x	0	1	2	10	...	20
Distance	None	None	1	0.101	...	0.050

5. a.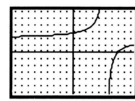

b. $y = 2$ and $x = 5$

c. Distance $= \left| 2 - \frac{2x - 14}{x - 5} \right|$

d.

x	0	3	5	10	...	20
Distance	0.8	2	None	0.8	...	0.27

6. Include $(x + 3)$ as a factor in both the numerator and denominator of the fraction.
$y = \frac{(2x - 14)(x + 3)}{(x - 5)(x + 3)}$

7. About 23.3 mi/hr and 43.3 mi/hr.

8. a. $y_1 = \frac{34}{x + 11} + \frac{13}{x}$

b.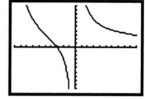

c. Answers will vary depending on how fast you think Eric can run (perhaps $2 < x < 10$ and $3 < y < 9$).

d. About 4.6 mi/hr

$[^-10, 10, 1, ^-10, 10, 1]$

There is a vertical asymptote at $x = ^-1$.
There is a horizontal asymptote at $y = 0$.

Chapter 13

Problem Set 13.1

1. a. sin 85° = 0.9962
reference angle = 85°

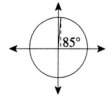

b. cos 147° = ⁻0.8387
reference angle = 33°

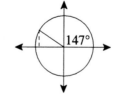

c. sin 280° = ⁻0.9848
reference angle = 80°

d. cos 310° = 0.6428
reference angle = 50°

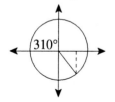

e. sin ⁻47° = ⁻0.7314
reference angle = 47°

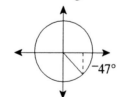

2. **a.** $y = \sin x$

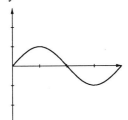

b. The graph will shift up 2 units.

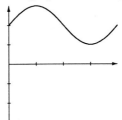

c. The graph will shift right 180°.

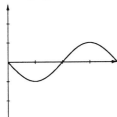

d. The graph will be stretched vertically by a factor of 2, shifted up 3 units, and shifted to the right 180°.

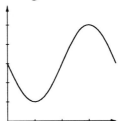

3. **a.–b.**

Angle A	0°	30°	60°	90°	120°	150°	180°
x-coordinate	1	0.8660	0.5	0	−0.5	−0.8660	−1
y-coordinate	0	0.5	0.8660	1	0.8660	0.5	0
Slope	0	0.5774	1.7321	Undefined	−1.7321	−0.5774	0
$\tan A$	0	0.5774	1.7321	Undefined	−1.7321	−0.5774	0

Angle A	210°	240°	270°	300°	315°	330°	360°
x-coordinate	−0.8660	−0.5	0	0.5	0.7071	0.8660	1
y-coordinate	−0.5	−0.8660	−1	−0.8660	−0.7071	−0.5	0
Slope	0.5774	1.7321	Undefined	−1.7321	−1	−0.5774	0
$\tan A$	0.5774	1.7321	Undefined	−1.7321	−1	−0.5774	0

c. The lengths of the legs of the reference triangle form the same ratio as the ratio of the x- and y-coordinates because lengths of the sides are the same as the coordinates, so the definition of a slope, $\frac{\text{rise}}{\text{run}}$, can be translated to $\frac{y\text{-coordinate}}{x\text{-coordinate}}$. Another name for the ratio of the legs is the tangent.

d. The tangents of the angles in the table in part a are the same as the slopes for the angles in the table.

e. $\tan A = \dfrac{\text{Height of lily pad}}{\text{Horizontal distance of lily pad from center}}$

5. **a.** Period = 360°

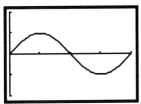

b. Period = 360°

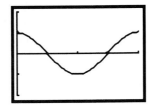

c. Period = 180°

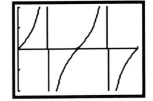

d. Period = 180°   **e.** Period = 60°

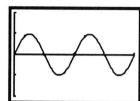 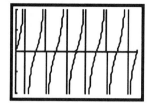

8. Answers will vary for the equations. Two possibilities are given for each.
   a. $y = 0.5 \csc x + 1$ or $y = 0.5 \sec (x - 90) + 1$
   b. $y = {}^-\cot \frac{1}{3}(x + 270)$ or $y = \tan \frac{1}{3}x$
   c. $y = \cot (x + 90) + 1$ or $y = {}^-\tan x + 1$
   d. $y = \sin 2 (x - 45) - 0.5$ or $y = {}^-\cos (2x) - 0.5$

Problem Set 13.2

1. a.

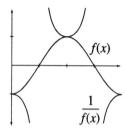

b. $y_1 = \sin (x - 90)$ or $y_1 = {}^-\cos x$

$y_2 = \dfrac{1}{\sin(x - 90)}$ or $y_2 = \dfrac{1}{{}^-\cos x}$

2. a. $y = 2 \csc (x + 360) + 1$ or $y = 2 \csc (x + 720) + 1$
   b. $y = {}^-\cot \frac{1}{3}(x + 270)$ or $y = {}^-\cot \frac{1}{3}(x - 270)$

3. a. The d-value shifts the graph of the function up or down; a positive d-value shifts the function up, and a negative d-value shifts the function down.
   b. The a-value represents the amplitude. A value of 1 for a gives an amplitude of 1, and a value of 5 gives an amplitude of 5.
   c. The b-value determines the period such that as b increases the period decreases; $\frac{360}{b} =$ period.
   d. The c-value shifts the graph; a positive c-value shifts the graph to the left, and a negative c-value shifts the graph to the right.

5. a. $h = 20 \tan A + 1.5$ **b.** 33.5 m   **c.** 16 m, 18.3 m   **d.** 23°

7. a.

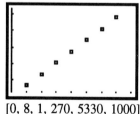

[0, 8, 1, 270, 5330, 1000]

b. $y = 10,000 \sin 4x$; the residuals imply that the accuracy of the function decreases as the size of the angle increases.
   c. $y = 39,250 \tan x$; the residuals show that the accuracy is much better than with the sine function.
   d. The maximum safe speed is ∞.

8. a. $x = 5 \cos 18(t - 10)$
$y = 5 \sin 18(t - 10)$

b. $y = 5 \sin (18x - 90) + 9.4$

c.

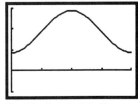

$[0, 20, 5, -5, 15, 5]$

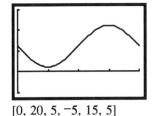

$[0, 20, 1, -9.4, 9.4, 1, -6.2, 6.2, 1]$

d. $y = -5 \sin (18x) + 6.2$

e.

$[0, 20, 5, -5, 15, 5]$

Problem Set 13.3

1. $y = \sin 8x$; $0° \le x \le 45°$, $-1 \le y \le 1$

2. b. Physical: $y = \sin 15.8695x$; emotional: $y = \sin 13.0357x$; intellectual: $y = \sin 11.0606x$
c. The plot depends on where your cycles are starting today.
d. 21,252 days or 58.22 yr

4. a. $y = 10 \sin 18(x + 15) + 12$
b. $y = 11 \sin 12(x + 22.5) + 23$
c. $y = (10 \sin 18(x + 15) + 12) + (11 \sin 12(x + 22.5) + 23) - 12$
d. 10 times

7. a. $y = 1 - \sin 2x$

b. $y = (\sin x - \cos x)^2 = \sin^2 x + \cos^2 x - 2 \sin x \cos x = 1 - \sin 2x$

Problem Set 13.4

1. a. $\triangle ABC$; $AB = 8.35$, $BC = 6.40$, $m\angle ABC = 25.5°$
b. $\triangle DEF$; $DF = 6.46$, $m\angle EDF = 81.22$, $m\angle EFD = 52.68°$
c. $\triangle GHI$; $m\angle HGI = 66.31°$, $m\angle GHI = 84.64°$, $m\angle GIH = 29.05°$
d. $\triangle LKJ$; $m\angle LJK = 38.81°$, $m\angle JLK = 33.29°$, $JK = 4.76$

3. 1659.8 mi

4. $m\angle B = 120°$; $m\angle C \approx 38.21°$; $m\angle A \approx 21.79°$

5. 57.85 cm

7. 149.3° from north

Problem Set 13.5

1. a. $m\angle A = 106.8°$ **b.** $m\angle B = 120.4°$

2. a. $x = t; y = \sin t$
$0 \le t \le 360$

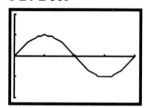

$x = \sin t; y = t$
$-90 \le t \le 90$

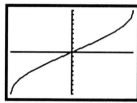

[0, 360, 10, 0, 360, 90, −2, 2, 1]   [−90, 90, 10, −1, 1, 1, −90, 90, 10]

b. $x = t; y = \sin 2t$
$0 \le t \le 360$

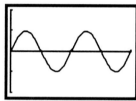

$x = \sin 2t; y = \sin t$
$-45 \le t \le 45$

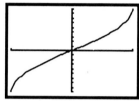

[0, 360, 10, 0, 360, 90, −2, 2, 1]   [−45, 45, 10, −1, 1, 1, −45, 45, 5]

c. $x = t; y = \sin \frac{1}{2}t$

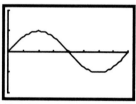

$x = \sin \frac{1}{2}t; y = t$

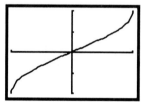

[0, 720, 10, 0, 720, 90, −2, 2, 1]   [−180, 180, 10, −1, 1, 1, −180, 180, 90]

d. The period changes in the same way as the range, that is, if the period doubles, so does the range.

3. $0 \le t \le 6.927$, $11.073 \le t \le 18.927$, $23.073 \le t \le 30.927$, $35.073 \le t \le 42.927$, $47.073 \le t \le 48$

4. a. $y = \sin 432x$ **b.** 144 times

6. a. Not including $t = 0$, 6 times   **b.** $\approx 29\%$ of the time

10. a. $y_1 = 5 \cos 25.7(x - 12) + 11$
     b. $16.42 \le x \le 21.58$ and $30.42 \le x \le 35.58$ or between 4:25 and 9:35 p.m. and again between 6:25 and 11:35 a.m. the next day

Problem Set 13.6

1. $(2, 390°)$ and $(-2, -510°)$

3. a.

θ	0°	5°	10°	15°	20°	25°	30°	35°	40°	45°	50°	55°
r	3	2.90	2.60	2.12	1.5	0.78	0	−0.78	−1.5	−2.12	−2.60	−2.9

60°	65°	70°	75°	80°	85°	90°	95°	100°	105°	110°	115°	120°
−3	−2.90	−2.60	−2.12	−1.5	−0.78	0	0.78	1.5	2.12	2.60	2.90	3

125°	130°	135°	140°	145°	150°	155°	160°	165°	170°	175°	180°	185°
2.90	2.60	2.12	1.5	0.78	0	−0.78	−1.5	−2.12	−2.60	−2.90	−3	−2.90

190°	195°	200°	205°	210°	215°	220°	225°	230°	235°	240°	245°	250°
−2.60	−2.12	−1.5	−0.78	0	0.78	1.5	2.12	2.60	2.90	3	2.90	2.60

255°	260°	265°	270°	275°	280°	285°	290°	295°	300°	305°	310°	315°
2.12	1.5	0.78	0	−0.78	−1.5	−2.12	−2.60	−2.9	−3	−2.9	−2.60	−2.12

320°	325°	330°	335°	340°	345°	350°	355°	360°
−1.5	−0.78	0	0.78	1.5	2.12	2.60	2.90	3

b.

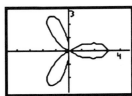

[0, 360, 10, −4.7, 4.7, 1, −3.1, 3.1, 1]

5. a. The graphs appear to be the same, but the starting point for each is different.

b. The graph is the same image rotated 90° counterclockwise.

c. The width at $y = 0$ is $2a$.

6. a. This is better for audience noise because it "listens" only to the area in front, where the performers are.

b. The edge performers are 3 units away. The center is 4, and the others are 3.732 units away.

7. a. $r = 3 \cos \theta: 0° \le \theta \le 180°$ **b.** $r = 3 \cos 2\theta,\ r = 2 \sin 2\theta: 0° \le \theta \le 360°$

Problem Set 13.7

1.

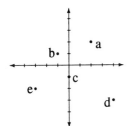

2. Answers will vary with different choices for θ.

a. $2.828(\cos 45° + i \sin 45°)$ **b.** $1.414(\cos 135° + i \sin 135°)$

c. $1(\cos {}^-90° + i \sin {}^-90°)$

3. $2 + 0i$, $^-1 + 1.732i$, $^-1 - 1.732i$

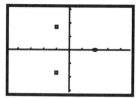

5. **a.** $5 + 2i$ **b.** $^-64 + 0i$ **c.** $0.223 - 0.114i$ **d.** $\frac{4}{3} + 0i$
   e. $^-0.125 - 0.125i$ **f.** $0 + 12i$

6. **a.** Points continue to spiral out.   **b.** Points spiral in to origin.

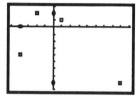 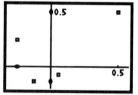

   c. Because the modulus of $1 + i$ is more than 1, raising it to increasing powers will make each result larger. Because the modulus of $0.5 + 0.5i$ is less than 1, raising it to increasing powers will make each result smaller.

11. The points iterate as shown below. Those colored black iterate to $(1, 0)$. Those left white iterate to $(^-0.5, 0.866)$. The others iterate to $(^-0.5, ^-0.866)$. If you try to find the point where it switches from one color to another, you will always find a point that goes to the other point. For example, while $^-1.6 + 0i$ iterates to $(1, 0)$ and $^-1.6 + 0i$ iterates to $(^-0.5, 0.866)$, if you iterate $^-1.6 + 0.0999i$, it goes to $(^-0.5, ^-0.866)$.

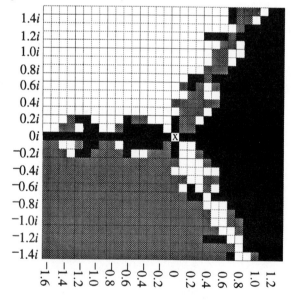

Chapter Review
Problem Set 13.8

1. **a.** Period = 120°, $y = -2 \cos 3(x - 120°)$ **b.** Period = 90°, $y = 3 \sin 4(x - 22.5°)$
   c. Period = 180°, $y = \csc 2(x + 45°)$ **d.** Period = $\frac{180}{2}$ = 90, $y = \cot 2(x - 45°) + 1$

2. **a.** $y = -2 \sin 2x - 1$ **b.** $y = \sin 0.5x + 1.5$ **c.** $y = 0.5 \tan(x - 45)$ **d.** $y = 0.5 \sec 2x$

3. **a.** The equation should be similar to $y = 1.92 \sin \frac{360}{365}(x - 80) + 12.13$.
   b. Approximately June 19; 14.05 hr
   c. Approximately March 17 and September 22.

4. **a.**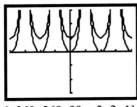

   $[-360, 360, 90, -3, 3, 1]$

   b. $\sec^2 x = \tan^2 x + 1$

5. **a.** $m\angle A \approx 74.5°$, $m\angle B \approx 58.4°$, $AB \approx 10.49$ cm **b.** $m\angle E = 52.55°$, $m\angle F = 17.45°$, $DE = 5.55$ cm

6. If the known parts include SAS or SSS, use the Law of Cosines. If the known parts include AAS, use the Law of Sines. If the known parts are SSA, you can use either law, but be careful if you use the Law of Sines to check whether you want an acute or obtuse angle.

7. $y = 100 \cos \frac{360}{105}(x - 10)$; 82.6 mi from the equator; passes over the launch site 41 times in 3 days.

8. $(5, -320°)$, $(5, 400°)$

9. **a.** $r = -2(\cos \theta + 1)$
   b. $r = 2(\sin \theta + 1)$

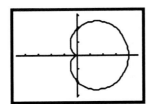

10.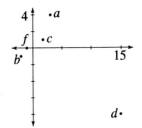

11. Points inside a circle of radius 1 centered at the origin iterate to $(0, 0)$. Points outside the circle become further and further away from the origin as they are iterated. Points on the circle stay on the circle. Some, such as $1 + i$, iterate to a single point. Others, such as $\left(\sqrt{0.3}, \sqrt{0.7}\right)$ keep bouncing around the circle hitting various points on the circle.

Glossary

absolute value   If x is the coordinate of a point on a number line, the distance from that point to the origin is called the absolute value of x, written $|x|$. This distance is always either positive or zero.

adjacent vertices   Two vertices that are joined by an edge.

antilog   The inverse function of a logarithm.

arithmetic sequence   A sequence in which each term is equal to the preceding term plus a constant. This constant is called the common difference.

asymptote   A boundary that a curve approaches but never quite reaches. A horizontal asymptote will represent the long-run value of a function.

best-fit line   The linear equation that meets the agreed-upon criteria for a set of data.

bifurcation   A process involving change whereby something divides in half or splits apart, then each of these parts divides in half, and so on.

binomial   A polynomial with two terms, for example, $2x + 3$.

box-and-whisker plot   Organization of data distribution represented by a rectangular-shaped graph that shows the minimum, first quartile, median, third quartile, and maximum values.

chromatic numbering   The process of grouping a graph network by identifying the least number of groups of vertices that are not connected to each other.

chunking   A simplification process whereby data are grouped and summarized into only a few values.

circle   A set of points, P, located a constant distance, r, from a fixed point, C, on a plane. The fixed point is called the **center**, and the constant distance is called the **radius**. Two equivalent symbolic descriptions of a circle are $|P - C| = r$ and $PC = r$.

coefficient of correlation   A measure of the strength of the linear dependency of y on x. It can be used to decide if a line is a good model of the data or of the accuracy of any prediction based on that linear model.

combination   A selection of objects from a set in which order is not important.

complete graph   (1) A network graph in which each vertex is connected to every other vertex. (2) A graph that displays all relevant features, including local extrema.

completing the square   The process of converting a quadratic expression in polynomial form into a form where the horizontal and vertical translations can be plainly seen, that is, center-vertex form.

complex conjugate pair   Two complex numbers of the form $a + bi$ and $a - bi$.

complex number   The sum of a real and an imaginary number written in the form $a + bi$.

composition of functions   The process of using the output of one function as the input for another function.

conic sections   The geometric shapes obtained by slicing a double-napped cone. Circles, ellipses, parabolas, and hyperbolas are conic sections.

conjugate pair   Binomials with the same terms but one sign different, for example, $2x + 4$ and $2x - 4$. See also **complex conjugate pair**. (Note: Nonreal answers always occur in pairs: $a + bi$ and $a - bi$. These are also called conjugate pairs.)

continuous function   A function whose graph has no breaks. It can be drawn without lifting your pencil.

cosecant   The reciprocal of the sine, abbreviated csc.

cosine   The cosine of an acute angle in a right triangle is the ratio of the length of the adjacent leg to the length of the hypotenuse.

cotangent   The reciprocal of the tangent, abbreviated cot.

counting principle   If there are n_1 ways to make a first choice, n_2 ways to make a second choice, n_3 ways to make a third choice, and so on, then the product $n_1 \cdot n_2 \cdot n_3 \cdot \cdots$ represents the total number of different ways (outcomes) in which the entire sequence of choices can be made.

data   A set of numerical information.

data analysis   A process of deriving information from data.

decay   The decreasing of some quantity over time. Usually decay describes a pattern of equal ratios for equal times. (Equal changes for equal times would be called linear decay.)

degree   The degree of a polynomial is the highest power of a variable in the expression. If the terms contain more than one variable, the degree is the highest value among the sums of the exponents in the individual terms.

dependent equations   A system of linear equations that has more than one solution.

determinant   A single value or measure associated with a square matrix that can be used to determine whether a matrix has an inverse.

deviation   The directed distance from each data value to the mean. Values below the mean have a negative deviation, and values above the mean have a positive deviation.

discrete graph   A graph containing unconnected points.

distance between two points   The distance between any two points located at (x_1, y_1) and (x_2, y_2) is $\sqrt{(x_2 - x_1)^2 + (y_2 - y_1)^2}$.

domain   The set of values for the independent variable. In a set of points the domain is discrete; for an equation the domain is the continuous set of values limited by those values that are reasonable and acceptable to the nature of the equation and the behavior that the equation models.

elimination method   The addition or subtraction of two equations or multiples of two equations to reduce the number of variables.

ellipse   A set of points, P, the sum of whose distances from two fixed points, F_1 and F_2, is always a constant length, d. That is, $F_1P + F_2P = d$. The two fixed points are called **foci**.

end behavior   The behavior or shape of a function for x-values that are large in absolute value.

escape set   Points with a modulus that grows infinitely large.

even function   A function that is symmetric to the y-axis; that is, $f(^-x) = f(x)$ for all defined values of x.

expected value   An average value found by multiplying the value of each event by its probability and then summing all of the products.

experimental probability   Probability that is based on trials and observations or simulation of the event.

explicit formula   A formula for a sequence or the sum of a series that defines a rule for calculating a term or sum based on the term's number.

exponential function   A function with a variable in the exponent that is used to model continuous growth or decay.

extrapolation   The process of using a model to find values beyond the present range of values.

factored form   The form of a polynomial equation written as the product of linear factors. In $y = A(x - R_1)(x - R_2)$ the roots are at R_1 and R_2.

feasible region   The portion of the coordinate plane that contains points that meet all conditions specified by a system of inequalities.

finite differences   Differences between consecutive values of the dependent variable when the independent-variable values form an arithmetic sequence.

fractal   A shape that is self-similar; that is, it contains infinitely many exact replicas of itself on various scales.

frequency   The number of times an event has occurred.

function   A function $y = f(x)$ is a description relating the variables x and y to each other. For each specified value of x, the description allows you to define a single value of y.

geometric sequence   A numeric sequence in which each term is equal to the preceding term multiplied by a constant, or $u_n = r \cdot u_{(n-1)}$. The constant r is called the **common ratio**.

graph theory   The use of diagrams involving vertices and edges in finding mathematical solutions to problems.

graphing window   The viewing screen of a calculator that is defined by specific values —Xmin, Xmax, Xscl, Ymin, Ymax, Yscl.

growth   The increasing of some quantity over time. Usually growth describes a pattern of equal ratios for equal times. (Equal changes for equal times would be called linear growth.)

half life   The length of time needed for a value to decrease to half of its original amount. This term often refers to the decay of a radioactive material.

heading   A compass direction given in degrees, measured clockwise from north. East is a heading of 90°, south is 180°, and west is 270°.

histogram   A data distribution showing the frequency of data elements within ranges of values.

hyperbola   A set of points, P, so located that the difference of the distances from two fixed points, F_1 and F_2, remains constant: $|F_1P - F_2P| = d$. The two fixed points are called **foci**.

identity   A mathematical statement that is always true.

identity matrix   One of a set of matrices that do not alter or transform the elements of any matrix A under multiplication.

imaginary number   The square root of a negative number.

inconsistent equations A system of equations with no solution.

interpolation The process of calculating a value between two given values.

interquartile range (IQR) The difference between the lower (first) and upper (third) quartiles (the length of the box in a box plot).

inverse matrix A matrix that when multiplied by another matrix produces an identity matrix. Not every matrix has a corresponding inverse.

inverse relation The relation obtained by exchanging the x- and y-coordinates of all points. The graph of an inverse relation will be a reflection of the original relation over the line $y = x$.

irrational number A number whose decimal expansion is nonrepeating and nonterminating, for example, $\sqrt{2}$ and π.

Julia set The set of points on the boundary between the prisoner and escape sets.

Law of Cosines A relationship between the sides of a triangle and the cosine of one of the angles. Specifically, the square of one side of a triangle is equal to the sum of the squares of the other two sides minus twice the product of those sides and the cosine of the included angle.

Law of Sines A relationship between the sides of a triangle and the sines of the angles opposite those sides. Specifically, the ratio of the sine of an angle in a triangle to the side opposite that angle is constant throughout a triangle.

least-squares line A best-fit line determined by calculating the line with the minimum sum of the squares of the residuals.

limit A value a function approaches but never attains.

limiting value The long-run value of a sequence or a series. The value as n grows infinitely large.

line of symmetry A line that divides a graph into two congruent pieces. If the graph could be folded along this line, the two halves would lie directly on top of each other.

linear Having to do with a line, a first-degree expression, an equation, or a polynomial.

linear function A first-degree function that can be put in either of the forms $y = mx + b$ or $y = m(x - x_1) + y_1$ where m is the **slope** of the line, b is the **y-intercept**, and (x_1, y_1) is a **point** on the line.

linear programming The process of finding a feasible region and then determining the point(s) in that region that gives a maximum or minimum value to a specific expression.

linearize The process of using mathematical operations to alter or transform data to fit a line.

local maximum point On a graph, the highest point in its immediate neighborhood of x-values.

local minimum point On a graph, the lowest point in its immediate neighborhood of x-values.

logarithm In the equation $a = b^x$, the logarithm base b of a provides the value of the exponent, $\log_b a = x$. The logarithm is the exponent that is put on b to give the value a.

logarithmic scale A measuring scale in which an increase in one unit means multiplying by a certain factor. For example, on a base 10 or common log scale, a measurement of 8.1 is ten times greater than a measurement of 7.1.

mathematical model   An equation or rule that describes a relationship that closely fits a set of data.

matrix   A rectangular array of numbers. The dimensions of a matrix are specified by the number of rows and columns it contains. A 2×3 matrix contains 2 rows and 3 columns.

mean   The average value calculated as the sum of all the values divided by the number of values in the set.

mean absolute deviation (MAD)   The sum of the absolute values of the deviations, divided by the number of values; the "average difference" between data values and the mean.

mean absolute residual   The mean of the absolute values of all the residuals. It is a measure of the accuracy of a particular model and may be used to give accuracy of predictions made with that model or to compare models.

measure of central tendency   A single value used to characterize or represent an entire set. Examples include the mean, the median, and the mode.

measure of spread   A single value used to characterize the distribution of a set. Examples include the interquartile range (IQR), the mean absolute deviation (MAD), and the standard deviation (σ).

median   The middle number of an ordered set. If the set has an even number of values, then the median is the average of the two middle values.

median-median line   A best-fit line determined by a process using a three point summary of a data set. The summary is based on medians of three groups of the data arranged by the independent variable.

mode   The value that occurs most frequently in a set. (Not all sets have a mode.)

modulus   The absolute value of a complex number; its distance from the origin.

multiplicative inverse   The reciprocal; for each nonzero real number, a, there exists a multiplicative inverse $\frac{1}{a}$, such that $\frac{1}{a} \cdot a = 1$.

nonplanar graph   A network graph in which it is impossible to draw all edges without forming at least one intersection that is not at a vertex.

normal distribution   A symmetric and "bell-shaped" distribution. It is the limiting shape of the binomial distribution as n grows increasingly large.

oblique triangle   A nonright triangle.

odd function   A function that is symmetric to the origin; that is, $^-f(x) = f(^-x)$ for all defined values of x.

outlier   A value in a data set that is uncharacteristic of most of the data. Typically those values that are at least 1.5 times the interquartile range less than the first quartile or 1.5 times the interquartile range greater than the third quartile are called outliers.

parabola   A set of points, P, that are equally distant from a fixed point, F, and a fixed line, l. The fixed point is called a **focus**, and the line is called a **directrix**.

parameter   The third variable in a set of parametric equations that is used to describe the other two.

parametric equations   A pair of equations in which the x- and y-variables are each written as a function of a third variable, t, called the **parameter**.

percentile rank   The percent of the scores that are below the given value.

perfect square trinomial A three-term polynomial that factors into two equal factors, for example,
$x^2 + 6x + 9 = (x + 3)(x + 3)$.

period The length of the x-interval required for the graph of one complete cycle before the graph begins to repeat itself.

periodic function Any function whose graph repeats over and over again.

permutation An arrangement or selection of objects from a set when order is important.

planar graph A network graph in which all edges can be drawn so that no intersections are formed other than at the vertices.

polar coordinates A system of identifying a point on the coordinate plane by specifying its distance, r, from the origin and an angle, θ, measured from the positive x-axis to the ray passing through the origin and the point.

polar form of a complex number Specification of a complex number in the form of $r \cos \theta + ri \sin \theta$ where r and θ are the polar coordinates of the point.

polynomial An expression made up of the sum of terms whose variables have only positive whole-number powers. The coefficients of these terms may be any type of number.

polynomial form The form of a polynomial equation without any parentheses.

prisoner set Points that under recursion tend toward the origin or never leave a finite region.

quartile Part of a data set that contains 25% of the data. The median of the entire set of data values is called the second quartile. The median of the data values below the median of the set is called the first quartile. The median of the data values above the median is called the third quartile.

random numbers Numbers that when generated are equally likely to occur and do not form a pattern in the sequence of numbers.

range The set of values for the dependent variable. In a set of points the range is discrete; for an equation the range is the set of values produced by an appropriate domain.

rational function A function that can be written as the quotient of two polynomials, $f(x) = \frac{p(x)}{q(x)}$. The denominator polynomial must be of degree one or more.

recursive definition A set of statements that specifies one or more initial terms and defines the nth term, u_n, in relation to one or more of the preceding terms.

reference angle An acute angle made with the x-axis that is used to calculate trigonometric functions for angles greater than 90°.

relation A correspondence between an independent variable and a dependent variable.

residual The difference between the y-value of a data point and the y-value of the equation with the same x-value. Points below the graph of the equation have negative residuals, and points above the graph have positive residuals.

root The x-value where the graph of an equation crosses the x-axis. Same as zeros.

rotation matrix A matrix for a rotation. The entries in the matrix are the sines and cosines of the angle of rotation.

scientific notation Any number written as a number between 1 and 10, multiplied by a power of 10.

secant The reciprocal of the cosine, abbreviated sec.

sequence   A set of elements in a specific order determined by a rule or formula.

series   The sum of the terms of a sequence. The nth partial sum, S_n, of a series is the sum of the first n terms of its companion sequence.

sine   The sine of an acute angle in a right triangle is the ratio of the length of the opposite leg to the length of the hypotenuse.

skewed   To be distributed, or stretched, in a nonsymmetric way.

slope   A ratio of the rate of increase (or decrease) of a line. The slope of a line is $\frac{\text{change in } y}{\text{change in } x}$ or $\frac{\text{rise}}{\text{run}}$.

standard deviation   The square root of the variance. It is a measure of spread used for single-variable data.

statistics   Various methods used to obtain numbers to characterize a data set.

substitution method   A method for solving a system of equations in which you substitute or replace a variable or an expression in one equation with an equivalent expression from the other equation.

synthetic division   A shortcut form of dividing a polynomial by a linear factor that involves only multiplication and division.

system of equations   Two or more equations that are solved or studied simultaneously.

tangent   The tangent of an acute angle in a right triangle is the ratio of the length of the opposite leg to the length of the adjacent leg.

theoretical probability   Probability that is based on calculation or physical properties of the event without actually performing or simulating the event.

trinomial   A polynomial with three terms, for example, $3x^2 + 2x - 4$.

unit circle   A circle with a radius of one unit.

unit hyperbola   The hyperbola with the equation $x^2 - y^2 = 1$.

variance   The mean value of the squares of the deviations from the mean of the data.

vertex form   The form of a quadratic equation, $y = A(x - H)^2 + K$, with the vertex at (H, K) and solutions at $x = H \pm \sqrt{\frac{-K}{A}}$.

vertex of a parabola   The turning point of a parabola. It is the intersection of the parabola with its line of symmetry.

x-intercept   The point where a graph crosses the x-axis.

y-intercept   The point where a graph crosses the y-axis.

zero   The x-values that make an expression have a zero value. Same as roots and x-intercept.

Index

The references that appear in bold refer to the Calculator Notes that accompany this book.

Essay on the Principle of Population (Malthus), 302
Euler, Leonhard, 206, 512, 574
even functions, 221
expected value, 395-397
experimental probability, 387, 388
explicit formulas
    arithmetic sequences, 58, 59-60, 77, **2A**
    arithmetic series, 64-66, 77
    defined, 58
    geometric sequences, 68-71, 77
    geometric series, 73-74, 77
Exploratory Data Analysis (Tukey), 97-98
exponential equations
    base as variable, 333-336
    exponent as variable, 341-343
    linearizing, 361-365
exponential functions, 302-306
    defined, 302
    linearizing, 362-364, **7I**
exponents
    calculator expression of, 6, **0B**
    division property of, 317-318
    multiplication property of, 316-317
    negative, 319-320
    nested power property of, 317
    of polynomials, 477
    power of a product property, 320-321
    power property of equality, 334
    rational, 310-313, **7B, 7C, 7D**
    zero as, 319-320
extraneous solution, 500
extrapolation, 146, 188-189

factored form of quadratics, 483, 488
factorials, 394, 533
factoring, 486-488, 491-492, 518-520
Fahrenheit, Daniel Gabriel, 206
Fahrenheit temperature scale, 206-207, 324-325, 434
fangcheng, 442
feasible region, 452, 455-456, 458, 463-464
Fechner, Gustav, 94, 97
Fibonacci, 530-531
finite differences, 478-479
first differences, 478
first quartile, 98
Fisher, Ronald Aymler, 553
fit. *See* mathematical models
flipping. *See* reflections
foci, 606, 610, 618
focus, 613, 614
Fractal Geometry of Nature (Mandelbrot), 524
fractals, 84-86, 524-525, **10F**
fractions. *See* rational numbers

France, 46, 167, 227, 343, 351, 546, 547, 688
frequency, 123
functions
    absolute value, 227, **0E**
    asymptotes of, 341, 582, 587-588, 620
    average value of, 234, 240, **5D**
    combining of, 661-663
    complex, 692-694
    compositions of, 243-245, 327-328, **5F, 7G**
    continuous, 205-206
    decreasing, 323
    defined, 205-206, 238-239
    distance and, 599-601
    domain of, 238
    end behavior of, 582
    even, 221
    exponential. *See* exponential functions
    greatest integer, 235, **5E**
    increasing, 323
    inverse. *See* inverse functions
    linear, 210, 213
    logarithmic. *See* logarithmic function
    notation of, 206, 210, 239
    odd, 221
    parabolas, 215-216, 219, 239
    parametric equivalents of, 262
    parent, 238, 581
    periodic. *See* periodic functions
    polar conversions and, 682-683
    polynomials and, 479
    power. *See* power functions
    projectile motion as, 496
    quadratic, 491
    range of, 238
    rational. *See* rational functions
    reciprocal, 652-654
    semicircle, 230-231
    square roots, 222-223, **5C**
    symmetry and, 221
    tables of, 479, 653
    transformations of. *See* transformations
    trigonometric. *See* trigonometry
    variable rates, 592-596
    vertical line test, 238
    See also equations; explicit formulas; matrix (matrices)

Galton, Francis, 94, 97, 119, 134, 152, 168, 561
garbage, 50, 150
Gauss, Karl Friedrich, 51, 64, 167, 442, 688
Gaussian elimination, 442
genealogy, 31
general term, 23, 24, 26, 35, 77

geology, 671
Geometer's Sketchpad Investigation
    Comparing the Mean and the Mean Absolute Deviation, 115
    Constructing an Ellipse, 633
    Constructing a Sequence, 54
    Constructing Trigonometric Curves, 659-660
    Inverse Functions, 332
    Largest Triangle, 510
    Least Squares, 174-175
    Linear Programming, 458-459
    Normal Curves, 568-569
    Random Points and Objects, 387
    Seeing the Infinite Sum, 83
    Transforming a Point and a Line, 236-237
    Trigonometric Ratios, 273
Geome Tree, 84-85
geometric sequences
    defined, 26
    explicit formulas for, 68-71, 77
    modeling growth with, 28-29
    recursively defined, 25-26
geometric series, 50, 51-52, 73-74, 77, 83
geometry
    angles. *See* angle(s)
    circumscribed circles, 166
    conic sections. *See* conic sections
    parametric equations and, 274-276
    polygons. *See* polygon(s)
    probability modeled with, 383-384
    relationships of, 211
    triangles. *See* triangle(s)
Germany, 51, 91, 94, 97, 227, 466, 688
government and politics, 208, 346, 372, 392, 467-468, 558, 570-571
Grandi, Guido, 682
Granville, Evelyn Boyd, 144
graphing
    best-fit lines and, 135-136
    binomial curves, **11D**
    complex functions, 692-694, 696, **13D, 13E**
    complex numbers, 687-688
    compositions of functions, 245-246
    dot mode, 382, **8C**
    fractals, 84-86, 524-525, **10F**
    inequalities, 451-453, **9C**
    inverse functions, 673-677
    lines, **4A, 4B**
    parametric equations, 254-258, 265, **6A, 6B**
    points, 38, 39, 49, **1A, 1B, 1E, 1F**
    polar curves, 680-683, **13B, 13C**
    polynomial equations, solving by, 478-479
    sequences, 38-40, 43, **1E**
    See also calculators

variation
- constant of, 213
- direct, 213
- inverse, 580-583

velocity and speed, 140, 241, 282-286, 299, 657

vertex form of quadratics, 482-483, 487-488, 492-493, 627-630

vertex (vertices)
- of a combination, 539
- corner-point principle and, 463-464
- graph theory and, 401, 408, 409
- of a parabola, 216, 239, 614

vertical asymptote, 582

vertical line test, 238

vertical parabola, 615

Volterra, Vito, 598

Wales, 5

water currents, 282-284

web graphs, 245, 331, **5G**

Weierstrass, Karl, 227

Wessel, Caspar, 688

Wiberg, Martin, 479

Wittich, Paul, 689

x-intercepts
- bisection method of, 522, **10A**
- defined (as roots), 486

finding, 487-488, 518-520, **10E**, **13A**

synonyms for, 506

y-intercept
- median-median line and, 153
- residuals and, 162
- slope-intercept form and, 210

zero
- of equations. *See* x-intercepts
- as exponent, 319-320

zero-factor property, 487

Zhu Shijie, 546

Photo Credits

CHAPTER 0

1: Bonnie Kamin. **2:** *parabolograph,* courtesy Charles Babbage Institute; *slide rule,* London Science Museum/Science and Society Picture Library; *Brunsviga calculator,* London Science Museum/Science and Society Picture Library; *abacus,* Bettmann; *21-column abacus,* London Science Museum/Science and Society Picture Library; *tide predicter,* London Science Museum/Science and Society Picture Library. **5:** Alex S. MacLean/Landslides.

CHAPTER 1

21: Alex S. MacLean/Landslides. **22:** *top,* ©1996 The Andy Warhol Foundation, Inc./Artists Rights Society (ARS), NYC; *bottom,* courtesy Don Albers. **27:** Stephen Simpson/FPG. **33:** *top,* © 1995 Comstock; *bottom,* Greg Ceo. **40:** John Nordell/The Picture Cube. **44:** *top,* Culver Pictures; *bottom,* Smithsonian Institution. **46:** Luis Shein/Key Curriculum Press. **51:** courtesy John G. White/Chess Collection, Special Collections, Cleveland Public Library.

CHAPTER 2

57: Alex S. MacLean/Landslides. **64:** Spencer Grant/Photo Researchers. **69:** *top,* Greg Ceo; *bottom,* ©Harold E. Edgerton 1992 Trust, courtesy of Palm Press Inc. **74:** Rod Planck/Photo Researchers. **76:** *left,* Erich Hartmann/Magnum Photos; *right,* Martin Rogers/Prism/FPG. **86:** Courtesy Springer-Verlag. **91:** Phoebe A. Hearst Museum of Anthropology, University of California at Berkeley.

CHAPTER 3

93: Comstock/Stuart Cohen **95:** Comstock/Russ Kinne. **97:** *left,* Science Photo Library/Photo Researchers; *center,* Culver Pictures; *right,* Corbis-Bettmann. **99:** Tony Freeman/PhotoEdit. **101:** FPG/Telegraph Colour Library. **110:** Karl V. Steinbrugge Collection, Earthquake Engineering Research Center, University of California at Berkeley. **112:** *top,* Jeff Greenberg/PhotoEdit; *bottom,* Comstock. **118:** David Young-Wolff/PhotoEdit. **120:** NASA/Johnson Space Center. **121:** Black Star. **126:** Knudsen/FPG. **130:** NASA.

CHAPTER 4

133: Wesley Bocxe/Photo Researchers. **135:** Bruce Forster/Tony Stone Images. **144:** from *Women and Numbers* by Teri Perl, ©1993. Reprinted by permission of Wide World Publishing/Tetra, San Carlos, CA. **147:** Heinz Kluetmeier/Sports Illustrated. **148:** Ken Biggs/Tony Stone Images. **149:** Bonnie Kamin. **151:** John Giordano/Saba. **155:** George Ceo. **161:** Michael Newman/PhotoEdit. **165:** Corbis-Bettmann. **167:** Giraudon/Art Resource, NY. **176:** courtesy Drive-Thru Tree Park, Inc., Leggett, CA. **177:** reprinted with permission of Biometrika Trustees. **184:** Richard Laird/FPG. **190:** Rod Planck/Tony Stone Images.

CHAPTER 5

197: David Butow/Saba. **201:** Comstock/Hartman-Dewitt. **204:** Heinz Kluetmeier/Sports Illustrated. **210:** Comstock/Henry Georgi. **211:** Corbis-Bettmann. **214:** Robert E. Daemmrich/Tony Stone Images. **222:** George Ceo. **227:** Jim Smalley/The Picture Cube. **230:** Comstock. **241:** Marc Asnin/Saba. **242:** Corbis-Bettmann.

CHAPTER 6

253: AP/Wide World Photos. **256:** Gary Conner/PhotoEdit. **264:** Lee Snider/The Image Works. **266:** Tom Carroll/FPG. **270:** C. K. Lorenz/Photo Researchers. **272:** Jack Thornell/AP/Wide World Photos. **282:** Bonnie Kamin. **290:** Alex S. MacLean/Landslides. **291:** Richard Stockton/FPG. **293:** Comstock/Art Gingert.

CHAPTER 7

301: Richard Megna/Fundamental Photographs, NYC. **304:** Jean Kugler/FPG. **305:** Bonnie Kamin. **307:** Comstock/George Gerster. **309:** *top,* UPI/Bettmann; *bottom,* Stephen Dunn/Allsport. **317:** P. Motta/Dept. of Anatomy/University "La Sapienza," Rome/Science Photo Library/Photo Researchers. **330:** *top,* UPI/Bettmann; *bottom,* Stock Montage. **335:** Richard Nowitz/FPG. **336:** Jim Pickerell/Tony Stone Images. **338:** Comstock. **340:** Jook Leung/FPG. **343:** Stock Montage. **346:** Jerry Driendl/FPG. **347:** Keystone/FPG. **352:** Roberta Hershenson/Photo Researchers. **355:** *top,* Reuters/Bettmann; *bottom,* Tim Brown/Tony Stone Images. **359:** David R. Frazier/Tony Stone Images. **363:** UPI/Bettmann **368:** Arnulf Husmo/Tony Stone Images. **369:** *top,* Michael Nichols/Magnum; *bottom,* Tony Freeman/PhotoEdit.

CHAPTER 8

375: Bob Daemmrich Photos. **376:** Metropolitan Museum of Art, the Carnarvon Collection, gift of Edward S. Harkness, 1926 (26.7.1287). **381:** Tony Freeman/PhotoEdit. **390:** Bonnie Kamin. **395:** Tim Davis/Photo Researchers. **400:** Bob Daemmrich Photos. **406:** Jeff Greenberg/PhotoEdit. **407:** courtesy Linda Valdés.

CHAPTER 9

423: Alex S. MacLean/Landslides. 427: UPI/Corbis-Bettmann. 437: Bonnie Kamin. 440: Michael Newman/PhotoEdit. 453: Georgia O'Keeffe, *Katchina,* 1936 (oil on canvas, 7X7") ©Georgia O'Keeffe Foundation/Artists Rights Society (ARS), NY/San Francisco Museum of Modern Art, gift of the Hamilton-Wells Collection. 457: Allan D. Cruickshank/National Audubon Society/Photo Researchers. 466: Stock Montage. 467: Bonnie Kamin.

CHAPTER 10

475: ©Harold E. Edgerton 1992 Trust, courtesy of Palm Press, Inc. 484: UPI/Bettmann. 496: Buddy Mays/FPG. 513: Comstock/Art Gingert. 521: Greg Ceo. 524: courtesy Don Albers. 525: Hank Morgan/Science Source/Photo Researchers.

CHAPTER 11

529: Comstock/Bill Ellzey. 533: Corbis-Bettmann. 536: reprinted by permission of Pacific Bell. ©1995 Pacific Bell. All Rights Reserved. 543: Reuters/Corbis-Bettmann. 544: Lawrence Migdale/Tony Stone Images. 559: Bonnie Kamin. 567: Tom McCarthy/PhotoEdit. 573: Arthur C. Smith III/Grant Heilman.

CHAPTER 12

579: Jim Brandenburg/Animals Animals. 580: Bonnie Kamin. 584: Paul S. Howell/Gamma Liaison. 585: Frederic Lewis/Archive Photos. 594: Jeanne Drake/Tony Stone Images. 597: E. R. Degginger/Earth Scenes 599: Stock Montage. 618: Stock Montage. 620: Science Photo Library/Photo Researchers. 624: courtesy St. Louis Science Center. 628: F. B. Grunzweig/Photo Researchers. 634: Brian Milne/Earth Scenes.

CHAPTER 13

643: Bruno De Hogues/Tony Stone Images. 644: Cathlyn Melloan/Tony Stone Images. 651: Vic Bider/Photo Network. 653: Bonnie Kamin. 656: Mark Newman/Photo Network. 661: Rhoda Sidney/PhotoEdit. 662: Jim Leynse/Saba. 673: London Science Museum/Science and Society Picture Library. 678: *both,* Andrew J. Martinez/Photo Researchers. 694: *all images,* Courtesy Springer-Verlag. 699: NASA.